Divine Teaching and the Way of the World

Divine Teaching and the Way of the World

A defense of revealed religion

Samuel Fleischacker

OXFORD
UNIVERSITY PRESS

OXFORD
UNIVERSITY PRESS

Great Clarendon Street, Oxford ox2 6dp

Oxford University Press is a department of the University of Oxford.
It furthers the University's objective of excellence in research, scholarship,
and education by publishing worldwide in

Oxford New York

Auckland Cape Town Dar es Salaam Hong Kong Karachi
Kuala Lumpur Madrid Melbourne Mexico City Nairobi
New Delhi Shanghai Taipei Toronto

With offices in

Argentina Austria Brazil Chile Czech Republic France Greece
Guatemala Hungary Italy Japan Poland Portugal Singapore
South Korea Switzerland Thailand Turkey Ukraine Vietnam

Oxford is a registered trade mark of Oxford University Press
in the UK and in certain other countries

Published in the United States
by Oxford University Press Inc., New York

© Samuel Fleischacker 2011

The moral rights of the author have been asserted
Database right Oxford University Press (maker)

First published 2011

British Library Cataloguing in Publication Data
Data available

Library of Congress Cataloging in Publication Data
Data available

Typeset by SPI Publisher Services, Pondicherry, India
Printed in Great Britain
on acid-free paper by
MPG Books Group, Bodmin and King's Lynn

ISBN 978–0–19–921736–6

10 9 8 7 6 5 4 3 2 1

Acknowledgments

Among the many people whose conversation and advice and encouragement have helped me over the 10 years in which I have worked on this book, I am particularly grateful to Andy Blom, Kyla Ebels Duggan, Anne Eaton, Bob Fischer, Jon Garthoff, Sandy Goldberg, Gordon Graham, Bill Hart, Andy Koppelman, Richard Kraut, Tony Laden, and Elijah Millgram, all of whom read and gave me extensive comments on large chunks of the manuscript.

I've also learned from discussions with audiences at Princeton Theological Seminary, Northwestern University, the University of Chicago, and the University of Illinois-Chicago (UIC), and from comments by, and conversations with, Ken Alder, Michael Balinsky, Tom Brockelman, Dan Brudney, Brad Cokelet, Becko Copenhaver, Mary Dietz, Stephen Engelmann, Robert Farley, Josh Feigelson, Patrick Frierson, Andrew Chignell, Paul Guyer, James Harris, Rachel Havrelock, Brian Hosmer, Nick Huggett, Peter Hylton, Robert Johnston, Michael Morgan, Burkay Ozturk, Mary Beth Rose, Mark Rosen, Sally Sedgwick, Ken Seeskin, Oliver Sensen, Danny Statman, Laurie Zoloth, and Rachel Zuckert. Several anonymous readers for Oxford University Press were also helpful, and Peter Momtchiloff has been a wonderfully supportive and encouraging editor.

I've received institutional support for work on this manuscript from the Institute for the Humanities at UIC. Mary Beth Rose and Linda Vavra make the Institute a terrific environment for friendly, constructive scholarly exchange—it is one of UIC's greatest treasures.

I find that environment also in my home. No list of thanks would be complete without mentioning my wife Amy, who supports and helps me in everything I do.

SF
15th of Av, 5770
July 26, 2010

Contents

Abbreviations

Ak	Immanuel Kant, *Gesammelte Schriften*: published by the Deutschen Akademie der Wissenschaften, 29 vols. (Berlin: Walter de Gruyter, 1902–).
AV	Alasdair MacIntyre, *After Virtue* (Notre Dame: Univ. of Notre Dame Press, 2nd edn, 1984).
BT	Babylonian Talmud. Unless otherwise noted, translations are from the Soncino edition edited by I. Epstein.
CPR	Immanuel Kant, *Critique of Pure Reason*, trans. Paul Guyer and Allen Wood (Cambridge: Cambridge Univ. Press, 1998). "A" designates the first edition; "B" the second.
CPrR	Immanuel Kant, *Critique of Practical Reason*, trans. Lewis White Beck (Indianapolis: Bobbs-Merrill, 1956). Pagination, for this and all other Kant works except CPR, will be to the German Akademie edition, given in all English translations.
CJ	Immanuel Kant, *Critique of the Power of Judgment*, trans. P. Guyer and E. Matthews (Cambridge: Cambridge University Press, 2000).
ELP	Bernard Williams, *Ethics and the Limits of Philosophy* (Cambridge, MA: Harvard University Press, 1985).
Enq	David Hume, *Enquiries*, ed. L. A. Selby-Bigge and P. H. Nidditch, 3rd edn (Oxford: Clarendon, 1975).
FE	John Finnis, *Fundamentals of Ethics* (Washington: Georgetown Univ. Press, 1983).
FIG	Robert Adams, *Finite and Infinite Goods* (Oxford: Oxford Univ. Press, 1999).
G	*Groundwork of the Metaphysics of Morals*, trans. Mary Gregor (Cambridge: Cambridge Univ. Press, 1997).
Guide	Moses Maimonides, *Guide for the Perplexed*, trans. M. Friedländer (New York: Dover, 1956).
LCC	Will Kymlicka, *Liberalism, Community, and Culture* (Oxford: Clarendon, 1989).
MER	Robert Tucker (ed.), *The Marx–Engels Reader*, 2nd edn (New York: WW Norton, 1978).
MT	Moses Maimonides, *Mishneh Torah*. Unless otherwise noted, translations from Moses Hyamson (trans.), *The Book of Knowledge* (Jerusalem: Feldheim, 1981).
NE	Aristotle, *Nicomachean Ethics*, as translated in Jonathan Barnes (ed.), *The Complete Works of Aristotle* (Princeton: Princeton University Press, 1984).
NLNR	John Finnis, *Natural Law and Natural Right* (Oxford: Clarendon Press, 1980).
OWA	Martin Heidegger, "Origin of the Work of Art," in *Poetry, Language, Thought*, trans. Albert Hofstadter (New York: Harper & Row, 1971).
PE	G. E. Moore, *Principia Ethica* (Cambridge: Cambridge Univ. Press, 1962).
PL	John Rawls, *Political Liberalism* (New York: Columbia University Press, 1993).

Rep   Plato, *Republic*, ed. G, R. F. Ferrari, trans. T. Griffith (Cambridge: Cambridge University Press, 2000).

RWB   Immanuel Kant, *Religion Within the Boundaries of Mere Reason*, trans. and ed. A. Wood and G. di Giovanni (Cambridge: Cambridge Univ. Press, 1998).

SN   Christine Korsgaard, *Sources of Normativity* (Cambridge: Cambridge University Press, 1996).

ST   John Locke, *Second Treatise of Government*.

T   David Hume, *Treatise of Human Nature*, ed. L. A. Selby-Bigge and P. H. Nidditch, 2nd edn (Oxford: Clarendon, 1978).

TJ   John Rawls, *A Theory of Justice* (Cambridge, MA: Harvard University Press, 1971).

TMS   Adam Smith, *Theory of Moral Sentiments*, ed. D. D. Raphael and A. L. Macfie (Oxford: Oxford University Press, 1976).

TT   Bernard Williams, *Truth and Truthfulness* (Princeton: Princeton University Press, 2002).

VN   Thomas Nagel, *The View from Nowhere* (Oxford: Oxford University Press, 1986).

WO?   Immanuel Kant, "What Does It Mean To Orient Oneself In Thinking?" In *Religion Within the Boundaries of Mere Reason And Other Writings*, trans. and ed. A. Wood and G. di Giovanni (Cambridge: Cambridge University Press, 1998).

Introduction

"Beautiful is the study of Torah together with *derekh eretz*."

Avot 2:2

The Talmudic tractate *Avot*, which contains advice for would-be rabbis, recommends combining Torah—a word that literally means "teaching" but is used by Jews to designate certain specific teachings that they regard as coming from God—with "*derekh eretz*": a phrase that literally means "the way of the world," but connotes something like common decency. If we now take "Torah" to represent all purportedly divine teachings and "the way of the world" to designate all principles held by religious and non-religious people alike, we get: "Beautiful is divine teaching together with the way of the world." Hence the title of this book, and its thesis: that revealed religions can offer us something of great importance, but stand in danger of corruption or fanaticism unless they are combined with secular scientific practices and a secular morality. I'll give an overview of what I mean by that in this introduction.

1. I take my bearings from two sorts of sources: traditional Jewish texts, and the philosophy of the Enlightenment. It will be helpful to start with examples of both.

First, a series of rabbinic texts on *derekh eretz*. *Derekh eretz* means a number of different things in rabbinic literature. Sometimes it is used as a euphemism for sexual intercourse (it's "the way of the world" to procreate).[1] Elsewhere, it means having a job; the most common interpretation of my epigraph understands it as calling for Jewish scholars to combine their studies with a worldly occupation. On still other occasions, it is best translated as "decency," a way of behaving that human beings in all societies expect of one another. The Talmudic tractates entitled *Derekh Eretz* consist of a hodgepodge of ethical and prudential advice—mostly independent of Judaism's specific teachings.[2] I want to focus on this last, ethical meaning of the phrase, but we should bear the others in mind.[3]

To get the ethical meaning in clear view, consider three passages in which it is used. First, a delightful, bizarre passage that sketches a sort of mini natural law theory:

Rabbi Johanan said, "If the Torah had not been given, we would have learned modesty from the cat, [what is wrong with] robbery from the ant, [what is wrong with] adultery from the dove, [and] *derekh eretz* from the cock, who first coaxes and then mates."[4]

Here, *derekh eretz* seems to mean something like "good manners"—good sexual manners at least. It is a virtue that transforms the sexual act from an act of force into an expression of affection. (The context is a discussion of how husbands should speak to their wives when they want to have sex.) Like the other virtues mentioned in the passage, it is presented here as having biological roots—as built into the natural functions of animals. There is an odd wrinkle in the passage: it implies that these virtues are hard-wired into *other* species, but not into human beings. If the Torah had not been given, says Rabbi Johanan, we would have *learned* virtues from the behavior of other species, not followed virtuous instincts of our own. I'm not sure how much sense this makes. We might take Rabbi Johanan to anticipate a point that the contemporary moral philosopher Christine Korsgaard likes to make, that the very fact of human self-consciousness divides us from our impulses, such that nothing can be hard-wired into us in the way it is in other animals.[5] Or we might read it as saying that our observing these behaviors in other animal species, and the way they help those species flourish, can help confirm our inclination to regard them as a good thing. Either way, I think it best to avoid reading the passage such that humans alone among the animals lack a biological basis for modesty, *derekh eretz*, and the rest. (How then would we know that the other animals' behavior is something to emulate?) Rather, the point is surely that by looking at the cat and the ant and the dove and the cock we can be assured that our own modesty, *derekh eretz*, etc., are natural dispositions, rather than products of social convention. We don't need revelation to learn the value of these tendencies.

2. Let's turn now to the second passage:

Rabbi Jannai [once brought a man he had met on the road] to his house and entertained him with food and drink. He tested [his knowledge of] Talmud, and found none, in *Aggadah*, and found none, in Mishnah, and found none, in Scripture, and found none.... Said R. Jannai: "... A dog has eaten of Jannai's bread." The man rose and caught hold of him ... Said R. Jannai to the man: "How have you merited to eat at table with me?" The man answered: "Never in my life have I, after hearing slander, repeated it to the person spoken of, nor have I ever seen two persons quarrelling without making peace between them." Said R. Jannai: "That I should have called you 'dog,' when you possess such *derekh eretz*!" ... R. Samuel b. Nahman said: "*Derekh eretz* preceded the Torah by twenty-six generations [i.e.: it dates from Adam, according to Biblical chronology]. This is [implied in], *To keep the way to the tree of life* (Gen. 3: 24). [First Scripture mentions] 'the way' (*derekh*), which means *derekh eretz*, and afterwards [it mentions] *the tree of life*, which means the Torah."[6]

Here *derekh eretz* clearly means ethical behavior in a broad sense—it's certainly not limited to good sexual manners—and here it clearly designates norms independent of what Jews consider divine teaching. Indeed, it is supposed to be something that a very uneducated person might know. Here also, in sharp contrast to the previous passage, it is something that *distinguishes* human beings from animals: Rabbi Jannai withdraws the epithet "dog" when he sees that his guest has it.[7] But there are at least two different ways in which the passage may be trying to draw that distinction. On the one hand, it may be stressing the social structures of human beings, and the fact that our modes of socialization are passed down in a tradition, from parents to children. The *derekh eretz* of R. Jannai's guest comes out in his trying to mend rifts in his society, and has been passed down, supposedly, from generation to generation since the time of Adam. On the other hand, the passage may mean to trace *derekh eretz* to the human capacity for reason—what the Greeks called "logos." Logos means both speech and reason, and the two are often linked in ancient sources. Here, the virtues given as examples of *derekh eretz* are virtues of speech, and concerned to prevent or cure, by way of speech, types of evil to which only speaking animals are prone. So we can plausibly see this passage as promoting a rationalist *derekh eretz*, as opposed to the biological *derekh eretz* of the previous passage.

We thus have intimations in rabbinic writings of both the biological and the rationalist ways in which codes of natural law have standardly been drawn up. Aristotle defined human beings as "rational animals," and the Western natural law tradition, which relies heavily on Aristotle, has tended to draw the laws binding all human beings either from our rational aspect or from our animal aspect. Rationalist natural law thinkers argue, in more or less Kantian vein (Kant is himself an heir to the natural law tradition), that *reason* shows us we must be honest, avoid violence, and the like, that an order in which human beings deceived or tried to destroy each other would involve some sort of self-contradiction. Biologically-oriented natural law theorists tend to say that an impulse to heed certain laws is built into our instincts, and necessary for our survival as a species; not coincidentally, they tend to identify natural law more with sexual prohibitions than the rationalist tradition does. I prefer the rationalist tradition, but don't want to get into the details of that debate here. My point is just that attempts to draw morality from our nature can go in two different directions. In fact, that's an understatement. Aristotle also defined human beings as "polis animals"—animals that are naturally social or political—and the natural law tradition has also drawn its basic list of moral principles from the conditions necessary to maintain a society. As we saw, the same goes for the rabbinic understanding of *derekh eretz*. So *derekh eretz*, like natural law, can be given two or three quite different origins and justifications. This eclecticism, this plurality of ways to justify a moral code, will be of interest later.

One more thing to note about our second passage is that it ends by giving *derekh eretz* priority over the Torah. I take that to imply that the Torah must be read through a lens of human decency. Every effort should be taken to interpret it such that its demands accord with what any human being would recognize as decency, even at the cost of radically re-reading certain verses. Many sections of the Talmud engage in this sort of morally-oriented re-reading;[8] I take this passage to offer support for that. The way to the tree of life is through the virtues of human decency—God doesn't make His revelation available to people who lack those virtues.

3. The third passage can be found, once again, in *Pirkei Avot*: "Rabbi Elazar ben Azaryah said: If there is no Torah, there is no *derekh eretz*; if there is no *derekh eretz*, there is no Torah." (Avot 3:1) Unlike the passage from which I draw my title, this one establishes a reciprocal relationship between Torah and *derekh eretz*. There is no *derekh eretz*—no ordinary human decency—without Torah, even if there is also no Torah without *derekh eretz*. We might reconcile the two texts by saying that, for the second one, there is no *true* or *full* or *lasting derekh eretz* without divine teaching, not that the former cannot exist at all without the latter.[9] Something about Torah—about divine teaching—may bring out the point or fullest nature of *derekh eretz*, or give people the strongest motivation to maintain it.

That, at any rate, comes close to the biconditional I will try to defend here. I argue that there can be no proper devotion to or interpretation of divine teachings independent of a commitment to ordinary human decency, but also that divine teaching can offer something to a secular ethic that it needs, but cannot itself provide. Ordinary human decency can exist and be justified in a fully secular way, but a conception of what we live *for*, what the point of all this decent behavior might be, cannot be brought out without a divine teaching. The way of the world breaks down, I maintain, when it comes to the question of what makes our lives worth living. If so, however, there will be a certain emptiness to *derekh eretz*. And to the extent that it is difficult for human beings to pursue courses of action they find empty or pointless, there may well be a sense in which the way of the world is unsustainable without a divine teaching. This may not be quite as direct a dependency as our third rabbinic passage wants—it is certainly not a claim that one cannot be decent without believing in revelation—but it is nevertheless a claim that, in some important respects, the way of the world requires divine teaching.

4. Turning away from the rabbis, now, let's consider some themes in 18th-century reflections on religion. In the 18th century, more or less for the first time in European history, many prominent intellectuals were strongly critical of religion, and critics of religion could make their case unafraid. A century earlier, the Catholic church had had heretics burned at the stake; now a bitterly anti-clerical writer like Voltaire could become the toast of high society. In America, a new nation was formed that made no reference to God in its Constitution, and that deliberately allowed people of any religion and no religion to hold high office.[10] In Britain, Adam Smith called for a political system that might eventually lead all traditional religions, including Christianity, to transform themselves into "that pure and rational religion, free from every mixture of absurdity, imposture, or fanaticism, such as wise men have in all ages of the world wished to see established."[11] In France, the revolution at the close of the century

attempted to substitute a religion of reason for Christianity. And in Germany, the greatest philosopher of the age, Immanuel Kant, wrote up an extended defense of a religion of reason, which played down or rejected every aspect of Christianity that seemed irremediably irrational to him. The word "Enlightenment" was indeed coined to describe people who saw themselves as having left the darkness of religious dogma for the light of reason. Admittedly, many 18th-century intellectuals didn't fit that mold, and today historians would be leery of identifying this tendency with the Enlightenment as a whole, but it is surely true that one major element of the Enlightenment was an attack on the received religions of Europe: a variety of philosophies united by their invention of what Peter Gay has called a "modern paganism."[12]

And that modern paganism has had long-lasting effects. It is by now the accepted outlook of most of Europe and the nations that trace their heritage to Europe, and is fast spreading through the rest of the globe—although that process has triggered a violent backlash in recent years. So there is reason to think that a productive re-thinking of the place we today give to religion might begin with the debates of the 18th century.

With that in mind, I'd like to elaborate two themes from the Enlightenment's discussions of religion. The kinds of religion that the Enlighteners were particularly concerned to criticize were a) revealed or positive or historical religion, as opposed to "natural" religion, and b) fanatical or enthusiastic, as opposed to "cool" or "moderate" religion. When we see what they meant by these distinctions, it will be clearer what I mean by saying that I am defending revealed religion, and what the stakes are in attempting such a project.

5. When Adam Smith speaks of the "wise men in all ages" who advocated a "pure and rational religion," he probably means to refer above all to the Stoics. In any case, the religion he describes in his *Theory of Moral Sentiments* looks a good deal like Stoicism. There he tells us that it is helpful to morality to believe in a benevolent deity who created this world for the happiness of its sentient creatures, and whom we worship by developing moral virtues.[13] Smith is not entirely clear about *how* belief in God is morally helpful. At one point, he appears to suggest that a belief in reward and punishment after death keeps people more committed to morality than they would otherwise be (TMS 170). He also hints at a rather different view: that it helps us regard the rules of morality as "sacred" if we see them as established by God (TMS 161–163). And he combines all this with indications of yet a third view: that it is inspiring to see ourselves, when we act morally, as "co-operat[ing] with the Deity, and advanc[ing] as far as in our power the plan of Providence" (TMS 166).[14]

In any case, this is a religion in which belief in God provides some sort of spur to moral action, but the point is the moral action itself, not the belief inspiring it. An atheist who acts virtuously will achieve the point of the religion regardless of his beliefs (that's how Smith thought of his friend David Hume), and it will be unnecessary to have any specific view of God's nature, or to engage in any non-moral rituals. To the extent that Smith's view of how religion aids morality runs along the lines of the last of the three I mentioned, moreover—by which we just see our moral actions as aligning our wills with the governing power of the universe—it is compatible with a wholly naturalistic outlook, that does without miracles and revelation and is uncommitted to the existence of an afterlife. Such a religion doesn't differ much from irreligion, except perhaps in a certain optimism it imparts about the hospitality of the universe to our moral deeds.

I use Smith as a source for rational or natural religion because he explains the idea relatively clearly and concisely, but much the same thing can be found in Lord Shaftesbury, Kant and Gotthold Lessing. It is also only this much religion that Francis Hutcheson thought states needed to teach their subjects,[15] and it is this much religion that many political figures, including some of the American Founders, considered necessary for good citizenship. Most of these 18th-century thinkers included within natural religion belief in the existence of a transcendent God and the immortality of the soul, which they thought were justifiable on rational grounds. The contrasting category to rational or natural religion, for them, was positive or historical or revealed religion, to which belonged the specific claims about God's nature or will or actions that characterize Christianity, Judaism, Hinduism, and the like—about Jesus being God's son or the Torah being God's word or the need for certain sacrifices to be offered at certain times. For the Enlighteners, these claims, if believable at all, were made believable by miracles and revelations: by an *experience* of the supernatural, rather than by reason alone. Even David Hume maintained a distinction of this sort—while holding that even natural religion is not justifiable by reason, and that nothing can justify belief in a miracle.

And it is this distinction that enables us to see the force of an argument that Lessing made, late in the century, to the effect that revelation, even if it occurred, could add nothing to the credibility of any religious claim. If true at all, Lessing said, religious claims must be truths of reason rather than historical truths. No matter how firmly one might establish the historical accuracy of the Gospels, for instance, that would not prove that there is a God, that God has a son whose death atones for our sins, or any of the other metaphysical claims that define Christianity. "Accidental truths of history can never become the proof of necessary truths of reason," says Lessing,[16] summing up a line of argument according to which truths of history are of a different *kind* from truths of religion—established by different sorts of argument and evidence (inferences from empirical facts, in the one case, rational proofs in the other), expected to hold in different ways (contingently in the one case, necessarily in the other), and accompanied by different sorts of implications for our lives.

Now Lessing was an admirer of Hume, and interwoven with his insight into the difference between historical and religious claims is a distrust of miracles that owes much to Hume. Lessing also, at least by the end of his life, was willing to live with a radical deism shorn of supernatural doctrines. Nevertheless, he thought there was some place for revealed religion. As he saw it, revealed religions serve as useful carriers for certain moral beliefs—such as the importance of acting for the sake of virtue rather than for an external reward—which people would be unlikely to learn, or learn as readily, were they presented in purely rational terms. Kant followed him in this, laying out a detailed account of how Christianity could be re-read as a metaphor for moral doctrines in his *Religion Within the Limits of Reason Alone*. Neither Lessing nor Kant meant, I think, that Christian churches should be abandoned, but they did hope that over time religious people of all specific faiths would see their non-rational doctrines more and more as useful metaphors, make morality more and more the core of their religious practice, and transform their churches into something like moral support groups.

It is in this context that I say I am writing a defense of revealed religion. I think Smith and Lessing and Kant were all in an important respect *wrong*, that historical or positive or revealed religion has an importance that cannot be reduced to morality, and that indeed is misconceived when regarded as a matter of moral teaching. I also think that if religion has something to offer us at all, that something comes in its historical or revealed, not its natural, form. Nevertheless, I agree with Lessing that religious claims differ radically from ordinary historical ones, and that it cannot be historical *evidence* that establishes the truth of a historical religion. For which reason, I prefer to describe what I am talking about as "revealed" religion, rather than "historical" religion: revelations may take an ineliminably historical form, but what is true in them, if anything, is not an historical matter. Sometimes I will also use the phrase "traditional religion," by which I mean to highlight the fact that revealed religions get passed down by a set of social structures.[17]

One consequence of this approach to the subject is that I will not argue for the central tenets of any religion—even the existence of God.[18] Instead, I want to defend precisely the *non-argumentative mode* in which revealed or traditional religions offer their visions of how to live. This has advantages, I think, even for natural religion. I suspect that natural religion is not defensible as such, only to the degree that it supports revealed religion.

6. The second Enlightenment theme I want to stress is its critique of what it called "superstition" and "enthusiasm." "Superstition" referred to the falsehoods that, the Enlighteners maintained, clerical authorities spread in order to maintain their power; it was usually associated with the Catholic church. "Enthusiasm"—literally, having a god in oneself—is a state in which one feels one has direct, incorrigible knowledge of God's will, a state, therefore, of great passion for one's religion and of unshakeable conviction; it was generally associated with radical Protestant sects, especially the early Quakers. We might today use the term "fanaticism" for what the Enlighteners called "enthusiasm"—they often did so themselves.[19] And on the subject of superstition and enthusiasm, I think the Enlighteners' concerns were entirely justified.

The Enlightenment's opposition to enthusiasm appears in many places.[20] Once again, Smith makes a good starting point. In his *Wealth of Nations*, he mentions the political dangers posed by the "popular and bold, though perhaps stupid and ignorant enthusiasts" who arise from time to time to challenge more established church hierarchies, and looks forward to a time in which a climate of "good temper and moderation" in religious matters might replace "popular superstition and enthusiasm."[21] The rational religion he describes is supposed to be free of both "absurdity" (superstition) and "fanaticism," and his treatment of religion is concerned throughout with how best to tamp down the potentially dangerous "zeal" of teachers of new religions. In his *Theory of Moral Sentiments*, he argues that religious fanaticism can lead us to commit great evil in the name of goodness, illustrating his point with a Voltaire play in which two young people kill a kindly old man because their religious leaders tell them to. "False notions of religion," Smith says, "are almost the only causes which can occasion any gross perversion of our natural sentiments in this way" (TMS 176).

Again, Smith echoes Hume and foreshadows Kant. Hume had distinguished between superstition and enthusiasm, and shown how both threaten our political lives. Superstition, Hume says, derives from our fears, and consists in rituals we conduct to ward off evils. Because it draws on our weaknesses rather than our strengths, it is a state of mind that inclines us to seek guidance from other people, and to rely on them unquestioningly; it therefore helps priestly hierarchies gain power over us. Enthusiasm, by contrast, is a state of self-exaltation, of confidence and "presumption" in ourselves, which leads us into "raptures, transports, and surprising flights of fancy." We then convince ourselves that these come from God, and suppose them to be signs that God prefers us to the more ordinary people around us. In a state of enthusiasm, says Hume, "human reason, and even morality, are rejected as fallacious guides, and the fanatic madman delivers himself over, blindly and without reserve, to the supposed illapses of the Spirit, and to inspiration from above." Hume adds that superstition, because it favors priestly authority, tends to be opposed to civil liberty, while enthusiasm, since it breeds contempt for all authority, unites those in its throes with the most radical defenders of liberty. For this reason, he rather prefers enthusiasm to superstition. Enthusiasm, he says, initially "produces the most cruel disorders in human society," but it fades quickly and leaves fairly libertarian institutions in its wake, while superstition "steals in gradually and insensibly; renders men tame and submissive; is acceptable to the magistrate ... till at last the priest, having firmly established his authority, becomes the tyrant and disturber of human society, by his endless contentions, persecutions, and religious wars."[22]

Kant worries about the same issues, but he gives an epistemological rather than psychological analysis of the sources of enthusiasm and superstition, and considers them equally dangerous to liberty. In his *Critique of Pure Reason*, he claims that the cure for both enthusiasm and superstition is the establishment of the limits of reason: the very project to which the book is devoted. He is particularly worried about enthusiasm, which he regards as a grave intellectual and moral vice, even aside from its political dangers.[23] Kant claims that Locke's epistemology, by allowing for knowledge of things beyond experience, opens the door to enthusiasm; a properly critical understanding of reason will help us see that we could never have knowledge of the nature of our selves, or of the nature or existence of God (CPR B 127). In his *Critique of Practical Reason*, Kant coins the phrase "moral enthusiasm" for the state of mind in which a person imagines herself to have a "holy" will: imagines herself to will nothing but the good. Virtue, Kant says, is properly understood as "moral disposition *in conflict*," a striving to be good in full awareness of our temptations to evil. Those who "flatter[...] themselves with a spontaneous goodness of heart" are in danger of falling into "arrogance" or "self-conceit," dispositions which can be devastating to morality (CPrR 84–86). Finally, in an intriguing essay called "What does it mean to orient oneself in thinking?," Kant rejects the idea that reason may ever be guided by a non-rational faith—it must instead, he says, always be its own guide—largely because the alternative would open the floodgates of enthusiasm.[24] No inspiration or revelation can be the source of a belief in God, says Kant; reason alone must supply us with that belief.[25] If we don't follow this rule, not only will we fail in any case to achieve knowledge of God, but we will give everyone who supposes himself to be inspired license to regard his "daring flights" of fancy to be divine illumination. The supposed inspirations of these various "geniuses" will in all likelihood conflict, however, which will sow the seed for political strife, and if that strife is then settled by further, non-rational means, the result will be the predominance of systems of superstition, and the "subjugation of reason" that comes with such systems.[26] Thus, the end-result of giving license to enthusiasm, wonderfully free as that mode of thinking may at first appear, is a suppression of the freedom of thought, which Kant regards as our "holiest" possession.[27]

I think all these figures are right to see enthusiasm as dangerous, and I agree with Kant that those dangers are rooted in a failure to understand the nature of reason. Religious believers need squarely to face the fact that their beliefs can never amount to *knowledge*. That is one meaning of Kant's famous insistence that we must restrict the claims of knowledge to make room for the claims of faith. And claims of faith properly bring with them a humility, an attitude of uncertainty, that can serve as a bar to extremism and source of moderation.

I can now state my project more precisely: I'm trying to defend revealed religion without falling into enthusiasm. I endorse the Enlightenment's critique of the latter, but reject its view of the former. The point is to defend faith while being alert to the danger that it can arise out of, or be mixed with, a state of fear or arrogance or madness—to defend a faith consonant with decency and moderation: with what the Jewish tradition calls *derekh eretz*.

7. Very briefly, the defense of such faith I'll be offering runs as follows: I argue in the first two parts of this book that our notion of truth, and our moral norms, can and should be independent of religious underwriting: that they belong to the way of the world. Our cognitive and moral practices depend on a sort of social contract, I argue, allowing human beings to work together regardless of their religious differences. I then

try to show that a conception of ultimate worth—of why, if at all, life is worth living—cannot be determined on a secular basis. The way of the world breaks down when it comes to why we should value our lives (our social contracts do not suffice to answer that question) and it is this that revealed religions can illumine. The rest of the book explores what revelation is, why it can do better with the question of worth than secular worldviews do, and how the revealed and the way-of-the-world elements of a religious tradition can be brought together.

In a little more detail:

1. The concept of truth belongs wholly to the way of the world. The meaning it has in religious contexts must be the same as a meaning it bears in secular contexts as well; there can be no "special truth" for religious contexts alone. This is a point on which religious believers themselves should insist, if they understand themselves properly. To accept a revealed religion is to regard it *as true*. But we never call anything "true" unless we have an independent measure by which to assess it. Truth is also basic to how human beings construct any way of the world, and if we cannot share an understanding of what to do in this regard, we will be unable to share any activities at all. People of all religions and no religion use truth for a large number of shared purposes, to which, for the most part, religious commitments are irrelevant.

2. A similar point can be made about morality. We consider our revelations to be good as well as true, and to do that we need standards of goodness independent of revelation. When I call my revealed religion "good," I don't mean just that it is good in its own terms, but that it is so in an absolute sense. How far this point goes towards establishing the independence of morality from religion is a long-contested question.[28] I argue for a strong version of the independence thesis, for a view of morality on which it can rest on a number of different bases—on utilitarian, Kantian or Aristotelian grounds, among others—that may, but need not, include religious principles. The rabbinic sources we considered earlier were right to offer several different bases for *derekh eretz*. They were also right to keep those bases independent of religious teaching. That allows people of different religions to co-operate with and respect one another.

3. But the word "good" is ambiguous. It has purely moral uses, but can also be used to evaluate things relative to our personal goals, or to evaluate those goals relative to some measure of the worth of our life as a whole. In principle, these uses can come apart. It is meaningful, if perhaps never correct, to say, "That is a bad thing to do, even if it is good for you," or "The best life I can imagine would not be a morally good one." At the end of my discussion of morality, I distinguish between these two notions of goodness, and in Part III I suggest that secular proposals about what makes for a good life in the second sense—what makes for a life worth living—are far less successful than secular proposals about how to

understand moral goodness. My overall strategy, as regards these proposals, is to treat them as certain critics of religion, especially in the Marxist and Freudian traditions, have treated claims for the existence of God: to show both that they rest on dubious arguments and that intelligent people may cling to them anyway out of psychological needs or indoctrination by social institutions. The point is to show that secular views of the worth of our lives are on par with religious views on that subject. And the point of putting religious and secular views of worth on par with one another is to argue that if we are going to hold what is in any case a *faith* in, a non-rational love for or commitment to, some goal or vision of our lives, it is more appropriate that we openly recognize that commitment *as* a faith than that we suppose it to be rational. It is also more appropriate that the object of our faith be something that *calls* for faith, rather than something that purports to be accessible by reason alone. Finally, the objects of religious faith, I shall argue, are better suited than secular conceptions of a worthwhile life to answer the needs that lead us to seek such a conception.

4. This brings us to the door of revealed religion. It is of the nature of revelations to call for faith, to address our imaginations rather than our reason alone and to present a telos to us that we love, and that orients everything else we do, without our being able fully to articulate it. The very form of revealed texts shows this: a central feature of such texts is that they are obscure and poetic, favoring story-telling or enigmatic aphorisms over philosophical discourse. This is the case even in religious traditions that later give rise to a rich tradition of philosophical debate. I spend part IV of this book explaining why this feature is suited to the presentation of a goal for our lives in which we can appropriately put faith, and relating it to the moral, ritual, and communal features that also mark revealed religions.

5. I conclude by considering how believers in different revealed religions, and in none, can share a public realm. The main point here is that the independence of morality from questions of worth, and consequently from the answers to those questions that may be found in revelation, means that religious believers can take up a wholly secular approach to politics. If *derekh eretz* is sufficient to define and ground morality, then it is sufficient to define and ground politics. Moreover, the religious believer, as I understand her, is well aware that she has reached her commitments, not by a universally sharable form of reasoning, but by affections and experiences that other people may not share. Once she puts this realization together with the fact that she needs to share a political community with these other people, she has reason to conclude that she should elide her faith commitments when she enters the political arena. She is more likely to reach mutually acceptable compromises on policy with her neighbors if she does that, and she has principled reasons for wanting to live in a political community of free and equal individuals: only that preserves her own ability to maintain her faith and gives others the opportunity to come to a similar faith. One can thus get from a

religious route to what John Rawls calls "political liberalism": an approach to politics that prescinds from religious commitments.

From a secular point of view, of course, the religious person may be wrong or self-deluded to hold the faith she does. But the secular person needs to recognize that a religion rooted in an explicitly non-rational faith is not easily open to rational refutation. Some secular people may also accept the claim that all views of what makes life worth living are based on faith. These considerations are enough to give secular people reason not to work towards the elimination of religion, at least as long as they can co-operate with religious believers, in the public sphere, on the basis of a shared commitment to the way of the world. Again, we arrive at Rawlsian conclusions from an understanding of the nature of religious commitment. What secular people can and should ask of religious believers is that they recognize the need to accord with *derekh eretz*, not that they give up their Torah.

8. In some ways this is a very Jewish book, but it is not a book on Judaism. I do not enter into debate with contemporary Jewish philosophers,[29] nor do I comment more than glancingly on the great figures in medieval Jewish thought. And the view I present is meant to fit a wide range of religions. That said, I generally draw my examples of religious belief and practice from Jewish sources. I do this in the name of the old advice to authors of all kinds: write what you know. Perhaps that advice might be irrelevant to some works of philosophy—an abstract field if ever there was one—but a central strand of my position is that revealed religions speak to us through our personal histories, and the imaginations shaped by those histories, and I accordingly illustrate the workings of revealed religion with examples familiar to me from my own religious experience. Sometimes I also add in reflections, separated off from the main flow of the text, that have an autobiographical cast. It seems unlikely to me that one can understand other people's religious commitments without entering into them imaginatively to some extent, entering imaginatively into the way religion works in their lives.

My Jewish commitments may also help counter the strong Christian bias that otherwise dominates most scholarly discussion of religion.[30] Theorists of religion tend to take Christianity as the paradigm religion and then pinch and squeeze other traditions to fit that mold. Two features of this bias are (1) an over-emphasis on *belief* as opposed to practice—ritual is seen as adorning religious commitments, rather than being essential to them—and (2) a view of religions as always proclaiming themselves to be the one right view for all humanity. These points are related. If religions, like scientific theories, primarily offer beliefs, then one of them must be the correct set of such beliefs, or the best approximation thereto. If they are instead primarily ways of living, there may be many equally good ones, suited to different individuals or peoples depending on their interests or circumstances.

Consider, in this light, the definition of "religion" offered by Keith Yandell, in an introductory text on the subject that is intended to be pluralistic:

A religion proposes a *diagnosis* (an account of what it takes the basic problem facing human beings to be) and a *cure* (a way of permanently and desirably solving that problem): one basic problem shared by every human person and one fundamental solution that . . . is essentially the same across the board. . . . Different religions offer differing diagnoses and cures. Given that criterion, there are a good many religions. The diagnosis that a particular religion articulates asserts that every human person has a basic non-physical illness so deep that, unless it is cured, one's potential is unfulfilled and one's nature cripplingly flawed. Then a cure is proffered.[31]

Now I don't wholly disagree with this. Yandell locates the common ground across religions (what enables us to label them *as* "religions") in features of their form rather than their content and I will do something similar in this book. But the language he uses to describe these formal properties is markedly Christian. For *Christians*, we are all "ill" or "crippled" or "flawed" without faith in Christ, and that faith is the one cure, for everyone, for the problem so diagnosed. But these terms do not fit other traditions very well.

More precisely, there are three problems with Yandell's description. The first is the language of "illness" and "cure." Christians characteristically see non-Christians as having a deeply marred life, and perhaps such language is appropriate for Buddhists as well. In many other religions, however, believers hold that one's life will be *improved* if one follows their religious path, but not that it will be "cripplingly flawed" otherwise. We might think of how Aristotelians see the life of virtue. The fully virtuous person is certainly leading a *better* life than other people, but a person of incomplete or inadequately phronetic virtue need not be sick or failed or crippled. Similarly, many religions offer a path that they think makes for a better human life without holding that life on a different path is necessarily a failure.

Second, not every religion represents its vision or path as the right one for everyone. Christianity and Buddhism and Islam do, but they are not typical of religions across the board. Jews have long held that there are different legitimate paths to God, even if theirs is the only right one for members for the Jewish community. Other more tribally-oriented religions, including most variants of Hinduism, either hold a similar view or have little to say about what sort of religious commitment people outside their communities should have. This point is connected to the previous one. If one regards one's path as something that improves human life, but not something that cures a deep illness or removes a crippling flaw from our lives, then one is less likely to think it imperative that everyone follow one's path.

Third, Yandell's description makes religion look too intellectual. Each religion, for Yandell, is a doctor, with a "diagnosis" of what is wrong with us and a "cure" related to that diagnosis, or else a philosopher, recognizing a "problem" and proposing a "solution." Again, this fits religions with a central doctrine, like Christianity or Buddhism; it doesn't fit religions like Judaism or Hinduism or Taoism, in which stories and rituals take precedence over doctrine, and there may be no doctrine that all the adherents share. (A Maimonidean and a kabbalistic understanding of Judaism can be almost exact opposites of each other.) Again, this point goes along with the other two. To the extent that a religion emphasizes practice or story-telling over doctrine, it need not have a view about human nature in general, and may be able to recognize—given how linked to history practices and stories tend to be—that other ways of life are more suited to communities with other histories.

One might respond to all this by saying that if Yandell's description fits Christianity, Islam, and Buddhism, it covers the majority of the world's population, so the fact that it fails to fit, say, Judaism, Zoroastrianism, and the beliefs of various aboriginal groups doesn't matter much. But, in coming up with the relevant instances of "religion," why count individuals, rather than groups? There are hundreds, perhaps thousands, of small religions that do not fit Yandell's pattern, so even if several large groups do, it's not clear what that proves. Size is surely not a sign of intrinsic superiority: religions generally become large by way of conquest and oppression. Moreover, if we look to human history as a whole, it will almost certainly not be true that the majority of the world's people have seen their religions as something that ought to hold for everyone, or as a cure for a disease from which all human beings suffer. The polytheistic cults of ancient Egypt and Assyria and Greece did not see themselves that way, nor did they expect all human beings to share their mode of worship.

Finally, Yandell's description gives us a misleading picture even of its paradigm cases. Christian and Buddhist leaders may represent their religions as he describes them, but ordinary Christians and Buddhists often feel attached to their religion as much because they associate its practices with their parents and community as for any doctrinal reason, and are, consequently, as attached to practices or ideas sanctioned by local custom as to what they are "supposed" to believe and do. A Tibetan Buddhist may hold many beliefs, and carry out many practices, that a learned monk in his community would condemn as barriers to enlightenment. Many Christians identify Christmas as much with its pagan tree as with the legend of the Christ child. Many Muslims, across Africa and Asia, don't distinguish their tribal practices from Islam proper, and a Hindu in Bali may have little in common with a Hindu in New Delhi. To come to all these people and tell them that *really* the core of their religion is its solution to a problem from which all human beings suffer, and that the local beliefs and practices they cherish are just so much window-dressing, is not only condescending, but, as a descriptive matter, very likely false. What Yandell has done, like many a Christian (and particularly a Protestant) theologian before him, is take a peculiarly Christian (and again even more peculiarly Protestant) view of religion as essentially addressed to the private, mental space of everyone's individual conscience, and project that onto the vast variety of actual religious traditions. One can certainly find *elements* of this view in many traditions, but those elements do not define every such tradition—even, indeed, every Christian tradition.

The sense in which this book represents a "Jewish" view of religion is thus a sense in which it may speak for the many forms of religion, including local forms of Christianity, that fail to satisfy the dominant Christian model for what religions should look like. Perhaps that can help widen our understanding of religion. In any case, I am trying to construct a view that fits many different religious traditions.

Accordingly, my central point is to defend the *idea* of revealed religion rather than any particular such religion. Although I use Judaism as my main example, I mean what I say to be of value to all religions, including non-theistic ones, that employ the notion of a revealed or sacred text. I do not even mean by this to cover just literate traditions: an oral teaching passed down from generation to generation will count as a "text" for my purposes.[32] It is the idea that one might find one's primary guide to life in an authoritative text or set of sayings, the idea—as Kant put it contemptuously (RWB 107)—that "it is written" is sufficient to justify some of one's main choices in life, that I want to defend. That notion alone is considered by many to be anathema to rational thought, the antithesis of what the 18th century called "enlightenment." Yet without it, I will suggest, we may be unable to establish a view of our lives as worth living.

But there is a certain oddity in defending the idea of revelation without defending any particular revelation. Many revealed religions, after all, do teach that they possess the only, or at least best, revelation. So to defend the fact *that* one should submit to revelation without defending any particular revelation might seem to undermine what it is that revelations have to teach. It is presumably for that reason that when I say I am defending revelations generally, friends often ask, "But how can you? They contradict one another."[33]

My response to that challenge is as follows: first, to defend a religious tradition is not to defend everything said in the name of that tradition. That would be impossible. Virtually every religious tradition contains conflicting strands and to make a case for its plausibility, one inevitably stresses some of these strands over others. To defend Maimonides's view of Judaism is to reject Kabbalistic understandings of Judaism; to defend Calvinist Christianity is to reject Catholicism; to defend Theravada Buddhism is to reject Mahayana versions of that tradition. So there should be no problem in principle about defending a religious tradition while rejecting its claim to exclusive truth or goodness. One could in principle defend all revealed religions while insisting that the claim, made by many of them, that there is only one true revelation must be reinterpreted or rejected.

But I have put the phrase "in principle" in the last two sentences because in fact the exclusivist claims of most religious traditions are hard to elide. That their vision of the good is the only correct one has been fundamental to Christianity, Buddhism, and Islam, and tied to the morally attractive universalism of these traditions: they can welcome each and every human being precisely because they claim to offer the best way of life for all human beings. Judaism, Hinduism, Confucianism, and most small tribal religions are more pluralistic (and, correlatively, more provincial), but it is essential to them, too, to reject some other religious traditions. It is crucial to Judaism to reject idolatry, for instance.

So it is not so easy in practice to defend revelation without defending some forms of revelation against others, and it may be impossible to show that any revealed religion offers a good way to live if a condition on its doing that is accepting all other revealed religions as equally good. Fortunately, my aspirations are not as radically pluralistic as all that. I want to make sense of the notion of revelation, while leaving *open* the question of whether any particular revealed religion, or set of such religions, has reason to proclaim itself the best or only good way to live. A believer who accepts the claims I make could go on to add that all revealed religions essentially contain the same core of truth or goodness and it doesn't matter which a person adheres to. Other believers might accept my argument, while holding that only some revealed religions are good or true—perhaps only one—but that those adhering to false or improper revealed religions, as long as they are morally decent, may be forgiven by God for making such a mistake. And still other believers could accept my claims on behalf of the idea of revelation, while adding that those who adhere to any revelation but their own are condemned to perdition. The thesis of my book is compatible with both pluralistic and monistic religious convictions. These convictions come with the *content* of particular revelations, while my thesis is about the *form* of revelation, about what it is to accept a scripture or set of sayings as the primary guide to one's life, and why that can be a good thing. This formal point has no direct implications for the content of revelation, although I will eventually suggest that it fits especially well with a certain degree of pluralism.

9. A natural question about my project concerns the extent to which it is historically conditioned. Am I offering a defense of revealed religion that is relevant just to people who take the European Enlightenment seriously? Is there not something very new, dating perhaps just to the European Enlightenment, about the very idea of divided "secular" and "religious" realms?[34]

The answer to these questions is both yes and no. Yes, in that I think any religious believer today needs to face the severe challenges to the intellectual underpinning of religion that have been accruing over the past three or four centuries. A world in which a naturalistic account can be given for practically every physical and psychical occurrence, in which all appearance of natural design can be explained instead by causal mechanisms, and in which the historical claims underlying most religious scriptures have been thoroughly debunked, is a world in which it is far harder to believe in a God, let alone the God proclaimed by a traditional scripture, than it ever was before. The fact that the scientific enterprise that began in the 17th century severely challenges the distinctive claims of traditional religious systems is something that adherents of those systems cannot afford to ignore. The novelty of this challenge is sometimes exaggerated—the Aristotelian science that dominated Europe and the Arab world in the medieval period was also in severe tension with traditional Christian, Muslim, and Jewish beliefs—but modern science does pose a more comprehensive and radical threat to traditional religious belief than any prior approach to the explanation of nature.

We may add to this the fact that the post-Enlightenment world, for the first time in human history, includes many large countries in which the vast majority of the population regard themselves as having no religion, and that those countries have nevertheless remained politically stable, and not experienced a notable decline in everyday moral behavior. Indeed, in many ways the Enlightenment seems to have fostered a notable *improvement* in moral attitudes: an increase in tolerant and cosmopolitan attitudes, especially. This gives the lie to the predictions of those who have resisted the Enlightenment by claiming that an abandonment of traditional religion leads to moral and political collapse.

So yes, the Enlightenment poses a serious challenge to traditional religious belief and this book is a response to that challenge. In that sense, what I say here is conditioned by historical contingencies. But I am also trying to sketch features that I believe religions generally need to have, and to respond to problems that arise for any religious believer anywhere and anywhen. In particular, the idea that there is or should be a distinction between a secular and a religious realm, for all that it may have been formulated particularly clearly in recent centuries, is neither altogether new nor something that any religious community can afford to do without. To be sure, in the past the "secular" (worldly) realm[35] was often conceived as one in which people might retain some belief in a God or other supernatural principle—one way in which the modern age differs from its predecessors is that we no longer think even the existence of God can be shown by reason alone. But the idea that there should be some part of human life, and some public arena, in which people hold at a distance the thick commitments of their religious traditions can be found in many premodern societies. We have seen intimations of this idea in the rabbis' talk of "the way of the world," and their reflections on that topic are in turn a response to the realities of the Roman Empire, where a variety of religious groups, along with some atheists, lived side by side and shared a good number of moral and epistemic principles. Augustine's description of the "city of man" is but one, late way of characterizing that social reality, and his distinction between this city and the city of God is one version of the secular/religious division.

Elsewhere, we find religions that share a social space with one another setting up neutral arenas in which their distinctive beliefs can be laid aside for the purposes of dialogue. In 10th-century Baghdad, there were philosophical discussion groups that included Muslims of different sects as well as "Magians, materialists, atheists, Jews and Christians"—"in short," as one displeased Muslim observer said, "unbelievers of all kinds." This observer went on to describe the discussions as follows:

One of the unbelievers rose and said to the assembly: we are meeting here for a discussion. Its conditions are known to all. You, Muslims, are not allowed to argue from your books and prophetic traditions since we deny both. Everybody, therefore, has to limit himself to rational arguments. The whole assembly applauded these words ... They proposed to me that I should attend another meeting in a different hall, but I found the same calamity there.[36]

Similarly, in 6th-century India the epistemological writings of Dignaga are said by scholars to have inaugurated the development of a "relatively neutral framework within which competing claims of Indian philosophical schools, such as Nyaya, Mimamsa, Jain, and Buddhist, could be assessed."[37] And the great Buddhist emperor

Ashoka, almost half a millenium earlier, proclaimed a minimal set of moral standards for all people to uphold regardless of religious commitment, and recognized, as part of that minimal morality, the importance of respecting people with different religious beliefs.[38]

So the idea of a realm that suspends religious premises is not wholly new with the Enlightenment, nor is the idea that religious believers need both to draw on that realm and to keep a certain distance from it. To be sure, the secular world that opened up in the Enlightenment was more threatening to traditional religious belief than any prior such realm had been. But these are differences of degree, not kind. The idea of a realm unmarked by religious traditions was already around in far more religious ages; it is an idea that arises naturally as soon as people who live with religious difference start to reflect on their epistemic and moral practices. It is also a notion, I shall argue, that religious believers need, if they are to achieve what they themselves regard as the ends of their faith.

Of course, this last claim is controversial. The possibility of separating the secular from the sacred has never been accepted by all religious believers. The Baghdadi debates I cited above were repudiated as heretical by many Muslims. Augustine regarded the city of man, in isolation from the city of God, as a place of vice and corruption. And many believers today—from sophisticated religious philosophers who argue that faith penetrates into all areas of life to the so-called "fundamentalists," in Christian, Muslim, Jewish, and Hindu communities, who abjure modern science and liberal ethical principles—regard the distinction as either incoherent or a temptation to evil. So the mode of faith in revealed religion I will be defending is not a mode that all believers in such religions share. But I am not engaged in a purely descriptive project, or an attempt to vindicate all types of religious belief. I would not venture to assert that the type of belief I am defending is even the average or dominant one, in my own or any other religious community. What I am trying to lay out is a type of revealed religious faith that I think is *defensible*, in general and especially in light of the powerful criticisms of such faith that arose in the Enlightenment.[39] My project is a normative one, meant to show how I think religious believers *should* regard their traditions and not just to explain those traditions.

There are other ways to defend revealed religion. Some begin from an attempt to prove certain metaphysical propositions and then demonstrate that a particular revealed text, or canonical creed, captures those propositions well. Others strip religious belief more fully of cognitive content than I am willing to do, and then defend a commitment to religion as something that has moral or political value, or that people rightly take to be important because of the affective goods—the joy or comfort—it brings them. I am skeptical of the arguments offered by those who take the first approach, and inclined to find the kind of religion defended by the second approach too thin to accomplish what I think religions should accomplish. But I think there is some merit to these alternative approaches, and will not on the whole be arguing against them here. My concern is to show that the view of religion I propose is *a* defensible one, not the only defensible one. I do of course regard some views as indefensible. For one thing, any acceptable mode of religious faith must on my account accept the legitimacy of modern science and modern, liberal morality.

10. Finally, when I describe my project as a "defense," I mean by that more what used to be called an "apologia" than an argument designed to show the superiority of religious to secular ways of life. My hope is to help those of us who are religious to explain to ourselves what we are doing, and the non-religious to see it as, at least, not dangerous, foolish, or insane. Following a revealed religion is widely thought today to be illiberal, to constitute a rejection of the freedom and common humanity for which the Enlightenment stood. I hope to show that that need not be so.

Of course, the commitments of some religious believers *are* illiberal—are indeed dangerous, foolish, and insane. Indeed, many religious believers today pose a grave threat to freedom and international peace. But that threat, I believe, is not inherent to revealed religion. Most Enlightenment intellectuals thought otherwise. They held that the faith in texts that defines revealed religion—the idea that a text can be "sacred"—leads people to resist critical scrutiny of their beliefs, substitute a blind acceptance of what the text prescribes for ordinary decency and moral reasoning, and fight with followers of other texts. I don't think any of these things needs to come along with faith in a text, and I try here to work out a view of such faith that embraces critical reasoning, a sharing of moral principles with people of all religions and none, and an openness to the goodness of faiths other than one's own. By arguing that these broadly liberal points follow from the way revelation is best understood, I hope to offer a model of a properly *religious* liberalism, a liberalism that grows out of religious commitment rather than being grafted on to it from the outside. In short, I try to develop a liberal, Enlightened understanding of religion from within the very type of religion that the Enlightenment rejected.

PART I

The Way of the World (I)

TRUTH

For what merit can there be in believing God or his Providence upon frivolous and weak grounds?...Excellent character of the God of Truth! that he should be offended at us for having refused to put the lie upon our understandings,...and be satisfied with us for having believed...what might have been the greatest falsehood in the world, for anything we could bring as a proof or evidence to the contrary!

—Lord Shaftesbury, *Letter Concerning Enthusiasm*

1

Introductory

1. David Hare's intriguing recent play *Gethsemane,* which touches at a number of points on the role of religion in contemporary life, opens with the following monologue:

For some reason I can't explain to you people believe in a book. They choose to believe in one book. They find a book and they decide they believe in it. In this book, they say, all wisdom resides. Different people choose different books, most of them according to where they were born. They hold up the book. "Everything that is true," they say, "is in this book."

Who, then, are we? The rest of us? The people who say, "Perhaps." Or "Explain to me, please." Or, "Well, I'm not sure"? Who are we?

We are the people without a book.[1]

The character delivering this monologue is the most sympathetic one in the play, and may represent the author. If so, the point of having her begin the play with this speech would seem to be to invite the audience into an "us vs. them" attitude towards traditionally religious people.[2] The tone of the monologue, as regards those who "believe in a book," is a sharply critical one, and the audience is clearly expected to identify with the "we" who do without "a book." Nevertheless, the monologue presents the central aim of my defense of revealed religions quite nicely: I'd like to help show people like this character why people do believe in a book—even if they choose it according to where they were born. The character says she can't explain this; I'd like to explain it to her, give reasons that make some sense of why one might hold up a book and say, "In this book . . . all wisdom resides."

Nevertheless, some elements of the way Hare presents revealed religions give me pause and I do not mean to defend them. Not everyone who tries to follow the vision or path laid out in a book will refuse doubt. Many believers say "Perhaps" and "Well, I'm not sure" about the doctrines of their religious tradition, even while trying to maintain a faith in those doctrines, and ask their religious leaders and fellow believers to "Explain to them, please" how troubling passages in the sacred text should be understood or what it means for the text to be sacred. Secular people do not have a monopoly on skepticism and humility, and religious believers are not necessarily unquestioning or arrogant.

More deeply, not everyone committed to a scripture will say, "Everything that is true . . . is in this book." One can be committed to a scripture, but recognize other sources of truth as well (for medieval Christians, God wrote two books: the Bible and the book of nature). Or one might say that all "wisdom", but not all "truth" resides there; one might distinguish wisdom and truth.

What difference might there be between wisdom and truth? Well, "wisdom" is a word often used for particularly *important* or *profound* truths, truths that have great significance for how we lead our lives. A person of wisdom might, indeed, be someone who *fails* to grasp everyday, trivial truths about, say, fashion or the best way to clean vegetables. To employ terms I will come back to later, we might take wisdom to be a grasp of truths about the purpose or worth of our lives as a whole. I will argue that a traditional religious believer is necessarily committed to seeing a particular book as containing the best or fullest guide to *this* sort of truth. But she need not see her sacred text as the repository or source of *all* truth. She may instead see scientific and most moral truths as quite independent of her book. I will, in fact, argue that she *must* see science and morality this way if she is to make sense of the very wisdom that she attributes to her sacred guide. She will need to fit her divine teaching in with a science and morality that belong to the way of the world, if she is to be able to persuade even herself, over the long run, that her chosen book is the font of all wisdom. Regarding her book as containing all wisdom will entail regarding it as *not* containing all *truth*. Scientific truth, especially, will have to lie outside the book.

2. Many people hold today that there is an irreconcilable conflict between religion and science. Many religious believers are skeptical of theories of biology and astrophysics that seem to contradict their sacred scriptures; many non-believers point to the same tensions as evidence that science has refuted religion. And modern science certainly poses a host of challenges for those who want to regard the Bible and Quran as true.

Still, it's tempting to make short work of the idea that scientific evidence could demonstrate either the truth or the falsehood of a sacred text. What makes us regard such texts as "revealed" at all is that we suppose them to uncover for us something *super-natural*, a being or condition beyond what we experience in the natural world. But science is geared to study precisely the natural world, and makes presuppositions that make it impossible for it to judge either that there does or that there does not exist anything beyond nature. This, in essence, is David Hume's point in his famous essay on miracles.[3] Inductive evidence—the kind of evidence that establishes scientific claims—works by assimilating particular observation claims to what we believe more generally about experience.[4] Consequently, the reasons in favor of a claim purporting to show that the entire course of nature has at some point been suspended or overturned will always be outweighed by the reasons against it. To tweak Hume's famous conclusion a little: "[N]o [empirical evidence] is sufficient to establish a miracle, unless the [evidence] be of such a kind, that its falsehood would be more miraculous, than the fact, which it endeavors to establish; and even in that case there is a mutual destruction of arguments."[5]

We might approach the same point from an ontological direction: by considering where a supernatural being or event would fit among the natural ones. Can God be placed among the things in space and time? Is He next to one thing, or around the corner from another? (Could MapQuest tell me how to find Him?) Does He show up on Tuesdays at Mount Sinai, and on Thursdays in Mecca or Varanasi? These are ridiculous questions, but they suggest that the idea of an *experience* of God, at least the sort of experience that a scientist could use—the object of which the scientist might locate, even probabilistically, in space and time—is also ridiculous. Nor does it help to switch our attention to non-theistic religions. If the *tao* is really beyond all the particular things in the world, and if Buddhist enlightenment is really unlike any state human beings arrive at naturally, then how could there possibly be scientific evidence that there is a *tao*, or that anyone has ever achieved Buddhist enlightenment?

From here it should be fairly obvious that what a sacred text is supposed to show us cannot possibly be something science could either prove or disprove. Even if one found evidence that the Israelites came out of Egypt just as the Torah says they did, and the Red Sea split for them, that wouldn't show that *God* was behind these events. Conversely, it could be true that God wants the Jewish people to keep the laws of the Torah even if none of the historical events described therein ever occurred. The same goes for all other sacred texts. The history recounted in the Gospels, even the existence of Jesus of Nazareth, is neither necessary nor sufficient for the truth of the claims that the Gospels make about God's relationship to us, nor is historical evidence of any sort either necessary or sufficient for the truth of the claim that the Quran is the best source for understanding God's nature, and how we should submit to Him. Gotthold Lessing noted that "accidental truths of history can never become the proof of necessary truths of [religion]."[6] Even if Jesus of Nazareth was resurrected, Lessing asks, why "should I form all my metaphysical and moral ideas accordingly"? Between the historical claims of the Gospels (or those of any other revealed text) and the metaphysical and moral beliefs that we properly designate as "religious" ones, there is a great gulf fixed—an "ugly, broad ditch which I cannot get across, however often and however earnestly I have tried to make the leap."[7] It is this passage that gave rise to the phrase, "leap of faith": it is Lessing who set up the challenge that Kierkegaard tried to respond to, with his weird, brilliant defense of Christianity, seventy years later. And Kierkegaard provides an excellent model for how to distinguish religious from historical teachings—from metaphysical and moral ones too, actually—which I follow here to a considerable extent.

3. Perhaps it should be fairly obvious that the truths of history are one thing and the truths of religion another, but to many people, it is not. Prominent Jewish scholars and rabbinic leaders are prone to making pronouncements of the sort, "We now know that the Torah was not, historically, given at Sinai to Moses: therefore it is not the word of God," or "We must believe that the Torah is the word of God: therefore we must regard it as having been given, historically, by God to Moses at Sinai."[8] Similarly, even the sophisticated Christian theologian C. Stephen Evans, a Kierkegaard scholar who

mostly defends a thoughtful fideism, insists that some historical claims are essential to Christianity: that, for example, one would be wrong to remain a Christian in the face of "overwhelmingly powerful evidence that Jesus never existed."[9] These are signs of a scientistic prejudice so deep and widespread that no quick attempt to separate historical from religious truths is likely to make much headway against it. Let that be my excuse for elaborating the point a little.

Historical facts fit within the course of nature and are verified in the same way as other natural facts. Did a large meteor collide with the earth millions of years ago? We find out by examining geological formations, analyzing soils, and fitting the possible collision into our general physical, chemical, and biological theories. We think, if we had been there and seen it, we would know for certain. Did Julius Caesar have an affair with Cleopatra? Did Giuseppe Verdi complete part of an opera based on *King Lear*? We use different sorts of sources as evidence for these claims, and assess their likelihood by fitting them in with different sorts of general knowledge (about human psychology, rather than geology, for instance). But the *type* of investigation is broadly similar, and the status of the evidence that will settle it is, in principle, identical. We again think, if we had been at Caesar's or Verdi's side, we would know the answers to our questions for certain.

Nor are these merely epistemic points. To be an historical fact is to be the sort of *thing* that can be investigated historically. Epistemology and ontology are linked. We use certain methods of investigation to determine historical facts because we believe that those methods track the nature of these kinds of facts (we use different methods to determine mathematical facts, because we are tracking different kind of *things*), and we identify certain things as historical facts because we see them as suitably investigated by historical means.

So, to call God's speaking on Sinai (or as Jesus in the Galilee, or, through the angel Gibreel, to Muhammad) an "historical fact" is to say that historical methods of investigation would suffice to establish it. But they would not. The very idea of God is the idea of a being beyond all of nature, who can control nature itself. No amount of historical evidence could prove that *that* being appeared at a point within the natural course of things. Indeed, the mere idea that they *could* prove such a thing is a betrayal of the idea of God, a suggestion that God is just one being in the universe among others. For God's appearance in history to be pinned down by scientific investigation would be for God to be subject to the forces of the universe, rather than to be the source of or governor of those forces. A god who can be studied by science is an idol, rather than God, even if there is just one such god, and to believe that the unique God in or on whom the universe is supposed to rest can be known scientifically is to reduce monotheism to idolatry.

It follows that the entire modern debate over the historical veracity of sacred texts is confused. Neither those who say that we know now that the Torah (or Gospels or Quran) is not God's word, since historical evidence indicates that the events at Sinai never took place, nor those who purport to have proof that God did speak at Sinai (or in the Galilee or outside Medina)—from spurious historical evidence to the faux science on display in books like *The Bible Code*—properly understand what it means for God to "speak" at all. Evidence that God spoke as one human being to another would not be evidence that *God* spoke. Even if, say, an apparently disembodied voice, accompanied by thunder and mysterious trumpet blasts, once uttered remarkably accurate prophecies and deep nuggets of moral wisdom, that would indicate just that there are powers in the universe beyond those with which we are acquainted. Erich von Däniken's hypothesis, in *Chariots of the Gods*, that all supposed religious revelations are really records of visits to earth by intelligent creatures from outer space is very silly, but *as an empirical explanation* of Sinai, it is better than the hypothesis that the speaker was God. (A better explanation is, of course, the Humean one: that the very event attested to by the Torah is excellent reason to disbelieve the testimony.) At best, evidence that the event at Sinai took place as described might be evidence for a superhero god. It is very unlikely, but we just might be able to show that a creature rather like Spiderman or Dumbledore killed all the Egyptian firstborn, split the Red Sea for the Israelites, and produced a grand sound and light show at Mount Sinai. That would fall far short of showing that *an all-powerful, all-wise and all-good source of the universe* had done these things, or had spoken to human beings. The notion of a power over-turning the usual course of events, whose presence can yet be determined by scientific means, is just a notion of an unusual, surprising power *within* the universe, a sort of magic or a force hitherto relegated to science fiction. The notion of *God* speaking, or otherwise intervening in human history, defies our very conception of how nature works, and of what a historical event is. So the hypothesis that God has spoken to us can neither be confirmed nor disconfirmed by the findings of historians, or other scientists.

4. The presupposition of everything I have said so far is that "science" means modern science, the approach to understanding the universe that has developed in the West since the early 17th century or so. Both the idea that religion and science conflict with one another, and the idea that they are talking about wholly different things, are quite new, not to be found to anything like the same degree in the West before the 17th century, or anywhere outside the West until the scientific project that began in 17th-century Europe spread through the rest of the globe. Arguably, this is because "science," in the sense we use that word today, did not exist until Europe's scientific revolution. And it is certainly true that the thoroughgoing mechanical, rather than teleological, modes of explanation insisted upon by Bacon and Descartes, the highly mathematized physics initiated by Newton, the use of sophisticated instruments like the telescope and microscope to make observations, and the notion of controlled experimentation developed in the 18th century, constitute a radically new way of acquiring knowledge about nature. But the idea that we can improve our knowledge of nature by investigating it systematically, rather than relying on the information gleaned casually in common life, and the idea that mathematics, and

a particular kind of observation, is essential to that sort of investigation, have been around in many cultures, for a very long time. The biology of Aristotle, and the astronomy and medicine of ancient China, certainly deserve the title "science," and it is not inappropriate to use that term for the general theories about nature used to correct ordinary observation in any culture.

And in that sense of "science," the relationship between science and religion today is quite different from what it has been in the past. Earlier scientific theories usually claimed to give evidence *for* the existence of a God or gods, and often to accommodate large parts of their host culture's more specific religious beliefs as well. A well-educated person who lived in the Muslim world of Ibn Sina and Ibn Rushd, the Christian world of Anselm or Aquinas, or the Jewish world of Maimonides, would have had every reason to think that science *supported* the foundations of his religious beliefs, that only fools did not believe in God, and that the histories recounted in the Muslim, Christian, and Jewish sacred texts were at least by and large accurate. This is not to deny that there was tension between science and religion in the pre-modern world. The Aristotelian physics that dominated Muslim, Christian and Jewish civilization had little room for miracles and free will, for instance, and generally promoted a view of the world as eternal, rather than created. Maimonides, for one, struggled mightily to reconcile the picture of God that he got from Aristotelian science with the one he found in Hebrew Scripture and the writings of the rabbis. Indeed, in a remarkable passage—used by some Jews today as a model for how one might respond to evolution—he says that if the creation were shown to be scientifically impossible, we would have to reinterpret Genesis.[10]

But in the pre-modern world there were simply *moments* of tension between religious systems and a science on the whole amenable to the idea that the universe is shaped by a divine being. Today, we have a science whose practitioners leave God wholly out of their work, whose basic principles are widely and reasonably understood to require no such hypothesis, and whose application to history has thoroughly undermined the credibility of most supposedly sacred scriptures—especially the ancient Hebrew stories so important to Judaism, Christianity, and Islam. A well-educated modern person reasonably believes that science does *not* support the foundations of any religion, and that there is nothing foolish about the many people who see no reason to believe in a God, or any other supernatural entity or structure.

Exactly why modern science is so different from its predecessors is a complicated and controversial story, to which I cannot devote much attention here. Of the various distinctive features of modern science I have listed, I think the insistence on mechanical, rather than teleological, modes of explanation is the most important, and I will occasionally touch on the implications of that shift when I take up the subject of the telos, if any, of our own lives. But for the moment, all we need to bear in mind is that modern science—the most successful attempt to predict and control nature in human history—is almost universally regarded as not requiring the metaphysical propositions so important to religious believers, and undermining many of their central historical claims.

To which one response, on the part of the believers, is to reject modern science, despite its great successes. This is a move I think we need firmly to disallow. Not that it can be clearly and decisively refuted. Time was when scientists and philosophers of science thought they could show that anyone who did not accept the results of modern science was irrational, in a strict sense of that word. Few would make such strong claims today. The idea that the norms validating modern science are built into the structure of reason itself, the idea that modern science can essentially be *deduced* from observational data, has gone by the board, as having been based on a naive philosophy of language, and a metaphysics that could not substantiate its own supposedly anti-metaphysical first principles. In its place have come demonstrations of the cultural-embeddedness of scientific practice, arguments that we can never defend science as a whole, just particular scientific models, and investigations of the centrality of testimony to the way all of us, including scientists, form our beliefs. In this context it is not flatly irrational for a religious believer to say, "You have your practices and models and experts and I have mine. You accept scientific paradigms and experts as your arbiters of factual matters, and I accept the word of my scripture and religious teachers." If there is something wrong with this attitude, it is not a matter of logic, a violation of the law of non-contradiction.

My main concern in this Part of my book is to show that there nevertheless is something wrong with this attitude—that religious believers have as much reason as everyone else to accept the word of scientific experts on empirical matters, even when those experts contradict their religious texts and teachers. Religious believers who challenge modern science are right to stress the fact that science depends on testimony and trust just as religion does. But they are wrong to treat testimony and trust in empirical matters as just like testimony and trust in religious matters. Almost all believers in the theory of evolution rely on the word of scientists, rather than carrying out the relevant experiments and model-building themselves. That may look like a kind of faith in scientists, analogous to the faith that religious people put in their scriptures. There are important differences between the two, however. They need to be teased apart, and given their different respective due in the different spheres of our lives to which they are relevant. Anything else will corrupt both religion and science.

5. We may sum up the discussion thus far, and indicate the burden of my argument in the rest of this Part, by way of three interconnected points. First, there is a great mistake in thinking that religious scriptures can either be validated by scientific means or used to show that scientific results are wrong. The best science human beings have developed to date tends to show that all known scriptures are filled with falsehoods, if read literally, and that the traditional doctrines upheld by their followers on subjects like astrophysics, biology, and history are largely false. This matters less than it may seem, however, because science is not the right sort of discipline to validate

religious claims. So there is a mistaken scientism both in trying to defend scriptural claims with scientific evidence and in insisting that a scripture must be false because it fails scientific tests.

Which brings us to the second point: that our secular ("way-of-the-world") practices and beliefs endorse modes of establishing truth other than scientific ones, and that it is to some of them, and not to science, that we should look when trying to establish whether or not to regard a religious scripture as true. The model for religious truth is secular ethical or other evaluative truth, and we need to be clear about how that sort of truth functions, and differs from scientific truth, if we are to understand the proper basis on which to accept or reject a scripture.

And third, it goes with any attempt to claim a non-scientific truth for scriptural claims that those claims, insofar as they look like scientific ones, need to be reinterpreted. In general, the idea that a god or supernaturally enlightened human being is the author of a certain text radically changes how we read that text. Ordinarily, we assume that a text means something its human author might have intended to say; we take the worldview accepted in his or her time to delimit what he or she is likely to have meant. An author writing in the 8th century CE is unlikely to have believed in a heliocentric universe and could not possibly have had views on the structure of DNA. We go wrong, consequently, if we interpret something he says by attributing beliefs of this sort to him. But once we regard a text as ultimately authored by God, or by a person with a wisdom beyond that of all ordinary human beings, these limits on interpretation fall away. If there is an all-wise Being in the universe, that Being *could* have intended a text composed by human beings in the 2nd century BCE to present truths that can be fully appreciated only in the 21st century CE. And the Buddha, if he achieved what his followers think he achieved, could also have meant to teach humankind something that no-one would properly understand for millennia. A supernaturally wise author could also compose a text whose true meaning differs from generation to generation. So it makes sense in these cases, as it does not in ordinary interpretation, to seek meanings for the text that an ordinary human author could not possibly have intended. In particular, we need not give a scientific meaning even to claims that, when originally written down, were surely meant by their *human* authors to describe the natural world.

6. We turn now to why truth must belong to the way of the world—why secular and religious people must share ways of determining truth.

One might think that we should define truth first, before moving to ways people determine truth. But truth is exceedingly hard to define, and for our purposes, we can avoid most of the debates over its definition. Philosophers have wrangled for millennia over its meaning, proposing correspondence, coherence, and pragmatic accounts of it and more recently suggesting that it may be virtually empty—that saying "p is true" amounts to little more than just saying "p."[11] These debates tend to be too abstract to affect ordinary disagreements over *what* is true, however, whether between religious and secular people or anyone else. I therefore propose on the whole to finesse debates over what "truth" properly means—although I will try to suggest that one use of that word makes better sense of what we mean when we apply it to revelations than other uses—and focus instead on the question of how we should *determine* truths. And the view I want to defend is that people committed to revealed religion must determine scientific truths in the same way that secular people do, and that the distinctive mode they have for determining some ethical truths must also be legitimized, in the first instance, by practices they share with everyone else.

I will proceed by first surveying a variety of commonsensical considerations that support this view, and then turn to a more formal way of defending it.

7. Here are a number of points indicating that religious and secular people either in fact share ways of determining truth or should do so, from the religious point of view itself:

- First, it seems to be a brute fact about human beings that we have no trouble agreeing on the truth of some claims—ordinary empirical ones, especially— regardless of the deep differences we may have in our worldviews as a whole. Even across vast gaps in religious commitment, culture and ideology, we are likely to come to quick and easy agreement on whether the fruit before us is an apple or a fig, whether a house is collapsing or not, whether a person holding a spear is dangerous or not. Different scientific and religious theories will account for this convergence in different ways, but the point for now is just that they all need to recognize that we *do* converge on many ordinary empirical facts, and their implications.

- Second, religious and secular people share many purposes for which they need to agree about facts. To get food, make clothes, build houses, and fend off threats, human beings need to work together, and therefore reach agreement on where the deer or apple trees are, what makes for a warm coat or stable house, which animals and other people are dangerous, etc. This is a point that sometimes gets lost in debates over truth. When followers of certain academic ideologies insist that the notion of truth is endlessly contestable, it is useful to remind them that they would be annoyed if their spouses argued that the claim "We're having pizza for dinner" could be made true by serving up goulash. The words "true" and "false" are used in everyday life largely in straightforward ways for straightforward purposes, to which philosophical theories are irrelevant. Theories about how we should determine truth need to account for the readily determinable truths and falsehoods we employ everyday, and usually do best if they start with these uses of truth, and work out from there.

- Third, most religions have some interest in converting secular people to their worldview. Christians and Muslims see themselves as having a mission to bring everyone to their faith, but even Jews and Hindus, who do not see themselves that way, often strive to bring members of their community who have become secular back into the religion, and prefer outsiders to convert first if they want to marry into the community. Now one does not convert or re-convert people wholly by way of argument—showing love and respect to the would-be convert, and sharing rituals with them, is also important—but the process inevitably involves some argument. The would-be convert needs, after all, to come to *believe* certain things, and not merely to be fond of people who hold those beliefs. And to engage in argument, to persuade people of one's religious precepts, one needs to start from common ground, from truths both parties accept independently of what the religion has to say. So a religion that converts people, even people who once were themselves attached to it, must uphold some notion of truth that non-believers can share.

• Finally, secular ways of determining truth, when they are successful in helping people predict and control their natural environments, draw people away from religions that do less well in these respects. Notoriously, when isolated tribal groups encounter modern science and technology the authority of their erstwhile religious leaders wanes drastically, and many of their adherents lose interest in the tradition. Nor is this merely a matter of the power wielded by the colonialists who brought these ways of thinking to pre-modern tribes (although that surely plays a role in it): the ability of modern science to solve the ordinary problems for which people seek truth-tellers is so spectacular that it tends almost always to win out, in the cognitive marketplace, over traditional worldviews.[12] Nor, again, is this wholly a modern phenomenon: the sciences developed in ancient Greece and Rome also tended to spread to other cultures once the latter became aware of them, and to replace aspects of those other cultures' worldviews where they were clearly more successful in predicting and controlling nature. The best explanation of this phenomenon, both in ancient and in modern times, draws on our first and second points. Human beings the world over are impressed by empirical prediction, and the technology made possible thereby, and tend to bestow the compliment "truth" on views that are regularly successful in this respect.

These four points are reflected in the narratives of most religious traditions. In the Jewish Bible, many non-Jews (Jethro, Balaam) are presented as worldly-wise—knowledgeable about everyday things, and how to use them—and non-Jews are never presented as failing to know things of this sort simply because they don't share the Israelite religion (points 1 and 2). In addition, the various heroes of the Torah come to their faith in God in part by way of success in navigating their way through the ordinary empirical world. Jacob asks for God to help him achieve worldly success (Genesis 28: 20–22), and is strengthened in his faith when he does achieve this. Moses performs miracles—shows an extraordinary ability to control the empirical world—that impress both his fellow Israelites and the Egyptians; later, Elijah brings the Israelites back to faith in one God by showing greater control over the world than his pagan competitors (I Kings 18: 20–39).

In the Christian Bible, Jesus attracts followers by way of a number of miracles. He tells "doubting Thomas" that it would have been better for him to believe without having had to gain ocular proof of Jesus' supernatural status (John 20:29), but seems, at the same time, to acknowledge a natural human tendency to believe on the basis of empirical evidence. The Christian Bible also presents non-Christians as having a firm grasp on the ordinary empirical truths around them and, indeed, contains one famous passage, much used in later Christian theology, according to which human beings should all be able to recognize God by way of "the things that have been made" (Romans 1: 18–23): should be able to use the mode of grasping truth they have independently of religious faith to come to a faith in God.

One can make similar points about Islam, as well as religions outside of the Abrahamic tradition. Hindus and Buddhists in India, and Confucians and Taoists in China, debated the merits of their respective religious views for centuries, and recognized, in the course of these debates, that they had to start from common ground to do so. Hence, their discussions begin with ordinary empirical points, and justify elaborate epistemological or metaphysical schemes in terms of their ability to account for these starting points. The Buddha and his followers generally begin by talking about jugs or pieces of cloth or human bodies, and move only from accepted views about these ordinary objects to the epistemological or metaphysical point they want the listener to grasp. Chuang Tzu, whether tilting against Confucius or addressing a general reader, similarly makes his points by starting out from observations and beliefs he could expect any member of his audience to accept.

There may well be less evidence of a recognition that all human beings share basic ways of determining truth in the myths and cognitive procedures of relatively isolated groups like the Australian aborigines, or small tribes in the Americas or sub-Saharan Africa—but if so, that is probably because these groups were until recently rarely in situations in which that point might come up (and were never, or hardly ever, faced with either the opportunity to win new members from other groups or the danger of losing their members to other groups). But here our fourth point comes into play— these are precisely the religions that have most dramatically lost members when they have come into contact with modern Europeans, and the easiest explanation of that loss is that the interest all human beings have in empirical facts, and prediction of or control over those facts, has made modern science more attractive than the traditional world-views with which it competes.

So I think it is pretty clear that most religions already recognize that they share their way of determining ordinary, empirical truths with the non-religious and with people of different faiths. This point may seem trivial, however. Surely, the problems about truth start, not when we consider ways of establishing ordinary empirical claims, but when we ask about much more abstract matters—matters of metaphysics (Is there a God? A self?) or scientific theory (How did the universe begin?). What I would like to claim, and what I hope the points made thus far begin to make plausible, is that any persuasive procedure for establishing truths of metaphysics or scientific theory will have to be *grafted onto* the way we establish ordinary, empirical truths. It will have to be made sense of and defended in terms of these ordinary judgments, or the presuppositions of the way we make them (we will have to get at the invisible things by way of the things that have been made). So our ordinary, empirical methods of determining truth will form a core of all science and any metaphysics that purports to be based on science.

8. We can begin to see the significance of this point by considering the claim made by some religious believers, when modern science seems to confute their theology or scriptures, that the way we rely on our senses when doing science may be corrupt. Sometimes they mean by this that we misuse our bodily senses when we don't employ them in a context of faith, and sometimes they suggest that we have a sense of God's presence independently of our bodily senses—John Calvin called this the "sensus divinitatis"—which we willfully refuse to heed when we conclude that there is no God, or that God cannot take the form of a Trinity, or that the development of life can be explained without positing an intelligent designer.[13] They say, in short, that we are not using the full range of our observational faculties when we disagree with them, that a more adequate use of the very faculties that lead us to the core ordinary, empirical beliefs that we all affirm should lead us to religious belief as well.

But how can such a claim be defended? Take Calvin's *sensus divinitatis*. What might convince an unbeliever that he has such a sense? Well, as C. A. J. Coady has pointed out, our senses are integrated with one another, and we generally trust the evidence of one sense if, and only if, it coheres with the information we receive from our other senses. Consequently, any claim that there is some sense other than the ones we're used to must be made in terms of what we learn from our more familiar senses:

[W]e are sensory investigators and not mere sensory receptors. Hearing certain sounds I look to the skies, expecting some sorts of birds to be passing overhead, and see a flock of parrots, or hearing other sounds I look around in time to take effective steps to avoid an oncoming car. We can see the force of this if we ask what would be involved in considering seriously the case for some alien creature's having a perceptual sense beyond our own. A crucial determinant of any such claim is surely the criterion of achievement. A new sense must both add something distinctive to the range of achievements possible to the organism and cohere with the existing achievement capacities it has. The sighted man in the land of the blind can convince them that he has a further sensory power just because he can *do* so much more than they in handling the environment, though there is also a range of recognizable achievements common to them and to him. (Coady, p. 169)

This seems to me exactly right. There could be senses other than our familiar ones—whether in the form of the "extra-sensory" powers described in science fiction or in the form of a religious "sense for the divine"—but the case for them has to be made in terms of capabilities that can be recognized by those familiar senses. But in that case, it's hard to imagine what would lead any impartial and sound observer of the world as we know it to suppose that there *is* a sensus divinitatis, or at least that the religious people who claim to exercise it actually do. For it is simply not *true* that religious people walk among us like Coady's "sighted man in the land of the blind," that they are able to achieve more, in terms that can be recognized by those of us who use just the five ordinary senses, than the rest of us. The great scientific achievements of the past two centuries have not tended to be made by religious people—or at least the scientists who made them have rarely if ever cited their religious faith as helping them in this process—and it is, indeed, largely secular people (or, again, people whose scientific procedures are wholly secular) who generally fill the successful laboratories around us.

To be fair, those who have made a case for a sensus divinitatis in recent years have not tried to show that it enables achievements that even secular people should be able to recognize as such. They have been engaged in a more apologetic project, arguing, against those who think religious experience is impossible, that there *could* be such a sense, that if there is, it could be treated as a source of legitimate information just like our other senses, and that people of faith therefore need not rely just on information gleaned from their bodily senses to validate what they believe. Put this way, the position is not vulnerable to the objection I have just offered, but it speaks only to those who already have faith, giving them an answer to those who would urge them to give it up; it's not a position likely to lead anyone to faith who does not already have it. It is placed "offline," as it were; it does not count as a move *within* the way-of-the-world science that religious and secular people share.

Much the same goes for claims that our ordinary senses are corrupted. A challenge to our ordinary modes of observation must proceed along the same lines as a suggestion that we consider a new, extraordinary sense. We need to fit the challenge into the beliefs we already have, to see how the proposed way of correcting or bypassing our ordinary modes of proceeding can add to human achievement. To quote Coady, again, the rejection of an old sense, like the acceptance of a new one, "must both add something distinctive to the range of achievements possible to the organism and cohere with the existing achievement capacities it has." A blind man in a land of the sighted might be able to persuade the latter that seeing gets in the way of their ability to perceive properly, but only if he can "do . . . more than they in handling the environment." Similarly, a religious person who tells us to ignore our senses in some respect, to disregard or be suspicious of the science to which they lead us, will be persuasive only if the alternative science he proposes is more successful than ours in terms we can all accept. And, once again, the record speaks against a case for faith-based science—scientists who rely on their religious faith as part of their investigative arsenal have tended virtually without exception to be far *less* successful, in predicting and controlling our environment, than those who proceed in a purely secular way.

The religious person who wants to challenge the reliability of ordinary sensory evidence could presumably respond that the truth of what he asserts will be made clear only after our deaths, or in a messianic age. But then he is again speaking only to those who already share his faith, not so much as beginning to make a case that his theory best fits the ordinary, empirical truths that are at the core of what everyone believes.

9. I hope what I have said thus far begins to make clear what I mean by suggesting that religious and secular people share a core way of establishing truth, and that other ways of doing that must be grafted on to the core. But thus far I have largely appealed to intuitions we have about truth. In the following chapter, I will try to supplement my appeal to intuitions with a bit of philosophical apparatus.

The philosophical apparatus in question is the device known as the social contract. In both Part I and Part II of this book, I will make considerable use of this device. Social contract theories have their home primarily in political philosophy, but they have been recently used to good effect in epistemology as well, and I will argue that they have a place also in moral philosophy. They are well-suited to the explication of what I call the way of the world, since they are concerned precisely to show how human beings might agree to certain things regardless of their religious or other ideological commitments. The condition of human beings who relate to one another purely as free and rational equals, either in a co-operative search for the truth about how to live overall, or independently of their beliefs about how to live overall, is well characterized by the idea of a social contract.

2

Truth in the State of Nature

10. Social contract theories help us understand, above all, why human beings agree to heed authorities. We look around and see people wielding power in all sorts of ways, many of which at least appear to be arbitrary or unfair. "What right do these people have to order us about?" we ask. To which the social contract theorist responds by asking us to imagine, first, what life might be like without government—in the "state of nature"—and then why, if we lived like that, we might come to set up governments. The purposes we thereby uncover for government establish a benchmark against which we can measure our political leaders. When we do so, we find that some of what they do is acceptable to us—something to which we might, implicitly, have agreed—although some of it is not. And we have a better idea of *which* of their actions are unacceptable, and why: how these uses of power violate what we now see as the proper purposes of government.

   Something very similar holds in our epistemic practices. We look around and see many people claiming things to be true that strike us as wildly untrue and wonder how they get away with their claims. Or we can't begin to figure out whether certain claims—made obscurely or in the name of complicated theories that we don't under-stand—are true or not; the purported authorities who utter them nevertheless claim and receive a right to shape policies that affect our lives on the basis of their obscure pronouncements. Some people respond to these phenomena by throwing up their hands and, supposing that all uses of "truth" are illegitimate, a means of manipulation, or that there is no such thing as legitimacy or illegitimacy when it comes to claiming truth. These are the equivalents of the cynics in the political realm who suppose that all power is illegitimate, or that there is no difference between legitimate and illegitimate kinds of rule. An alternative to their position is to consider why, in a world without experts and authorities, we might come to use the word "true." Given the purposes we thereby find for the word, we can then ask whether we can justify some of the uses of it, in our actual world, that struck us as questionable before—whether we can identify them as extensions of our state-of-nature uses of the term—and if not, why not. Both the legitimate and the illegitimate uses of our actual truth language become clearer in this way. Again, that is because we understand better what uses we can *accept*, can *agree to*, as opposed to the ones that have been simply foisted upon us by manipulative experts and authorities.

At the same time, social contract theory can be problematic, and we should take up some objections to it before proceeding.

First, the founders of social contract theory—Thomas Hobbes and John Locke—insisted that human beings actually lived in a pre-social condition before coming together in communities. There is good reason to doubt this. Modern biological theories suggest that our primate ancestors were already social creatures. In addition, we might not want to count any animal as fully human unless it can talk: in which case it must already belong to a society. But even if there were a pre-social state of nature, we would need to ask why we should draw normative conclusions from it. How does anything about what we *should* be like follow from what we *are* like, much less what we once were like? Suppose human beings are, by nature, as deeply fearful and violent as Hobbes describes them. It may still be possible to overcome those tendencies, rather than simply limiting their baleful effects. Moreover, perhaps our distant ancestors were more violent or fearful than we are—they may have differed from us genetically in certain ways and they certainly lived in very different physical circumstances. But then nothing derived from these aspects of their nature would bear on what we should agree to today: the reasons there might be for *those* people to agree to, say, severe punishments for violence would not necessarily apply to us. Again, perhaps our early ancestors labored under various illusions and superstitions that we can now see through. Any agreements they made under the influence of those errors would now be void, because not made in a properly free way.

So what the social contract theorist really needs to describe, to get useful mileage from the idea that we implicitly agree to institutions around us, is an *idealized* state of nature, in which the individuals entering the contract have just those features that we take to be essential to our identity as human beings, or to our freedom. That was understood by the time of the second or third generation of contract theorists. Rousseau and Kant, for instance, presented the social contract as a theoretical construct, drawn from a hypothetical picture of pre-social people. It remains important when the social contract is revived today that it not get confused with a story about the actual development of early human societies.

Second, there is a special danger in using social contract theory to understand our epistemic practices. For any agreement human beings enter about what sorts of social institutions they want to have, must presuppose the truth of many things. People cannot make an agreement unless they already know what "agreements" are, and the difference between agreeing, and being coerced or manipulated into something. They need also to know what they are agreeing about. So we cannot say that human beings simply agree to call some sentences "true" and others "false"; the notion of agreement already pre-supposes a notion of truth.

At the same time, in some respects we clearly do enter agreements about what to count as truth. In a jury trial, evidence may be deemed impermissible, and the vote of the jury establishes the right answer, for legal purposes, to the question of whether the defendant is guilty. In news sources and political debates, some argumentative moves are acceptable and some are not, and some claims will not get so much as examined for truth. And for the purposes of ordinary decision-making, most people in modern Western societies assume that they can afford to ignore those who speak for the "spirit world," check entrails for omens, or otherwise depart from our accepted modes of empirical investigation.

It is this last example that especially interests me. In the past, of course, people did widely turn to spirit-seers and entrail-examiners in the course of their ordinary decision-making, but even then they also relied on the sorts of empirical observation we use today. Indeed, the spirit-seers and entrail-readers gained credibility because it was thought they were often successful in predicting and controlling the things that everyone could observe for themselves. And one good way of putting the question about whether people *should* rely on spirit-seers and the like, or turn instead to scientific expertise, is to ask what sorts of cognitive experts and authorities we might agree on if we set up practices of truth-gathering in a state of nature. Some notion of truth must be taken for granted even to raise this question—that pre-supposition shows up in the model I'll offer insofar as the denizens of my state of nature have an array of cognitive practices before entering their agreement—but it remains reasonable to ask, given a minimal notion of truth, how people might most reasonably establish the specialized, hierarchical modes of truth-gathering that give rise to experts and autho-rities. It is these modes of truth-gathering, after all, and the institutions that represent them (church, academy, media), that lead to the disputes over religious truth that concern us today: whether science has shown the Bible or other scriptures to be false; whether, on the contrary, the word of scripture and the clerical authorities who interpret it should trump the word of scientists. And if the central point of this book is to defend the idea, contra Kant, that "It is written" can be a good basis on which to make some of one's main choices in life,[1] then the question of where, if anywhere, it is reasonable to rely on an authority is essential to our enterprise.

So social contract theory, which focuses on why we accept authorities in various aspects of our lives, is a promising avenue for us. To repeat: a social contract theory about truth, as opposed to one about politics or morality, cannot treat truth as simply *constituted* by what people agree to. (One might indeed take it as a condition on any agreement about how to pursue truth that it includes the recognition that truth can transcend whatever we agree to.) It's not unreasonable to see legitimate political authority as wholly dependent on an agreement we make to accept that authority, and it is at least possible that what we call "morality" is constituted by such an agreement. But we cannot coherently say just that about truth. We can, however, use social contract theory to delineate a baseline of socially-acceptable methods for *seeking* truth, from which we start our individual investigations of the world and which we employ when we want to persuade others of our results. Kant maintained that there can be no purely private truth, that truth is always and necessarily something shareable with a public. I think this is a bit too strong,[2] but something close to it must be right. We've seen reasons to suppose that human beings, in fact, share a core notion of truth, and that any further truth-claims need somehow to be grafted on to that core. The social contract approach to truth will make clearer why that is so. It will make clear in particular why any kind of truth that might deserve the appellation "private," that might not be wholly shareable with other human beings, will have to be made sense of in terms of the sorts of truth, and truth-gathering, that we do share with one another.

11. One more preliminary, before turning to the social contract model of truth. This concerns the relation between what I hope to accomplish with this model and the uses made of it by Bernard Williams, on whom I draw heavily for its basic features. Williams, taking a hint from an account of knowledge proposed by Edward Craig, shows beautifully how a state of nature story about truth fits in with some of the most sophisticated philosophical treatments of that notion, accords, at the same time, with the bulk of our ordinary intuitions, and provides a powerful tool for addressing the public controversies we face over how to establish truth.[3] Nevertheless, I do not mean to endorse all of Williams' reasons for favoring this approach. (Indeed, after recounting his basic state of nature story, I will take it directions of which he would probably disapprove.) Williams says that state of nature theories, whether in politics or episte-mology, are part of a broader naturalism, and he melds his own use of such a theory with an attempt to debunk appeals to the supernatural. By "naturalism," as regards truth, he seems to mean a view that eschews both the attribution of truth to claims about non-natural objects and the idea that truth itself might be a non-natural property. I do not want to rule out these possibilities, of course, but it in any case seems to me a clear methodological failing, on Williams's part, to allow naturalistic commitments to drive his project. No view about truth itself should be committed to the truth of naturalism in particular. Among other things, that would make it impossible for us to find a substantial answer to the question, "Is naturalism true?" If our account of truth presupposes naturalism, then "naturalism is true" will turn out to be a tautology, and it is certainly not *that*.

12. Without further ado, here is the social contract story about truth. We begin with a cognitive state of nature. For our purposes, this means a condition in which the claims that are made are simple enough that each individual can check their truth or falsehood on his or her own, in which there are no experts whose insistence that a claim is true has weight with other people even when they fail to understand it. The truths uttered in this condition are straightforward ones; there are no truth-claims whose difficulty might lead people to worry about what "truth" itself might mean. This idealization may help us see how our own worries about truth arise.

Bearing in mind that no actual group of early human beings is likely to have resembled our model, we may nevertheless make the model more concrete by representing it in the form of a group of people in the early stages of language use, whose language consequently consists primarily of factual reporting. Speech, for these people, serves just as a way for the group to help its members satisfy their needs better than they would do on their own. Thus, Joe might use his own eyes and ears to determine that there is a ripe pineapple on that tree, or a tiger coming through the undergrowth, but he might also learn some of these things from Amanda or Balthazar—who are perhaps better at spotting tigers or ripe pineapples, or who are better positioned, at a given moment, to see them. As Craig says:

Human beings . . . have 'on-board' sources, eyes and ears, powers of reasoning, which give them a primary stock of beliefs. It will be highly advantageous to them if they can also tap the primary stocks of their fellows—the tiger that Fred can see and I can't may be after me and not Fred—that is to say, if they act as informants for each other. On any issue, some informants will be better than others, more likely to supply a true belief. (Fred, who is up in a tree, is more likely to tell me the truth as to the whereabouts of the tiger than Mabel, who is in a cave).[4]

Williams describes this way of drawing on one another's stock of knowledge as a "division of epistemic labour," and the feature of other people that may lead us to rely on them as "positional advantage" (TT 43). The economic analogy is apt.

But once the acquisition of knowledge becomes a social project, even to the minimal extent we have allowed thus far, it becomes important for each member of the society to distinguish between reliable and unreliable informants. If Fred can't tell the difference between a tiger and a house cat, or is a conniving fellow with an interest in Joe's wife, then Joe may want to disregard any information he proffers. If Fred, on the other hand, is a person who has both great integrity and superb eye-sight, then Joe may want to trust Fred's tiger-sightings even where he would not trust his own. And if Joe doesn't know Fred well, then he may want information about whether Fred is a reliable or unreliable informant. So having Balthazar, Joe's friend, say, "Fred's a truth-teller," will be helpful.

Here we have the place for truth. I am on the ground and can't see whether there are tigers coming through the undergrowth; Fred, up in a tree, says, "There's a tiger!"; and Balthazar, down here with me, but knowing more about Fred than I do, says, "That's probably true." After *both* these announcements, I rely on what Fred says to supplement my own observations. Fred becomes an informant for me on tigers, and Balthazar becomes an informant for me on informants. Both kinds of information are necessary if I am to draw on other people's primary stocks in forming true beliefs, and the concept of truth is essential to the second one. Until we get to the question of how to evaluate informants, the concept of truth may be unnecessary. If Balthazar is merely another informant about tigers, up in the tree across from Fred, he can say "I see a tiger too" after Fred does, rather than, "That's true." If Balthazar is in no better position to see tigers than I am, however, then he can't inform me about that. But he may be in a position to inform me about Fred's qualities as an informant. In that case, his saying, "That's probably true" after Fred speaks cannot be replaced merely with another iteration of "There's a tiger!" The latter would wrongly imply that Balthazar's sentence is meant as a report on tigers. It isn't that. It's a report on *Fred*, and only thereby, indirectly, on tigers. The concept of truth cannot be removed from this sort of report—Balthazar cannot merely utter Fred's own sentence, even though he endorses it—and it is in this sort of report that it finds its first, and paradigmatic, home.

It is perhaps obvious, but worth mentioning since it will play a large role in what I say later on, that the information provided by both Fred and Balthazar would be considerably more important to me if I was concerned, not with tiger-spotting, but cases in which it is difficult for me even in principle to pick out the relevant facts on my own. Fred's positional advantage as regards tiger-spotting is just that he is up in a tree and I am not. The "position" in question is literally a spatial one, and I know perfectly well what would lead me to think *I* had spotted a tiger if I were in Fred's place. But suppose now that I am looking for safe mushrooms, without any prior experience in distinguishing between poisonous and non-poisonous ones. Then, if Françoise is an expert on mushrooms, her positional advantage over me is such that I cannot just stand where she is and make the same observations: "position" is now a metaphor for having certain sorts of background knowledge, and/or observational skills, that I lack. Here, the informant supplies facts that I could not pick up on my own, and I will rely on her, and on those who give me information about her, more heavily and more unquestioningly than I would if I were out tiger-spotting. Nevertheless, there is an analogue in this case, too, if I accept Françoise's word, to my having the thought "if I were in Françoise's position, I would observe the same thing." I know what is significant about poisonous mushrooms, and I can imagine the sorts of sensory evidence that might correlate with that feature. I can imagine, that is, what it *would be like* to be in Françoise's position, and use that to flesh out my counterfactual same-saying of her sentences when I regard them as true. I believe her sentences to be true just in case I would affirm the same ones, were I in her position. So the structure of truth remains the same, even in cases like this one, where I cannot simply switch places with Françoise. It will remain the same even in cases where, say, a complicated mathematical claim is at stake, in which it is doubtful that I could ever occupy the speaker's position. We regard the speaker's utterances as true if and only if we think we would utter the same ones if we occupied his position, and we use the word "truth," paradigmatically, when we do not occupy that position, but want to give or receive some assurance that the speaker does, and is the sort of person, or is in the sort of circumstances, to use her position responsibly. "That's true" gives us some assurance that the speaker is knowledgeable and honest: that we can rely on her word.

13. One noteworthy feature of the state of nature story is that the word "truth" is used in it more to assure us of the trustworthiness of certain speakers than to give us confidence in what in particular they say. I want assurance that I can rely on Fred or

Françoise—that these people are, in general, truth-tellers—and that assurance gives me reason to trust a particular sentence they utter. Much contemporary philosophy, especially in the analytic tradition, treats "truth" as if it were a property solely of sentences, but in many circumstances it is used of speakers, rather than sentences. In this respect, we are led astray when we take sentences like "It is true that snow is white" as our paradigm for the use of truth-language. In ordinary life, we hardly ever say anything like "It is true that snow is white." If we do, we say it in response to some *challenge* to that claim. We are in Fiji, perhaps, and someone who has never seen snow doubts my friend Joe's claim that it is white. Even here, we are more likely to say "What Joe says is true," or "Joe's telling the truth," than to attach "truth" to the sentence he utters; we are likely to vouch for *Joe*, more than for his utterance. Occasionally, we might vouch for Joe's utterance while acknowledging that Joe is not generally reliable. Joe is a notorious liar or jokester, but he says "It's snowing" one day when it really is snowing. I say, "Joe's telling the truth," perhaps with a bit of surprise in my voice, in order to *substitute* myself for Joe as a reliable witness for the statement. But in that case, I am still implicitly making reference to a speaker—myself—not just to a sentence. Saying that a sentence is true is not literally saying that its speaker is reliable, or that I, who vouch for it, am reliable, but that is the *effect* of saying it, its illocutionary force.

The word "truth" in many traditions is connected to words for "reliable," "trust-worthy," etc., and in pre-modern times was often applied first and foremost to people, rather than sentences. Williams notes the historical relationship between "truth" and "troth" in English (TT 93–94, and note 12 on 290), and says that "truth" originally meant "fidelity, loyalty, or reliability." "Truthfulness is a form of trustworthiness" even today, he points out (94), and originally a truthful person was by definition one whose pledge of "troth" could be relied on, rather than one who merely reported states of affairs accurately. In ancient Hebrew, the word generally translated as "true" (*emet*) almost always means something like "trustworthy." Abraham's servant says that God led him on "a way of truth" in his quest to find a wife for Isaac, and then asks Laban and Bethuel, Rebecca's brother and father, whether they mean to deal with him "in kindness and truth" (Genesis 24:48, 49). Jethro tells Moses to choose "people of truth" as judges (Exodus 18: 21). King David tells his son that God made a promise to keep the kingship in their family line as long as David and his sons "walk before [God] in truth" (I Kings 2: 4). At a central moment in Jewish public prayer, even today, the leader exclaims, "The Lord your God is true." In all these cases, a *person*, or way for a person to conduct him or herself, not a sentence, is called "true," and the quality thus designated seems to have far more to do with keeping promises, or showing integrity or loyalty, than accurately reporting facts. A person of truth is a person one can *rely on*, and a way of truth is a way one can proceed along in trust.[5]

Of course, a person who is careless about accuracy, or who tells outright lies, is unlikely to be trustworthy. But trustworthiness may on occasion require a person to say something false, at least if taken literally (see § 29, below), and in any case involves many actions and attitudes in addition to uttering, and intending to utter, accurate reports. So the virtue of truth in a person or way is not identical with the virtue of truth in a sentence. I shall suggest as we go along that the primary locus of truth may well be persons rather than sentences. For most of human history the truth of sentences has been secondary to the truth of persons, and the importance we place in the modern age on the truth of sentences alone may derive less from epistemology than from a certain ethical outlook according to which it is best for all people to walk their own paths by themselves, and in which what we want from "truth," therefore, is a way of assessing sentences without anyone else's help—without having to trust in the reliability of their speakers.[6]

Why does the prayer leader call out "The Lord your God is true"? Well, the passage we have been reciting at that point—the Shema—at its end comes dangerously close to telling the individual reciting it that he or she is God. Its first paragraph affirms God's unity and calls on us to devote ourselves, in internal unity ("with all your heart, with all your soul, and with all your might"), to that unified Being—a call that would have us love God whether or not we understand the goodness in what He does. Having wrung that commitment from us, the second paragraph promises that God in fact does act in a way we can recognize as good (produces a world in which reward—"rain in its season"— ultimately comes to the righteous and punishment to the wicked). And the final paragraph circles back to our internal devotion to God. But now it approaches that devotion by way of a reminder that God frees us (from Egypt, and from desires that enslave us as Egypt did) and a command to clothe ourselves in a symbol of all God's commandments—the four-cornered, blue-fringed garment in which we are wrapped as we recite all three of these paragraphs. By way of this symbol, the passage tells us, we can tear ourselves from our empirical desires, from the temptations of our eyes and hearts, and become "holy": separated off from the world and close to its God. And this hint that full devotion to God may bring us directly into God's presence ends with the words, whispered by the worshipper to herself: "I am the Lord your God. True."—which can be read, with just a little stretch of the Hebrew, as: "I am the Lord your true [or faithful] God.

But I am saying these words to myself. I can therefore hear them as declaring that my true or faithful God is in me—or, indeed, is me. Mystics might love that thought, and even non-mystics may agree that we are meant to feel God's presence coming closer and closer to us as we proceed through the Shema—there are few moments in my liturgical experience in which I have felt closer to God than when holding the four fringes of my tallit together, after the Shema, and waiting for the prayer leader to repeat its conclusion—but it is crucial, for the normative Jewish tradition, that God is not identical with any of us.

So we need to hear the last words spoken aloud to us, by someone else; we need to hear the liturgical unit end with the sentence "The Lord your God is true," rather than the sentence "I am the Lord your [true] God." The objectivity of God's true words to us, the gap between what we seek to know and our attempts to know it, must be brought out even as we come closer and closer to God. We may feel identified with what we believe to be the source of our universe, in the Shema, but we must remember that that feeling of identification is just momentary, and that a permanent unity with God is out of our reach. To speak of "truth," here and everywhere else, is to allow that we can go wrong—can err, make mistakes—and that God, therefore, can lead us: can be a true (faithful) guide to us.

14. Our story fits well with the emphasis in contemporary accounts of truth on "same-saying." Many modern theorists of truth have insisted that the predicate " . . . is true" cannot add anything to the meaning of a sentence—otherwise we could not hold fixed what we are evaluating for truth—and consequently suggested that those who utter "p" and those who utter "p is true" are saying the same thing. Taken to an extreme, this leads to a redundancy view of truth: to the view that we could do without truth, and just assert the sentences to which we are inclined to apply it. This is implausible,[7] but there is surely something right about the idea that one asserts "That's true" only when one is willing also to assert the sentence to which the "that" refers. And this idea is reflected in our state of nature story.

At the same time our state of nature story, unlike redundancy theories of truth, shows how and why a truth-attributor is not *merely* same-saying the p to which she attributes truth. Rather, the truth-attributor is *endorsing another speaker's claim that p*, either implying that the speaker is in a good position to assert p or bringing in his own reputation for veracity to buttress the speaker's. The truth-attributor is saying, in effect, either that he too would assert p if he were in the p-sayer's position or that he is in, or has been in, a position from which he can also assert p. In the first case, at least, straightforward same-saying gives way to counterfactual same-saying: I call a sentence "true" when I think I *would* utter the same sentence *were* I in the same position as the speaker. This is an endorsement of the p-sayer's authority as an informant about p, not directly an assertion of p, and it leads listeners, if they accept the truth-attribution, to believe p for *different reasons* than they would have if they witnessed the truth-conditions of p themselves. This complex structure, by which attributions of truth implicitly set up a situation containing at least three different people—a speaker, an endorser of that speaker, and a listener, trying to decide whether to accept what the speaker says—characterizes the idea of truth in all its uses.

15. Williams describes the claims characteristically made in the state of nature as "plain truths."[8] What he primarily has in mind here are empirical truths, about objects all observers in a conversation can readily observe. But the notion ranges more widely than this, to anything the denizens of our state of nature might regard as easy to establish. Many, but not all, will concern empirical matters. Language itself makes it possible to conceive of new kinds of entities; it is not merely a tool for noticing the same objects we noticed before it came on the scene. Rather, language *transforms* the scene, changes what we count as an object and what we think we are doing, or want to do, among the objects around us. We cannot introduce language to our state of nature without allowing at least the following kinds of reports to become part of the repertoire of sentences that get evaluated for truth or falsehood:

(a) "89 can't be evenly divided by 3." Human beings eventually recognize a difference between numbers and the results of counting a group of objects. At that point they don't have to count the members of every group in order to figure out how much one group added to another will make, or whether a group can be divided evenly into some number of parts. At that point, however, sentences like "89 can't be evenly divided by 3" will no longer simply replace sentences of the form, "I've tried dividing these 89 cattle into 3 groups, but can't get them to come out even." Rather, the former becomes a *norm* for sentences like the latter. If someone claims that he *has* made the division come out even, we look for the mistake in his counting; we aren't even tempted to suppose he might be right. And the way people test the properly mathematical sentences will not rely on observation. So same-saying the sentence will not amount to endorsing the observational position or powers of the original speaker, and attributing truth to it will not amount to saying that observation will confirm it.

(b) "That pineapple is delicious." Utterers of sentences like these need not suppose that what they are saying reflects a subjective take on the world. They instead regard themselves as imparting information, no different in kind from "Pine-apples grow on trees." Lacking any theory about objective and subjective qualities, they have no reason to separate their observation of the pleasant and unpleasant features of things from their observations of anything else. In fact, since many human tastes are widely shared, people both in our imagined state of nature and in the most sophisticated of modern societies will have reason to rely on some reports of this form. There will therefore also be reason for people to endorse what others say on these subjects, to say "That's true (false)," or "He's a truth-teller (liar)," in response to such utterances.

(c) "Killing people is bad." "Helping the tribe find food is good." We might model this kind of talk on the taste discourse we just considered. The speaker may mean, "Killing is despicable" and "Helping the tribe find food is admirable." Or perhaps he means that the tribe punishes killings and rewards those who help it find food. Primitive ethical statements—"proto-ethical" statements, perhaps—may be of a piece with pragmatic advice, and go along with the purposes for which people announce tigers and pineapples. If I get mad at Joe and want to kill him, Fred's saying "It would be wrong to kill Joe" may mean: "Joe's friends will come after you if you kill him." And on this construal, if Balthazar says "That's true" in response to Fred's remark, he means to endorse Fred's reliability as an informant about the dangers involved in killing Joe. Suppose, however, that a policy of punishing killers has been announced and enforced for some time in our tribe. One result of such a policy may be that many tribespeople come to feel that killing is somehow shameful, or guilt-inducing, even when there are no enforcers about. That is, announcing a group policy to prevent individuals killing others might eventually bring about a *norm* against such killing. Then, while "It's wrong to kill Joe" *may* still just mean "It's dangerous to kill Joe," it may also be a way of announcing that a certain norm is in place, or of expressing one's adherence to that norm. If Fred announces that it's wrong to kill under these circumstances, Balthazar's saying "That's true" may be an endorsement of Fred as an informant on local norms, or an expression of agreement with the norms that Fred upholds, a suggestion on Balthazar's part that I will, or should, feel guilty or ashamed if I kill Joe.

There is yet another way of interpreting at least some of the (proto-)ethical discourse we have been considering. In some cases, the announcement that an action or general way of behaving is "good" may mean that it will lead the hearer in the long run to be happier, or to approve of himself more fully. A speaker may say "Restraining one's desires is good," and mean: "If you try it, over time you will find that you are happier." Here, positional advantage consists in having greater experience than others, or moral tastes that others have not yet achieved. The speaker does not occupy a spatial or temporal position one could simply move into and out of again, so others cannot try out the speaker's position and see whether they make the same observations. One cannot occupy *this* speaker's position unless one becomes *like* her, and develops the same moral tastes. But in that case endorsing the speaker's say-so invites the audience to a far higher level of reliance on her than in our simple observational cases. One may need to rely on the speaker for a long time, and in the course of a wide variety of one's activities, to be able to occupy her position. Accordingly, those who say "That's true" about her utterances, or "She's a truth-teller" about her, may think of their remarks as having more gravity, and the trustworthiness they attribute to her as being deeper and more comprehensive, than in the simpler cases. The word "truth" will, however, continue to function in the same way: as a marker that a speaker occupies the right sort of position to give information on a certain subject, with which the endorser believes he himself, and the audience, would agree were they to occupy that position. Truth language remains a way of endorsing an informant, as a reliable guide to what the audience might in principle find on their own. Filling out the "in principle" has just become a lot more difficult.

16. So there are different kinds of plain truths.[9] A plain truth may report on or predict an empirical state of affairs; it may report the result of a calculation or other reasoning process; or it may announce, or express the speaker's agreement with, an ethical norm. And it may describe something one can perceive, or an experience one can have, only after passing through some sort of training or discipline.

Will religious claims belong among the plain truths?

Joe says, "Zeus spoke to me yesterday." In the first instance, this will appear as a plain truth (or plain falsehood) to the denizens of our state of nature, on par with "I saw a tiger yesterday." It will probably be correlated with some sort of empirical occurrence—but only *we*, looking in on the state of nature with our scientific theories in hand, not the inhabitants of the state of nature itself, will be able to see why Zeus is irrelevant to that occurrence. "Zeus told me you should take this herb for your stomach-ache" will also be seen as a plain truth, if the herb does cure my stomach-ache, and "Zeus told me your dead grandfather is suffering for his adulteries" may be treated as a plain truth if I find evidence that my grandfather did commit adultery.

Nor need the positional factor central to truth language be missing from these cases. Once there are claims about gods, there will presumably be agreed-on ways for determining what sorts of people, in what sorts of circumstances, can communicate with the gods. A report of the "Zeus spoke to me" variety might be backed up by an informant who witnessed a certain oracular procedure ("That's true: I saw Joe go into a trance and start speaking in the Zeus voice"), or perhaps giving correct medical information, or demonstrating a knowledge of adulterous affairs and other secret social goings-on, will count as evidence that a person was in position to hear from other-worldly beings.

Williams resists including this sort of speech among the plain truths. He says it is natural to suppose that many of the sentences uttered in the state of nature "will concern everyday features of the environment which we ourselves readily pick out— people, animals, trees, fruits, bodies of water, the sun and the moon, and such things," but that it is unnecessary to include "references to gods or supernatural agencies" among these sentences (TT 52–53). This move is part of the broader naturalist project for which Williams wants to employ the state of nature story, and he makes clear that he regards the "whole dimension of...speech" that makes reference to gods and supernatural agencies as "systematically false," radically "ill-founded." A sentence such as "some god has passed [this] way" therefore cannot possibly count as a plain truth for Williams, or even a plain falsehood: it cannot count as the sort of thing to which the word "truth" is paradigmatically applied (51).

But even for the purposes of Williams's own project, this is surely the wrong point at which to eliminate supernatural references from the discourse one is interpreting. As Williams himself admits (51), the people in the state of nature may themselves regard statements like "Some god has passed this way" as plain truths. If we want first to describe their use of these terms, and only then to draw a theory of truth out of that usage, we need to accept this parity between (what we would call) naturalistic and supernaturalistic sentences. The elimination of certain sorts of speech as systematically ill-founded should come after we see how, within the practices of the state of nature itself, systematic falsehood might be recognized. We want an immanent rather than a transcendent critique of state-of-nature practices: that is the whole point of setting up such a story. If we could agree on general principles allowing us to pick out systematically true from systematically false kinds of discourse, then we would hardly need the state-of-nature story. We could derive our account of truth from those principles instead. Williams turns to the state of nature, as I do, to *finesse* the seemingly interminable philosophical search for such foundational principles. But then he should not endorse naturalism until he can draw it *out* of his state of nature story.

17. How might the denizens of our state of nature come to recognize whole types of purported entities as non-existent? Or (what is in the end the same thing) how might they come to see a whole swathe of their discourse as systematically false?

There will inevitably be mention, in our state of nature, of creatures that do not exist, but resemble those that do. Someone spots a fierce lizard with a long red tongue from a distance, and the legend of the dragon is born. Others catch a glimpse of a rhinoceros, or tell visitors from afar about rhinoceri, and the legend of the unicorn is born. Or people's dreams, or fantasies, get mixed with real perceptions and they start to think they have seen centaurs or chimeras. On an eerie night, one might see a bush as one's dead grandfather. Nor will one necessarily correct this impression upon getting close enough to see that it is just a bush. One may instead suppose that it was briefly transformed into one's grandfather, or that one's grandfather's spirit wafted through it. And the people one speaks with, having had similar experiences, may be inclined to believe these reports.

Falsehoods of this sort come along with the mere fact of having language. One of the features of language is that figures of imagination can be named and thereby shared. Even if there is some sort of communication among birds and apes and porpoises, they cannot communicate about imaginary entities. Their calls and gestures are too vague for that, and can function to summon other members of the species, or warn them away, only if they substitute for the other animals' own eyes and ears, for the noting of opportunities or dangers that those other animals might pick up on their own. A non-talking animal may be able to *mislead* another animal—calling out danger where there is none, making a noise or gesture that signals food only to lure another animal to its death—but could not invent something that neither it nor the other animal has ever experienced. The possibility of referring to a type of entity that does not exist can come in only once one has the highly sophisticated kind of communication that we do: including, among other things, universal terms. Language makes possible both a more extensive sharing of truths and massive, systematic falsehood.

This feature of language explains how marking the truthfulness of informants can gain a function beyond establishing the reliability of tiger-spotters. The people in our state of nature might want to rule out not a particular utterance, but a particular *kind* of utterance, and perhaps to regard those who make that kind of utterance as generally unreliable, worthy of suspicion at least, whatever they happen to be talking about.

Suppose Sylvester begins to report the existence of a creature unlike those anyone else has seen: a striped dog with sharp horns, say, that screams like a sick child. Eventually, others accompany him to the spot where he claims to see this animal, and he points it out to them. They say, "But that's not a dog," or "It's only the shade from the trees that makes you see stripes," or "The sound you're hearing is the wind in the trees." If he responds, "Oh yes, you're right," the matter is over. But perhaps he instead continues to insist that he sees and hears what he claimed to see and hear. Then the others may say that his eyes or ears are shot, or that he has too strong an imagination (the idea of an "imagination," and of some people having one that's too strong, may arise in such a context), and report back to the community that what he says on this subject is not true. They have occupied his position, found that he possesses no observational advantage from there, and refuse, therefore, to same-say him.

Note the form of this account. It is not just that Sylvester's fellow tribespeople do not observe what he does. They also have an *explanation* for what they regard as his observational failings. If they could not find such an explanation, his reports might seem a mystery to them, hence might—if he is otherwise trustworthy—retain a certain authority. As is, the informants on Sylvester's status as an informant see something of what Sylvester sees and can report back a revised version of his observations, minus the entity they hold to be non-existent.

This is still not systematic falsehood. Sylvester's fellow tribespeople do not rule out an entire *kind* of entity and way of speaking, just a *particular* entity and speaker. Nor does it make much sense that generalizations over kinds of entities and discourse would be possible in a condition that contains as yet no theories, just particular observations. It is hard to see how one could discern systematic error without theory—to discern *patterns* of truth and falsehood just is to engage in theory. Still, Sylvester's illusion goes beyond ordinary error, and it is reasonable to anticipate that systematic falsehood, once we do find a place for it, will take something of the same form: will be, minimally, a pattern of falsehood with a core of truth, of claims about non-existent entities for which there is a good explanation of how those entities came to be added on to what does exist.

This fits nicely with some of what Williams says about the elimination of gods and supernatural agencies from a society's discourse:

[O]ne reason we might have for saying that some of [these people's] statements refer to 'gods' or similar agents, and that all those statements are false, is that they seem to imply a certain kind of explanation of happenings (happenings which we ourselves recognize) . . . Why should we think that they imply such an explanation? One reason might be that when, with our arrival, these people become familiar with our explanations of those happenings, and with the technology that our explanations make possible, their statements of that kind go out of business, or at least go underground. (TT 51–52)

What Williams calls "our explanations" can hardly belong among the things uttered and understood in the state of nature: they do not consist of plain truths, and the kind of wholesale elimination they entail does not, as we have seen, fit with the demonstrations of falsehood we expect in the state of nature. But it is true that when people with naturalistic explanations for disease and crop failure arrive in places where those sort of happenings are given supernaturalistic explanations, the latter often "go out of business." And it is reasonable to suppose that the naturalistic style of explanation comes to replace the supernaturalistic one because the spokespeople for the former are able to predict and control the happenings in question better than the local experts on the supernatural, and to give a plausible account of why the latter wrongly suppose that supernatural forces are at work.

As Williams himself concedes, however, when he acknowledges that the supernatural explanations may "go underground," rather than disappearing, this replacement shows only that supernaturalistic *explanations of empirical phenomena* tend to be defeated by naturalistic ones, not that appeals to the supernatural disappear altogether. The supernatural cannot be eliminated as easily as Sylvester's monster. After the discovery that gods are unnecessary for explaining ordinary observables, a society may, and often does, reinterpret its view of the gods as a part of ethics, or as relevant to realms less accessible to ordinary observation (to the workings of our souls, perhaps). The society may, indeed, radically reinterpret what it understands the supernatural to *be*, moving from animism, or an anthropomorphic polytheism, to a view in which everything supernatural is ultimately an expression of a moral force of some sort, governing the natural universe without resembling any item *in* that universe.

We will get to this sort of shift in the meaning of religious discourse in chapter 4. First, we need to pursue systematic error more fully. Do the challenges that some religious believers pose today to scientific experts, in support of creationism or the historical veracity of the Bible, represent systematic error? To answer that question, we will need to explore how expertise arises in our state of nature—a development that, we will see, also spells the end of the state of nature.

3

Socialized Truth

18. The very idea of systematic falsehood takes us beyond the state of nature. So does the idea of "the natural" and "the supernatural," which make sense only if one has already organized nature into a whole. Before we can address these ideas, therefore, we need to figure out how the denizens of our state of nature might get beyond the plain truths to which their discourse has thus far been limited. We need to complete our social contract theory by seeing how our state of nature might come to an end.

We noted earlier (§ 10) that state-of-nature stories serve in political philosophy as a background for determining the legitimate role of government. In Locke's political theory, the state is legitimate to the extent that it protects the ability of individuals to enjoy the liberties they had in the state of nature. In Hobbes's theory, we institute government to ensure that we never return to the state of nature, but again the measure of legitimacy depends upon a comparison between the governed state and the natural one. Arbitrary uses of authority, and power grabs disguised as exercises of authority, can be described as such only once a political structure is in place, although we sift out the illegitimate from the legitimate uses by looking back to the state of nature. Legitimate appeals to authority satisfy needs we already had in the state of nature; appeals to authority that do not meet that test are illegitimate.

We can use our epistemic state of nature, similarly, as a touchstone for sifting out legitimate from illegitimate appeals to truth. Once "truth" becomes an honorific signaling that one should hearken to what a particular speaker says, it can be used thoughtlessly or manipulatively, or in the service of fantasy. Mystical doctrines, quirky philosophical theories, and wildly false and dangerous political theories can all gain a veneer of legitimacy if an authoritative figure calls them true. Our state of nature story can help us test these claims against more basic, unexceptionable uses of truth.

Let us adopt "socialized truth" as our term for the sort of truth that comes into play when we leave the epistemic state of nature.[1] The word "socialized" allows us to exploit the ambiguity between (a) what arises *in* society, and (b) what is instilled *by* society, which is useful since the two are closely, if problematically, intertwined.

Socialized truth will include all state of nature plain truths, as well as the arbitrary, manipulative, and confused uses of truth-language that lead us to ask after the legitimate use of "truth." But socialized truth will also include a third category: uses of "truth" that arise *by reflection upon* first-order, state-of-nature truth claims. It is this category that makes the distinction between the two levels useful and provides an analogy to what happens, in political theory, when governments are seen as having been added on to a state of nature. In the epistemic case, as in the political one, there is a kind of normative authority that both arises out of the first-order modes of evaluation in the state of nature and reflects back upon them, so that they come to have a different status than they had initially. In the political case, especially as Locke sets it up, the state rationalizes an enforcement of norms that had already gone on haphazardly in the state of nature.[2] The state sets up procedures to enforce norms more dispassionately and fairly. But that means that the state does a better job at defining and carrying out certain norms *about* enforcing norms to which the inhabitants of the state of nature were already committed. In the state of nature, people punish others for battery, and a first-order norm against battery arises. Over time, however, they find that the very attempt to punish violators of such norms shades into practices of vengeance that can be as destructive as the original violations themselves. This leads to the setting up of a state, where punishment is more orderly, and where the punishers are watched by the people, and removed or punished themselves if they violate the second-order norms about punishment. So the coming of the state is the coming of a second-order level of norms, the need for which is present within the state of nature, but which the state of nature cannot itself supply.

The analogy in the epistemic case is a close one. In the state of nature, people report on a variety of readily ascertainable facts, and endorse one another's reports with words like "true." But these endorsements are haphazard and unreflective, and often a whole group of people, each of whom endorses the others' reports, may be jointly and systematically mistaken or deceitful. The breakdown in epistemic authority to which such incidents can lead provides the impetus to search for more systematic ways of ascertaining truth. Upon encountering members of another tribe, the people of one tribe discover that their belief that all mushrooms are dangerous is false, or they see, after a devastating volcanic eruption, that the priests who claimed to control volcanoes are charlatans. On coming out of their errors or illusions, they wonder how they might avoid such mistakes in the future. The failure of some truth practices leads them to seek more systematic ways of determining who is a truth-teller, just as the failure of some ways of enforcing norms leads them to seek a more systematic type of enforcement. In both cases, problems in the use of first-order norms give rise to higher-order norms. Remember that the very coming of language, and the concomitant coming of same-saying and endorsement, make possible *both* an extensive sharing of information *and* massive error and deception. So we inevitably have to figure out, eventually, how massive error arises, and how massive deception can be avoided. This is the main impetus behind our coming to reflect on our practices of gathering and sharing truth, and to ask questions like "How do we know when we have grasped the nature of a thing?," "Is there a non-observable reality that affects what we observe?" and "What is reality?" or "What is truth?"

There is an impetus within our first-order practices of reporting facts, that is, to move towards theory: about our first-order reports, about entities or laws or forces that may explain or lie behind such reports, as well as about theory itself, and what might make some theories true and others not, or some truer than others. We eliminate some entities we thought existed on the first order—we may say now that there are no dragons and couldn't possibly be gods or spirits of the sort we once thought we experienced—and add others: numbers, forces, perhaps moral and aesthetic values. We also introduce distinctions between subjective and objective qualities, or primary and secondary ones. If ethics proper requires general reasons—reasons that, say, distinguish between what satisfies our selfish desires and what is good from an impartial perspective—then our proto-ethical discourse now becomes properly ethical for the first time. We are capable of science proper at this point, too: and of having a naturalistic, *or* supernaturalistic, outlook. The idea of "nature," a whole that orders everything we observe and by which we judge that some observations are misleading or illusory, first gets its place here.

And inextricable from all these developments is theorizing *about* theorizing, which is to say theorizing about what makes theories, as opposed to first-order reports, true. Here, the attribution of truth no longer means, "If you could see (hear, taste ...) what I do, you would say the same thing," if only because the claims that need to be evaluated as true or false will include ones about the adequacy of observation itself. Something will remain from the first-order use of "truth," however, since that was how the word acquired meaning at all, and since the second-order uses grow out of problems that arise within the first-order ones. Someone who says "That's true" about sentences of scientific theory, or epistemology, continues to endorse the speakers of those sentences, and continues to mean, "If you could occupy the speaker's position, you would say the same thing." It is just that "position" now has to do with skill in argumentation, rather than spatiotemporal position. There is also a substantive carry-over from the first-order uses of truth. Saying "That's true" about a theory of truth suggests that the theory will help us resolve the problems that arose with first-order truths, will help us sift out systematically meaningless or ill-formed discourse from real candidates for truth and falsehood, and expressions of dogma or fantasy from honest attempts to convey truth. It will thereby, albeit indirectly, help us sift out reliable from unreliable first-order informants.

Theories about the non-observable forces, entities and principles that might govern the things we observe, thus bring with them theories about what makes these theories themselves true.[3] The latter include theories of scientific method, ontological theories—theories about the fundamental elements of reality—and theories of truth:

correspondence, coherence, and pragmatic theories of truth, as well as redundancy theories and the social contract model I am currently laying out. We decide what we should count as "real," whether that be complex numbers or gravity or quantum particles or God, in accordance with what we regard as a good theory about reality. Our ontological theories are inextricably intertwined with our theories of scientific method and of truth.

And it is at this level that endless arguments break out about what counts as truth, and whether the very word is useful. I think we can finesse most such debates here, although of course we can't avoid the question of whether claims attributing reality to supernatural entities could possibly be true. One guide we can use to wend our way through the thickets surrounding that issue is the fact that any successful second-order use of truth will have to mesh with the way we use the word on the first order. A constraint on any plausible theory of truth, given the need from which such theories arise, is that it endorse our uses of truth to assess first-order reports made from positions of comparative advantage, that it account for the paradigmatic role of such uses in what we mean by "truth," and that it carry the broad structure of first-order truth language over into its uses on the second order. These points, as we will see, are sufficient to ground a view of expertise that will answer the challenge posed by those who uphold creationism and the historical veracity of the Bible, and to illuminate the difference between scientific expertise and ethical or religious authority. We will be concerned in this chapter primarily with scientific expertise and scientific theory—the second-order institutions and discourse that grow out of observational and mathematical plain truths. The next chapter will consider the truth claims of ethics and religion.

19. How might we justify scientific theory, and expertise, from the perspective of our state of nature? There are two questions here: What *legitimizes* such ways of claiming empirical truth, and the institutions that make the claims? And what makes such institutions *reliable*? In political philosophy, we distinguish between merely legitimate and good government; we should distinguish similarly, in epistemology, between merely legitimate and effective or reliable ways of pursuing truth. A legitimate truth regime[4] will be one that acknowledges the need for socialized or higher-level truth discourse to be responsible to plain truths, one in which the experts on a theory make a good-faith effort to justify their claims as extensions or explanations of plain truths, rather than proclamations that need to be taken on faith. But a reliable truth regime will not *just* be legitimate: there will be good reason to see the way it systematizes and explains plain truths as generally adequate. The experts and theorists in reliable truth regimes will make not just good-faith, but generally *successful* efforts to justify themselves by way of plain truths. They will bear the relationship to merely legitimate experts and theorists that successful politicians do to merely legitimate ones. Of course, this is not an entirely hard and fast distinction. In politics, rulers who are unsuccessful in carrying out the most basic tasks of government are rightly suspected of not making a good-faith effort to rule legitimately and, in any case, wind up fostering

conditions (anarchy, mob rule, criminal gangs) that are little better than tyranny. Similarly, experts and theorists who are utterly unsuccessful in justifying themselves by way of plain truths do not differ materially from experts and theorists who make no effort to justify themselves at all. For the most part, we are interested far more in the reliability than the mere legitimacy of a truth regime. But especially where it is hard to tell whether a truth regime is reliable or not—as is the case on religious matters—we need to insist at least on legitimacy: on an approach to the justification of theory and expertise that keeps the paradigmatic status of plain truths firmly in view.

With this in mind, let's examine how a legitimate truth regime might arise from our state of nature.

We have already seen that the people in our state of nature may include experts on various subjects (e.g. Françoise, the mushroom connoisseur: § 12). This is a feature of their life that is likely to increase dramatically as that life becomes more complicated. At a very simple stage, advantages as regards truth may be purely a matter of spatio-temporal position. I know better than you that there is a lion approaching because I am in the tree and you are on the ground, or I know better than you that there are fresh berries on the mulberry bush because I went there this morning. Even here, it is possible that some people—with sharper eyesight, or more patience, or a better ability to draw inferences—will prove more likely than others to be right. And as the society becomes more sophisticated, more opportunities will arise for differences in skill to show up as differences in reliability about truth. As there come to be complicated irrigation systems or methods of accounting, let alone scientific theories to explain and guide such technology, there will be more occasions in which one person has intellectual or observational advantages over others, rather than mere spatiotemporal advantages. Moreover, the division of labor that comes with such advances in technology will *create* differences in skill, and corresponding differences in knowledge.[5] So one will not use the language of truth just to pick out people with advantageous positions in time or space, but start to invest some people with a better *ability* to access truth than others, at least on some subjects. A class of experts will arise, people whose job it is to provide information wherever others don't have it, and they will be regarded as having a better sense of how to pursue truth in general than other people do.

This provides a natural model for how truth systems on factual matters come to be hierarchical and why there are good reasons to turn to experts, over the opinions of just anybody, in many areas. But the model also brings out why such hierarchies can be dangerous. For the very fact that other people trust you to lead them to the truth on a variety of issues opens up opportunities for you to mislead them. After all, positional advantages due to skill, or greater knowledge, are not nearly as easy to correct as positional advantages due to literal place. Others may be unable to acquire your understanding of irrigation or accounting, or unable to do so in time to correct your misleading statements before they are acted upon. So your expertise gives you an opportunity to exploit those who turn to you, and over time many experts will make use of that opportunity. All human beings are subject to desires that would be most readily satisfied by manipulating their fellows, and the sorts of skill that make for cognitive expertise do not have any special tendency to correlate with nobility of character. In addition, some of the desires that lead to manipulation are ideological desires—desires to realize visions that one believes will benefit everyone—and experts, looked up to as models of wisdom, are rather more likely than other people to become convinced that their ideological visions are correct, to find clever ways of rebutting criticism of those visions, or to refuse to heed such criticism. Finally, the position of being regarded as an expert conduces to laziness (why bother to check one's facts when nobody can catch one out if one doesn't?). As a result of all this, some experts become *worse* guides to truth than those who know less than they do. It follows that a tribe that wants the best possible access it can have to truth will need its experts to keep a sharp, critical eye on one another, and its non-experts to keep a sharp eye on the whole class of experts.

These considerations allow us to sketch a model of a reliable truth regime. Any moderately sophisticated society needs to have both experts and critics of those experts, and it needs generally to rely on the experts, while at the same time listening intently for the moments when the critics make a good case for the experts' corruption or laziness or dogmatism. We may picture this as a "center and periphery" model—as opposed both to purely hierarchical, expert-focused models, and to deconstructive models that reject any distinction between center and periphery, or see knowledge as conducted entirely on the periphery—in which the members of a society consider it generally appropriate to turn to experts, and to reject opinions that experts tell them are ridiculous, but also protect a periphery of critical voices against the sneers and power plays of the experts, and give them a close hearing whenever they make good sense, or the experts seem to be obviously betraying or abandoning their proper role. One thing to note about the critics is that they will perforce appeal to plain truths as a way of undermining the experts' claims. Theories will be accepted and rejected in accordance with their ability to help us predict or manage the non-theoretical truths of the state of nature. And non-experts will make their case for corruption or laziness among, say, experts in irrigation or accounting by pointing to canals fouled with excrement or governments that are broke, while their advisors get rich. Expertise, and the theories that breed expertise, will be judged by their mesh with plain truth.

20. There are other aspects of the expert/non-expert relationship that come out when we consider theory as a practice of its own. It has been widely recognized since the work of Thomas Kuhn that training in any sort of theoretical expertise takes place within "paradigms" of how knowledge in that area should be pursued.[6] A paradigm is a concrete model of how to work—often, as Kuhn explains it, a particular experiment or type of experimental procedure—held up as an example to apprentices in the enterprise, which the budding expert is supposed to follow, and the presuppositions of which she is supposed to accept, as she develops her own research agenda; the paradigm

also helps set the questions she explores. Kuhn calls work within the paradigm "normal science," and work that proposes a new paradigm, "revolutionary science." He adds, although this often goes missing among his followers, that *most* science will, of necessity, be normal science.[7] Paradigms allow different scientists to co-ordinate their investigations, share results, and check each other's work: the social space of science would not exist without them. Paradigms also provide a concrete model for how to instantiate theoretical laws and concepts, without which we would have no criteria for judging theories. They provide the "middle term," the link between the abstract and the concrete, giving content to theories. Without paradigms, we cannot derive plain truths from theory, and we cannot accumulate theoretical knowledge, add one discovery to another. Without paradigms, there would not even be revolutions. Paradigms set the terms for their own overturning, and there is no revolution without a paradigm to overturn and a new one to propose in its place. Continuous revolution would not be revolution at all, and would certainly not be science.

The importance of paradigms gives us yet another reason to foster expertise. A paradigm is something we cannot understand or make use of without training. In her training, the budding expert learns what a paradigm means—how it represents the going theory—and how to see out from within it, to absorb its terms: to make judgments and set questions for herself, in those terms. So the apprentice comes, once again, but now for somewhat different reasons, to a type of knowledge that others can't obtain on their own. We have seen that societies can grow to a point in which differences in mental ability, whether inborn or a product of the division of labor, lead some to have knowledge that others lack, but in that case the knowledge is something that people of the right psychological constitution could, in principle, acquire on their own. Now an intrinsically social feature of knowledge produces a difference between experts and non-experts. And since this feature is *intrinsically* social, no-one can achieve the relevant expertise on his or her own. In theoretical knowledge, as opposed to knowledge of plain truths, progress depends on learning a paradigm accepted by an established group of experts: on being "socialized" into a discipline, as the process of learning paradigms is often described. But that process further extends the difference between experts and non-experts. It has the consequence that revolutions in a theoretical discipline will almost always come from within—from experts who know the going paradigm well enough to overturn it.

It also has the consequence that the pursuit of knowledge in the theoretical realm is structured by a feature that limits one's ability to view rival theories clearly. What makes a truth-teller reliable, here, makes him potentially unreliable as well: an intrinsic part of the growth of knowledge is also a potential obstacle to that knowledge. Investigators in a well-developed theoretical discipline can't work without a paradigm. They can choose only between working in one paradigm and working in another. To the extent that specific features of a going paradigm are unrepresentative of what needs to be explored, or its presuppositions are misleading, one can opt only for another concrete model, blocking from view other aspects of the field, and having presuppositions that are misleading in other ways. Experts in a field will therefore have good reason to resist any proposed overthrow of their paradigm. At the same time, knowing that their investigations are guided by models with these intrinsic limitations, every responsible investigator needs to be on the lookout for good reasons to *endorse* such a revolution, to decide that another model will advance her field better than the one in which she is working. Experts must keep an especially wary eye out for the flaws of their fellow experts, and the limitations of the mode of investigation in which they are jointly engaged. No-one else will know when their paradigms have failed.

21. We have now seen a variety of reasons why cognitive experts may be useful to the pursuit of truth while simultaneously posing dangers to it. Just as the very factors that enable government to enhance our liberty also allow it to destroy that liberty (on Locke's account and in fact), so the very factors that enable the growth of expertise to expand what we know also make possible widespread and devastating forms of misinformation and superstition.

Which makes it crucial that experts be constantly scrutinized for dogmatism, corruption or laziness. Without, not just free speech, but an array of independent truth-gathering institutions—competing news media, universities and publishing houses, and private as well as public research centers—and a wide variety of protections for dissidents, we have no reason to consider our truth regime a reliable one. So we have reason to tolerate, even to foster, a range of anti-establishment voices, where even cranks can make themselves heard. Only a vigorous periphery, which can challenge and sometimes overturn well-entrenched centrist figures and views, gives us reason to have confidence in our truth regime as a whole.

At the same time, our picture allows us to posit an asymmetry between the center and the periphery. If the truth regime is a reliable one, with a healthy mode of checking and questioning experts, then everyone has reason to trust the center far more than the periphery, to assume that those in the center are correct, when they speak in their areas of expertise, unless there is strong evidence to the contrary. Even if we have not investigated any of these things ourselves, we are exercising our cognitive capacities correctly when we assume that JFK was not assassinated by a conspiracy reaching into the upper echelons of the US government, that Elvis is not still alive, that the theory of evolution by natural selection is broadly sound, and that biblical accounts of history are ridden with falsehood. There need to be experts in areas like these—we cannot, for many reasons, each investigate them for ourselves—and we live in a society with a reliable truth regime, so even if a few of the accepted views on these subjects turn out to be incorrect, it is far more likely that the experts are right, on most of them, than the cranks.

22. To complete our picture of legitimate and healthy truth regimes, let's briefly consider illegitimate and unhealthy ones.[8] A truth regime will be obviously illegitimate

where the state or some other powerful body prosecutes people who dissent from an official political or religious line. Political tyrannies in which dissenters are killed or imprisoned, and religious tyrannies in which heretics are sent to the stake, are paradigm examples of regimes in which one has no reason to trust what one hears from the experts. But a similar effect can be achieved where an authoritarian state, or powerful church, is simply the sole or primary owner of news media, or controls most education. Here, dissenters need not be imprisoned or executed; they need just be kept from educating the young, and disseminating their views widely. Again, one has reason to distrust all experts under such a regime, even when they appear intelligent and sincere.

An unreliable if not precisely illegitimate truth regime is also possible without anyone explicitly controlling the flow of information. Where most people are too uneducated to judge effectively of what they hear, much less to provide evidence or arguments against it, few skeptics and dissenters will arise. Those few will, moreover, be a motley crew of the thoughtful and the lunatic, will probably not get much of an audience, and will find it difficult to co-ordinate their efforts effectively. A person who lived in such a society would have reason to doubt the word of anyone around her who purported to speak with expert authority.

Something similar goes for societies where there are few universities and independent news sources, where there is no tenure or other protection for unpopular scholars, or where universities and research centers hire their friends and students to every position. What is officially put out and accepted as knowledge in such a truth regime is unlikely to have been well investigated, much less to have been checked properly by others for accuracy. Those doing the checking put their own job at risk, after all, if they contradict their teachers or friends.

These are just a few examples of illegitimate truth regimes. In each case, an individual who came to understand the nature of the truth regime in her society might suppose she had reason to doubt the testimony of its experts altogether, and try to reconstruct her knowledge base, as much as possible, from scratch. I suggest that this is a good way of understanding the epistemological projects of Descartes, Hume, and Kant. Descartes was frustrated by the dogmatic, old-fashioned scientific teachings that dominated European education at the time, including the schools at which he had studied, and he frequently indicates that this frustration was a motivation for his philosophical work.[9] Hume tells us in the opening section of his *Enquiry Concerning Human Understanding* that his investigation of the limits of our thought is meant to help undermine "popular superstition," "religious fears and prejudices," and the "abstruse philosophy and metaphysical jargon" that supports such confused ways of thinking.[10] And Kant uses his account of how we ought to reason as a ground for rejecting the supposed authority of religious teachers and texts.[11] But that is to say that these philosophical projects were not inspired by epistemological concerns that might have occurred to anyone at any time. They had, rather, a particular *political* setting, and were intended, as much as anything, to help individuals overcome the baleful effects of powerful institutions that had corrupted the societal search for truth. Had these philosophers respected the social means of truth-gathering around them, they might have attended more to the social component of epistemology instead of making the search for knowledge appear an entirely individualist matter.[12]

I don't mean by saying this to denigrate epistemology and put politics in its stead. I mean, instead, to suggest that *epistemology and politics are intertwined*, that improving our cognitive situation may require us in part to improve our politics, and that endorsing the soundness of the knowledge claims around us requires us, in part, to make a political judgment. I have good reason to trust an expert claim, and better reason to trust a consensus among experts, when I know that the truth regime under which I live is subject to a healthy balance of credentialing and rigorous questioning, that there are appropriate courses of training through which would-be experts must pass before they are given positions of trust, and that at the same time all experts, including those doing the training, are subject to vigorous scrutiny. As W. K. Clifford rightly observed, the authority of an expert "is valid because there are those who question it and verify it."[13]

23. We may use this account of expertise to respond to creationists and other religious questioners of modern science. Contemporary opponents of evolution often represent themselves as opposing a dogmatic scientific establishment in much the way that Descartes opposed a dogmatic Church. What do we say to this challenge? Well, one thing we cannot say is that the Ptolemaic establishment in Descartes' time based its claims on authority, while we base our belief in evolution on empirical evidence. Not only do laypeople today trust scientists in much the way that the laity trusted the clergy in Descartes' time—not only do almost all of us believe in evolution, if we do, on the authority of scientists and not on the basis of our own observations— but scientists themselves contribute to the building of a theory only by taking an enormous number of empirical and theoretical beliefs on authority. There is no point in investigating the reasons why the Neanderthals died out, and no way to set up experiments or archeological digs to test hypotheses on the subject, without taking on trust many theories in chemistry, physics, and biology, and many factual claims made by other parts of the theory of evolution itself. Each scientist fits whatever she discovers on her own into a given theoretical context. So authority relations are as crucial to modern science as they were to theology in the medieval church.

What we can say to the opponent of evolution is that our modern authority structures are much more open and much more responsive to empirical evidence than any religious establishment has ever been—certainly more so than the church in Descartes' day. One may fail to get tenure if one disagrees with widely-held beliefs in one's scientific community, but even that is often not the case, and one will certainly not be burned at the stake. Nor does any scientist, even a head of a prestigious scientific association, have the power to declare a set of views anathema, and forbid people from proclaiming them or trying to prove them. And the work of most scientists consists in projects that are designed to correct as much as possible for subjective biases, and that are closely scrutinized by colleagues who get rewarded for raising good skeptical questions. So while today we may rely as much on authority as our ancestors did in Descartes' day, there is excellent reason to believe that our authority structures are more reliable, on factual matters, than the Catholic authorities that Descartes criticized.

This may seem a disappointing response to the creationist; many defenders of modern science would prefer to do that by showing the correctness of scientific principles than by appealing to the health of the scientific establishment. But it is hard to find *a priori* arguments for the correctness of the principles underlying science,[14] and even if one did, they would not vindicate any particular scientific theory. Even if evolution by natural selection could be shown to be true by the principles of scientific method alone, moreover, that would not be the reason why we believe in it. No, we believe in evolution, when we do, because we *trust the scientific authorities* who have built that theory. We have very good reason to trust them, very good reason to think they have built the theory on a massive collection of data, and a judicious, responsible analysis of those data. But in the end it is the trustworthiness of scientific authorities on which our biological beliefs rest, not a direct inference from things we can all observe, or a direct application of scientific canons to such observations.

24. Let us return at this point to Bernard Williams' claims about the eliminability of supernatural forces. It should now be clear that the proper place to consider such an elimination is on the second-order, socialized level of discourse, not in the state of nature. In the state of nature, reports of spirit- or god-sightings will be treated much like reports of pineapple- or tiger-sightings, and while any particular report of this kind might be undermined by the unreliability of the informant announcing it, there is no reason to suppose that the entire *kind* of report would be rejected. That move requires a theory about what sorts of entity the world contains—a theory of nature, against which the supernatural can be contrasted—and such theories, and the more abstract positional advantage for assessing truth that goes with them, arise only on our second level of discourse. So supernatural entities will be eliminated, if at all, only on this second level.

Will they be eliminated there? There is no guarantee that they will. Second-order theories, and the notion of truth that goes with them, are far more contestable than first-order empirical reports, and there will not be nearly as straightforward, universally acceptable a way of showing that an entity posited on that level does not exist. What *will* presumably happen is that a second-order theory *that claims to improve first-order empirical reports* will be rejected if it fails to do that. Thus, a claim to the effect that "prayer to Zeus cures illnesses" will generally fall out of favor in the face of an alternative theory about what cures illnesses, should the latter have more predictive success than the former. This gibes with Williams' point about supernatural forces disappearing from a society's discourse once more successful naturalistic explanations take their place (TT 51–52). By extension, supposed empirical evidence for the existence of God may fail by the lights of a successful scientific theory. Design proofs for the existence of God, and their creationist descendants, have come to fail for this sort of reason. And the ontological and cosmological proofs of God have come to fail for reasons more loosely tied to scientific theory: reasons that follow from the metaphysical and logical theories generally held, by our truth regime, to make best sense in the light of modern science. All of these are much more contestable bases on which to refute a claim than the sort of thing that refutes plain truths in our state of nature; they leave out, in any case, the possibility that theories tied to *ethical* plain truths, rather than empirical ones, might vindicate a belief in God (or other supernatural being or principle). Theoretical discourse about God is not subject to easy empirical or logical refutation. Certainly, our state of nature theory alone does not tell us which theories of science and metaphysics are correct, just that generally accepted theories of this kind will be the measure of socialized—second-order—truth claims. Still, these theories as a whole are largely judged by how well they help us produce or assess plain truths, so a scientific or metaphysical theory that appeals to God may well lose legitimacy, in the eyes of the public, if rival theories are better at explaining or producing plain truths. When presented *as* a matter of science, or the philosophy of science, claims for the existence of God may be defeated, at a particular time, by the science of that day.

And if we ask today whether we have reason to accept religious claims on a scientific basis, or by inference from the philosophy of science, the answer I think is clearly "no." Our going science and philosophy of science makes the idea of experiencing supernatural entities seem virtually incoherent, while also giving us an error theory to explain why societies in an earlier day included claims of such experience among their plain truths. Our scientific theories also show how we can explain practically every supposedly mysterious feature of our universe without making reference to supernatural entities. And the theories of logic and metaphysics we have developed in conjunction with modern science are held by almost all experts neither to depend on a belief in God nor to favor proofs of God. Neither on the level of plain truth, then, nor on the level of theory, do we have scientific reason to believe in God, or any other entity beyond the realm of naturalistic explanation; on the contrary, we have reason to *exclude* such entities from our empirical beliefs. Granted, what encourages us to carry out this exclusion is theory, but sifting out real from unreal kinds of entities is a primary function of theory—plain truths themselves, as we have seen, cannot do this—and theory is, moreover, in no way more suspect than plain truth. Theory is something that our state-of-nature truth practices themselves demand we develop, and it corrects many claims once taken to be plain truths. There is thus nothing less certain about a claim that follows from a well-entrenched scientific theory than about a well-attested plain truth. And our most well-entrenched scientific theories today firmly rule out belief in supernatural entities as at best unnecessary to the explanation of the empirical world, at worst obviously false. We have every reason to trust our experts on this.[15]

25. But we have no reason to trust these experts when they insist that science alone can delineate reality. Science can give us good reasons against believing that a God is part of nature, that the supposed empirical evidence for miracles is ever trustworthy,

and that the history recounted in sacred texts is true. Science cannot tell us that there is no God, or other being or principle beyond nature, or that it is impossible for the natural order to be suspended or complemented. Pace Richard Dawkins, these are not scientific hypotheses.[16] Nor is the idea that science could rule out the existence of a God, or other supernatural entity or principle, a scientific hypothesis: the fact that no empirical evidence can possibly count for these sorts of claims entails that no empirical evidence can count against them either. Science cannot tell us that the natural order (what it studies) is all there is. Scientism—the idea that science tells us all there is to tell about reality—does not follow from science; naturalism, the idea that nature is all there is, is not a scientific hypothesis.

Indeed, the philosopher of religion Alvin Plantinga has recently argued that naturalism is self-defeating, that the premises of evolutionary biology, in particular, render it unlikely that any of our beliefs, including our belief in evolutionary biology, are reliable guides to truth.[17] Evolutionary theory suggests that we will develop beliefs that adapt us well to our environments, not true beliefs. Adaptive beliefs need not be true, and may indeed be more successful, in some circumstances, if they are not true: a false belief that all snakes are dangerous may for instance be a better guide to survival than a more accurate belief that could lead us to interact with the wrong sort of snake.[18] I like this argument, although I would revise it a bit,[19] but even if it is wrong there is no scientific reason to suppose that naturalism is true. Naturalism is a metaphysical view, not a scientific one; many alternative metaphysical views could be true without the facts that scientists consider being any different.

Now one might argue, on grounds independent of science, that metaphysical views should be rooted as much as possible in empirical facts, and that metaphysics is or must be continuous with scientific theories about such facts. But there is no principle of deductive or inductive logic that would dictate such an approach to metaphysics, and empirical evidence cannot be used to support it without circularity. It could perhaps be supported by an "inference to the best explanation" of what metaphysics seems to accomplish, but what counts as a "best explanation," in this area, is likely to be highly contested. It is contested, after all, even when scientific theories are in question: how to balance simplicity against empirical adequacy, how to define both of those terms, and whether other considerations should be taken into account when evaluating scientific theories, remain, and probably always will remain, subjects of great controversy among scientists and philosophers of science. When we turn, now, from scientific theories to theories *about* science, all of these problems will be vastly exacerbated: and one will, in addition, have to determine how hypotheses about supernatural entities or principles can be assessed without circularity. So the likelihood that experts will ever be able to agree on an answer to the metaphysical question of how, in general, to define "reality" is very remote. Experts on metaphysics and experts in science are very different sorts of creatures, and there is no reason to expect convergence among the former, nor to take even convergence among them to be validated by the mesh with plain truths that can validate our acceptance of scientific experts. Nothing that I have said in favor of accepting our reigning scientific experts, as against creationists and believers in the historical accuracy of the Bible, therefore tells in favor of accepting the word of *philosophers* of science (or scientists, when they try to do philosophy) on metaphysical questions like whether a God exists.

For what it's worth, my personal view is that metaphysical arguments based solely on logical and scientific considerations will forever leave the question of whether there is or is not a God, or any other supernatural principle or entity, indeterminate. It is a metaphysics based on *ethical* considerations—in a broad sense of "ethics," which I will define in Part II (§ 38)—that can support belief in God (or the *tao*, or a number of other religious views), and even then we come to these beliefs in the first instance by way of an embrace, in faith, of a certain text or teaching as revealed. We begin to believe in a God, and perhaps certain miracles, or in the possibility that we can transcend our human nature and grasp something that, naturalistically speaking, seems impossible to grasp, *because* we believe in (trust) certain teachers and teachings. And we then endorse the truth of these texts and teachings because they help us make sense of our notions of the good: of the purposes we think we had best pursue in our lives, and of the place of morality in that pursuit. So we come to our considered beliefs in certain supernatural entities or principles because we are trying to make metaphysical sense of certain ethical notions, not scientific ones. And these ethical beliefs may lead us to complement or override some of what we believed on the basis of science alone (we have no reason to believe in an afterlife, much less in miracles, if we trust just our best theories about what the natural order is like, but might have such reason if our ethical metaphysics allows us to see the natural order as rooted in a supernatural one).[20] But such beliefs, by hypothesis, will not be *scientific* beliefs, nor beliefs that can be grounded in the metaphysics of science. We will mistake their nature, and corrupt both our ethics and our science, if we treat them as if we had scientific evidence for them.

26. This completes my case against creationism, claims for the historical veracity of the Bible, and other attempts to underwrite religion, in the modern day, by way of science or the presuppositions of science. Our reliance on scientific theories that challenge religiously-based empirical claims is a reliance on fallible experts, of course, but that is as solid a basis for empirical belief as we can have—reasonable to question only when there are signs that the whole truth regime of which the experts are a part is improperly structured. There is no justification for challenging such a regime simply because it threatens one's pet religious beliefs. And since the modern scientific truth regime, in Western countries, is as well structured as any truth regime in human history, and since it is virtually unanimous in its rejection of the empirical claims made by traditional religions, we have reason to accept that consensus unless and until it is challenged from within.

Two points, in conclusion. First, it may seem inappropriate to lump the metaphysical and logical considerations that have dismantled traditional arguments for the existence of God together with scientific challenges to creationism and the historical claims of the Bible: to lump together metaphysical and scientific experts. And as I indicated in the previous section, I certainly don't mean to imply that metaphysics enjoys or should enjoy the credibility of scientific theories, or that its experts converge in a similar way. But the metaphysics *of* science develops its canons of argument in tandem with developments in science. When final causes seem to have an important scientific use, they are also respected as a tool for metaphysical argument. When science is understood to require *a priori* laws, the settling of fundamental questions of ontology also relies on a priori principles. It is no accident that traditional arguments for the existence of God began to fall out of favor just as scientists began to feel that the hypothesis of a God was unnecessary to their work.

Second, my case is an unabashedly historical one, not an argument that religion was never reasonably seen as supported by science. As we noted earlier (§ 4), the truth regime in many premodern worlds converged strongly on the view that reason can show the existence of God, and it seems that those truth regimes were often both legitimate and reliable. It was therefore reasonable for people then to trust the experts who argued for God's existence. By exactly the same token, however, it is reasonable for people now to trust the experts who say there is no good scientific argument for God's existence. It is implausible to me both that Maimonides' or Thomas Aquinas' proofs of God were a mere mistake and that they remain reasonable today because they were reasonable then. An argument against the empirical or logical foundations of religious belief need not make that belief look equally unwarranted at all times. In other circumstances, with different experts and theories, it was reasonable to believe in God as a matter of science. Today, under a regime of experts who have shown what is wrong with Aristotelian and neo-Platonic science, and produced outstandingly successful theories of nature that have no room for God, it is unreasonable.

In general, it is reasonable to trust one's experts on empirical matters as long as one knows that they are working within a system in which theory and expertise are held responsible to plain truth, and, as far one knows, there is no better truth regime out there in that respect. It is therefore reasonable for us, today, to trust the scientific establishment when it tells us that the empirical claims on which our religions are based are unproven or false. That doesn't mean that there is no reason to believe in traditional religions. It just means that any reasons we might have for that belief will not be empirical ones, and we cannot look to scientific experts to underwrite them. What other sorts of reasons there may be is the subject of our next chapter. There we will also consider the attitude that religious people call "faith," which is very different from the kind of trust we put in scientific experts. Religion certainly requires trust, but it requires trust for different reasons, and in different sorts of people, than science does.

4

Experts and Authorities

27. I take the previous two chapters to have made a case for the first broad thesis I'd like to draw from our investigation into truth: that religious people have reason to respect the same scientific experts and theories as everyone else does, and today have reason, therefore, to reject a scientific basis for their religious claims. If treated as scientific hypotheses, these claims are almost certainly false.

The second broad thesis I'd like to establish goes in the opposite direction: that religious claims may be true if treated as part of ethics, rather than science. We will need to draw on a different aspect of our state of nature story to defend this second thesis. As long as we look at observational plain truths and the theories based on them, Williams is quite right: religious claims will fade from the scene as more successful naturalistic ones take their place. But Williams plays down the fact that observational reporting is not the only form of discourse in the state of nature, and ignores the fact that empirical evidence is not the only source of support for truth claims in religion. He also ignores the fact that, once second-order discourse comes on the scene, claims can shift their register, can cease being observational reports and become, instead, elements of ethical or other evaluative discourse. We'll begin this chapter by exploring such shifts, then turn to the types of truth claims that appear in ethical discourse, and how some such claims may underwrite a religion.

28. What might it mean for a sentence to "shift register"?

An 18th century biologist writes, "Eye-color gets passed down in the blood." Prima facie this utterance is false: nothing gets passed down in the blood. But we can also regard it as *essentially* true. Suppose the 18th-century biologist was directing his remark against views that eye-color is a product of the environment. We may presume that if we could bring the biologist back to life today, and teach him genetic theory, he would say "Well, that's what I meant." And we can easily allow this, even though he surely anticipated nothing quite like genetic theory when he originally made his remark, and even though "in the blood" does not literally mean "in the genes." We allow for a broad interpretation of the remark, perhaps turning the originally literal language into a metaphor. Dead metaphors can become literal, according to Donald Davidson[1]—why shouldn't dead literal language become metaphorical? That seems exactly what has happened to words like "melancholic" and "hysterical."

Elsewhere I have argued that we do this for reasons analogous to those that make for the doctrine of "frustrated contracts" in law.[2] When a contract cannot be fulfilled for reasons that neither party to the contract could have foreseen, legal systems often allow the party who loses thereby to collect something for its losses.[3] The point is that contracts take place against a set of background expectations that are taken for granted by both parties to the agreement. When those background expectations fail—where the parties are both, as jurists say, "surprised by the facts"—exactly what the contract commits the parties to is unclear. But it may well give them *some* commitments. Something analogous happens in conversation. Our utterances normally commit us to a claim given a set of reasonable background expectations. Where those expectations fail, it will be unclear exactly what we remain committed to, but we may remain committed to *something*. This is a good framework with which to understand our biologist: the facts have surprised both him and those he was engaging in conversation enough to render the meaning of their debate indeterminate. Whether traits are passed down by blood or by genes was not in question in the debate between him and his opponents; his opponents would have granted that *if* eye-color is passed down, it is passed down in the blood. Hence, no participant in the conversation would have known what literal language to use in the new circumstances. And *we*, looking back on their argument, are entitled to see one of the two parties as committed to something closer to the truth than his opponents were.

Another example: Pythagoras seems to have believed that numbers were real entities, more perfect than anything in the material world, and that he was able to discover relations among them by way of a mystical, direct connection to this ideal world. Mathematics was, for him, a kind of religion. Today, we reject his religion while accepting his mathematics. So sentences that for Pythagoras may have meant one thing—may have had, for instance, religious implications—mean something quite different to us. We say that the Pythagorean theorem is true, while being aware that we would not necessarily regard it as true under his interpretation of it. His sentences have *shifted*, have *swerved*, from the realm of religion to the realm of mathematics (or from a realm in which religion and mathematics were intertwined to one of "mere" mathematics). In the process, his non-naturalistic understanding of what he was doing has been reinterpreted as a recognition that mathematics is an *a priori* rather than an empirical science; his religious language may accordingly be reinterpreted as metaphorical for a Kantian understanding of the status of mathematics.

Both of these cases concern what I have called the socialized or theoretical realm: they have to do with how, in the course of doing the history of science, we interpret past scientific theories. Neither would arise in our state of nature, and it may seem as if shifting or swerving occurs only where theory is in play, and truth attributed to claims *about* truth-claims, rather than to first-order statements alone.

I expect this phenomenon will, indeed, be more part of socialized or theoretical discourse than of the discourse we attributed to the state of nature. But there is every reason to suppose that discourse could also shift or swerve in the state of nature. Suppose Fred, in that simpler world, sees an animal in the distance and comes rushing into the village to proclaim that a crash of rhinoceros is approaching. People barricade themselves in their homes or make tracks for another village. Meanwhile, others go out to a sighting post, and eventually more careful observers than Fred, or observers with better eye-sight, report that there are, in fact, some large animals moving toward us, but they are elephants, not rhinoceri. Fred says: "Well, I meant that there were animals stampeding toward us; it doesn't matter whether they are rhinoceri or not."

Will Fred be regarded as having told the truth? That depends on a number of things, such as how much the fierceness of the approaching animals matters to his fellow villagers. If they were mainly worried about the fierceness of the animals, then it will matter a great deal that they are elephants, rather than rhinoceri, and Fred will be regarded as having not told the truth. But if they were mainly worried about being trampled, then his report may well be regarded as true—or true *enough*, true "for all intents and purposes." Of course, his report was not *as* true as those of the better observers who came after him, but the difference may be unimportant, not worth mentioning or investigating. (As when a pedantic person says, "he's not really in the *bath*room" because there's no bath in that room.) An attempt of other observers to find out exactly what animal is approaching could, indeed, endanger the village, in many circumstances. The search for precise reports would then defeat the purposes for which the villagers gather reports at all.

By the same token, the search for precision would defeat the purposes for which the villagers attribute truth and falsehood to reports. A reliable reporter will be one who gets things as right as they need to be for the purposes for which the report is made; one who tries to be more precise than that may well be a reporter on whom the villagers do *not* want to rely. Imagine that Balthazar responds to Fred's outcry by saying, simply, "Fred's not telling the truth." The effect of that might be to stop all preparations against a stampede, and the villagers—if they survive—might prefer in future to rely on Fred's reports than Balthazar's. A refusal to jump to a possibly inaccurate conclusion, when a report of some kind is needed, may be a terrible failure to contribute to a society's pool of information, and the society might therefore be reluctant to regard people with such scruples as excellent truth-tellers.

29. So the function of truth-telling even in the state of nature allows people to claim a slightly different sentence from the one they uttered as what they "meant." But in the rhinoceros case, the literal meaning of a sentence shifts, while the sentence remains within the same type of discourse. What about attempts to shift a sentence from a literal to a non-literal meaning, or from one mode of discourse to another? Is there room for that in the state of nature?

Well, there are certainly different registers of speech in our state of nature, and I see no reason why a sentence couldn't sometimes preserve its truth by shifting from one of these registers to another. Suppose Aloysius tells me that in the village over the mountain I will find a great treasure. Greedy fellow that I am, I dash off to look for it. But what I actually find is a terrible famine. Having brought along a lot of food to keep me going while I looked for the treasure, I am in a position to alleviate the suffering, and I set to work doing that. As it happens, seeing suffering and being able to help end some of it has a powerful impact on me, so I come back from the village surprised to find myself feeling rather good about life. I am, however, still annoyed that there was no treasure when I had been told there was. When I tax Aloysius with this, I become even more annoyed, because it turns out that he knew perfectly well that people were starving in the village, and there was nothing for me to acquire. "But," he says, "the opportunity for you to help others—and to discover the joy of doing that— was that not a great 'treasure'?" If I agree that it was, as I might, I will surely not regard Aloysius as a liar. (If I also ruefully acknowledge, as I might, that I would never have gone to the village had Aloysius not used the word "treasure," then I may even admit that he told me the truth in the only way I could have heard it.) Here, a sentence retains its truth by shifting from a prudential to a moral key. And its central term, correspondingly, shifts from a literal to a metaphorical meaning.

Why should this not happen in our state of nature? No reflection on modes of truth-gathering is needed to set up the story, and allowing for such shifts could enhance how people give advice, even in a very simple society. Indeed, the resemblance of the story I have told to many traditional folktales suggests that it represents precisely how people in relatively simple communities get a reputation for dispensing "wisdom": how people like Aloysius come to be regarded as the highest kind of truth-teller.

30. The Aloysius case is a model for understanding a central event in the history of many religious traditions. In fifth-century Athens, Socrates and Plato insisted that "god" must mean a perfect being and that traditional Greek myths about the gods must accordingly be reworked, to eliminate the bits suggesting that gods fight with one another, or engage in lusty or other unvirtuous behaviour. A bit earlier, in Israel and Judea, prophets like Amos and Isaiah insisted, against the plain meaning of older Hebrew traditions, that God will not accept our sacrifices unless they are accompanied by a compassionate and righteous way of life; a view of this kind also informs much Talmudic interpretation of the Torah, and is explicit in Maimonides. And a similar moralizing of practices that may once have been intended to get amoral gods and spirits on one's side can be seen in the teachings of Confucius, and of a series of Hindu reformers. One way to understand these patterns is to say that religious teachings generally tend to shift or swerve over time from the realm of magic to the realm of ethics: from being pragmatic suggestions about how to harness supernatural powers for one's selfish ends to being moral prescriptions, or suggestions for how we can transform ourselves so that we have less selfish ends. In the process, the meaning of key terms in

the original sentences shifts from a literal to a metaphorical one. Maimonides says for instance that God's "anger" must be understood as God's meting out just punishment, not as an emotional state.[4] A belief that the Torah was literally spoken by God on Mount Sinai might similarly shift to a belief in which "spoken by God" becomes metaphorical for "ethically authoritative," and a belief that Jesus of Nazareth was literally crucified and resurrected may change over time into a symbol for God's willingness to suffer with the victims of cruelty, and forgive the agents of it.[5] The historical claims on which a religion relies can thus be transformed into elements of a different mode of discourse.

Why retain the original sentences, in that case? Surely the best thing to do, when a sentence shifts registers, is to replace it with a new sentence, better suited to the new mode of discourse. Instead of saying "God is angry," we should say "God punishes justly," and instead of saying "There's a treasure in the village over the mountain," we should say, "There's an opportunity to do good in the village over the mountain."

Sometimes that will be exactly what we should say. There is every reason to replace "Eye-color gets passed down in the blood" with "Eye-color gets passed down genetically." In other cases, however, including the ones about God's anger and the treasure over the mountain, there is reason to hold on to the original sentence even as it shifts meaning. The original sentence may be more emotionally powerful. "Sacrifice purifies the soul" is more dramatic than "Giving charity improves your character," even if the kind of sacrifice you have in mind is giving charity and the kind of soul-purification you have in mind is improvement of character. "God is angry" may similarly capture the evil in cruelty or oppression more effectively than "Wrongdoing must be punished." Or we may have no alternative language that does a better job of conveying what we were trying to say. Maimonides regards "God punishes justly" as only somewhat less problematic, theologically, than "God is angry." But in that case, it may be preferable to stick with an *obviously* anthropomorphic expression, which cries out for a metaphorical reading, than move to a translation like "God punishes justly," which will appear to many to be literally true. Finally, the original sentence, in its original key, may be the only or the best way to lead a listener into using the higher key that we would like him to employ. "There's a treasure in the village over the mountain," taken literally, may be the only thing that will get a selfish person to go to that village, and if he then learns something of the joys of altruism, there may be no better way to express what he has learned than to say he has come to see the many meanings of "treasure." Indeed, we underplay the point if we say that he comes to take "treasure" as metaphorical once he hears the original sentence in its new key: he really comes to see a new *literal* meaning that the word can bear.

We replace the original sentence with a new, more accurate one when the purposes of the type of discourse in which we are engaged call for such replacement. "Eye-color gets passed down in the blood" needs replacement because it is a sentence of *science*, an enterprise in which precision is essential, and metaphorical language largely unhelpful.

To assume that all modes of discourse similarly require precise and literal language is to assume that all modes of discourse take science as their model. That is not true. Rather, the level of metaphor and obscurity we can tolerate varies with our mode of discourse. The question we need to ask, when we wonder whether we should allow a sentence to swerve in meaning rather than replacing it with a different one, is whether it is useful or necessary, in *this* mode of discourse, to continue to endorse a sentence even after we have come to regard its literal meaning as false. But this question can arise, as we have seen, in the state of nature as well as in conditions of socialized truth-gathering. That sentences can swerve from one realm of discourse to another, and the meaning of their terms shift correspondingly, is a basic feature of language.[6]

31. Let's return to Aloysius. It would be a mistake to treat Aloysius as an expert on ordinary factual matters. If you want to know where to find treasure in the ordinary sense, Aloysius is not your man. Indeed, Aloysius is probably not your man if you seek any sort of information with a clear notion of what your goals are, of what you want to do with the information. He may be your man if you seek precisely to *change* your goals, however, or are open to doing that. And even in the state of nature, there is no reason why people might not sometimes want to do that. It's an ordinary fact, a "plain truth," that some people find themselves burdened by their own desires and want, above all, to *want* different sorts of things.

I say "even in the state of nature," since once reflection on the practices of the state of nature begins, once people begin asking what their practices accomplish and wondering whether they should have different ones, it becomes yet more likely that they may come to feel that they are pointed in the wrong direction, and seek to be oriented differently. Ethical theory, certainly, brings with it the possibility that we need to be transformed, re-oriented, converted from one set of desires and aims to another. The first known forms of ethical theory—the teachings of Confucius and the Buddha, and Socrates and Plato—were programs for the transformation of character. And one feature of many of these theories was a suggestion that people need a guide, a master or guru, to lead them toward transformation. The process that the guide helps initiate brings about a change of perception, moreover, as well as a change of desire: one comes literally to see things differently, to see one's ends differently at least, or to see different things as one's ends. And with this role for perception comes a role for truth-language. In transformative ethical theories, there is a straightforward sense in which some people occupy positions from which they can see what the rest of us cannot, and we need ways of endorsing some of the people who claim this positional advantage and refusing that endorsement to others.

Plato provides the perfect metaphor for this point in his story of the cave, where people are turned around by a philosopher and led to a place where all that seemed real before appears as mere shadows, while the abstractions that seemed shadowy stand out as the true reality. The centrality of a change in perception to his account of the good has been beautifully brought out by Iris Murdoch, in her Platonic meditation *The Sovereignty of Good*, and John McDowell has shown how a similar sort of position can be found even in Aristotle, for whom ethics was not radically transformative.[7] McDowell makes clear that Aristotle carries over from Plato the idea that virtues are ways of perceiving the world—picking out what is salient to our decisions, among the many facts around us—and that perception is shaped by emotion. People with different emotional structures will, therefore, literally see the world differently, and there will be no way to show the non-virtuous person what she would see were she to become virtuous until she actually develops the virtues. It would seem to go along with this position, although neither McDowell nor Aristotle stresses this point, that people need to be led toward virtue in part by silent role modeling or a prescribed discipline, not simply given reasons for pursuing it.

Now the idea that we might need some sort of non-rational guidance in ethics, might need more to trust a teacher than to reason along with him or her, goes uncomfortably with naturalistic ethical theories. It fits in better with the idea that there is something supernatural, something beyond what we can grasp in our natural state, to be encountered if one transforms oneself ethically. The idea of revelation hooks on nicely to such a transformative conception of ethics. It is no accident that Plato was of great importance to the founders of Christianity, or that religious traditions grew out of the teachings of Confucius and the Buddha. Nevertheless, to call the revealed or sacred teaching true, in these cases, is to use the word "true" in a way that a secular ethicist can recognize. If this is the sort of truth to which revealed religion appeals, then it is a sort of truth that has a place in secular ethical thought as well, that can be justified in terms of the plain truths of our state of nature, even if we restrict those plain truths to those that make no mention of gods or spirits. Revealed religions, when they ask us to put faith in their teachings so that we can see something we would never see without that faith, appeal to a mode of validation shared by non-religious practices of truth-telling, and it is only *because* they can appeal to such practices that we understand what it means to call them true.

32. The practice of transformation is significantly different when it becomes part of a religious rather than a secular ethical system. I'll say more about that difference later, but roughly speaking, if transformative experiences are to support a religious view they must be taken as of the presence of God (or of a supernatural enlightenment). One takes them to show what it would be like for an all-good being to govern or produce the universe, what it would be like for the universe to be a fundamentally good place. Or one thinks they show how, from a position beyond ordinary human nature, we could transcend our attachment to ourselves, and thereby no longer experience suffering.[8] An ethical vision that one can attain only via a certain discipline and mode of trust thus shades over into a properly religious vision.

And a religious vision of this sort just is revelation, is what religious believers take to be a communication from God. This is not the same as taking the vision as *evidence* for God's existence: it is not grist for the mill of science. (Only if one already believes in God can one interpret it as the religious believer does.) The fact that experiences of this sort are supposed to be reached only through a relationship of trust in a person or text or discipline separates them off from other experiences. This segregation from ordinary experience makes their apparent content something that cannot be used in scientific arguments,[9] but also makes it impossible for science to refute that content. They are not *evidence* for the supernatural goodness we think we see in them. When we give them central importance in our ethical beliefs, they serve, not as a way of *arguing for* a view, but as *a condition for grasping* that view—a condition for seeing or understanding something, as in the Aloysius case, that we would not have understood otherwise. And this segregation of what we see in such moments from what we learn from ordinary experience serves to insulate it from either contributing to or being refuted by arguments based on what we learn from ordinary experience. We preserve the content of these experiences strictly within the ethical sphere and it contributes to faith, rather than knowledge. In the terms I used when responding to the opening of David Hare's *Gethsemane* (§§ 1–2): it contributes to wisdom, rather than to ordinary or scientific truth.

33. At this point we can draw a distinction between two kinds of cognitive authority. One kind of authority—the kind relevant to our scientific concerns—gets its justification from the pooling of information that helps us meet our material needs in the state of nature. Reliance upon authority here expands what we could find out about nature for ourselves, and although we need not test each authority we rely on for accuracy, we do expect their reports to mesh with our own, to be about objects that fit in with ones we already believe in, and to help us achieve purposes we already have. I don't mean by this to reduce reliance on scientific authority to what we know individually, but we must always *stand ready* to test authorities of this sort by our own observations or by authoritative claims that we feel have already withstood such tests. C. A. J. Coady has shown that reliance on testimony cannot be reduced to what we learn on the basis of our individual cognitive resources alone, that instead our very learning of language, and development, consequently, of individual cognitive capacities, depends on our accepting testimony as a basic, irreducible source of knowledge. Nevertheless, even Coady grants that, having begun "with an inevitable commitment to some degree of [testimony]'s reliability, we find this commitment strongly enforced and supported by the facts of [its] cohesion [with what we know by memory, inference, and perception]."[10] So we are inclined to test bits of testimony, and willing to reject it when it fails such tests, even if we can never test all our testimony-based beliefs at once. Which is to say that, on Coady's picture, we are in principle all *equals*, in the scientific realm, with our authorities. Scientific authorities are to us as witnesses are to a jury; they serve our purposes and need to accord with our standards of truth-telling. "Witness and audience are active explorers of a common world,"[11] Coady says, working together to produce a communal store of knowledge.

This is an attractive and I think accurate picture of knowledge in the realm of observational plain truths and the theories built on them. But given even this very rough characterization of our relationship to authority in that realm, we see a sharp contrast when we come to the ethical realm. For in some parts of the ethical realm, at least, we rely on authorities precisely to *change* our purposes, to lead us to a place where we might come to want different things. Here, we are *not* equal with our authorities, not capable even in principle of occupying their position when we rely upon them, and here we cannot test them by measuring what they say against the purposes that bring us to them: those purposes are as much in question as any of our other purposes. As we have seen, there is a state of nature basis for this relationship, but even in the state of nature it is distinct from the sort of relationship that helps us gather plain truths for purposes we are holding fixed. (Again, Aloysius is not your man if you know what you mean by "treasure" and want the plain truth about how to find it.)

I have spoken thus far of two kinds of authority, but perhaps it would be better to distinguish between expertise and authority. We rely on an *expert* when we seek information within a structure of purposes that we have no immediate plans to change, and when we believe we could, in principle, occupy the expert's position ourselves; we are equals with our experts. We rely on an *authority* when we are out precisely to change our overall orientation or structure of ends, when we are willing to be led to a new way of looking at things; we are, essentially, *not* equals with our authorities. Experts help us refine and expand science; authorities offer wisdom rather than science. Aloysius is an example of an authority, an ethical or spiritual guide—a "guru" or "rabbi," as such people are called in some traditions.[12] He is not an expert and should not be assessed in the way an expert would be. Conversely, experts should not be assessed as if they were authorities, nor relied upon as if they were.

A confusion between faith in an ethical authority and faith in scientific expertise lies at the heart of the attack on science carried out by many religious believers today (and of the response of their scientistic opponents). It is authority, not expertise, to which we may properly respond with religious faith; it is that sort of trust that is called for by revealed texts and those who speak for them. And it is just as important to religious faith *not* to trust authorities as if they were scientific experts as it is *to* trust authorities ethically. After all, religious trust is essentially directed toward *changing* our purposes, opening up new ways of living to us, rather than giving us more effective ways of continuing in the selfish, idolatrous, or deluded paths we already have. So if the practice of science presupposes and reinforces each individual's readiness to use claims for ends she has no plans to change, it is vital that the practice of religion not be confused with it. To treat scientific experts as if they were religious authorities, or religious authorities as if they were scientific experts, will be religiously dangerous.[13]

The religious person should therefore be at the forefront of those who understand and accept the scientific process for what it is, should insist on the need for scientific experts to live up to scientific and not religious standards of excellence. To suppose that an appeal to religious doctrine could count as a trump card against the correctness of a scientific claim is to mistake the nature of religious doctrine, as well as the nature of science. The religious person should instead be as skeptical and detached as the most hard-boiled scientist when it comes to matters of empirical fact. That helps sharpen the distinction between religion and science, which is good for both. Only when we recognize this distinction sharply do we understand what we are doing when we put faith in a religious teacher or text. Only when we recognize this distinction sharply do we open ourselves up to the need to change our nature, and our ends, in the course of religious practice.

34. It is, then, something of a betrayal of religion itself that religious believers frequently oppose healthy truth regimes. From fundamentalist Christians who reject the theory of evolution, to traditional Jews or Muslims who suppose that the Torah or Quran is historically accurate, to the many people, all over the world, who try to block medical or other scientific progress when it conflicts with their religious teachings, it is religious believers above all who today resist the modes of thought characteristic of the Enlightenment, and refuse to accept the fallibilist, open, self-critical truth regime it introduced. On my account, they thereby corrupt their religions, as well as the pursuit of science. If they think through their commitments, religious people not only may, but must strive to be as intellectually honest and open as possible.[14] Policing the borders of faith, ensuring that we do *not* have faith where faith is out of place, is just as important as maintaining faith in its proper sphere. Otherwise we lose the distinctive objects and character of faith, and it becomes instead a cover for a refusal to think.

But the constant risk that faith will degenerate like this means that religious people will rarely find the best model of a healthy cognitive temperament among their fellow religionists. Neither the individual religious life nor the institutions to which religious belief give rise are well-suited to an open-ended, probing search for scientific or philosophical truths. Rather, it is followers of the Enlightenment, with all the skepticism about religion that that movement brought in its wake, who provide the best models for truth-seeking. Here, the way of the world has something to offer divine teaching, and the followers of a divine teaching ignore that offer at their peril. We might say that God Himself wants us to look to the ways of the world, not to divine teaching, for our understanding of truth and how to pursue it. Only then, after all, can we truly judge that—and in what sense—God's own teaching is true. (Only then can we appreciate its *wisdom*: the profundity and importance of its truth.) Moreover, if there is a God, a Creator of the universe, He is also the Creator of skeptics about His existence and teachings, and surely intended them to play a useful role in human life. The rabbinic text from which I have drawn the title for this book also includes the following admonition: "Despise no thing and no person, because every thing has its place and every person has his hour" (*Avot* 4: 3). As regards the nature of truth-seeking, the atheist and agnostic, and certainly the religious skeptic, emphatically "have their hour," and we had better not despise them.

PART II

The Way of the World (II)

ETHICS

If we hear that a man is religious, we still ask, "What are his morals?" But if we hear at first that he has honest moral principles and is a man of natural justice and good temper, we seldom think of the other question, "Whether he be religious and devout?"

—Shaftesbury, *Inquiry Concerning Virtue or Merit*, section 1

1

Introductory

1. Many people think we need religion in order to have a moral code. Indeed, in American popular discourse, religion and morality tend to be identified. When American voters tell pollsters they are concerned with "moral issues," they usually mean by that that they hold certain views—against gay marriage and abortion, for instance—that their religious traditions characterize as "moral" ones. One has only to take a small step back from this way of speaking to find it very strange. *Support* for gay marriage and abortion rights are surely also moral views: even to one who thinks they are incorrect moral views. In fact, not a few people oppose religion, of all sorts, on moral grounds. So it can't be right to *identify* morality with what traditional religions regard as such.

But the point of those who see religion as necessary to morality can be made without this tendentious reinterpretation of language. They mean to say, essentially, that without revealed religious traditions we wouldn't know which moral claims were correct; we would be at sea on moral matters, or misled into unsound or vile moral beliefs. Some maintain that religious traditions first introduced morality to people. All moral views, they say, even if now cast in a secular light, were originally presented to us by religious teachings. On this line of thinking, secular liberals who promote such non- or anti-Biblical causes as pacifism or gay rights really derive their ideals from Christian or Jewish sources, and would clarify their own beliefs if they returned to the Bible. Others eschew these historical claims and hold, instead, that the morality promoted by their religious tradition, or perhaps by all believers in God, is a true morality—a code that promotes true human ideals—while other moral views are instruments of human selfishness that will, in the end, degrade human beings or make them miserable. Those who follow this line of thinking tell secular liberals that their values are hollow, selfish ones, rather than that they stand on grounds established originally by religious teachers. They say that secular people apply the term "morality" to codes that are really excuses for selfishness. Without faith in God, people serve themselves alone, they maintain; any ideal faithless people purport to uphold *must* be an excuse for selfishness.

The claims underlying both of these lines of thinking seem clearly false to me. Human beings did not need to wait for the Ten Commandments or any other religious teaching to learn that there was something wrong with murder and theft—that is not even a very good reading of the Bible, which holds its characters responsible to moral norms long before it introduces the Ten Commandments—nor are non-religious people generally more selfish or morally misguided than religious ones. Indeed, religious believers have been responsible for many of the worst atrocities in human history, often committed in the name of their religion.

One might look for a weaker version of the claim that morality depends on religion. Perhaps the *general outlines* of morality are clear to us even without religious teachings, but religious revelation is necessary to settle many moral details. Secular moral systems, on this view, might have an adequate general grounding and definition, but they are incomplete: God reveals to us how we should complete them. The function of revealed religion is to fill in the gaps in secular morality: sacred texts offer their followers a decision-procedure by which to settle cases that secular moral principles cannot handle.

There are many problems with this view, too, however. The most obvious is that sacred texts do *not*, in fact, provide clear answers to most of the detailed moral problems we worry about, nor any answer to many of them. The Torah contains an extensive code of conduct, but says little about marriage and divorce, nothing, of course, about intellectual property or cloning, and even its apparently clear endorsement of war and capital punishment doesn't necessarily apply in political circumstances very different from the theocracy it envisions. (Some devout Jews cite the Bible as a source for their *opposition* to war and capital punishment: stressing the fact that the biblical guidelines for administering capital punishment aren't followed anywhere today.) This is to say nothing of the difficulty of interpreting the rules it does contain. Something similar can be said about every other revealed text. No code of conduct, revealed or otherwise, covers all moral difficulties. Nor can a code, by itself, tell its users how it should be extrapolated to situations far removed from the ones it describes, or how it should be interpreted when it uses unclear or ambiguous language. No purported revelation of which I am aware even tries to do these things—not the Gospels or Quran or Book of Mormon—and the followers of revealed traditions find themselves on different sides on many moral issues, with people on each side citing passages of their sacred text in support of their position.

> I confess that my own attraction to religion, as I was growing up, initially arose from the view that secular ways of being ethical are weakly grounded. incomplete, and hypocritical. Few of the secular people around me seemed to have especially inspiring ideals, or to live up to the ideals they did proclaim. In addition, I found myself without any clear sense of how I should act: with, instead, an unnervingly astute ability to argue for and against almost any moral claim, to find justifications even for courses of action that at first sight seemed appalling or against the importance of actions that at first sight seemed morally required. The Torah seemed to compensate for this uncertainty about how to act, and to provide moral motivation to boot. A sense of duty to and fear of God kept me in line with conventional

moral norms more than anything else did, and I tried to figure out what norms everyone should hold as best I could by extrapolation from the Torah. I could see no good reason for moral norms other than a desire to accord with God's will, no justification, in purely secular terms, for acting against one's own desires, and I presumed that the right norms were consequently to be found, if at all, in the book I regarded as most likely to express God's will.

And it seemed to me that that was precisely the conclusion to which the Torah wanted me to come: I saw it, for instance, in the relationship between Genesis and the other four books. In Genesis, again and again, the characters who are supposed to be the heroes do things that Sinaitic law would later forbid. Set aside the actions of which the narrator seems clearly to disapprove, such as Jacob's lying to his father, or the sale of Joseph. Without any clear hint of disapproval, we are shown Lot sleeping with his daughters, Abraham and Isaac offering up their wives to other men, Jacob marrying two sisters, and Judah having sex with an apparent prostitute. All these things will be forbidden by Sinaitic law. The most dramatic example is of course Abraham's willingness to bring his son as a human sacrifice. What does this tell us? Perhaps that without revelation, human beings lack crucial kinds of moral knowledge. Perhaps we are supposed to draw a line between the actions of our forefathers that merely **happen** *to violate later, Sinaitic law (e.g. the marrying of sisters) and the evils that the narrator condemns in some manner (e.g. the sale of Joseph): perhaps there is a suggestion that what is wrong with (say) certain marital practices, although hidden, will show itself when the family that results has a later history of vice or feuding.*

So a God-given law comes in to give us answers in cases where, on secular views, several conflicting options all seem justifiable. This points up the hollowness of secular morality in general. Without Sinai, we would flounder helplessly when wondering whom we may or may not marry, when a "white lie" might be acceptable, or even whether sacrificing our children is a supreme sign of piety or the worst of evils. Now we can look up the answers to these problems in a divinely-given Book. And the fact that we can do that shows that only this Book provides a deep and comprehensive morality, as opposed to the shallow moral systems, constructed to serve selfish ends, upheld by secular people.

It took me a long time to work my way out of this view. But the bald fact that many secular people are extremely decent, and many religious people malicious and deceitful (often using their religion to further their malice and deceit) became more and more apparent to me over time, until at last the idea that the Torah is uniquely capable of making us **morally** *good seemed untenable.*

2. Nevertheless, religion certainly has a special relationship of some sort to morality. The relationship may, in part, go in the opposite direction from the one we just considered: religion may depend on morality, rather than the other way around. After all, some moral norms and ideals are necessary to get the central vision of any religion off the ground. We could not recognize God as good, could not grasp that, let alone why, we are supposed to worship Him, had we no notion of goodness independent of teachings about God. If calling God "good" is not a tautology, the meaning of "good" must not, in the first instance, depend on God. Of course, one might learn more fully or deeply what goodness is by committing oneself to a religious vision, but that is still to say that one learns, in such a case, a fuller or deeper version of the same concept that one brought *to* the vision in the first place. Any fuller or deeper meaning for "goodness" that we learn by worshipping God must graft on to the ordinary, secular meaning of the term that we use when we first come to understand it.[1]

In any case, religious believers normally take being a good person, in the ordinary sense, to be an essential requirement of their faith, even if that is not all the faith requires, and indeed see themselves as obliged to be rather more serious about this ordinary morality than their secular peers. I think they often misconstrue this commitment, misunderstand the proper relationship between their religious beliefs and their moral ones, but understanding how and why religion tends to give morality a special urgency is essential if we are to understand religious faith at all.

With that in mind, my goal in this section is to tread the delicate line between showing the degree to which morality can be constituted independently of religion, on the one hand, and showing the way in which religious traditions may legitimately contribute to moral discourse, on the other. That is one reason why I will not simply embrace one of the many secular moral theories on the contemporary philosophical scene. The decline of traditional religions, in late 17th-century Europe, led to a remarkable flowering of secular moral philosophy, with writers all over Britain and Germany, especially, trying to show how morality could be established on a purely secular basis. This project has continued without abatement for 300 years now, and today the academic world boasts a wide variety of utilitarian and Kantian and neo-Aristotelian moral systems that all do without religious premises. To make the claim that morality does not depend on religion, I could simply defend one of these systems. I think there is somewhat more to be said for the use of religious norms in the course of moral deliberation than most of my secular colleagues generally acknowledge, however, and the model I will present allows for that—while still maintaining that a wholly secular morality is intelligible, and can reasonably guide anyone who disavows religious commitment.

There is also another reason, built into secular moral philosophy itself, for the somewhat unusual approach to morality that I shall recommend. As noted, utilitarian *and* Kantian, *and* neo-Aristotelian moral systems all have wide followings in the modern philosophical world; there are, indeed, several other such systems. But these systems sharply contradict one another in many ways. There is nothing like the theoretical consensus that one can find in the scientific world. So to present just one of these systems as if it were "the" secular way of understanding morality would be tendentious, and make the overall view I defend in this book more controversial than it needs to be. That is one reason why the account of morality I defend finesses some of the crucial differences among moral theories—offers a reasonable explanation, moreover, of *why* they differ—and maintains simply that *one or more* of such systems can adequately meet our moral needs without relying on religion. My account explicitly endorses eclecticism in morality, sees moral discourse as in fact and properly marked by attempts to defend claims from several standpoints at once. I happen to believe that this is the *right* account of morality, but philosophers who disagree with that, and endorse a single secular moral system instead (utilitarianism *or* Kantianism *or* neo-Aristotelianism, etc.), should see that they could substitute their view for mine without much affecting the overall argument of this book. For that argument maintains just that morality can be satisfactorily constituted without an appeal to religious premises. That claim can be true regardless of whether it takes an eclectic mix of secular arguments, or a single secular system, to do the constituting.

3. We should not expect too much similarity between the argument of this Part of this book and the argument of the previous Part. There is a close parallel in general structure between the claim that a secular conception of the good must precede religious commitment and the claim that a secular notion of truth must precede religious commitment. When we move from the general to the particular, however, this parallel becomes more remote. For there is far more disagreement, in ordinary practice, on what properly counts as "good" than on what properly counts as "true." When a neighbor approves of an act I consider cruel or dishonest, I may think he is vicious or insensitive or badly brought up, but I don't think he is mad. I think exactly that if he mistakes a tree for a dog, or a fire hydrant for a human being. We rarely encounter the latter sort of disagreement; we often encounter the former. Across cultures, especially, we find deep disagreement on moral norms: there have, notoriously, been whole societies that practiced infanticide and cannibalism. To be sure, there are plausible explanations of how societies come to approve of such practices. It is, indeed, virtually a criterion of good anthropological work to offer such explanations: the bare report of moral attitudes and actions extremely unlike our own is unconvincing unless we can see how a human being might have come to develop such attitudes, or rationalize such actions. And that fact itself testifies to the basic morality that we expect to find, and normally do find, across humanity. But this is a very thin level of morality, far less capable of underwriting a theory about what to count as good than our ordinary empirical beliefs are of underwriting a theory about what to count as (scientifically) true.

So we will not proceed in quite the same way as we did in Part I. Instead, the deep and wide disagreements human beings have about the good will be one of our starting points, a fact about morality with which any adequate moral theory must come to grips. Nevertheless, the social contract approach has at least as much of a role to play here as it does in relation to science. We need some agreement on morality to enable us so much as to negotiate how we are going to live with our moral disagreements. It is that level of agreement that the social contract model can help us find and, in so doing, it has considerable advantages over other approaches to moral theory. As indicated above, moral philosophers disagree vehemently to this day on the proper explanation and defense of morality; the differences we have about everyday moral problems are reproduced on the level of theory. These disputes are not easily settled, but they can be finessed. My contention in the next two chapters will be that various moral philosophies work together to explain and justify what we ought to do. While none is as comprehensive and persuasive as its advocates believe, we can cobble together an adequate morality out of a combination of them. In practice, we arrive at a tacit social contract about how to act and that is as firm a foundation as morality needs.

Still, there is something unsatisfying about seeing goodness as grounded in a contract of any sort. We have strong intuitions that goodness must transcend anything we agree on—must be able to be *turned on* such agreements, for one thing, and find them wanting. One major source of this dissatisfaction is a sense that ethics should be able to hold out a possibility that we might radically transform our desires and goals: including the desires and goals that lead us to agree to any contract we may have entered. With this possibility in mind, I turn in Chapter 4 to reasons why many people, whether secular or religious, are uneasy about the secular moral systems that play into the social contract I have described. And Chapter 5 begins the process of moving us from this unease toward what it is that revealed religions may legitimately contribute to our views of how we should live. Ethics belongs to the way of the world first of all and most of the time, but not entirely or ultimately.

4. To begin our investigation into secular moral systems, we might ask what the words "morality" and "ethics" mean. It's hard to find a clear and uncontroversial definition for them. The root of "ethics" is the Greek "ethos," which means "charac-ter," but we need to be wary of using that fact alone to underwrite an approach to our practice that emphasizes virtue. The root of the word "morality" is a Latin word for "custom," but to stress *that* fact runs the risk of collapsing the moral into the conven-tional. While providing interesting insights into the milieu in which a word arose, etymology is often a poor guide to its use at later dates, and we surely do not want to insist, in the case of a term we use for normative purposes, that what it should mean is just what it originally happened to mean.

When we turn instead to the common uses of "ethics" and "morality" today, we find that they are generally supposed to pick out norms that (1) govern our relations with other human beings,[2] and (2) have priority over all other guides to practice. Harry Frankfurt says that "[t]he basic concern of morality is with how to conduct ourselves in our relations with other people."[3] Moral or ethical norms are also supposed to be supremely important. They are supposed to trump other considerations when we deliberate, and a person who violates them is supposed to feel guilt and self-contempt. Many people take for granted that these two features are essentially linked, and jointly capture the essence of morality and ethics: that moral norms are supremely important *because* they govern our relations with other people and that anything governing our relationships with other people would by that fact be supremely important. But it is not obvious that this is so. As Frankfurt asks, immediately after identifying morality with interpersonal relations, "Now why should *that* be, always and in all circumstances, the most important thing in our lives? No doubt it is important; but . . . there is no convincing argument that it must invariably override everything else." We may have duties or obligations to ourselves, or rights to please or express or fulfill ourselves, that sometimes take priority over our duties and obligations to others, or we may have responsibilities to God or nature or art that take precedence, on some occasions, over our concern for other people. Perhaps there are no duties to self or God or nature;

perhaps nothing is more important than respecting and caring for other people. That needs to be shown by an argument, however, not assumed in a definition.

The question of whether our most important norms should also be our norms about how to treat other people is one I want to keep in play for the next few chapters, and I therefore want to exploit the ambiguities of words like "moral" and "ethical," rather than attempting to get rid of them. For the most part, I will use both words for virtues and norms about treating other people, but without taking for granted that that makes those virtues and norms what is most important to our lives. In Chapter 5 I will distinguish between the "moral" and the "ethical," along lines in which the ethical is necessarily identical with what is most important to our lives and the moral is not. But in ordinary usage the two terms are more or less interchangeable, and that is how I shall use them until then.

5. For all the controversy over whether morality and ethics concern just our relationships with other people, or also our relationship with ourselves and perhaps God, the *general* function of both terms is fairly clear. They are ways of deciding how and why to act, of answering the two questions:

(1) What should we do? and
(2) Why should we do it?

There is also a third question:

(3) Why do we so often fail to do what we think we should do?

But most philosophers treat this as an afterthought, to be handled only after the first two questions have been settled, and we will accordingly set it aside for the moment.

The trouble we encounter in delineating moral systems starts when we try to spell out what exactly the first two questions mean, and what the relationship between them ought to be. The first question might, for instance, be asking what specific things we ought to do or it might be asking for a general procedure for making decisions. Or, again, it might be asking what type of person we should aim at being, regardless of the specific things we do. Finally, it might be asking either about actions that we take as individuals or about what the collective "we"—we as a society or as all human beings—should do.

The second question is similarly open to multiple interpretations. Above all, it can be subdivided in accordance with two meanings of the word "why":

(2a) What is ethical action *for*? (what *purpose* does it serve)? and
(2b) What is the proper *motivation* for ethical action?

2a may provide us with an answer to 2b: the proper motivation for ethical action may be a desire to achieve the purpose of ethical action. If the purpose of ethics is to foster universal happiness, for instance, then the proper motivation for ethics may be to desire universal happiness. But 2a and 2b may also come apart. The goal of ethics might be best achieved if one does *not* aim directly at it. Some indirect utilitarians, for instance, have maintained that the greatest possible happiness is best fostered if people cultivate certain virtues, or follow certain general rules, rather than assessing each action as a possible contribution to the greatest possible happiness. Or ethics may have no goal—no single, overall goal at least. It may, instead, express constraints on action that we should follow regardless of our goals, or provide the conditions for us to reflect on our goals. In that case, what motivates us to be ethical could be quite different from what motivates us to pursue our goals.

Finally, there are difficult issues about which of our two questions is more fundamental. Should we figure out the purpose of ethics first, as utilitarians do, and derive how to act from that? Or should we determine how to act first—gleaning our duties up from common sense, perhaps, or deriving them from a formal rule like Kant's categorical imperative—and only then seek the purpose of moral action? Quite different views of the nature and function of ethics hang on how one settles the priority relations between our two questions.

6. I imagine some readers getting restless by this point. Surely, what morality entails is *obvious*! Such readers may be among the many people who take exactly the opposite tack from the one that leads others (including the younger version of myself) to assume that religion is necessary for morality. Morality is *not* a difficult thing, they say, not something for which we need to develop complicated philosophies. Indeed, developing a complicated approach to the subject is often just an excusing for clouding one's intuitive access to right and wrong. The right and wrong way to behave, in most situations, is obvious to anyone who is halfway honest with herself; common sense tells us what it is. It's common sense that taking bribes and killing and assaulting people are bad things to do, and telling the truth, taking care of one's family, and helping those in need are good things to do. A child and a day-laborer know that, as 18th-century common-sense philosophers used to say.

But some of the same people who think ethics obviously involves telling the truth, etc., also think it obviously involves not having gay sex, while others find it equally obvious that *disapproving* of gay sex is unethical, and that gay sex itself is ethically neutral, or good and beautiful when it expresses a loving relationship. Similarly, some of the same people who think that killing is obviously unethical also believe that capital punishment, and much or all war, is obviously wrong for that reason, while others believe that ethics (obviously) *requires* capital punishment, and many of the wars that the first group would rule out.

Again, some of the people who think ethics is obvious think that telling the truth means *always* telling the truth while others think that that is—obviously—ridiculous. Similarly, some think that ethical obligations to one's family obviously involve being around a lot while one's children are young, to an extent that may preclude a career with long hours, while others think that it is necessary just for one parent, or specifically the mother, to be around a lot. And still others think ethics has nothing to say about parenting at this level, and that both giving one's career priority over spending time with one's children and giving time with one's children priority over one's career can be justified ethically.

Pretty much the same thing can be said about every issue that stirs up ethical controversy. People tend to think their own side is not just right, but obviously right, and those who believe that what is ethical can be known by common sense think that common sense unproblematically delivers their own verdict on the matter. They also disagree, but consider their own views obvious, on the question of *why* we should be ethical. Are we ethical, ultimately, for egoistic reasons: because we need each other's help and can only get it if we are nice to each other? Or because it is objectively good to make others happy? Or because ethics enables us to keep our dignity and help others keep theirs? Or because being ethical is what God wants? Many who think ethics is obvious also think one of these answers is obviously right. But they disagree vehemently on *which* answer is the obviously right one.

7. It therefore cannot be *simply* common sense what ethics is, or why we should care about it. Philosophers who regard the question about the nature of ethics as easy usually do not appeal to common sense for the whole of their answer to that question. They tend to say instead that the *general purpose or form* of ethical action can be readily seen, and that the rest of ethics, including the controversies I listed previously, can be settled by way of this purpose or form. Consequentialists, at least of the most common, utilitarian stripe, say that the purpose of ethics is to maximize human happiness; deontologists, at least of the most common Kantian stripe, say that the form of ethical action expresses our freedom, our capacity for rationally determining how to act. Many in each camp believe that their basic characterization of ethics is obviously correct (they think they are bringing out a notion of ethics that is already contained, albeit confusedly, in ordinary thought), and that once it has been clarified, the way to resolve specific ethical problems will be fairly straightforward.

But utilitarians and Kantians *disagree* in their characterizations of ethics. They also disagree, within their own camps, about many specific moral issues. Nor does either camp have a single answer to the question about *why* we should be ethical. Utilitarians include in their ranks both rational egoists and people who believe in a natural human altruism, while Kantians include both those who, like Kant himself, insist that the goodness of rational action is absolute but cannot be further defended, and people who see rational action as conducing to or helping to constitute another good: mutual respect among rational beings, say, and relationships based on such respect.

So it is hard to see how the philosophical answers to our question, even if correct, are obvious either.

8. The question "What is ethics?" is interwoven with the question "What is ethical philosophy?" I don't mean just that ethical philosophy is about ethics—that much really *is* obvious!—but that ethics itself often is, and may necessarily be, defined

by ethical philosophy. Answers to the question, "what is ethics?," tend to depend heavily on one's ethical philosophy. If one believes norms for conduct always and primarily concern human welfare, then many questions others have traditionally considered to be ethical ones—are we responsible for our actions if there is no free will? what should we do when justice conflicts with benevolence?—may appear meaningless or empty, while questions others have considered matters of prudence or technological expertise—how can AIDS be cured? how can poverty be abolished?—will occupy the heart of ethics. If one's philosophical views lead one to believe that norms for conduct express our identity as rational agents, on the other hand, then technical questions about how to solve human ills do not focus on properly ethical issues, while questions about the nature of free will and responsibility will be central to ethics. A virtue ethicist may divide the territory yet differently, considering it a mistake to regard particular actions of any sort, rather than ongoing characters, as the locus of ethical evaluation.

Along a different dimension, there are those who define "ethics" as having to do with ways one human being affects another (or perhaps other rational or sentient beings) and, therefore, consider the very notion of self-regarding duties to be incoherent, while others define ethics as a matter of how we each achieve "excellence" as a human being, and consider self-regarding duties to be the most important of all our duties.[4] Those who hold the first view also tend to regard any norms having to do solely with an individual's relationship to God, or her ability to achieve some sort of supernatural enlightenment, as lying beyond the scope of ethics, while those who identify ethics with the pursuit of excellence may incorporate religious rituals within its sphere.

There is yet a third philosophical dimension along which to carve up the territory of ethics. This has to do with the way ethical philosophy may serve to help combat evil, and thereby contribute to ethical practice. Here, we can imagine a number of possibilities, all of which have been proposed by canonical figures in moral philosophy. Some suppose that the great problem with human life is our ignorance of technical facts that would help us overcome sources of misery like cancer or war or poverty. If one thinks that, one is likely to become a utilitarian, direct attention towards social activism or progress in the social sciences rather than matters of abstract speculation, and be impatient with norms and practices that seem unconnected to human welfare. Others suppose that some sort of metaphysical mistake lies at the heart of the wrong that humans commit—that a lack of belief in our own free will provides people with an excuse for weakness of the will (Kant seems to have thought something like this), or leads them to manipulate one another rather than showing proper respect for all free beings (contemporary Kantians often think something like this), or again that a metaphysical error about the nature of the universe, or our own nature, leads people to grasp at vanities, and suffer and inflict suffering as a result (Hindu and Buddhist philosophers, as well as Plato, the Stoics, and Spinoza, have thought something like this). Someone with any of these latter views is likely to think that a focus on social science, or on societal projects that alleviate misery, will not do human beings much good as long as their metaphysical illusions remain intact, and that the work of moral philosophers should focus precisely on metaphysical issues.

Again, one may think that the great source of evil in human life is self-deception, or some other form of mental cloudiness that prevents us from properly recognizing the harm we inflict on others. Someone with this view is likely to think that social activism will be inadequate to solve our problems, but that clarifying metaphysical positions is also fairly useless: that the work of the philosopher should be to help us understand ourselves better, and to develop a finer ability to see what we really do. Adam Smith, Nietzsche, Iris Murdoch and John McDowell are examples of philosophers who have proposed views of this sort. (Freud held much the same view of self-deception, but didn't think that *philosophy* was the cure for it.)

And different views about ethics itself come along with these different views about the point of ethical philosophy. Ethics is a way of solving problems, for the utilitarian, but a way of seeing the universe, for our metaphysicians, and a discipline in seeing ourselves aright, for those who emphasize cloudiness in our self-understanding. There are yet other ethical philosophies and other views, correspondingly, of ethics. The emotivist may come to his view, as Francis Hutcheson did, from the thought that all would be well if we would just feel more kindly towards one another, and see ethical practice correspondingly as the cultivation of a set of emotional dispositions. Radical social reformers, like Marx, may see the central problem in human life in the illusions and false doctrines propagated by various institutions, and regard the proper cure— "ethics," if they accept that word—to lie in the abolition or wholescale restructuring of those institutions, not in personal discipline, or social projects that leave the basic shape of society unchanged, or metaphysical investigations of any kind.

The definition of "ethics," consequently, is not just hotly contested, but contested on grounds that are themselves largely ethical ones. Nor does philosophy provide a neutral spot from which to construct such a definition. On the contrary: the work of philosophers concerned with ethics tends itself to be largely driven by ethical commitments. Ethical philosophers generally set out to *reform* how we understand ethics, not just to reflect it,[5] and their reforms tend themselves to be ethically motivated.

9. That we have trouble pinning down exactly what "ethics" and "morality" mean should alone suggest that finding a fully satisfactory ethical or moral system will be difficult. But the problems we have encountered arise mostly in marginal cases: the definition of "ethics" or "morality" becomes problematic if we want it to be *comprehensive*, to cover all possible cases that might be brought under those terms. We do agree on core moral cases—it *is* usually obvious that we should not kill and should

help the needy—and on the general questions that anything we can count as a moral or ethical system needs to answer. I will therefore set aside the problem of how exactly to define "ethics" and "morality," and consider whether we can develop systems that give a plausible answer to our general questions on most of the occasions on which we ask them. The idea is to see whether we can develop such systems without making use of religious premises—whether secular moralities can suffice to help us figure out what to do and why to do it. In combination, if not on their own, I believe that they do.

2

Application

10. What secular moral systems do we have? Those of us who teach moral philosophy generally tell our students that there are two major approaches to the subject, one emphasizing the purpose of our actions (consequentialism, and in particular utilitarianism) and one emphasizing the form of our actions (deontology, and in particular, Kantianism). Recently, such courses have also come, often, to include a segment on virtue ethics, which focuses on character—habits of feeling and dispositions to act—rather than particular actions. But these are not the only alternatives. Here are some others:

- *Emotivism.* Emotivists (sometimes also called "sentimentalists") hold that moral language expresses certain emotions we have about one another. Some emotivists, notably Frances Hutcheson, believe that only one kind of emotion—benevolence, for Hutcheson—constitutes properly moral motivation, and only one kind of emotion is expressed by properly moral evaluation; others say that a wide variety of feelings are appropriate sources of moral motivation, and a similar variety of feelings can go to compose moral approval. But almost all draw some distinction between moral and, say, aesthetic approval: disliking Chopin or spinach is not normally a moral matter.

  The emotivist position has often been regarded as a purely meta-ethical view, appended to larger metaphysical or epistemological programs such as logical positivism, but it can be developed into a full-fledged normative system of its own.[1] To the question, "what should we do?", the emotivist responds that we should do whatever the appropriate motivating emotion inclines us to do, or whatever will win us approving emotions from those around us. To the question, "why should we do it?" the emotivist responds that it is part of our nature to seek approval from others, or that such approval brings us a special kind of pleasure.

- *Conventionalism.* I use this name for a cluster of views according to which morality consists of whatever norms the members of a society treat as decisive in their deliberations. Norms in general, on this view, are guides to action instilled in us by our societies; moral norms, as opposed to norms of etiquette, business procedure, etc., are those norms that are regarded as of the highest importance. We are good if we conform to our society's moral norms, bad if we do not—although "conformity" must be construed broadly enough to allow for some immanent criticism of these norms. Most societies consider criticism of their norms to be at times a good thing.

I call this a cluster of views, rather than a single one, and use the term "conventionalism" for it rather than "cultural relativism," because the latter is not the only view that belongs in this category. Not everyone who holds a view of this sort focuses on norms held by *cultures*, as opposed to other sorts of society (states, clubs, neighborhoods). Nor is everyone who holds a view of this sort a relativist. Anthropologists often claim that moral norms are relative to cultures as a matter of *fact*—that there is nothing else for them to be, or that only the socialization process instilled by cultures can explain the hold moral norms have over us—and then get into trouble if they try to add to these factual claims the normative view that people *ought* to obey the norms of their own culture, or that outsiders to a culture ought not interfere in it.[2] But the fallacies of relativism can be avoided if one instead argues, say, that the conventions of society implicitly reflect an agreement of its members, and thus express their wills, or that human beings need societies in order to be happy, and that those societies cannot survive unless their conventions are observed. One can defend the conventionalist position, that is, on Kantian or utilitarian grounds, holding up a meta-norm that transcends convention as a ground for following conventions. This position avoids relativism, but can also remain distinct from Kantianism and utilitarianism proper by insisting that its meta-norm is thin and cannot be used as a concrete guide to action. Where the Kantian has a rational procedure that is supposed to determine the *right* expression of our will in concrete situations, the Kantian conventionalist says that reason cannot reach so far and instead tells us only that we have already agreed to, and should therefore follow, the norms of the society in which we choose to live. Where the utilitarian has a procedure to tell us what conduces to human happiness, the utilitarian conventionalist insists that no-one knows that and our best bet for maximizing happiness, in most cases, is to uphold the conventions of the society around us.

- *Rational egoism.* Rational egoists start from the premise that we all aim (or reasonably aim) at nothing more than the satisfaction of our selfish preferences. "Good," for them, is applied by each of us first and foremost to what we want for ourselves alone, and "right" to the actions that will help us attain this good. Morality is then built up from our need, as selfish individuals, to work within a society.[3] Unlike some other animals, human beings can get little of what they want without help from other human beings. But if we pursue our selfish wants with no regard to the needs and wants of others, we will end up in civil war, and no-one will get what they want. So we compromise, and agree to certain norms that enable a society to survive. "Good" and "right" now acquire extended meanings, by which to approve of actions conforming with, or helping to preserve, these norms.[4] Often identified with Hobbes's picture of the social contract, this view of ethics has no room for there being anything intrinsically good about freedom, or the welfare of people other than oneself, or the achievement of virtues. The appeal of the view is, indeed, that it cuts away the illusions and hypocrisy that may seem attached to utilitarianism or Kantianism or virtue ethics, that it seems rooted in scientific facts about human beings, and healthily skeptical of claims that cannot be established scientifically.

Rational egoism does not coincide with conventionalism or utilitarianism, although it can be used to support both. It does not coincide with conventionalism because it is perfectly possible, and in some cases clearly true, that a norm is upheld by a society, but nonetheless likely to be harmful to the society's survival. (Zoroastrians and Jews favor in-group marriage, for instance, even though that cuts down the pool of marriage-partners and increases the prevalence of genetic defects.) The rational egoist may also dissent from, or ignore, norms that he considers unnecessary for his society's survival.

And rational egoism differs from utilitarianism when the latter sets up the welfare of all human beings (much less all sentient beings) as a good in itself. The rational egoist can endorse norms that foster the welfare of all human beings out of a belief that those norms benefit him, but he cannot see a reason to pursue the good of others independently of its relationship to him. The assumption, made by many utilitarians, that we can and should care about the happiness of everyone, is not one that egoists share.[5]

11. These are just three alternatives to Kantian, utilitarian, and virtue-based ethical theories. There are others: the intuitionism of G.E. Moore and David Ross, for instance, doesn't quite map on to any position we have considered, and popular divine command moralities, which appeal to a purported revelation as the proper source for moral rules, are different from all these positions.[6] I set aside divine command moralities for the moment since we are concerned precisely with the degree to which morality can be established without reference to the divine, and I won't say much about other secular moral philosophies because I think the six we have before us adequately represent the range. They are quite a varied bunch, and I don't think we would gain by spending time on more variants.

Now these philosophical systems have a lot to say about human life in general— arguably, what they most deeply give us is a picture of human nature, and a better understanding of why we are creatures who make moral claims on one another[7]—but for our purposes in this chapter we need to focus just on how they deal with the first of our basic ethical questions: what should we do? To some extent, this involves a thinning out of what they have to say (we will see that such thinning out is indeed essential to their ability to answer our basic question), but over the past two centuries, moral philosophers have in fact presented themselves largely as offering a way of resolving concrete moral problems: helping us cut through controversies, and reform those aspects of our mores and legal codes that reflect prejudice, rather than real moral insight. So to emphasize their answer to the bottom line question about how we should act is not entirely unfair to their view of themselves.

In principle, our six systems answer that question in very different ways. Some utilitarians consider us obliged to give very large amounts of charity; Kantians and virtue ethicists usually consider such giving meritorious, but supererogatory; emotivists and conventionalists join the Kantians and virtue ethicists on this (we neither feel, ordinarily, that such giving is required of anyone nor have conventions mandating such giving); and rational egoists are likely to consider large charitable gifts ridiculous. Strict Kantians find themselves isolated, on the other hand, in their absolutism about lying and other duties of justice: utilitarians, emotivists, conventionalists, virtue ethicists, and rational egoists all justify lies in some circumstances ("white lies," for instance, or lies to would-be murderers). Conventionalists may find themselves ranged against all the others when they endorse societal taboos—against homosexuality, say, or eating pork or mocking religious figures. And virtue ethicists tend to resist taking definite stands about particular acts, but their picture of good character usually mixes enough of the elements of the other five positions (a strong emphasis on reasoning, but also on cultivating certain feelings, and on being concerned for general welfare) that they will be disinclined to agree with any single one of them in every case. So no two of the positions I have listed will agree on every act.

Nevertheless, the six positions we are considering, and all other widely held moral philosophies, agree on the vast majority of the most common and most important moral issues. Murder is similarly defined on all the views, and regarded as always or almost always a great wrong. It almost always causes great disutility to a number of people; it violates the freedom of a rational being; almost all of us, almost always, feel horrified at it; all societies forbid it (albeit with variations about what to count as murder and when it can be excused); it almost always offends against the virtues and harms our ability to maintain them; and a societal prohibition of murder is essential for the rational egoist to pursue his interests comfortably. Something similar can be said about rape, battery, torture, kidnapping, deception, and theft. It may be a bit harder to reach agreement on the definition or serious wrongness of adultery, but there are plausible utilitarian, Kantian, virtue-based, emotivist, conventionalist, and rational egoist arguments in favor of some sort of stable sexual pairing, and some degree of fidelity in those pairings. Similarly, there are arguments from each position for at least a vague ideal of mutual aid, and a norm against acts that show gross indifference to suffering.

The different positions that philosophers hold about the nature of morality, therefore, do not yield radically different answers to the question of what we should do.

12. We are faced, then, with two striking facts about systematic attempts to tell us what we should do: first, that we have many, very different such systems; and second, that those different systems nevertheless agree in the central cases in which we worry about what to do. How to reconcile these facts is, I think, the core question in moral theory. Let's approach it by first considering each fact in more detail.

So, to begin with, why do we have such different ways of arriving at moral conclusions?

Well, there are plausible historical answers to that question. What we call "morality" has elements that trace back to medieval natural law systems, to the emphasis on love, conscience, and other internal states that Christianity, especially in its Protestant forms, has often favored over law, to Greek and Roman virtue theories, and to the bureaucratic rules of procedure, aimed at satisfying the needs of as many people as possible, that have become more and more important with the growth of large, anonymous societies in the past two centuries. Kantian moral theory is a descendant of the first of these traditions (although it owes something to the second as well); sentimentalist moral theories have a clear root in the second; neo-Aristotelian systems draw on the third; and utilitarian and rational egoist theories have been constructed in large part as a response to the fourth. So these modern moral views come out of historical traditions that arose to serve very different purposes. It is unsurprising, then, if they talk past each other much of the time and cannot easily be reconciled.

A view of this sort has been championed in recent decades by Alasdair MacIntyre, and I think there is a lot to it. But it is not wholly satisfying. For one thing, it suggests that there are times and places without the divisions over morality we face; MacIntyre himself has argued that a far more unified approach to morality can be found in the pre-modern West, especially in the Aristotelian tradition that was taken up by Thomism. I am not sure how realistic this is. Aristotle's approach to morality was just one of many in the pre-modern West, contested by, for instance, the Stoics and Epicureans, who anticipate modern Kantians and utilitarians. And parallel divisions among styles of moral thinking can be found in other cultures. The Mohists in ancient China, for instance, developed a view very like utilitarianism, while Confucius and his followers held a virtue theory similar in many ways to Aristotle's. There are also deontological— "Kantian"—elements to Confucianism. A similar range can be found in classical Indian thought and we saw earlier that ancient rabbinic teachings contain a variety of approaches to morality that parallel our modern ones.[8] So I am inclined to suspect that the idea of a social world with a unified approach to moral thinking is a fantasy that has never been realized, at least in any large society.[9]

In any case, there are systematic reasons to resist purely historical explanations of why we have such different modes of moral thinking. Historical explanations of these differences make them look like surds, accidental consequences of contingent facts. But then it is hard to understand why different traditions about morality *argue* with one another: they are not merely *different*, but *competing* views of how to live. Pace

MacIntyre, utilitarians, Kantians, neo-Aristotelians, and the like are not really talking past each other most of the time. They are, rather, debating a common subject matter: addressing one another's claims and offering reasons for rejecting them.

So we have reason to look for a deeper, more philosophical explanation of the differences among kinds of moral discourse. There are probably several such explanations, but a plausible one is that our moral traditions all represent different views of the ultimate or overall human good, and that there is something reasonable about each of these views because the nature of our ultimate good is extremely hard to pin down. Utilitarians see pleasure as our ultimate good; virtue ethicists see expressing our sociability as a supreme and intrinsic good, independent of the pleasure it may bring; intuitionists see intrinsic value or goodness in a great many things, like knowledge and aesthetic appreciation, in addition to pleasure and sociability. Kantianism may seem not to fit this picture, since it draws its prescriptions for action from a procedure that abjures any dependency on our ends.[10] But this very setting aside of ends can be seen as following from a certain view of them. One way of understanding Kantianism is to say that it acknowledges the fact that we cannot determine our ultimate good definitively and focuses, for that reason, on constraints on action that people can agree on whatever they aim at: on a condition for right action that holds regardless of our ends. Alternatively, one can understand Kantianism as taking rational deliberation—coming to action out of a process of reasoning—to be an intrinsic and crucial good whatever other goods we may have. Kant himself seems to have believed this: he begins his *Groundwork* with the premise that a properly-formed will is the one thing we can all agree is unqualifiedly good.

All these views seem to have something right about them. Pleasure does seem to be an intrinsic good, and, in some moods, many of us presume that it is our only intrinsic good. But expressing our social nature also seems an intrinsic good, and in some moods also seems our most important one. The same goes for knowledge and aesthetic appreciation and rational deliberation. So it is no wonder that we feel drawn to some degree by many different moral systems: pulled now to utilitarianism, now to Kantianism, now to virtue ethics or intuitionism. We might try to put all the various claims about our ultimate good together, and declare *the* good to be a tapestry woven out of all the various things that sometimes appear intrinsically good—and seeing our various moral systems, then, as like the legendary blind men who grab different parts of an elephant and, consequently, come up with entirely different notions of what elephants are like. But this would again miss the degree to which our views of the good *compete* with one another, each having enough reason on its side that in some circumstances we think it rightly claims to be the one view to which the others can be reduced. The idea that we can simply throw all our intuitions about what is good together into one pot presupposes far too easily that they are harmonious with one another (can a Kantian and a hedonist really agree about our ultimate good?), that we have no need to choose among them.

So I think the correct thing to say is that we have many different intuitions about what is good without any clear idea about how to settle the differences among them. Moreover, the differences we have over the good are deep ones. Among those with purely secular views, hedonists, Kantians, Marxists, and radical individualists disagree sharply with one another over what human self-realization ideally looks like. And these differences are intensified once religious claims are added to the discussion.

13. Let's turn now to the second striking fact about our different moral systems: that in spite of their differences, they agree in a great many of their prescriptions.

Finding similarities among seemingly disparate moral systems is a popular sport among moral philosophers. The past two or three decades have witnessed an out-pouring of work demonstrating the sentimentalist elements in Kant and the Kantian elements in sentimentalist theories,[11] as well as the many affinities between Kant's moral theory and Aristotle's.[12] In the 1950s, R. M. Hare showed how rule-utilitarianism and Kantianism could be brought close to one another, and Bernard Williams brought them together in his critique of both systems in the 1970s. Scholars love to find similarities where others have long seen only differences, but I am not aware of any equivalent amount of scholarly effort devoted to the reconciliation of, say, empiricist and rationalist epistemologies, or realist and anti-realist metaphysical systems.

Still, one may find these conciliatory projects, on the level of theory, fairly uninteresting, if the moral systems in question yield different prescriptions for how to act. To a remarkable degree, however, they do not do that. Bernard Williams once noted the tendency of utilitarians, in particular, to conform their position to what most of us already believe about morality:

[O]ne feature of much modern utilitarian theory is that it is surprisingly conformist. Bentham and Mill regarded the Greatest Happiness Principle as an instrument of criticism, and thought that by appeal to it they could show that many Victorian moral beliefs were mistaken and irrational... But, except for the well-established areas of sexual and penal reform, themselves inherited from Bentham and Mill, modern utilitarian theorists tend to spend more effort in reconciling utilitarianism with existing moral beliefs than in rejecting those beliefs on the strength of utilitarianism.[13]

Williams complained about this tendency, saying that if utilitarianism "can be got going at all," then "it is a special doctrine, not necessarily coincident with contemporary Western moral ideas in all respects." But his complaint has not been much heeded.

Williams could have raised a similar complaint about the defenders of the other positions I have listed. Contemporary Kantians expend a great deal of effort showing that Kant's theory need not issue in the more counter-intuitive results to which Kant himself came. Qualifications are placed on his absolute prohibition of lying, to rule out his notorious claim that one needs to tell the truth to a potential murderer looking for his victim, and on his prohibition of suicide, to allow for euthanasia on some occasions;

duties to animals are wrung from his position; and not only do Kantians never understand their position anymore to rule out such things as masturbation, but they tend to use it to underwrite the most up-to-date positions, in the intellectual set, on sexual freedom.[14] And emotivists and virtue ethicists similarly expend much of their energy on showing that they have resources allowing us to criticize entrenched racism and other prejudices, as against those who think their position must lead them to accept any reigning social attitude; they also occasionally try to show how their views can yield a nuanced, but basically liberal position on such hot topics as abortion.[15]

Now one might say, as Williams does about the conformist utilitarians, that each of the positions these moral philosophers represent, if it is worth representing, should lead to some distinctive conclusions, and not just endorse "contemporary Western moral ideas in all respects," or the subset of those ideas fashionable among academics. But there are philosophical pressures that favor massaging one's favored moral view to yield the moral conclusions that most people, or most people one respects, already hold. For what is supposed to show that a position explains *moral* principles at all? As we have seen (§ 4), there are sharp disagreements over the very words "moral" and "ethical," and no obvious way of resolving those disagreements. So in practice we normally define them by pointing to core cases on which we agree. It therefore counts in favor of a position about the nature of morality or ethics if it issues in conclusions we can already recognize as moral (ethical) ones.[16]

In addition, given the deeply social nature of human beings, our core moral judgments will very likely converge on those norms necessary to keep our societies together. That means that we will uphold norms necessary for societies to survive in general—against murder, assault and dishonesty, above all, and in favor of co-operation—but also that we will tend to be wary of norms or ideals that might seriously threaten the consensus keeping our particular society peaceful, free, and co-operative. A peaceful, free, and co-operative society is essential to our pursuit, as individuals, of what seems to us to be the ultimate or complete human good, and also seems intuitively to be a core example of a human good. And it is reasonable to suppose that most of what most societies value will promote their ability to achieve such a condition: they would otherwise be torn apart by strife. So advocates of different moral systems, whatever differences they have in principle, will have good reason to justify most of the widely accepted ideals and norms around them. Of course, some of a society's practices may conflict with its own ideals and norms, and all moral theorists except conventionalists believe that the right moral path can in principle conflict radically with that of their society. But only rarely will they be able to make the case that this possibility has been realized without threatening the philosophical and social conditions enabling them to promote their moral systems at all.

We should therefore expect a large area of agreement among ethical positions over what to do, and that area to overlap with the large area in which actual societies agree about how to act. And, in fact, major moral philosophers have generally recognized the need to align their systems with the accepted moralities around them. Plato takes great efforts to "save the phenomena," after proposing a view of morality that might seem to run sharply contrary to established moral views.[17] Aristotle takes it to be the job of moral philosophers to address only those who have already been brought up well: which is to say, socialized into the conventional morality of Aristotle's day. Kant says that he is merely drawing out the metaphysical substructure of "common human reason" as regards morality, which knows well enough on its own what in fact is good and bad (G 404). And Mill tells us that human beings have been in effect figuring out how to implement utilitarianism for the entirety of their history.[18]

14. How should we bring together our two striking facts about moral systems? What account of morality as a whole can respect both our deep disagreements about how to systematize our moral beliefs, and the fact that our different systems converge so strongly—and converge, for the most part, on the norms and ideals we already uphold?

I suggest that in practice what generally happens is the following: We have many shared intuitions about what is good in an everyday sense, which we use when we attempt to come up with a view of our ultimate good and, in that light, systematize our moral beliefs. But the systems at which we arrive disagree sharply and deeply—for many reasons, which include disagreements over virtually unsettleable metaphysical questions (Is there a God? Free will?). So we maintain different moral systems, and different telic views, as I would like to call our beliefs about our ultimate or overall good. But because we have reason to try to share modes of moral argument with our neighbors, because we can minimize the differences among our moral systems by bracketing our telic beliefs, and because most of us are quite tentative about the latter in any case, and realize how difficult it is to persuade others of them, we abstract from our telic views as much as possible when making everyday moral decisions. Sometimes that is very difficult, as when we have to consider whether it is worth trying to extend the life of a gravely ill person. Here, the question, "Is her life still worth living?" may seem forced on us, and it is hard to give that an answer without saying something about the question, "What makes any human being's life worth living?"[19] (At which point our moral differences come vividly to the fore.). And the fact that this *can* happen tempts some moral theorists to suppose that a telic view must settle all moral disputes. I think that that is not true, but that telic views do *hover in the background* of all moral reasoning. Our moral views depend on intuitions that we also consider when asking about our ultimate good, and sometimes they impel us to ask after that good. But they also give us reason, most of the time, to abstract from any answer we might have to that most difficult question. This leads to a separation, if not a sharply delineated separation, between our moral and our telic beliefs.[20]

Assuming this is right as a descriptive matter, we still face normative questions. Should we *accept* the fact that we normally abstract from telic questions when trying to resolve moral ones? And if so, how should we argue morally—especially when we confront people with quite different moral systems? I suggest that the answer to the first question is a resounding "yes," and that, in answer to the second one, we should respond as for the most part we already do respond: we should try to convince each other about how to act as much as possible from a variety of moral positions, try to defend the claims we want to make by way of utilitarian *and* Kantian *and* neo-Aristotelian arguments, and an appeal to widely accepted intuitions to boot. We should, in short, embrace moral eclecticism. Instead of showing one moral position to be correct, or seeking a least common denominator morality that would elide the distinctive features of our various moral systems, we should take morality to be a realm in which positions are rightly defended by an eclectic mix of arguments. On the eclectic view, variety in moral systems is ineliminable, and we should make our case for particular decisions from many different perspectives.[21]

Why embrace moral eclecticism? Well, in the first place there is a certain honesty, realism, and humility in embracing a condition that is not going to go away however hard we struggle against it, and honesty, realism, and humility are all generally considered virtues. In the second place, there are good reasons for accepting an eclectic approach to moral argument from the perspective of each moral system that goes into our eclectic mix. And in the third place, an eclectic approach to moral argument helps keep alive the disagreements over our ultimate good that lie at the root of our differences over moral systems, and we all have reason to want to keep those disagreements alive.

I take the first of these points to be fairly obvious, if not terribly compelling on its own, but the second and third could use some elaboration. We may demonstrate the second point from a perspective like that of John Rawls's original position, in which advocates of each theory consider how they might think moral discourse in their society should be structured if they didn't know which theory they themselves upheld.[22] Bearing in mind that none of these theories is so strongly anchored in reason or human nature that it is likely to surpass all the others in commanding everyone's allegiance, it seems obvious that, in such a position, all moral theorists would favor eclecticism as the dominant mode of such discourse. Otherwise they run the risk of having their favored system wholly ignored. Only eclecticism allows each moral system to keep alive its claims to the full truth about morality, and to have a chance of deciding at least some moral debates. Eclecticism allows us to continue our debates over the relative importance of freedom and pleasure, character and action, social convention and universal principle—to avoid settling them too quickly and without adequately thinking through why both sides in these debates have a lot to say for themselves.

Relatedly, eclecticism keeps alive debate over the nature of our ultimate good. This is its main advantage. For reasons we've already touched on (which I will also explore in detail in Part III), it is extremely hard to see how human beings could ever reach rational agreement on their ultimate aim in life. To settle what we are all living for would seem to require having definitive answers to the questions of what we are like, and what our universe is like, which in turn would seem to require having a definitive answer—*inter alia*—to the questions of whether we have free will and whether there is a God. But definitive answers to these latter questions may be impossible. If so, however, it would be oppressive and dishonest for any society to settle on just one view of the good to the exclusion of all others. If we cannot pin down the nature of our ultimate good, then to enshrine one view of the good—as freedom, as pleasure, as wisdom or virtue—above all others is to misrepresent the real state of our knowledge, and to oppress dissenters. We might ask anyone who resists having an eclectic mix of views dominate the moral discussions of his society to consider whether he would prefer it if the view he considers most wrong-headed (utilitarianism, if he is a Kantian; Kantianism, if he is a utilitarian) were to dominate those discussions instead. In the absence of a rational process to determine which moral system is the correct or best one, however, there is no reason to expect the victory of one system over the others to be anything but arbitrary. Advocates of each system will thus be rolling the dice if they push for just one system to dominate their society's moral discourse, and will have to live with a mode of discourse that they find confused or corrupt or evil if luck is not with them. Far better—for one's ideals themselves—that one's view continue to be heard, even if the price of its doing so is to be but one voice among others.

We might add that disagreement over the nature of the ultimate good is the deepest factor differentiating human beings, and the one that most directly reflects human freedom. We are attached to nothing as strongly as our views of what our lives are for. We tend to hold up views on these questions as prime markers of our identity: what makes us distinct people, who have thought freely and come to distinctive conclusions as a result. We are Jews or Jains, atheists or theists, devotees of politics or eros or art, far more ardently than we are anything else, and we choose or embrace these identities because we have certain views, however inchoate, of how, overall, we think life should be led. It is hard to imagine that human beings could differ in any interesting way without differing over the ultimate good. But it is also hard to imagine a world without human difference as a world in which anyone would be very happy, even harder to imagine it as one in which anyone would be free, and impossible to imagine it as one in which anyone would be admirable. So neither utilitarians nor Kantians nor virtue ethicists should welcome such a world. On practically any moral view, if preserving debate over the good helps keep us from oppression and homogeneity, then preserving debate over the good is a very good thing.

Advocates of each of our moral systems thus have moral reasons for endorsing an eclectic approach to everyday moral debate. They have moral reasons, that is, for not insisting that their own system dominate moral argument, for endorsing a way of coming to moral decisions that does not rely exclusively on their own comprehensive view. Instead of "eclecticism," we might call this an "overlapping consensus" approach to morality, borrowing Rawls's term for the mode of political justification that he thinks properly arises when we recognize what is problematic about using our com-prehensive views of life as a basis for political argument.[23]

15. We can now return to the social contract apparatus that helped us make sense of the cognitive way of the world in Part I. The mention of Rawls already points us in

that direction: Rawls is perhaps the leading recent spokesperson in political theory for something like what the 18th century called a "social contract." And the kind of social contract appropriate to the moral way of the world, I shall suggest, bears a number of similarities to the overlapping consensus that Rawls uses to arrive at liberal political principles.

A social contract approach to morality has to be quite different from the social contract approach we developed for cognition. In the first place, as we've seen, there are far more common and more significant disagreements about moral plain truths than about empirical ones. In the second place, there is a far more limited and qualified role for expertise in ethics than in empirical fact-gathering. People will not as readily turn to an expert to figure out what they ought to do as they will to find tigers and pineapples. In part, that is *because* there is more dispute over moral than empirical plain truths— there is more dispute, for that reason, over who is a good moral expert. In part, it is because "positional advantage" has less of a role to play in ethics than in empirical matters. There isn't anything in ethics quite like seeing better because one is up a tree, nor is it at all obvious that those with highly developed logical skills, say, do better than the rest of us at figuring out the right thing to do. There can of course be experts on what the norms are in a particular group, but that is less than a properly ethical matter; ethics always concerns what norms *should* be, not just what they are.

Finally, it is much harder to identify moral than empirical plain truths, harder to find a similar, non-theoretical baseline for assessing moral theories and expertise. On many conceptions of ethics, I do the right thing only if I act for the right reasons, and that requires me to have already come to some conception *of* morality—to have *reflected* on moral discourse. If my act seems to show you respect, or give you happiness, but I do not understand it as showing you respect or giving you happiness, I am acting less well than I should, and perhaps not acting well at all; it is a part, perhaps an essential part, of moral action to recognize *that* people should show each other respect or make each other happy. But reflection on first-order discourse is precisely what defines the move from plain truth to socialized truth (Part I, § 18): to theories and truth regimes. So ethics may not properly exist until we have already reached a reflective and socialized level— which would deprive us of an unsocialized "plain" level of discourse against which we could judge our moral theories and truth regimes.

Nevertheless, we can understand morality as grounded in a social contract of sorts. It is just that this contract must expressly leave open some of our most profound moral disagreements, especially our disagreements in moral theory—it will be justified, indeed, in good part *by* the fact that it leaves these disagreements open. That is what brings it close to Rawls's overlapping consensus.

16.   There is a problem, however, in adapting Rawls's overlapping consensus to the moral realm. Rawls's consensus is supposed to apply to the political *as opposed* to the moral realm, to be something on which people with different moral views can agree.

How can we push the consensus back into morality without destroying the basis on which Rawls thinks he can draw, for reasons that justify his political principles?

To begin answering this question, we might note that morality can be seen as an extension of politics. Rawls distinguishes the political realm by way of the "coercive power" of government—its "use of sanctions"—noting that "government alone has the authority to use force in upholding its laws" (PL 136). Government is not the only body that uses sanctions, however, nor are coercion and force properly limited to the threat of physical violence that we permit only to governments. If you tell me that you will discredit me with my employer or friends unless I stop my foul language, then I may well feel coerced into changing my behavior, and I will certainly feel sanctioned if you carry out your threat. Mill points out that the idea of sanctions, or punishment, enters into our understanding of any kind of wrong: "We do not call anything wrong unless we mean to imply that a person ought to be punished in some way or other for doing it—if not by law, by the opinion of his fellow creatures; if not by opinion, by the reproaches of his own conscience."[24] In the political realm, legal sanctions are applied to wrongdoing, but the violation of non-political moral norms is also punished: by "the opinion of our fellow creatures" or the "reproaches of our conscience." (And moral but non-political goodness earns analogous rewards: the approval of our fellow creatures, and/or a pleasurable sense of self-approval.) We don't put people in jail for everyday dishonesty or rudeness, but we do rebuke them or shun them or otherwise display a sense that they deserve some sort of penalty—some distance from us, some deprivation of the full status they might otherwise have had, as a neighbor or friend.[25] Or we think they should rebuke themselves, or see themselves as less than fully worthy of friendship or honor. On this picture, legal sanctions are a model for how we maintain all moral norms. It will usually be ineffective or inconvenient for us to jail the mildly dishonest or unkind, so we sanction them informally instead. And it is often ineffective or inconvenient for us even to sanction them informally, so we hope they will sanction themselves. But in principle all violations of moral norms, and failures to live up to moral ideals, are of the same kind. It is utilitarian considerations, primarily, that lead us to seek different sorts of sanctions for them.

Contrast the way we hold aesthetic and intellectual and religious norms and ideals. We may feel a certain contempt for those who don't have what we consider good taste in art or music. Normally, however, not only do we not rebuke them for that, but we feel a little ashamed of or guilty about our judgmental tendencies in this regard. Similarly, we may look down on people who don't live up to our intellectual norms and ideals, but we tend to keep these feelings to ourselves. And followers of religions that hold out just one path to salvation tend to feel sad or worried about people who don't accept that path, but not to condemn them with the anger suitable to moral violations. We feel we have a *right* to get angry at the unkind and dishonest and cowardly—the proper reaction to immorality is often dubbed "righteous anger"—which we don't feel about people who fail to live up to our non-moral values.

Why do we feel that we have this right? The best answer, it seems to me, is that in the case of morality we think the people we are criticizing have, at least implicitly, *already accepted* the ideals and norms to which we are holding them.[26] We regard those ideals and norms as embedded, that is, in some sort of implicit social contract. If the view of morality that uses a legal paradigm is even roughly correct, the informal sanctions we bestow on moral violations must have a justification analogous to the one given for legal sanctions. Informal sanctions are normally far less painful and damaging, and easier to reverse, than the sanctions of a state, so we need not set the bar of justification as high as we do for laws. Still, the question of how to justify moral norms and ideals amounts to a question about how to justify our being willing, as a society, to inflict certain serious costs on each other, and most of us feel we need to be operating against the background of some sort of agreement to do that. This is the opening for a social contract conception of morality.

17. The social contract about morality, as I understand it, makes room for significant disagreement to endure over our fundamental views of value: that is why it urges us to embrace an eclectic mode of moral discourse, rather than a single moral system. Rawls's overlapping consensus similarly allows people to agree on political norms and ideals even while they not only disagree on other values, but ground their very agreement in different moral systems. An advantage of this basis for political argument is precisely that its grounding is shallow, that it is not rooted in any comprehensive vision. The idea that our public discourse should appeal just to a limited set of political values "can seem shallow," Rawls says, "because it does not set out the most basic grounds on which we believe our view rests" (PL 242). But this very shallowness is a plus, because our fellow citizens will "share with us the same sense of its imperfection, though on different grounds." We are all in the same boat, then, all equally deprived of a "deep" grounding for our political principles. And the recognition of this equality is what allows us to treat one another with respect. In coming to recognize "that politics in a democratic society can never be guided by what we see as the whole truth" (PL 243), we also recognize that our political ideal is to live together with other people on equal terms. So the very structure of Rawlsian political discourse displays our equality—while simultaneously displaying the incompleteness of political values, the reasonableness of holding more comprehensive views from which our political values can flow. The principles of public reason, Rawls says, form a "module" that can be fitted into many different comprehensive moral views (PL 12–13, 144–145). And the shallowness of that module enables it to display on its surface the need for more comprehensive moral views, and the legitimacy of continued debate over them.

Now Rawls constructs this picture of political discourse against a background of comprehensive, non-consensus-based, moral doctrines.[27] As I have indicated, I want to push the consensus one step back. I am arguing that even morality is best understood, not as a comprehensive view of how to live, but as a module that can be fitted into a variety of such views, on which we agree for different kinds of reasons. The Millian points we considered in the previous section suggest that morality shadows politics, in its importance to our ability to hold societies together, its (consequent) reliance on sanctions of some sort, and its (again consequent) implicit appeal to reasons we can share, for justifying those sanctions. It differs from politics in that we don't use outright force to keep people in line with purely moral norms, or in pursuit of purely moral ideals. That allows for a more fluid set of norms and ideals, and of justifications for them. Because the sanctions we inflict for immoral but legal acts are relatively mild, we needn't establish as strong or clear an agreement on how to justify those sanctions, or exactly what to count as moral. But otherwise there will be a close analogy between our grounds for calling acts morally right and wrong, and our grounds for calling laws, or political structures, just and unjust. Above all, it will be important that the discourse in which we offer such grounds be structured so as to keep open, and make clear *that* it is keeping open, continued disagreement over our most fundamental values: that it keep open the nature of the ultimate good.

The differences between Rawls's political overlapping consensus and the moral overlapping consensus I am describing are not insignificant. For one thing, in politics we need one set of laws for everyone; in morality, we can afford to be more flexible, with the standards upheld in one part of a society not necessarily being upheld in other parts of the society, or with standards upheld within close relationships (between husband and wife, parents and children, etc.) being somewhat different from the standards upheld among strangers. For another thing, even if morality is not yet the most comprehensive sphere of value, it concerns a far broader swathe of our lives than politics does. It is therefore more important to preserve disagreement in the moral than in the political sphere. If there is to be room for substantial disagreement over ultimate value, we cannot be stifled by a demand that all our actions and attitudes conform to a social consensus. Taken together, these considerations give us reason to seek a unified model of discourse in the political realm—Rawls sketches such a model—while allowing the discourse proper to the moral realm to be a hodge-podge: where moral claims are defended from many different points of view, drawing as much as possible on all the sources of value that flow into the moral realm.

One thing this means is that there is more room for religious principles in a moral overlapping consensus than in a political one. If two people share a religious commitment, especially, it makes eminent sense for one of them to quote Scripture to the other in order to buttress a claim that some action is mean-spirited or unfair. It also makes sense for a religious person to make a case, to a non-religious one, that her grasp of morality will be enhanced if she turns to a particular scripture—that she will discover a deeper or more nuanced version of Kantian or Aristotelian norms and ideals in the Upanishads or Gospels or Quran, or will be inspired to live up to them more fervently. In politics, where our debates conclude with the establishment of rules backed up by force, such appeals run a grave risk of imposing a view on people against their will. In morality, where the sanctions behind a claim are much milder, and a single rule for everyone is unnecessary, we can welcome a variegated kind of discourse, which includes appeals to religious sources.

But it is important that such appeals be *grafted onto* other kinds of moral reasons. A claim based on a scripture only becomes a moral claim at all—something we can expect anyone to heed, and blame anyone for dismissing—when we can show how it promotes human welfare, protects individual freedom or dignity, or enhances virtues like courage and generosity. We may be able to scare each other with the possibility that a powerful supernatural being will hurt us if we don't carry out some action, or inspire each other with the hope that such a being will reward us if we do perform some other action, but neither of these is a moral argument. For religious arguments to be moral arguments, they need to be endorsed by the secular strands in our discourse that allow for wide human agreement on conduct.

18. Four central features of this overlapping consensus view of morality:

(1) It should not be confused with conventionalism. The conventionalist sees norms and ideals as justified by the mere fact that they are endorsed by a society that appeals to them. On the overlapping consensus view, norms and ideals are justified by a variety of moral *theories*—utilitarianism, Kantianism, virtue ethics, etc.—which may include, but will certainly not be limited to, a conventionalist view. So the legitimacy of each norm or ideal will depend, not on its simply being accepted in the society in which it circulates, but on *why* it is accepted: on the fact that a variety of plausible absolutist moral theories, which together underwrite the society's moral discourse, can agree on it. Indeed, if it finds justification in a conventionalist view of morality alone—if no justification can be found for it other than the fact that it is broadly accepted—then it will likely seem *illegitimate* on reflection. The upholder of an overlapping consensus view of morality has reason to reject, not embrace, cultural relativism.

(2) Relatedly, the overlapping consensus is an agreement about the *sources of moral justification*—the range of positions from which moral argument can be launched—not on the justifiability of specific actions. At the same time, an agreement on modes of justification will to some extent include an agreement on the merits of specific actions. All moral theorists give their views plausibility in part by showing how they account for our intuitions about the wrongness of killing innocent people, for instance, or the goodness in helping others in distress. One mode of moral justification—intuitionism—indeed, works entirely by taking paradigm cases of right and wrong actions, and trying to map more controversial cases onto those paradigms: by showing how economic oppression resembles slavery, say, or why someone who supports interracial marriage should support gay marriage as well. For this mode of moral argument to work, the rightness or wrongness of many specific moral claims must be held fixed. But even here what allows us to hold the paradigm claims fixed is not just the fact *that* we agree on them. It is the fact that our other modes of moral

argument *lead us* to agree on them, that we have no good basis on which to challenge our agreement on them. Otherwise the claim that our intuitions in these cases are reliable would be very much open to question, and couldn't do the work it is supposed to do. The mere fact that people in general agree that, say, eating meat is morally acceptable, or that one need not give more than modest amounts of charity—to take two claims that seem plausible to many people, but are challenged by certain moral theorists—is not enough to give these claims the paradigmatic status by which they could support an intuitionist argument.

(3) Third, and again relatedly, the overlapping consensus is an agreement in large part to preserve a certain kind of disagreement. Recognizing that our freedom and well-being and ability to develop virtues require that debate over the ultimate good be kept open, we allow an eclectic collection of theories to co-exist in our moral discourse, even while seeking enough agreement on specific cases that we can live together peacefully, retain our basic freedoms, and help each other achieve basic forms of well-being. The overlapping consensus thus treads a delicate line between seeking agreement and preserving disagreement. That is one reason why it does not endorse conventionalism—for the conventionalist, every case we agree on would by that fact *be* good or right—and why it is strongest when all the varying modes of argument that feed into it converge. When only utilitarians consider something good (e.g. giving away large amounts of one's money), or only Kantians demand something (e.g. telling lies that badly hurt people), then most of us will be reluctant to say that morality entails such claims, or call someone who violates them immoral.

(4) Finally, unlike Rawls's political overlapping consensus, the moral overlapping consensus does not converge on a distinctive mode of argument. The Rawlsian consensus focuses on a set of principles about the nature of justice and citizenship that are supposed to be used as premises throughout our discussions about fundamental political issues. Rawls presents these principles as cohering, and having clear enough implications that they can form a self-sufficient module to guide political debate and deliberation. People with different comprehensive moral or religious or philosophical views will accept the module for different reasons, but once they accept it, they can use it without alluding further to their broader views. The moral consensus I am describing does not work the same way. Rather than converging on a particular mode of argument, it converges precisely on a way of settling questions by employing many different modes of argumentation. It converges precisely on an effort to seek different kinds of grounds for the same position. We are most confident that a claim is a moral one when we can defend it from the standpoint of all our moral theories, and uneasy about the morality of positions that only a utilitarian or only a Kantian can hold. Consequently, we converge on an effort precisely *not* to employ a self-sufficient module of moral argument—to preserve instead an eclecticism in which the

variety of directions from which people come to the consensus remains in view even as we agree on particular conclusions.

19. With these clarifications in place, it should I hope be clear how the overlapping consensus model tracks our actual use of moral terms. When I say "That's a *terrible* thing to do" or "That's immoral" or "She's a good person," I normally expect widespread agreement on the reasons for which I say that; I expect that I can give a number of different such reasons, and thereby convince practically anyone. Thus I may call a dishonest announcement by a Federal official "wrong" and find that the person I am talking to doesn't accept my Kantian reasons for condemning dishonesty in general— but nevertheless win his or her assent when I switch course and point out the likely environmental damage, or risk to workers, that this announcement may cause. Or I may find it hard to see the great good in a person whose praises are being sung to me if that person's attempts to help others are not very successful, yet recognize that this is a reasonable moral claim when the eulogist shows me evidence of the person's virtuous dispositions, or rigorously Kantian integrity.

By contrast, I'll be reluctant to call something "immoral" when I know that my basis for thinking so is not shared by others. Even thoroughgoing utilitarians rarely use that term, in ordinary conversation at least, of people who fail to live up to their extreme demands for charitable giving. Similarly, Kantians tend to withhold strong forms of moral condemnation from the sorts of lies that they know people with different moral views regard as wholly acceptable. (When have you heard a Kantian say "That was a terrible thing to do" about a false compliment to an elderly or unattractive person?)

Sometimes we do use "good" and "bad," or "right" and "wrong," when we approve or disapprove of things for reasons we can't widely share, but we tend in that case to signal that the words are not being used in a strictly moral way. I may say, "As a Jew, I think it's wrong for fellow Jews to eat pork," or "As a Catholic, I think it's terrible if people remain outside the true Church," but I will normally be reluctant to substitute "immoral" in for "wrong" and "terrible" here: the values underlying such judgments are not, even in my own eyes, properly moral ones. Similarly, I may say "As a White Sox fan, I think it's terrible for anyone to root for the Cubs," or "As a music-lover, I think it's wrong for orchestras to shun contemporary composers," but I would never suggest that these are *moral* claims.

At the same time, the overlapping consensus view allows, as it must, for people to make moral claims that defy some of the norms upheld in the society around them. Early opponents of slavery thought that slavery was morally wrong, and that everyone should agree with them on that, even if few did; contemporary vegetarians, and opponents of abortion, similarly take themselves to be making moral claims even if few share their views. Such people believe that others share the grounds for their claims even if they don't share the claims themselves: they believe that the bases for moral argument widely shared in their society entail the wrongness of these practices, and that those who fail to see this have missed an implication of their own moral views. So these are properly moral claims. What takes a claim out of the properly moral realm, on the overlapping consensus view, is that the *grounds* for it can't be generally shared, not that people disagree about the claim itself.

Nevertheless, I think we do tend to be more cautious about using our moral vocabulary in an unqualified way as regards specific claims that are widely disputed. Few vegetarians, no matter how strongly they condemn meat-eating, limit their friends to fellow vegetarians. Few opponents of abortion call for mothers who have abortions, or their doctors, to be punished like ordinary murderers. And even fervent opponents of slavery in the late 18th century couldn't quite bring themselves to shun their slave-holding neighbors the way they would a thief or kidnapper.[28] We might say that people with dissenting views of this sort hold up *candidate* moral norms to us, without investing those norms with the emotional content that actual moral norms carry. They urge their societies to accept their claims as moral ones, but acknowledge, in their behavior if not always in their language, that those claims do not as yet belong to a properly moral mode of discourse. They do not actually expect all reasonable people around them to agree yet to the norm they propose, or guide their behavior by it. As a consequence they withhold the full force of the attitudes and actions that normally accompany our use of a moral vocabulary, that come with judgments that we are confident are already ratified by our overlapping moral consensus. They express in their attitudes, if not their words, an implicit acknowledgement that an actual moral norm needs actual acceptance in its society.

Think here of how we regard comprehensive moral systems other than our own when they are taken to their logical extremes. Kantians who condemn even the fictions we tell in order to give a friend a surprise birthday party seem to be more in the grip of some kind of obsession than holding up so much as a plausible candidate for a moral claim. Something similar goes for utilitarians who say that we ought to give charity to the point at which we would be poor ourselves if we gave any more, or who regard even gross deception as legitimate—nay, *required* of us—if it will make people happier than the truth. And the same sort of doubts arise when conventionalists insist that seemingly arbitrary, cruel, or unjust practices—ritual taboos, infanticide, human sacrifice—must be regarded as morally legitimate if a society is strongly attached to them. To one not in the grip of the system in question, claims of this sort do not appear to be serious contributions to moral discourse; one can see how they follow from the system, but that just raises doubts about whether that system is really a system of *morality*.[29]

In the end, however, what matters most about the overlapping consensus model I am proposing is not that it tracks our actual way of discussing moral issues, but that it is better justified than other attempts to ground that discourse. No philosophical attempt to establish just one comprehensive moral system has come anywhere near persuading most people, and there are good reasons to think that no such attempt will ever succeed (see § 8, above). Meanwhile we need to share some mode of bestowing moral approval and disapproval, and the only way we can do that without compromising our comprehensive systems is to maintain an eclectic mode of moral discourse. Moral eclecticism is the best way for all plausible systems both to continue to have a say in how moral decisions get made and to keep debate over the foundations of morality open enough that they have a chance of winning over their opponents. An eclectic mix of moral arguments is therefore preferable, from the point of view of each moral system, to a grounding of moral discourse in just one such system.

20. One feature of the moral overlapping consensus is that it issues in clear verdicts on questions that will not be at the top of anyone's moral agenda, while leaving unsettled some issues that most people would regard as crucial. Our various moral views will converge clearly and emphatically on the claim that I am obliged to pay $19.95 to my butcher if I buy 19 dollars and 95 cents of meat from him. The overlapping consensus among these views will also clearly endorse our being kind to children in pain and doing what it takes to patch over arguments with our friends and relatives. But the consensus comes apart over whether abortion or capital punishment is permissible, what duties, if any, we have to animals, and whether there is anything wrong with homosexuality. How can a consensus like this, which unravels on issues of great importance, be a satisfactory basis for moral decision-making?

Well, first, I have been exaggerating a bit, to bring out a concern. The overlapping moral consensus will cover most core moral cases. Murder, theft, and adultery will be forbidden, at least in paradigm cases, and approval will be bestowed on kindness and courage, and refused to cruelty and cowardice. It's just that difficult cases arise at the margins of each of the concepts whose cores we share—when we deal with the beginning and end of human life, for instance, or with human beings who have very limited rational capacities—as well as where one important value must be balanced against others, or where we need to consider the value, if any, of the non-human world. These are cases in which we are pushed to settle why we value human life so highly, or to put all our values into a clear hierarchy, or on which a consensus shaped by the need of human beings to get along has little bearing. When we have to probe the basis of the value we place on human life, or of our valuing in general, it becomes difficult to avoid questions about what, overall or ultimately, we consider good: it becomes difficult to rely on a consensus that finesses such questions.

But other approaches to morality do not necessarily fare better with these issues. Kantians have long argued furiously, among themselves, over whether capital punishment is morally wrong, or, on the contrary, *required* of us in response to murder. (Kant himself held the latter view.) There are also Kantians who oppose and Kantians who favor abortion, Kantians with all sorts of positions on our duties to the non-human world, and Kantians who oppose homosexuality, as well as Kantians who favor gay marriage.

If this is the case even among Kantians, who usually present themselves as having a clear decision-procedure to settle ethical questions, we should expect it to be all the more true among utilitarians and rational egoists, who notoriously find it hard to settle what makes for happiness or displays our true preferences, and among conventionalists, who have few resources for responding to situations in which conventional norms clash. And among people with each of these views, we do in fact find almost every imaginable position on abortion and capital punishment and homosexuality, and our duties to the environment. Moral systems are too coarse-grained to issue in clear answers to these questions and the questions turn, besides, on how we interpret evidence, or define the borders of vague concepts, rather than on matters that any system alone could settle.

Indeed, our overlapping consensus is more likely to produce a compromise that everyone in a given society can live with, even on contentious moral issues, than the systems that contribute to it. What drives the consensus, after all, is that we need as a society to agree on policies so that we do not tear the society apart, and thereby deprive ourselves of a necessary condition for making any moral principles effective. So the rational egoist finds himself willing to make do with a society that disapproves of cruelty to animals, even though he himself couldn't care less about it, and he and the pro-choice utilitarian or Kantian may be willing to cluck sympathetically when people talk about needing to show concern for the life of a fetus as long as the pro-life utilitarians and Kantians agree that the status of the fetus is too hard to agree on for a prohibition of abortion to be written into law. In this way, sometimes by law and sometimes by the evolution of social attitudes, we work our way into compromises on controversial issues that all our different moral views can more or less accept. This preserves each of them better than if we had to decide that just one of them had the right response to the issue. It is therefore in the interest of each view to have the overlapping consensus provide the dominant answer to even our most controversial moral questions. The same reasons that justify our consensus in the first place justify having it respond to difficult cases.

So we muddle along, with our paradigmatic moral norms and attitudes being drawn from cases in which two or more mature, fully rational human beings encounter one another and need to help each other or respect each other's rights. A mostly libertarian code of law, prohibiting violence and deceit above all, arises out of these cases, but also a preference in daily life for kindness and generosity over selfishness. From here we can work our way out to a complex set of duties to infants, people with severe mental deficiencies, and animals, and to more elaborate codes of conduct, among the fully free and equal human beings involved in our paradigm cases, for matters of sexuality, behavior in the workplace, respect for cultural or religious symbols, and questions about the end of life. But not all these questions will receive an answer from the overlapping moral consensus, any more than they would from any element within that consensus. It is no surprise, and should not be a mark against the overlapping consensus view of morality, that we find ourselves differing irremediably over medical intervention at the end of life even while we can agree that we should pay a debt of $19.95 to our butcher. The one kind of case involves challenges to our entire conception of morality that the other does not, and no moral system is in a good position to handle such challenges.

21. What, now, is the relation of religious views to an overlapping consensus on morality? Well, in the first place, religious views tend not to form coherent moral systems on their own. Rather, different believers in the same religious tradition have different views on concrete moral questions—there are, and have long been, Christians, Jews, Muslims, and Buddhists on both sides of almost every moral debate—and find themselves all over the map of philosophical moral systems I have laid out. There are Christian utilitarians and Christian Kantians, Christian virtue ethicists and Christian conventionalists, even some Christian rational egoists. The same goes for every other religious tradition. So it is not clear what it would mean to add a *distinctively* Christian (or Jewish or Muslim) moral system to the mix I have described, and many Christians would be upset if one kind of Christian morality were regarded as "the" moral voice of Christianity. Conservative Christians would be horrified if moral discourse was dominated by voices who insist that gay love is blessed by Christ, and liberal Christians would be just as horrified if conservative Christianity dominated moral discourse. Better, again, for all Christians (and Jews, Muslims, and other religious people), if the voices entering into their society's moral consensus are mixed enough that each can find some support for the moral reading he is inclined to give of his religion.

In the second place, to the extent that religions do claim to have distinctive moral views, what is distinctive in those views tends to consist in the *role* they give morality in their conception of the ultimate or overall human good, not in what specifically they think morality permits or proscribes. Religions place morality in a telic context, understanding it as helping us attain holiness or nirvana, or express our love for Christ, or align ourselves with the fundamental structure (*tao*) of the universe. Sometimes such placement, according to the religious tradition, helps believers see moral demands more perspicuously than a secular person would, and sometimes religious believers indeed seem to have a particularly thoughtful or deep commitment to morality. At other times, the telic vision comes into *conflict* with morality: it may seem to the believer that he can express his commitment to God, or attain holiness or nirvana, only by violating the demands of ordinary justice or kindness. (We will see more of this possibility, under the heading of "the teleological suspension of the ethical," in Chapter 4 of this Part.) But what is distinctive about a Christian or Jewish or Buddhist morality has in any case more to do with the place of morality, in the life of the believer, than with its content.

Finally, to the extent that religious communities put forward moral norms that cannot be integrated into the overlapping consensus in which human beings more generally can participate, they undermine what most of us regard as morality, rather than supporting it. Insofar as people insist that their norms cannot be justified in a variety of ways, including ways that abstract from their religious commitment, insofar as they refuse to seek compromise norms that they can share with human beings outside their faith community, they make demands on others that the latter cannot themselves see as reasonable. Then their demands appear, to those outside their

community, not even to belong to morality—they seem, like the outlandish utilitarians, Kantians, or conventionalists mentioned above (§ 19), not to be speaking the
language of morality at all.[30] Moreover, to the extent that they, or the rest of us, are
tempted to think that they *are* using moral language, they threaten the central functions
of morality. The hope for a shared moral way of the world that enables us to maintain
peaceful, free, and co-operative societies, and keep alive debate over the ultimate good,
diminishes to the extent that we replace our eclectic moral discourse with views that
refuse to seek integration into such discourse. Either a single such view will dominate,
and oppress those with different views (again, any religious person tempted by such a
scenario should imagine the religion she most opposes coming to dominate her
society), or several conflicting such views will vie with one another, refuse compromise, and destroy the peace that societies need to survive.[31]

As a result, in practice even people who officially proclaim that morality stems
wholly from their religious tradition tend to make their case for the moral norms they
propose in terms that do not depend on that tradition. Consider the way religious
opponents of abortion generally argue for their position. They may cite Scriptural
verses,[32] but most of the time they produce pictures designed to arouse disgust or shock
at the act of abortion, or help us see the fetus as human. Or they appeal to analogies
with slavery or the Holocaust to suggest that ignoring the humanity of the fetus is like
ignoring the humanity of black people or Jews. Sometimes they add claims about the
need to uphold an absolute prohibition on the taking of life or assert that abortion
harms the women who have them. They appeal, that is, to emotivist, intuitionist,
Kantian, and utilitarian conceptions of morality: they appeal to *secular* moral systems.[33]
And while they may do this in part because, in liberal democracies, it is problematic to
offer a purely religious basis for law, they also use these sorts of arguments among
themselves, as part of their case for the claim that abortion really must be wrong in the
eyes of God. In addition, of course, they want to convince people outside their
religious fold, and they recognize that they can only do that by using arguments that
do not depend on their particular tradition. De facto, then, they recognize the secular
cast of moral discourse, and rely on it even in their reading of their religious sources.

All of which is not to deny that religious traditions can be a source of moral insight.
"Love your neighbor" has had a profound impact on the way moral issues are framed
in the West, as has Jesus' admonition to turn the other cheek. Some would claim that
the idea of social justice was first invented in the Hebrew scriptures.[34] Others find
insights in Taoist or Buddhist texts that help them develop virtues they need for moral
practice, and that they think no purely secular moral system would have produced. All
these people may be right; what I want to stress is just that the religious insights they
prize *become* part of morality only when they get integrated into the mix of utilitarian,
Kantian, and other non-faith-based views that make up our moral overlapping consensus. They become something we can designate as "moral," and invest with the
emotional charge and practical consequences that go with that designation, only when
we can show that they help us promote one another's welfare or freedom, or clarify our

duties of respect for one another, or enhance social harmony or our individual virtues—that they have grounds that any human being could accept, regardless of faith. Religious traditions can and often do pour something into the moral river from which we all drink, but they are not in themselves moral except insofar as they enhance the norms and ideals we share.

Again, this is a normative point, not merely a descriptive one. Religious language in fact comes to be seen as moral language, ordinarily, if and only if it can be integrated with secular forms of moral argument, but religious believers should also welcome that fact, rather than trying to change it. For each religious believer has the same sorts of reasons as an advocate of a secular moral system does to prefer an eclectic mix of moral vocabularies over any single basis for making moral claims. She does not, after all, want the discourse of her society to be dominated by a moral view other than her own, even (perhaps especially) a rival moral view that claims the mantle of her own religious community. Far better, for the flourishing of her ideals, to preserve a variety of voices. Short of a resolution of the deepest metaphysical problems that human beings face, a way of making normative claims to which we can all agree—because it preserves our *dis*agreements—is better for the idealistic, as well as the materialistic, ends of all of us.

22. The distinction I've drawn between candidate and actual moral norms, between what people merely propose as a moral norm and what actually functions as such, suggests that actual, fully-functioning moral norms will vary to some extent from one society to another. I think that that is in fact the case. The consequences, intention, and meaning of most human actions will vary from one set of historical circumstances to another, and the rightness or wrongness of what look at first like similar actions will vary accordingly. Polygamy, for instance, may be a reasonable practice in one society, but not another, and to rebuke one's friends frankly may be a mark of respect in one society while even mild reproof is a gross affront in another. Of course—as noted earlier (§ 10)—the higher-level principles allowing for such cultural variation may have to be themselves invariant across time and place, but we guide our daily actions by concrete norms, rather than abstract principles, and the former will inevitably be informed by history.

We may now define concrete or actual moral norms as rules or ideals that are taken to be of over-riding importance in a particular society (that trump norms of decorum or business procedure, for instance) and are well-rooted in their society's overlapping consensus on morality: ones for which good grounds can be given from within most if not all the moral views going into that consensus. This definition is vague in a number of respects. It leaves open what exactly will count as "good grounds," as well as how many of the moral perspectives need to be satisfied. But that is an advantage, rather than a disadvantage: it fits the facts of morality as we know it. The boundaries of the moral sphere are not precise. Debates often rage over whether a particular norm or ideal is properly a moral one or not, especially when it can be defended from some perspectives, but not others (e.g. it promotes well-being, but violates Kantian constraints).

The definition also allows for some moral norms and ideals to have a grip on a society even if it does not acknowledge them as such, and for a society wrongly to bestow the compliment "moral" on other norms and ideals. This again fits the phenomenological facts about morality. Sometimes the modes of argument that ground moral claims in a society converge on a principle that it has yet to formally acknowledge as such—everything the founders of the American republic believed should have led them to see that slavery ought to be forbidden, even if most could not bring themselves to admit that—and sometimes they do not support a principle that is so acknowledged. A greater understanding of the nature of sexual orientation has led norms against homosexuality, for instance, even where they are still proclaimed, to lose the moral grounding they once seemed to have. In most cases, however, especially since modes of moral argument work so heavily through widely-accepted intuitions about morality, a norm or ideal well-grounded in a society's dominant moral views will be recognized as moral by that society, and norms and ideals that cannot be so defended will be abandoned, or shunted off into the realm of taste or custom or religious ritual.

To repeat: this view allows for a certain degree of pluralism, in concrete moral norms, across cultures. That does not mean the view is relativistic, but it does mean that members of one society may often find it hard to persuade members of other societies to share their norms. Because what makes a norm moral is its grounding in modes of argument accepted by our society, not its mere acceptance by that society, we are in principle capable of using those modes of argument to criticize the practices of other societies. But we are unlikely to be persuasive unless we can show the people in those other societies how the positions we hold are rooted in views they share. That, however, is a fact that every account of morality must face. On my model, intercultural disagreement will be resolved much as intra-cultural disagreement is: by conversations, when people of different cultures encounter one another, in which they begin to develop an overlapping consensus to govern their inter-cultural relationship.

From here, we might be tempted to define the *ideal* morality as that set of norms and ideals on which all reasonable people concerned to find general rules to govern their shared practices would converge if they engaged in a fair and reasonable discussion with one another for as long as it takes to reach such agreement. This proposal, which combines elements of the philosophies of T. M. Scanlon and Jürgen Habermas, would make clear that my overlapping consensus model is underwritten by an absolutist conception of moral justification, at least on the formal level.[35] But I would stress:

(1) that we need not anticipate that any such agreement will actually be reached, over historical time;

(2) that even the ideal morality could have room within it for some degree of pluralism, indexed to the different histories and circumstances of different societies; and

(3) that the notion of an ideal morality will not tell us much about how to resolve the moral disagreements we actually face, in our concrete historical circumstances.

The third point is crucial. The conditions for reaching the ideal are formal ones, and do not say anything about which modes of moral argument reasonable people should employ to resolve their disagreements. In practice, what will and should happen in a world that has yet to achieve the ideal is that different reasonable people in different societies will work out from the overlapping consensus that happens to be in place in their society—or the makings of consensus that have thus far been built across their societies, if the dispute crosses societal borders—not look to an ideal that abstracts from such historically achieved agreements.[36]

23. Finally, I'd like to address a potential objection to both my epistemic and my moral uses of social contract theory. When it comes to politics, one might say, the social contract seems not just a nice theoretical model, but something that has practical application. There are real political institutions around us to which we consent or fail to consent: we vote for our leaders, for instance, and can throw them out if they fail to live up to the purposes for which we have chosen them. What analogy is there to that in the epistemic and moral domains? We don't vote for the leaders of scientific institutions, much less get a say in what they publish, nor do we vote for a particular kind of moral discourse. In what sense can we say, then, that anyone ever *withdraws* consent from the regime of scientific experts, or type of moral discourse, around her? If people never withdraw consent, however, how can it be meaningful to say that they give it?

Two responses:

First, the objection presumes that "we" live in a democracy, or perhaps that social contract theory implicitly demands that every government become a democracy. But social contract theory was first developed in a non-democratic age, was meant to apply to monarchies as much as to any other system, and found its first great champion in Thomas Hobbes, who preferred absolute monarchy to democracy. The point of the social contract, for Hobbes and even, in part, for Locke, was not so much that one saw when to withdraw consent from *illegitimate* governments, but that one understood better why governments are *legitimate* most of the time. The social contract provides us with a model that can help shape our attitudes towards our governments, even if we should not or cannot change them. And that model can similarly shape our attitudes towards the epistemic regimes and dominant modes of moral discourse around us, regardless of whether we can change them.

Second, to some degree there are real epistemic and moral institutions around us, and we do, on various occasions, have a chance to shape them. Expert fact-gathering goes on in newspapers, universities, police departments, and government commissions, among other places, and many of us help shape these institutions by addressing them or working in them. Even when we aren't directly involved with them, moreover, we can influence them: by reading one newspaper rather than another, going to or supporting one university rather than another, writing a letter to the editor, signing a petition, or joining a public protest against a police investigation. There are also institutions that have a strong influence on the moral discourse of a society—universities and the media, again, but also community organizations and churches—and many of us, much of the time, have a chance to shape them: again, either by working there, or by participating in their activities, or by pressuring them from the outside. So there is a significant sense in which we can consent to or withdraw consent from what goes on in the powerful epistemic and moral institutions around us, even if we don't vote for their leaders.

But more important than these modes of influence are the attitudes we hold towards such institutions in our private lives. Many people live under illegitimate governments, and that affects the degree of respect they show to laws and government officials when they can get away with being disrespectful. By the same token, people who live under legitimate political regimes, or regimes they regard as legitimate, tend to work actively to uphold the law, even when they could get away with flouting it. Similarly, people who live under an epistemic or moral regime they regard as illegitimate are likely to avoid paying more than lip service to the factual and moral claims made by the experts around them, while people who regard their epistemic and moral regimes as legitimate are likely to participate in them actively, and endorse their claims when conversing with their neighbors.

People who view their government as illegitimate, if they hold a Lockean view of the social contract at least, will leave or revolt if they can. People who view the cognitive or moral regime around them as illegitimate will likewise opt out from it or establish a new one if they can. People who live under the illegitimate truth regimes I described earlier (Part I § 22)[37] often try to get their information from alternative sources—the BBC has long served that purpose, for people all over the world, and the internet does today. People who feel that the people around them engage in a stifling or corrupt mode of moral discourse—dominated, say, by citations from religious texts or authorities that are interpreted in a way that ignores human welfare and dignity—may also look to teachings promoted in more liberal countries for moral guidance, or immigrate to such countries. And people who live under a secular epistemic or moral regime, but think that all truth or goodness is to be found in a particular religious teaching, form sects and cults with their own schools and newspapers, in which modern science and moral claims rejected by their religious leaders are treated as confused or evil. They are, as it were, epistemic and moral radicals, who would overturn, if they could, the social contract about truth and goodness that most of us accept.

But the fact that there are such people only brings home, once again, that my social contract model is a normative, not a descriptive one. It *is* possible to withhold consent, and therefore also to give consent, to the dominant cognitive and moral institutions around us, and what I am recommending is that we *should* consent to those institutions as long as they respect the social contract in which they are properly grounded. In the case of cognition, the heart of the argument for consenting to a particular regime has to do with the mesh between what its experts tell us and the plain truths we can all recognize. In the case of moral regimes, the reason we should consent to a particular regime turns on the degree to which it preserves an eclectic discourse of approval and disapproval, rather than pressuring us all towards a single moral system. People of various comprehensive views about the good all have reason to endorse an eclectic mix of modes of moral judgment as the best way of determining the right and the good, for ordinary purposes, that their society is likely to find. For each comprehensive view this may be only a second-best way of coming to such determinations in *principle*, but it will nevertheless—even in principle—be the best way to make moral judgments in prac-tice. For a religious person (or a devotee of a secular comprehensive view of the good) to regard all codes and sets of values as immoral if they do not coincide in every particular with his own prescriptions would be preposterous: it would amount to a rejection of the way morality must function in human societies.[38] In any and every society, morality ordinarily and perhaps necessarily falls short of the fullest expression of the values that we each hold, but nonetheless supplies the only standards to which we can hold everyone accountable.

What more is needed to compose a vision of the good that we can comprehensively embrace is a subject we will broach in Chapters 4 and 5 of this Part. First, however, we need to address the second of the basic questions about morality: why should one be moral? We need to consider what motivates us to heed the norms and ideals on which our overlapping consensus converges. One might think that even if moral norms and ideals can be supplied in a secular way, we need religious motivation to live up to them. That is a common claim, but not, I think, a correct one. I take up the reasons why not in the following chapter.

3

Motivation

24. So why should we be moral?

Let's start by noting that there are several different voices in which we might ask that question. We might ask it as people fully committed to ethics who merely want to understand ourselves better, for the sake of the understanding itself or to improve our practice. Here, learning that ethics is really the expression of our freedom will lead us to develop our characters in one way, while learning that ethics is a means to universal happiness, or a discipline for fulfilling our true nature, will lead us to quite different sorts of character development, and different particular actions in some cases.

We might also ask the question when morality requires a great and difficult sacrifice of us. Telling the truth about a crime I've witnessed may put my life or career in jeopardy. In other circumstances, doing the right thing may threaten my marriage. Here we might ask "why should we be moral?" because we are wondering why we should take such risks. Again, a utilitarian will give us one kind of answer, a Kantian another, and a virtue ethicist yet a third, even if they all agree on what we should do.

But in neither of these first two ways of asking our question is there any real doubt about *whether* we should be moral; the question about why we should be moral is, rather, a way of getting at the question of what being moral entails. In the third, and most common, way of putting this question—I have left it until last to remind us that it is not the only way of putting it—the questioner does want to know whether he or she should be moral. Here, the voice with which the question gets asked is the voice of the moral skeptic, the Thrasymachean voice, or the voice of what Hume calls "a sensible knave":

[A]ccording to the imperfect way in which human affairs are conducted, a sensible knave, in particular incidents, may think that an act of iniquity or infidelity will make a considerable addition to his fortune, without causing any considerable breach in the social union and confederacy. That *honesty is the best policy,* may be a good general rule, but is liable to many exceptions; and he, it may perhaps be thought, conducts himself with most wisdom, who observes the general rule, and takes advantage of all the exceptions. (Enq 282–283)

In Plato's *Republic*, Thrasymachus defends complete moral skepticism. The part of the prudent person, he suggests, is to break all moral rules if one can. Hume puts the skeptical challenge more effectively because he acknowledges the obvious ways in which morality is useful even to a completely selfish agent. His "sensible knave" (Thrasymachus, we may say, speaks for an *un*sensible knave) acknowledges the importance of "the social union and confederacy." He wants cakes and wines for his meals and beds for his orgies, and he's not about to make all that himself. Moreover, he needs a peaceful society if he's to go about his selfish business. And he knows that peaceful societies need rules against things like dishonesty, and that it is generally useful, to his own egoistic projects, for him to adhere to such rules. He merely doesn't see why he should keep the rules when they *aren't* useful to him: when he can get away with breaking them, his society will be little affected by the breach, and that breach would bring him something he'd really like to have. Hume's sensible knave is a rational egoist who doesn't think the argument for agreeing on moral rules goes all that far, or who sees reason to "free ride" on the agreement whenever he can. He is a *moderately* sleazy person—not very different from many actual people—who keeps to an ethical path as long as he's being watched, but is always on the lookout for opportunities to maximize his pleasures at the expense of the suckers who have internalized moral norms.

It is to *this* person's question about why we should be moral that many will say: only religion can answer that. Only if the sensible knave thinks he is always watched by God, and will be rewarded for morality and punished for immorality in another life, even if he gets away with it in this one, does he have good reason to keep moral rules when he could break the rules without getting caught, and without seriously harming the society that is otherwise so useful to him. This is not a good answer to the knave's question even from the perspective of religion, for reasons we will see shortly, but we need to take note of it, since it is a very common view and it has become so common precisely because many people think there is no good secular answer to the knave's question. That is not true.

25. Hume's own response to the knave's question, still one of the best to be found anywhere, begins as follows:

> I must confess that, if a man think that this reasoning much requires an answer, it will be a little difficult to find any which will to him appear satisfactory and convincing. If his heart rebel not against such pernicious maxims, if he feel no reluctance to the thoughts of villainy or baseness, he has indeed lost a considerable motive to virtue; and we may expect that his practice will be answerable to his speculation. But in all ingenuous natures, the antipathy to treachery and roguery is too strong to be counter-balanced by any views of profit or pecuniary advantage. Inward peace of mind, consciousness of integrity, a satisfactory review of our own conduct; these are circumstances, very requisite to happiness, and will be cherished and cultivated by every honest man, who feels the importance of them. (Enq 283)

Hume adds that knaves are likely to underestimate the chances that they will be caught when they practice villainy; that they are likely to be led from one small exception from morality to another until "they give into the snare, whence they can never extricate themselves, without a total loss of reputation, and the forfeiture of all future trust and confidence with mankind"; and that none of the expensive goods ("worthless toys and gewgaws," he calls them) one might gain by villainy are likely to outweigh, in point of pleasure alone, what one could get at almost no expense from good conscience, friendship, study, health, and "the common beauties of nature."

This is a very complete response to the knave, and it is worth slowing down the flow of Hume's beautiful prose to appreciate all its component parts. To begin with the end and move backwards:

(1) there are few pleasures for which villainy is necessary, and they tend to be less intensely pleasurable, or make for a less pleasurable life on the whole, than the inexpensive or free goods that do not require wrongdoing;

(2) we are very likely to be caught when we practice villainy, if not at the first attempt, then as we become more and more accustomed to it;

(3) good conscience—"inward peace of mind, consciousness of integrity"—is essential to happiness: few if any other goods will compensate for the loss of it; and

(4) since people inclined to good conduct are aware of (3), they don't really need an answer to the sensible knave's question, while anyone who has gotten to the point of seriously asking it has already gone too far along the path of villainy to grasp the answer to it properly.

I've done this backwards because the most interesting feature of Hume's response comes out best if we see that he reverses the order in which we might expect him to make these points. It may *seem* that Hume's strongest points are (1) and (2), the ones that appeal directly to the sensible knave's own point of view. The knave asks, "What's in it for me, if I'm good?" and "How would I suffer, if I'm bad?"—meaning, what *material goods* does decency bring me and villainy cost me. (1) answers the first question and (2) the second one. But Hume doesn't begin there. Why not? Because *he's not talking to the sensible knave*. He's talking to us, the readers of his book, who are unlikely to be knaves—real knaves, full-fledged egoists who are good only when we think it's useful to us—and who are asking questions on behalf of the knave in a voice that really represents one of the other two reasons I gave for raising the motivation issue: because we want to clarify the role of morality in our lives, or because we are in the situation, or fear being in the situation, in which morality demands heavy sacrifices of us.

And to us, speaking with one of these other two voices, the main point that needs to be made is that the kind of thinking to which (1) and (2) respond is already a kind of thinking that has largely abandoned morality. From within a morally committed life, the answer to the knave's question is obvious. If you know and treasure the comfort of a clean conscience and sense of integrity, would you seriously think of giving that up for a chance at some luxury goods, even where the probability that you will succeed is high? Anyone who sees the merits of this response doesn't really need to be told that the probability of success is likely not to be all that high, or that the goods are not likely to bring all that much pleasure. Hence, Hume puts these answers in almost as afterthoughts, despite the fact that they seem at first the most "sensible" responses to a sensible knave, the most "rational" responses to a rational skeptic. In essence, Hume's response to the question—a response that fits with his general view of ethics, and general view of skepticism, in theoretical as well as practical matters—is to say that *rationality* doesn't provide the proper answer to it: *nature* does. If our feelings do not show us the foolishness of the knave's question, then no rational argument will be of much help to us. And if our feelings do show us the foolishness of the question, then we will have little need of rational argument. When we ask about morality from the perspective of the sensible knave, we need to be reminded above all that we are *not* knaves, that we have in place an emotional structure to answer our question that the knave, *ex hypothesi*, lacks.

If we set Kantians aside, for a moment, there is very little that representatives of any of the moral positions we surveyed in the previous chapter would feel they need to add to Hume's response to the skeptic. The rational egoist is likely to agree at least with points (1) and (2), and perhaps also that, since moral norms in fact tend to get internalized, most people will be incapable of happiness if they are conscious of having committed gross immorality. The utilitarian may add that we take a great pleasure in fulfilling our kindly impulses, and the conventionalist may add that there is an intrinsic pleasure in living up to the conventional norms of our society, or that our projects tend to be enmeshed in those of our society. And virtue ethicists and emotivists are likely to agree fully with Hume (Hume himself is generally seen as both a virtue ethicist and an emotivist), stressing the feelings by which we are inclined to pursue good conduct as precisely the right source for a response to the skeptic.

But Kantians are likely to find all this unsatisfactory, as Kant himself did, for reasons that have probably occurred to the reader. What happens, we may ask, if we come across a person for whom villainy does *not* interfere with happiness, who is not much perturbed by bad conscience, who values luxury goods very highly and either doesn't care much for close friendship or manages to maintain some good friends despite his villainy? Are we supposed to say that such a person "ought not" be moral, that it is more reasonable, wiser, more judicious, of him to be immoral? Moreover, a small amount of wrongdoing, here and there, may not perturb the peace of mind of many people. Perhaps if one observes the general rules and takes advantage of just *a few* exceptions, one can escape the "snare" into which Hume believes his sensible knave will slip. A bit of self-deceit may also serve as an anodyne against the pangs of conscience for these small offenses. One tells oneself that the boss deserves to be cheated now and then, or that one's wife will prefer a happy husband who is occasionally unfaithful to a grumpy one who keeps to the straight and narrow. In this way, one may even maintain a "a satisfactory review of one's own conduct," while gaining some of the knave's pleasures. "Treachery" and "roguery" will still arouse one's outrage, of course, and one will cringe from committing them oneself. But need peccadilloes be ranged under such grave vices . . . ?

Finally, as we noted earlier, there are times when the price for being moral is very high. Here, it may be far less obvious that the good of a clean conscience outweighs the good to be gained by violating some moral norms. When our careers or central relationships are at stake, the calculus Hume proposed may come out in the opposite direction.

So we need to supplement the Humean answer. We can find materials for that in Kant's moral philosophy. Kantians aim to give the skeptic an answer that will hold in *all* cases, that cannot be defeated by any cost/benefit analysis of vice and virtue. In the end, I don't think that effort succeeds, but the Kantian position nevertheless adds to what we get from Hume alone.

26. Kant, on this as on virtually everything, was both impressed by Hume's views and dissatisfied by them. For a while, Kant was a moral sentimentalist himself, holding, with Hume, that moral beliefs express our sentiments, and that certain sentiments are the actual and proper source of moral motivation. On such a view, the desire to maintain one's self-approval, and the desire for the approval of one's friends and neighbors—the sorts of things to which Hume appeals—are the right sources of reasons to be moral. But Kant became more and more impressed with the unreliability of our sentiments, the fact that decent feelings come and go while we expect people to act morally whatever their feelings. In the *Groundwork* he repeatedly gives examples of people whose feelings conflict with what they themselves believe they should do, such as the "friend of mankind" who gets too immersed in his own troubles to feel kindly towards others, and is virtuous if he nevertheless continues to act in a kindly manner. (G 398–399, 422–423)

So Kant started off on the road toward his own, distinctive view of morality precisely because he wanted an answer to the sensible knave that would hold universally, not just in the limited way that Hume's answer does. But his views came to incorporate two other aspects, which go beyond any attempt to answer sensible knaves. First, he was concerned, not just that some people might value the gains from immorality highly enough to be unpersuaded by Hume's case for morality, but that, if they do, *we* are left having to concede that their behavior is rational. On Hume's response to the sensible knave, it would seem that the reasonable course for someone who doesn't much care for friendship, and does care a lot for "gewgaws," *requires* the abandonment of morality. Kant finds that conclusion bizarre, and it is, in any case, harmful to the ability of those of us who are not knaves to maintain our commitment to morality. For if it can be reasonable for the knave to be immoral, why should it not be reasonable for us? Granted, it is reasonable only for a *suitably situated* knave to be immoral, but we could try to occupy that situation: train ourselves to worry less about friendship and clean consciences, say, or learn how we might get away with criminal activity. We all have a bit of the knave in us, and we would like to tell ourselves that we keep to the straight and narrow in cases of temptation not just because we *happen* to prefer decency over indecency, nor just because our circumstances make decency more prudent for us than indecency, but because *no reasonable person* prefers indecency to decency—because one *ought*, if one is reasonable, to prefer decency to indecency. Hume could see no way to argue for such a view other than by accepting moral realism—the idea that something about decency inherently calls up approval in a rational person—which he considered unintelligible. Kant tried to find a non-realist argument for that view.[1]

Second, Kant thought that resting the case for morality on feelings made our being moral or immoral a deterministic fact about ourselves, rather than something we choose. It is an important part of morality that we are held accountable, and hold ourselves accountable, for our choices, not for facts about ourselves that we cannot help. But on Hume's view, it looks as though the decent person just happens to be structured to prefer the good over the bad, while the knave happens to be structured in the opposite way. Feelings are natural facts about ourselves, and as such, Kant would say that they are determined by strict causal laws, not something over which we have choice. Much of the argument of the *Critique of Pure Reason*, as well as Kant's works on moral philosophy, is devoted to showing that the exercise of our reason cannot be regarded in this way, cannot be regarded as (simply) a natural fact. Instead, it is the locus of our choices, our freedom. Hence, it is the proper source of morality.

What we get from Kant, consequently, is an argument that reason in all cases demands moral action of us, that morality is indeed the expression of reason, and of the freedom we have[2] when our actions flow from our reason. The "categorical" aspect of the categorical imperative is meant to rule out precisely the possibility that we might reasonably opt out of morality, as some sensible knaves might if given Hume's justification. There is no cost/benefit analysis for Kant, no appeal to how much peace of conscience outweighs the goods one might gain by villainy. We are told, rather, that reason demands moral action of us in all cases, and independently of what we might gain from it. Anything else will, in fact, not *be* action, in the proper sense of that word, or not action performed by "us."[3] To have a self, and to give it expression in the world, is to use reason; all else manifests mere impulses fixed in our bodies by nature. All else is certainly not something we can *respect* ourselves for doing. Kant argues persuasively that our respect for human beings—for ourselves and for others—is ultimately a respect for reason (and, once again, the freedom expressed in reason).[4]

The strong, metaphysical commitments to free will that were so important to Kant have not always been retained by his followers, but they do continue to argue that reason demands moral action in every case. Some say the very nature of thinking about what I ought to do leads me to think in universal terms—about what *one* ought to do, and what ought to be done not just here, but in all circumstances like these—hence, to formulate a universal principle for my action and regard myself as acting reasonably only if I follow it.[5] Others stress the similarities between practical and theoretical reason, and argue that in both cases, the reasoner needs to take up a "view from nowhere," removing himself in thought from the particular situation in which he finds himself and seeking something like a natural law to fit all situations like that one.[6] Still others, stressing precisely the *differences* between theoretical and practical reason, between theorizing and deliberating, argue that features peculiar to the deliberative stance require us to act on Kant's categorical imperative. One version of this view places the distinctive feature of practical reasoning in the fact that we need a specific identity in the practical realm, which we cannot have unless we act on reason.[7] Another version suggests that the distinctive feature of practical reasoning is that it is second-personal, that we find ourselves addressing or being addressed by a "you," another person, and that the presuppositions of second-person address require a Kantian form of reasoning.[8]

I find all these attempts to show the inescapability of morality fascinating, but ultimately unconvincing. The idea that morality must take the form of exceptionless laws seems rather implausible to me; I agree with those who think it is far more particularist than that.[9] The idea that we will not exist as agents if we do immoral things seems wholly implausible (and makes it notoriously difficult for Kantians to account for how people can be held responsible for immoral actions). And even if we could accept these claims, it seems to me just mistaken to identify morality with a structure built into reason. Harry Frankfurt brings out nicely how counter-intuitive it is to identify morality with reason:

The normative authority of reason . . . cannot be what accounts for the normative authority of morality. There must be some other explanation of why we should be moral. For one thing, our response to immoral conduct is very different from our response to errors in reasoning. Contradicting oneself or reasoning fallaciously is not, as such, a moral lapse. People who behave immorally incur a distinctive kind of opprobrium, which is quite unlike the normal attitude toward those who reason poorly. Our response to sinners is not the same as our response to fools.[10]

Instead, says Frankfurt, morality represents a vision that we *love*. This makes it easy to explain our reaction to immorality:

Attributing moral blame is . . . a way of being angry at the wrongdoer. . . . What makes moral anger understandable and appropriate is that the transgression of an immoral agent consists in his willfully rejecting and impeding the realization of our moral ideal. In other words, he deliberately injures something that we love. That is enough to make anyone angry.[11]

In terms that Stephen Darwall has recently used to defend his Kantian approach to morality, we may say that Kantians (including Darwall himself) give us the *wrong kind of reason* to be moral, give us reasons that do not fit the way morality looks from the inside.[12] It makes much more sense to understand morality as directed towards something for which we have strong feelings (perhaps love, as Frankfurt says, but not necessarily just love: we may, for instance, also *fear* immorality) than something we merely take, rationally, to be correct.

Nevertheless, the Kantian tradition adds dimensions to our thinking about morality that other positions, including Hume's, tend to miss. It is surely true that our freedom consists, at least in good part, in making reasoned decisions, rather than flinging ourselves about haphazardly, and that bringing particular cases under more general policies is part of making reasoned decisions. It is surely also true that our respect for ourselves and others consists in good part in our respect for freedom, and for the reason necessary to that freedom. So we can add to our response to the sensible knave, including the knave within ourselves, that the betrayal of morality can lead us to lose our freedom, to violate the respect that we like to show our friends, and to violate, and lose, our self-respect. In immorality, we can become literally enslaved to our desires, as Plato showed so vividly (Kant looks back to Plato, in this regard), and to treat others as such slaves as well. We have reason to be moral insofar as we want to maintain or express our freedom, and to respect others and ourselves. This is not a properly Kantian reason to be moral—it relies on what we *want*, rather than on reason alone—but it draws on Kantian materials. I suspect it is the most we can get from Kant, as far as moral motivation is concerned.

That said, it doesn't much matter for the purposes of this book whether Kantian views of morality are successful or not. All we need to establish is that there are good secular reasons to be moral. That can be done fairly well on the Humean grounds we surveyed before coming to Kant. The Kantian elements merely make those grounds stronger. If Kant is right, we have stronger secular reasons to be moral than if Hume alone is right. If Kant is not right, we still have a pretty good case for being moral, independent of religion.

27. Religious grounds for being moral don't add much to the secular ones. Crude religious reasons for morality are theologically problematic and more sophisticated ones presuppose that there are adequate secular grounds for morality. In practice, moreover, neither the crude nor the sophisticated religious reasons to be moral are more effective, in keeping would-be knaves from immorality, than the secular motivations we have considered.

The crudest religious argument for being moral is that God will mete out severe and eternal punishment to evil-doers, and great and eternal reward to the good. The calculations of the sensible knave are therefore mistaken if they ever make the wrong path appear to bring in greater rewards than the right one: the greatest possible rewards, in the long term, go with the right path and the worst possible costs go with the wrong one.

Less crude versions of this view hold not so much that we should act morally *in order* to reap God's rewards and avoid His punishments, as that God establishes a system of reward and punishment because justice demands it, and we can and should act morally out of respect for the justice of this order, or out of gratitude for the fact that the universe embodies a just order.

One thing wrong with this view in all its versions is that it represents God as simple-minded and cruel. Any God who would want us to be good just to reap selfish rewards, or avoid selfish punishments, is less noble than many human beings, and even the idea that justice requires reward and punishment presupposes that goodness is intrinsically tied to reward and badness to punishment. The thought that God would establish eternal punishments is, moreover, quite horrifying—seems indeed *unjust*, given human limitations—yet it is hard to make the response to the egoist effective if one relaxes that requirement.[13]

In addition, these styles of argument represent the goods of morality as external to it. You act honestly, or give charity to your neighbor, and are rewarded with health or a place in the heavenly choir; you do wrong and are punished with sickness or hellfire. The Humean picture contrasts favorably with this—at least there are pleasures built into acting rightly, or closely connected with it—and the Kantian picture makes morality good in itself, independent of reward. Of course, religious people can embrace the Humean and Kantian pictures of motivation alongside a story about heaven and hell, but in that case it is the secular part of their view that is the most admirable, not the religious part.[14]

In any case, it's a mistake to suppose that the notion of divine reward and punishment deters bad conduct better than secular pictures of the advantages of goodness. Throughout history, plenty of people who seem fervently to have believed in a Hell have nonetheless done things—adultery, rape, murder—that they themselves claim will bring on God's eternal wrath. Why they do things like this is an interesting question. Sometimes a few moments of earthly bliss seem to them worth an eternity of torment after death; sometimes they are probably not in the end all that convinced that there is a God, or that God will mete out eternal punishment; sometimes they are probably confused or acting unthinkingly. There are, of course, parallels to each of these cases in the way secular people fail to heed their own justifications for morality. The goods of immorality on occasion seem worth more to them than the goods of morality; they may not believe as wholeheartedly in the arguments they proclaim as they say; or they may be confused, or overwhelmed by a momentary impulse. But I know of no evidence that this weakness of will and self-deceit, or the immoral behavior it enables, is any more common among secular than among religious people.

28. A more sophisticated religious story about moral motivation says that the best reason to be good is *love* of God. In our gratitude for what God does for us, or simply in our love for God's goodness, we want to be good to all His creatures. Moral action consequently pours out of us.[15]

This is an admirable reason for being good, and can accompany a morally admirable picture of God, but it is hard to imagine that many people actually *are* motivated by such a rare and difficult religious achievement. Loving a Being one cannot directly sense is not easy and is usually pictured as the crown of the religious life, to be strived for by all, but fully achieved, in this life at least, only by religious virtuosi. Certainly, people are less likely to be motivated by an ideal love like this than by the Humean considerations we listed earlier.

It is also unclear whether we can properly love God without having the secular moral motivations canvassed earlier. To love God is after all to love *goodness*, and to do that one needs some or all of the desires for goodness put forward by the Humean, the utilitarian, the Kantian, etc. Love of God may then not add much to the moral motivations we have from secular sources. Loving goodness—being grateful for it, admiring it, or wanting to help preserve or foster it—includes loving the happiness of sentient beings, the freedom and self-respect of rational beings, and the like. Does it include anything else? Perhaps, if there is a kind of goodness in relation to God that transcends all merely moral goodness. But then that aspect of the love of God is unlikely to be the basis of *moral* motivation.

We may put this point in another, more theological way. God, as the supremely good being, surely wants us to love our fellow creatures *as such*, not just through our love for Him. It would be a less than supremely good being who would want us to reserve all our true love for Him, and care for other beings solely out of duty or gratitude to Him—at arm's length, as it were, without any real respect or concern for the human beings or animals and plants themselves. Having us act on such simulacra of respect and care would not be the best way for God to demonstrate His own love for his creatures, and would require us to be less than fully honest. So we must presume that a supremely good Being would want us to have direct, secular sources of moral motivation, rather than acquiring those motivations only when we come to recognize or care for Him. This is, indeed, the central problem with divine command theories of morality: that morality, first and foremost, concerns our relations *with our fellow human beings*, and the best motivations to heed it are therefore ones that draw on our attitudes toward those human beings, rather than taking a detour via a Being outside the human realm.[16]

Finally, we should note that love of God has historically not been much more effective than fear of God in preventing people from immoral behavior. Partly, perhaps, because loving God is so difficult, and partly for the same reasons that the threat of divine punishment is not that effective, there have been many religious people who seemed, both to others and to themselves, to be sincerely in love with God, but nevertheless engaged in adultery or sexual harassment or fraud, betraying their ultimate Beloved for more immediate, embodied loved ones. Love of God has also led, of course, to some remarkably noble and self-sacrificing behavior. But it needn't do that, and when it does, that is usually in part because the agent has a strong love or respect for his or her fellow human beings, as well as for God. Hillel, St Francis, and Gandhi stand out for their gentleness and respect for their fellow human beings even among other lovers of God, and they sometimes acted in ways that seemed drawn from them by their love for people, rather than any distinctively religious thoughts or feelings. Their love of God merely enhanced, and perhaps helped them to interpret, an attentiveness they had anyway to the good of God's creatures. Whether those of us with less humanity than these great teachers can do the same is doubtful, and it would certainly be a mistake to strip them of their humanity, when we present them as role models, as if their love for God were all that mattered.

29. To summarize, secular sources of moral motivation generally do as good a job as can be done in leading us toward moral action. If the desire for approval and self-approval, and for the honest friendships that are possible only among people who approve of one another, do not keep you a decent and generous person, if wanting the internal freedom, and respect and self-respect, that come of pursuing general polices, rather than being driven by whims or overpowering desires, do no more to keep you on a moral path, if even the fear of punishment by other human beings, through legal means or otherwise, and desire for their help in attaining your selfish goods, is of no use, then neither fear of God's punishment nor love of God's goodness is likely to be any more helpful. (Indeed, in that case you are unlikely to be capable of loving God). And if you do not fear God's punishment, or love His goodness, but have many of these other motivations, that alone is quite likely to keep you moral. All these motivations can fail, and often do. Nothing in human history suggests that religious motivations do so less often than secular ones. And there are plenty of admirable human beings who seem to have been motivated by secular considerations alone: David Hume himself, for example. At most, religious motivations can enhance a moral disposition already anchored in Humean sentiments or Kantian reason. Religious motivations can also redirect an already established moral disposition, such that one puts the energy or self-command one might otherwise use for purely humanistic ends towards religious ends as well. That can be a good thing, if one continues to respect one's fellow human beings and the religious ends enhance human life in a way that could not be achieved by the promotion of happiness or freedom alone. Or it can be a terrible thing, if the religious ends conflict with moral ones. In either case, however, the distinctively religious motivations will be grafted on to sentiments and beliefs that incline us toward morality regardless of our sentiments or beliefs about God. As with the search for truth, so with goodness: it makes sense, even from a religious point of view, that a good God would provide human beings with reasons to be moral independently of any belief in Him. Since morality primarily serves to sustain human societies—to enable us to build a way of the world together—it is appropriate for our reasons to be moral to grow out of our attitudes towards each other, and crucial for them not to depend on controversial metaphysical views. And we do have purely humanistic reasons to be moral, and these reasons do keep us, most of the time, in accord with the demands of morality. Secular moral motivation is self-sufficient; we need not be religious in order to be moral.

4

Transformation

30. I said earlier (§ 5) that there were three main questions about ethical systems:

1. What should we do?
2. Why should we do it? and
3. Why do we so often fail to do what we think we should do?

We come now to the third of these questions. Our consideration of it will begin to bring out the limitations of morality, the reason we seek more comprehensive visions of value.

It is a well-known, perplexing feature of human beings that they often know quite well that they ought to act in one way, but nevertheless act differently. This is not by any means a neglected topic in moral philosophy, but it tends to be treated as a sort of addendum to the main issues. We come up with an account of what people should do, and the motives that properly lead them to do it, and then try to give an explanation of why those motives sometimes lack strength, why otherwise reasonable and well-intentioned people ignore them and pursue more selfish ends instead. Usually, philosophers explain this phenomenon by way of self-deceit or weakness of the will (akrasia). The person who doesn't do what is obviously the right thing either makes efforts to keep himself from recognizing the rightness of this choice or fails to make the requisite efforts to bring his will in accordance with his reason. We fail to live up to the demands of morality because of some sort of distortion or weakness in ourselves—some way in which our emotions overcome our reason, perhaps.

But one can approach this phenomenon in another way: perhaps the failing lies in morality itself, not in our ability to live up to it. In the past two chapters, I have described morality as a limited system of values that does not and cannot achieve the full range of things we consider good. There are tensions, in many circumstances, between what seems to us to be real goods and what morality tells us to do. These tensions range from the fairly trivial—keeping a promise may get in the way of spending time with one's family—to the danger that one will lose a great romantic love in order to remain faithful to an indifferent marriage, or that one's obligations to a spouse or child may get in the way of one's ability to serve one's country or religion. Sometimes it seems there are excellent reasons to suspend morality for a higher purpose. Perhaps that is what leads people to ignore moral demands, much of the time.

It is unlikely that this explains all failures to do our moral duty. Self-deceit and akrasia are real phenomena, and people often engage in them to pursue behavior that serves no value other than their crassest selfish interests. Often self-deceit comes along with akrasia. We commit actions of which we disapprove out of akrasia, then rationalize them to minimize our disapproval of ourselves.[1] But the third of our questions at least opens up the possibility that there is something limited, something cramped, about morality itself. I shall suggest that this idea gives us a lens by which to understand a number of influential modern critiques of morality. These views have both secular and religious variants; indeed, they are more commonly secular than religious. This is the arena in which religion finally begins to come into its own, however, to make legitimate claims be may more worthy of belief than their secular rivals. Which is to say that the opening in the way of the world for divine teaching is one that secular people can recognize and have themselves not infrequently exploited.

31. As noted above, the third of our basic ethical questions is generally treated as a separate and a lesser one, not requiring a solution before one tackles the other two. But a few philosophers have reversed that order, with intriguing results.

Suppose that whatever blocks us from *doing* what we should do also blocks us from properly *seeing* what we should do. This is not implausible. Most people who do something sleazy or cruel come up with excuses for their actions—"So what if I'm cheating my boss? That skinflint owes me back pay for years"; "She deserved a slap, the way she spoke to me"—and one effect of this sort of rationalization, over time, is likely to be a corruption of one's ethical principles. We deceive ourselves about what we are actually doing, and we then deceive ourselves about what we believe we should do. But if so, then perhaps it is our self-deception, and/or weakness of will, that leads us to suppose there is any problem about what we should do, or why we should do it. Part of the self-deception by which we avoid doing our ethical duty might be a pretense that we don't know what choice we should be making. We may excuse a listlessness about moral action, a laziness about overcoming our vices, by telling ourselves we're not sure what we should be doing. Or the vices and weaknesses that lead us into bad action may take up so much mental energy that we cannot think straight about the right and the good. In any case, it is surely possible that transforming myself into a fully virtuous person would make the questions of what to do, and why to do it, fade away. I might then just *see* what I should do—it would be obvious—and see why I should do it to boot.

For some aspects of the moral life, this seems quite plausible. Consider a person sunk in theft and dishonesty out of alcoholism. Overcoming the weaknesses that lead to his addiction, transforming his emotional profile, may well lead this person to find it obvious that he should not lie or cheat to raise the money for another bottle of vodka—obvious, also, that a life of sobriety is better than the life he has been leading until now.

But it is important that this is an extreme and a limited kind of case. Because it is extreme—because the vice in question is readily redescribed as an *illness*, or form of self-enslavement—we can make easy sense of how the person in question could be blind to what is obvious to the rest of us. And because it is limited, because recovery from the illness will solve some, but not all of one's ethical problems, agreeing that a certain clarity about the right and the good might come with such recovery does not commit us to viewing all of ethics as likely to become clear by an analogous emotional change.

Nevertheless, that is just what some philosophers have argued. Relying heavily on an analogy between vice and illness, and portraying the evil person as very much like an addict, Plato argued in the *Republic* that getting our emotions under firm rational control could solve all the other problems in ethics. The tyrant who seems to have such absolute power over others, says Plato, is in reality enslaved to the soldiers and courtiers who enable him to stay in power. And the tyrannical *personality*, who seems to pursue his own desires in complete freedom from moral or social constraint, is in reality similarly enslaved to those desires, and unable to establish a clear direction for his own choices. "[T]he soul which is ruled by a tyrant will...be least able to do what it wants," says Socrates: "Despite itself, it will be forever driven onward by the gadfly of desire, and filled with confusion and dissatisfaction" (Rep 577e)[2] Like a city ruled by a tyrant—poor, fearful, and full of misery—the tyrannical soul will be impoverished and insatiable, frightened and miserable. The cure for these evils is to put one's soul in proper order, which in part means to develop one's capacities for courage and moral reasoning to the point at which they can rule one's desires, and in part means to "convert," "re-orient" oneself (518c–d), so that one cares more about abstract ideals than the experiences offered by one's senses—to take a new telos, understand one's ultimate good in a new way.

Plato devotes the bulk of the *Republic* to explicating and defending this conception of moral character and moral education, as against what we today call "applied ethics." In a remarkable passage (425a–d), he has Socrates ask whether, in building an account of the good city and good soul, it is worthwhile to settle questions about business dealings, slander and assault, the nature of the legal system, or the treatment of parents and elders. Adeimantus answers that it isn't worthwhile: "If we've got the right sort of citizens, it's a waste of time telling them what to do. I imagine they can easily develop most of the necessary legislation for themselves." Socrates approves of this answer, and says that those who try to solve moral problems by settling specific moral issues are like those who, without changing their diet or general way of life, try to solve health problems with ever-new medical treatments:

What a delightful life those people lead! Their medical treatment achieves nothing, except to increase the complications and severity of their ailments, yet they live in constant hope that each new medicine recommended will be the one which will make them healthy.... [T]he truth ... is that until they give up drinking, over-eating, sex and idleness, no medicine, cauter-isation or surgery ... will do them the slightest good. (426a–b)

Trying to solve moral problems one by one, like trying to solve health problems one by one, is an effort at "cutting off the Hydra's head": each time one is removed, another pops up in its place. Both morality and health (for Plato, morality may well *be* mental health) can be achieved only in a holistic way, and once one has done that, one has no further need for specific ethical guidance. Good people need no case-by-case ethical advice to figure out how to act, and bad people cannot be helped by such advice.

We may miss how striking this view is if we think the *Republic* is simply *unconcerned* with the issues that come up in applied ethics. In fact, the beginning of the *Republic* reads as if it were a book precisely on applied ethics. In response to a proposed definition of "justice," Socrates offers a case, of exactly the sort given in applied ethics classes today, in which a person leaves you some weapons for safe-keeping, but has gone mad when he returns to claim them. Should you return the weapons or not, asks Socrates? Does *justice* demand the keeping of trust, in a case like this, or does it demand the opposite?

No direct solution is given to this question, nor are its details discussed at any length, but the possibility of encountering problems like it haunts the rest of the dialogue. Famously, a question later arises about whether it could be justifiable to found a political regime on a "noble lie." Again, the details of the question are not directly addressed. Instead, in both cases, Socrates indicates that *if* a breach of trust or lie is ever justified, only extremely wise and good people will know *when* it is justified—and can be relied on to "use" such a violation of justice, or apparent violation of justice, for good ends. Which brings us back to the passage about specific ethical issues that I discussed above: the reason Socrates fails to offer a direct answer to the questions about the weapons and the noble lie may well be that he has in mind all along to show that a certain kind of good character is the key to handling such questions. In any case, the *Republic* as a whole urges us to replace our questions about specific ethical issues with a concern to clarify and re-order our general mental structure. The idea seems to be precisely to resolve the third of the basic ethical questions with which I began—to overcome the delusions or weaknesses that lead us to fail to live up to our ethical ideals—and only thereby to resolve the other two.

Call this "therapy as ethics." Plato is far from its only proponent. Aristotle also dedicates his ethical work to an account of good character, albeit a different one from Plato's, and implies by his silence on specific questions that they are not the appropriate locus for deep thought on the subject. The Stoics explicitly hold that there is one, holistic cure for ethical difficulties of all kinds: to align our wills with the course of nature, and let go of the many desires that would put us out of alignment with it. Spinoza continues this Stoic line, the British moral sentimentalists maintain that shaping our emotional systems correctly is the key to ethical conduct, and even Kant primarily urges us to overcome the confusion caused by our desires, rather than giving us a method for resolving moral problems one by one. Freud also stands in this tradition of ethical philosophy, although he takes the tradition away from philosophy: extending Plato's comparison between virtue and mental health, he transforms ethics into a matter for doctors, rather than speculative thinkers. Psychoanalysis, by reintegrating parts of our psyche that have fallen into disarray, and by clarifying ourselves to ourselves, leads us to a position from which we can have more rational control over our lives, rather than being enslaved by illusions and obsessions—leads us, in Freud's wonderful phrase, "from neurosis into ordinary unhappiness."[3] And when we emerge from this process, we may find our specific moral questions far less pressing. We may come to see our ends differently or more clearly, and in the light of this picture of our overall good find it easier to solve the problems we face about the morally good.

32. Therapy as ethics is one important alternative to moral systems that purport to help us figure out, directly, what to do. There are other alternatives: revolution as ethics, for instance. I include under this heading all descendants of the Marxist approach to ethics: all claims that we can best change our emotional constellation, and everyday practices, by changing our social structure. If class hierarchies—or, in later versions, racial or gender hierarchies—pervasively corrupt human relations, such that some people feel servile while others think they deserve to be masters, and everyone pursues vain and selfish goods rather than working together in communal solidarity, then perhaps the abolition of the class system will get rid of the vices that lead us to think there are difficult moral problems. Perhaps, in a classless, truly communal society, we would simply *see* the best way to behave, and the right way to answer what now seem like tangled moral quandaries. And perhaps focusing on the quandaries, rather than dealing with the underlying corruption, is again like cutting off the heads of a hydra: each particular problem solved will simply give way to new particular problems, without any real progress. Like Plato's person with an unhealthy diet and lifestyle, we as a society can solve our moral problems only holistically, by abolishing classes and re-structuring our institutions in a fully egalitarian and communalist way. Only then will we find a morality that we will not fail regularly to satisfy: a morality we can embrace, wholeheartedly, as our own.

The *locus classicus* for this sort of position is the writings of Marx himself.[4] His early writings repeatedly suggest that human nature has been twisted out of its original, communal shape into an individualist, competitive one by capitalism and the division of labor. Our consciousness, which distinguishes us from other animals, is inherently oriented toward "species" or universals, including the species human being; we are free only when we act as conscious beings, thus free only when we act as members of the human species. But "estranged labour reverses this relationship, so that man . . . makes his . . . *essential* being a mere means to his *existence*" (MER 76). The worker in capitalist societies becomes estranged from his own activity and, as a result, feels at home only in his animalistic activities—"eating, drinking, procreating, or at most in his dwelling and in dressing-up, etc."—not in his truly conscious, truly free, truly human ones:

> The worker... only feels himself outside his work, and in his work feels outside himself. He is at home when he is not working, and when he is working, he is not at home. ... What is animal becomes human [in him] and what is human becomes animal. (MER 74)

Communism would change all this, would return us to our essential human nature. It would enable us to produce goods in true freedom, out of a love of making akin to the feeling of an artist for his creations (MER 76), restore the truly human, truly free and respectful, relationships that have been distorted by divisions between masters and workers, and transform sexual relationships from being based primarily on lust to being free and equal partnerships. Our very sense-perception would change. Communism would emancipate "all human senses and attributes" from being tools merely for individual purposes to being part of a truly human, which for Marx means truly social, approach to the world. (MER 87; on sex see 83–84).

This transformation of feelings and perceptions would make what we now call "morality" unnecessary. We would spontaneously act out of love and respect for our fellow human beings, and that would take care of the problems we now regard as moral ones. Marx generally talks of morality the way he talks of religion: as a projection of the alienating and oppressive socio-political structure under which we live, which contributes to its distortion of our lives. Religions project a god whose commands track whatever it is that the ruling class wants us to do. Moral systems do the same. Morality encourages enjoyment in some societies, asceticism in others, depending on what is useful for the ruling class. Kant's "good will" reflects nothing more than "the impotence, depression and wretchedness of the German burghers."[5] Communism will "shatter [...] the basis of all morality, whether... of asceticism or of enjoyment."[6] For Marx, as for Nietzsche, morality is a product of false consciousness, something that pretends to represent our highest ideals while actually serving the crass, selfish interests of an elite, and justifying a sociopolitical structure that de-humanizes us all. Some commentators maintain that a new, truly humanistic morality could arise, on Marx's view, once communism is in place.[7] I think a more consistent understanding of his teaching is that morality necessarily involves the presentation of norms or ideals as superior to us, something we should be awed by, and that that presentation itself represents our estrangement from our humanity. For Marx, as I understand him, norms get the label "moral" only when they appear to us as something alien, underwritten by God or some similarly supernatural being or principle standing over us. Even Kant's justification of morality by way of freedom removes moral norms too far from us, given the non-naturalistic character Kant attributed to freedom. And the fact that moral norms have this distant character makes them easy tools for domination: we use morality to beat each other over the head with, to coerce or cajole other people into doing what we want them to do.[8] A properly humanized set of social norms will appear to us as our *own* norms, something we create and daily shape, not something that comes to us from the outside—not, consequently, as *moral* norms. Communist revolution will bring about an emancipation *from* morality, in favor of a mode of life in which morality is unnecessary.

I find this vision very attractive, both because a world in which everyone was spontaneously kind to and respectful of everyone else would be a nice place to live, and because it provides a plausible explanation for why moral problems seem so intractable (as does the therapeutic view of ethics, which I find attractive for the same reason). It would also be a relief if one day these issues, rather than being solved, simply disappeared. Marx's utopia is attractive partly because it offers the hope that one day we will be able to breathe freely of the knotted *worry* that moral problems induce in us.

On the other hand, I don't find Marx's view of human nature as essentially communal very plausible, nor do I think communism of any sort can be maintained without great violence—without, therefore, making impossible the sort of utopian transformation Marx thinks it will bring about.[9] But *if* Marx were right on the facts about human beings, and *if*, therefore, his utopia were achievable, it does seem reasonable to expect that what we now take to be moral problems might simply fall away. Accordingly, it seems reasonable for people who accept Marx's anthropology to work on bringing about revolution, rather than trying to resolve specific moral problems one by one. A focus on such issues, from a Marxist perspective, is a distraction from the real solution to our problems, and a distraction that the ruling classes would like us to take up, since it is endless and encourages minor tinkering instead of significant social change.

33. Søren Kierkegaard is known for a philosophy that tried to draw its readers away from philosophy altogether—to a faith, against reason, in Christ. But he also had interesting things to say about ethics. One of those things, an extension of thoughts to be found in Kant, may be described as a third alternative to what we ordinarily think of as ethics: we may call it "inwardness as ethics." If what lies at the heart of being an ethical person is an internal commitment to being good that each individual must make for herself, then it is a distraction from that core ethical act, and a misleading way of presenting the ethical terrain, for anyone, including moral philosophers, to tell others what ethics requires. Suppose the essential ethical task is for each of us personally to commit ourselves to being ethical—for *me* to grasp for *myself* the nature and importance of being good and commit myself to trying to achieve that. Then if I am good only because *you* tell me I should be good, or if I try to be good to win your admiration, or because I trust you and think what you do is worth doing, I will fail in my central ethical task. But in that case, how do you communicate to me what I should do? If you tell me so much as that I need to appropriate ethics for myself, and I then do so because I trust or love or admire you, your communication will have done exactly what you didn't want it to do. You need to push me away from you, somehow, giving me space to see what I need to do for myself.

Kierkegaard calls this the problem of "indirect communication." With his usual sharp wit, he speaks of a teacher who comes to the conviction that no-one ought to have disciples, and in reward for his success in expressing and defending this conviction, gets "applications from at least ten candidates, offering to preach this doctrine, in return merely for a free shave once a week. That is to say, he would in . . . confirmation of his doctrine have experienced the peculiar good fortune of obtaining disciples to accept and disseminate this doctrine of not having any disciples."[10] Kierkegaard goes on to mock those who go about as "town criers of inwardness":

Suppose that someone wished to communicate the following conviction. Truth is inwardness;[11] there is no objective truth, but the truth consists in personal appropriation. Suppose him to display great zeal and enthusiasm for the propagation of this truth . . . Suppose he announced it on all possible occasions, and succeeded in moving not only those who perspire easily, but also the hard-boiled temperaments: what then? Why then, there would doubtless be found a few laborers, who had hitherto stood idle in the market-place, and only after hearing this call went to work in the vineyard—engaging themselves to proclaim this doctrine to all. And then what? Then he would have contradicted himself . . . The matter of prime importance was, of course, that he should be understood; the inwardness of the understanding would consist precisely in each individual coming to understand it by himself. Now he had even succeeded in obtaining town criers of inwardness, and a town crier of inwardness is quite a remarkable species of animal.[12]

The solution to this problem is to fit the form of one's communication to its content, and Kierkegaard urges anyone who shares his intensely subjective conception of the good life to adopt an indirect form of communication, to present her teaching in a hypothetical or ironic or obscure enough way that the reader or listener is pushed away from it unless and until he thinks it through, and assesses it, for himself. Exactly what this might amount to is very hard to say, and it leads Kierkegaard himself to adopt a variety of games and poses in his writing, but he picks out Socrates as an example of a philosopher who managed it reasonably well.

Kierkegaard's main concern, here as elsewhere, is with religious commitment, but the point applies to secular ethical commitments as well. If Kant's central teaching is that we must autonomously choose, each for ourselves, to be guided by the categorical imperative, then there is a danger that Kant's own writings will lead people away from his teaching rather than toward it: we may act in accordance with the categorical imperative because Kant said so, and we or our friends think that Kant was a very smart man, rather than because we see it as an expression of our freedom. Kant is often presented as saying simply that we need to follow the categorical imperative. If that were so, then people could be ethical regardless of whether they understood exactly why they should follow the categorical imperative, or saw it as an expression of their own freedom. But in a number of places, Kant suggests that the real ethical task is to see ourselves as *free*, and thereby to overcome the wayward and unruly desires that lead us into vice.[13] The categorical imperative then becomes just a way of expressing how we see ourselves as free, and useless if one follows it mechanically, rather than *as* an expression of freedom. On this reading of Kant, his ethical texts themselves run the risk of tempting us to ignore the task of appropriating our own freedom, or at least of distracting us from that task, and indirect communication might be a useful complement to Kantian ethics.

In any case, Kierkegaard directs us away from the social function of morality, from all accounts of it that focus on the way it enhances our social relationships, rather than expressing our individual ideals. Like the other views we have considered in this chapter, inwardness as ethics attempts to bring our ethical commitments more in line with our overall personal ends: to overcome the gap between moral demands and a broader sense of goodness that may lead us to reject morality as cramped and limited.

34. Finally, we might consider self-assertion as ethics. Once again, we can find a 19th-century philosopher who represents this view (the 19th century is the heyday of doubts about traditional ethical systems): Nietzsche, this time. Nietzsche has often been read as simply hostile to ethics, but more sympathetic readers have shown how he can be understood as, instead, making an important ethical point.[14] On this reading, he attacks *conventional* ethics, and standard philosophical theories of ethics, to make room for a healthier, more self-respecting kind of human being who would be honest and generous naturally—as a spontaneous product of his or her emotions, rather than under the constraint of peer pressure.

The problem with standard codes and theories of ethics, on this view, is that they attempt to move us by a sense of shame or guilt, or some other form of self-hatred. We are urged to feel terrible about ourselves, small in our own eyes, if we violate the codes of behavior our society wants us to keep. Nietzsche sees this as a "slave morality": we are given the consciousness of slaves, looking worshipfully up to others (priests, politicians, philosophers) for guidance about how to live. A truly free person would throw off the yoke of other people's opinion, be kind or cruel as he felt like it, and rejoice in his body and natural impulses, not restrain them out of fear of what other people may think, or superstitious faiths invented to buttress those opinions. Nietzsche thinks that only such a person would truly be honest, in the sense both that he would rarely bother to lie and in the deeper sense that he would express his own nature, rather than some construction foisted upon him. Nietzsche also thinks that only such a person would truly have courage, and that only such a person's generosity would be true generosity, rather than a wheedling simulacrum designed to win approval from others. These appeals to honesty, courage, and generosity make clear that he is launching an *ethical* critique of ethics, an argument that the burdens that come with thinking in standard ethical terms keep us from the psychological health by which we could actually attain our ideals.

There are obvious affinities between this view and the emphasis on inwardness in Kierkegaard, and psychological health in Plato and Freud. Certainly, all three views urge us, if we are really interested in acting well, to put our mental houses in order, rather than listen to those who tell us what we ought to do or what motivations we ought to have. Acting well requires not worrying about how to act well, but rather turning one's attention *away* from such matters and building up a healthy spirit within ourselves.[15] For all three of these views, acting well requires ignoring especially the conventional shibboleths that our society tries to thrust upon us. The conventional norms around us, and raised eyebrows, tongue-cluckings, or politically correct reprimands by which our friends and neighbors enforce those norms, *distract* us from taking responsibility for our own choices about how to live, from releasing or expressing our inward selves. People drawn to Plato, Kierkegaard, Nietzsche, or Freud may see great ethical value in, for instance, works of art that defy conventional norms, that shock or horrify the self-righteous moral bourgeoisie. Don Giovanni and Faust may seem more ethical to them, because more honest and /or freer, than respectable members of society. Artworks like Bertolucci's *Last Tango in Paris* or Andres Serrano's "Piss Christ" may similarly seem morally valuable, since they break us of the prison of conventional morality and thereby lead us to think through our moral beliefs on our own. The moral self, on these sorts of views, is necessarily a self that has gone through a stage of readiness to reject everything its society holds up as good—even if, in its new-found freedom, it comes to embrace similar beliefs and attitudes. Only the examined self can truly live up to moral ideals, but true self-examination requires us to be willing to suspend or reject precisely those ideals.

It's hard to imagine views further removed from a social contract model of morality—from ethics conceived as a means for people, ordinarily, to live together: as part of the way of the world.

35. All the positions we have considered in this chapter share something with a religious approach to ethics. They suggest that there is something unsatisfying about the ethical systems we normally encounter, that ethics thus conceived is somehow incomplete and needs help from outside. They advocate turning *away* from ethics for ethical reasons. I will call such approaches "transformative" ones—they believe a transformation of human nature, including the part of human nature that issues in ethical systems, is necessary if our ordinary ethical problems are to be solved. They oppose themselves to the immanent approaches to ethics we considered earlier, in which the point of ethics is thought to be more or less visible in what it actually does. Immanent ethicists tend to see ethical thinking as immanent also in human nature—a natural tendency—and in more or less good shape as it stands: some tweaking may be needed, but not a thorough overhaul. They are concerned to spell out clearly how ethics works, rather than replace it with something else.

We came across transformative ethical claims earlier, in connection with the truthfulness of characters like Aloysius (Part I, § 29). There we saw how the ordinary connotations of the word "truth" can be used to help us trust someone who takes us away from how we have been ordinarily living. Here, we begin to see how promises of transformation may take us out of the social contract approach to both knowledge and morality—how, if such promises can be redeemed, they may show us something other than what we see when we stay within the ways of gaining information, and living together, that we share with our neighbors in daily experience. They may take us out of the way of the world.

Note that this hint that we may need to go beyond the way of the world comes from *within* the way of the world. Perhaps promises of transformative ethical visions cannot be redeemed—perhaps they are all illusory, hold out vain hopes. But then a hope that many quite secular people—Spinozists, Marxists, Freudians—hold out would be vain, not just a religious hope. The transformative approach to ethics is by no means an exclusively religious one. Indeed, in the hands of a Marx or Nietzsche or Freud it can be strongly anti-religious: religion, for these thinkers, is one of the things from which we need to recover. We might say that the transformative approach requires what Kierkegaard calls a "teleological suspension of the ethical"—a willingness to suspend the ethical, or what is normally regarded as such, in the name of some higher purpose. Our highest end—telos—may conflict with ethics, as we ordinarily understand it, rather than being fulfilled by it. Both religious revelations and the systems of philosophers like Plato, Marx, and Nietzsche promise to transform us by a reorientation that will alter the meaning and purpose of ethics. So a religious ethic, far from being a way of settling ordinary ethical issues, consists centrally in a rejection of that sort of decision-making, a move to something else. We begin to explore this move in the next chapter.

5

Teleology

36. According to the views canvassed in the previous chapter, transforming ourselves goes together with grasping our real ends. Without an understanding of our true telos, we can't be the people we would really like to be—although we may also be incapable of grasping that telos properly until we are transformed into such people. In any case, on these views, standard moral systems don't capture our real ends. What Plato, Marx, Kierkegaard, and Nietzsche all suggest is that our conventional moralities are not really *ours*, that some part of our selves perceives, rightly, that we have important ends these moral systems do not help us achieve. If our real end is to participate in an abstract, obscure good, or be part of a universal human community that creates its own norms, or express or develop our radically individual subjectivities, then we will often feel thwarted when faced with overlapping-consensus moral demands that finesse questions about our ultimate ends. Perhaps this is the source of akrasia and self-deceit: we can't bring ourselves to do the morally right thing, and we delude ourselves about what is the morally right thing, because the very notion of the "morally right thing" arises out of a structure that distracts us or blocks us from our true ends—because the ends that morality serves are for good reason not that attractive to us. If we could be reoriented so that we see our true ends, and how morality fits into the pursuit of those ends (Plato), or if we could jointly determine what to count as our ends (Marx), then we could have norms and ideals that would be truly our own: ones we could wholeheartedly embrace, and no longer be tempted to betray. The reason we fail to do what we ourselves believe we should do, on this account, is that what we should do has yet to be brought together with our deepest ends, our telos. Ethics fails from the telic standpoint, and our vices implicitly reflect a yearning for what Kierkegaard calls a teleological suspension of the ethical.

> *Famously, Kierkegaard's prime example of the teleological suspension of the ethical is the Akedah: Abraham's attempt to sacrifice Isaac. Kierkegaard is clear-eyed about the fact that the sacrifice would have been murder, from the moral point of view; indeed, he emphasizes that aspect of the story.*[1]

Nevertheless, he regards it as God's command, admires Abraham for it—seems even to admire God for being willing to suspend the moral prohibition against murder. He longs, in any case, for something that would lift us out of the cage of morality. God, for Kierkegaard at this point in his career (he will have a somewhat different attitude when he introduces the category of the "ethico-religious" in the **Postscript***), frees us from all moral constraints. Kierkegaard's descendants, as regards this phase of his work, are al-Qaeda and the rabid Jewish settlers in Hebron. God may tell us even to kill innocents, and if he does, that is the right thing to do.*

I don't think I could continue to accept the Torah if I thought it taught us this.

37.   We'll return to Kierkegaard's phrase in a moment. Before we do that, we should note that telic failure is but one diagnosis of our tendency to betray our own moral standards, and not a wholly convincing one by itself. There are plenty of people— religious, as well as secular—who have a vision that incorporates morality into their overall ends but still act in sleazy ways of which they themselves in principle disapprove: think of Jimmy Swaggart or Eliot Spitzer. Akrasia and self-deceit, or whatever it is that leads us to betray our own norms and ideals, have complex roots that are unlikely to be traced to any one source, including the problem of interfering with our true ends. Nevertheless, it is plausible that a tension between morality and our pursuit of our individual ends is one source of this betrayal.

In any case, the fact that we are often tempted to betray our own moral principles is surely a *symptom* of a tension between morality and our telic aspirations. It is that tension that I want to explore. Many of the views we considered in the previous chapter offered a vision of the true human telos that we would not expect to find by rummaging around in moral common sense. Sometimes their advocates try to show how the pursuit of their favored end would yield actions that accord with morality, but they don't always say that (Nietzsche certainly doesn't) and, in any case, they make clear that morality and the pursuit of our telos are not identical. Morality enables human beings to form and sustain societies, but it is possible that each human being can achieve his or her highest end only by not caring much about the needs of society, not attending, much of the time, to the needs of others.

This is what raises the specter of a teleological suspension of the ethical. Not just religious commitment, but Platonic contemplation, Nietzschean self-expression, and Marxist revolution may all call on us to suspend what we ordinarily take to be ethical. This is a dangerous possibility, and one we all hope is unlikely, but it is intelligible, and that alone brings out the fact that ethics is not identical with the pursuit of our highest end.

At least that is true on some understandings of ethics. On others, ethics is *defined* as whatever enables us to achieve our highest ends. A "teleological suspension of the ethical" will then be a logical impossibility: it amounts to a teleological suspension of the teleological. Kierkegaard could use the phrase without worrying about this because he had a Kantian conception of ethics, in which what marks an action as ethical has to do with its form—whether it can be willed in accordance with a universal law—rather than its purpose. A utilitarian, and some virtue ethicists, will regard the phrase as nonsense.

We badly need a terminological distinction at this point. I turn to that below, adopting a distinction between the "moral" and the "ethical," and reworking Kierkegaard's phrase, such that it concerns a teleological suspension of the moral, rather than the ethical. With that bit of lexical housekeeping out of the way, we can begin to consider teleology proper: the question of what, if anything, makes our lives worth living. I will take up again a central argument of Chapter 2 of this Part, that our moral norms and ideals can accomplish their main role in our lives while finessing telic questions. But I will also argue that earnestly trying to fulfill the demands of morality can make questions about the worth of our lives especially pressing. Morality leads us toward ethics. Ethics, however, with its demand for an overall conception of our lives, may be incapable of adequate treatment within the way of the world. It is precisely a vision of our overall or highest end that revealed religions provide, and these visions may be more believable than the secular equivalents we find in Plato and Marx and Nietzsche. But if revealed religions alone satisfy our deepest ethical needs—if they alone provide an adequate conception of our highest or overall end—then they supply something that morality encourages us to yearn for, but cannot itself provide. That would be a good reason to put faith in them.

This, in a nutshell, is the view I'll be defending in the rest of this book. Its structure is based on the argument that Kant gives for what he calls "moral faith." I'll close this chapter by sketching Kant's argument and the degree to which I want to follow it.

38. A number of recent writers have proposed a distinction between morality and ethics. One of the best known is Bernard Williams, who uses "ethics" to denote any way of evaluating human conduct as good or right, while limiting "morality" to the specific type of ethical theory that focuses on obligations, and is centrally concerned with volition, responsibility, and blame: the type of ethical system given its "purest, deepest, and most thorough representation" by Kant (ELP 174).[2] Williams suggests an etymological basis for this distinction. He acknowledges that both words mean something like "custom," but says that "the Latin term from which 'moral' comes emphasizes, rather more the sense of social expectation [involved in customs], while the Greek favors that of individual character" (ELP 6).[3] The paradigmatic thinker of ethics as opposed to morality is Aristotle, for Williams, whose major treatise on the subject conveniently includes the word "ethics" in its title, while Kant's most famous work in the same area is known in English as providing a groundwork for the metaphysics of "morals."[4] One important difference between Aristotle's ethics and Kant's morality, as Williams presents them, is that the former is concerned with how each of us can lead an admirable and excellent life, while the latter focuses on the norms of interaction among us, the duties we owe to other people. Another important difference is that Aristotle looks at ongoing habits of character—virtues—and how they fit into our lives as a whole, while Kant looks at individual actions.

Williams's purported sources for his distinction do not bear much critical scrutiny. Both the Latin *mores* and the Greek *ethos* point us toward customs, as Williams admits, and in any case the two words have come to be virtually interchangeable in English. Certainly, anyone who talks of "business ethics" or "medical ethics" is likely to be concerned with norms for judging discrete actions, and when and how we should be held responsible for violating them. "Morality," on the other hand, as used in phrases like "moral teaching," can concern virtues as well as norms, and the way we ought to view our lives as a whole. Nor does Aristotle leave rules, much less volition and its bearing on blame, entirely out of his account of ethics, while recent readings of Kant have brought out how concerned he is with virtue as well as codes of conduct.[5] Moreover, Kant does not focus on our relationships with others to the exclusion of our relationship with ourselves: he always gives examples of duties to ourselves alongside duties to others and, indeed, sees the former as taking priority over the latter.[6]

Nevertheless, there is a distinction to be drawn here, and Williams' terms for it will do as well as any. It's particularly useful to distinguish between what goes into our obligations to others[7] and what we need to do in order to have an admirable or excellent life. I don't think this quite coincides with the distinction between a focus on actions or rules and a focus on virtues, but it is close enough to Williams's account that we can use "morality" for matters that concern solely our relations to others and "ethics" for a broader evaluation of our lives, which includes morality but is not limited to it. In addition to morality, ethics will include the arena—what I call the "telic" arena[8]—in which we raise the question of our overall or ultimate end: of whether our lives are worth living, and what, if so, makes them so. And all sorts of concerns will be relevant to that question that do not come up when we are concerned with morality alone. This provides us with a useful language for some key points: that morality, but not ethics, can be accounted for perfectly well within the way of the world, and that morality may lead us to ethics without itself being able to answer certain ethical questions.

Importantly, the telic arena is not by definition religious. There can be secular as well as religious conceptions of what makes life worth living, although I will try to show that religious conceptions have advantages over secular ones. My attempt to make that point would fail, however, if "telic" just *meant* "religious." Religious visions of our telos can be superior to secular ones only if both are in fact visions of our telos.

I can now put the general claim I shall try to defend as follows: Morality leads us to ask for, but does not depend upon, a vision of the human telos, which religions are in better position to provide than secular worldviews. A secular morality may therefore be complemented by a religious ethics. And while that secular morality will be transformed, as regards its function and justification, by being placed in this religious context—while it will acquire a new role in our lives and we will acquire new reasons to keep it—its content will not change. Consequently, the morality that secular and religious people share can be, as it should be, a constraint on the interpretation of any religious view of how to live.

39. But is it in fact possible to have morality without a notion of the ultimately good or worthwhile? I argued earlier (§ 14) that we arrive at an adequate mode of shared moral discourse only by finessing the question of what constitutes our ultimate or overall good, but I also acknowledged that this question haunts our moral thinking, and that at times we employ answers to it in making moral decisions. So perhaps I should say more about exactly what relationship our telic views bear to our moral ones.

There are certainly theories according to which everyday morality depends on a notion of the ultimately worthwhile. A number of moral philosophers refuse the distinction between morality and ethics I have just drawn, and regard both as the way human beings pursue their highest end. For them, we can have a morality only as long as we have a highest end. Aristotle presents practical reasoning as all of a piece, and so geared towards a hierarchy of ends that it makes no sense to engage in it unless we have a highest end.[9] He therefore tries to show that our activities are indeed intrinsically worthwhile, and bestow worth on the rest of our lives.

I don't think Aristotle is correct to tie morality to our telos, of course, but I do think a notion of the intrinsically worthwhile plays some role in our everyday moral lives. For one thing, failing to find anything intrinsically worthwhile in our lives can deprive us of a crucial source of moral motivation. If I find it difficult or impossible to see my own life as worthwhile, I may become listless and drift into my actions, rather than deliberating thoughtfully over them; *inter alia*, I may lose interest in fulfilling my moral obligations, and the shoddiness of my deliberations may lead me to be careless even when I do carry out such duties. Moreover, if I find it difficult or impossible to see *any* human life as worthwhile, then I may find it difficult to know how I should care for other people. How do I care for someone if I can't see her life as aiming at something worthwhile? What do I help her do—how can I guide her against, for instance, spending her life in an alcoholic haze, or an addiction to TV?

In this sense, a notion of the intrinsically worthwhile can contribute both to our reasons for taking morality seriously and to some of the moral decisions we take. My point is just that, on the whole, we don't *need* that notion to determine the content of morality, or give us adequate reasons for being moral. We may make do with limited goals that we enjoy without worrying about whether they bestow intrinsic worth on our lives (I may try to persuade the alcoholic, or TV-addict, that she is depriving herself of greater or more long-lasting pleasures). Or we may construe morality so that it can prescind from our overall goals. Rational egoists commonly start from the belief that notions of absolute or intrinsic worth are fraudulent, and that we need to see worth as instead always relative to our desires. Utilitarians start from the assumption that all human beings seek pleasure, without necessarily being committed to seeing pleasure as worthwhile. Some utilitarians would say that, while others regard the idea of intrinsic worth as meaningless; still others view pleasure as a proxy for whatever is worthwhile, but use it as their standard of moral judgment because it, and not the value for which it is a proxy, is intersubjectively observable and measurable.[10] Both rational egoists and all these utilitarians are, nevertheless, able to come up with full-bodied moral systems. The point of such systems is to enable us to satisfy our desires whether or not there is something worthwhile about doing that.

And Kantianism can be understood as motivated by the hope that we can develop norms for action while prescinding from questions about our ultimate goals. The whole point of Kantianism is that we can derive rules for how we should act from the form of what we plan to do rather than its end.[11] If rational egoists and many utilitarians finesse the question of whether our ends are worthwhile, Kantians finesse our ends altogether, telling us what principles we ought to follow regardless of our ends. Kant himself thought there was one end at which all rational action ought to aim—the promotion of rationality itself—and the second formulation of the categorical imperative is built around that end, but he recognized that that could not be our *only* end and said little about how our other ends could be integrated with this one.[12]

Even Alasdair MacIntyre, famous for complaining that modern moral thought has abandoned the notion of the human telos, proposes, as that telos, the life spent in *seeking for* our telos, and recommends that we understand virtues as the qualities of character we need to engage in this search.[13] Here, a quest for what might make life worth living takes the place of what, in ancient ethical systems, actually did make life worth living. This is still a way of defining virtue by avoiding the question of what makes life worth living, rather than answering it. Moreover, MacIntyre conflates morality with ethics, to use the distinction we have now introduced. He is right that the modern world is characterized by a loss of the notion that we have a clear telos, but not that this makes *morality* impossible. The point of modern moral philosophy is precisely that it shows how morality and notions of the worth of human life can be decoupled. We can know what it is to be moral, and have reasons for being moral, without having any clear idea of what makes our lives worthwhile. The ways that Kantians, utilitarians, and other modern philosophers define morality, and the reasons they give for being moral, differ widely, but their views of the content of morality overlap in large and crucial measure, and together they give reasons that suffice to convince most reasonable people to be moral. What MacIntyre laments is the loss of the *ethical* systems that flourished in ancient and medieval times. But that is not the same as a loss of morality.

In general, it seems possible to have an adequate moral system without a conception of ultimate worth if:

(1) the notion of ultimate worth is incoherent or empty yet we can find reason to be moral as a means of pursuing pleasure, or in our nature as rational beings;

(2) we need some notion of worth for moral purposes, but can make do with local, and conventional or relativistic, notions of worth; or

(3) we need some notion of ultimate worth for moral purposes, but don't need any particular conception of that worth: don't need to commit ourselves to the idea

that being free, or worshipping God, or achieving some political or intellectual goal, makes life worth living, just that some *one* of these does.

The first case we have already considered. The second we will examine in the beginning of Part III: it involves a Wittgensteinian dissolution of the questions that lead us to seek a worth for our lives as a whole. The third is the most intriguing. Here, we may see morality as a pre-condition for the *investigation* of worth, as consisting of those norms and/or virtues that help further our search for something that would make our lives worth living. We may define the moral life more or less as MacIntyre does: "the good life for man is the life spent in seeking for the good life for man, and the virtues necessary for the seeking are those which will enable us to understand what more and what else the good life for man is."[14] But to hold open "what more and what else" goes into our ultimate good like this is to deny that we know now what makes our lives worthwhile, and that we need such knowledge in order to know what morality demands of us, or have a motivation to abide by it.

These three strategies for dealing with worth differ, but any one of them will do to show that morality can get along without a conception of absolute or intrinsic worth. The rational egoist may deny that anything is absolutely or intrinsically worthwhile, the Wittgensteinian may affirm that *many* things are worthwhile, while denying that life as a whole can be described that way, and a person who sympathizes with MacIntyre may insist that morality needs to hold out some conception of ultimate or overall worth, while acknowledging that no-one knows what might fill in that conception. For our purposes, it doesn't matter which of these strategies one favors. Nor does it matter that on some other views—Aristotle's, for instance—morality will fail if we cannot find a conception of what makes life worth living. What matters is that there are eminently plausible strategies for defining morality and giving us reason to abide by it that bracket the question of worth. It is not unintelligible to uphold moral principles even while being agnostic about why, or whether, life is worth living.

The point we should be making may, indeed, be rather stronger than this. In Chapter 2 of this Part, I argued that morality succeeds best as an overlapping consensus among different accounts of how we should live. But we can arrive at such an overlapping moral consensus only if we *set aside* the question of what, if anything, makes life worth living. Any insistence that this question be settled, that we agree on a single answer to it, will make it impossible for utilitarians and Kantians, Aristotelians and rational egoists, as well as religious and secular people, to share a moral way of the world. Those who thought otherwise, in the ancient and medieval worlds, wrote many of their fellow human beings out of common morality. It is the achievement of modernity—a great achievement—to develop societies, and philosophies, that maintain a shared morality without expecting agreement on the telos of human life.

40. If morality doesn't provide us with a conception of life's worth, what does? That's the question of Parts III and IV of this book. Before getting there, I'd like to say more about how morality leads us to this question without being able to answer it.

People trying earnestly to pursue a moral life, deliberating over—say—how to balance their humanitarian against their personal projects or how best to care for their loved ones, are brought repeatedly before the question, "what ends should I have, or expect my loved ones to have?" This leads naturally to the further questions, "what ends should anyone have? what should human beings care about accomplishing before we die?" We confront such questions when we decide how to raise our children or care for a parent who has lost cognitive abilities, or whether to continue in a job or marriage. We confront them, also, when morality demands great sacrifices of us and we are tempted to give up on it. But we don't have to *answer* them in order to make these decisions responsibly. We can refrain from urging any view of life's worth on our children, and raise them simply to think judiciously about such matters; we can rely on what an aged parent in the past said he valued, when caring for him; we can consider only such factors as our feelings of comfort or oppression, in jobs or relationships, when deciding whether to continue in them; and we can consider only our interest in keeping our friends and our self-respect when reminding ourselves why we should remain committed to morality. Telic questions haunt such deliberations, however, and we often feel we could carry them out best if we had an answer to those questions. So morality leads us to telic questions, brings us to their doorstep, as it were, but morality need not, and for the most part does not, require that we answer them.[15]

What I call telic questions are thus much like the questions about the nature and existence of a highest good that Kant introduces at the end of his *Critique of Practical Reason*. And Kant also says that morality raises that question without answering it, or depending on our having an answer to it. He uses this point as the basis for what he calls a "rational faith" that there is a God who grants us eternal life, in which we will have happiness in accordance with our virtue. I shall use it as the basis for a faith, not wholly rational, that there is a God who makes it possible for us to have a life *worth living*, or that there is a supernatural condition from which we can see our lives as worth living. Kant calls his view a "moral faith"; I prefer the term "ethical faith," given the distinction between morality and ethics I have adopted. My slight variants on Kant's terminology represent ways in which my views of the content of religious faith differ from his, but his *strategy* for defending such faith—as unnecessary to ground either our theoretical or practical thinking, but something to which our practical thinking leads—is very much a model on which I want to draw. In the rest of this chapter, I'll examine Kant's argument for rational faith, and indicate how it provides a model for my own position.

41. Kant explains and defends his moral or rational faith[16] in several places. In a nutshell, the idea is that morality gives us reason to believe in a number of propositions on which science and the philosophy of science would leave us at best agnostic, including the existence of God and an afterlife. Kant says that although our motivation for moral action ought to be purely the notion of duty, and not an attempt to gain any

sort of reward, including happiness in an afterlife, the whole project of being moral would make little sense if there were no highest good (*summum bonum*) for us to achieve. He adds that this highest good consists in happiness in accordance with our virtue, and that it cannot be achieved unless there is a God who will reward us for our virtue in an eternal life. In our commitment to the project of being moral, then, we are implicitly committed to the possibility of our achieving such a highest good, and the God and eternal life that is necessary for it to be possible.

Much in this view is obscure. In particular, it is not easy to see how belief in a highest good is supposed to follow from our commitment to morality, what it means to say that that highest good is a combination of virtue and happiness, or why exactly it requires a God and an afterlife. I shall try to clarify these points, but at the end of the day I do not want to endorse all of Kant's arguments. For our purposes, we may usefully divide them into two main groups:

(1) A set of *formal* claims about the status of moral faith, according to which the practices to which we are committed, and not just empirical evidence, can give us reason for believing things; and

(2) A set of *substantial* claims, about the content of moral faith, according to which our highest good consists in happiness in accordance with virtue, this is not attainable within the confines of our life on earth, and we need therefore to assume there is a God and an afterlife if we hope to attain it.

With this division in hand, I can put my relationship to Kant's view by saying that I want strongly to defend (1) but to let go of much of (2), at least as Kant formulates and defends it. I want, that is, to defend the idea that moral faith—or, as I prefer to say, ethical faith—can indeed give us reason to maintain a view of our highest good and its presuppositions, even if science alone cannot support that view, but to leave far more widely open than Kant does *what* view of our highest good ethics demands. This will allow revealed texts to fill in the content of our ethical faith, and accordingly allow that content to vary, from person to person and society to society, far more than Kant would have countenanced.

Let me illustrate what I mean, and then return to Kant's arguments. For Buddhism, our highest good is a state of enlightenment conditioned by moral virtue (among other things), in which one is able to grasp the truth of "No-self" and experience the relinquishment of desires, and outflowing of compassion, that goes with this realization. So the Buddhist view of our highest good is also possible only given certain presuppositions: that there is, in fact, no self; that human beings are capable of grasping that fact; and perhaps that, as most Buddhist traditions teach, we need to go through a series of reincarnations in order to grasp that fact. Kant's formal claims about ethical faith allow us to conclude that *if* Buddhist-enlightenment-conditioned-by-virtue is the highest good, we have reason to believe in all its presuppositions—even though those presuppositions differ from, and in part contradict, the ones that Kant himself defends. On the Buddhist view, reincarnation replaces immortality, there is no God, and our ultimate goal is to relinquish our selves, rather than have them exist eternally. Yet nothing about Kant's overall strategy for defending ethical faith makes it less applicable to a Buddhist faith than to theism.[17] So this is an example of how Kant's formal claims about ethical faith could help ground a faith with a far different content than he had in mind. My aim is to show the legitimacy of such a move as regards a wide variety of revealed religions.

42. Let's turn now to Kant's argument for his formal claims.

Kant himself presents these formal claims by saying that practical reason takes priority over speculative reason. The kind of reasoning we use in the course of practice, which Kant believes to be governed by the demands of morality, takes priority over the kind of reasoning by which we merely "speculate"—"watch the world"—as we do when we try to figure out what is going on scientifically, or when we seek the underpinnings of, the transcendental conditions for, our scientific research. If it is practically necessary to believe in a proposition,[18] we have reason to believe it even though we cannot prove it to the satisfaction of speculative reason—as long as we also cannot *disprove* it.[19]

Why so? In essence, Kant's point is quite simple: speculative reason is itself a practice, and thus gains even its independence of our ends and moral demands only insofar as that independence itself *serves* our ends and moral demands. We must decide *why*, and to what extent, we should engage in speculative reason, and that decision will be a practical one, not a speculative one. Even speculative reason has an "interest," Kant says, and "every interest is ultimately practical" (CPrR 121). Practical reason therefore has priority over speculative reason, and if there are presuppositions to which practical reason is ineluctably committed, speculative reason must be committed to them too.

But there are at least two quite different ways of understanding this point. On one reading, speculative reason winds up underwriting one form of practical reason or another, whatever it says about the presuppositions of the highest good. If speculative reason rejects these presuppositions, if it refuses to entertain so much as the possible existence of free-will, and of a God or afterlife, because it insists on identifying the real with what we can sense, then, in effect, it endorses what Kant calls the "canon of Epicurus": a purely empiricist epistemology that can ground only an empiricist ethical theory, on which we can seek nothing except happiness.[20] So the choice speculative reason has to make is whether to endorse one kind of ethic or another, an ethic of freedom or an ethic of happiness,[21] not whether or not to endorse any ethical view at all. Speculative reason will inevitably throw its support behind the metaphysical presuppositions of some ethical system; it cannot remain ethically neutral.

On the other reading, Kant's point is just that speculative reason, like practical reason, has an "interest"; it is not an inert, interest-free reflection of the world. Speculative reason must be understood as *doing something,* as a *project* of some sort; we are motivated to engage in it, are interested in it. It is practical reason that sets and examines all interests, so *inter alia* it must set and examine the interest of speculative reason.[22] On this view, we pursue even science and the philosophy of science in the end for ethical purposes: we use them to help us figure out what to do with our lives. But in that case the ultimate end of what we do is an end for *both* practical and speculative reason. And speculative reason, which does not have resources to examine ends on its own (no facts, by themselves, will determine our ends), must defer to practical reason in this matter. Simply put: if we have no highest end, or the highest end we set for ourselves is impossible, then there is no point in doing anything, including science and speculative philosophy. But science and speculative philosophy cannot tell us whether we have such an end, or what it is if we do. So we have reason to accept a view of our ultimate end, and the presuppositions necessary for that end to be attainable, even for the purposes of doing science and speculative philosophy. As long as this view can't be shown *false* by science and speculative philosophy, we ought to accept it even in our speculative capacity.

Kant says that this line of argument does not license beliefs whenever they might be useful: it applies only to the question over our ultimate end.[23] Practical reason cannot insist that a particular moral end (e.g. the cure for a child's illness) must be possible, just that the end of *all* moral action must be possible. Only in connection with our ultimate end are we forced to consider the possible existence of things that transcend experience. When we think about human life as a whole, we necessarily view it as if from a position beyond all our experience, and must take up at least the possibility that our lives might extend beyond our existence in the natural world. So speculative reason cannot insist here, as it does elsewhere, that all factual claims be grounded in experience. It also makes sense for speculative reason to defer to practical reason at this ultimate point, since the interest of reason as a whole is settled here: without that interest, we have no reason to do anything, even to try to determine the difference between facts and fictions. Hence, Kant says, "this is the *only* case where my interest inevitably determines my judgment" (CPrR 143; my emphasis). Simply put, again: our reasons for allowing science and the philosophy of science to yield to ethics when it comes to belief in the highest good that guides all our practice do not allow us to posit entities that seem good to us in the *course* of that science or philosophy of science. Once the enterprise of science gets going, it must abstract from all particular interests. But the enterprise as a whole is interest-driven, and cannot, on pain of irrationality, use its results as a basis for undermining its own interests. So if a conception of our ultimate end sets those interests, then science cannot rationally undermine that conception.

43. Thus far, Kant's position seems to me very plausible; the idea that science, and the philosophy of science, are not the right sorts of enterprises to determine the truth about our ultimate purposes was, indeed, one of my own points in Part I of this book. But we have yet to see why our moral practice might demand any particular view of our ultimate end, let alone one with presuppositions that stick in the craw of science. Why does Kant say that morality requires us to believe in the *summum bonum* he describes?

We can't answer that question without taking up a prior one: what does Kant *mean* by saying that morality requires us to believe in the *summum bonum* and its presuppositions? In what sense is this belief "morally necessary"?

I think Kant is torn among a number of different answers to this question. Some read him as saying that we will cease to be moral if we lack a belief in the highest good—we won't see the point of doing our duty, anymore, and will lose all motivation to keep it up. But although Kant does say things along these lines in some relatively early writings on morality, he stops doing so once he arrives at his mature view of moral motivation in the *Groundwork of the Metaphysics of Morals*: that reason alone motivates us to follow its demands, without our having to expect any reward for so doing in this life or the next.[24] Kant also says explicitly, in all his writings after this point, that atheists like Epicurus, Spinoza, and Hume, who rejected the beliefs in an afterlife and a transcendent God that undergird Kant's highest good, were nonetheless fully moral people—better, indeed, at living up to what duty demands than many people who do hold the relevant telic views.[25]

Then there is the possibility that Kant regards the attainability of the highest good as he does free will: as something presupposed by the logic of moral decision-making. And again, there are texts supporting such an interpretation. There are also places in which he distinguishes the two, however, saying that a belief in the highest good is not as essential to moral deliberation as a belief in freedom,[26] and I think his considered view has to be the latter one. That deliberation presupposes freedom is a very plausible claim. That deliberation presupposes a belief in the highest good is not nearly so plausible.

The most charitable reading of what Kant means by describing a faith in the highest good as morally necessary is, I think, that the best *second-order account* of our moral practice—what makes best sense to us when we *reflect on* our commitment to morality—involves a faith in the attainability of the highest good. Consider two intriguing features of what Kant says about moral faith. First, it is supposed to provide us with an answer to the third of the great questions to which, in Kant's view, all philosophy is directed: what may we hope for? Moral faith characterizes how we *hope*, rather than what we know or what we do. It thus comes in at a point "after" or "beyond" our engagement in actual moral decision-making—a point at which we wonder, perhaps, why we care about such decisions as we do.

Second, as we saw a moment ago, Kant recognizes Epicurus, Spinoza, and Hume as virtuous people despite their rejection of the moral faith that he regards as necessary. Clearly, then, it is not necessary to our *being* virtuous. In what sense, then, is it necessary? Well, right after one of his encomia to Spinoza, Kant says that a person who, like Spinoza, commits his life to virtue will eventually realize that all human beings, even the righteous ones, are subject in our world to evils that make the whole project of being virtuous seem pointless: "to all the evils of poverty, illnesses, and untimely death, just like all the other animals on earth" (CJ 452). He then adds, in one of the most remarkable passages in his entire oeuvre, that as far as we can tell empirically, people will always remain subject to such evils

until one wide grave engulfs them all together (whether honest or dishonest, it makes no difference here) and flings them, who were capable of having believed themselves to be the final end of creation, back into the abyss of the purposeless chaos of matter from which they were drawn.

Epicurus, Spinoza, and Hume, if they recognized this truth, were people who had to live without hope, for Kant. They had no good answer to the question, "what may we hope?" and there is something bizarre, if noble, about being virtuous without hope, something that makes the whole project of morality look absurd. On a second-order level, the level in which we reflect on the entire project of engaging in moral deliberation, we find that that project does not make much sense unless our highest good is attainable—even if, on the first-order, when we deliberate over particular actions, we have every reason to be moral.

There is, admittedly, something strange about this view.[27] I used the word "absurd" to characterize it as a deliberate gesture toward certain affinities between Kant, in this respect, and such 20th-century writers as Franz Kafka, Albert Camus, or Samuel Beckett. A characteristic mark of these writers is that their characters reason carefully about how to carry out projects even though the projects themselves seem utterly unreasonable. Despite having turned into a giant insect, Gregor Samsa worries about how to excuse his absence from his office.[28] Meursault, in Camus's *The Stranger*, deliberates skillfully over such things as how best to enjoy himself on a given day, while seeming incapable of rational thought about his life as a whole. Beckett's Estragon can give good reasons for why he mistook Pozzo for Godot, but can't explain why he is waiting for Godot.[29] The end of Beckett's novel *The Unnamable* provides what could be the motto for this view, a view on which we have reasons for our local actions without any overall reason to live at all: "you must go on, I can't go on, I'll go on."[30]

Kant may seem as far from this attitude as one can possibly get, and in one sense he certainly is: he believes that there *is* or at least might be a highest good, and that morality, and our other projects, are therefore justified. But in another sense his resolutely unteleological picture of practical rationality is not an implausible ancestor of the absurdist one.[31] And in the "purposeless chaos" passage, he comes startlingly close to the very language of the absurdists.

It is with these affinities in mind that I suggest that the highest good is "necessary" to morality, for Kant: it is necessary in a sense that appears only when we reflect on the whole project of moral deliberation. Kant asks, in the third *Critique*'s Spinoza passage, how a righteous person "would *judge* his own inner purposive determination by the moral law." Judgment about purposiveness, for Kant, is always an act of reflection on something that has already been constituted by other cognitive faculties, always a sort of meta-thinking about an object or system in which we already have reason to believe.

And the idea that finding a purpose for morality must be the result of a meta- or second-order reflection is also suggested by Kant's remark in his book on religion that a commitment to the highest good "exceeds the concept of [our] duties in this world," that it "adds a consequence of these duties...not contained in the moral laws" themselves (RWB 7n). Religious commitment arises from our reflections *on* morality, not from our moral deliberations themselves. At its best, religion consists of a hope that morality awakens. It does not belong to morality itself.

This interpretation of Kant's moral faith fits nicely with my own view that morality gives rise to, but is not identical, with telic convictions—and that religion has something distinctive to offer us on the telic level, not the moral one.

44. We might characterize the interpretation of Kant I've just offered as an "inference to the best explanation" (IBE) account of the ethical realm: we posit the attainability of the highest good, and the conditions making it attainable, when we seek the best explanation of what we are committed to in morality. The fact that we use IBE to describe a mode of argument common in science makes it a little misleading in this context, however, since Kant emphatically rejects the idea that there could be a legitimate *scientific* inference to the existence of God, and consequently places his view of the highest good in the realm of faith, rather than knowledge. In addition, the notion of inference to the best explanation is seriously vague even in science,[32] and almost impossible to delineate clearly in metaphysics—especially in ethical metaphysics, where the idea of a "best" explanation would seem to require us already to have defined the good.

Nevertheless, we do have at least a rough and ready idea of what it means for one account to provide a more satisfying explanation of a range of phenomena than its rivals, and it seems not inappropriate to say that Kant's picture of the two components of the highest good, and the metaphysical principles they presuppose, is supposed to convince us if and only if we see it as providing the most plausible overall account of what we are committed to, in moral practice. That is the sense in which it is supposed to be a *rational* faith. But it is still a faith: we cannot know that it is correct, as we can know scientific or logical propositions, cannot even make it more probable, as we can make scientific beliefs for which we have inadequate evidence. Perhaps we should say it is a faith based in *part* on an IBE, or a faith that has been rationally scrutinized by an IBE.

In any case, it is in this sense that I will want to suggest that our telic views depend on a rational faith. We start with a non-rational faith that certain texts or teachings reveal our highest good, but then endorse that faith only if it fits into some sort of "best account" of the ethical realm. We seek the account of the ethical realm that makes best overall sense to us—again, in a rough and ready way—and we accept a telic view in accordance with its place in such an account. What we consider to be the ultimate or highest good depends on how well the telic component of that good fits with what, in general, we have reason to expect our telos to look like, how well the telic and the moral components of that good are integrated, and perhaps also how well we can integrate the entire picture of ethics we thereby get with our scientific beliefs. This attempt to fit one's faith into a best account of the ethical, which checks the faith against and adjusts it to moral and scientific considerations that are not based on faith, ensures that it is not *just* a faith: it is a faith that one holds reasonably, a rational faith.

The form of the view I am advancing is thus recognizably Kantian, and the process of scrutinizing one's faith by, or adjusting it to, a best account of the ethical is a legitimate heir, I think, to what he and others in his time called "natural" or "rational" religion: a rational investigation into the conditions of religious belief that brackets the truth of any particular revelation. As I conceive it, however, this kind of investigation is always subordinate to a particular revelation, coming after we have already put faith in a specific text or teaching, and serving to delineate how the interpretation of *that* text or teaching can best fit in with our other moral and scientific beliefs. There are really two roles for faith on my view: first, in the text that we think reveals our telos and, second, in the supernatural entities that our best account of the ethical, once it incorporates our revealed telos, presupposes. The first of these kinds of faith differentiates my view from Kant's, as does the idea that natural religion is carried along by revealed religion, rather than the other way around. What is Kantian in my view is simply the idea that faith, whatever its objects, needs rational scrutiny, and that it is properly scrutinized in the course of our second-order reflections on morality, our reflections on what we are committed to when we try to lead a virtuous life: on the telos of morality, its place in the ethical realm as a whole.

One thing that follows from my version of Kant's view is that a belief in God or an afterlife or miracles may be reasonable without being demonstrable to people who do not share one's telic vision. There will be no neutral way of showing such a thing, no reason one could use to convince others independently of the telic vision one holds to be revealed. Religious beliefs will depend in a twofold way on faith, rather than rational argument; even the arguments of ethical metaphysics, stripped of a particular telic commitment, will not yield such beliefs. The idea that our faith may fit into a "best account" of the ethical realm merely keeps it from being *irrational*, and gives us rational criteria by which to evaluate some kinds of faith as more belief-worthy than others. (A religious faith will for instance be implausible if it flies in the face of our overlapping-consensus morality.) On my view, we can have faith-based ethical views from which to derive a belief, or reasonable hope, that certain supernatural entities or conditions exist, but nothing like scientific evidence, or even religiously-neutral metaphysical arguments, for their existence.[33]

45. Turning now to the content of Kant's moral faith (2, in my division of his views in § 41), we come to a number of claims that I do not want to accept. Kant says that our highest good consists in happiness in proportion to virtue; that we cannot attain the proper level of virtue for this except in an eternal life; and that only a God will know how to apportion happiness correctly to each person's degree of virtue, and will have the power to carry out that apportionment. Parts of this view are poorly defined; parts

are poorly defended; and parts seem arbitrary and shallow. Nevertheless, some of it helps clarify the place of what I have been calling the telic aspects of an ethical faith. I would therefore like to spend a little time separating the wheat from the chaff.

To begin with the latter: Kant's official arguments for the necessity of immortality and God to the highest good are remarkably weak. In particular, his argument for immortality depends on a baroque theory about what it takes to be virtuous enough to deserve the highest good. In being virtuous, he says, we aim at being perfectly good, but in practice we can never do more than approximate that goal, so only over eternity could we be counted as having reached it. Just as the limit of $1/x$ equals 0 as x approaches infinity, even though at any given point $1/x$ will be greater than zero, so our progress towards virtue, although at every point only closer to the goal than at the previous point, coincides with the ideal over infinite time. But why accept the idea that the goal of being virtuous is perfection? And how does Kant imagine that we can continue progressing towards virtue in a bodiless afterlife?[34] Answers can be given to these objections,[35] but it is fair to say that the idea that eternal life, if necessary to us at all, is necessary only so that we can improve our characters, is quite bizarre.

Kant does rather better, I think, when he simply *posits* that immortality is part of our highest good—one of the things we most deeply seek, or a condition for everything we deeply seek. Towards the end of the first *Critique*, he tells us that, if the universe is structured by divine wisdom, "the magnificent equipment of human nature and the shortness of life which is so ill suited to it" give us "sufficient ground for a doctrinal belief in the future life of the human soul" (CPR A827 = B855). In the preface to the second edition of the same work, he says that the hope of a future life is aroused by "that remarkable predisposition of our nature, noticeable to every human being, never to be capable of being satisfied by what is temporal (since the temporal is always insufficient for the predispositions of our whole vocation)" (CPR B xxxii). And in the *Critique of Judgment*, as we have seen, what most seems to make the life of virtuous non-believers like Spinoza absurd is that on their views "one wide grave" eventually engulfs all human beings, "and flings them, who were capable of having believed themselves to be the final end of creation, back into the abyss of the purposeless chaos of matter from which they were drawn." The fact of death defeats the fundamental yearnings of our nature, defies our "whole vocation," and renders our lives as purposeless as chaotic matter. I don't know that Kant has a real argument for this claim, but it seems nevertheless a plausible one to me, as it does to many, and I see no reason why those who do find it plausible shouldn't include immortality in the second component of the highest good for which they hope.

With that belief in place, it seems reasonable also to believe in (hope for?) a God: it's hard to see how we could have eternal life if there is no God.[36] We may also understand our highest good as requiring the existence of God for other reasons. We may, for instance, see the vision of God, or the ability to stand in His presence, as itself the deepest or fullest happiness we can achieve. These seem like better reasons to postulate the existence of God than the one Kant gives: that God is necessary to give us happiness, understood as a sum of pleasures, in precise proportion to our virtue. It is not unreasonable that God might be necessary to guarantee, in some manner, that virtue achieve a good beyond itself. But that God should be a sort of Santa Claus with an accountant's mentality, ensuring that every virtuous person gets exactly the reward she deserves, is ridiculous.

46. My revisions to Kant's arguments for immortality, and the existence of God, suggest a rather different conception of the highest good than the one he proposes. If immortality, or the vision of God, are basic *elements* of our highest good, then we may not want to accept Kant's definition of it as a combination of virtue and happiness.

How does Kant defend his definition? It's not easy to answer that question. Much of his energy is devoted to the relationship between the two components of the highest good, rather than to what those components are: to the claim that the highest good consists in happiness *in proportion to* virtue, rather than in virtue plus an unlimited amount of happiness. While not entirely unexceptionable,[37] this claim is plausible. Surely we could not regard any ultimate end as truly good unless we achieved it in a virtuous way. Kant argues throughout his moral writings that for this reason happiness cannot be our only real good, that happiness enjoyed by way of moral evil is not good at all. The worthiness to be happy, he insists, must precede happiness in any account of the human good.[38]

But this polemic presumes that happiness, when deserved, is of course a good thing. That may be why, when he comes to the definition of our highest good, Kant thinks we will accept the idea that it consists of happiness in proportion to virtue without much argument. To the extent that he does argue for it, he relies on something like Adam Smith's impartial spectator test for moral claims. The fact that virtue is our supreme good does not mean that it is "the entire and perfect good," he says: "For this, happiness is also required, and indeed not merely in the partial eyes of a person who makes himself his end, but even in the judgment of an impartial reason."[39] Similarly, in the *Critique of Pure Reason*, he follows up the claim that happiness is necessary to "the complete good" by saying that "Even reason free from all private aims [i.e.: from all partiality] cannot judge otherwise if . . . it puts itself in the place of a being who would have to distribute all happiness to others" (CPR A813= B841). And in RWB Kant tries to make the highest good plausible with a thought experiment in which we picture creating a world in accordance with practical reason. It is clear, he says, that everyone in such a world should receive happiness in proportion to his or her virtue, even if we ourselves thereby get less happiness than we might have wanted: we have to "acknowledge this judgment with complete impartiality" (RWB 6). In all three cases, Kant has us engage in an imagined switch of positions, by which we regard our ends or our world as if we were outside them, very much as one is supposed to do in Smith's impartial spectator procedure. And in all three cases he uses the language of "judgment," which for him as for Smith is the kind of utterance characteristically issued from the spectatorial position.[40] The point seems to be that the propriety of regarding happiness as the second component of the highest good cannot be *argued* for, strictly speaking. It can only be *seen*—although the seeing, if it is to win the approval of reason, must be an impartial one, the sort of seeing we expect from a good judge.[41]

But why suppose that every impartial spectator or judge will see happiness, understood as a sum of anything we happen to enjoy, as the second component of the highest good? It's worth noting here that there are resources within Kant's own thought for seeing the second component of the highest good as something rather different from happiness in this sense. Kant could, for instance, have said that only "rational" or intellectual pleasures belong in the highest good. By this I mean not just the pleasurable consciousness of having acted virtuously, which Kant calls "contentment" and criticizes the Stoics for having regarded as the whole of happiness (CPrR 126–127), but any pleasure that comes with the use of our minds. This might include the pleasure of scientific discovery, which Kant mentions in the *Critique of Judgment* (CJ 184), aesthetic pleasure, which he discusses there at great length, as well as the pleasure of doing philosophy itself. It's not clear why a life of *such* pleasures—the pleasures of virtue and art and natural beauty and science and philosophy—if achieved in accordance with virtue, could not constitute a wholly good life, and we might have expected a highest good willed from the perspective of practical reason to set an end of this sort for us. Indeed, at one point in the *Critique of Judgment*, Kant comes close to such a view: he suggests that "culture"—the development of all our talents—not mere happiness, is our final end, and indeed the final end of the universe (CJ 430–431). But that is not his general position. He generally regards *all* pleasures, whether rational or purely sensual, as belonging to happiness[42]—hence, part of our highest end as long as we have earned them by virtue.

I am not saying that the second component of the highest good *should* consist of intellectual instead of full-bodied happiness. My point is rather that the impartial spectator test by which Kant sets up his highest good can easily yield a number of different results, even within Kant's own philosophical system. It can yield yet more varied results if we allow it to consider ethical intuitions beyond those that appealed to Kant. If the second component of the highest good could be intellectual, rather than full-bodied happiness, why could it not instead be nirvana, or the beatific vision of Christ, or what Jews call *kedushah* ("holiness")? Smith's impartial spectator procedure ties ethical judgment closely to the intuitions we share with our culture, even if it allows us also to correct those intuitions by being more impartial or better informed than our neighbors.[43] It is hard to see how an increase in impartiality or empirical knowledge will have much impact on our views about our final end, however, so even an impartial spectator in a devoutly Buddhist, Christian, or Jewish society is unlikely to see the highest good the way an Enlightenment rationalist does. Kant's way of defining the highest good, then, lends legitimacy to a number of alternative understandings of that concept. As long as the second component of the highest good can be willed from the perspective of practical reason—as long as it accords with virtue, and can plausibly be seen as conditioned on virtue—it should be a legitimate candidate for our ultimate end.[44]

With this in mind, I want to suggest that we may learn what counts as the second component of our highest good by way of revelation, rather than by relying on any naturalistic conception of happiness. Of course, this suggestion allows for views of the highest good very different from Kant's: nirvana, kedushah, or Christian salvation may supply its telic component, rather than happiness. But that good will still have two components; its second component will still be conditioned on virtue;[45] we will still have reason to believe in it only insofar as our reflections on morality require it; we will still hope for it, rather than being able to know that it exists or control its coming into existence; and we will still have reason, in the course of the hope we place in it, to put faith in supernatural entities or conditions, if it is unattainable without them. So, in form and general outline, if not in detail, my picture of the highest good will remain a Kantian one.

47. We can bring out the role that revelation might play in a telic view by moving away from Kant's term "happiness" to characterize the second component of our highest good. As we have already seen, it is very hard to understand why Kant himself insists that practical reason wills happiness as a crown of virtue—given, at least, Kant's characterization of happiness as a sum of pleasures we just happen to have. Why, from the perspective of Kantian virtue, should we care about a sum of pleasures at all? And why from the perspective of Kantian happiness, should we care about virtue: about whether our pleasures are merited or not? The lumping together of virtue and happiness seems a return to the egoistic reward-and-punishment models of goodness that Kant's moral system otherwise does so much to overcome. The desire for what Kant regards as happiness seems an amoral one, and it is hard to see any reason why our practical reason should regard it as bound up with morality.

I'd like therefore to propose that we characterize the highest good, in general, as composed of virtue plus *a life worth living*, rather than virtue plus happiness. It is, I will argue, far easier to see how morality might demand that our moral efforts enable us to achieve a worthwhile life than a happy one, and easier also to see why virtue might be a condition for having a worthwhile life—although virtue and worth will not be identical, nor will worth and happiness.

I don't mean by saying this to presume that we know what would make a life worthwhile—on the contrary, I will argue in Part III that that is or should be a highly contentious notion. A religious faith in the highest good, if we have one, will indeed be a faith in a revelation that tells us what would make life worthwhile, as well as how to achieve that worth. There are, however, some formal points about the notion of a worthwhile life on which practically everyone, religious and non-religious, will agree. To begin with, although happiness could be equated by definition with a worthwhile life—if, for instance, we stuck closely to the Greek word, *eudaimonia*, which is often translated as "happiness"—that is not how Kant, and most other modern moral philosophers, use the term. Happiness in modern thought primarily connotes some sum of pleasures, and it is not to be assumed that a worthwhile life is a pleasurable one. Many lives of great suffering seem worthwhile: few would want to deny that Mother Teresa's life, and Gandhi's and Lincoln's, were worthwhile, for all the pain they involved. Of course, the whole point of Kant's moral faith is to introduce something that can compensate for the suffering involved in moral commitment, and we may want to insist that some level of contentment with one's life will be a component of any worthwhile life. Still, this is quite different from the role pleasure plays in happiness. Notoriously, *all* pleasures have a *prima facie* claim to being counted as contributing to happiness, and eudaimonistic theorists who resist that fact have to proffer all sorts of strained arguments to rule some pleasures off the table. When we talk of what goes into a worthwhile life, by contrast, there is no reason to include any particular pleasure. To say nothing of outright immoral pleasures, like those taken in inflicting cruelty, we need not count trivial pleasures. We may also not want to count purely selfish pleasures: the notion of a worthwhile life is plausibly understood as an intrinsically social one.[46] Nor need we count pleasure as the only component of worth, or measure the worth of a life in proportion to the amount of pleasure in it. There could be, and may need to be, experiences to which pleasure is irrelevant that feature in a worthwhile life. To be worthwhile, a life may, for instance, need to be admirable, or intellectually interesting, and there is no reason to think those qualities are reducible to pleasures that the agent experiences. The only pleasure that will necessarily figure in a worthwhile life is the pleasure of reflective self-approval, the pleasure that we can take, if we have such a life, when viewing it as if we were impartial spectators of it.[47] This is a pleasure inseparable from regarding our lives as worthwhile, a pleasure that may, indeed, distinguish a worthwhile life from a hedonistic one: many of us find, on reflection, a life of pure pleasure displeasing.

A worthwhile life is thus not identical with a happy one, although it includes some elements of happiness. It is not identical with a virtuous life, either. Of course, one might re-define "virtue," as one might re-define "happiness," such that it consists of just the activities or character traits that make a life worth living. But our ordinary use of the term makes it perfectly possible for a person to be virtuous—honest, generous, courageous, and the like—while at the same time leading an empty life. This is something on which Kant insisted: that is precisely why he introduced the *summum bonum*, and refused to identity it with virtue alone.[48] I want to replace the second component of his *summum bonum* with something different from happiness, but I agree with him that the *summum bonum* should have two parts, with virtue being one of those parts, but emphatically not the whole. We cannot *care* about, cannot *love*, a life that consists solely of virtue. Hence, as impartial spectators, we cannot regard such a life as fully good. In Adam Smith's original use of the phrase "impartial spectator," that figure has feelings, not just a capacity to reason, and our feelings need to be aroused for us to care about something. So Kant's use of an impartial spectator test invites us to consider whether we can *care*—impartially—about anything proposed to us as a *summum bonum*. And he was right to think that a life of virtue alone will fail that test.

With these clarifications in place, it is not hard to see how my version of the *summum bonum* might clarify better than Kant does how the two components of the highest good go together. If we appeal baldly to our intuitions, it seems hard to deny that virtuous people deserve a life worth living, hard to see how an impartial spectator could approve of a virtuous being having something other than a worthwhile life. Gandhi may or may not have deserved (or, indeed, wanted) a great sum of pleasures, but it would be cruelly unfair if he worked so nobly for so long without achieving a life worth living. A weaker claim is surely unimpeachable: that morality will be empty unless *some* people have a worthwhile life. If *no* human lives are worthwhile, if the whole idea of a worthwhile life is confused, then virtuous people like Gandhi are making a mistake about what to do with their time. Why should anyone bother working to improve human life if none of us has a life worth living? We aim at increasing the worth of other people's lives when we help them, and what we most want ourselves, as a reward for virtue, is a worthwhile life.

We can, moreover, supplement this appeal to intuitions with a modicum of argument. On the Kantian account of ethical faith, the second component of the highest good should be systematically related to virtue: otherwise we can't have moral reasons to set it as our goal.[49] But it is easier to see the two components this way if we think of the second component under the rubric of a life worth living than under the rubric of happiness. On many conceptions of what goes into a worthwhile life, virtue is a necessary condition for the attainment, sometimes even the perception, of that worth. Aristotle, for whom philosophical contemplation made life worth living, held that virtue tames the passions of those who would philosophize sufficiently that they can focus on contemplation, and reason well when they do. Stoics believe that one can bring oneself into harmony with the universe only by way of the self-control won by virtue. For a Buddhist, one can grasp the truth of selflessness only after one has been disciplined by virtue; for a Jew, one can enter the presence of God only after fulfilling one's obligations to other human beings. In these and many other cases, virtue, in addition to helping or respecting the people around us, is essential to our achievement of the ultimate human goal.

And if virtue is, as Kant would have it, the expression and preservation of freedom, this makes perfect sense. As freedom, virtue is an essential condition for our being able wholeheartedly to endorse metaphysical truths, or pursue religious paths, just as it is the condition for our choosing freely in the everyday moral sphere. But if we see virtue as a condition for our freely endorsing something outside of itself, then it makes far more sense that that something be a belief or practice that enhances our freedom (which is what Aristotelians think about contemplation, Stoics and Buddhists think about recognizing their central metaphysical claims, and Jews think about coming into the presence of God) than that it be just a sum of pleasures, which can be experienced in a purely passive way. On his own account of virtue, then, Kant's picture of the *summum bonum* looks more plausible if it is understood to consist of a life worth living earned by virtue, rather than a life of happiness earned by virtue.

48. An additional reason favoring this conception of the *summum bonum* over Kant's is that "worthwhile" and "life worth living" are ill-defined. I have said little about the content of these terms, and that was not an oversight. I think little *can* be said about how to define them properly; that will, indeed, be a theme to which we will return. But there are advantages to this resistance of our central terms to clear definition.

First, and most importantly, the exact nature of the highest good simply *is* an open question. Are we seeking happiness (and if so, what kind of happiness—any sum of pleasures or only certain types of pleasures)? If not, are we seeking some kind of intellectual achievement? Artistic expression of some sort? An erotic union that will take us "out of ourselves"? A union or sense of union with a political entity? Does just *one* of these alternatives make a life worth living, to the exclusion of the others, or will any do, or do we need some combination of them? We will look at these and many other possibilities in Part III.

Relatedly, by calling the second component of the highest good "a worthwhile life," we are able to keep more open than Kant does debates over whether the attainability of the highest good requires supernatural conditions or not. Could virtue actually be enough for a worthwhile life? I have resisted that claim, but the definition of the highest good I have given does not entirely rule it out, as Kant's definition seems to do, and the resolution of the question will presumably turn, as it should, on whether defenders of virtue-as-ultimate-worth are able to make their case convincing to us in our capacity as (caring) impartial spectators. Is immortality necessary for a life to be worth living, or could a contribution we make to human progress, in a finite life, suffice to imbue our existence with worth? Again, my definition allows us to leave that debate open, and again a convincing case would be one that leads us to feel on impartial reflection either that we can care only about a life that extends infinitely or that we can love a finite life. I think this is the way such debates should be resolved (importantly, they are not then resolved by *proofs*). Moreover, to make the case for immortality, if we want to do that, we need not appeal to Kant's strained argument that immortality makes it possible for us to approximate ever closer to perfect virtue. We can, instead, rely just on the point he also makes that it is a "notable characteristic of our nature never to be capable of being satisfied by what is temporal" (CPR Bxxxii).

Finally, if we move from "happiness," which is a fairly well-defined term, to "a worthwhile life," which is not, we open the way for revealed religion to take priority over natural religion. (Kant would not consider this an advantage.) What revelation centrally does, I shall suggest, is provide us with a vision of a worthwhile existence we can embrace, and a way of living that can help us grasp that vision more fervently and in more detail. Revelation tells us what ultimate worth is as well as how to achieve it. But then our faith in God and immortality, if we have one, will come along as a condition for *a particular revelation's presentation* of the highest good. The postulates of what Kant calls natural religion will be carried along by revealed religion. There will be no natural religion without revealed religion.

49. So ethical faith is a faith that arises from morality, but leads us to a telic vision that may require religion. In this sense, ethics transcends the moral, and we can entertain the possibility of a Kierkegaardian teleological suspension of the moral. We have reason to put faith in our telic vision only because morality demands some notion of the highest good, however; morality also remains the ground and core of ethics, and the paradigm for all other norms and ideals it may contain. So there is no reason to expect the Kierkegaardian possibility to be realized: it brings out a structural feature of ethics, but not something that could, in practice, call on us to defy morality. The norms and ideals that require us to respect other human beings, and work together with them to meet the needs we share, are a necessary part of our highest good, and a condition for recognizing any vision of it as such. This is especially true of the norms and ideals at the core of morality, the ones on which the views in our moral overlapping consensus fully converge, such as the prohibition of murder. In that sense, even after being distinguished from morality, ethics continues to belong mostly to the way of the world.

A reading of Genesis opposed to the one with which I began my religious life: throughout the book people are held responsible for moral actions even though they have had no revelation. Cain is supposed to know that he shouldn't have killed his brother. The people of Noah's generation are supposed to know that they are acting corruptly—they wouldn't deserve punishment otherwise (compare BT Sanhedrin 56b). Abraham calls God Himself to account when he fears that God may be acting unjustly, and God seems to approve of this independent moral conscience: just before Abraham's rebuke (Genesis 18: 19). He expresses His intention for Abraham and his children to keep precisely the path of "justice and righteousness" to which Abraham holds Him. Later, Jacob realizes without revelation that he must reconcile with the brother whose birthright he stole, and Joseph, without revelation, comes up with a way of bringing his brothers to repentance.

So the Torah sees human beings as quite capable of knowing right and wrong on their own. God appears to the patriarchs, and to the people of Israel, only after they have gone through a long process of moral development. The Ten Commandments bring a religious framework to a moral code that the Israelites already hold—folding rituals like the sabbath into that code, and adding details to it that they may not have previously considered, but not presenting any radical moral news. In one intriguing story (BT Sanhedrin 56b), the Talmud says that 10 commandments were given to the Israelites at Marah (Exodus 15: 25): before they came to Sinai. The fact that the story uses the number 10 is striking— the Talmud seems to want to displace or demote, certainly to foreshadow, Sinaitic revelation—and the 10 include such central elements of the Sinaitic 10 as the prohibition of theft, murder, and idolatry.

Indeed, it is possible to understand 8 of the 10 as overlapping with the middle 8 at Sinai. What, then, does the Sinaitic revelation add? Two things: a statement (in the first commandment) of **Whose** *law this is, and an exhortation (in the final commandment) to transform one's appetitive structure. According to this Talmudic story, then, Sinai supplies a religious and transformatively ethical frame for a set of moral laws* **that we already knew.** *Sinai changes the context, but not the content of morality.*

PART III

Beyond the Way of the World

WORTH

I could not ascribe any sensible meaning . . . to my whole life. . . . Sooner or later there would come diseases and death . . . to my dear ones and to me, and there would be nothing left but stench and worms. All my affairs, no matter what they might be, would sooner or later be forgotten, and I myself should not exist. So why should I worry about all these things? How could a man fail to see that and live—that was surprising! A person could live only so long as he was drunk; but the moment he sobered up, he could not help seeing that all that was only a deception, and a stupid deception at that!

Leo Tolstoy, "My Confession"

My point in this section is at bottom quite simple: that secular conceptions of life as worthwhile are rationally flawed in just the way that religious views are generally said to be. So those who regard science as ruling out the existence of a God, or some other supernatural entity or condition, should also deny that life is worth living. At best, a secular perspective may be able to show that the notion of life's being *either* worthwhile *or* not worthwhile is meaningless, that the very idea of life as having "worth" is confused. At worst—and this is I think more likely—there are secular criteria for what would make life worthwhile, but our lives do not in fact meet those criteria: on secular grounds alone, the claim that life is worth living seems to be intelligible, but false. So those who think religious faith is a matter of superstition should regard the notion of a worthwhile life as superstition as well. Richard Dawkins and Christopher Hitchens and Sam Harris and Daniel Dennett should reject the notion that life can be worthwhile, along with the notion of God.

They don't do that, of course, and most secular people believe there are good naturalistic reasons to regard life as worthwhile. I shall try to persuade my readers that this is not so. My arguments for this point will not be definitive—no argument for or against the worth of life can be that, I will maintain, for reasons built into the notion of worth—but it is unlikely that even definitive arguments would, on their own, persuade people of the conclusion I am trying to establish. For the resistance people put up to the idea that life might lack worth does not come from reason alone. It comes from other, more personal places, above all from the affective and pictorial dispositions that I shall sum up under the heading of "imagination." And to deal with this source of resistance, I will need to approach my central point from many different directions, and to present pictures of various sorts along with arguments. We put up a great variety of imaginative defense mechanisms against seeing our lives as pointless, against finding an empty space where we had hoped the value of our lives would be. Nevertheless, I suspect that most of us, in secular mode, are on some level aware that the view of our lives presented to us by modern science is not one we can care much about, and my efforts in bringing out this point are aimed not so much at presenting something new as at removing the obstacles to recognizing it honestly.

The imagination is also the faculty, or set of dispositions, that initiates and directs religious faith, and to which revelation appeals. After the critical work to which this section of my book is devoted, I hope to show how the visions of a worthwhile life presented to us by revealed religions are adequate to the demands of our imaginations, while secular conceptions of worth are not. With this thought in mind, I will return to the ethical faith discussed at the end of the previous section, and give it a more precise content.

I begin by taking up two potential obstacles to the investigation of questions about worth. The very question about whether life is worthwhile may be malformed, even meaningless, or it may have such an obvious, common-sense answer that attempts to address it philosophically are ridiculous. I'll offer a response to these two challenges in the first two chapters of this Part. With a firmer sense of our question in hand, and of why we can't easily dismiss it, we'll consider in Chapter 3 various specific activities that many modern secular people believe make life worth living, then look in Chapters 4 and 5 at strategies employed by modern secular philosophers to bring out general features of life that might ensure its value. I give reasons to reject both the specific and the general visions of the worth of life, and in Chapter 6 begin the process of turning away from secular conceptions of a worthwhile life, to a religious alternative. It is important to bear in mind—I'll remind the reader of this at various points—that before we get to Chapter 6, I'll be writing as if religious views are clearly false and a view of our lives as worthwhile, if available to us at all, should be derivable from wholly secular, scientifically acceptable premises (from within the way of the world). It is by way of the failure of that approach to the question that I hope to make room for religious faith. But we will see that failure only if we first give the approach an adequate chance to play itself out.

Finally, I'd like to make clear that in speaking of the importance of religious faith, and the failure of secular approaches, to a grasp of the worth of our lives, I do not mean to suggest that one must be religious to have a worthwhile life. Some religious people do believe that; I do not, and do not think it follows from anything I'll be saying.[1] My point is rather that, if we must accept a secular approach to worth, we will have no reason to think that *any* life—religious or secular—is worth living, while on religious accounts, some, many, or even all human lives will be worth living. This is quite similar to the view that advocates of different secular ethical theories take of one another. Utilitarians and Kantians often think that the view of life promoted by the other group entails that life has no value: Kant himself certainly thought that about utilitarianism.[2] *If* life has value, for a Kantian, it is because we express our freedom in it. Even the utilitarian's life will be valuable because she expresses her freedom in it, not—whatever she may think—because she achieves a certain amount or kind of pleasure. (Similarly, the Kantian's life will be worthwhile in the eyes of the utilitarian because and insofar as the Kantian achieves certain kinds or amounts of pleasure, not because he expresses his metaphysical freedom.) From the Kantian's perspective, a view that reduces all our ends to pleasure entails that *no* life has value, including his own, while his own view entails that *any* life, including that of a utilitarian, may be valuable: although not for the reasons that utilitarians themselves give for that value. What I want to say about the dispute between secular and religious people about the worth of life is exactly like this. If secularism is true, I believe, *no* life is worthwhile, including the lives of religious people, while the truth of many religious views allows for *any* life, including the lives of secular people, to be worthwhile: although not for the reasons that secular people themselves give for that worth.[3]

1

Dissolving the Question

1. When I told some friends that I was working on whether life is worth living, one of them said, "Surely the jury isn't still out on *that* question!" To which I thought: no. the jury isn't out on that question, but it should be. It's not as though we've reflected deeply on the question and determined that yes, life is worth living. Rather, most of us assume that the answer to the question must be "yes," then push it aside and treat the attempt to reflect on it as faintly ridiculous. Discussion of the question, if it begins at all, closes down quickly. We laugh at it, or put it out of mind by declaring how wonderful it is to watch the sunset and saying that that's surely enough to show that life is worth living. There are plenty of jokes about philosophers who ask whether life is worth living; there aren't plenty of philosophers who do ask that question.[1] I would like in this chapter to open the question up to reflection, to send the jury back out on it.

That said, a good philosophical case can be made for saying that this question is not a well-formed one, and that the attempt to reflect on it is a mistake. The trick is to separate this philosophical move from an unreflective refusal to think about the worth of life. The *natural* reasons why we may be disinclined to engage in this sort of reflection—fear, perhaps, that we will be unable to live with the results of our reflections—are not good ones; if we have good reasons to put the question aside. they should come after we have overcome the simple desire to ignore it. We may put this point in terms of another remark that my friend made about my project, after the one about the jury: she suggested that the momentum with which we are carried forward in life may remove the need to answer any question about its worth. We simply go forward with our various projects and never find an opportunity to ask whether we should be doing that or not. Her husband added, in much the same spirit, that it was the curse of intelligent animals, of human beings and especially of philosophers, to be able to raise a question about the worth of life. He seemed genuinely sorry for me, that I should be in a profession where such questions came up.

Much as I love the response of my friends to my project, I think the willingness simply to go along with the momentum of life is a mistake. At the same time, it's certainly true that once we start asking on what terms, if any, life is worth living, it's not easy to find a satisfactory answer. In Chapters 3–5 of this Part, I will take up a series of suggestions about what makes life worth living, and argue that they are all problematic. In this chapter, I want simply to address the charge that the question about the worth of life is framed badly. This methodological issue takes priority over any attempt to provide a substantive answer to the question. There is no point in taking up concrete suggestions about the worth of life, after all, if the very notion is unintelligible. I don't believe it is. The sentence, "Life is worth living," is meaningful, I think, although it may be false.

2. In premodern times, the question "Is life worth living?" often had a clear meaning, and received a definite answer. For most traditional Christians, your life was worth living if you put your faith in Christ; otherwise, it would have been better if you had never been born. For a Buddhist, you were doomed to an endless, painful striving after vain goods unless you grasped the Four Noble Truths and followed the corresponding path to self-annihilation; the only life worth living—the only life, at least, in which the question of the worth of life ceased to be a pressing one—was a Buddhist life. For Jews, Confucians, and Taoists, the life *most* worth living was a life sacralized by a certain discipline and set of ceremonies; other kinds of life were at best worthwhile to a far lesser degree. And for many ancient philosophers—Pythagoreans, Stoics, Cynics—there was similarly one realization or discipline that constituted a life truly worth living. Socrates, famously, said that the unexamined life was not worth living, and that was not meant as hyperbole.

A few features of these sorts of answer to our question:

To begin with, they are monistic—one way of living is said alone to make life worthwhile—and they are counter-intuitive, opposed, at least at their introduction, to common sense. None of the first Christians or Buddhists believed that the truth about Christ or suffering was obvious to anyone with eyes to see, or followed readily from the science of their day. (On the contrary: they understood full well that it was "an offense to the Jews and folly to the Greeks" (1 Corinthians 1: 23).) No early Stoic, and certainly no Pythagorean, thought their telic doctrines were obvious either, and while Socrates may have believed that what he was doing followed from the logic of common sense, rightly understood, he would have been the first to insist that most people do not rightly understand that logic.

By contrast, contemporary answers to the question of what makes life worth living, among secular philosophers at least, tend to be pluralistic and commonsensical.[2] Practically any morally decent life is supposed to be worth living—there is certainly not thought to be a single teaching one needs to grasp, or discipline one needs to follow, in order to have a worthwhile life—and both *that* life is worth living and *why* it is are supposed to be matters of common sense. At a minimum, these assumptions need more defense than they generally get, since they conflict radically with the views held by both the many and the wise in the past.

We will get back to these issues in a bit. Before we do, here are two other features of the premodern answers to our question. First, they do not generally say that their answers to the question about what makes life worth living are necessary for any *moral* system to get off the ground. Christians could grant that many non-Christians were decent people, if we appeal to human standards of decency alone. They just added that that kind of decency is not good enough in God's eyes. Buddhists allowed that the ordinary level of thinking in which most people are enmeshed contains a reasonably adequate morality, even if it blinds us to the metaphysical truths we need to see. Neither Socrates nor Plato nor Aristotle denied that the hoi polloi had many correct opinions about virtue, and managed to some degree to live up to those opinions, even if they failed to attain the highest human good. Premodern cultures across the world agreed that human beings share at least some minimal set of moral standards no matter how misguided their conceptions of the ultimate good: otherwise their societies would fall apart. A worthwhile life was supposed to be something *more* than a moral life, and to call a life decent but worthless was not a contradiction in terms. The distinction I have drawn between the telic and the moral aspects of ethics has long been recognized, if only implicitly.

Second, most if not all premodern views about what makes life worth living depend on either a belief in God or some equivalently strong metaphysical commitment that sits ill with modern science. This is, indeed, the most obvious explanation of the difference between modern and premodern responses to our question. With the fall of the metaphysical systems that purported to prove the existence of a God, abstract "Forms" in which we can participate, or an underlying structure of the universe with which we can align ourselves, the monistic, anti-commonsensical answers once given to our question have lost their underpinning and the only plausible answer left to us is one that affirms the worth of whatever kind of life we ordinarily deem worthwhile. At least, that seems to be the view of this question generally held among modern intellectuals. It is an inadequate view, however. If the metaphysics that upheld earlier, religious views about what makes life worth living has now failed, that doesn't mean that a secular, common sense view of that worth is correct. We may just as well be mistaken to suppose that life is worth living, or we may need a new metaphysics—or a return to religion—to tell us how to find the value of life. One might have expected the modern reaction to the ancient and medieval link between religion and life's value to be a denial of the value of life along with the truth of religion; one might have expected that there would at least be a significant philosophical tradition to that effect. But in fact, few philosophers have held such a view.[3]

3. What do we want out of the notion of a worthwhile life? One thing I think we want is to organize the many goods that claim our attention, to help us set priorities. We wonder whether we should be spending more time on politics, or on our families or our hobbies, and we hope that an idea of what makes life worthwhile overall will

help guide us in these decisions. Hence the appeal of monistic answers to our question. The idea that doing philosophy or worshipping God or renouncing our attachment to our selves is the most important activity in life provides us with a hierarchy of priorities, in which political or family obligations, or a fondness for art, can either receive a clear place or be removed from what we bother about.

The other main thing we want is to counter certain feelings that make it difficult to go on living at all—to go on, certainly, with a life that requires us to sacrifice, or expend great energy. The most important of these feelings are a sense of disappointment or frustration—a feeling that one has lost, or failed to achieved, what one most deeply wanted—a sense of boredom, which can be brought on precisely by a *surfeit* of getting what one wants, and of course a fear of death, a feeling that no accomplishment or experience is enough to outweigh the horrific fact that at some point we will permanently cease to exist. The anti-commonsensical feature of the premodern answers to our question arises largely from an attempt to address these feelings. The premodern answers defy the intuition, which has been part of common sense in practically all cultures, that pleasure alone is every human being's ultimate goal, providing instead a more interesting object for us to seek, and they claim, contrary to appearances and to much common sense, either that death is not the end of our existence or that a proper understanding of the self can lead us to overcome the fear of death.

Contemporary philosophical accounts of the worthwhile life tend to respond to the first motivation for such an account, but not the second. I don't think this will work. It is the second set of issues that most drives people to ask about the worth of life, and it is the appeal of a good response to these issues that leads them to take seriously what it has to say about setting priorities. The question of how to prioritize our activities is not in itself something we care that much about, unless and until we ask it in the face of a despair prompted by great disappointment or boredom, or by the fear of death.[4] If we are told that one way of living will resolve our dissatisfaction with life or enable us to overcome our fear of death, the priorities set by that way of living will become very important priorities for us indeed. But if we are told that there is no solution to our despair, or that such solutions as there are (taking Prozac, seeing a therapist) do not favor one way of life over the others, we are likely to lose interest in any advice we are given about how to organize our activities.

> *Like many people, I find survival after death extremely important; I can imagine nothing worse than being "snuffed out." There may be other things that are intrinsically important, but not disappearing from existence seems to me unquestionably one such thing. Many other people I know—including quite a few religious people—seem not to feel this way. Those who share my attitude often say that the others are fooling themselves or have never properly thought about death. The others tend to say that people like me are making a fuss about nothing, being childish, instead of learning to live within the limitations that define human life. I have no idea what could resolve these differences.*

I do wonder how far down indifference to an afterlife goes in anyone. Many people who officially proclaim disbelief in an afterlife seem nevertheless to have a sense that their spirit will survive after death. Some say they work for a variety of political causes because they want to "be part of something larger than themselves," or they justify an artistic career by saying they want to create "something lasting." But why, if we don't last ourselves, should we care about other things that last? One possibility is that even when we avow that the death of our bodies is the end of our existence, we still retain a picture by which we will somehow be aware, after we die, of what goes on. We picture our own funerals, imagining what our friends will say, and think of them thinking of us after that, concerned that they speak well of us. Our language about death also encourages a sense that it is more a sort of sleep than an absolute end to our existence. We say we'll "rest easy" if we accomplish some goal, or we describe someone who dies as "passing away," as if she has gone on a journey. The picture here is one of slipping gently into a sleep, with the dim awareness of one's surroundings that one retains to some extent during sleep.

For a secular person, such hints of further existence after death must be illusions. And if we firmly strip away all such illusions, we should stop talking about wanting to be part of "something lasting."

4. Let's move now to the circumstances in which the question "Is life worth living?" might actually arise. Here is a series of cases in which people might be driven to ask such a question:

1. Jones has a difficult marriage and works hard at a dull or strenuous job, passing up many opportunities to relax, grab a friendly drink here or a vacation there, let alone to abandon his family and career altogether. All this virtuous energy is aimed at allowing his children to have a better life, or promoting a political cause. Periodically, when the work is particularly hard or the temptation to relax particularly strong, he asks himself, "Is this effort really worthwhile? I am not enjoying myself—why do this, unless I am contributing to something worthwhile?" If Jones ever came to the conclusion that life is not worthwhile, or that the notion of a worthwhile life is unintelligible, he would lose all motivation to pass up pleasures, to sacrifice as he does. We may frame Jones's version of our issue as: "Is life worth living even if it is not pleasurable?"

2. Smith is at the point of suicide. He is not ill or disabled or facing disgrace—on the contrary, he is rich, healthy, and has been having what others would regard as a delightful time: exotic vacations, cutting-edge artistic experiences, affairs with beautiful people, etc. But he sees no point to living, and in that light all the pleasures in the world seem bleak and empty to him. Having more of them strikes him, indeed, as so boring that he is afraid he will be in despair as long as he realizes that that is why he is alive. Unless he can find his life worthwhile, he fears he will not really enjoy anything and doesn't want to continue. Smith's version of our question gets at the same distinction as Jones's, but from the opposite direction: "Can anything make life worth living *other than* pleasure?"

3. Brown does little with her life, but she is satisfied with it. Most of the time, she lies on the couch and watches TV. She has no familial or political or intellectual commitments, nothing she believes in or cares deeply about. Generally, this

doesn't bother her: the TV-watching keeps her content—sedated, at least. Nevertheless, at moments, she wonders whether she should be doing something different with her life, whether she *should* have a career or raise a family or get involved with a political cause, or at least get off her couch and do more with her days. She may wonder this because other people suggest she is wasting her time. Or perhaps at some level, despite her day-to-day contentment, she feels a twinge of the same despair that overwhelms Smith. The question, "Is this all there is?" nags at her a little, and when it does, her daily pleasures seem shabby. Brown's question differs somewhat from Smith's: "Can a life be pleasurable and still not worthwhile?"

4. Green encounters a charismatic young man, neatly dressed and with fire in his eyes, who claims to see through the futile lives that the rest of us lead, to be able to explain why we fritter away our time on shallow pleasures. He also claims to have a truly worthwhile way of living to replace our ordinary ones: a program for radical personal or political change, a discipline that goes along with that change, and a community that practices the discipline and pursues the program. Needless to say, the program involves practices utterly different from those with which Green has been brought up, and rests on beliefs and attitudes that defy the ones approved of by her society. Green has, in short, met a member of a cult, promoting religious salvation, or herbal medicine, or Marxism or the return of the Caliphate. The cult member claims that Green's life is not worthwhile now, but will be so once she joins the group. Green wants to know whether this is true. Of course, she wouldn't even ask that question if there weren't something appealing to her about the young man's presentation. She could, after all, have dismissed him as a nut or a charlatan. But there is something that seems right to her about the suggestion that the ordinary ways of living around her are shallow. She asks: "Could there be something that made life worthwhile utterly different from what we ordinarily we take to do that?"

5. A variant on Green (call her Olive): This time we have someone who has been *raised* in a cult, or a group similarly set off from mainstream modern society, and now asks herself whether she should leave it to join the mainstream. In one sense, her situation is exactly like Green's: she has to ask whether the beliefs and attitudes around her, about what is worthwhile, could be fundamentally mistaken. She needs to evaluate her local common sense from the outside, as it were, and either vindicate it or reject it. But in another sense, her situation is the reverse of Green's: if she abandons her local way of life for the modern, secular mainstream, she will be leaving a group that has a *theory* about what is worthwhile, and regards individuals as incorrect when they disagree with that theory, for a world in which, for the most part, no theory is considered necessary to determine value, and individuals are encouraged to endorse most of the intuitions about worth that they already happen to have. She asks a question that looks like Green's, except that what for her has thus far been the ordinary way of

establishing worth was not supposed to be correct merely *because* it was ordinary. If she is to adopt what *we* would call a commonsensical approach to worth, she will, paradoxically, have to reject what has thus far been common sense for her. She will need *reasons* to adopt what we call "common sense," and that itself will mean that she will not be adopting it in a commonsensical way.

I will call these five cases the "prompting scenarios" for my investigation of worth. They prompt the investigation in the sense that they raise the main questions we need to pursue—What is the relationship between worth and pleasure? What is the relationship between what really has worth and what we ordinarily take to do so?—but they also prompt the investigation in that they remind us that there is an investigation to be carried out here at all. They push the investigation forward when it stalls.

And this is an investigation that has a tendency to stall. The question, "Is life worth living?" can seem a mere philosopher's worry, with no place in ordinary life: the sort of thing that Wittgenstein calls "language going on holiday."[5] We have a strong inclination not to raise any such question as long as we feel satisfied with our lives, and to suppose, if it does get raised, that a feeling of satisfaction with one's life is enough of an answer to it. What my prompting scenarios have in common is that they actually arise for many people—they are not mere philosopher's counterfactuals—and that asking, "Well, do you feel satisfied with your life?" does not so much as address the questions that their characters ask. Jones does *not* feel satisfied with his life, and wants assurance that that is OK, that a good life need not *feel* good; Smith is dissatisfied, but has a view by which feelings of satisfaction, alone, would not be enough to overcome his dissatisfaction (he is dissatisfied with merely being satisfied); Brown does feel satisfied, but worries, with good reason, whether that feeling is sufficient to justify her particular life; and Green and Olive may or may not feel satisfied with their lives, but what concerns them is whether there is a reason to *take* any such feeling as enough to tell them how to live. All these characters want to know whether the feeling of satisfaction with one's life might be just a symptom of self-delusion, and in that light the philosophical investigation of worth has real bite, is not a holiday for language at all. Of course the investigation is prompted in most of my scenarios, as I think it generally is in fact, by a crisis of some sort, a moment that suspends our daily routine and puts that routine in question. Moments of this sort are the characteristic starting points for philosophy, and there is a long tradition of dismissing them because of the way they stand outside the ordinary. But whatever the merits of that dismissal in relation to, say, the metaphysical speculations that Hume found so "cold and strain'd and ridiculous," when he came home from a night of billiards (T 269), it has no place when we inquire into how we should be leading our lives. For the answer to this question is not irrelevant, as metaphysical speculations may be, to what we actually do in our lives, even if we ask it while suspending those doings. Moreover, the question appears to us, when it does, as urgent and unavoidable, not strained and ridiculous at all. And if we want to answer it reflectively, rather than by simply ignoring it, we can't avoid suspending what we have been doing to some extent, inquiring from a position removed from the course of our daily activities.

5. Why give so many scenarios? First, to fend off the tendency to imagine that our question comes up only among people considering suicide, to make sure we keep in mind the variety of situations that might prompt such a question. There are, indeed, several interesting kinds of cases I left out. We could, for instance, consider a person in the midst of great suffering, who wonders whether it is worth going on—a case that reminds us that some degree of pleasure must be part of what makes life worth living, even if it is not the whole story—or someone who asks herself whether she should leave her pleasant, but socially irresponsible job in favor of doing something "better for humanity." It's hard to remember the cases if we have too many of them, and for our purposes we won't need all these variations, but it is worth bearing in mind that our question takes even more forms than the ones I have listed, and affects very different kinds of real-life deliberations.

An additional reason for giving so many scenarios is to bring out the fact that they are inter-related. The answer that each character gives to the question about the worth of life is likely to draw on what he or she thinks about the other scenarios. Jones, for instance, will find it hard to justify his choices without implicitly condemning the kind of life that Smith and Brown lead, and Brown will be unable to maintain her belief that satisfaction is a sufficient criterion for a worthwhile life without implicitly dismissing Jones's way of living.[6] A question about what would make *my* life worthwhile quickly leads to the question, "what would make *human life in general* worthwhile?" No matter how much we might like to avoid issuing judgments on the worth of other people's lives, we have to do that in order to figure out what we ourselves are living for.[7] (Of course, we don't have to issue those judgments out loud.) Whether I find your life worth living is a significant factor in my assessment of my own life.

6. In the remainder of this chapter, I'd like to draw out four implications of my prompting scenarios. The first is that they help us see what is problematic about my friends' suggestion that we allow ourselves simply to be carried along by the momentum of life, rather than asking questions about its value. The problem is that that momentum may *not*, in fact, carry us along; it may dissipate instead, in crisis situations like the ones I have described. Moreover, to a certain extent, these crisis situations haunt all of us, even if we are not currently in one. The possibility of seeing our lives the way Jones or Smith does stands ever at our side, and affects choices we make about what jobs to take, whom to marry, whether to devote time to political causes or religious commitments, and practically every other large-scale decision we face. We are constantly choosing a largely self-sacrificing over a largely hedonistic life or vice versa, for instance, and if we do not actually explore the questions that I have put in the mouth of my characters, that is either because we feel we have already answered them

or because we are too unreflective, too lazy, or too frightened to ask them. We need an answer to the questions of the prompting scenarios, whether we have one or not.

7. The second implication of my prompting scenarios—to which I will return in later chapters—is that they make certain standard answers to the question, "Is life worthwhile?" seem rather implausible. It's hard to see how a hedonistic or a subjectivist answer to the question, in particular, will be able to get off the ground. The attempt to equate worth with pleasure will not satisfy any of our questioners except Brown—and the fact that she might accept the equation tells against its plausibility. Indeed, for Smith the fear that life is worthless arises precisely from the thought that pleasure may be worthless. We certainly cannot adequately respond to that thought by telling him that "worth" is by definition identical with "pleasure"—it's bizarre to suppose he has made a mistake about the meaning of our words—and we probably need to concede that the thought has some plausibility.[8] There is an irony, but not a confusion, in feeling displeasure at the thought of living for pleasure.

It's similarly difficult to see how subjectivism could answer our question adequately. When a would-be suicide or an alcoholic couch potato is worried that his life is worthless, it's not much of a response to say, "It will be worthwhile if you regard it as worthwhile." He does *not* regard his current life as worthwhile, and wants some *reason* either to regard it differently or to value some other way of living. We do not help him settle on either of these alternatives by telling him that worth is established by subjective attitudes, rather than by reason.[9] The notion of a worthwhile life functions for him, as it does for most people who employ it, to help *correct*, and thereby re-direct, his subjective feelings about how he is living, and saying "your life is worthwhile whenever you feel that it is" is equivalent to getting rid of this function. The people in our prompting scenarios want to know whether they are *wrong* to regard their life as worthwhile or worthless, whether their feelings on this matter are misguided. If the language of worth doesn't allow for any right or wrong on the matter, we might as well abandon it.

We might say: our subjective powers are not great enough to approve their own projections, when seen solely as such. They do not approve of their being the source of all worth.[10] Our subjective attitudes about worth do not themselves aim at the construction of value. They seek instead a value that can be *discovered*, that is objective.[11]

8. A third implication of my prompting scenarios is that we cannot rely simply on common sense in our investigation of worth. Much recent philosophy has taken common sense to show the worth of life, but I think this is a mistake. The Green and Olive stories, in particular, are meant to illustrate why. To persuade Green not to join the cult, and Olive to leave it, we need at the very least to give a *defense* of what we consider to be common sense and a defense of common sense cannot itself depend on common sense. Moreover, the Green and Olive cases bring out the fact that there is

not just *one* common sense, with one set of implications for how we should live. Rather, common sense varies with cultures.[12]

Philosophy needs in general to be wary of common sense, and there are particular reasons to distrust it on the question about the worth of life. In the first place, common sense answers this question in radically different ways in different times and places. It was common sense that endorsed the view, in most of the West until a few centuries ago, that life here on earth was worthless unless one used it to gain a good place in a life after death. It is also common sense that tells us, in most of the West today, that the value of our lives here on earth is independent of what happens to us after death. (Here, as in many other cases, the common sense of a culture came to incorporate views that started out by opposing the common sense of their day.) Common sense also answers other questions about the value of life in contrasting ways. Some cultures hold that only a small elite will ever live a fully worthwhile life; others insist that everyone must be equally capable of a worthwhile life. Some cultures take for granted that sensual enjoyment is an essential part of what makes life worth living; others treat it as equally obvious that *separating* oneself from sensual pleasures is a condition for achieving a worthwhile life. So appealing to common sense on this matter is likely to lead just to confusion, to intuitions that cannot be reconciled.

In addition, there are structural reasons for common sense to answer "yes" to the question "is life worthwhile?" even if that is not true, and to locate the value of life in something that favors the preservation of a particular society, even if that is not true.[13] Common sense, by definition, is a mode of cognition shared widely in a society, and it is hard to imagine how any belief or attitude could come to be part of such a sense if it worked against the society's continued existence. But if individuals came to believe that life has no intrinsic value, they would lose much of their motivation to stick with their families, their jobs, and their civic responsibilities, and if they came to see the value of life in a radical transformation of their society, they might join dangerous terror groups or cults. Societies therefore make strenuous efforts—in training school-children, in religious sermons, in the speeches of politicians and cultural icons—to indoctrinate everyone with the thought that life is *of course* worth living, and that the society's own way of life is especially worthwhile. This is not to say that some powerful cabal deliberately shapes common sense on this subject, just that there are strong tendencies pushing everyone who addresses the young to fall into platitudes about how wonderful life is. The social need for these platitudes, and for a general attitude by which anyone questioning the platitudes will be made to feel like a scoundrel or an idiot, is a good reason for regarding them as expressions of a prejudice.

Finally, common sense is well-structured to answer limited, concrete questions we have about objects we encounter or activities we carry out in the course of daily life, but not to answer grand, abstract philosophical questions, about the nature of objects in general, or the goal of our activities as a whole. Common sense is directed towards practice and it is rarely helpful to practice to stop and reflect for a long time. Common sense therefore tends to resist philosophical reflection, especially of the more strenuous kind. But questions that require us to step back from everything we are doing and consider the universe, or our lives, as a whole are questions that inevitably do require strenuous reflection. So there is no reason to suppose that the answers to these questions that get incorporated into common sense are particularly well grounded. And there is excellent reason to suppose that if what makes life worth living is itself some sort of philosophical reflection—as many premodern thinkers supposed— common sense will resist or submerge that fact in its teachings.

9. The fourth implication that I want to draw from my prompting scenarios is that, by giving our question a location within ordinary practices, they help us respond to an important challenge to the very intelligibility of the question—the challenge, which I will characterize as a broadly Wittgensteinian one, that the word "worth" gets wrenched out of its ordinary use and thereby loses its meaning when we try to apply it to life as a whole. If we attend to ordinary usage, says the Wittgensteinian challenger, we will find either that life is *obviously* worthwhile or that both the sentence "life is worthwhile" and the sentence "life is not worthwhile" are meaningless.

There is one way to understand this challenge such that it provides an interesting response to our question. On this view, the answer to the question, "Is life worthwhile?" appears exactly when one realizes that the question need not be asked. Suppose a person has reached a stage in which she is willing wholeheartedly to retract the question about worth. It simply doesn't arise for her any more—she has thought long and hard about it in the past, but it now seems unnecessary, undeserving of an answer. We might say that this is precisely a person who has *achieved* a worthwhile life, although that is, of course, badly put, since anyone who has reached the enviable stage we are describing will, *ex hypothesi*, no longer speak either of worthwhile or of worthless lives. She will no longer use that sort of vocabulary. And those of us who do use that vocabulary show by that very fact that we have not yet reached the appropriately exalted stage. Once we do reach it, if we ever do, we can regard our earlier way of speaking as a ladder to be kicked away.

The ladder imagery recalls the early Wittgenstein, who presented a view of exactly this kind:

The solution of the problem of life is seen in the vanishing of the problem.

(Is not this the reason why those who have found after a long period of doubt that the sense of life became clear to them have then been unable to say what constituted that sense?)[14]

But this aspect of the early Wittgenstein is, as he himself indicates in the very next paragraph, something *mystical*. Indeed, the ladder imagery that comes in a half page later appears explicitly in medieval mystical writings (Bonaventura's *The Mind's Road to God*, for instance). The people Wittgenstein describes as having "found after a long period of doubt that the sense of life became clear to them" are not analytic philosophers who argue that questions about the worth of life are literally meaningless, but figures like the Buddha, or certain Christian mystics, who found a way of reconciling themselves to the universe, or to their lives in it, that enabled "the problem of life" to vanish. Wittgenstein, of course, denies that any Buddhist or Christian *beliefs* adequately explain this reconciliation—he admires the silence that is often said to come at the highest point of a mystical revelation, the point at which one is "unable to say what constitutes" one's understanding of life—but pretty much everyone who fits the description he gives at some point reported coming to a belief of some sort: that the evils we face must be accepted, in stoic fashion; that they will evaporate once we let go of the illusion of the self; that they are compensated for by Christ's all-embracing love; or something else along these lines. They also engaged in a variety of disciplines—practices designed to lessen the pull of their bodily appetites and enhance their willingness to serve others—without which, they claimed, one could not reach the position of reconciliation. So while it may be true that the question, "Is life worth living?," disappears when one achieves a level of reconciliation with the universe that an outsider would describe as finding a positive answer to that question, it is hard to see how one could arrive at that point without a mystical faith, a set of metaphysical beliefs, and a series of practices, that are not part of any modern, secular philosopher's toolbox. There is certainly no reason to suppose one could arrive at the serene top of Wittgenstein's ladder by way of a straightforward argument about the nature of language.

That said, this sort of mysticism does provide a real response to the prompting scenarios I have given. If it is true, and Jones or Smith or any of our other characters approaches us for advice on whether life is worth living, or what makes it worth living, we can introduce him to the discipline leading people to the point at which these questions disappear, and once he reaches that point, or agrees that embarking on the ladder will lead him to such a point, there is every reason to think that he will no longer be tempted by suicide or dangerous cults (assuming that the path I am describing need not be carried out in a cult). Nor is he likely, from then on, to believe that one should live for pleasure alone. The discipline itself will probably lead him away from pursuing pleasure alone, and towards the sort of self-sacrifice that Jones already engages in. So the mystical response is one that engages with our prompting scenarios, and offers a satisfying solution to the problems they present—*if* one can accept the metaphysical propositions, or achieve the faith, on which it depends. The mystical response, that is, cannot reasonably be construed as a form of the sort of philosophy that the later Wittgenstein characterizes as "leaving everything where it is."[15] Instead, it is a radically revisionary proposal, which requires us to change the way we speak as well as the way we lead our lives. It is, indeed, a proposal that presupposes something very much like religious faith.

So if there is a good secular argument that the question, "Is life worthwhile?" is ill-formed, we will need to look elsewhere for it. And if there is a Wittgensteinian version of that argument, we will need to look to Wittgenstein's later work, not his early work, to find it.

10. Followers of the later Wittgenstein might lodge a number of complaints against the way I have put my question.[16] One such follower might say that there is a perfectly good sense of "worth" by which many ordinary activities can be called worthwhile, and that I have gone wrong by infusing the word with a metaphysical meaning that is unintelligible. If we look to the places where the word is at home in our language, this Wittgensteinian might say, we will find that all sorts of things are described as being "worthwhile"—art, knowledge, erotic love—and nothing except metaphysical illusions would lead us to regard this way of speaking as problematic. Life, then, *is* worthwhile as a whole: insofar as it is filled with all these worthwhile activities.

Another follower of the later Wittgenstein might hold that we know perfectly well what "worth" means when we say, "It's worth seeing a specialist about your foot," or "Going to the opera is really worth your while," but that none of these uses gives us any clue about what it might mean to say "life as a whole is (or is not) worthwhile." Questions about worth always arise in a local context, and are answered with reference to the standards of worth that apply in that context (one standard in health contexts, a different one for aesthetic appreciation). The question, "Is life as a whole worthwhile?," on this view, should simply not be asked.[17]

Neither version of these complaints can possibly be meant to deny that people do ask themselves whether their life is worth living, at least as they are currently living it. Rather, the first Wittgensteinian presumably says that when we come to such junctures in our lives—to our prompting scenarios, for example—we should simply conclude that life *is* worthwhile, because love and politics and art and the rest are all worthwhile,[18] while the second Wittgensteinian maintains that people who ask such questions are under the spell of bad philosophy. Both call on us to give up any notion of worth other than the ordinary one.

I call this approach "Wittgensteinian" because it resembles the way Wittgenstein dealt with such issues as rule-following and our language for sensations. There are metaphysical illusions (the idea of Platonic "rails" that determine how rules should be used;[19] the idea of an essentially private access to our sensations) that lead us to be skeptical about whether rules can ever be followed, or sensations can ever be put into language. At the same time, there are ordinary practices of rule-following, and ordinary ways of talking about pain that seem to be in perfectly good order. Banish the illusions, and the skepticism disappears as well. We need have no doubt that we can use rules, and talk about pain, as long as we look to ordinary usage, rather than any supposedly higher-order philosophical analysis.

But there is a crucial disanalogy between these cases and the problem with the language of worth. The "Platonic rails" model of rule-following and the private access model of sensation language turn out to be *unintelligible* when Wittgenstein is done with them. The ideas that my life on earth might be worthwhile because it enables me to live up to an objective telos, or to achieve a union with God in a life to come, by contrast, may be *false*, but they are hardly unintelligible. So when people hold up these notions of what worth should be and then find that nothing they do will, in fact, achieve such worth, we cannot say they are confused in the *terms* they use. Rather, we should say that the notion they are employing has turned out to have no referent, like "witch" or "phlogiston." It is a factual discovery, or perhaps a change in the way we make factual discoveries, that has led to the disappearance of Aristotelian teloi, and traditional beliefs about God and an afterlife from our world, not the realization that we have been employing meaningless terms.[20]

To come back, now, to the plane of ordinary language, what would our Wittgensteinian objectors have us respond when a person considering suicide, or radical changes in her lifestyle, asks if life is worth living? Should we say, as the first of my imagined objectors would seem to want us to do, that, since this person has often said that this visit to a specialist or that night at the opera was "worthwhile," she *must* think that life as a whole is worthwhile? But when she came back from the doctor or the opera she used "worthwhile" in one key, and now she is using it in a different one. She then felt that a thing was worthwhile because it was conducive to her survival, or was pleasurable and interesting, on the assumption that survival and the pleasurable or interesting are good measures for the worth of local projects. Now she is asking about the whole in which those local projects figure, and questioning the assumption about local measures that she earlier took for granted. She does not feel, now, that the doctor's visit and the opera, or other experiences of that sort, are enough to give her *life* worth. Is she wrong about that? There is something blank and unresponsive in an insistence that she is not just wrong, but *obviously* wrong, that the standards she used to assess her local projects guarantee—as a matter of logic —that her life as a whole has worth.[21]

Should we therefore say, as the second of my imagined Wittgensteinians would, that our character is mistaken even to ask this question, that she needs to get over the philosophical illusions that lead her to think it is well framed? This is a better answer, I think, if only in that it recognizes that the question being asked is not of the same kind as the question, "Is it worth my while to go to the doctor?," or "Is it worth my while to see *Aïda*?" Instead, says this objector, the local questions are meaningful while the global question—"Is my life worth my while?"—is not. That itself distinguishes the two. This objector does not try to get the questioner to accept the value of doctor's visits and nights at the opera as adding up to the value of a whole life; rather, the objector tries to get the questioner to recognize that the global question is meaningless, and refrain from asking it.

But is the question meaningless? Why should it be? Because it is not an ordinary one? Our ordinary practices themselves allow extraordinary sentences to be formulated, however; otherwise there would be no poetry, no scientific breakthroughs, no radical transformations of politics or moral attitudes. Our ordinary practices are open: they allow for radical challenges to themselves, and revisions if necessary. And one move they have clearly allowed for, since at least the days of Socrates, is the one that questions whether the entire array of ordinary practices in which we engage is the right way to pursue a life that we can endorse on reflection—a life we can regard, reflectively, as worthwhile. Socrates was a *threat* to many people in his society; he was not unintelligible. It is true, I believe, that the question "Is life worth living?" can have an answer only if it arises out of our ordinary thought and practice, but it does so arise. At the same time, it sets us against our ordinary thought and practice, or at least requires us to suspend our commitment to that ordinary way of doing things. It represents a point at which ordinary thought and practice *is at odds with itself*, in which ordinary thought itself demands that we step beyond it.

Are there, then, metaphysical illusions that inform the question? If my diagnosis is correct, the question is fundamentally inspired by a horror at death and a despair about pleasure. Is there a mistake involved in having such feelings? It's not easy to see what that mistake would be—at least on the plane of ordinary thought, as opposed to the plane, which Wittgensteinians presumably want to avoid, of metaphysical argument. There may, for instance, be some sort of mistake involved in fearing death,[22] but if so, it is a mistake that can be exorcised only by engaging in precisely the sort of metaphysical debates that Wittgensteinians of the sort I have been discussing tend to regard as meaningless: debates that involve claims much further removed from ordinary discourse and practice than the claim that life is, or is not, worthwhile.

Finally, what does this Wittgensteinian dismissal of our question amount to in practice? What kind of response does it allow us to give to the people in our prompting scenarios? Does it mean that we should refuse to judge between Brown's life and the life of a person with a family and an interesting job and some projects that help other people? Does it mean that we should say, whenever a person faces a major choice about how to live, "It doesn't matter"? Surely not. Does it mean that we have no answer to the would-be suicide, or should say, "Your life thus far will have been neither worthwhile nor worthless if you kill yourself and your life, henceforth, will be no more worthwhile or worthless if you don't kill yourself"? Again, surely not—surely the Wittgensteinian would rather point out some ways of improving life to a potential suicide, or of finding things worth doing that he or she has overlooked. But then the Wittgensteinian *does* endorse some ways of living over others, implicitly at least, does act as though some kinds of life are more worthwhile than others.

I conclude that there is no reason to regard the question about the worth of life as unintelligible. On the contrary, the question arises in the course of ordinary discourse, even if it does not receive a satisfactory answer there. Whether there is any more satisfactory answer to be had at the hands of philosophers depends on whether there is a good argument that could lead us either to withdraw the question, as the early Wittgenstein encouraged us to do, or find something about life that compensates for the discomfort many of us feel about living for pleasure and the horror most of us feel about our deaths. Or perhaps a good philosophical account could help us embrace pleasure, and our limited life-span, as good things.

There is yet another alternative. We may be able to provide a good argument that life *would* be worthwhile if there *were* something to aim at other than pleasure, and/or if we were to continue on after death, but in fact there is no such something, and we do not survive our deaths, so life is not worthwhile. The fear that this last alternative is correct is, I suspect, a major reason why modern philosophers tend to avoid the question. It is not a good reason. To the extent that traditional views of what made life worth living depended on the belief that we have a soul that survives after our bodies die, or that there is a God, those views may, now, stand refuted. That does not make the traditional notion of ultimate worth unintelligible, however. On the contrary, it makes that notion all *too* intelligible. Precisely because we can make good sense of what people used to mean when they said that life is worth living, we can also say that they were *wrong*. Or we can say that we should now reconstrue the notion, such that the value of life no longer depends on our living forever or the existence of God. It is possible that we could find life worth living while holding up a different standard for what such worth should be. It is also possible that we could get ourselves to a point where we are so deeply satisfied with our lives that we no longer question their worth. And that might be an eminently good thing. But in neither case would the notion of worth we held in the past be unintelligible. The ordinary-language approach to making the question about the worth of life disappear does not succeed. We cannot show that that question is unintelligible, merely that it might be better for us to redefine its terms so that it *becomes* unintelligible. That is a pragmatic or an ethical recommendation, not a conclusion from semantics. We need reasons to accept it, if we are going to do that, and to find such reasons we need to reopen the question about the worth of life, rather than dissolving it.

We will try to do that shortly, taking our cue from the way the question appeared to us in our prompting scenarios. First, however, we need to take up another challenge to any such investigation, one that allows the question to open up, but then prevents it from receiving any extended hearing. According to this view, our question is a meaningful one: but it can be given a quick and easy answer by way of "intuition."

2

Dismissing the Question

11. Some ways of opening the question about the worth of life immediately close it down again. One way of doing that, not uncommon on the contemporary philosophical scene, is to hold that we can see the worth of life, or of certain ways of leading our lives, intuitively.[1] This position has something in common with the appeals to common sense and ordinary language that we considered in the previous chapter, but here the point is not that the very question about the worth of life is malformed. Rather, intuition is thought to give us an adequate *answer* to that question. Again, the possibility that life is not worthwhile gets dismissed; intuition serves as a barrier to serious investigation of that possibility. We need therefore to consider this view before launching any such investigation.

A widely acclaimed example of this approach is a little thought experiment Robert Nozick proposed, in which we consider whether we would be willing to plug ourselves into an "experience machine" that would give us all the sensations of an enjoyable life without our actually living that life. Our aversion to such a machine, Nozick suggested, shows that we value things other than pleasure, and many philosophers since have drawn on this thought experiment as evidence that we intuitively regard aspects of our lives as having an intrinsic and non-hedonic value. I am puzzled by the acclaim given to this thought experiment and will devote some time in this chapter to what strikes me as misleading about it, but it is just one example of a broad basket of strategies for showing the value of our lives by way of intuition.

I will approach this basket of strategies by way of three case studies. The first focuses on Nozick's thought experiment, and what I think are its antecedents in G. E. Moore and J. J. C. Smart. The second takes up the notion of basic human goods to be found in John Finnis and Martha Nussbaum, and the appeal to self-evidence that Finnis, especially, uses to defend that notion. And the third addresses those who explicitly call themselves "intuitionists" among contemporary moral philosophers. These case studies illustrate a variety of problems in relying on ethical intuition, at least to settle questions in the telic sphere. Together, I hope they will convince the reader that intuitionism is an unattractive route by which to address our question.

12. G. E. Moore pioneered a test for objective goodness that has made its way into much contemporary ethical theory, even while other aspects of his thought have faded away. He called it the "method of absolute isolation,"[2] and it involved taking anything whose intrinsic worth was in question and considering how good we would consider a world that contained it and nothing else.[3] We thereby abstract from the goodness a thing may have in our world just because it is a means to some other good—chemotherapy would clearly not be a good in any world that did not contain cancer—or because it is part of a good whole (what Moore called an "organic unity"). Moore asks, for instance, "if consciousness of pleasure existed absolutely by itself, would a sober judgment be able to attribute much value to it?" and feels he can answer with some confidence that we would give a number of other states, similarly isolated, greater value: "a pleasurable Contemplation of Beauty," for instance, has "an immeasurably greater value than mere Consciousness of Pleasure" (PE § 57). Moore thought his method showed us that there are many goods independent of pleasure and irreducible to it, even if those goods might generally be accompanied by pleasure and made yet better by it.

Moore was writing in respectful response to and revision of Henry Sidgwick, who had appealed to intuitions to ground his utilitarianism. The method of absolute isolation is a more rigorous kind of intuitionism as well as a way of demonstrating flaws in Sidgwick's emphasis on pleasure. And when W. D. Ross, a generation later, wrote in respectful response to and revision of Moore, it is unsurprising that he took over Moore's conception of intrinsic value[4] and a version of Moore's isolation method in the course of making his case for his four intrinsic goods (virtue, pleasure, a distribution of pleasure in accordance with virtue, and knowledge).[5]

What is more surprising is that J. J. C. Smart, writing again a generation later in response to and criticism of both Moore and Ross,[6] but this time with a far less respectful tone—indeed, implying strongly that their entire mode of ethical thinking should be rejected—would also make use of a version of the Moorean test. Nevertheless, when he comes to the question of whether a life of pleasure alone might be good enough for us (precisely the question that inspired Moore to introduce the absolute isolation test: PE §§ 55, 57, 112), Smart invites us to engage in a thought experiment in which we imagine a life of pleasure isolated from all its normal surroundings. We are to imagine a future in which we can plug into machines that will give us all the pleasures we could possibly want by pressing a few switches, without cost to health, ability to work, or future pleasure.[7] Smart teases the reader with the thought that perhaps this "pleasant picture of the voluptuary of the future, a bald-headed man with a number of electrodes protruding from his skull" really does represent the ideal human condition, but concludes, with uncharacteristic deference to our ordinary intuitions, that because we *now* are not contented with the prospect of becoming electrode operators, electrode operation would not, in fact, be happiness.[8] The word "happiness," he says, has an ineliminably evaluative component to it, by which pleasures we shudder from in advance do not count as fully part of it. A recognizable descendant of Moore's isolation method thus leads Smart to judge the purely hedonic life as less than ideal.

But if this is a descendant of Moore's isolation method, then so is Nozick's question about whether we would enter an experience machine in which we could seem to have any life we chose.[9] So, also, is the thought experiment proposed by a professor I assisted in graduate school, which invited the students in an Introductory Ethics class to imagine choosing between a life in which, although they never knew it, their friends secretly despised them and a life in which the outward warmth of their friends was sincere. The fact that we would all opt for the latter, this philosopher maintained, shows that pleasure is not our only value—that true intimacy, whether or not we ever know that we have achieved it, is something we value as well.[10] Again, pleasure and its alternatives are represented so that we can judge them in isolation.

The central problem with this tradition already appears in Moore, although it can be brought out more clearly in his successors. I can put it abstractly by saying that the word "good" loses much if not all its meaning when stripped of its normal uses and applied to a scenario wholly alien to our actual experience.[11] But the point is better made concretely.

Begin with my last example of the isolation method, the one given by the Introductory Ethics professor. To make our intuitions quite clear, suppose that the story were yet worse than the one he told. Not only do your friends secretly despise you, but your spouse does so as well, and is having a running affair with someone else. You, however, never find out any of this, and get through your life receiving every indication of love and warmth from your spouse and friends. Would it be better to have exactly the same apparent experiences of love and warmth backed by *real* love and warmth? *Of course* it would! Or so we are strongly inclined to say.

But *why*, exactly, do we say that? Well, perhaps because we see friendship and love as intrinsic goods, independent of any pleasures they bring us. That, certainly, is what the Ethics professor hoped his students would conclude. We shouldn't rush to this conclusion, however. After all, we are subject to very strong social pressures urging us to say, and even think, that we believe in the intrinsic good of intimate relationships. We will be made to feel shallow or nastily egoistic if we do not say this. Most of us feel uncomfortable about ourselves if we so much as suspect that we value our friends only instrumentally. These pressures on us give us reason, however, to wonder whether our belief in the intrinsic goodness of friendship is well-grounded, or only a prejudice, a pretty platitude that we dare not question. So before conceding that a real insight into intrinsic goodness motivates our answer to the professor's thought experiment, we should look around a little for other possibilities.[12] Could our response to the professor's scenario be interpreted, for instance, in terms of an *instrumental* value we see in genuine intimacy, rather than an intrinsic value?

Well, yes. In the first place, even in philosophy class most of us find it hard to take seriously the hypothesis that sham intimacy will last. We think that there is a good chance we will one day find out the truth, and that that revelation would be so devastating as to wipe out all the pleasure we took in the sham relationships—to turn that pleasure, indeed, into a source of suffering, for having been such a fool. For all that our professor may assure us that "by hypothesis" we will not find out that we are being duped, a doubt about how we could ever be certain of such a thing creeps into our imaginings, and many of us will be inclined, even in imagination, to shrink from such a risky option.

We also find it difficult to accept, even as a hypothesis, that sham love and friendship could be just like the real thing. We expect, instead, that our experience of sham love and warmth will *not* be exactly as it would be if our spouse or friends really felt what they seem to feel, that no-one could fake love convincingly for that long, and that we would have to be very poor judges of love to suppose, all through our lives, that we were loved by people who were only shamming. The idea of a sham love or friendship that one will never detect as such, that will appear in experience as exactly like the real thing, is difficult to imagine.

In addition, there is something inappropriate about asking people to choose between having just the appearance of love and having the appearance of love plus the real thing as a way of determining the value of the latter. Normally, we make choices when there are costs, as well as benefits to our options. Our faculties of choice are not really aroused when we are faced with an option that brings us a potential benefit at no cost. Of course, we would rather be rich and healthy than poor and sick, as my father used to say; there is no real choice to be made here. Choice comes into the picture when our options are being rich and sick or poor and healthy. Similarly, our sham-love scenario gets much more difficult if we transform it into a choice between having all the appearances of love without the reality and having the reality without the appearances, or between having sham love or friendship and having nothing of that sort at all. Suppose you were given a choice between being loved by someone, but experiencing that love miserably—you'll be too jealous to enjoy it, or unable to consummate it sexually, or you'll spend your whole life apart from your beloved— and having a life full of something that seemed like love, but was really a sham. Which would you take? I suspect that in this case, many people would opt for the second.

Exactly the same sorts of points can be made about Smart's electronic pleasures and Nozick's experience machine. Many readers' aversion to a life of electrode operation or in an experience machine is almost certainly due to a fear that the scenarios will not turn out as promised, that the electrodes will inflict physical or mental damage on the operator, or will fail, leaving the operator with such an addiction to electrode opera- tion, and such atrophied skills, that he will no longer be able to hold a job or maintain a relationship. Smart and Nozick, of course, tell us to suppose that such things will not happen, but only the hardiest of philosophical readers is likely to avoid a lingering suspicion of such assurances. Our affective capacities are built to resist this sort of philosophical game, and it is well that they are—people would do all sorts of self-destructive things if they were not instinctively guided to be chary of wildly unrealistic presuppositions.

In addition, if we can have a reasonably pleasant life outside the machine, then of course we would all prefer to do that, but if the choice is between misery outside the machine and pleasure within it, many of us might opt for the latter.[13] Just how strongly do we value the experience of reality, in that case? If we choose pleasure minus real experience over real experience minus pleasure, don't we, at bottom, value pleasure *over* being in touch with reality?

We can now return to the general problem in the method Moore invented. What happens when I am asked to consider the goodness of a world that contains only *x*, or compare its goodness with one that contains *y* in addition to *x*? Well, first, in ordinary discourse the word "good" is used to mark a possible object of choice, within an at least implicit array of other possibilities, not to mark something for disinterested approval or admiration alone. We therefore normally make a comparative judgment when we describe something as "good," evaluating the advantages and disadvantages of having or experiencing this thing vis-à-vis other things. "Good" directs our choices, and since to choose is to pick one thing out of a range of alternatives, we use the word at least implicitly to value one thing *over* others. It is therefore difficult to know how to evaluate a thing as good that by hypothesis exists in a world where no choices need to be made, where there is nothing else we could have or experience.[14] Moore's method asks us to set aside all thought of risk or cost: these are irrelevant in a world that contains just one isolated good. But we may be importing them anyway. How do we so much as know whether we are doing that or not? We are asked how we *feel* about these various possible worlds.[15] Our feelings are, however, informed heavily by the circumstances in which they normally operate: where they help us make choices.

Second, in our ordinary world, where goodness is linked to choice, any cost-free item that might be useful is generally chosen, rather than rejected—hence, marked as "good"—because we never know when we might want it in the future, and then it might be unavailable or expensive.[16] That doesn't mean we consider it intrinsically good. We just can't rule out its future instrumental value. This is especially true when the good in question is something like knowledge, or access to reality, which has all sorts of instrumental uses, and without which we might easily lose our ability to achieve any other goods, including pleasure. So it is a mistake to suppose that our inclination to think that knowledge plus pleasure is better than pleasure alone necessarily reflects any belief that the former is intrinsically good. Rather, the attempt to isolate this good creates a scenario in which our intuitive judgments of good and bad are untrustworthy. "Wouldn't you prefer a world that contained *x* plus *y* over a world that contained only *y*?" means one thing when we are situated in a context where every *x* and every *y* comes with some cost, and having *x* may one day help us get more

y. It means something quite different—if anything at all—in a context where you can have as much x and as much y as you like, without worrying about the cost.

We therefore have strong reason to doubt that any version of the Moorean thought experiment shows that we see intrinsic value in anything other than pleasure. For all we know, we may be inclined to answer "yes" when Moore or Smart or Nozick offers us knowledge, or sincere intimate affections, along with our pleasures only because we are unable to pull our evaluative language out of the usual contexts in which such extra goods might one day pay dividends in terms of pleasure.

One other point about Moore's intuitionism, as a clue to objective value. Recall that we are trying to find an account of the worth of life that does not make the strong metaphysical assumptions that religious views do. We are trying to see whether a person who regards belief in God as incoherent or metaphysically extravagant can make sense of how life can be worth living without committing himself to presuppositions that are just as metaphysically extravagant. But it is hard to see how Moore's assumption that our intuitions track objective goods can avoid the accusation of metaphysical extravagance. Surely, the idea that we can directly intuit the goodness of things is at least as little supported by natural science, or logic or mathematics, as the belief in God, and surely there are at least as plausible reductive explanations of the experiences that Moore understood as intuitions of objective goods as there are of the experiences that religious people understand as perceptions of God's presence. Some Mooreans might respond that the posit of objective goods is necessary to make sense of our moral beliefs: that there is an "inference to the best explanation" from the way we settle moral issues to the existence of objective goods. I suspect this is false, but if it were true, it would open up an equally rational path to belief in God— there is an "inference to the best explanation" from moral practice to God's existence that is at least as convincing as the argument that purports to establish objective goods.[17]

It is, of course, no accident that there are parallels between arguments for objective goods and arguments for God. God, on most theological accounts, is the Objective Good par excellence. And, indeed, it makes far more sense to believe in objective goods if there is a God—an all-good Being who transcends the universe and thus can endow it, or aspects of it, with goodness, and us with the power to perceive that goodness—than if they are supposed to exist on their own, non-naturally, alongside the natural things. Moore's goods are yet *more* metaphysically extravagant than the posit of a transcendent God. Anyone who eschews religious views because they posit metaphysical entities on weak or non-existent grounds should have exactly the same reaction to Moore's intrinsic goods.

*People who like Moorean thought experiments often also note that we care about what happens after we die, and say that that shows we regard things as good independently of whether we are conscious of them. But it may be a **mistake**, a product of some kind of illusion, that we care what happens after we die. Certainly the fact that we care, now, about what will happen after we die doesn't mean that what*

*happens then will actually be good or bad for us. While we are alive we are immersed in projects that
we expect will keep going after we die—political movements, artistic institutions, intellectual investigations, etc.—and we would be very disappointed, now, if we found out otherwise. So we need a sense,
while alive, that our efforts will bear fruit after we die. And that sense had better be a realistic one, else
our hopes may well be disappointed even during our lifetimes. That certainly would be bad for us. But
it doesn't follow that the failure of our hopes to be realized after our deaths would be bad for us. It's hard
to see how that could even make sense without supposing that our consciousness somehow survives after
our bodily deaths. The idea that what is good for me could somehow float out there in an ethereal space
of reasons, independently of my consciousness, is a remarkably unnaturalistic view for a person to hold
who finds it hard to believe in gods and afterlives. It seems reasonable to suppose that people cling to
metaphysical pictures like this mostly out of fear that their lives might otherwise lack meaning.*

12. Both John Finnis and Martha Nussbaum develop lists of what they call "basic
goods" or "basic values" largely by way of intuition.[18] Aside from a shared fondness for
Aristotle, you could hardly find two more different philosophers. Finnis is a political
conservative, with a strong commitment to a conservative Catholicism; Nussbaum is
extremely liberal, and writes thoroughly secular philosophical work although she is
committed personally to a liberal form of Judaism. Perhaps unsurprisingly, Finnis's list
of basic goods does not have any separate place for sexual satisfaction while Nussbaum's
does, and Nussbaum's list does not have any separate place for religion while Finnis's
does.[19] This gives us some reason to suspect that what seems intuitively good to them
may depend significantly on their cultural and religious backgrounds. I'll come back to
that thought later, but for the moment we can set it aside. For it is not obvious that this
potential bias affects the rest of what they say. With this one striking difference, their lists
are quite similar, and, if one is to give a list of basic human goods at all, quite plausible.
Finnis and Nussbaum agree that human beings value life, play, knowledge, practical
reasoning, and having relationships with other human beings. It's hard to gainsay that,
hard to deny that Finnis is right when he says that the obvious answer to the question,
" _____ is a good in itself, don't you think?," where any of the above fills in the blank, is
"yes" (NLNR 86).

The question I want to press is *why* we are so strongly inclined to answer "yes" to
that question. In particular, do we do so out of some sort of insight into the true good
or because we are under biological or social pressures to feel that these things are good?
There is some reason to suppose that these are the only alternatives. The fact that we
have such a quick and clear response to Finnis's question, that we indeed find it hard to
see how one could *not* see basic value in most of the things on his or Nussbaum's list,
and the fact that we all tend to agree in this, are good reasons to think our answers
derive from a veridical perception of some sort. In empirical matters, the apparent
clarity and indubitability of a perception, and the convergence of many different
witnesses on it, are always taken as strong indications that the perception is veridical.
We are likely to consider a clear empirical perception, on which all witnesses agree, to
be illusory only if we know that people are biologically structured or socially

conditioned to be subject to an illusion as regards this type of perception. (Thus, we discount our strong and widely shared inclination to succumb to the Müller-Lyer illusion because we know the biological tendencies that lead us to make errors in these matters.) So it is not unreasonable to suppose that, in ethical matters as well, a strong and widely shared inclination to "see" something as good should be taken as veridical unless it can be shown to arise from a biologically or culturally implanted prejudice.

Finnis strenuously rejects the possibility that prejudice is responsible for our agreement to his list of goods. He does not, however, offer much argument for this rejection. He dismisses anti-realists about goodness, from David Hume to J. L. Mackie, in fairly peremptory fashion, describing them as simply making "mistakes," or being "confused."[20] "What reason is there," he asks rhetorically, "to doubt the objectivity, or truth, of [our basic] practical judgments? What reason is there to seek to reduce ... them to the status of mere 'objectifications' of some 'subjective response' that we ... are supposed to have to a 'stimulus' provided by the 'natural features' ... of the world?" (FE 60). It seems clear to him that explanations that take the goodness of objects we seek to be primary, and our inclinations to pursue those objects as brought about by our perception of their goodness, make better sense than explanations that work in the opposite direction (FE 31–35). This is, however, just to use one intuition—about good explanations—in defense of his other intuitions, and one who doubts the reliability of all intuitions in these matters is free to reject the whole package.

To be fair, Finnis's view of the status of our basic ethical intuitions does not allow him to defend them much. According to Finnis, the goodness of his basic goods is *self-evident*, where "self-evidence" is not a feeling, but a property of statements by which their truth is grasped from themselves alone. Now this is a rather mysterious property and Finnis doesn't make clear why we should believe there are any statements of this sort. Nevertheless, it is true that *if* there are self-evident statements in this sense, then they neither need to be nor can be defended by argument. Accordingly, Finnis refuses to argue for the claims he regards as self-evident, telling us that even the anthropological evidence that his basic goods are widely shared should be taken as merely "an assemblage of reminders of the range" of what may be intrinsically good (NLNR 81) or something that can "aid our reflective identification of [the] basic goods" (FE 51).

Central to Finnis's own view of what he is doing, therefore, is that there are self-evident truths in ethics. This is, indeed, the core claim of ethical intuitionism, and I want to probe it extensively in a moment. But let's first consider some other ways of defending a list of basic goods like the ones Finnis and Nussbaum give us. For in Nussbaum, certainly, and I think implicitly even in Finnis, there are arguments that supplement the core intuitionist claim. I would identify at least four of these:

1. *The Anthropological Argument*: The basic goods are agreed on across cultures, and therefore represent, if not the objective truth about how to live, at least a reasonable basis on which to construct a universally acceptable view on that subject.

2. *The Biological Argument*: Any highest good for all human beings must reflect deep features of human nature, and according to our best biological evidence, all human beings desire the basic goods.
3. *The Axiomatic Argument*: The logic of every discipline, and mode of argument, requires that it have some non-derivable starting point, and the list of basic goods is the best candidate for this starting point in ethics.
4. *The Pragmatic Argument*: We will be unable to agree on any ethical issues unless we take some principles for granted, and a relatively uncontroversial list of basic goods is as good a set of such principles as we're likely to get.

Nussbaum and Finnis make different uses of these arguments. Nussbaum explicitly presents arguments (1), (2), and (4) as part of a package of reasons to accept her list. Finnis explicitly *denies* that he derives his list from either anthropological or biological evidence, saying that that would be a fallacious attempt to draw "ought" from "is." Nussbaum, on the other hand, doesn't bother with the Axiomatic argument, while Finnis offers it as an indirect argument for his basic goods: an argument *that* we need no further argument for them. And the Pragmatic argument gets more or less absorbed into the Axiomatic argument for Finnis, if he accepts it at all, while it provides an independent, important element of Nussbaum's position.

The Axiomatic and Pragmatic arguments differ interestingly. The Axiomatic argument depends on an analogy between ethics and cognition; the Pragmatic argument is compatible with both a cognitivist and a projectivist approach to ethics. This difference between them explains, I think, why Nussbaum's view of basic goods is more plausible than Finnis's. Starting with the Pragmatic argument, Nussbaum's view, which she has developed in the course of an attempt to define a list of ideals and rights for public policy, may be reconstructed as follows:

For a variety of public purposes,[21] we need to agree on some goods that all human beings need and deserve (4). It will be difficult to reach such agreement, or likely that the agreement will reflect the imposition of one culture's values on people in other cultures, if we start from controversial views about the nature or importance of free will or happiness, let alone views derived from a specific religion. We are much more likely to reach an agreement that people from all cultures can accept if we start from values on which all cultures in fact already agree (1) and that reflect uncontroversial facts about human nature (2).

That we may have clear, hard-to-challenge intuitions in favor of the values on Nussbaum's list is almost an afterthought. Nor does it matter, to her view, whether the intuitions express our emotions or reflect an insight into the true good for human beings. Either way, as long as they are reasonably uncontroversial, they can function as a basis for constructing a list of shared human ideals. Nussbaum's position is neutral in the debate between realism and antirealism in ethics: it must be, to serve the political purposes she wants it to serve.

I therefore see no difficulty in accepting Nussbaum's version of the list idea for the purposes for which she develops it. If we want to launch international efforts to combat the oppression of women, help the poor, and protect the environment, then we need some universally acceptable standard of the human good to guide us, and Nussbaum's list, and the way she develops it, is as reasonable a basis for that standard as any of which I am aware. Whether that list enables us to answer questions about what is of intrinsic value to our lives when we turn away from politics and ask those questions of ourselves is another matter. I don't see any reason to suppose that Nussbaum's list describes the highest human good *absolutely* or *objectively*, to suppose that either what all human cultures agree on or what our biology leads us to desire, let alone my own or Nussbaum's intuitions, will provide a reliable answer to the question I ask myself about whether my life is worth living, or why.

Finnis, on the other hand, promises to answer precisely that question. If his basic goods are, indeed, self-evident in the sense he gives to that term, then it is self-evident that, and why, my life is worth living. If not, there is no reason to accept Finnis's version of the list project at all. The fact that his position is not driven by pragmatic purposes, and that he strips it—officially, at least—of any defense except self-evidence, makes it simultaneously harder to accept than Nussbaum's and more exciting if one does accept it.

Let's return, then, to his claims about self-evidence. Consider, to begin with, the Axiomatic argument for relying on self-evidence in ethics. That argument turns on a comparison between ethics and the sciences—all of which, Finnis says, rest on some non-derived principles (NLNR 68, 70). Now this claim is controversial, as Finnis admits (NLNR 67), and Finnis has a tendency to slide between elementary *logical* principles, which may indeed be self-evident, and the more informative, but far more questionable, principles taken for granted in particular empirical disciplines. The Axiomatic argument works beautifully for the law of non-contradiction, and quite well for such metaphysical beliefs as that there is a material world, but is considerably less persuasive as a basis for accepting the contingent claims that specific sciences take for granted. Suppose we grant that it does hold for the sciences, however. Why, even then, should we think it holds in *ethics*? . . . unless we already suppose that ethics is a science. Finnis thus seems to presuppose ethical realism in the course of his defense of ethical realism.

Perhaps this is because Finnis thinks there is no reason *not* to be a realist. Recall the set of rhetorical questions I quoted earlier:

What reason is there to doubt the objectivity, or truth, of [our basic] practical judgments? What reason is there to seek to reduce . . . them to the status of mere 'objectifications' of some 'subjective response' that we . . . are supposed to have to a 'stimulus' provided by the 'natural features' . . . of the world? (FE 60)

But there *is* reason for such doubts and reductions: that the stimulus/response account of our reactions fits better into our empirical sciences, and philosophy of science, than the posit of abstract normative entities; that people's responses alter when their social situation changes—their responses seem to track features of their conditioning—which gives empirical support to the projectivist view; that many of us have experienced cases in which we, or others, had ethical intuitions that we later regarded as completely misguided (disvaluing other races or ethnic groups, say). There are, in short, a host of arguments making it seem very likely that our intuitions are really projections of biologically or socially instilled attitudes. It is much harder to make that case as regards our empirical perceptions, at least the more basic ones, on which human beings of all sorts agree. There is nothing metaphysically odd about empirical perceptions, nor does a scientific account of their etiology undermine their veridicality, nor do they vary, to anything like the same degree, with social conditioning. At best, if we already believe that a God created us, we can reasonably maintain a faith that our faculty of ethical perceptions tracks an objective good—but then it is the reasonableness of such faith, rather than the perceptions themselves, that does the work in committing us to this good.

In addition, although I have been writing thus far as if we are likely to agree with Finnis's list, that is not entirely the case. Finnis himself at one point imagines a "scholar [who] may have little taste or capacity for friendship" and feels that "life for him would have no savour" if he had to pursue friendship at the cost of his scholarly work. "None the less," Finnis goes on, "it would be unreasonable for him to deny that, objectively, . . . friendship [is] good in [itself]" (NLNR 105). But why would that be unreasonable? Perhaps the scholar believes friendship requires a lot of hypocrisy or that it's a threat to autonomy (William Godwin thought something like this). How does reason tell us that this is wrong? Finnis says it's "stupid or arbitrary to think or speak" as if friendship—or scholarship, "physical heroism," or "sanctity"—were not a real good. That's the language of someone who *lacks* reasons for his beliefs, however, who is firmly convinced of something that he cannot properly defend. Finnis's reliance on non-inferential understanding seems here to have carried him into precisely the arbitrary dogmatism, and cultural prejudice, of which intuitionism is so often accused. This reawakens the suspicion that his leaving sexual satisfaction off his list of basic goods and putting religion on it may reflect the eyes of faith or socialization, rather than reason. And, of course, the inclusion of religion on his list presents us with another case in which people's intuitions are likely to vary, in which we will not all respond "yes" to the question, "_____ is a real good, is it not?" Finnis tells us not to worry about "the opinions of other men" (NLNR 73) in these matters, just about what we ourselves see when we "attend [. . .] carefully and honestly" to what might be good, but we can't just dismiss the fact that intuitions vary: that's something we naturally take as a cue to wonder whether we *have* been attending carefully and honestly. Finnis's method works best when his conclusions seem uncontroversial; variation leads us to worry that we are confusing cultural prejudice with real insight.

I conclude that Finnis's intuitionism does not secure the worth of our lives, or the ways in which they may be worthwhile, unless one already has faith that intuitions can yield that result. Finnis takes himself to a considerable extent to be giving an exposition of the natural law tradition (NLNR v–vii), and in the hands of its primary exponents that tradition included a proof of God, a claim that objective good is established by God, and a claim that our God-given reason is capable of perceiving the main contours of that good. Within such a picture, intuitions of the sort Finnis presents would, indeed, be best explained as real perceptions of the good. For Aquinas and Vitoria and Suarez, however, a rich theology is needed to vindicate moral intuition. Finnis thinks he can get the same result without the theology. That seems very unlikely.

13. A number of different positions in contemporary moral philosophy can be grouped together under the heading of intuitionism. There are people who explicitly use that name for their position, meaning by it that we know what is good and bad, in concrete cases, by direct insight, rather than by inference from general principles; there are also moral perception theorists like John McDowell who regard our grasp of the right thing to do in particular cases as formed by a complex of educated feelings. Some of these theorists like to test our intuitions against outlandish counterfactuals; others believe we have trustworthy intuitions only in response to realistic scenarios. These differences are deep and important, but we can set them aside here and focus on two commitments shared by all intuitionists: (1) to the priority of our judgment of specific cases over any rule- or principle-based moral thought, and (2) to the claim that bracketing such particular judgments leads to moral skepticism. For the first of these points, we may take a famous line of John McDowell's as a motto: "[T]o an unprejudiced eye it should seem quite implausible that any reasonably adult moral outlook admits of . . . codification."[22] For the second, we might take our cue from Aristotle, who famously said that there was no point in listening to lectures on ethics unless one has been properly brought up. Those who believe that our sense that this particular person is courageous or miserly, or that that particular act is noble or indecent, should serve as the first premises of moral philosophy, rather than any general view of the human end or the nature of practical reasoning, also usually offer arguments to show that such moral perceptions are as trustworthy as the empirical perceptions on which science is based, or at least counter-arguments against those who would maintain an asymmetry between scientific and evaluative perceptions, by which the former are veridical, but the latter are not.

I am quite drawn to this view of morality. It fits the phenomenology of our moral thinking very well: most people, most of the time, do not derive moral conclusions from what conduces to universal happiness, or from the conditions for practical reasoning, but work out from a collection of concrete intuitions about what sorts of acts are noble or generous or sleazy. And the case that defenders of this position make against granting science a monopoly on veridical perceptions strikes me as largely persuasive. McDowell's point, that no sophisticated moral view can be fully codified also seems right to me, and it seems right that moral theory is impossible unless it starts with certain intuitions. In addition, there are moral advantages to attributing people's moral judgments to a faculty of intuition, rather than to a capacity for abstract reasoning. Our intuitions seem closer to who we are than our ability to carry out algorithms; it seems more appropriate to hold someone responsible for having a good or bad intuition than for coming to a correct or faulty conclusion. That Joe sees adultery as a good thing seems blameable, and that he sees self-sacrifice as a good thing seems praiseworthy, in a way that Joe's coming to these conclusions via a Kantian or utilitarian decision-procedure does not. Similarly, it is easier to conceive of a faculty of moral intuition than a faculty of moral reasoning as being corrupted by vice, or improved by virtue. Moral reasoning, like non-moral reasoning, seems a *neutral* faculty. Moral intuition, by contrast, can hardly be understood except as part of an entire character, as a set of attitudes that already expresses virtue or vice.

Now it is possible for intuitionists to give us a fairly easy answer to our questions about what makes life worth living. We have many intuitions encouraging us to see this or that activity as intrinsically worthwhile, and these intuitions can be as strong, and can seem as objective, as any intuition we might have on purely moral matters.[23] Our intuition that going to a production of *King Lear* is more worthwhile than watching *Rocky III* is, for instance, just as strong as our intuition that we shouldn't steal. We also have the moral intuition that Frances Kamm describes, according to which there is something wrong—something churlish, or immature—about denying the value of our experiences once they are over.[24]

But there are problems with this intuitionist approach and they are more severe when we come to questions about the worth of life than when we deal purely with morality.

The problems are well-known. First, to say that we intuit the goodness of a thing or rightness of an act is to resist calls to argue for that claim, or at least to suggest that argument will not go all the way down, that in the end others will either see the same thing or not. This can be an invitation to arbitrariness and dogmatism, and critics of intuitionism say that that is precisely what comes in its train. Rawls stressed that on issues of public moment, like the issues of justice with which he was primarily concerned, a reliance on intuition is a barrier to achieving reasoned agreement (TJ §§ 7–8).

Second, intuitions tend to track acculturation closely, such that even if there is a distinction between a real intuition into the right and the good, and a mere conventional dogma, it will be hard for most of us to tell where that distinction lies. People with different upbringings can have radically different intuitions about important moral issues, in a way that has no parallel when we are dealing with empirical intuitions. They may disagree about the application of various norms and virtues: agreeing, perhaps, that murder is a great wrong, or that justice is a great good, but disagreeing sharply on what counts as murder and justice.[25] Or they may disagree about the norms and virtues themselves. Some see military valor or sexual chastity as great goods, for instance, while others don't see them as goods at all. There is no real equivalent to this when it comes to seeing trees and animals, cars and stones. Moreover, the best explanations of our differences in evaluative perception appeal to socialization: most of the differences correlate so closely with differences in moral education that the relationship can hardly be accidental. Intuitionists have very little they can say by way of offering an alternative explanation of these differences. They are pretty much forced to insist, without argument, that some people's moral perceptions are correct and others are incorrect.

Finally, the posit of objective values is metaphysically extravagant—certainly, no-one who thinks the posit of a God is untenable should be comfortable with it—and there are good naturalistic explanations that enable us to do without it: that show very plausibly how moral and spiritual values might seem objective to us even if they are not. We are well aware that social pressures of various sorts can lead us to see things as real that are not so, and that this phenomenon is especially common in the sphere of values.[26] We watch with bemusement as each new cohort of teenagers finds a new musical phenomenon "cool" or "hot," and is confident that they will feel this way forever, and that all past generations have been mistaken in their tastes. We are aware that a spate of movies on war themes or young love will be better explained by some need in the culture from which Hollywood is hoping to make money than by the objective value of the subject. And we are aware, in our individual lives, of how deep longing or intense fantasy can lead us to project value onto a person or cause. So we know that the appearance of objectivity in values can easily be a mirage. Once we bear that in mind, however, it is hard to remain confident that even our firmest moral and telic intuitions are objective.

These are excellent reasons not to trust intuitions too far in morality, and certainly not to abandon all rule-based or other more systematic thinking for the deliverances of intuition. I suspect that intuitionism will never make much sense as a free-standing account of morality, only as an element contributing to other moral systems. But let's say, for the purposes of argument, that a full-blown moral intuitionism could be successfully defended. It still would not follow that a *telic* intuitionism, an intuitionism about our ultimate ends, will be defensible.

Telic intuitionism holds that certain things have intrinsic value, and that these things help provide ultimate ends for us. Our own lives may have intrinsic value, and other species and certain works of art and intellectual achievements may have it as well. Many moral theorists find it useful to speak this way. Some environmentalists believe that it helps us avoid anthropocentrism if we see wilderness as having an intrinsic value, not merely a value relative to our concerns or attitudes.[27] Some people working on end-of-life issues hold that there is something admirable about regarding one's life as having intrinsic value, whatever we decide about the circumstances in which the value of a life may be overridden. So telic claims come up in the course of moral investigations, although they are supposed to be independently justifiable.

And insofar as they serve moral investigations, I have no problem with such claims. Sometimes they clarify or enrich the way we think about the relevant moral issues, and in any case we use such language in ordinary moral talk. So we may be able to improve our understanding of our moral views by paying heed to talk about intrinsic value.

Saying that wilderness has intrinsic value is a common move in discussions about preserving the wild, and many people accept the intuition to which the move appeals.

But none of this means that intrinsic value talk makes much sense *outside* of a moral context—that we can start a hunt for our ultimate ends, for instance, by accepting our intuitions about what has intrinsic value. There is a sharp difference between using intuitions in moral context and using them in a telic one. When our debates are located within moral discourse, we presuppose that there is good reason to engage in moral deliberation at all. That reason may be very much *not* an intuitionist one—we may think morality is justified on rational egoist or utilitarian grounds, or as the expression of our freedom or respect for one another. But once we do engage in moral deliberation, for whatever reason, it makes sense to try to find something intelligible and useful in our moral intuitions. In an eclectic model of moral discourse, certainly, intuition-talk has a role to play, and can fruitfully complement the other modes of moral argumentation we have considered. Appeals to intuition are held in place, as it were, by our other modes of moral reasoning. Moral intuitionists like Kamm and Jeff McMahan may justify the premises of their arguments differently from a Kantian or utilitarian, but chances are that the premises themselves will be more or less the same. We saw in Part II that there are many alternative ways of justifying morality, and that they converge on a largely similar core of views about which actions are right and wrong. The intuitionist, the Kantian and the utilitarian are all likely to condemn murder and theft, cruelty and cowardice, albeit for different reasons. So those who are not intuitionists can let the intuitionists be when it comes to moral theory.

But we can't do that on telic issues. In this realm the intuitionist story comes off as just a dogmatic insistence on the rightness of one or another culture's views about the human good. As we saw in the previous chapter (§§ 2, 8), views of our overall goals that seem obviously right in one place and time—that are part of a local "common sense"—may seem obviously wrong in another, and there are in addition structural reasons why the platitudes about the value of life that are taken as intuitively obvious in each culture may serve just to support that culture's survival. This makes the answers that intuition gives to our question about worth useless as a response to the people in our prompting scenarios. The would-be suicide who is told it is intuitively obvious that life is worthwhile has good reason to distrust the objectivity of this source of information, and the TV-watching couch potato who is told it is intuitively obvious that hers is a selfish waste of a life can respond that intuitions urging us to serve other people are just products of society's interest in getting us to preserve it. And why should the preservation of her society give her reason to find her own life worthwhile?

This question becomes particularly sharp when we recall that our moral overlapping consensus abstracts from the question of what goals individuals ought to have. The moral discourse we share focuses on what enables us to live together, and therefore brackets questions about the purposes for which we live. But why should I take a way of thinking that abstracts from my purposes as having anything useful to say about those purposes? The fact that a thing or type of activity is said to have intrinsic value in the context of moral talk—talk about what *we*, as a community, should do or approve of being done—isn't much to lean on as a source for my telic investigations. When I ask whether my life is worth living, I stand outside the conventions of my society, and am among other things afraid that conforming to those conventions blinds me to a certain emptiness in my life. I am in precisely the opposite condition from the one I take up when I help my society maintain or justify a moral code.

Telic intuitionism therefore seems to me an unprepossessing project, whatever the merits of moral intuitionism. Moral intuitionism can deliver insights of great value even if intuitions are reflections of our feelings or conventions. *Only* if the most radical claims for the veridicality of intuition are correct, however, only if we have a faculty for direct insight into the truth on evaluative matters, will it begin to look remotely plausible that intuition could determine what makes a life worthwhile. The most radical claims for intuition are virtually indefensible, however: the fact that the position claims access to a truth that cannot be reached by ordinary methods of observation and inference makes it very difficult to show that there is any truth to be accessed here at all. (Only intuition, we might say, can support radical intuitionism.) So those who uphold intuitionism in this radical form are relying on a sort of faith. But the point of my investigation into secular accounts of ultimate worth is precisely that they depend on faith as much as religious views do. So if telic intuitionism is a faith, it will not offer us a real alternative to religion. I propose therefore to set it aside, as we proceed in our search for a view of life's value anchored in the way of the world: in reason, rather than faith.

> *Here's a life—not I think an atypical one:*
>
> *As a boy, everything seems open to him. He does well in swimming competitions and wonders idly whether he might someday swim professionally. He is smart, and dreams also of coming up with a great scientific discovery. He is a bit shy with women, but gets enough encouragement to hope that one day he will experience deep love. All these possibilities seem tremendously exciting to him; life looks like it will be a great adventure, even if (as on any adventure) he will face obstacles and setbacks.*
>
> *Then he comes into adulthood, and meets with the usual run of disappointments. He is not a good enough athlete to compete beyond the high-school level, and eventually becomes overweight. He winds up in a job marked mostly by the need to kowtow to those above him, and to follow a humdrum daily routine; after many years in it, the company rewards him by making his position redundant. Love, appearing first to him in the guise of ecstatic affairs that end in bitterness and humiliation, eventually leads him into a dull and quarrelsome marriage that endures mostly on the basis of a mutual fear of loneliness, and of the shame and ugliness of divorce. His children are a source of joy but also of irritation and pain; he is eventually alienated from one of them and disappointed in the other.*
>
> *He doesn't worry too much about any of this during his working years because he is too busy with daily chores and crises. He also has various hobbies, which he expects to pursue further in his retirement—he hopes that he'll then look back on his working years with serenity. But in his retirement his working life appears instead in the yellowed, sad light in which I have portrayed it here, and he is too busy with health problems to pursue his hobbies. He did little in his career to earn honor, and nobody remembers what good he did accomplish. His parents and siblings die; his friends die. He loses his hair, and some of his sight, and his taste for sports and sex. He loses much of his mental capacity.*

His wife and children eventually put up with him out of a sense of duty, and stoic patience; they think he doesn't notice this attitude, but he does. He comes not to care much whether he lives longer or not, so he puts up little resistance when one day he gets the 'flu, and he dies.

What in this life is worthwhile? Why should its protagonist, whether in his active years or looking back on them in old age, be proud or pleased with his life or care that he had it rather than never having been born?

One response to that challenge is to tell a different story—an uplifting Samuel Smiles sort of story, or the unlikely but true stories of people like Abe Lincoln. But I think most readers will agree that my story is in fact more typical than the Abe Lincoln one, and that even "rags to riches" lives often have a dark side that makes them less joyful to the person going through them than to those who merely read about them.

My story depicts a life with what some present-day theorists would regard as the wrong sort of narrative arc. For a life to be worthwhile, they say, it should move from disappointment to success rather than vice versa.[28] My protagonist's life doesn't do that. But nor do most lives. Biologically, indeed, we should expect a life to have the shape I have described. Of course we have unrealistically high hopes of life when we are young, else we wouldn't put energy into surviving and reproducing, and of course we decline into disappointment and impotence in old age: otherwise we would fight too hard against death.

If this is indeed a typical life, the case against life being worthwhile is better than the case for. At the very least, there is a strong case to be rebutted here, and no-one should assume that "obviously" or "intuitively" life is worthwhile.

3

Worth as Attached to Specific Activities

14. Having set aside attempts to dissolve or dismiss our question, we can now come back to it. To regain our bearings, let's return to a point with which we started: that at one time, before the modern age, people held a variety of clear pictures of what would make life worth living. When I imagine existing eternally in a condition of calm or joy, and being able to look back on my bodily life as somehow enabling or enhancing this condition, it seems to me that that would certainly make my bodily life worth living. My bodily life would have served a purpose that I could endorse from a position in which I wouldn't have to worry about further purposes. I can also imagine that if my bodily life enables me to achieve a state of enlightenment in which I feel wholly reconciled to the universe, I could declare that my life as a whole has been worth living. In general, if I could someday enter a state that satisfies my deepest aspirations, and in which, therefore, I have no further purposes to fulfill, I can see how I might regard all the purposes I had up to that point as aimed at and fulfilled by my securing that condition. When I am told that this condition is impossible, however—that there is no afterlife, and no position of supernatural enlightenment[1]—then it seems most reasonable to say that life *might have been* worth living, but is in fact not so. The challenge for the secular theorist of ultimate worth is thus to show that life is worth living even if there is no afterlife and no position in which we transcend our desires. That is a tall order. It will, I shall argue, be hard to answer it without relying on a non-rational faith every bit as rich as that of a religious believer.

Our original question thus appears at this point as follows: Is there a satisfactory secular account—an account that presupposes no supernatural entities and requires no non-rational faith—by which we can see our lives as worth living? The modern, secular person does not ask, "Are there any views on which life could appear as worthwhile?" Of course there are: there are Christian and Jewish and Muslim and Buddhist views, and views to be found in the writings of ancient philosophers, and the commonsensical view we considered in the previous chapter, on which any morally decent life is worthwhile. But the sort of person we have in mind is troubled precisely because she does not find these sorts of answers persuasive. Her question takes the form, "Are there views of life as worthwhile that a scientifically minded person, who keeps her distance from religion, doesn't accept ancient metaphysical systems, and is skeptical of common-sense when it is likely to reflect prejudice, can reasonably believe?"

That is the position from which I will begin here. I hope to show in this chapter that the secular views that circulate in everyday discourse about what makes life worth living are grounded in much the same mixture of empirical falsehood and metaphysical confusion as religious beliefs are generally said to be.[2] Indeed, my strategy will be to treat claims about worth on analogy with religious claims, arguing that the sorts of reasons commonly given to undermine the latter will undermine the former as well. Even if successful, such an argument would not show that the secular views are false. But it should help remove the impression that they are more rational than religious views. We may need to rely on a non-rational faith to uphold *either* a secular *or* a religious account of a worthwhile life.

Given that my strategy is to bring out the failings of secular views of ultimate worth as measured against the failings generally attributed to religious beliefs, I will assume, as we pursue this investigation, that religious faith is false: that there is no God, no afterlife, and no spiritual experience to give life value. It is important to bear in mind that I make these assumptions in the next few chapters, since many of the candidates for worth that I canvas might play that role more plausibly if seen within a religious framework. Many believers in God see God at work in erotic love, politics, art, the pursuit of knowledge, and the other human activities that today get promoted, in place of religion, as making life worthwhile. But my point is to see whether a purely secular case can be made out for that worth, and to do that, I will need to bracket religious claims, to treat them as false.

What do I mean by treating belief in the value of life on analogy with belief in God? Well, belief in God generally comes under attack in three linked ways. First, there are direct attacks on the standard arguments for God's existence. Second, error theories are proposed for why people, nevertheless, persistently believe in God. Belief in God is a tool used by the ruling classes to maintain their power, say Marxists of various sorts. Belief in God grows out of our feelings about our parents, say Freudians of various sorts.[3] Belief in God is a distraction from our fear of death, say existentialists of various sorts. Finally, the case for what Kant called a "moral faith" in God gets undermined by arguments to the effect that belief in God commonly and perhaps inevitably encourages a host of *vices*: intolerance, arrogance, self-hatred, and unhealthy attitudes about sexuality. There are, that is, a variety of moral and pragmatic arguments *against* believing in God; belief in God, the supposed source of all goodness, may make it harder, not easier, for us actually to be good.

These three modes of critique work together. If the arguments for God are weak, but many intelligent people believe in Him nonetheless, one might think that there must be some good reason for the belief. Persuasive explanations for how intelligent people could hold onto a false belief help dispel that notion. At the same time, the error theories encourage us to think that there must be fallacies in the direct arguments for belief in God. And the moral and pragmatic arguments against that belief encourage us not merely to suspend our commitment to it, but to reject it. Kant offered a moral argument for maintaining a faith in God even after we see that there is no theoretical way of proving His existence. But that argument depends on such a faith being morally useful. If belief in God, on the contrary, works against morality, Kantian grounds would require us to reject it.

What I hope to show is that secular claims about what gives value to life—about the importance of love, or art, or political activity, or knowledge—can be defeated by a similar trio of arguments. The direct arguments for the claims are weak; the passion with which the claims are upheld, by otherwise intelligent people, can be well explained by a variety of social and psychological functions that that passion serves; and the claims are at least as likely to block as to further our moral or pragmatic purposes.

I am particularly inclined to think that secular answers to the question about worth serve as a distraction from our fear of death.

When I was about eleven, I spent a year worrying almost nonstop about death, and whether there could be any point to our lives if we stop existing at some point. The thought of my consciousness terminating abruptly, after a few quick decades, and then endless ages passing of which I will never have an inkling, horrified me and made anything I might experience in my lifetime look trivial. I felt literally sick to my stomach, and tried in vain to find some way either to show myself that the problem was not so serious or to slough it off. At first it plagued me mostly at night and I could forget about it in the bright light of day, but eventually I woke up fearing the day, spent my daytime hours trying to push the problem off, and then became yet more anxious as darkness came on, longing in the evening for a morning that would bring no relief.

I couldn't solve the worry but I did find ways to avoid it periodically. Schoolwork provided a distraction; music sometimes absorbed me enough that I could forget about everything else; occasionally, infatuation with a pretty girl kept my mind otherwise occupied. But I began to notice that I was throwing myself into these activities—even into hopeless and painful infatuations—in order to distract myself from my fears, and the very fact that they served as distractions made them increasingly look hollow. They seemed no longer intrinsically absorbing, merely things that I was trying to pretend could absorb me enough that I might forget about death.

One evening, I came to my parents in great distress and told them what I had been worrying about. I had almost never talked to them about anything emotionally important before, but I thought they might know something I didn't about the nature of death (had science perhaps proved that we do go on afterwards?) that explained why everyone else seemed to go on their way quite cheerfully, and be whole-heartedly committed to all sorts of activities. My parents were sympathetic, but also surprised at the question. They laughed a little, not unkindly, saying that death was nothing to worry about: "Everyone dies, and it's a long way off." That was not comforting, but their calm and good humor led me to think that somehow they had made peace with what horrified me and that I might do the same someday.

They had not, however, made peace with death. As they approached their own deaths many years later, in fear and great anger, I thought back often on the moment they had tried to cheer me up by pushing off the question and realized that they had simply succeeded in distracting themselves better than I did. My father's obsession with collecting classical music (he had 11,000 records by the end), my mother's absorption in soap operas and romance novels, made sudden, sharp sense in this light. And now I often wonder, when I see someone passionate about baseball or politics or social status or almost anything else, "Are they just distracting themselves from having to think about the abyss that awaits them in a few years? Is all this frantic busy-ness, this enthusiasm, not just perhaps a way of keeping their eyes off of questions and thoughts that they know would be paralyzing, if they ever turned their attention to them?"

I don't know, of course. Perhaps what I am calling "distraction" is just absorption in the activities that make life worth living—perhaps I can't see that aright because of my own focus on a pointless question. But it seems to me that if I am wholly wrong, people would have better answers, not the platitudes they usually come out with, when you ask them what makes life worth living.

15. Let's begin with the belief—widespread in literature over the past two centuries, and a part of common discourse—that deep erotic love can make one's life worth living. We seek a soul mate, and if we find him or her, think we are complete in a way we have never been before. We see movies or read books, from Dickens' *David Copperfield* to any of the enormous number of pulp romances that are churned out every year, in which finding someone to love makes up for a lifetime of unhappiness, and guarantees a richly satisfying life from the moment our love is consummated onwards. Erotic love is seen as the equivalent of religious salvation by many people, and the ability to seek and enjoy it is increasingly seen as a central political right that states ought to protect.

There are many different kinds of considerations one can use to defend this view. One could, for instance, make the case that sexual love is our telos on biological grounds, arguing that all animals are structured such that reproduction is the goal and source of orientation for their activities and that humans, especially, are built so that sexual union can feel like a moment towards which the rest of their life has been heading. But most people who see life as primarily directed toward a great love hold that view on the basis of their experience of love, or fantasies about it. Most of us, at least in societies in which we are allowed to choose our erotic partners, experience our first erotic loves as shining a joyous light through the entirety of our lives, as a delight that seems able to compensate for virtually all other suffering, and as something that inspires us to want to fill our lives with all sorts of projects, to be shared with the object of our affections. "I want to learn the guitar, for her sake." Or: "I want to go everywhere with her." Or: "*Now* I feel like finishing my college degree." It's easy to see this passion as the source of energy for all of life, something that motivates all our projects and bestows meaning on them. It's also easy to see it as fostering virtue: I feel larger, with her, as if I have transcended my own boundaries and as if her wants and needs have become my own. If we bring our passion into a longer relationship, the expanded self we now seem to have can spill over into a yet more expanded self that embraces our children. Erotic love might therefore seem to teach us general benevolence. A passion like this, compensating for suffering, bestowing joy on everything we do, and inspiring us to transcend our selfishness, is surely a reasonable candidate for the be-all and end-all of our existence.

But these views all rely on empirical premises, and there is very good reason to think those premises false. Most of us, again, at least in societies where erotic passion can be freely bestowed, learn quickly that the promises of this passion are illusory. If we are unfortunate enough, as many are, to have a number of "first loves," we see that the fervent avowals we make, or have made to us, in the throes of early infatuation—to be together forever, to do unprecedented things together, to be honest with each other to a degree we've never been with anyone else—turn out to be false, that the joy we start with ebbs after a while and turns into a bleak despair at the end of each relationship, as enervating as the initial passion was energizing, and that the sense of great altruism we felt in the beginning of these relationships can and often does turn out to be just another expression of selfishness: a tool for making ourselves look good in the other's eyes. If we are among the more fortunate few to transform a first love into a lifelong partnership, we may not see all the early expressions of our passion turn out to be quite so hollow, or experience the despair that comes when the tide of eros goes out, but we will also almost certainly find that our passion fades after a few years and that the relationship underlying the ensuing partnership is grounded in more humdrum feelings: a desire for companionship, an unwillingness to run one's household alone, a fear of the legal and emotional difficulties that come with separation or divorce. Only a very few couples—I think I know two or three, and am not sure even about them— experience erotic love as illuminating and bestowing value on everything else they do throughout their lives.

Compare, now, erotic love with the experience many religious believers say they have when they first come to their religious commitments.[4] At first the believer feels a great joy, relieving her of other sufferings (many people testify that religious belief enabled them to break an addiction or overcome a terrible loss), illuminating and bestowing value on everything else she does, and seeming to promise that it will continue forever. This stage of feeling and commitment can last quite a while, but in every case I have known it eventually fades. The everyday problems the believer originally faced return to some degree (the addiction is gone, perhaps, but the psychological needs that fueled it re-appear); the joy no longer comes back, in part because the promises it seemed to hold out have failed again and again; and the person continues being religious, if she does, for other reasons.

Of course, both the religious believer and the votary of erotic love may cite their ecstatic experiences, even after they have long faded, as evidence of the power of God or love. But as secularists (we are, remember, all secularists in this Part), consider how we tend to respond to these claims on the part of the religious believer. She thought the experience she had was empirical evidence of God. We say that, even if there can be empirical evidence of God, this experience surely wasn't that, since the promises it seemed to contain have failed. It was not everlasting, as she thought it would be; it did not help her overcome all her personal problems, as she thought it would; it does not, any longer, inspire her to act, or bestow her actions with an aura of importance. She comes back to us insisting that the feelings may eventually return and achieve all they seemed to promise, or she points to other people (her priest, or a saint she has read about) who, she says, have the religious experience in a deeper and longer-lasting way. We point out the gap between the avowals of personal transformation many priests and supposed saints make and the poor moral behavior they display. She refuses to accept our claims about these moral failures or acknowledges them in the cases we bring up, but insists there are yet other cases, with which we are less well acquainted, where the experience of God's presence really is both long-lasting and morally transformative. In the end, we say she is deluded, clinging to her faith despite its refutation by experience, or on the basis of cases that none of us can verify.

Now apply all this to the person who continues to believe in the transformative and enduring power of erotic love, despite its failure in his own life. He acknowledges the disappointments he has experienced in the past, but insists every time that a true love awaits him in the future. Or he points to other people who, he claims, are experiencing a lasting and properly transformative true love, and either refuses to listen to any evidence we bring that the love is not as true as it seems (they fight constantly; she cheats on him), or accepts every particular refutation of his claims, but then points to other couples, with whom we are less well acquainted, who, he says, *really* demonstrate how love can make one's life worthwhile. We point to the high levels of divorce in societies where erotic love is freely chosen, and the reasons to suppose that couples who do stick together for their whole lives do so for financial or religious reasons, or out of inertia or fear of disapproval. We note the evidence, amassed by biologists and psychologists who have studied erotic love, that the initial feelings of passion are driven by hormonal changes that fade after a few months or years. None of this shakes our believer; he simply comes back with counter-claims designed to avoid empirical refutation. This is not the way a rational believer responds to empirical counter-evidence; we have every reason to suppose we are in the presence of a non-rational faith.

On the basis of discussions like these—typical, in my experience, of debates with people who hold up erotic love as the be-all and end-all of life—the first of our three strategies for debunking religious faith should work equally well against erotic faith. The grounds on which it is held do not stand up to much scrutiny. How about the rest of our anti-religious triumvirate? Well, we have an obvious candidate for an error theory about the experiences that purport to present love's endurance and transformative powers: the biological account of the emotions leading to such impressions as induced in us by a series of temporary hormonal changes, which last for just the amount of time needed to bear and raise a minimally independent toddler and, therefore, make best sense as part of the human animal's reproductive strategy. On this naturalistic explanation, the promises our initial feelings of love seem to hold out to us are strictly illusory. We feel we will want to be with this person forever, but we won't; we feel that the joy we are experiencing will infuse our whole lives from now on, but it won't; we feel that we are becoming far more interesting and benevolent, but we are not. These are illusions, useful for the survival of our genes or species, but untrue.

The social error theories we used against theistic belief also apply nicely to belief in love. A belief in the supreme importance of love between two people is useful to the powers that be in any hierarchical society, since it distracts and deters people from revolution. Communists have for that reason often opposed enduring romantic liaisons, and promoted free love in its stead. For a Freudian, enduring romantic love is easily understood as a vain attempt to regain the security we experienced at our mother's breasts. And for an existentialist, romantic love is an obvious source of distraction from our fear of death.

Finally, faith in erotic love has largely baleful moral consequences. It often leads people to being unfaithful to a long series of erotic partners, in the conviction that each partner was not "the one" as the initial passion burns off. Love can also blind one to evils in the beloved, and it not infrequently leads those in its throes to behave in nasty, sometimes criminal, ways to people outside the relationship. While lovers in the early stages of their delight in each other may be so happy that they spontaneously do generous things, they also even then tend to neglect many of the other people they know. Once the initial passion begins to burn off, and work needs to be done to keep the relationship going, the anxiety or anger that overwhelms the lovers can lead them to be yet more selfish to their friends and family. Erotic love is attended with at least as many moral dangers as religious belief; there is no good moral reason to maintain a faith in it.

All three of our strategies for atheism therefore militate against faith in erotic love as well. Every type of reason we have for abandoning faith in God also gives us a reason for abandoning faith in love.

16. Before going on to our next candidate for what makes life worthwhile, we should pause over two features of the account I have given of the promises and failures of love.

First, I have construed faith in love as a state that involves propositional attitudes. One might think that it is instead a purely emotive state, a feeling of satisfaction with the world that involves no beliefs. But I think this would be a mistake. There is a difference between *being* in love and *taking* love to make one's life worthwhile.[5] One might be in love while feeling that something other than love makes life worthwhile. One might be in love with someone in part *because* she shares a commitment to a religion, political cause, or artistic project that one considers far more important than love.[6] One can also be committed to love as making life worthwhile without actually being in love. The commitment to love as what makes life worthwhile clearly involves certain beliefs, however much feeling may come into it: belief that the joyful feelings love initially brings will last, for one thing, and that one should commit one's primary energy to one's love relationship, sacrificing other things for it, rather than sacrificing it for other things. One will also not normally think that these latter things can be sacrificed to love unless one has beliefs about them as well (that politics and art are unimportant, say, or that religion is an illusion or fulfilled in erotic love), nor value the feelings of love so highly unless one holds at least some of the beliefs I listed above: that the joys of love can make up for past sorrows, improve us morally, and inspire us to other projects. So a supreme commitment to the importance of love really does deserve the title "faith." To endorse one's satisfaction with one's life as a mark of its worth is not simply to enjoy a non-cognitive state. It is to commit oneself to a set of propositions about that state.

Second, in my account of love I did not deny that *some* people might experience a lifelong, transformative love. Statistics, anecdotal evidence, and what we know of the biology underpinning erotic love all suggest that this is extremely rare, and it is possible that even people who say that they have such a love are deluding themselves. The claim that their relationship is so wonderful may be but a pretence the two uphold to cover over disappointments, about other aspects of their lives or indeed about each other. But some couples may truly experience, lifelong, something like the joyous passion in one another that most of us feel only fleetingly. This raises two, linked questions: (1) Are these people then deluded to think that love makes life worthwhile for *them*? And (2) could love be what makes life worthwhile for everyone, even though only these few people actually achieve it?

To the first question, we can say that it is of course possible that ultimate worth will turn out to be a quality that many different relationships or projects enable us to achieve. Then it would be perfectly possible that some people's lives are made worthwhile by romantic love, while others are made worthwhile by political activities, a good relationship with their children, the experience or creation of art, etc. What is worrying is the possibility that *only* true love can make life worthwhile, even though only a few people will ever experience it.

Which brings us to the second question. Could the worth of life lie in something that only a few experience? Or does worth need to be a broadly egalitarian concept, something any human being can attain? I am not sure of the proper answer to this, but there are reasons to favor an egalitarian construal of worth: a construal on which whatever makes life worthwhile is something that every human being at least *can* achieve. We don't want to deny that some people in fact fail to lead worthwhile lives. If we denied that, we would deprive the question, "Is my life worthwhile?" of any punch. Brown, the couch potato I described earlier who is trying to motivate herself to do something less selfish, and more interesting, with her life will hardly find that motivation if we tell her that whatever she does—even if she continues just to watch TV—her life will be equally worthwhile. So we don't want to be fully egalitarian in our construal of worth. (Ironically, we would thereby just *defeat* some egalitarian political and moral hopes: we would deprive ourselves of reasons to improve the life of the poor and oppressed.) But there are reasons to suppose that any achievement or experience that most of us cannot hope to have could not possibly be what makes life worth living for human beings.

Why? Most generally, because anything that could reasonably be considered the purpose of *human* life, as opposed to the purpose of this or that human being's life, should be something to which the interests and abilities of human beings in general are fitted. But this intuition is unpersuasive as long as it looks merely like a bit of semantics. Let's try to illustrate the point concretely by way of our love example. Suppose a person in a romantic relationship that does seem to fall among those exceptional cases in which passion lasts for a lifetime nevertheless asks herself one day whether this love of hers is enough to make her life worthwhile. Perhaps her love, delightful as it is, has certain costs. Her partner doesn't want to have children, or prefers that they not spend time with their other friends, or wants her to suspend her career or leave her hometown. So she asks herself, "Is it worth it, this love of mine? Is it worth giving up the other things that I care about?"[7] It can't be a very good answer to these questions to say, "It's worth it if I feel that it is." What she wants to know is precisely whether her feelings are enough to tell her what makes life worth living, or whether they are deluding her and she should take more seriously some of the things she is being asked to sacrifice. Her feelings are not in question; she *feels* as though her love is indeed enough to outweigh all other costs. Her question, then, is precisely whether her feelings are a good guide to worth or whether she needs some more objective test. And once she does seek a more objective test for value, even one that might validate the use of feelings to determine value—*objectively*, it might turn out, our feelings are the correct criterion for what is worthwhile—she will have moved from her private experience to a criterion of value that holds for human beings on the whole. Her questions, that is, are directed to what makes human life *in general* worth living, to whether her feelings about her specific situation are clouding her judgment about what, qua human being, she most needs or wants. So unless she finds either that there is no worth to human life, or that human life is given worth by whatever people feel gives it worth, her desire to maintain her love relationship will not answer her question. Unless there is some general answer to the question of what makes life worth living, some answer that applies to all human beings, she can't call her life in particular worthwhile.[8]

Could there be some general criterion for the worth of life that is satisfied in the experience of just a few people? That's not logically impossible, but it's very difficult to see how it could be justified, especially if we want to avoid relying on a non-rational faith. In some societies, religious adepts—priests, elders, gurus—tell others that anyone who achieves their level of philosophical understanding, or mystical insight, would see why life is worth living, and the others take it on faith that this is true. A naturalistic account of worth should not depend on any such faith, however, and anything it holds up as making life worthwhile should be visible as such to everyone. How else could it make sense as the telos of everyone's life? Anything for which a convincing case can be made that it makes life worthwhile must be something with which many human beings are acquainted. But it's hard to imagine how they could be acquainted with it unless they experienced it.

Perhaps this is too strong: perhaps it is possible that only the *type* of experience making life worthwhile must be something with which most human beings are acquainted, while a small minority of us experience a token of that type. But even this will be enough to throw suspicion on any claim that an experience available only to a small elite can meet the criteria for worth. Suppose a defender of love says, "Only a small elite ever fully experiences the transformative nature of erotic love, as I do, from the inside, and therefore only that elite realizes how and why it gives worth to all of life." We have every reason to come back with the reminder that a great many of us *think* we have experienced erotic love from the inside, and that the meaning of both the word "love" and the word "worth" derives from their use among the great many, so it is likely that fully experiencing love, and assessing its connection to worth, is something that most of us do. A type of experience closed to a small elite is like the purely private experience that Wittgenstein showed to be unintelligible.

Again, we might return to our comparison with the way religious believers justify themselves. If someone says, "I know that when the rest of you think you experience God's presence, it turns out, afterwards or on cooler reflection, that you were deluding yourselves. But when *I* think I experience God's presence, I perceive things you can't so much as understand, and it is those aspects of my experience that assure me that it is veridical," most of us have no trouble writing off this claim as an appeal to private experience that borders on the nonsensical, and treating it as a symptom of an irrational faith. Why should we not do the same with someone who makes analogous claims for his experience of erotic love?

17. Let's try another candidate for an activity or project that might give our lives worth. Many people say that social and political activism has ultimate as well as instrumental value, that by participating in, and improving, our polis, we can find our proper role and greatest fulfillment. Activists for various causes report that they find fighting for the poor, or freedom of speech, or women's rights, to take them beyond their selfish concerns and show them the intrinsic value of their lives. They often also suggest that the feeling that life is not worth living arises out of baleful social conditions. It is a product of misery or oppression, they say, and if we could ever reach a world without poverty, or sexism or racism, we would all begin to realize our true human potential. Not infrequently, they also wag a reproving finger at people more removed from politics. They tell us we have a duty "to get involved," and they remind us that we are "put on earth to help others."

More sophisticated arguments for this sort of view include Aristotelian or Hegelian claims that by nature we are social beings, that the private thoughts of any individual are thoroughly shaped by his or her social environment, so we cannot fully achieve even our own individual freedom unless we participate in the shaping of that environment. Upholders of this view sometimes add that a person engaged in promoting the good of her society may find herself transformed, developing virtues and a wider array of unselfish feelings for others than she had ever had before. The

212 WORTH AS ATTACHED TO SPECIFIC ACTIVITIES

strongest versions of this view maintain, with Marx, that a society whose governance was shared equally by everyone would transform the very *senses* of all human beings, and that the experience we would then have would be fulfilling in a way that we can barely even imagine in our current, egoistic condition; the very pleasures we would have would feel worthwhile in a way they never do now.[9]

How good are these arguments? Well, to the informal hopes and dreams of those who think that political reform can bring about human self-realization, I would point, first, to the great rarity of significant political change, especially of the transforming kind that might end poverty and oppression—in the US, only the administrations of FDR and Lyndon Johnson moved the country even minimally in this direction—and second, to the continuing malaise and world-weariness of people even in successful social democracies: suicide rates in Denmark and Switzerland are, for instance, higher than those in the United States. And Charles M. Schulz offered the best response to the informal bit of moralizing that we are "put on earth to help others." In one *Peanuts* strip, Charlie Brown offers Lucy precisely this platitude. This is followed by one of the wonderful, meditative, but also bewildered pauses that mark the *Peanuts* strip. Then Lucy asks, "What are the others here for?"[10] It may sound noble to dedicate one's life to the good of others, but as an answer to the question, "What makes life worthwhile?," this is simply buck-passing. Unless someone out there has a life intrinsically worth living, there is no point to helping others. Indeed, we will not even succeed in helping anyone; "help," strictly speaking, is a contribution to making a life more worthwhile.[11] And if I cannot find anything intrinsically worthwhile about *my* life, I have no reason to believe other people's lives can be worthwhile. So I had better locate some way for my life to be intrinsically worthwhile, independently of any help I give others, before I set out to give such help.

The more sophisticated arguments tend to depend, explicitly or implicitly, on metaphysical views fully as robust and controversial as any argument for the existence of God. For Hegel, precisely the same sorts of arguments that were supposed to lead one from the belief that one's individual consciousness is self-sufficient to the realization that it is but a part or epiphenomenon of a social mind were also supposed to lead one from treating this social mind as self-sufficient to the realization that it is but a part or epiphenomenon of a divine mind. For Aristotle, the idea that we are essentially social beings rests on a set of metaphysical views about essences. Modern, secular Hegelians and Aristotelians, uncomfortable with these metaphysical considerations, argue for our dependence on our society by pointing to the nature of reasons: showing the extent to which reason-giving is always and necessarily a social activity.[12] When we reflect on our identity as reasoning beings, we are supposed to see that we are ineluctably social beings. And from this it is supposed to follow that we cannot properly be free, cannot properly express our identities, except by pursuing the good of our societies. Presumably, this lack of freedom is what accounts for our feeling that our lives are not worthwhile. When fully free, which here means fully shapers of our societies, we will find our lives worthwhile.

Now it is of course true that reason-giving is a social activity. It is a linguistic activity, for one thing, and language is a social product. What counts as a reason in a given context is also often defined by particular social practices, which determine (a) the aim of reason-giving in that context, (b) the background beliefs that each participant may take for granted, (c) the authority figures, if any, whose opinions structure the conversation, and (d) the issues in play, the questions to which reasons should be relevant. That a player has touched the ball is good reason to give the other side a penalty kick in the practice of soccer, and not a reason at all in the practice of American football; that seven is a sacred number counts as a good reason for believing there are seven planets in one social context, while not counting as a reason at all in another.[13]

But it is not essential to giving reasons that we address someone else—we give ourselves reasons in many situations—and there is nothing about the social background needed in order to become a reason-user, or that determines what counts as a reason in many specific contexts, that requires us to try to maintain the society that has enabled us to reason. Once we have learned how to reason, we can reason on our own: sometimes to greater success than if we paid heed to our society's norms for reasoning (the medieval astronomer who ignored the notion that sacred numbers have anything to do with the number of the planets might have come a lot closer to the truth than one who followed the norm). There may be something ungrateful about accepting our society's help in learning how to reason and then turning away from, or against, that society, but it is certainly possible to do that. We are indebted to our society for our ability to reason at all, but we are indebted similarly to our physical environment for the fact that we exist at all, and that debt does not prove that our essence is to be found in the physical environment. Indeed, the idea that my identity is to be found in something that *distinguishes* me from the universe as a whole is far more plausible than the idea that I am identical with the universe. But how much more plausible is it that my identity is to be found in what I share with my society, rather than in what distinguishes me from it?

Moreover, the claim that we find our identity in our society leaves open *which* society we are supposed to identify with. I belong to a family, a neighborhood, a religious group, a nation, the community of humankind. Which social group should I promote? Their aims may not cohere. My family may dislike my neighborhood; my religion may struggle with my nation. So helping one group may harm the other. Yet all these groups shape me, protect me, further my aims, etc. Nor is this merely a pragmatic problem. The fact that the votaries of social and political commitment have no good answer to the question of which social/political group counts as truly mine suggests that their fundamental terms are ill-defined, that there is no definition of "polis" one could use to prove that we are, in essence, "polis beings."

Let's now apply the other two members of our triumvirate to the claim that politics is the be-all and end-all of life. The Marxist, Freudian, and existentialist styles of explanation can easily make that claim look like an illusion. Freudians have no trouble making out our attachment to our societies, much like our worship of God, to be a derivation from our awe for our parents. Existentialists can argue, very plausibly, that devotion to politics is a distraction from the fear of our own deaths, or from taking responsibility for our individual lives; Heidegger's critique of "das Man" and of "idle talk" indeed seems aimed precisely at the blather of the political realm. And Marxists, for all their own commitment to politics, can note that practically all societies have an interest in promoting the importance of political participation: even authoritarian regimes like the populations over which they rule to believe that being a certain type of good citizen (one who faithfully obeys the laws, reports other lawbreakers to the authorities, and dutifully pays her taxes) is supremely important. Every sub-group in society, moreover, including a group of Marxists, has an interest in encouraging us to devote our energies to its programs. In sum, there is good reason to suppose that belief in the importance of politics is more a product of our early childhood attachments, our existential anxieties, or the indoctrination we receive from our society, than of good argument.

There is also good reason to doubt that political participation really inculcates virtues in us. Political participation is said to help us develop a more expansive self, with virtues like civic courage and feelings of sympathy that go out to a wide range of humanity. The empirical evidence for these claims is weak, however. People who hold office are notoriously hypocritical and sycophantic to their supporters, when not openly corrupt, cruel, or abusive of power. Political activists tend to be purer in their political visions—they can afford to be, not having much power to lose—but many of them suffer from what we may call the "Mrs. Jellyby syndrome." Dickens's Mrs. Jellyby suffered from a peculiar ocular failing: she could see nothing nearer than Africa.[14] While promoting "the Brotherhood of Humanity" and working vigorously on behalf of African causes, she neglected her own children. And Dickens' characterization of her is famous to this day because most of us know plenty of people who avidly pursue the good of all humanity while displaying thoughtlessness, arrogance, or coldness to their families and friends. Political activism fills those engaged in it with a sense of righteousness, which works against the humility one needs in order to accept correction, or respond sensitively to individuals one has injured. In my own experience, I would say it is the exception rather than the rule that people who work for humanitarian causes display an especially decent, open, or humble demeanor in ordinary personal relations.

Again, nothing I have said rules out the possibility that political participation might *contribute* to an objectively worthwhile life, if something other than politics grounds that worth, or that it may be necessary for a just or liberal political system to thrive. But the claim that political participation is itself the ultimate telos of our lives, that we can find our lives worthwhile by making it our primary concern, cannot easily be given a better justification than the claim that we live to do God's will. The worship of politics is no easier to uphold on the basis of reason than the worship of God.

18. Perhaps the enjoyment or creation of art gives life worth? In premodern times, art mostly served religious purposes. Greek festival dramas, Islamic architecture,

Balinese dance, Christian liturgical music—in all these cases, art was supposed to serve the greater glory of God, to enhance a religious experience. But in the West since the late eighteenth century, art has been seen more and more as a *replacement* for religion, and artists as a replacement for prophets. Some insist that we are all artists, deep inside, and find our fulfillment when that artistic core gets properly expressed. Others say that art reveals truths that we cannot find in science and philosophy: that it alone shows us, in particular, why our lives are worth living.[15] Still others have supposed that the experience of art can give us the "higher" pleasures that utilitarians like J. S. Mill and G. E. Moore say should fill a properly human life. Both creating and experiencing art involve intellectual skills as well as our senses, and the pleasures we get from them therefore draw on more of what makes us distinctively human than do the pleasures of food or drink or sex.

To begin, this time, with the second and third of our debunking strategies: It is easy to find explanations for the value people place on art that work against the claims that the apostles of art make for it. Devotion to art once again distracts people from radical political or religious movements and, in addition, serves to reinforce class hierarchies (having "refined taste" is a ticket of admission to high status in many societies). Devotion to art also functions, notoriously, as a sublimation of frustrated erotic desires. And for obvious reasons the feeling of eternity people claim to have in the presence of art can distract them from their mortality. Finally, people who devote their lives to making or experiencing art often use that as an excuse for sleazy behavior towards those around them, and for not even trying to strengthen their capacities for honesty, courage, and other virtues.

What about the direct arguments for this view? Well, as in the case of erotic love, these arguments often rest heavily on experience—one is supposed simply to see, in the presence of great art, or when expressing oneself artistically, that the experience one has is what the rest of life is for—and it's not easy to refute an argument that appeals to experience. But again as in the case of erotic love, the appeal to perception is bound up with a number of empirical claims, and some metaphysical ones, about the nature of this experience. The following points shed some doubt on those claims:

1. The fact that standards for what counts as art shift so much over the years, and that one of the few fixed points about these standards is that they are used to confer status on the supposed artists and their followers, should lead us to wonder whether art is a well-defined category at all. Some people have argued that art consists of nothing but what certain institutions choose to call "art,"[16] and that position has enough plausibility that we ought at least to wonder whether the great experience we think we have in front of artworks really reflects just our pride in attaining a certain social status.

2. Even if the institutional theory of art is incorrect, there is an explanation for what leads us to bestow the honorific "art" on some works, and value the experience they give us, that undercuts the deep meaning we like to attribute to that

experience. This is an explanation in Darwinian style: For good evolutionary reasons, human beings have a tendency to enjoy anything that takes great skill to make or appreciate. Being able to differentiate close shades of color and tone, or create ever-subtler compositions of color or tone, could well be an offshoot of the skills that enabled us to be good hunters, and escape dangers, in jungles and deserts. It is helpful to our survival that we enjoy developing the skills that we need to survive, and the refinement of our perceptions has long been one of those skills. As a consequence, we have all sorts of practices—sports and games, as well as art forms—that require a high level of skill both to engage in and to appreciate. The pleasure in using these skills is then simply an overflow of the sorts of pleasure we are hard-wired to take in whatever helps us survive. We may suppose that our fine ability to craft or appreciate a sonata has to do with some ineffable truth it reveals, but really a genetic pattern that once helped us kill deer has the ability to make and enjoy music as one of its side-effects.

3. What counts as "properly" human—an ineliminable element of the Millian argument for higher pleasures—is difficult if not impossible to establish without an appeal to Aristotelian metaphysics.[17] Moreover, while art does both call on and enhance our intellectual capacities, so do chess and video games and assembling rifles. The mere fact that we need to use our minds to enjoy or create art does not distinguish it from many other human activities. We also need some argument to show that using our minds is, in itself, such a wonderful thing. There are of course instrumental reasons why one wants to keep one's mind in good shape, but we are looking here for something of *intrinsic* worth and it is not obvious why the intellectual pleasure of interpreting Joyce's *Ulysses* should be *intrinsically* better than the non-intellectual pleasure of body-surfing in the Caribbean.

4. The idea that everyone is capable of producing art has now been pretty well refuted as an empirical matter. For over a century, educational programs all over Europe and North America have tried to encourage all children to bring out the little poet or painter or musician within, and the result has just been to provide evidence that the ability to make art is a rare gift, and that most people will produce banalities when they try to connect with their inner artist. It is somewhat more plausible that everyone is capable of *enjoying* art, but the undying popularity of bathetic novels, shallow music, and kitschy painting should give pause to those who believe even this. Tchaikovsky's *1812 Overture* is a concert staple, which Beethoven's late quartets will never be.

Again, nothing I have said is meant to deny that art can be a source of intensely joyous experiences, or that, if we can defend an account linking intense joy to objective worth, art may be a prime source of such worth. But the case for the idea that art in *itself* could make life worthwhile is weak. Few of us would be ready to embrace death as long as we had listened to enough Bach or read enough Thomas Hardy. Few can see the experience of art as the point of all the work we do, the relationships we have, and the political programs we champion, much less be willing to sacrifice those relationships and causes so that we could experience more art. The value of art doesn't bear this much weight. As with the other candidates we have considered, our ordinary willingness to say, "of course, art is intrinsically good" wavers once we are asked whether it is *good enough* to serve as the point of our existence.

The devotee of art begins by finding in childhood that certain films or novels or music take him out of the empty and stiflingly dull world of his parents, to an undreamt-of excitement and joy. Religion seems to him hypocritical and silly; politics seems boring and ineffectual; philosophy is far too abstract. Only art transfigures his life as the preacher, the politician, and the philosopher promises to do. As he gets older, he is drawn towards friends who find a similar excitement in art. He needs such friends since he finds it difficult to talk about anything but his current objects of aesthetic devotion—a film that uses camera angles he has never seen before, an author all of whose work he wants to read, a new development in painting or theater or dance. He looks down on people who don't appreciate Shostakovich or Morandi or Pynchon. He also looks down on those who take an interest in art only to show off; he is a true lover of art, not a snob, and is concerned to make sure that his passion remains a real response to aesthetic values, rather than allowing it to drift into snobbery.

Mingling as he does with like-minded aesthetes, he eventually marries a partner who shares his passions, and together they begin to collect paintings, if they can afford it, or go on pilgrimages to festivals and artistic "events." As they grow older, these activities have to be fitted into spaces in their work and childcare schedules, and become to some extent routine; the paintings and festivals and events themselves also come more and more to seem similar; and the initial excitement with which they threw themselves into an aesthetic life fades to a considerable extent. While they often still really enjoy a film or concert, the affirmations of the transforming importance of art that they made when they were young begin to sound, even to them, like tired mantras. Occasionally they find themselves, in the middle of dressing up for an artistic outing, unnerved by how much of a ritual these things have become. They certainly no longer debate the nature or importance of aesthetic experience any more, with each other or any of their friends. On the contrary, they are upset or irritated if anyone questions that—it has become a dogma, for them, not unlike the religious beliefs they used to mock in their parents or grandparents. It eventually also becomes hard for them to draw a sharp line between true aesthetic experience and snobbery: their taste now follows certain fairly set patterns, and conforms for the most part to the taste of their friends, and at times they uneasily catch themselves more concerned to live up to the expectations set by these patterns than to respond, directly, to what they see or hear in the work before them. To outsiders, they look quite a bit like snobs; their children certainly do, and their grandchildren abandon art for politics or philosophy or religion.

19. We have now twice appealed to evolutionary biology to debunk claims for the intrinsic worth of certain experiences (§§ 15, 18). Is this an appropriate use of Darwinism?

There are a number of ways in which Darwinian evolution might be seen as bearing on the idea that life has an intrinsic worth, not all of which deserve to be taken seriously. In the late nineteenth and early twentieth centuries figures like Herbert Spencer believed that the theory of evolution requires us to regard human survival as our ultimate goal,[18] and that this had all sorts of implications for how societies should structure themselves: we should, for instance, let the weaker among us die off. In fact, no such thing follows from Darwinian evolution. What we learn from Darwin is not that our telos is to survive, but that we need not have *any* telos, that our features can be explained without understanding our nature as having any purpose.[19] (We have certain features because we *have* survived; we do not have them *in order to* survive.) More recently, sociobiologists have sometimes suggested that we really do not love anyone other than ourselves, and do not care about knowledge or politics or art for their own sake, that instead we are structured by our genes, for *their* survival, to *appear* to be loving, intellectual, political, or artistic beings. This is silly, as Simon Blackburn points out.[20] The mother who cares so much about the well-being of her child that she is willing to die for it most certainly does love the child, even if her feelings are hard-wired into her. So what if the love serves to propagate her genes? That doesn't make it any less genuinely love, or suggest that it lacks any of the characteristics that we expect motherly love to have. The mere fact that features of human life help us survive does not prevent them from serving whatever other purposes we take them to have.

But a reasonable Darwinian challenge to our ordinary notion of the worthwhile lurks within the sociobiologist's point.[21] If we can show that features of our lives that we take, from the "inside" of those lives, to serve this or that purpose will in fact *fail* to achieve that purpose whenever doing so conflicts with the survival of our genes, then we do have reason to say that the real purpose of those features is to help our genes survive and the other purposes we took them to serve are merely apparent ones. If a thing is structured so as to serve purpose x, that does not show that it fails to serve purpose y unless x conflicts with y. One cannot debunk the claim that it serves y just by showing it serves another purpose as well, but one can do so if one can demonstrate an asymmetry between the way it serves the two purposes, such that one of them, in cases of conflict, regularly takes priority over the other. If I am your political advisor and you discover that I am also making a film about your campaign, that does not show that I have been giving you bad advice, but if you find that the film is meant to be a *satire* of your skills or program, then you do have reason to say that my real purpose conflicts with yours. Similarly, if the survival of my genes leads my motherly love regularly or in important cases to falter or go astray, or my interest in art to vanish when it is not useful to my genes, then it is reasonable to say that the commitments I think I have are illusory, and serve the propagation of my genes instead of the purposes they seem to promote.

One might object to this claim by saying that my feelings or interests cannot deceive me, that deception can only take place where there is a deceiver: an intelligent agent, independent of me, attempting to manipulate what I think. But this is not so. I can be deceived—I can certainly be under an illusion—even if there is no-one out to deceive me. We use the word "illusion" in cases when we misrepresent things to ourselves, as when we see an apparently bent stick in water. Here, a part of our cognitive apparatus represents something as other than what the rest of that apparatus knows it to be. It doesn't matter that the illusory setup arises naturally, without anyone setting out to fool us. The question is simply whether the thing is what we take it to be. And it is quite intelligible that we can fool ourselves in what we take our feelings or desires to signify in just the way we fool ourselves when we take our watery image to represent a bent stick.

But now it is intelligible that Darwinian evolution can show our notions of worth to be illusory. If illusion arises when a thing is other than what we take it to be, then we can ask whether we are under such an illusion when we take things to be of ultimate worth—whether the features of our lives that we take to be ultimately worthwhile are really aimed at the purposes we take them to have, or whether they merely appear to have such purposes, while actually serving just to propagate our genes. Darwinism teaches that individual living things have many features that are useful to the survival of their species (in modern versions: of their genes), but not necessarily to that of the individuals themselves. It is an illusion, then, if an individual takes them to be useful to him or herself. If there are features of our lives that we take to enhance those lives, but that in fact serve our genes *as against* our individual selves—defeating our individual ends whenever that will help propagate our genes—we can see our normal view of those features as illusory.

And many of the commitments that we ordinarily take to represent ultimate ends are properly regarded as illusions of this kind. Take the feeling we have, in the throes of a first love, that we will delight in our lover forever. That is almost certainly *not* true; yet we feel convinced of it. The effect is quite similar to that of the stick in water. Or at least it is for those who come to realize that the feeling is misleading—others, when the feeling wears off, may just feel, "that wasn't true love, after all; someone else must be the one meant for me"—and Darwinism helps us realize that. Darwinism gives us a good explanation of the feelings that come with first love, and of why those feelings fade. So we *think* the feeling we have about our lover is directed to the good of ourselves and our lover, but in *fact* it is directed to the good of our genes. There is a mismatch here, between expectation and reality, such that the feelings can rightly be called illusory. Moreover, Darwinism is likely to say that being under the illusion is itself conducive to the survival of our species, that the false belief that we will delight in this other person forever is more useful than a true appreciation of the situation would be.

There are similar Darwinian ways to debunk the value that art, politics, and many other things seem to have for us. In addition, Darwinism undermines both traditional religious and Aristotelian arguments for our having an objective purpose. Darwinian evolution notoriously challenges the idea that we have been designed by an intelligent being, and it also makes nonsense of the idea that species have a particular form that each individual needs to realize in order to flourish. Rather, the more varied the lives of different members of a species, the better the chance that species has of survival in a varied and changing environment. If vegetarianism was natural for a particular kind of animal up till now, but the plant life around it gets suddenly devastated, at the same time that large, ill-defended prey moves into the area, then members of that species that develop a quick taste for meat will do well, however much they may violate the "form" that their species has hitherto taken. One day it may be good for a type of animal to be tall and straight-backed; the next day, it may turn out that only the hump-backed, "stunted" members of the species survive (they hide under trees better, say, from tall hunters that move into the area). In this context, there is no fixed notion of flourishing for any life form to have, nothing that could be used, in the human case, as a norm for the good life. Rather, the notions of flourishing we may derive from the normal ways in which human beings have thus far survived are illusions, false impressions encouraged by the fact that the environment in which we have lived over the past 3000 to 4000 years has been relatively stable.

20. One more concrete candidate for worth. Many professors think that the pursuit of knowledge is intrinsically worthwhile. Once, when a distinguished historian gave a presentation at my university decrying political threats to the continuation of a thriving scholarly culture, he was visibly disconcerted when a questioner suggested that research might be a less important function of universities than teaching. "Throw this man out!" he said, only half-jokingly; "He doesn't believe in scholarship." But he couldn't say *why* scholarship was so important. The moment was very much like one in which a heretic presses a religious believer on an article of dogma to which the latter is fervently attached, but cannot defend.

Now, of course scholarship can be *useful* for a wide variety of purposes, from enabling us to cure diseases to helping us develop more just and peaceful states. The idea that knowledge is a good thing in itself does not have any obvious justification, however, once the religious or metaphysical doctrines that used to support it have fallen away. Plato and Aristotle provided powerful reasons for the intrinsic value of knowledge, and the Muslim, Jewish, and Christian thinkers who followed them fit those reasons into an account of what it is to love God. But if we don't accept the metaphysical premises underwriting these views, it is hard to see any good reason for them. Suppose the increase of scientific knowledge no longer helped improve human lives, and that any effort spent on it had serious *costs* for the cure of disease, alleviation of poverty, or prevention of war: would the belief that we should carry out further research anyway then seem more than a blind prejudice?

And, of course, the pursuit of knowledge not infrequently comes at the cost of many ordinary virtues and duties: the self-centered professor who sets friends or family aside for his scholarship is not to be found in fiction alone. We can also again easily find social and psychological interests—along the same lines that we've seen in other cases—that encourage us to believe in the intrinsic value of knowledge whether knowledge has such a value or not.

I think our speaker was discomfited by what I call "the mocker through the window" effect. One of the few experiences that will lead a person to question his own passions is having other people make light of them. Normally, passions are incorrigible: if you take joy in something, nothing anyone else says about it will change your mind. But there is a certain kind of experience that can destroy your pleasure. Imagine that you are immersed in something—reading a novel or work of philosophy, or listening to a romantic opera, or arranging some collection you've been keeping—and in your immersion find it tremendously moving and important. You are wrapped up in what you are doing, humming to yourself or smiling or nodding along or feeling a chill of joy run down your back. Then suddenly you notice, through a window, a friend laughing and pointing at you, amused at your fervor. Perhaps also, when the friend comes in to join you, he makes a casual but devastating remark about the shallowness of the book you were reading, or the overwrought character of opera, or the silliness of collecting. Even if you don't fully believe him, the pleasure may flee abruptly, leaving shame for your own inept sensibility in its wake, and an inclination to rewrite the pleasure you felt before, in memory, as an embarrassing rather than a joyous experience.

The point here is not that some people like some things and others like other things. We are content to let there be no arguing over many tastes, to find other people's fondness for something just as intelligible as our own distaste for it, but there are striking cases in which the people involved in an activity (stamp collecting, watching Star Trek re-runs, listening to country music) think it the most important and exciting thing in the world, while outsiders find it ridiculous that any human being could take the activity seriously. Here, each sees the other as blind to some objective source of value—but here also we all tend to think that the outsider, because dispassionate, is more likely to be right than the insider, and the insiders themselves can feel deflated by the outsider's contempt. (The outsider never feels deflated by contempt from the insider.) The insiders therefore find it difficult to let the outsiders be, in their contempt: they feel a need to persuade the outsiders to share their own passion, and can get angry or upset if they fail.

I suspect that almost any human activity can be subjected to the scrutiny of the mocker through the window, and deflated thereby. But this raises the specter that all apparent value, everything that seems to us truly exciting and worthy of commitment, could turn out, if we take up the outsider's position, to be an illusion.

21. There are a host of other candidate activities for what gives worth to life—raising children,[22] participating in sports, identifying with a culture—but I hope the reader will take my word for it that similar sorts of arguments can point up the hollowness of the claims made for them as well, and show that the faith people put in such claims is best explained in terms of psychological need and social indoctrination.[23] This raises the question, however, of whether the strategy I have been using works too easily. Undermining the pretensions of candidates for ultimate worth has been like shooting fish in a barrel. The claims made on their behalf look quite silly after a little prodding and we are never at a loss to find social or psychological explanations for why belief in these claims may persist nonetheless. There is something suspicious about this. A method of argument that succeeds too easily is rightly suspected of having stacked the deck so that it will win every debate, defining its terms so that its conclusions follow tautologously, or insulating its apparently empirical methods against any real possibility of empirical refutation. (Both Marxism and Freudianism have, with reason, been accused of doing something like this.) Our very success should prompt the thought, "Have we framed our question properly? Have we defined 'worth', implicitly or explicitly, such that nothing could *count* as giving worth to life as a whole?"

The suspicion is just that—a suspicion, not a proof that there is something wrong with our method. It is possible that we have framed our question badly, but it is also possible that our strategies work so well because life is not worth living. Or perhaps the notion of life as worth living is intimately bound up with the religious and metaphysical systems we are setting aside, and collapses if they are rejected. Many activities we regard today as making our lives worthwhile derive, after all, from premodern religious and metaphysical systems in which they were supposed to help us realize our true essence or satisfy the will of a God or gods. Perhaps we continue to regard these activities as so important today only because we are tacitly employing remnants of these religious and metaphysical views. The transformative role we attribute to erotic love, for instance, probably derives from elements of the medieval cult of the Virgin Mary, together with arguments from Plato's *Symposium*, widely used in the Christian world to show that earthly love is a shadow of and means to love of the divine. We don't believe in these Christian and Platonic views anymore, but we may, nevertheless, be clinging to their erotic components, and hiding ourselves from the fact that these components have lost their grounding. The same could be true for the importance placed on the political realm, the creation and appreciation of art, and the pursuit of knowledge. They may all be remnants of comprehensive views we no longer hold, in which politics, art, or knowledge were means to the worship of God, or ways of attaining the objective human telos. The remnants don't stand up to close scrutiny on their own, however, and are either propped up by bad arguments or continue to rest, implicitly, on beliefs that their devotees can't admit to holding.[24]

Finally, all these conceptions of ultimate worth may survive, despite the loss of their grounding, for psychological or sociological reasons. Any candidate for what makes life worth living will inevitably satisfy some basic psychological needs: serving as an object of intense affection and thus replacing, in our crude Freudian schema, either the security we sought from our mothers or the approval we sought from our fathers, and distracting us from our fear of death. (*Of course* anything that makes life seem worth living will mitigate our fear of death!) And our societies will have a stake in our believing that *something* makes life worth living, whatever it may be, and will be particularly inclined to foster beliefs according to which that something can be found in some stable feature of life, that its institutions can easily support. Love and art and political participation and knowledge all fit that bill, since they have instrumental uses in practically every society. Nevertheless, every candidate for what makes life worth living will have certain moral costs. For one thing, obsession with any one activity takes us away from other things our societies need us to carry out. For another, if the belief that these activities make life worth living is false, as I have been suggesting, then holding the belief, against contrary evidence, is likely to lead the believer into self-deception.

So one conclusion we might reasonably draw from the ease with which our strategy disposes of common secular candidates for what gives life value is that nothing gives life value, that only flimsy arguments ever led us to think otherwise, and that the reason we don't see through these arguments ordinarily is that the belief that life has value is a psychologically and socially useful delusion.

An alternative conclusion is that it is a mistake to seek a good secular account of worth in our ordinary, unreflective views, that what we need is a philosophical reconstruction of that notion suited to modern science and philosophy. We will consider a series of proposals along these lines in the next chapter.

4

Worth as Attached to General Features of Life

22. When we turn from ordinary views of the sorts of things that make life worth living to a philosophical reconstruction of the notion of worth, one of the first things we are likely to do is reject the assumption that there is a single type of event or activity around which our whole lives should be structured. Most philosophers today favor a pluralistic over a monistic approach to our question, to return to some terms we used earlier (§ 2).

On this approach, life is or can be worthwhile, but that worth emanates from general features of our lives, which can be manifested in many different activities. Perhaps the quantity or kind of pleasure we get, from a variety of activities, is what gives worth to life, or perhaps a person has a worthwhile life if he develops a variety of skills—if he "flourishes," in current Aristotelian parlance—or perhaps we project worth onto what we do and our lives are worthwhile if we live up to our own standards of worth. We might say that I have put the question thus far too much as though life took a narrative form, in which everything we do contributes to a particular achievement and our assessment of the whole depends on whether our expectations of that focal activity are fulfilled or not. Perhaps worth is spread out more broadly across the course of a life filled with different activities, no one of which takes priority over the others.

We'll take up these possibilities in a moment, but we should first stop to emphasize the fact that, if it is a mistake to see life as taking a narrative form, it is not simply my mistake. People characteristically do view their lives that way, especially when they ask themselves whether their lives are worth living.[1] If this is a mistake, it is a widely shared one, and understanding worth such that it does not require life to take a narrative form itself entails a significant reconstruction of common sense on the subject. My narrative candidates are, on the whole, better suited to the inside view of our common thoughts about worth. We find ourselves in the prompting scenarios I described when we worry that we have failed, or missed something, in our love life, career, or political commitments, and we are relieved if we find a teaching or practice that gives our life a new focus. Worth, we think, gives structure to a life, shows us how to prioritize what we do and select among competing projects that claim our attention. We see our lives as hierarchically organized, with many of our activities serving to make possible certain highlight experiences. People who think they have found something that makes their life worthwhile generally see the value of what they are doing as built into *that* particular activity, not as an instantiation of some more general value that could equally be found elsewhere. Those in the throes of romantic love ("I would die for her!"), or a commitment to art ("I'd give up anything for my painting!"), or to a political cause, do not normally see their projects as just one among many things that might make life worthwhile. "If this doesn't work out, I'll take up gardening," is not the expression of a committed lover, artist, or activist.

But we have seen reason to regard the lover and the activist as mistaken, and it is possible that the mistake lies with the inside view of worth. Perhaps we will do better if we approach the language of worth more from its outside. Each of the accounts I consider below—locating the worth of our lives, respectively, in pleasure, happiness, flourishing, the exercise of judgment, and the successful carrying out of whatever we ourselves take to be worthwhile—does just that, taking the many different activities in which people find ultimate worth and looking for some feature that those activities have in common, rather than taking seriously the claim we are inclined to make when immersed in one of these activities: that it alone has a value that should outweigh all competitors.

23. The first outside account of worth I want to take up is one we have encountered before—the equation of worth with pleasure. We seem to pursue pleasure, directly or indirectly, much if not all of the time. We also generally pursue pleasure as an end-state, not a means to something else. And some degree of pleasure is surely, on any account, at least a necessary condition of what can count as worth. It is hard to imagine how our lives could possibly be worthwhile if we found them unremittingly repulsive, painful, or boring.[2]

These considerations make a good presumptive case for identifying worth with pleasure. But pleasure alone fails miserably when brought in as a response to our prompting scenarios. What argument could persuade Jones or Smith that pleasure makes life worthwhile—or persuade Brown of that, once she is willing to entertain the thought that being satisfied with her life doesn't necessarily make it worthwhile? We can imagine Jones or Smith or Brown turning, or returning, to a life of pleasure alone *if they were persuaded that life has no worth*, but as long as they think that lives may have worth, it is hard to see how they could see pleasure as constituting that worth. A clue to why not may be found in how we think about past pleasures. A person asking whether her life is worthwhile is unlikely to regard any past pleasures she has had as giving her, at the moment of asking, an answer with which she can be satisfied. Once they are over, past pleasures do nothing for us, unless they are renewed in the present, or we have a promise of renewing them in the future. It may be a bit ungrateful of us, but we don't *care* about our past pleasures unless something about those pleasures has an effect on an experience or relationship we are enjoying in the present.

The reason for this, I suggest, is that the temporal shape of pleasure is ill-suited to the temporal shape of our consciousness.[3] Pleasures have discrete beginnings and endings in time, and we neither expect nor want them to extend beyond these limits. We may wish a particular concert or vacation would go on a bit longer, but we would become impatient if it went on for too long; we want the pleasurable moment to be succeeded by a different sort of experience, and sometimes find it preferable to have boring or moderately painful moments sprinkled in among our pleasurable ones. Our consciousness, by contrast, seems to traverse time continuously, and to yearn to extend beyond any limits it encounters.[4] Consequently, at any given moment we regard past pleasures as having little to do with who we are now—as not really "ours," in a sense.[5] Sometimes the memory of a pleasure is itself pleasurable, but often we look back unmoved, or even with some envy of our past selves, when we remember joyous moments.[6] *I* am the conscious being who is currently reflecting, and while my memories of certain experiences may be important to my identity as this reflecting being, the pleasure or pain I went through while having those experiences is not. I do not identify with my past pleasures and pains. What could give *my* life worth, as this reflecting being, would be something commensurate with my consciousness: something that can accumulate continuously—knowledge, for example—and that I can gather in a cumulative fashion. Only then can I feel, as I deeply want to feel, that each successive moment can add to the value of my past moments.[7]

In addition, at the point when I reflect on my pleasures, rather than simply have them, they are likely to bore me, and I have reason to fear that a life of pleasure alone would eventually bore me even in the having of them. One more art event, one more exotic vacation, one more love affair—eventually these become routine events, and the pleasure one takes in them, although real enough as a matter of bodily stimulation, will be flat, lacking the intensity it once had and accompanied by a sense that one wouldn't really have cared if one had lacked it. People rich enough to fill their lives with endless pleasures often attest to how boring this becomes. The threat of boredom may well be tied to the issue about consciousness: the reason we find pleasures, on their own, eventually uninteresting is that we want our pleasures to have a *point*, to have cognitive content that could leave a trace on our consciousness.

There is, furthermore, something disturbing about allowing pleasure to serve as the be-all and end-all of our lives now that we understand how much it functions as an instrument for our genes and species. Seen in a Darwinian light, pleasure appears as a manipulative device moving us around for ends other than our individual good. The impression that it does serve our good—that it is an end in itself and, indeed, an end that we have set for ourselves—is, in this light, an illusion. Again, it is inadequate to respond to this objection by saying that we should not regard anything that naturally occurs as an illusion. As long as we have one set of beliefs when going through an experience, but realize that those beliefs are false upon considering the experience from the outside, we have every reason to consider the beliefs illusory. Otherwise we could not use that term for mirages, or the bent appearance of straight sticks in water. We are under the impression that pleasure is an end in itself for us, while all the time, if evolutionary theory is correct, it really functions to keep us moving towards the reproduction of our genes: to the extent, indeed, that it ceases to come once we are too old and weak to serve the needs of our sub- and super-structure any longer. (This is presumably part of the mechanism by which we are built, according to biologists, to ensure that we die after a certain point.) And it is essential to the success of this biological process that we not, most of the time, *realize* that our pleasures serve something other than our own good. We are built so as to be under the illusion that our pleasures are "our own"—chosen by us, or directed at our individual good—while in reality they serve our genes.

Some philosophers, in recent years, have given yet further reasons for distinguishing goodness from pleasure. We all ordinarily acknowledge, for instance, that there are bad pleasures, pleasures we would prefer to give up for the sake of such goods as truth, freedom, or dignity.[8] We also value many things, in ordinary life, independently of the pleasure they bring. These are points made from the perspective of common sense, which I have suggested we should hold at a distance in an investigation of worth, but the case *for* identifying worth with pleasure is itself generally made by appeal to common sense, so an attack from common sense has a force here that it does not always have. Moreover, the commonsensical points against hedonism concur nicely in this case with the more philosophical analysis given above.

What do we say, now, to a person who insists, in the face of all these considerations, that for *him* life does seem worthwhile as long as it is pleasurable, and that he is under no illusions? I don't think there is any clear refutation of such a claim, but his confidence that he is free of illusions surely amounts to a kind of non-rational faith. It certainly gives no-one else a reason to share his hedonism, gives no reason, in particular, to one who is agonizing over whether the pleasures in her life are sufficient to give it worth. On the contrary, the language of worth is so much at odds with the language of pleasure, the considerations that might lead us to regard an activity as worthwhile are so easily used *against* the claims of pleasure ("that was fun even though it wasn't worthwhile"), that it makes far more sense to view hedonism as a call for the *abandonment* of the notion of worth than as an interpretation of that notion. If we can and should live for pleasure alone, then the questions of the couch potato and would-be suicide are confused. To say there is nothing to worth but pleasure is to say that the question of the worth of pleasure itself cannot arise, to tell the people in our prompting scenarios that it is a mistake even to ask their questions. So there is really no difference between reducing worth to pleasure and abandoning the notion of worth.

Or so it looks, from the perspective of one who does not feel satisfied by pleasure alone.

   - These are the musings of a depressive!

    - Perhaps they are. What of it? Have you never heard of depressive realism? Many psychologists believe that depressives are more realistic than "healthy" people.

24. We are on somewhat firmer ground if we identify worth with happiness or well-being or flourishing. Happiness is generally thought to extend over time, and to include a series of pleasures without being identical with them, so it is more commensurate than pleasure with the shape of our consciousness. Happiness has also long been used by philosophers to translate the Greek word "eudaimonia," which designated the highest human good for Aristotle, and which in his hands had an objective component that enabled it to avoid the problems that come of identifying our telos with pleasure. "Well-being" and "flourishing" are other terms used to translate that word, for which reason I have coupled them here with happiness.

But we lose as much as we gain by turning to happiness or flourishing. For what makes these translations of "eudaimonia" seem a better candidate for ultimate worth is that the idea of worth is built into them: to say a life is "eudaimon" is just to say that it is pleasurable *in a worthwhile way*. John Stuart Mill was explicit about this. Happiness, he said, consists in a life that is filled more with "higher pleasures" than lower ones, but what earns a pleasure the designation "higher" is that it is intrinsically worthwhile. A life of higher pleasures will then of course be worthwhile—*if* some pleasures really are "higher" than others. It is tautologous, that is, to call a happy or flourishing life worthwhile if we use those terms in their philosophical sense.[9] One who denies that our lives are worthwhile can then just deny that any life is a happy or flourishing one.

Perhaps this is a bit unfair. When Aristotle tells us in NE I.7 that eudaimonia must be an excellent activity that extends over a lifetime, we learn *something* more about the meaning of that term than that it describes an intrinsically good state. "A worthwhile life is a life of eudaimonia" is not a *mere* tautology; it tells us, rather, something about the structure that worth needs to have. Still, what it tells us concerns at most the formal conditions of worth, not its content. (Hence, this chapter needs to be complemented by NE X.7–8.)[10] The conditions are reasonable ones, but they do not alone tell us what kinds of activities might satisfy them. And Aristotle's later arguments for why contemplation or practical virtue fit the bill depend on teleological premises that no longer seem plausible today.

Some of the many recent writers who have appealed to Aristotle, or the notion of flourishing, to make sense of the human good—Alasdair MacIntyre, John McDowell, Martha Nussbaum, Richard Kraut—think that we don't need Aristotle's arguments to see how the exercise of our characteristic capacities is an intrinsic good. MacIntyre thinks we can substitute a sociological teleology for Aristotle's biological one. For McDowell, the person who has been brought up to practical virtue will just *see* that exercising his capacities is intrinsically worthwhile. Kraut compares goodness to health, and seems to think it obvious that health is an intrinsic good for us.[11] And Kraut and Nussbaum and many others appeal also to the fact that we ordinarily regard the activities that exercise our characteristic capabilities as obviously good.

But all of these views seem to me to provide blank and question-begging responses to someone who seriously wonders whether her life, virtuous as it may be, is worth living. *Ex hypothesi*, she does not see serving her society or the exercise of her characteristic capabilities, or even health, as *obviously* good. Perhaps McDowell would say that she *will* find this obvious, and not be inclined to ask such questions, if she is truly virtuous, that truly virtuous people do not face such questions, but this is either an empirical falsehood or a tendentious redefinition of what sorts of people count as "virtuous." Without the metaphysical arguments that Aristotle makes for seeing certain activities as our objective telos, it is hard to understand why we must accept any human activity, no matter how characteristic of our species, as something with which we ought to be satisfied.

Imagine actually telling a person worried about whether her life is worthwhile— thinking about giving up her high-paying job to work for the homeless, say, or, like Green, to join a religious cult—"Don't worry: you are flourishing." Do we really expect her to take that as reason to endorse her life if she doesn't already feel like doing so, reason *not* to work for the homeless or join the cult? Suppose her capabilities would not be well served by the charitable work or the cult. If she thinks this activity would give her life a value it currently lacks, will she care about that? If we convince her that her hope to imbue her life with worth at the shelter or in the cult is an illusory one, on the other hand, will she really be comforted by the fact that her high-paying job allows her to exercise her capabilities? We do not find it unreasonable if a person loses enthusiasm for politics because she comes to think it impossible to challenge the plutocracy around her, or loses her enthusiasm for art because she comes to think it does not transform people as she once believed it did. If an activity does not achieve its purported end, one has reason to withdraw one's commitment from it. But then why should it be unreasonable to lose interest in the development of our capabilities once we learn that there is no metaphysical end for them to achieve? Why should that objective discovery be any less enervating than the discovery that more local projects hold out false hopes to us?

25. In *A Third Concept of Liberty*, I myself proposed a version of the "flourishing" answer to a question about how to assess people's lives.[12] Human beings seek to carry out "phronetic activities," I said there, skilled activities that require us to exercise our phronesis or good judgment, and when we exercise it successfully, when we achieve a good proper to that activity, we take a pleasure in that success. Unlike other pleasures, however, this one arises from the use of a mental process that, I argued, could be seen as the primary locus of our freedom. A life of these pleasures therefore feels dignified, free, and properly human to us where a life of mere animal pleasures does not. I suggested that we could understand in this way what Aristotle means by "proper pleasures" (NE X.3–5) and Mill by "higher pleasures." I also suggested that the question of the overall value of life might disappear if we could be satisfied with the small, achievement-oriented pleasures that come of participating in phronetic tasks.

Even when I wrote this, however, I left open the possibility that an over-arching goal might be necessary in addition to the small phronetic activities, if one is to regard one's life as worthwhile, and I am returning to the question now, in part, because I have not myself found that phronetic activities alone are enough to give me a sense of worth about life. Why not? Well, one answer is that even proper pleasures, once they are over, don't add up to something that my consciousness can easily regard as belonging to it, let alone take as its goal. Proper pleasures, and the phronetic activities they crown, have the same temporal shape as other pleasures, and remain, therefore, incommensurate with the temporal structure of consciousness. I look back at my phronetic activities, at a moment of reflection, and they don't add up to anything with which I can identify *now*. They don't answer the question of whether it is worth continuing to live or not, or give me much guidance as to what I should do with my life from now on. They don't *organize* my life in any way; they don't give me something to aim for. Of course, even if I had an over-arching goal, I would need to pursue that goal through some set of activities, and those had better be phronetic ones if I am to preserve my freedom and dignity, but the phronetic activities themselves won't give me such a goal.

In addition, my point in *Third Concept* was primarily a political one: that *governments* should regard the happiness, and worth, of each of their individual citizens as resting in his or her phronetic activities, since if the government protects the citizen's ability to engage in those activities, it will perforce protect that individual's freedom. My argument for protecting phronetic activities therefore depended on an attempt to *sidestep* the question of what makes individual lives worthwhile, on the presumption that it is essential to liberal politics that that question be left up to individuals to decide for themselves. When we now come precisely to the ethical question elided by these political considerations—to the question that the individual is supposed to decide for herself—it is by no means so clear that a focus on phronetic activities will be helpful. It is, indeed, unclear from this perspective that life *is* worthwhile, as we have seen.

26. Let's now consider the flaws shared by the pluralistic accounts of worth we have reviewed, as we did earlier with the monistic ones. I have given reasons for rejecting pleasure, happiness, and phronetic activity as adequate bases on which to ground the claim that life is worthwhile. But why should we think that all such accounts will fail? Well, one reason to think that can be found, again, in the modern move away from Aristotelian teloi. Pluralistic accounts of worth take some features of our lives to be fundamental to human nature and then see our lives as worthwhile to the extent that we express or exercise these features. But it's hard to see how we could be brought by reason to any single account of human nature, once we abandon Aristotelian teloi in our investigations of nature in general. For Aristotle, each kind of thing has its own specific essence, which defines it and which it strives to realize. Human beings too, therefore, have an essence which can be determined objectively and which we all strive to realize whether we know it or not. Modern science does away with essences and correspondingly with any strong notion of kinds, looking for a basic structure of nature

in particles and forces that underlie *all* things, not for specific structures for each kind of thing. When we ask now, in our practical capacities, after a specific "nature" we might try to realize, we cannot expect science to have much to say to us. The scientific answers we get will be vague and conflicting ("It depends what you mean by 'nature' ..."), and ultimately we will need to *choose* what to regard as our nature. (We also have to choose whether to accept a scientific answer to this question.) For that reason, Kant and his followers give pride of place to choice itself; they identify our nature or essence with our capacity for choice. But it is possible to choose not to choose, or to choose in a whimsical, irresponsible way, so even our ability to choose does not unequivocally yield a nature or essence for us to realize.

Again, an Alasdair MacIntyre might say we have gone wrong in abandoning essences and we should restore an Aristotelian conception of who we are. But now that we have a very successful science of nature that does not follow Aristotle on essences in general—a science whose success, moreover, in good part *depends* on this rejection of essentialism—it is hard to see how we could have reason for returning to Aristotle in our view of human nature in particular. We could perhaps say that the very ability of such a view to underwrite a belief that life is worth living is a reason for adopting it. But that itself would be to take it on as a faith, a presumption we cannot prove, but adopt anyway because we need it to guide our lives.

27. If not Aristotle, as MacIntyre might say, are we left with Nietzsche?[13] Doesn't everything I have said thus far reinforce Nietzsche's famous critique of objective values? But Nietzsche, and his twentieth-century followers, seemed to want us simply to embrace, subjectively, the space where objective values had been—to use his critique as inspiration for a projection of our own desires on to the world. Perhaps that's right— perhaps we *make* our lives worth living, constitute the worth of our lives. There's a purely subjectivist version of this claim that I'll take up in the next section, but there's also a view, associated with existentialism, on which we are supposed to see self-creation or self-constitution as itself worthwhile.[14] Could this be a good way to answer, or dismiss, our telic questions?

Well, first I'd like to draw a distinction between existentialists like Nietzsche and Sartre, on the one hand, and absurdists like Kafka and Camus and Beckett, on the other. The absurdists may well be saying just what I have been saying—that life, viewed in a wholly secular light, is pointless. The existentialists make this very claim, or the willingness to acknowledge it, look heroic.[15] And if it is, indeed, heroic to embrace the pointlessness of our lives, or to use that as the starting point for a life both shaped and valued as we see fit, then we might be able to relinquish our telic questions: to stop worrying about worth. But I think the heroism that the existentialists claim for themselves rests on some confusion.

Many people in the twentieth century were attracted to the idea that we determine, each for ourselves, what kind of story about worth we tell ourselves. There seems something delightfully free about such a view—light-hearted, whimsical, unstuffy, released from the constraints of Victorian conventionality and the fears of traditional religions—and something brave and honest as well. Existentialists are heroes, who see the objective pointlessness of life for what it is and keep right on going. They are also mature and independent, able to do without the crutch of religion or conventional moralism. They are clear-eyed, where others are murky or self-deceived; strong, where others are weak; courageous, where others are fearful. And they are sexy, both in their courage and honesty, and in the literal sense that their views seemed to mean that anything goes when it comes to sex.

Such, at least, is the common view of them, the view that fills classes on existentialism in American universities. But there is reason to be suspicious of this view. In the first place, it is empirically false, much of the time. Many existentialists are neither particularly honest nor particularly independent-minded. Nor have they tended to stand out for their strength or courage; it doesn't take much strength or courage, after all, to espouse a view that is very popular, and sells books or fills classrooms—certainly not more courage than it takes, say, to espouse Victorian morality in today's academy. Perhaps Nietzsche himself was a great risk-taker, but his followers, strutting up and down university hallways proclaiming "God is dead" as if nobody had ever heard such a thing before, exemplify what he would have called "the herd mentality" more than they do his super-heroes.

Nor is the conformism of these would-be non-conformists an accident. For there is a confusion hidden in the appeal of existentialism. The idea that self-constitution is the source of all value depends on the claim that there are no objective values, but the *attractiveness* of this idea depends on a belief that qualities like honesty, courage, or sexiness *have* an objective value. If we are really to clear the deck of objective values, and let our values depend entirely on our subjective projections, then the objective value of honesty and heroism falls away as well and there should be nothing wrong with choosing, say, to bury one's head in the sand and embrace Victorian morality, rather than existentialism. In short, existentialism trades on an implicit acceptance of certain traditional values, even as it claims to do without all such values.

It also trades on some deeper confusions. For one thing, normally we value creativity because we value its products, and it is unclear how we are supposed to measure the "product" of self-creation. We are far less keen on aesthetic creativity when it leads to dull or silly art than when it leads to stuff we admire, and we value creativity in business because we think that at least some of the people with this trait will wind up producing something useful. So when it comes to creating a whole life, one might think we would assess the creativity that enables someone to do that well against a model of what a good human life looks like. But, *ex hypothesi*, we can't do that. It's therefore hard to see why we should care about the creativity itself, or even how we could figure out exactly what sort of creativity it is. Is a person who devotes his life to counting blades of grass, to borrow an example from Rawls,[16] exercising his power of self-creation? Or is he hiding from himself, refusing to face his existential situation authentically? I have no idea how one is supposed to answer that question: there's not enough in the notion of worth as self-created to tell me.

Finally—and here we get to a point that affects subjectivism generally, not just existentialism—it's not clear that there can be any project of self-creation shorn of objective norms about what one is trying to create. Creation, in ordinary human life, aims at an end of some sort. An idea of what I want to bring into being, or of the values I am trying to realize in the creative process itself, guides how I paint a picture, compose a sonata, make a machine or piece of furniture. I can therefore succeed or fail in my efforts, and can assess my success or failure in accordance with the criteria that guided me. But if I am making up the very criteria for success or failure even as I claim to be trying to "succeed" in creating something, I will essentially have *no* criteria anymore: anything will count as my succeeding or failing, hence nothing will. The idea of succeeding and failing will no longer be operative; there will be nothing, outside of my will, to mark whether I have achieved anything. And that means that I will no longer have use for the idea of creativity: the very difference between trying to create something and actually creating it will no longer be intelligible. Creation takes place where a subject brings about something at least notionally independent of itself. Self-creation, then, makes sense where one brings oneself into line with qualities whose nature and value can be established independently. It doesn't make sense if one must make up the nature and value of one's benchmarks themselves.

28. I conclude this chapter with three clearly subjectivist views of worth, by which life is worthwhile if and only if we take up a certain attitude toward it. Subjectivism, in which my feeling content with my life is not just a necessary, but also a sufficient condition for its having value, is pretty much all that is left to us if we cannot appeal to an objective account of the human essence, and these are some of the most plausible versions of subjectivism.

I begin with Bernard Williams's notion of a "ground project," which is a type of monistic conception of worth, but with an important twist: instead of marking one particular kind of activity as giving worth to *everyone's* life, Williams leaves it up to each of us to pick out some such activity for ourselves. This ground project then becomes the source of worth for the particular person who selects it. We might say: Williams is a pluralist who allows each of us to be monists (thereby recognizing the need for a conception of worth to organize our lives).

Williams sometimes talks of ground projects as "categorical desires."[17] A categorical desire, he says, is one which provides us with a reason for going on, for continuing to exist at all.[18] It does not have to be a very grand desire—wanting to complete my stamp collection, or to attend next season's production of *Macbeth*, will do. Our categorical desires may also change over time, but each one suffices to make life seem worth living to us while we have it. Williams presents these desires as answering the question about whether to go on living to a rational person contemplating suicide.[19] He grants that there are plenty of non-rational suicides, but suggests that there are rational ones as well, and rational people who contemplate it and decide against it. And he maintains that it may be perfectly rational for a person in such a position to decide to go on living in order to satisfy even a fairly small desire. In that case, he says, the project of satisfying the desire suffices to give the person's life a point, a meaning: the person exists at that moment in order to satisfy the desire, rather than seeking satisfaction in order to go on existing. No such desire could be conditional on the person's continuing to exist, since it settles the question of *whether* he is to continue to exist.

As is often the case with Williams, it is a bit unclear exactly what he is arguing against. I think he is giving at least a partial answer to the question of whether life is worthwhile, and of what might make it worthwhile, but his more immediate target is probably someone who, faced with Aristotle's question about "whether we choose life for the sake of pleasure or pleasure for the sake of life" (NE X.4; 1175^{a}17–19), opts for the latter alternative, someone who holds that pleasure is nothing more than a means that has evolved to keep animals, including human animals, seeking the things they need in order to survive and reproduce. In that case, as we have seen, there would be a sort of illusion in the impression that pleasures could possibly give any meaning or value to life. All desires would merely serve life, and it would be an error to suppose that we lived in order to satisfy some of our desires. Williams says that this cannot be right, else a person contemplating suicide could not rationally decide that it is worth living in order to satisfy one of her desires.

But it is not as clear as Williams suggests that the satisfaction of a particular desire settles the question of whether to live, even for Williams's rational contemplator of suicide. Suppose the would-be suicide does not see any good reason for going on—she has gotten to this place, perhaps, after the failure of some important ground project— but cannot bring herself to the point of taking her own life out of religious and moral qualms about committing suicide, or a fear of death.[20] As long as any of her qualms or fears are rational, however, it is also rational for her to treat a very little desire to go on as enough to put aside the contemplation of suicide. Indeed, it would be rational for her to *cultivate* such a desire in herself if she lacks one. She might, for instance, picture vividly how tasty tomorrow's croissant will be, to try to arouse in herself a desire to live until breakfast. If she fears death, or thinks she ought not bring about her own death, one problem she faces is that her lack of interest in living may make her virtually *unable* to go on, and to get over that she needs some desire to see the next day. A desire to meet a friend, teach a class, eat at a cafe can suffice for that purpose. That doesn't make them categorical desires. She needn't by any means think that the satisfaction of these desires makes life worth living. They just provide that "little extra" to get her over the hump to the next day, once she has independent reasons to reject suicide. They are, in short, precisely desires that have a function *if* she is to go on living, not desires that, by themselves, make it reasonable *for* her to live.

Of course, it is possible to see her desire for a tasty breakfast as a reason to live, rather than just part of the causal mechanism helping her go on living. But that need not be how it figures in her deliberations. She may not see any reason to live, just a reason not to die (or to die *that* way), which is a very different thing. The desire that enables her to go on living is in that case an instrumental desire, not a categorical one.

The point here is that even someone who supposes that he or she has been led away from suicide by a categorical desire may actually be acting on an instrumental desire instead. To know, even of oneself, that one has not thus confused the status of one's own desire, one would have to know that one's reasons for not committing suicide were *not* fear of death, or a lingering moral or religious qualm about taking one's own life. But these sorts of thoughts can seem cowardly or confused, so it's very easy to delude oneself about whether one is acting on them. Consequently, it's very difficult to know, even in one's own case, whether anyone ever has categorical desires.

There is an additional doubt to be raised about Williams's ground projects, even supposing that we have them. In his "Critique of Utilitarianism," Williams distinguishes a ground project, which he here calls a "commitment," from a run-of-the-mill project.[21] Commitments are projects "with which one is more deeply and extensively involved and identified," he says, projects "round which [a person] has built his life."[22] The idea seems to be that we can measure the value of our everyday projects, and determine whether it might be reasonable to give them up, in the light of our commitments. It will rarely if ever be reasonable to give up a commitment, Williams says; to do that is to give up one's integrity. We can infer, I think, that for Williams the worth of our lives will depend on how well we think we have fulfilled our commitments.

But it is not easy to see how we are supposed to draw the distinction between commitments and other projects. Williams does not explain what "deeply and extensively involved" is supposed to mean,[23] and he rejects Kantian theories of free will and philosophical views that give human nature an objective telos, like virtue or happiness or freedom. But without criteria to distinguish authentic from inauthentic choices, or to measure projects according to whether they really meet our purposes or not, it becomes impossible to determine so much as what it *means* to say that a particular project reflects a "deep and extensive" identification, or just a passing whim. Imagine an agent trying to decide whether a particular project is one of her commitments or not, at a point when she needs to invest more resources if she wants to maintain her involvement in it (whether to get another degree to continue her career, say, or whether to go into therapy with her lover, rather than ending the relationship). Absent any appeal to authentic and inauthentic ways of making choices, and of purposes that her choices ought to serve, what will tell her that the time and energy she has spent thus far on this project reflects a deep identification with it or not? How can she so much as predict whether she is likely to want to spend similar time and energy on it in the future? Williams' work as a whole can be characterized as an attempt to replace traditional groundings for ethics with what he calls "commitments": we are supposed to be able to do away with utilitarian and Kantian and Aristotelian theories about how people ought to live while still having a basis, in our commitments, for reasonable evaluative judgments. That the resulting judgments are reasonable is important to

Williams; he has no patience for the rhetoric of anti-rationalists or radical subjectivists, and always presents his doctrine of commitments as if it offers us a reasonable starting point for deliberation. But if we cannot tell so much as what our commitments *are*, cannot distinguish them from projects for which we feel (what we ourselves later regard as) a foolish and temporary enthusiasm, then this sort of grounding will yield arbitrary whimsy, not anything resembling reasonable deliberation.

29. Our second subjectivist candidate is Stoicism, which I treat here as a type of doctrine, rather than an historical school. According to this doctrine, we can see our lives as worthwhile—or relinquish the terminology of "worth"—as soon as we recognize that everything in the world must be just the way it is, and consequently give up all resentment against what happens to us, along with all hope that things will turn out differently from the way they do. The fullest expression of this sort of view is to be found in Spinoza, although the discipline needed for achieving it is better described in Epictetus or Seneca.

It may seem surprising to describe this as a subjectivist view about worth, since it depends on an objective view about the nature of the universe. It is because we cannot alter the universe that we are supposed to adjust to it, and give up on the hope that things could be other than they are. Nevertheless, in its conception of worth the view is subjectivist, for it takes the worth of our lives to rest in an *attitude* we take towards the world: an acceptance of it that allows us to see it as good. Classical Stoics added the idea that the world was run by a benevolent God, but this muddies what is distinctive in the view, which is why I take Spinoza to have spelled it out most fully. Spinoza also maintained that God exists, but for him God was identical with the universe and His goodness was not our goodness, not relative to human needs and desires. All the evil, from a human perspective, that the world contains must for Spinoza be considered as much a consequence of divine goodness as the parts of the world we ordinarily consider good. This might be seen as an abandonment of the thought that the universe is good at all, and of the notion of God. An all-powerful, eternal and all-knowing being, but one that is not "good" in the human sense of that word, seems not to fit the ordinary definition of "God." Spinoza has, therefore, often been regarded as an atheist.

But he need not be regarded quite that way. The Spinozist God or universe can be considered good in an intelligible sense as long as we can reconcile ourselves to it—and that we can do that, to a large extent at least, is Spinoza's point. If we reconcile ourselves to the universe, accept everything that happens to us and other human beings as inevitable and thus not to be regretted, then we can regard the universe as good. And coming to the position where we can do this is, Spinoza argues, the best way to achieve good moral character, the best way to calm one's lusts, anger, and impatience to the point at which one will never be inclined to harm anybody. So it is good, even in human terms, to adopt what Spinoza considers the divine perspective on goodness.

The stoic view can give plausible answers to the sorts of questions that a despairing person might ask about whether her life is worthwhile or how it should be changed to become worthwhile. The view shows how any life, no matter how externally miserable, can be accepted if the person living it understands the causal sequence that has led to her circumstances and accepts that it could not have been different. At the same time, the stoic can tell a despairing person *why* she feels the way she does. So the stoics have both a diagnosis of why we sometimes feel our lives are not worth living and a discipline to overcome that feeling. This is as much of an answer to our question about intrinsic worth as any we have seen.

Does this answer depend on faith? Spinoza doesn't think so. He believes that reason alone can answer every question human beings have, and that he himself has given a fully rational argument for both his metaphysical views and their ethical implications. And it does seem true that if we can reconcile ourselves to the universe in the way Spinoza urges us to do, we will be able to regard our lives as worthwhile, or at least to find any further question about the value of life meaningless.

But that is a big "if," and the element of the stoic view that is least well defended, in Spinoza and his predecessors, is the claim that it is *possible* for our emotions fully to follow our reason. The stoic view of emotions deserves credit for recognizing that emotions can be shaped by reason, a point that has only recently been brought back into mainstream Western philosophy.[24] Learning new facts about a situation, or seeing the motivation of the agents in that situation in a new light, will in many cases change our emotional response to it. To some extent, our emotions track facts and respond to arguments. But the stoics put too much stock—put, indeed, a non-rational faith—in the ability of reason to guide emotions. Our emotions are built to struggle with the world, to motivate us to change circumstances that cause us suffering, not to accept them. And if death really is final, and there is no compensation for the sufferings we experience in life, it may simply not be possible for us to achieve the full reconciliation with the universe that the stoics recommend. I certainly have never met anyone who has come close to such a reconciliation. So it seems to me that the stoic view, too, rests on an unargued faith—this time, in our ability to get ourselves to accept the view itself.[25]

30. We come, finally, to radical projectivism, according to which all value is spread onto the world by us, and life is consequently worthwhile if and only if we view it as such. This is probably the most common secular view of worth today, both in the general population and among philosophers.

But is there really much left to say in favour of this view—at least as an answer to our questions about the worth of life, rather than a way of dismissing them? We can offer the same objection to it that we did to the stoic: that our subjective powers are not great enough to approve their own projections, when seen solely as such, that when we turn them on themselves, they are not satisfied to find that they alone are supposed to be the source of all worth.[26] Or we could hearken back to our prompting scenarios, and recall that we fail to engage with the question asked by a couch potato or would-be suicide worried that her life is worthless if we say, "It'll be worthwhile *if you regard it* as worthwhile."

The projectivist can do better than this, however. She can say (a) that it is the projection of our *long-term* or *dispositional* desires and attitudes, not our short-term, occurrent ones that sets the standard for the intrinsically worthwhile, or (b) that the worthwhile is determined by a social, not an individual, projection. Both versions of projectivism allow for some check on our immediate subjective attitude towards our lives, for at least a quasi-objective answer to the questions of our prompting scenarios. On strategy (b) it is obvious that if, say, I projected a notion of worth based on my fondness for a life spent entirely in wild parties, I could be shown that this projection does not mesh with my society's approval of marriage, hard work, and civic engagement, and therefore have reason to regard it as mistaken. But on strategy (a), too, an individual can go wrong in particular cases about the worth of his life. I project worth, let us say, onto a life that consists in helping to bring about communism, and regard my life as worthwhile because I think I have been contributing successfully to the communist movement. Now I am shown that my contributions have been feebler than I thought, or the movement is less successful than I thought, or the goals of communism fit my basic ideals (my fundamental attitudes) more poorly than I thought. So I regard my life thus far as a failure, and my attitude that it was worthwhile as mistaken. And this possibility of error allows for a meaningful answer to the questions of our prompting scenarios. We can give content to the suggestion that Jones or Smith or Brown or Green may be making a mistake about his or her life.

Ultimately, however, these more sophisticated versions of projectivism collapse into the cruder version. To take strategy (a) first this time: what happens when I ask myself why I *should* value my long-term attitudes over my immediate ones, or my long-term projects over living for the moment? I have no higher court to appeal to than my own feelings, no basis for saying that long-term attitudes are superior to short-term ones if I don't currently feel that way. So it is hard to see why I should not switch my basis of evaluation from my long-term to my short-term attitudes, if—in the short-term— I feel like it.

Under pressure, then, the appeal to long-term attitudes against which to measure short-term ones proves to be a weak dam against the onslaught of skeptical questions about our attitudes. If I realize that my activism is not bringing communism any closer, but insist on regarding my life as worthwhile anyway, I can re-define my standards for worth such that activism itself makes life worth living, and if I realize that communism would defeat some of my own ideals, I can eliminate or redefine those ideals. Nor will this be self-delusion, since on the projectivist account, there is nothing to be deluded about. My attitudes determine what counts as worth, so when they change, what is worthwhile changes with them.

As for strategy (b), it is unclear why someone tempted to subjectivism should accept social rather than individual attitudes as the proper source of the projection that constitutes value. It is important to note a disanalogy with morality here. If we want to be projectivists in morality, we do have reason to look to socially-held rather than individually-held attitudes as the source of the relevant projection. Morality concerns how we relate to one another, and it is reasonable to suppose that attitudes widely shared in our society will generally track what is helpful and harmful to such getting along, and that sharing those attitudes will itself help us get along. The situation is entirely different when it comes to evaluating the worth of our individual lives. If I find a life my society approves of repugnant, another person might try to point out features of that life I have overlooked, or put those features in a new light for me, but if I am not convinced by any of that, it is ridiculous to say, "Well, your society approves of it so you must take it as worthwhile." My society's positive attitude towards a particular kind of life is not enough to make it worthwhile *to* me—and lives, ultimately, must be worthwhile to those who live them if they are to be worthwhile at all.

In the end, then, even sophisticated versions of projectivism reduce to a position in which there is nothing further to be said if, right now, I regard my life as worthwhile, or refuse to do so, and that amounts to a position in which there is nothing to say to a person who wonders whether her feelings on the matter are wrong-headed. But in that case it is pointless, perhaps literally meaningless, to talk of worth in application to our lives.

I have left out one very powerful modern response to our question that deserves a chapter to itself: that freedom, construed as Kant would have us construe it, bestows worth on life. I don't think Kant himself clearly held this view, but he certainly provided the materials for it—the materials, indeed, for a view of freedom that could allow it to stand in, on Aristotle's own terms, for what Aristotle regarded as our essence or telos. Although I do not think in the end it succeeds, we should not abandon our quest for a secular account of ultimate worth without considering this possibility. The following chapter, accordingly, is devoted to it.

5

Kantian Accounts of Worth

31. Part of what makes Kant an important resource for us is that he provided the materials for the most plausible secular account of ultimate worth since the demise of Aristotelian teleology. Understanding where it goes wrong will therefore help clear the way for the central claim of this book—that reason alone cannot establish the worth of life. But the materials we can glean from Kant are also useful because they help us lay out, more precisely than we have done thus far, what the criteria for an adequate account of worth might look like.

I speak of "materials we can glean from Kant's writings," and the title of this chapter refers to Kant*ian* approaches to worth, because I am not sure that Kant himself thought we could rationally demonstrate that life was worth living. Often, he indicates instead that this is one of the things reserved for faith, for reasons not unlike my own.

Of course, Kant does say that every rational being has absolute worth. But is that meant to be an answer to the question we have been asking, about the worth of a rational being's *life*? Does the absolute worth that we assume for the purposes of morality also help us answer telic questions? I shall argue here that to the extent that Kant intends the moral absolute worth of persons to answer telic questions, his answer depends on the most controversial, metaphysically-laden aspects of his system. As we have seen earlier (Part II, Chapter 5), Kant is also uneasy about resting the value of our lives on rationality alone, and sometimes suggests that life cannot be worthwhile unless some form of religious teaching is true. So even if one accepts Kant's metaphysics, one may not be able to see rationality alone as making our lives worthwhile.

32. Kant's claim that all rational beings have absolute worth is one of the most famous elements of his *Groundwork* (G 428, 435). He is not precisely concerned with the *life led* by a rational being when he says this, however, and it is not impossible that a being of absolute worth could have a life that lacks worth. What Kant means by saying that rational beings have absolute worth may be just that respect for rational beings

must constrain what we do to them; his point may just be another way of putting the importance of treating rational beings always as ends and not merely as means.

But it is unlikely that Kant's point is so restricted. For his claim that rational beings have absolute worth arises in the course of a search for the proper end of rational action, and is meant to show us that we can and must take the fostering of our own rational agency as an end in everything we do. We have seen that one of the main functions of the claim that a quality or activity makes our lives worthwhile is to set us an ultimate end, and thereby organize our other ends. Kant clearly wants his claim that rationality has absolute worth to function that way. So it seems fair to say that for Kant the mere fact that we are rational makes our lives worth living. We might add that his argument for the absolute worth of rational beings closely resembles Aristotle's argument for why we need a telos. Both Kant and Aristotle say that since we have relative ends, and relative ends make no sense unless they back up to an absolute end, we must also have an absolute end. The similarity of these arguments suggests that practical reason is for Kant what contemplative reason is for Aristotle: the characteristic human activity that is worth carrying out in itself and that gives worth to the rest of our lives.[1]

In addition, Kant tells us explicitly in a number of other places that fostering our capacity for rational agency must be a central goal of all our activity, and that realizing that capacity gives our lives worth. In the *Critique of Judgment,* human rationality is indeed described as the ultimate purpose not just of our lives, but of the universe, as what makes the entire universe worthwhile (CJ § 82, 426–427). And in RWB, becoming moral, bringing one's inclinations as fully as possible under the control of practical reason, is presented as the true meaning of salvation in Christ. Indeed, Kant sometimes hints, here and in the first two *Critiques,* that insofar as we act purely on practical reason, we are identical with God.[2] Again, the echo of Aristotle is striking: practical reason is a divine as well as a human activity, as contemplative reason is for Aristotle. And it is reasonable to suppose that for Kant, as for Aristotle, divine activity is the very model of intrinsically worthwhile activity.

Of course, Kant makes clear that the mere *possession* of reason does not suffice to bestow worth on one's life. We need to *cultivate* our rationality, to develop it and give it mastery over our desires, in order to achieve our proper telos. So the absolute worth of every rational being does not immediately entail that every rational being leads an equally worthwhile life. Some people live for happiness, for instance, yet Kant holds that "The value life has for us if it is assessed merely by what one enjoys . . . [is l]ess than zero" (CJ 434n). Only a life that strives to "liberat[e] the will from the despotism of desires" can be intrinsically worthwhile (ibid. 432). But even a person who doesn't conduct his life in this way—whose life has a sub-zero value—is of absolute worth. The mere possession of a capacity to reason is sufficient to earn a rational being respect as an end in himself, but not sufficient to give his life absolute worth. Rather, the worth of our capacity to reason seems to be an indication, for Kant, that the worth of our lives depends on the development of that capacity: he takes absolute value in its moral sense to be the basis for absolute value in its telic sense.

Thus, the absolute worth of rationality in the *Groundwork* does in part function to help answer the telic questions we have been exploring. Nevertheless, it is far from clear whether Kant regards rationality as constituting the value of our lives by itself. As we saw at the end of Part II, he speaks of the highest good as consisting in more than rationality. Even if we allow that our highest good has components other than rationality, however, developing our rational capacities certainly seems to be enough, for Kant, to give our lives *some* value. I will argue that Kant is not entitled to this conclusion. Rationality may be a necessary condition for the worth of life, but it is not a sufficient one; our lives may lack worth even if we have fully developed our rational capacities.

33. Critics of Kantianism often begin with a contemporary defender of Kant and then move back to Kant's own position.[3] Their point is to show that Kant's views actually fare worse, not better, when they are stripped of the metaphysical baggage that his contemporary defenders like to unload. I think this is a useful strategy, and will therefore address the account of worth in Christine Korsgaard's *Sources of Normativity*, before returning to the *Groundwork*.

Korsgaard has written what may well be the deepest and most exciting defense of Kantian morality since Kant's own writings. She also revises Kant in ways that seem very appealing. She gives pain and pleasure a direct role in moral deliberation, for instance, by understanding them as expressions of reasons. Relatedly, she gives life, not only rationality, an absolute value, drawing on Aristotle to suggest that rationality is just the way the basic drive of living things to preserve their identity expresses itself in us (SN 152, 156). All claims of value, for Korsgaard as for Kant, flow from our identity as rational beings. But our rationality depends on our being alive, so our claims of value also flow from our identity as living things. Indeed, life now becomes the ultimate source of value: and for that reason valuable in itself. We must regard life as valuable, on pain of losing our ability to make sense of the notion of value at all. Korsgaard uses this line of argument to gloss Wittgenstein's remark, "If suicide is allowed then everything is allowed" (SN 131, 162–163). Life is the condition for all value, so anyone willing to take his own life must have abandoned evaluation altogether: "[R]emaining alive is not so much a value as a condition of all value" (SN 162).

Korsgaard's point here in part dovetails nicely with the position I defend in this book. No-one can be argued into seeing life as valuable, she suggests; the value of life lies instead at a point beyond the reach of reason. But she wants to add, as I do not, that there is, nonetheless, a certain irrationality in not valuing our lives, at least if we value anything else. She denies the possibility of separating local from global ends on which I have been relying (see especially Part II, § 43). Ends belong together in a single hierarchy, for her, so anyone who rejects the value of rationality, and life, must be a "complete . . . normative sceptic" (SN 163). And a complete normative sceptic cannot so much as properly act, cannot direct his movements by rational deliberation. A complete value skeptic "does not really have any *ends*, since his desires do not provide him with reasons" (SN 163; her italics). The life of a value skeptic turns out to be one of utter aimlessness and thoughtlessness, a life in which we lose all ability to direct ourselves—cease, perhaps, to *have* a self at all.[4]

But this seems just false. Surely there are many value skeptics who nevertheless pursue ends in their everyday activities, and reason about how to achieve those ends. Other people keep going in life just because they are afraid to die; that does not mean they lose the ability to reason about what to do. Or we keep going because we are willing to follow our local desires, accept them without questioning them further; that again does not mean that we cease to deliberate rationally. Korsgaard's brilliant rhetorical and argumentative skills can lead one to forget these points, but anyone who steps out of her framework for a moment is likely to suspect that there must be something about her use of the terms "value," "reason," and "end" that is too heavily front-loaded with the conclusion she expects to reach, obscuring some of the meanings those words have in ordinary life. Only on some understandings of those terms, not on all, does reasonably holding one value, or pursuing one end, entail that we integrate all our values and ends into a systematic whole. Only on some understandings of those terms, therefore, do we have to accept the regresses into which Korsgaard wants to draw us.

34. Are Korsgaard's regresses then not built into the very nature of reason?

Korsgaard tells us that we can't stop, in our reflections, at the notion that we simply care about this or that desire or project. We need reasons to endorse the desires and projects themselves, and when we find such reasons in our practical identities, we need further reasons to endorse those identities. So the process of reflecting on our actions pulls us back from endorsing a particular action, to endorsing a practical identity, to endorsing the rational nature that has enabled us to reflect at all. Reason itself demands that we keep reasoning, for Korsgaard, until we find intrinsic value in our nature as rational beings.

But does reason really make these demands? Questions *can* keep being asked at each level of reflection, but they *need* not be asked. Our reasoning can just come to an end. Wittgenstein, one of Korsgaard's favorite philosophers, famously gave reasons *for* reason to come to an end if we are to justify anything.[5] Perhaps reasoning needs to be grounded in something non-rational, or perhaps it simply can and should stop at some point. No non-circular argument can be given for taking each reason to require a further reason behind it.[6]

In practice, this point has significant implications for whether a person who refuses to endorse the value of humanity is being irrational or not (see SN 120–123). Korsgaard says that rational action would be impossible if we didn't endorse our humanity:

If you had no normative conception of your identity, you could have no reasons for action, and because your consciousness is reflective, you could then not act at all. Since you cannot act without reasons and your humanity is the source of your reasons, you must value your own humanity if you are to act all. (SN 123; see also 164)

But like the analogous claim about rational deliberation being impossible if we don't value our lives, this can't be true. Or if it is, it must mean something different from what it seems to mean. For it seems to mean either that people who don't value their own humanity literally cannot act, cannot direct their movements by reason—and the cannibalistic murderer Jeffrey Dahmer would seem to be evidence enough that *that's* not true—or that they, in fact, value their humanity even if everything they say and do suggests that they do not. If a Jeffrey Dahmer wishes he were a man-eating animal of some other species, says and thinks that he hates his humanity and expresses that hatred in as full an attack on human beings as one could imagine, do we still have to say that his actions, by being actions at all, show that he values his humanity? If so, "value" will have lost its meaning.

But if not, then we need an argument to show that even a Jeffrey Dahmer, insofar as he is rational, *ought* to value his humanity.[7] We need to show he is irrational unless he engages in "a further stretch of reflection" (119, 152), that he has "stop[ped] too soon" (161) in his reflective work. What could possibly show this? Does reflection intrinsically require more reflection? Certainly not, if by "reflection" we mean the ordinary empirical process we engage in when we think about what to do. Often, reflection tells us precisely to break off reflection, to go out and act instead. If reflection is constituted by reason in the full-bodied Kantian sense, on the other hand, perhaps it does have a requirement to continue reasoning built into it. (Although Kant himself suggests, in CPR, that the search for the unconditioned leads us to antinomies.[8]) But why suppose that ordinary practical reflection, the sort of reflection that is supposed to issue in decisions, should take this full-bodied, potentially endless form?

What we need is a distinction between the minimal rationality that even a Jeffrey Dahmer must have and the full-blown rationality that would condemn that minimal rationality as inadequate. And with that in hand we would need an argument for why anyone engaging in minimal rationality should step back to the more full-blown version instead. Korsgaard implies that reason alone *forces* us to take that step, that minimal rationality itself demands that we adopt full-blown rationality. But that seems just untrue.

35. At the most fundamental level, what leads Korsgaard to represent us as forced into her regresses, what leads her to represent the Kantian position as entailed by a strict logical argument from premises assumed by anyone who values anything, is that she cannot appeal, as Kant himself does, to the attractiveness of free will. Korsgaard is a compatibilist. Unlike Kant, she thinks we can see ourselves as free from the perspective of deliberation while simultaneously granting that we are determined from the perspective of scientific explanation (SN 94–97, 124–125). "Determinism is no threat to freedom," she says (95). But this overlooks the power of a thought that suggests itself quite naturally *within* the deliberative perspective. We may put that thought as follows:

"I know that my reason tells me to follow the moral law rather than just grabbing objects of my immediate desires. But why should I listen to my reason? Scientists tell me that what I call 'reason' is just a mechanism that has developed within me in order to help my species survive. If so, however, then the idea that my reason expresses who I truly am is surely just one more illusion to get me to pursue the goals that my biology has set for me. A sort of 'trick' is being played on me (perhaps by my own biology, but that doesn't make it less of a trick): I am being led to think that I am pursuing various lofty ends while I am really doing nothing more than helping the human species keep going. Why should I give up what immediately appeals to me for *that*?"[9] Kant worries a great deal about thoughts of this kind, noting that we may suspect that all the justifications we can give for the importance of reason are "only high-flown fancy" if reason is really nothing more than a tool implanted in us by nature (G 394–395). We want some assurance that reason is, or at least might be, independent of all other ends, that it expresses a freedom transcending all the purposes that science may tell us are implanted within us. The scientific viewpoint, by the evidence it provides for the heteronomous function of reason, as well as by its general support for determinism, threatens our ability to continue endorsing our reflective norms. What we learn from the theoretical standpoint can leach into the deliberative one, undermining our confidence in reason's very claim to be intrinsically valuable. That is why Kant rejects compatibilism,[10] arguing by way of his Third Antinomy, and other arguments in the *Groundwork* and second *Critique*, for the reasonableness of positing a radically incompatibilist conception of free will, which transcends and can trump all our biologically implanted purposes. A freedom that appeared to us from the deliberative standpoint, but could be shown theoretically to be part of nature would, he says, be "no better than the freedom of a turnspit, which when once wound up also carries out its motions of itself." The grip of morality is impossible without "transcendental freedom in its proper meaning" (CPrR 97). Kant considers the practical and the theoretical perspectives to be far more deeply intertwined with one another than they are for Korsgaard.

Accordingly, Kant has a better answer to the temptations that might lead us not to care about our freedom. Freedom is far more plausibly conceived as an intrinsic good when we see it as something transcendental than when we treat it in the common-sense way that Korsgaard does. Transcendental freedom appears noble, exciting, something we can be proud to express. The limited freedom, or appearance of freedom, that even a determinist can allow us is much harder to see that way. Transcendental freedom is therefore far more plausibly an ultimate value and source of other values than is Korsgaard's compatibilist freedom. Accordingly, Kant's own views are more appealing than Korsgaard's. Korsgaard's attempt to move us from minimal rationality to reason in the full-blown sense is unconvincing because it is hard to endorse full-blown reason unless we can *care* about it. To value something is at least in essential part to care about it, and what we need, to give reason ultimate value, is to care more about it than about anything else.[11] Korsgaard makes the importance of reason to us seem instead to be a matter of inevitability: once we have embarked on the course of rational reflection, we will be led inexorably to seeing ourselves as rational beings first and foremost. On this picture, we feel compelled to identify with reason, not drawn to do so; reason forces us to follow it. But reason does not have to work that way, especially in the practical sphere. It can cajole us, present us with ways of seeing things as good, rather than compelling us.[12] And if we are to endorse reason as the source of our deepest identity, it would help if we could find some way of being drawn to it, of seeing it as the object of our deepest yearnings. Kant himself comes much closer to doing this than Korsgaard does. It is time to turn to him.

36. Here is the passage from the *Groundwork* in which Kant says that rational beings have an absolute worth:

The ends that a rational being proposes at his discretion . . . (material ends) are all only relative; for only their . . . relation to a . . . faculty of desire on the part of the subject gives them their worth[. This worth] can therefore furnish no universal principles, no principles valid and necessary for all rational beings . . . But suppose there were something the existence of which in itself has an absolute worth, something which as an end in itself could be a ground of determinate laws; then in it, and in it alone, would lie the ground of a possible categorical imperative, that is, of a practical law. Now, I say, . . . every rational being exists as an end in itself and not merely as a means . . . All objects of inclinations have only a conditional worth; for if there were not inclinations and the needs based on them, their object would be without worth. . . . [On the other hand], rational beings are called "persons" because their nature already marks them out as an end in itself, that is, as something that may not be used merely as a means . . . These, therefore, are not merely subjective ends . . . but rather objective ends, that is, beings the existence of which is in itself an end, and indeed such that no other end, to which they would serve merely as means, can be put in its place, since without it nothing of absolute worth would be found anywhere; but if all worth were conditional and therefore contingent, then no supreme practical principle for reason could be found. (G 428)

There is a parallel passage, a few pages later (G 434–436). Here, Kant says that material things have a "price" or a "relative worth," while morality has "dignity" or an "intrinsic worth," which is "infinitely beyond any price." He defends this claim with a little argument that clarifies 428 as well: "[N]othing can have a worth other than that which the law determines for it. But the lawgiving itself, which determines all worth, must for that very reason have a dignity, that is, an unconditional, incomparable worth."

In the first passage, the value of rational beings seems to be at stake; in the second, value is attributed to a certain process—lawgiving—in which rational beings engage. But it is essential to rational beings that they give laws, for Kant, so I think we can set aside this difference. More importantly, in the first passage rationality alone seems to be of absolute worth, while in the second, rational beings get that worth only if they are moral. But we learn, at the beginning of *Groundwork* III, that rationality and morality reciprocally imply one another, so this difference too doesn't make much difference. Insofar as we are rational, which is to say insofar as we are moral, our existence is absolutely worthwhile. We need not learn anything, love anything, or experience anything outside ourselves to achieve such worth.

I leave unquestioned here the equation between rationality and morality. What interests me is whether either one suffices to bestow absolute worth on our lives. Since Kant's argument focuses on the rational side of the equation, I will explore whether simply being rational is enough to give our lives absolute worth.

37. Two main arguments, it seems to me, run through the above passages. They are not clearly presented, and it is unclear whether both are needed to make the point Kant wants to make. It is also unclear whether Kant was aware that he had two separate arguments. And both these arguments yield a position with problems similar to the ones we saw in Korsgaard.

But in addition to the two main arguments, there is an appeal to the "dignity," the "incomparable" value of reason, which is I think tied to the sublimity that Kant sees in transcendental freedom. We shall see in a while that this appeal may do more work for Kant than do his official arguments.[13]

The first of the official arguments runs as follows:

(1) Morality needs something of absolute worth to take as an absolute end. The end of every act determines how it ought to be carried out. So without an absolute end, there could be no absolute law for action. If the absolute end at which the law of rational action aimed lay outside the process of morality itself, however— if it depended on our inclinations, for instance—then the law would be heteronomous.[14] So the only thing that can play the morally necessary role of being an absolute end is the process of moral thinking itself—the process of rationally determining how to act.

The second argument at first sight looks quite independent of the first:

(2) Things have worth (value), ordinarily, if they are prized by a valuing being; without valuing beings, they would have no worth. But the worth of such things is then always *relative to* the favorable view of that thing held by a valuing being; they have "relative worth" or "price," bestowed by a "faculty of desire in the subject." It might seem, then, that there can be no absolute worth. The notion of worth would seem to require relativity to worth-bestowing beings, and "absolute worth" would seem to be an oxymoron. But it turns out also to be part of the notion of worth that without something of absolute worth, there can be no worth at all. Unless there is something of absolute worth, there will be nothing with even relative worth. But by hypothesis there are things with relative worth. So there must be something of absolute worth. By definition, that thing, whatever it is, cannot get its worth merely by relation to a subjective faculty; otherwise its value would again be relative rather than absolute. Where, then, could absolute worth possibly lie except in the process of bestowing worth

itself, the faculty by which other things get their relative worth? Again, absolute worth consists in the process of rationality itself, but here considered as the process that evaluates things, rather than the process that determines action.[15]

One advantage this second argument has over the first one is that it does not depend on any strictly moral premises, only on premises about what is needed for evaluation.

38. How good are these arguments? At first glance, (1) seems quite weak. If morality depends on there being something of absolute worth, the conclusion we should draw if we have trouble finding such a thing might just as reasonably be that morality is illusory as that there is in fact something of absolute worth. But Kant regards morality as equivalent to rational action, and his point in both (1) and (2) might be put by saying that without something of absolute worth, no *rational action* would be possible. "If all worth is conditional and thus contingent, no supreme practical principle for reason could be found anywhere," he says. Since he thinks that all practical principles must ultimately be grounded in a supreme such principle, that implies that reason could then find no guide for itself at all. The idea is roughly this: To call something an end is to say that it has worth. This worth can be either relative or absolute, but all relative worth must ultimately be grounded in something of absolute worth. So if there is nothing of absolute worth, there is nothing of worth at all. But if there is nothing of worth at all, there are no ends for us to pursue. Reason, however, must always act for an end,[16] so if there are no ends, there is no rational action. Since there is rational action, there must also be rational ends. Hence there must also be some end of absolute worth. QED.[17]

Understood this way, the argument looks invincible—but also smacks of sleight of hand. Can the mere fact that we reason about what to do be enough to show that there is something of absolute worth in the world? Surely not—surely it is possible that we could discover that there is nothing of absolute worth, or that the idea of absolute worth makes no sense, but still reason about what to do after coming to that conclusion. The amoralist who decides that only superstition leads people to believe in morality still seems to use his reason when he deliberates about how to grab pleasures that come his way.

Kant might respond by stipulating that a plan of action will *count* as rational only if it sets ends for itself that are grounded in an end of absolute worth—so the amoralist will count as irrational despite appearances to the contrary—or he might say that the amoralist, despite appearances, implicitly *does* believe there is something of absolute worth. But to retreat to stipulation would be to concede that there is no good argument for tying reason to worth, and to insist that all rational beings implicitly believe in absolute worth even if they deny it, and provide arguments against it, is to run up against the normal uses of the word "believe" enough that the thesis, thus defended, becomes empty.

Kant's position as we have described it thus far is much like Korsgaard's (unsurprisingly, since Korsgaard's derives from it), and I suggest we respond to it by distinguishing again between weaker and stronger senses of "rational." In the full-blown Kantian sense of that word, it certainly cannot be applied to an action with an end the agent herself regards as worthless. Nor does one have to be a committed Kantian to find the intuitions behind this use of the word plausible. There is something bizarre about pursuing something one regards as worthless, and one would expect a fully rational person who had a choice between doing that and pursuing an end she regards as worthwhile to go for the latter. But there is a weaker sense of rationality in which the person who chooses the worthless over the worthwhile can be called "rational": that is why we *blame* her for that choice, why indeed we describe her as "choosing," instead of viewing her action as we might the movements of a tree, a fly, or a neonate.[18] It may follow that fully rational action is impossible without something to regard as of absolute worth—but then fully rational action may just *be* impossible. More weakly rational action—action steered by reason in some sense, but with an ineliminably arbitrary component—will still be possible, and that is all we need to make sense of how people behave. If rational action, and the deliberation that precedes it, require that every aspect of one's actions meet with reason's approval, then many ordinary actions are not rational, and rational action may be impossible. If our ordinary doings do count as rational actions, and thereby prove that reason can guide action, then reason demands far less of us than Kant would like to insist.

39. It is not just plausible but I think correct to say that rationality in the weak sense is a necessary condition for worth; this is a Kantian insight that we will want to take with us in our further explorations of the subject. Surely nothing could make my life worth living of which I was unaware, or of which I resolutely disapproved. If my body were to participate in an event while I was asleep or in a coma, that event, by itself, could not possibly give my life value; it could do so only if I someday became aware of it or its effects. And if I know that an event of some sort is happening to me, but disapprove of it—before it happens, while it is happening, and after it happens, to the end of my existence as a conscious being—then it is foisted on me, rather than something I value; it is not of worth *to me*. Nothing can be of worth to me unless *I* value it. Certainly, I could not take it as my end otherwise, could not orient my life around it.[19] Kant puts this point very well: "I can . . . be constrained by others to perform *actions* that are directed as means to an end, but I can never be constrained by others *to have an end*; only I myself can *make* something my end."[20] And the "I" in this passage is a rational being, at least in the weak sense of rationality: a being who can argue, and whose choices, including the choice to approve or disapprove, depend in some measure on argument.

But this point shows only that I must *endorse* any end if it is to be my end, not that I must invent it, let alone constitute it out of my rational capacity. I don't even have to choose it, strictly speaking. Someone else could propose it to me, or I could be led to it by happenstance, and it could yet become my end if at some point I decide to take it as such. I could have a marriage forced on me, but later take the marriage to be my own end. I could wind up in a job by accident, but eventually come to regard it as my own end—even choose to remain in it when other jobs, more like the ones I had been hoping for, open up to me. That "only I myself can make something my end" does not mean I must initially select it and certainly not that I must create it. So it is possible that my rationality must endorse my ends, but cannot give me any ends: that it is a necessary, but not sufficient condition for something's being my end.

Perhaps we should not grant even this much? Could our ultimate end not be an extinction of our selves, or perhaps a pleasant, half-dreaming state like the one we occupy as we are about to fall asleep, in which the point is precisely the *abandonment* of conscious thought—and *a fortiori* of rationality?[21] I don't want to rule out these possibilities, but it seems to me we can insist that even an end that involves the extinction of my conscious self can only be *my* end if I endorse it at some point (here, presumably, before I experience it). I am inclined to think that we can insist on a stronger claim: that rationality—discursive consciousness—must be present throughout our experience of whatever it is that might constitute absolute worth, that nothing can be absolutely worthwhile for us unless we, as rational beings, are there to experience it. But I will not insist on this, since the weaker claim already entails that our rationality is absolutely worthwhile if anything is, which is what I think Kant got right.

40. We've now arrived at the conditional claim that rationality is absolutely worthwhile if anything is. This is considerably weaker than Kant's claims. It could still turn out that nothing, including rationality, is absolutely worthwhile, or that what is *most* worthwhile is not rationality itself.

Some Kantians might want to say that *only* rationality can be absolutely worthwhile. Kant himself did not say this. But understanding rationality alone to be absolutely worthwhile would have the Kantian advantage of making it not depend on anything outside itself for its worth, of making worth autonomous, just as choice and evaluation are supposed to be. One might also defend such a position by noting that absolute worth is supposed to set an ultimate goal for all choices, a goal that would settle conflicts among our other goals. It would seem to follow that absolute worth should be located in just one thing. So if rationality is absolutely worthwhile, then it should be the only thing that is absolutely worthwhile. All worth should bottom out in it.

I doubt that the sort of irreducible pluralism about ends advocated by Isaiah Berlin and Charles Taylor, among others, can be so easily dismissed,[22] but even if we could rule out pluralism about final ends, it would take an oddly narrow understanding of monism to end up in the position described above. Even if there can be only one condition with absolute worth, so as to settle disputes over other things of worth, rationality might be just a component of that condition, rather than the whole of it. Rationality itself has components of a sort. It comprises the ability to formulate propositions as well as the ability to draw inferences from them; it comprises different kinds of inferential skills; it probably also includes the ability to form concepts and perhaps to notice certain kinds of empirical data and grasp their salience. So to posit rationality as having absolute worth is already to understand the worthwhile as composite. Why, then, could the composition not be a larger whole, of which rationality was but one part? Why could rational love, say, or the rational love *of* God or art or philosophy, not serve as an adequately unified end?

Of course with such an end we would not be autonomous in the full Kantian sense. As long as we chose the love in question, we would be autonomous in *some* sense—the more minimal sense I have proposed—but our end-setting would not be self-sufficient in the way that advocates of "rationality alone" want our ends to be. I would not achieve my end just by *being* rational. If my end were rational love of God, say, I would fail of my end if there were no God to love. If my end were the rational love of art, I would fail of it if there were no art. My rationality would be a part of the absolute end I sought, but if the other part did not exist, I would have no absolute end. And in that case, my rationality would not retain its absolute worth. Its absolute worth would be contingent on the existence of the whole of which it was a part. It would be absolutely valuable *if* anything was, but it could turn out that nothing was.

It is this position that I think we should hold, and it is this position, only, to which Kant is entitled.

41. In his moral theory, Kant characteristically turns necessary conditions into sufficient ones. Kant took the process of rational deliberation that many theorists before him had agreed was a necessary condition for moral agency and insisted that it was also a sufficient condition. *Voilà*: autonomous ethics, a moral system for which religions, traditions, and theories of human nature are all unnecessary.

But can reason really provide the whole content of morality? That's hard to say. Debate over whether Kant's categorical imperative can yield significant moral pre-scriptions or not has been going on for 200 years now. Let's suppose that it can. Even then, trouble will arise when we ask after the point of the moral realm as a whole. A complete moral system includes deliberation, assessment, and end-setting. We need to choose our actions; we need to evaluate them (and those of others) after they have been taken; and we need for each of these actions, and the whole they form, to have ends. And the last of these tasks requires a holistic perspective for which reason is poorly suited. It seems at least possible to deliberate over individual actions, and to assess them after they have been taken, using the categorical imperative alone. The idea that that imperative, or any other expression of reason, could alone give us our ends, is harder to swallow.

Of course, the three tasks are not easy to separate. Deliberation and assessment are tightly interwoven. Our judgments of past actions inform our deliberations over actions now before us, and the outcomes of our deliberations affect how we will judge similar acts in the future. Deliberation and assessment are also interwoven with end-setting: it is hard to deliberate over an action that seems pointless, and we assess pointless actions negatively.

But the interweaving with end-setting is not all that tight. Rationality can suspend the point of an action in its deliberations and assessments; this is, in fact, crucial to the way Kant arrives at the categorical imperative. We often suspend the point of actions in everyday life. My boss tells me to fill out a certain form and I do it without seeing the point of what I'm doing. Or I work for a political campaign and carry out chores passed down to me by higher-ups without knowing, let alone agreeing to, the purposes of many of these tasks. I carry out religious duties, or do favors for friends, in much the same spirit. In all these cases, I of course still have purposes for acceding to my boss, my religion, or my friends, but those are not the purposes of the tasks in question. Alone they would not give a point to those tasks, and in some cases (when, say, the tasks could reasonably be expected to hurt my company or religion) might even lead me not to carry out the tasks. What happens when we are given tasks in such contexts, generally, is that we *defer* the question of whether a particular action properly has a point and perform it anyway as an expression of a professional or political or personal loyalty. So purposes can be deferred, put out of sight, at particular moments, and some acts can fairly be described as performed out of duty, rather than for a purpose.

This does not mean that deliberation ever loses sight of purposes altogether. I use the word "deferred" advisedly. It may be rational not to look for the purpose of many particular acts, but at some point the roles or commitments that lead us to particular acts do deserve questioning, and a rational person cannot forever defer the question of what roles and commitments belong in her life. Otherwise, these roles and commitments are not properly hers; she has not freely chosen them.

It is this last sort of concern that leads Kant to his categorical imperative. For Kant, duties to bosses and religious communities and even friends are, as such, merely heteronomous. Truly autonomous duties must spring from freedom, and our ultimate duty should be to freedom alone. But with this alteration, Kant's argument for the first formulation of the categorical imperative looks much like the kind of consideration that leads us to perform a task for a job or campaign without questioning its purpose. I must decide whether to keep a particular promise or not—say, a promise to have dinner with a friend. I *may* think about the likely effects of keeping my promise versus the likely effects of not keeping it: the effects on my relationship with my friend, on my character, even on promise-keeping in general. I *may* do this, but I need not. It is not irrational to set all these effects aside, and according to Kant, I can only be truly free— free of the coerciveness of external, merely desired purposes—if I do suspend consideration of these effects. I think instead about the form of my action, and whether it is such that it could accord with a universal law of action for rational beings. According to some Kant interpreters, I cannot rationally assess whether anything could be a universal law of action for rational beings without considering the purposes such a law would serve. But even if that is true, there is a great difference between thinking about the *hypothetical* purposes a *law* would serve if it were universally followed and thinking about the *actual* purposes a *particular action* will serve. The hypothetical purposes that figure in my thinking about the former are not actual purposes I can promote by my actions. So in an important sense, just as Kant says, I can deliberate rationally over each action I perform, and assess it or a similar act performed by others, without considering the purposes it serves.

But again, the deferral of purposes must come to an end somewhere. Purposes come nested within one another, in hierarchical systems in which each serves another one further down the road, so if I feel I can endorse the entire system in which I am immersed—whether that be a system of politics or religion or a system that expresses pure rationality itself—then I do not need to find an end for each particular bit of the system.[23] One cannot rationally endorse the system as a whole, however, without asking after its ends. In the case of the Kantian system, which is conceived as embracing all other roles we inhabit and ensuring that they are taken on autonomously, the relevant whole may be *all* our actions, or the totality of actions taken by the totality of rational beings. But then that whole of rational action must have a purpose. What could that purpose possibly be? A purpose is something set over against the events or things for which it is a purpose, something at which those events or things can aim. So we cannot answer our last question by saying that the purpose of the whole of rational action is rational action itself. That would be the same as saying that rational action has *no* purpose.

It is at this point that I think Kant's attempt to draw the whole content of morality out of rationality runs into trouble. Purely rational deliberation and evaluation may be alright, but purely rational end-setting is not alright. Purposes are set, at some point, by what we *love*, what we can commit ourselves to; they are, necessarily, heteronomous: something given to us rather than made up by us. Perhaps it is true that we must autonomously endorse even these given purposes if they are truly to be ours—that much I want to accept from Kant—but that does not remove their givenness. In the end, we need rational love if we are to have purposes, and the love is no more eliminable than the rationality.[24]

42. We may reinforce this point by considering Kant's relationship to the Scottish moral sentiment theorists—Hutcheson, Hume, and Smith—who talk of moral ideals as something beautiful, something we can love. Kant admired the Scots greatly, and followed them in the structure of his moral theory, while substituting rationality in every place that they put sentiment. Thus, he agrees with the Scots that we should assess actions in accordance with the way they are intended, rather than the results they bring about, but instead of saying that those intentions should reflect benevolence, or the feelings approved by the impartial spectator, Kant says they should consist in maxims approved by reason. Relatedly, the proper way to deliberate depends for Kant on an exercise of reason, rather than on arousing any constellation of feelings within oneself (benevolent ones, as Hutcheson would have it, or the feelings required by the impartial spectator, as Smith would have it). Finally, the goal of morality as a whole is something we simply desire—happiness—for Hutcheson and Hume and Smith, while it is something that reason tells us we *ought* to desire for Kant. But the

only thing reason can tell us to desire is the furtherance of reason itself, so that must be our absolute telos, our ultimate goal.

As we have seen earlier (Part II, Chapter 5), this conclusion makes Kant himself uncomfortable; he declares, albeit without much argument, that our *full* good (*summum bonum*) must include happiness, as well as rationality. Then, in the *Critique of Judgment*, he attempts to revive at least a hope of seeing nature as purposive, and claims that we seek above all the full development of our powers (what he calls "culture" [CJ 429–430]): a higher state of ourselves that looks quite like an Aristotelian final cause. I take these moves to indicate a profound dissatisfaction with the idea that rationality alone could be the telos of our lives.

The parallel with the Scots helps explain this dissatisfaction. Kant substitutes reason for sentiment in the way we make decisions, the way we assess decisions, and the way we determine the goal of our decisions and assessments. But while it is not so hard to see how choice and assessment might be entirely rational processes, it is extremely hard to see how anything could serve as our ultimate end unless it satisfied every aspect of our selves, not just our reason. Choice and assessment can be piecemeal, as we have seen, considering actions one at a time while deferring the ends of those actions, or setting provisional ends for them in accordance with the demands of duty. Correspondingly, they can rely on one aspect of our identity—reason, for instance—and leave the question of who we are as a whole up to our end-setting capacity. End-setting cannot be piecemeal in this way, is not tied to the taking of any particular action, and must consider the demands of our entire identity, not just our identity as rational beings. Among other things, our sentiments must come into the picture: indeed, it is hard to find a better term for the relationship we want to have to our ultimate end than "love." At the end of the day, we will not see our lives as worthwhile unless we can love them. But love is in crucial part passive, a reaction to something given: it cannot simply be willed. So the idea that we could love the bare process of making choices and assessing them, that we could love our own wills, is implausible in a way that the idea that we can act on that process is not. Love is essentially other-directed, essentially heteronomous, in a way that deliberation and assessment are not. To compose an adequate picture of our ends, Kant needs to retain some of the Scots' sentimentalism, even if he can manage without that for an adequate picture of action. We need a rational love in relation to our overall purpose, and there will have to be an affective, passive component to this love.[25]

43. Let's return now to the passage from the *Groundwork* quoted in § 36. It may be that Kant misses the weakness of his main arguments for the absolute value of rationality (1 and 2 in § 37) because he is implicitly appealing to one or both of two subsidiary considerations, showing that rationality is indeed something we can love:

(3) The first is a view of freedom as good in itself that Kant shared with, indeed helped to inspire among, many late 18th and early 19th-century writers, artists,

and political activists. Rationality simply *is* freedom, for Kant, and has absolute worth because freedom has absolute worth. It is a mistake, however, to try to explain why we value freedom absolutely, because any such explanation, by the very nature of explanation, will have to posit a condition that leads us to take an interest in freedom, and any such posit would reduce freedom to something unfree, make it serve something outside of itself (G 432–433, 463). Instead of seeking such an explanation, we should realize that every time we make clear to ourselves what freedom is we can *see* that it is the one thing above all we most admire and want. Kant either says things along these lines or tries to bring us to say them for ourselves in his tale of the criminal who wishes to be free of the inclinations that have led him to act badly (G 454–455), his account of respect for the law in the second *Critique* and of sublimity in the third *Critique*, his interpretation of the resurrected Christ in RWB as freedom rising out of the death of our emotion-driven selves, and his hints, beginning with the Third Antinomy in the *Critique of Pure Reason* and running throughout his writings, that to act freely is to act like God.[26] These purple passages anticipate, and helped to inspire, Schiller's glorification of fighters for political freedom in *William Tell*, Goethe's description of humanity as "the little god of the world" in *Faust* (Part I, l, 281), and Beethoven's odes to freedom in the overture and Prisoners' Chorus of *Fidelio*. For all of these figures—as for the early Marx, who was indebted to both Kant and Goethe[27]—freedom releases everything exciting and admirable in human nature; if one has it alone, the whole of one's life is worthwhile. It's interesting that Mozart's *Don Giovanni* was almost exactly contemporaneous with Kant's *Groundwork*. *Don Giovanni* was another important source for Goethe and Beethoven, and a work that Kierkegaard and Bernard Shaw later saw, rightly I think, as providing its defiantly autonomous antihero (not autonomous in Kant's sense, of course!) with music suggestive of a supernatural power. It also contains a short but spirited paean to freedom ("*Viva la liberta!*"). The idea was in the air that, if we could all just free ourselves from political and social oppression, we would see our existence as having infinite and absolute value.

Indeed, it was virtually dogma, by this point in the Enlightenment, to regard freedom as the key to all other human goods. What Kant adds is that freedom is valuable in *itself*, not just instrumentally so. One can imagine him arguing, "If Mozart could stir us so powerfully to share Don Giovanni's joy in what he called '*liberta*,' which consisted in nothing but drinking and promiscuity, how much more should we celebrate the freedom to govern ourselves intelligently?" Or suppose he had had a chance to hear the prisoners slowly hail the light as they emerge from their dungeons in *Fidelio*, or the unearthly hymn, as Switzerland first tastes independence, that closes Rossini's *William Tell* (based on the Schiller play). We might imagine him arguing that if mere *political* freedom can so move us, how much the more must we revere *moral* freedom. If we can love libertinism and political liberty, then we must be able to love metaphysical freedom as well.

I think this a very appealing suggestion, which takes Kant beyond the dry inevitability with which we are supposed to endorse our rational nature for Korsgaard. But it depends on a series of empirical claims and, like the ones we considered when we took up erotic love and art and knowledge as possible purposes for our lives, these may well be false. Today the Romantics' love of liberty seems excessive. After a vast increase in political and social freedom that has made room, mostly, for dreary lives in pursuit of material and status goods, it seems naïve of Schiller and Beethoven and Marx to have supposed that being politically free would make life worthwhile, would lead us to create a new and wondrous human universe, and it is correspondingly harder to accept that a life of properly Kantian freedom would be absolutely valuable simply as such. An absolutely worthwhile life should be a life we could love and, unlike Kant and Beethoven, we are not inclined to love bare freedom.

(4) Kant seems to accept a version of the argument Hobbes and Spinoza had used to suggest that self-preservation was our end. This is itself a modern, metaphysically trimmed-down version of the *ergon* argument by which Aristotle established the contours of the human telos (NE I.7). If there is to be an objective human purpose against which all our subjective purposes can be measured, it seems reasonable to locate that purpose in some activity characteristic of all human beings. But once one abandons Aristotelian final causes as a part of scientific explanation, it is hard to find any activity characteristic of all human beings except the attempt to preserve oneself. So perhaps self-preservation, the effort merely to survive, should count as our telos. Human beings, like other animals, clearly take many of their actions in order to fend off death, and modern biological explanation generally assumes that the drive for survival can explain practically everything we do. One can go further, with Spinoza: it is virtually a tautology that every thing, living or not, seeks to remain that thing as long as it in fact does remain that thing.[28] And the general rule that everything seeks to maintain itself fits nicely with the laws of inertia that characterize modern physics.

Now Kant of course denies that biological survival is the be-all and end-all of our existence. Biological survival may be the end of our *human* nature, but Kant is concerned throughout his moral philosophy to show us that our *rational* nature, rather than our human nature, is what matters most to us. That said, however, Kant's moral system can be seen as giving rational survival the role that Hobbesians and Spinozists give biological survival. The fundamental law of rational nature, says Kant, is to follow rational laws, and the fundamental value, the one thing of absolute worth, for a rational being is to foster rationality itself:

rational self-preservation is the governing principle of this natural system. So, as for Hobbes and Spinoza, the goal of a thing is its own preservation; the goal is already to be found in the starting point. Such a goal is of course very different from an Aristotelian telos, although for Aristotle too, anything pursuing a telos must already contain that telos *in potentia.* The crucial difference—and it makes a great deal of difference—is that the Hobbesian, Spinozist, and Kantian teloi are contained *actually* in the thing, not merely potentially.

Which raises the question: can a true goal, a telos, take such a circular form? Is a goal not, essentially, something *outside* that of which it is the goal, something the goal-seeker can work towards rather than something it already has? If we say that our goal is just to maintain ourselves as we are, how is that different from saying we have no goal?

44. This brings us to the reaction most people today have to Kantian accounts of worth. We are free (rational) just in order to be free (rational)? That's it? How is this better than having no goal at all? Normally, we think of freedom as a condition for our ability to make choices. We think of rationality in much the same way, which gives plausibility to Kant's equation of the two. But that's to say we think of freedom, and rationality, as setting up our ability to choose *other things*; we don't think of them as what, by themselves, we choose. To be told now that nothing other than freedom/ rationality is ultimately choiceworthy seems equivalent to being told that nothing is ultimately choiceworthy, that our provisional goals are backed up by no ultimate goal. Movement only in a circle is movement towards nothing, and choosing only to preserve the state that permits choices is a choice of nothing.

Of course, for Aristotle movement in a circle was the very opposite of pointless: it was the only intrinsically worthwhile kind of motion. Similarly, for him the pure exercise of rationality was the very opposite of pointless activity: it was instead the only intrinsically worthwhile kind of activity. Kant comes close to echoing Aristotle at one point in the *Groundwork* —the "proper self" of a human being is intelligence, he says (G 457), which sounds much like Aristotle's claim that intellect "would seem . . . to be each man himself" (NE X.7, 1178a1–2)—and although I think this is a mistake on Kant's part (we are not supposed to know anything about the nature of our "real" selves, according to the first *Critique*), it suggests that he may have seen himself as following Aristotle. At the same time, there are obvious and important differences between the two. For one thing, the kind of reason that Aristotle considers worthwhile in itself is *theoretical* reason, while Kant locates our absolute worth in *practical* reason. For another, there are subtle but crucial differences in what they count as reason, whether theoretical or practical. Aristotle understands reason as always seeking a final cause, a telos; no thing or event is properly explained without reference to its final cause. The final cause is the fully actualized form of the thing, and it may, and often does, lie outside the thing's state at any given moment. We see an acorn or a sapling, and we know that the final cause of this thing is not what it currently is. So the thing strives to be something beyond its current self. Now our own final cause is a fully active reason, a reason seeking and finding the final causes of everything else in the universe. Hence our use of reason is thoroughly goal-directed, in the sense both that we seek the goals of the things we reason *about* and that our reason itself—in part because it is never finished with the search for the goals of other things—is always reaching for a goal beyond itself, always in an unfinished state of its own form. To identify our selves with our reason, for Aristotle, is therefore not to identify ourselves with what we already are: it is to identify ourselves with something that prods us always to become *other* than what we are. It is to identify ourselves with a goal-oriented process, constantly reaching beyond itself. If this is circular motion, it is circular motion guided by the focus of the circle, and indeed Aristotle's argument for the divinity of circular motion, in the *Metaphysics*, depends on the fact that the eternal spheres that move in a circle have the ideal, unmoved mover as their focus (itself mentally turning, cyclically, around its own thought).

We might add that Aristotle's forms, while significantly different from Plato's, play some of the same roles that Plato's do, and that Plato's arguments for why we love the forms may therefore carry over to the way Aristotle conceives the movement of reason. Plato provided a number of plausible reasons for why we might love the forms: why all human love, in fact, might be ultimately directed to the forms. All love, we are told in the *Symposium*, yearns for participation in eternity, for the extension of our temporal being—by procreation, in heterosexual love; by the sharing of feelings and ideas, in homosexual love; by participation in low-level forms, when we grasp the beauty of an artwork; and by participation in high-level forms, when we grasp philosophical arguments. The forms themselves, because abstract, can be neither created nor destroyed; they are eternal and incorruptible. We, terrified of our mortality ("corruption"), admire the eternity of the forms and yearn to partake of it. And to the extent that we reason, to the extent that we understand the forms, we become like them and share in their incorruptibility.[29] Hence, we love knowledge, and love it more the more we understand how it works. Philosophy, the engagement with the deepest kinds of knowledge, is therefore the greatest and most fundamental love we can have, the love whose satisfaction takes us closest to what we most deeply want.

This is an extremely plausible account of the value of philosophy to anyone who accepts Plato's ontology.[30] Aristotle does not fully share that ontology. Crucially, his forms are integrated into the things of which they are forms; they do not exist in a separate world of their own. But they still represent what is most lasting about each thing—what a divine knower would know about each thing—so it still makes sense to suppose that grasping the forms of things, and especially of ourselves, will take us beyond our own temporality to some extent. At any rate, although Aristotle never explicitly responds to Plato's account of love in the *Symposium*, it seems reasonable to see some version of that account behind his view that the rational soul is just as naturally driven to discover the forms of things as the appetitive soul is to seek reproduction. "All men by nature desire to know," begins the *Metaphysics*, and that is not a casual remark expressing a philosopher's fondness for what he does, but a claim with deep roots in Aristotle's metaphysics and epistemology.

But it is exactly these metaphysical and epistemological roots that any parallel claim by Kant must lack. For Kant, as for most modern philosophers before and after him, reason is not teleological. Kant wrestles in a number of writings to preserve a reasonable place for "purposiveness" in our overall view of the world, but it is fundamental to his epistemology that no reference to the purposes of things is ever necessary to scientific explanation. Reason seeks laws connecting events to one another across time— "mechanical laws," Kant called them: as opposed, precisely, to "teleological laws."[31] We may still yearn to find purposes in nature, but we no longer have any guarantee that we will find them. We certainly should not suppose that we will lack knowledge of nature unless we find purposes for things.

This change has the following three consequences for our investigation of worth:

(1) To the extent that the value of our lives depends on finding purposes in the world (one large purpose for everything or separate purposes for each thing), that value is now contingent: we have no guarantee, as Plato and Aristotle thought they had, that the goal we set for ourselves is achievable.

(2) We no longer know that we ourselves have any purpose, any more than we know that of other things. *Inter alia*, we no longer have scientific or metaphysical reason to claim that using reason is our purpose. Kant's suggestion that our essence, our real self, lies in our intelligence, in *Groundwork* III (457), must be taken as, at best, an expression of rational faith, not a statement of physical or metaphysical fact.

(3) We can no longer see our reason as becoming a higher version of itself when it grasps the purposes of things. Kant doesn't see reason as becoming identical with its objects—it sets rules, rather, that order our *representations* of objects—and he sees it as forming a complete system in itself, independent of and logically prior to its acts of cognition or deliberation. Reason is autonomous for him, both speculatively and practically. So it is hard to see how it could possibly grow, achieve a higher state of itself, by way of its engagement with the world.

But it is therefore also hard to see how Kantian reason could possibly constitute an ultimate goal for us, something we could strive to achieve, in the way that we do for Aristotle. If there is anything that can make our entire lives seem worthwhile, pull them along the way erotic and aesthetic love pulls along pieces of our lives, Kantian reason may provide a condition for our love of that thing, but cannot, alone, be the object of that love. It does not hold out the promise of transforming our desires, let alone opening up the eternal existence for our deepest selves that we were offered by Plato and Aristotle.

45. Our examination of Kantian reason has helped bring out some useful general criteria for how we might recognize an adequate conception of the worth of our lives if

we ever came across one. We have seen, in the first place, that a necessary condition on the adequacy of an answer to our question about worth is that it be able to survive reflective scrutiny. Anything that happened to us when we were unaware of it, or had lost our capacity to reason, would not count as happening to *us*, nor would we continue to endorse any feeling we had that a certain activity or state was worthwhile were we to discover that we came to the feeling by way of manipulation or coercion or false beliefs.

And we have seen, in the second place, that we need to love the world, and/or our existence in the world, in order to regard our lives as worthwhile. Each of these is a necessary but not sufficient condition for regarding our lives as worthwhile. Loving our lives under the sway of an illusion or on the basis of false beliefs will not uncover any true ultimate worth, nor will seeing good reasons to value our lives while being unable to love them. Together, however, the two conditions may well be enough to constitute an attitude that picks out ultimate worth. So we may take it as at least a good working assumption that a reflective love of our lives, a love that survives rational scrutiny and can be endorsed on reflection, is the right state in which to say they are truly worthwhile. And my point thus far may then be put by saying that I do not think the secular candidates we have surveyed for activities or conditions that might make our lives worthwhile are reflectively lovable. They either depend on false premises, and therefore do not survive reflection, or they do not evoke love—appeal instead to a dry rationality that cannot bring us to love anything.

> *What we want is a vision of our lives we could love, along with ever new reasons to support that love: reasons to see the vision as beautiful and good, ways in which it extends or fits with or explains other things we regard as beautiful and good.*
>
> *Such a vision is akin to the richest dreams of romantic love, and to what it is said to be like to stand in the presence of God.*
>
> *There may be nothing that fits this vision.*
>
> *I don't think there can be any such thing unless we have eternal life, and unless the world can eternally be made new for us. Others may not see these as necessary conditions for it, or set other necessary conditions. That may just mean that we love different things.*

6

Secular versus Religious Visions of Worth

46. Let us take stock. We have seen that the question about whether life is worthwhile cannot be dismissed as meaningless, nor adequately answered with intuitions to the effect that of course life is worthwhile. That would seem to leave three possibilities for a secular account of worth: either (1) the value of our life is somehow inscribed in the world around us, or (2) our life gains value when we project value onto it, or (3) the very fact that we *can* project value onto things, our very faculty for ascribing value, itself gives our life value. But none of these possibilities yielded a particularly plausible account of the value of our lives, once we scrutinized them with the same skeptical empiricism with which we normally approach religious hypotheses. So we are back now to the practical argument for religious faith that we considered at the end of Part II: if, for practical purposes, we need to be able to regard our lives as worth living, and if secular attempts to ascribe such a worth for our lives fail, then we have reason to put faith in a religious account of such worth instead.

This is not quite as straightforward as it sounds, however. In particular, what we have really argued thus far is that secular accounts of ultimate worth require some sort of faith, not that they are incoherent or clearly false. But that would seem to make them equivalent, not inferior, to religious accounts of worth. It will be the burden of this chapter to suggest reasons for putting our faith in a religious rather than a secular vision of worth.

First, however, we have to get from "reflective love" to faith. The last chapter concluded by suggesting that a vision of worth ought to evoke reflective love in us. What relationship is there between that and faith? To say that we need a reflective love for our lives in order to regard them as worthwhile — is that the same as saying that we cannot prove they are worthwhile, that we hold our views of ultimate worth by faith?

To begin answering that question, consider how a person seeking an adequate view of ultimate worth might react to the investigations of the past few chapters. A prominent feature of those investigations is that the arguments against our various candidates for worth were not knock-down refutations. They consisted more of considerations that might lead a reflective observer, removed a bit from the view under investigation, to find it implausible, unlikely to bring about what it promises, than a demonstration that they are incoherent or empty.

There are a number of reasons why that may be the most one can do, in this arena. For one thing, the notion of ultimate worth is vague enough that no argument that life does or does not have it is likely to be definitive. For another thing, our perceptions of the worth of activities we care about are rife with self-deception. All sorts of factors lead us to convince ourselves that one thing or another is worthwhile, and to cling to weak arguments in its favor, rather than face the dreadful possibility that we have been pouring our energies into something pointless, let alone that there is nothing worth living for at all. As is often pointed out in relation to religious belief, it is hard to make any argument persuasive to people with a strong psychological investment in denying the conclusion of that argument.

So the difficulty we had determining whether our lives are worth living may be inherent to the subject matter. In any case, we have repeatedly arrived at a stand-off between defenders and critics of particular conceptions of worth, finding that while the arguments in defense of each conception are not as strong as its defenders think and, in particular, not strong enough to convince a skeptic of that view, the skeptics also cannot show conclusively that the view is false. What is the status of arguments that end on such an inconclusive note? What are we entitled to draw from such arguments?

Well, one possibility is that we can take the inconclusiveness of the arguments to be reason for embracing a view of ultimate worth on a basis other than reason. We may find ourselves simply drawn to a view – experiencing a love of some sort for it – without being able to say exactly why, and perhaps this being "drawn to" a view of worth is as good a way of coming to it as any.[1] Perhaps reason itself licenses us to go beyond reason, in this context. If we need to hold some belief about worth—to avoid absurdity, in our reflections on morality (see Part II, § 43), and to plan our lives, organize them, and steer them—we may have reason to endorse even a non-rational attachment to such views. We may have reason to replace reason, in this arena, with faith.

Consider someone who holds onto a hedonistic view in spite of all the arguments against hedonism. He may simply insist that he is satisfied with his hedonistic life—and satisfied with it over time, in a sober, well-informed way—even in the face of everything I have said about boredom, the mismatch between the time-span of pleasure and the time-span of consciousness, or the common sense reasons to distinguish pleasure from worth. Perhaps he spurns my account of consciousness, saying that he does not believe in continuous selves or that *his* continuous self can embrace its past as well as its present pleasures and does not demand to go on beyond death. Perhaps he has some other objection to what I said or just isn't moved by philosophical argument on this subject. It doesn't much matter what his reasons for rejecting my account are: if he *feels* satisfied with his life on an ongoing basis—if he reflectively loves his life, or thinks he does—then he has good *prima facie* reason to regard his life as worthwhile and it will be very hard to prove that he must be wrong. I may insist, if I like, that he has arrived at his feeling of satisfaction by way of a delusion, but I have no obvious delusion to point to, and the fact that I have no better grounded account of worth to offer makes it easy for the accusation to rebound on me.

The same goes for someone who insists that erotic love or art or Aristotelian flourishing makes his life worthwhile, or that he can achieve a stoic standpoint, or is content to live up to his own subjective standards of worth. I may warn such a person that these accounts will be unable to handle the sorts of questions that come up in our prompting scenarios—that he will not remain satisfied with his outlook if the course of his life breaks down and he feels the need for an objective check on his views, or a reasonable way of revising them. But he may never run into such a breakdown, or refuse to change his mind if he does. What do I say then? Surely at this point we both have to recognize that we simply have very different ways of imagining the good life. What I imagine to be the highest good is not what he imagines. As a consequence, he feels satisfied with his life and satisfied, on reflection, with his feeling of satisfaction. I am unlikely to be able to do much by way of argument, at this point, to change his mind.

That said, his satisfaction is unlikely to persuade *me* that he has solved the problem about the worth of life. It is helpful here to distinguish the circumstances in which we might be brought to evaluate someone else's feeling of satisfaction with life. If Jimmy tells me he is satisfied with his life, and Jimmy is sober and thoughtful, and has not just fallen in love or had a book favorably reviewed by the *New York Times*, then who am I to tell him he is deluded? The question, "is his life *really* worthwhile?" need not arise, either for me or for Jimmy. But if *I* am wondering whether my own life is worthwhile, and do not take my own feeling of satisfaction with it as sufficient to tell me that, then the question of whether feelings of satisfaction with one's life may be deluded does arise for me. And in this situation I may need to question Jimmy's feeling of satisfaction: I may need to ask myself whether he is deluded in order to help myself figure out whether *I* am deluded. In general, the question of the worth of other people's lives arises for us because we are trying to evaluate our own. When we're not sure what to think of our lives, one thing we often do is suppose that perhaps we would have a worthwhile life if we were like Ms X, or a worthless one if we were like Mr Y. As in many other areas of ethics, we take others as models and find it easier to reflect calmly on them than on ourselves. Perhaps I feel comfortable with my life, but am unsure whether I should take that feeling of comfort to be an adequate test for worth. So I look at Jimmy as a sort of "control," to see whether his feeling of comfort is deluded. Or I feel dissatisfied with life, and wonder why Jimmy, who is externally fitted out much as I am, should be satisfied. In either case, I may have to conclude that Jimmy and I simply differ in our emotional makeup: he is satisfied with many things, and satisfied to be so satisfied, while I, more darkly constituted, am not. Since feelings are deeply tied to modes of imagination, this amounts, we may say, once more to the conclusion that different attitudes towards ultimate worth result from different ways of imagining the good life, rather than different beliefs, or modes of reasoning.

But what we imagine is rarely entirely independent of what we believe, and I may also conclude that there is some difference on metaphysical issues between Jimmy and me that explains the difference in our attitudes. He believes and I don't, say, that our selves are but epiphenomena of a larger social being, which he serves in his political activities, or he believes that he participates in eternity by appreciating art or having a great love, or he doesn't believe, and I do, in an ongoing consciousness that wants never to die or an objective telos that all human beings yearn to achieve or express. If we have differences of this sort, our difference in feelings may be but a symptom of a difference in beliefs. But since the beliefs on which we differ concern issues that resist clear definition, and that depend on the most difficult and controversial questions about how factual truths should be sought, it remains unlikely, to say the least, that we would ever come to a purely rational resolution of these differences. What we might now want to say, however, is that Jimmy and I differ, not (simply) in our feelings or imaginings, but in our faith.

Nor need this faith differ in any interesting way from religious faith. Since I've been talking thus far about secular views on worth, I left out belief in a God or an afterlife from the metaphysical issues that may separate Jimmy from me, but belief in God is a metaphysical stance not unlike belief in a social self or an ongoing individual consciousness or objective human telos. It raises the same difficulties of definition and argumentation, and is unlikely, therefore, ever to be resolved by rational means alone. Moreover, our feelings of satisfaction with our lives may depend on belief in God or an afterlife in just the way they may depend on beliefs we have about social selves or ongoing consciousnesses. I may be simply dissatisfied with life in a universe where there is no God or no afterlife, just as I may be dissatisfied with a life in which political communities will always be hierarchical and manipulative, or where there is no lasting great love, or no objective purpose for human beings beyond survival. Others may by contrast be rather pleased not to have a God around and content with a life that terminates absolutely with the death of their bodies. This emotional difference may remain even if we could definitively show that there is or is not a God or an afterlife. So differences in faith may depend heavily on differences in feelings or imaginings.

47. We'll come back to this possibility in a little while. First, let's consider the implications of saying that our attachment to a vision of ultimate worth depends on faith, rather than reason.

The main implication is that secular commitments to politics, art, love, etc., as giving life value are on all fours with religious beliefs, as far as their grounding is concerned. Religious faith has long been accused of being an "opiate," an illusion with which people comfort themselves, rather than facing the disappointments of life, but exactly this can equally well be said of the secular views that are supposed to replace religious teachings. Many people comfort themselves with the illusion that their intuitions reflect real values, rather than mere instinct and social conditioning, or that political action will one day bring about freedom and equality for everyone, or that they experience something unutterably deep in art, but they have not a whit more reason for any of these beliefs than for a belief in God. The empirical and metaphysical arguments by which people defend such secular views of what gives life value are no better than the empirical and metaphysical arguments people give for believing in God; both religious and secular telic conceptions depend, not on reason, but on faith.

One might be tempted to take this conclusion in our stride. After all, we quite often say that we take something "on faith" without meaning by that to impugn its rationality. I may say that I take something you tell me on faith, or that I take it on faith that I will run into a grocery store sooner or later if I walk along the streets of a big city, and mean merely that I have good but not conclusive empirical reason for these beliefs, and pragmatic reasons for not seeking more conclusive evidence before I proceed. Similarly, a scientist may have faith in his research program in the sense that he has good but not conclusive grounds for thinking he is on the right track, and excellent pragmatic reason to proceed in confidence, rather than doubt, to keep running experiments and applying for grants, rather than constantly questioning the underpinnings of what he is doing. In each of these cases, "faith" refers to something based on less than fully adequate reason, but that reason would probably recommend, all things considered.

This is not what people mean when they criticize religious believers for holding views based on faith, however, nor what religious believers themselves mean by that claim. The faith in these cases is in *tension* with what reason alone might tell us. The religious believer holds views that seem either ungrounded or false—views that conflict with what the scientific use of reason, at least, tells us that we should believe. And my claim about the secular telic views we have canvassed is similarly not just that there is no good reason *for* them, but that there are reasons *against* them. Each view we examined explicitly or implicitly relied on claims more likely to be false than true. That is the point of saying that religious and secular telic views are on all fours as regards their grounding: to put faith in them is in part to believe something we have good reason not to believe. There may yet be reasons of some sort to hold the faith, but there is no getting away from the fact that we will need, at least, a division in kinds of reasoning if we want to make rational sense of it. We need reasons to suspend our normal requirements for rationally grounded belief, if we are to justify a telic faith, ethical reasons to hold true a view that we cannot defend by way of our normal fact-gathering processes.[2]

With these thoughts in mind, we can return to the question of whether we should prefer a religious to a secular faith or vice versa. If both secular and religious telic views depend on faith, we might think there is nothing to choose between them—or that, since secular views at least endorse our normal modes of gathering facts, we should opt for a secular faith. If there are reasons of some sort to prefer a religious to a secular faith, on the other hand, we will be able to fill in our Kantian argument for religious faith quite nicely (Part II, §§ 41–48): the moral life leads inevitably to a demand to resolve certain telic questions; those questions can be satisfactorily answered only by claims in which we may put faith, not claims we can prove; the most appropriate kind of faith to respond to these questions is a religious, rather than a secular faith; hence, religious faith is ethically justifiable. So the point of drawing out the similarity in grounding between religious and secular telic views is to set up the question of whether there are any advantages to holding a religious over a secular faith. I turn to that question below.

48. At first glance, secular views would seem not to run up against reason as badly as religious views do. Secular views generally rely at most on false empirical claims, after all, rather than metaphysical claims that challenge the entire structure of empirical investigation.

That, however, is not wholly true—we have seen that many secular views rely implicitly on metaphysical claims—and even where true is not necessarily an advantage. A colleague once told me a wonderful story of a class on Kant's notion of the highest good, taught by a secular Kantian who believed that Kant's faith in historical progress is better grounded than his faith in a traditional God, but attended by a Kantian who found the religious faith more persuasive than the political one. At the end of one session, the professor looked at the auditor and said incredulously, "Eternal life?!" To which the auditor responded, with equal incredulity, "Perpetual peace?!"

This encapsulates our issue perfectly. Is it more reasonable to believe in a possibility for which there are metaphysical arguments, but no empirical evidence, or in something which is empirically possible, but seems in fact extremely unlikely? Well, there is, of course, a sense in which it is always better to believe in something that appears unlikely than something that appears impossible. But in another sense, the metaphysically grounded belief may be preferable. There, at least, empirical evidence is irrelevant—the claim is not being made on such a basis.[3] In the other case, we have something that requires empirical support, but fails to get it. The religious believer, positing a super-natural realm that undergirds the natural one, can give an argument for why we need not rely on empirical evidence for some of his central claims; the secular believer cannot. Of course, the secular believer may say that his favored claims are not strictly *ruled out* by empirical evidence. But empirical evidence rarely rules things out, strictly speaking, and no-one who respects such evidence can rationally hold on to a belief that goes against the overwhelming preponderance of the evidence available to him or her. Hume remarks that "The raising of a house or ship into the air is a visible miracle, [but t]he raising of a feather, when the wind wants ever so little of a force requisite for that purpose, is as real a miracle, though not so sensible with regard to us" (Enq 115n). If miracles consist, as Hume says they do, in any violation of the uniform course of nature, then votaries of utopian political redemption or transformative romantic love may—literally—believe in miracles.[4] And this sort of belief is particularly unsuited to one who thinks of herself as a naturalist. To challenge the right of science to serve as the final arbiter of truth, as religious believers do, makes some sense of why one might dare to contradict a scientific claim. To maintain that science ought to determine the truth on all matters of fact, on the other hand, while also holding the opposite of what it says on a particular fact, is incoherent.

The staunch secularist may reply to all this that it is better to stick with empirical beliefs, no matter how unlikely, than to believe something that commits one to metaphysical views. *Any* view that appeals to empirical evidence for its support remains at least within the general territory of reason, he may say, while non-empirical views— metaphysical claims that can be neither proven nor disproven by empirical evidence— have *ipso facto* cut themselves off from rational support. This response involves a confusion, however, for the claim that empirical beliefs constitute the whole of what there is to know about the universe is itself a metaphysical one. There is no way to show that the universe consists solely of facts that can be known empirically without, as it were, standing beyond the universe and trying to ascertain a fact about it without employing one's sensory faculties. Positivism is as much a metaphysical view as the non-empiricist outlooks it rejects. To hold an empirical belief that runs against the overwhelming weight of the empirical evidence we have is therefore in no way epistemically better than to hold a belief on the basis of metaphysical arguments, without relying on empirical evidence at all.

49. So we might take our investigation into ultimate worth to provide the basis for a "companions in crime" defense of religious faith: a ground for claiming that religious faith is no worse than the secular alternatives to it. If any view of the value of life requires a faith, then religious views are no more and no less rational than their secular rivals. Perhaps we can go a step further and say that religious views of the value of life, because they openly acknowledge the importance of faith, are to that extent superior to secular views. If we are going to hold what is in any case a faith, a non-rational belief, in some project or vision, it is more appropriate that we openly recognize that commitment *as* a faith than that we suppose it to be based on good reasons. Someone who holds a faith without being able to admit to himself that he holds a faith is bound to wind up in self-deception; someone who knows she lacks a proper rational defense for some of her beliefs, but openly holds those beliefs as a faith, is able to be more honest with herself and others. We have moral reasons, therefore, for replacing a blind and self-obfuscating faith with a clear-eyed recognition that at the heart of all our projects and beliefs lies a commitment that is absurd, beyond rational argumentation.

On its own, however, this response to our investigation of worth grants both too much and too little. Too much, because the properly philosophical response to discovering that all our views of the value of life are based on faith, if faith is something that a rational person should avoid, would seem to be to renounce all such views, secular and religious alike.[5] Too little, because what makes a religion convincing, to its followers, is not its seeming *just like* certain secular views, but its seeming to *fill a gap* that secular views cannot fill. A revelation comes in to meet a need that secular beliefs cannot meet. It is not supposed to be one among many equally non-rational choices for how to see our lives as worth living. To the believer, the religious teaching in which she has faith is supposed to be, not just more open or honest than a secular one, but *true*, or more likely to be true, than its secular alternatives. Moreover, if the idea is simply to hold a view that confesses its own absurdity, then any religious view will do, no matter what it has to say. So a companions-in-crime argument is not enough to establish the legitimacy of holding religious views of ultimate worth. We need some reason, instead, to *prefer* religious over secular kinds of faith—and a reason that pertains to the content of religious views, not merely to the fact that they openly call for faith.

One reason that may do the trick is that religious views, if true, would satisfy the yearnings that motivate our questions about ultimate worth, while secular views would not. If we ever did achieve perpetual peace, as our secular Kantian hoped, human beings would still worry about whether their lives were worth living (more acutely, perhaps, since the struggle to end war gives us an urgent goal that allows us to push telic questions aside). Religious views provide responses to the worries that make it difficult for many of us to accept secular answers to our question: they tell us, for one thing, that we will either live eternally or stop wanting to live eternally. But surely it makes sense, if we are to have faith at all, to have it in something adequate to the needs that demand faith, not something that falls short of those needs. So the ethical basis for faith, the Kantian argument for withholding our normal demand for speculative proof when we come to issues on which a certain view is ethically necessary, would seem to favor religious over secular kinds of faith.

50. We might put this point by considering how we hope. Recall that in Part II we described Kant's ethical faith as answering the third of the great questions to which, he believed, philosophy is directed: what may we hope for? That implies that hoping, and not just believing or deliberating, is a rational activity.[6] We cannot hope for just anything, after all—cannot reasonably or sanely hope for just anything, at least. It makes no sense to hope that $2 + 2$ will someday equal 5 (what could that possibly mean?), nor does a sane person hope that he will sprout wings one day. In general, we do not hope for what we consider impossible.[7]

There are also ethical limits on how we hope. For moral reasons, it is inappropriate to hope for, say, the death of one's rival in love or the subordination of people of another race. It seems inappropriate, in a somewhat different sense, to hope intensely for something silly, or shallow, or pointless, especially if one allows such hopes a role in one's more important choices. Thus, to hope over a long period of time that a person will return one's feelings of romantic love, when he or she shows no inclination to do so, can blight one's chances of having a healthy union with someone else. Thus, also, to hope that one will someday achieve extraordinary wealth or fame can direct one towards vain efforts and ruin one's pleasure in the life one has. A hope can also be too trivial to satisfy the desires that inspire it. To hope that I will be able to visit Disneyworld someday—to hope for that as a solution to any deep or long-term unhappiness, at least—may be inappropriate because achieving it will not satisfy me nearly as much as I expect it to. And to hope that my life will feel worthwhile if I achieve a high level of moral virtue may be a similarly inadequate hope, if virtue is insufficient to give people a life they can love on impartial reflection.

These features of hope give us reason to resist the claims of secular faiths. If the considerations I have proposed in this Part are on target, those who seek political utopia, or supreme or endless erotic satisfaction, or a life that can be fulfilled by aesthetic experiences, are all guided by *false hopes*, yearnings that are bound to lead to disappointment or a blinding of oneself to what one has really achieved. In our telic searches, we are looking for an appropriate place in which to put hope—for something we can unequivocally yearn for, because, if we achieved it, we could wholeheartedly love our lives. Our ultimate hopes must be for something both achievable and appropriate to the yearnings that inspire it: neither too big nor too small, neither impossible nor shallow.

Secular hopes, I have suggested, cannot meet these criteria.

51. But religious hopes will also not meet these criteria unless they are achievable. Are they? What reason do we have to think so?

Well, this is precisely the issue on which religious views demand faith, but one advantage they have over secular views is that they can offer plausible explanations for why faith might be needed on this subject. More precisely, they can explain why we might have to have faith both that the end they posit is or can become real, and that it would satisfy our telic yearnings if we reached it.

As regards the first of these aspects of achievability, the main question is why we should consider possible something that science tells us is impossible. But religious views provide explanations of why they conflict with science—they give reasons why the supernatural Creator of the natural world might not want us to be able to perceive His presence too directly, might want us, for our own good, not to pick up the full truth of our universe by empirical means alone. Relatedly, religious revelations are intrinsically obscure, couched in poetry, and the traditions receiving them offer reasonable accounts of why we can't understand their central terms fully, or prove the claims in which they figure. We are supposed to understand them better the more we have faith in them—the more we rely on them to orient our practice (see Part IV, Chapter 5) and the more we are willing to live without proof that what they tell us is true: the more we relax the demand, central to secular, naturalistic views of the world and raised to a level of moral principle by W. K. Clifford, that "it is wrong always, everywhere, and for anyone, to believe anything upon insufficient evidence."[8]

And as regards the second aspect of achievability, it is not implausible that we will also be unable to grasp what exactly our telos is, or how it will satisfy the yearnings that lead us to seek it, until we approach it in faith, relax the grip of the secular views that demand clarity and proof. One inference suggested by the investigation we have carried out in this Part is that there is something about the world as understood from a purely secular, naturalistic standpoint that makes it impossible for us to regard our lives as having ultimate worth. Plato and other ancient writers worried about nature because it constantly changes, and thought we needed to direct our attention to a stable, eternal world of abstractions in order to locate value—thought also that we partake of this supernatural world when we attend to it. The obsession with change and stability has faded from modern concerns, but a parallel view may be launched on the grounds that our modern understanding of nature does without final causes; value or purpose may therefore have to lie somehow beyond nature, rather than within it. A number of secular philosophers accept this point, but say that value is projected by us onto nature, or perceived, in a quasi-objective way, because of an interaction between us and the things around us. This, however, supports largely subjective conceptions of worth, and I argued earlier that what we seek, when we ask after the worth of our lives, is *objective* worth, not something we have ourselves spread onto the world. That may be impossible unless we can see the world as shaped—created—by an intelligent Being, unless we can see it, or some of its components, as really having purposes.[9] Objective purposiveness would then require the existence of a supernatural God—faith in such a God would be a prerequisite of faith in our having an objective purpose.[10] The best account of the telic realm, we might say, presupposes the existence of a God.[11]

52. We can, therefore, construct an argument that the best account of the telic realm must be a religious rather than a secular one. So we might suppose that reason alone properly leads us to a religious telic view.

I want to resist that conclusion, while allowing some place for a best account of the good to help us distinguish between rational and irrational kinds of faith. A number of prominent philosophers in recent years have used the notion of a best account of the good as part of an argument for religious conceptions of it. The argument I have just sketched is close to one Charles Taylor has offered,[12] and Robert Adams uses an inference to the best explanation (IBE) to argue that our ordinary beliefs about goodness make best sense if the good is identified with God.[13] But I have reservations about how much any IBE can accomplish. In addition to what I said earlier on this subject (Part II, § 44), people are likely to disagree irremediably on the relevant inputs to such an explanation. Appealing to an IBE, or best account, can however help us organize our beliefs—bring out their connections with one another and show the lines of implication among them. It can also strengthen them—*by* showing that they hang together—and help us prune away those that do not fit well with the rest. Religious people may thus use a best account of the telic, or of ethics as a whole, to strengthen and shape their faith, even if it is unlikely to convince someone who does not already share their starting points. Accordingly, as we will see in Part IV, there are a variety of religious best accounts of our telos, and the ethical realm as a whole, none of which can easily be shown to be superior to the others. Different religious people begin with a faith in different revealed texts and traditions (different inputs to their IBE) and come as a result to different views of our telos, and its relationship to morality.[14] Religious people do not come to their faith by seeing that a best account of the telic appeals to God or the *tao*; they begin, rather, *with* a faith in God or the *tao*, or a revealed text or teaching about God or the *tao*, and then see that a best account of ethics can give them rational support for such faith. I think it highly unlikely that any rational argument, including an IBE, could bring a person to faith in a God, let alone a revealed teaching about God, *ab initio*. But one can find oneself with a certain faith, in a teacher or text or tradition, and then be relieved to find that rational reflection confirms the reasonableness of one's faith, rather than giving one reason to reject it. It is that purpose that a best account of the ethical can serve.[15]

53. With this caveat in mind, let me play out a little more what a best-account approach to the telic might look like. The considerations we have explored in this Part suggest, I believe, that a satisfactory account of our highest good is unlikely to be either naturalistic or wholly graspable by reason. Which is to say that, if we have any telos at all, a teaching about that telos that explicitly represents itself as dependent on a supernatural being or principle, and as graspable only if one is willing to put some kind of faith or trust in that being or principle—and follow the teaching about the being or principle with a certain degree of faith or trust—may best fit our understanding of how that telos needs to be represented. We could of course alternatively reject the idea that we have any telos, and accept the practical difficulties that come with such a stance.[16] But if we are unwilling to do that, we have good reason to allow that our telos is dependent on something supernatural, and cannot be grasped by us without faith in a teaching about that supernatural entity. Our practical reason itself, that is, may allow us to hold a best account of the telic that requires a non-rational faith.[17]

At the same time, the considerations we have surveyed in this Part, along with the argument at the end of Part II, give us certain rational criteria by which to assess any faith we might have. We have seen that any view of our highest good should be something we can endorse from a position of rational reflection, and something that makes it possible for us to love our lives. We have also seen that rational reflection is unlikely to constitute our highest good by itself: we can't love a life of rational reflection alone. And we have seen, for similar reasons, that we must be able to love the highest good, but it cannot be constituted by the fact that we love it (we can't love an object whose only claim to being lovable is the fact that we love it), and that our highest good must somehow give us pleasure, but not be constituted by the mere fact that it gives us pleasure. In short, anything we can accept as our highest good needs to speak to us as reflective and loving and pleasure-seeking beings, but cannot satisfy the yearnings that lead us to seek such a thing if it is reduced to reflection or what we love or what gives us pleasure.

Finally, we saw in Part II that views of the telic need to be grafted onto the morality we uphold independently of telic considerations. The eclectic overlap of concerns for welfare, freedom, virtue, etc., that we identified with morality is what leads us reasonably to posit (hope) that we may have a highest good at all—it is our pursuit of virtue that seems most vain unless we have a life worth living—and nothing can be our highest good unless it is something to which morality might lead, and help us earn. So a plausible candidate for our highest good must be something that moral efforts can preserve and promote, that endorses morality and can be plausibly understood as something at which morality might aim. Ideally, it should also explain why morality alone can seem so empty to us: why we are so often torn between our moral duties and a sense that non-moral goods can be more important than moral ones.

The appeal to a best account thus gives us constraints on what we can reasonably regard as making our lives worth living. It doesn't give us an *answer* to that problem, but it helps us determine criteria for an answer to it. In the previous two paragraphs, we have laid out at least five conditions that a candidate for our highest good should meet: it should (a) depend in some way on principles or beings or conditions beyond the natural order, (b) require faith in such principles, etc., and in teachings about them, (c) be something we can reflect on or that enhances our reflective capacities, but not be reducible to reflection, (d) give us some kind of joy or pleasure, but not be reducible to joy or pleasure, and (e) endorse morality, but transcend it, and we should be able to see how and why it transcends morality. Traditional religious views can meet all five of these criteria, as we will see in Part IV, and seem to believers that they are revealed by a supernatural being, or teacher with access to a supernatural position, *because* they meet these criteria. At the same time, precisely which of the many purported revelations appears best to satisfy our reflective nature, or promise a true, lasting, and properly human joy, or explain the place and limits of morality, will vary from believer to believer, in accordance with their different religious upbringings and experiences, and different ways of being inspired, accordingly, to reflective love. So different teachings will call up faith—appear as revelation—to different believers, and reason alone will be unable to resolve these differences. But any believer who attempts to scrutinize her candidate for revelation against the five criteria I have listed (and others, perhaps), and to interpret it in accordance with those criteria, has reason to maintain her faith in it: has not only faith, but a reflective, a rational faith. The idea that the ultimate end posited by her religious tradition gives her a best account of the highest good has real content and she may reject the tradition if she comes to feel it fails to meet the relevant criteria: if its conception of the highest good comes to seem silly or unsuited to her reflective capacities, or if it endorses norms that blatantly violate morality as she understands it. People lose their faith, or convert to a different one, when they think their tradition does not offer the best account of the highest good, and they endorse it with fervor when convinced that it does accomplish that. These broadly ethical considerations are, indeed, far more important to most people than either the purported scientific evidence they sometimes offer for the truth of their sacred texts, or the idea that their religion alone captures the proper content of morality.

54. Nothing I have said about best accounts of the ethical is meant to suggest that reason *requires* us to take up a religious approach to the highest good. Given the essential role I've given to a non-rational faith in such best accounts, I couldn't possibly suggest that. My point is rather that reason can *allow* us to accept a religious view of the ethical—in spite of, or indeed because of, its non-rational element. We will also find the best-account approach useful to us when it comes to the question of how revealed texts and teachings should be interpreted. The five criteria, and the best account that they enable us to endorse, set terms for the reception of revelation (see Part IV, Chapter 6). In particular, they demand that every revelation be interpreted in accordance with common morality. No best account of the ethical realm can afford to ignore the moral values on which we converge independently of our telic views, or to distort those values so that they can no longer be recognized from within our overlapping consensus. Although revealed religions on my view have something considerably richer to offer us than Kant allowed—a distinctive conception of our telos that is more powerful and convincing than anything we could find by reason alone—I agree with Kant that they must answer to the morality that we come to independently of revelation. Even if revealed religions do not properly reduce to morality, they can rightly be rejected if they do not conform to it.

55. So believers in revealed religions use a best account of the ethical to check and shape their faith in a particular text or teaching. But what is it, exactly, to put faith in a text or teaching? How, exactly, do people come to accept a text or teaching as revealing their true telos, as an authoritative guide for their lives? And how does this differ from the faith in the value of an activity, or type of experience, that a secular person may have?

At various points, I have indicated that faith may be connected to love and to imagination. Revelation speaks to us, if it does, through our imaginations more than our reason—it *shows* us something worth living for, rather than defending a conception of worth by argument—and a commitment to it is something that can be rationally defended only in the way that we defend, say, a commitment to the power or value of an artwork. Some find Verdi's *Requiem* compelling; others do not. Some can spend hours in front of a Rothko or Mondrian; others find that a waste of time. And there is only a limited amount of argument that can get members of one camp into the other. Much the same can be said about the gap between those who find religious views of worth appealing and those who find secular ones appealing: it arises from different modes of imagining, not of reasoning.

Phenomenologically, I think this captures very well what goes on when we attach ourselves to a view of ultimate worth, or are torn between different such views. We try to picture to ourselves what would make our lives worth living, and find some pictures compelling while others put us off. I have therefore spoken often of "views" or "visions" of worth, and it seems to me that we do concern ourselves more with *visions* of a truly worthwhile life, when we commit ourselves to a religion or to the importance of politics, love, art, etc., than with a set of propositions. Moreover, the importance of such visions, such imaginative pictures, would go a long way towards explaining why good and thoughtful people are unable to convince one another to share their rival commitments about how to live. Not just pervasive self-deception, or the inherent obscurity in the notion of a worthwhile life, but the importance of imagination vis-a-vis reasoning makes argument over such matters ultimately unsatisfactory.

56. But a difference in imagination is not a trivial difference. Our imaginations do more to constitute who we are, individually, than any other element of our psyche. Nor should we regard the way imagination brings us to a view as necessarily a non-cognitive one. The imagination, although importantly distinct from reason, plays a crucial role in much cognition.

To see this, we need a richer account of what "imagination" means.

The eighteenth century developed an elaborate theory of elements of the mind, dividing it into such parts as "sensibility," "imagination," "understanding," and "reason," and describing each part as if it corresponded to a separate organ, just as our physical senses are divided up among eyes, ears, nose, etc. Modern psychology does not support such sharp distinctions among parts of the mind, and modern epistemology and philosophy of mind tends to do without "faculty psychology," as the eighteenth-century theories are called. But some contemporary philosophers have argued persuasively that we can continue to use the theories that Hume, Kant, and others developed about the imagination, understanding, etc. as long as we interpret them in terms of mental *activities* rather than elements of the mind.[18] There are many reasons for distinguishing among the ways we use our minds, and the types of evidence or inference or attitude appropriate to these different activities. No compartmentalization of the mind is thereby implied, nor need one suppose that any of these activities can be carried out in isolation from the others. It is in that sense that I will be using the word "imagination." Even when I speak of "*the* imagination," this should be taken as shorthand for imaginative activity, not as a reference to a mental organ that might be isolated scientifically.

We say commonly of people that they have "a great imagination" when they are good at coming up with stories, but the creative function of imagination is not the only one. Our imaginative activity includes our treatment of all sensory images, whether fantastical or real. It should not be identified with the process by which we merely receive sensory images (what Kant calls "sensibility")—that can be done without leaving enough of a trace on our consciousness that we register the images when asked about them[19]—and it is also distinct from the activity by which we come up with or use abstract concepts: what Kant and other eighteenth-century writers call "understanding" or "reason." Imaginative activity concerns the concrete rather than the abstract. It presents us with particulars that can at least in principle be located in space and time, rather than ideas, which have no spatiotemporal location.

Imagination is a conscious and potentially self-conscious process, in which we present images to ourselves and are able to ask ourselves whether the image represents a real object or was, in whole or part, created by us.[20] It includes memory—images that we take to represent past events—the attentive consideration of images currently before us, and the projection of images into the future or past, or into parts of the present we are not currently experiencing, as well as the creation of images in fantasy. Adam Smith argued that sympathy, our fellow-feeling with the joys and sorrows of others, depends on our projecting ourselves, in imagination, into their situation.[21] Our other feelings also depend on the imagination. How we feel even about inanimate objects depends as much on what images we associate with them, or project into them, as on any direct impact they have on our senses. I see a dark wood and love or feel afraid of it because of images I project into it, associations I make between it and my past experiences, or the stories I have read. Imagination is thus a crucial source of many of our feelings, and dispositions to feel, whether about other human beings or anything else.

We use imagination all the time, far more than we may think we do. We project before ourselves, in imagination, what is likely to happen next whenever we plan. That's fairly obvious when my imagining life with you leads me to ask you to marry me (or decide against doing that), or when my picturing myself as a Senator leads me to run for that office, but we also rely on imagination in the most humdrum of everyday actions. I pick up a spoon at the beginning of the cafeteria line because I imagine that I am likely to find a soup or custard I want to have somewhere further down the line. I imagine what is likely to be around the corner, as I proceed down a street, in the course of deciding whether I want to turn the corner or not.[22] I imagine myself in other people's shoes throughout the time I speak to them, if I make even the slightest attempt to keep up with their feelings. I project myself similarly into everyone I read about, in order to try to figure out the feelings motivating what they do. I am imagining even as I sense: I project a fuller image before me of a tree or box than what I could glean from the parts I see. I anticipate what I will see or hear on the basis of what my memory tells me usually goes with what I am currently seeing or hearing. And I figure out what I am currently sensing in good part by way of these images. Without imagination, I would not be able to figure out so much as the proportions of physical objects, and I would not be able to use the sensory similarities between objects to forge concepts. I could not understand the world around me, or move through it.

Nevertheless, imagination on its own is insufficient for knowledge. Insofar as we merely imagine, we do not know: that is, indeed, part of how we *define* "imagining." The contents of the imagination float unmoored, as it were, without making claims about reality. Or if they do make such claims—seem so vivid as to be real—we are apt to treat those claims with suspicion. We do not accept images that float into our mind as, by that fact alone, representations of reality. First we need to figure out how we got them—were we manipulated? Drunk? Fantasizing? Do they come from eyes or ears we know to be faulty?—and how they fit with the rest of what we regard as real.

Meanwhile, there is a certain pleasure, and many cognitive uses, in entertaining images, while suspending questions about their relation to reality.

Again, imagination is not, on its own, a way of making moral decisions, but it is essential to moral decision-making. Without imagination, we would not be able to share other people's feelings, and we would not, consequently, have any idea how to alleviate their suffering, make them happy, or express our gratitude or remorse effectively to them. But the mere presentation of an image to ourselves, the mere imagining of a kind gesture we might make to a friend in pain, or a way we could display our gratitude or remorse, is not itself a moral act, nor is it immoral to entertain an image of doing something cruel. And the moral neutrality of imagining is a good thing. It means we can feel free to present a variety of imagined scenarios to ourselves, and figure out how the people in each of them are likely to feel, before actively trying to bring one of them about. Once again, the suspended animation, the lack of commitment, that marks imaginative activity is useful. Decisions cannot be responsible unless they are preceded by a non-decisive imaginative play among alternative possibilities.

Still, we can have what I'd like to call "an imaginative commitment": a choice to focus our imagination on someone or something that affects our disposition towards that person or thing, or our way of acting as a whole. Romantic love is an imaginative commitment. We picture our beloved in certain ways, and we take efforts to cultivate this picture, so as to maintain a way of acting with regards to him or her. A love central to our lives will also affect our ways of imagining, hence of acting, towards everyone and everything aside from our beloved.

Faith is another imaginative commitment. We picture our lives, in relation to a certain realization of ourselves, or a certain state of humanity, or a God. And, again, we take efforts to cultivate this picture so as to sustain a way of acting towards this end or being, which in turn shapes all the rest of our lives. Faith is not a state of knowledge, nor, on its own, an ethical program; it is a state of imagistic and affective orientation *to* knowledge and ethics.[23] It is, fundamentally, a state of the imagination. It depends on how we visualize the unknown, and project ourselves into it, in concrete images. This process of imagination is essential to our acceptance or rejection of visions of worth, and it is a process appropriately aroused, I will argue, by imaginative texts: by the poetic outpourings that religious people call "revelation."

57. I will say more about this understanding of faith in Part IV, but it should be obvious already that to link faith to the imagination is to suggest that it may be guided, in good part, by what we ordinarily think of as aesthetic values—by beauty or sublimity. And, indeed, I will want to suggest that what revelation gives us, above all, is a vision of the world as beautiful. We might almost want to identify the second element of the Kantian highest good, as we are reworking it, with a life in a beautiful world.

Exactly what this means will also require considerable clarification later on, but we can fill in the point a little by considering our intuitions about the relationship between a good world and a beautiful one. There seem clearly to be good conditions that are not beautiful—communities of people who are free, healthy, and comfortable, but lead dull lives, or works of art that promote admirable values, but are trite or clunky. There are also beautiful conditions—sublime ones, at least, like a performance of *Othello* or *King Lear*, or the moonscapes one may come across in the aftermath of a flood or volcanic eruption—that are not good. In some ways, a world entirely like the first of these conditions is more dreadful than a world entirely like the second. I can imagine finding a terrible world fascinating enough that I would want to continue existing in it. But when I picture a world that is merely "good"—a world in which people are free and happy, but utterly boring—I imagine that I would quickly be unable to stand it.

There is, of course, a sense in which an extremely boring world could not, for that reason, *be* a good world. But in ordinary use, we would not readily deny the word "goodness" to a world in which, say, all human beings are free of great illness, natural disaster, violence and oppression, and able to satisfy their basic desires. Picture a comfortable suburb where everyone has a job, a house, three square meals a day, and a TV to watch when the day is done. Suppose, moreover, that these things more or less satisfy the people in this suburb, and that when they want a bit more—a vacation, a fancy car—they can usually get it. Finally, suppose that they have peaceful marriages and healthy children. How could one possibly say that this suburb is a "bad" or "evil" place? The only moral complaint we ordinarily lodge against such communities is that not enough people have access to them. If this problem were solved, if everyone in the world were able to live in a comfortable suburb like the one I have described, it would be hard to see how we could deny their goodness. Certainly, standard moral theories would have little to say against them. Most utilitarians would consider the people in such a community to be happy, most Kantians would regard them as free, and they could possess enough temperance and generosity and friendship to count as virtuous in the eyes of Aristotelians.

But such a community would not be beautiful. It would be boring in the way that many real suburbs are, and would remain so even if it overcame the exclusiveness that makes suburbs politically problematic today. Indeed, we can take the scenario we have been considering one step further and picture all the people in our suburb as playing out a life-plan that consists largely in an activity that seems entirely pointless, like that of the person John Rawls asks us to imagine, "whose only pleasure is to count blades of grass in various geometrically shaped areas such as park squares and well-trimmed lawns" (TJ 432). Rawls says that, from a political point of view, we are forced to allow that his grass-counter's life is a good one,[24] and, from both a political and a moral standpoint, we might similarly have to approve of a whole community that counts blades of grass. But we would not have to call such a community beautiful, and it would be hard to see how human life could possibly have a point if it culminated in such communities. Of course, we could redefine "moral" such that it is concerned with every kind of goodness, and "good" such that it is concerned with every human goal. Then, we could resist calling our community of grass-counters, or TV-watchers, good in any sense. But then we would be building the beautiful and the worthwhile into the meaning of the word "good," and depriving moral theory of its independence from telic value. We might say that a morally good world is minimally good, while a morally good world that is also beautiful—admirable, fascinating, lovable—is maximally good. (We will later substitute "holy" for maximally good.)

Using this terminology, we may say that Kant's *summum bonum* is in fact but minimally good.[25] The kingdom of ends is a realm of rational beings and whatever ends they happen to set, not a realm in which rational beings necessarily have and achieve the end of living in a beautiful world. On Kant's own description, it is a realm that consists of freedom plus happiness, where happiness is the satisfaction of whatever desires we happen to have, or the subset of those desires that can be morally endorsed; Kant doesn't include wanting the world to be beautiful among the desires we have or ought to have.

This I think is at the heart of why Kant's rational faith is so unconvincing. It's not easy to see why a God is necessary to bring about *Kant's* good world, or, indeed, why the reality of a good world along his lines is so important that morality would be pointless if it did not come about. Kant, of course, says that we will achieve our *summum bonum* only if we are immortal, and for that a supernatural God would seem necessary. But why would we care to be immortal if we had to live forever in Kant's boring, minimally good world?

By contrast, a beautiful as well as good world—an endlessly fascinating, endlessly new world—would be worth living in eternally. And its existence can in principle not be guaranteed by human action: we are fascinated by, find ever new, only something that transcends our own creations, eludes our grasp. A God is necessary to bring about such a world, as well as our eternal existence in it. And faith in such a God would I think be a faith in the God of Jewish, Christian, Muslim, and other theistic scriptures. What is revealed, in revealed religions, is precisely a vision of a maximally good world, and a path for humanity to earn a place in it. That is how revelation offers something to ethics that our reason alone cannot supply.

Or so I will suggest.

PART IV

Divine Teaching

Dora was . . . moved by the pictures [in the National Gallery]. . . . It occurred to her that here at last was something real and something perfect. . . . [T]he pictures were something real outside herself, which spoke to her kindly and yet in sovereign tones, something superior and good whose presence destroyed the dreary trance-like solipsism of her earlier mood. When the world had seemed to be subjective it had seemed to be without interest or value. But now there was something else in it after all.

These thoughts, not clearly articulated, flitted through Dora's mind. She had never thought about the pictures in this way before; nor did she draw now any very explicit moral. Yet she felt that she had had a revelation.

Iris Murdoch, *The Bell*

Revelation is the reach of a supernatural being or force into the natural order, the way something maximally good, beyond the natural world, breaks into that world to let us know of its existence, or what it wants from us. This being or force must be supernatural: nothing in the natural order, as we know it, suggests that it is maximally good, that we could reflectively and wholeheartedly love it. Nor is anything in human nature capable of making the rest of nature lovable. We are led to revelation when we are convinced that by our own efforts we can neither create the maximal goodness we seek nor transform ourselves into beings who, without delusion, can wholeheartedly love the world in which we find ourselves. Revelation must come from beyond us and beyond nature as we know it.

There can, accordingly, never be scientific evidence that a revelation has taken place. Scientific evidence establishes empirical facts: facts within nature. Revelation discloses a realm or entity beyond nature. So what matters about revelation cannot rest in any naturalistic, merely sensible properties of the circumstances in which it is supposed to have occurred. Apparent voices from heaven, marvelous thunderings, and extra helpings of bread and fish are of no help in establishing that a revelation has taken place. By the same token, naturalistic explanations of these supposed miracles cannot prove that a revelation has *not* taken place. Whether an event or text is revelatory or not depends, rather, on how it appears to those inclined to have faith in it. And it is ethical, not empirical, evidence that draws the commitment of religious believers; it is an ethical, not a scientific, best account that undergirds their telic faith.

So to what should the faithful person look, when trying to decide whether a particular event or text, as interpreted by its tradition, is revelatory? What reasons, if not scientific ones, appropriately lead us to regard a text or teaching as revealed?

Well, revelation is supposed to give us a vision of the highest good, so the reasons to believe that a text or teaching is revelatory should reflect features of the highest good. One mark of that good, as we have understood it, is that it be eternally fascinating, something we can enjoy reflectively and that holds out the promise, at each moment, of ever deeper reflective enjoyment in the future. Another mark is that it depend on our achievement of full moral virtue. And a third mark is that it orient our lives, that we be able to see it as a focus for all our activities. This suggests three general marks of the revelation of the highest good:

(1) that it be itself fascinating, moving, beautiful, in the way a great artwork is, and/
    or direct us towards seeing our world as fascinating, moving, and beautiful;
(2) that it require us to live up to the highest moral ideals, and show how doing that
    is a condition for the experience of beauty it makes possible;
(3) that it issue in a set of practices and norms by which its moral-beautiful vision
    can infuse and structure our daily lives.

After laying out a general account of revelation, I will develop each of these marks of it in detail. I'll turn from there to the process by which we receive revelation, which I argue is integral to how a text or saying comes to count as revealed at all. And in the final chapter of this section, I consider the implications of an understanding of revelation that can allow for many different, even contradictory, texts and sayings all to have been revealed.

I begin, however, with a chapter examining faith in greater detail. Faith is the commitment awakened in us by revelation. So one way to make sense of revelation is to understand better what sort of utterance or vision might call for faith. We can clarify revelation by considering the subjective condition that it evokes.

1

Models of Faith: Trust, Orientation, Receptivity

1. I've used the word "faith" often in this book, but I'm not altogether fond of it. It's a Christian term, usually contrasted, in early Christianity, with the law central to Judaism and the reason favored by philosophies like Stoicism. Since the Jewish tradition, with its emphasis on law, is my prime exemplar of a revealed religion, and since I want to stress that religious commitments, while not based on reason, are also not antagonistic to it, I am uncomfortable with both these polemical connotations. I prefer the word "trust," and will offer other terms as well for what Christians call "faith" as we proceed in this chapter.

One advantage of "trust" over "faith" is that the former is primarily oriented towards persons, rather than propositions. We trust a person, or the text or oral teaching passed down by certain people, and ultimately, if we are theists, we take ourselves to be trusting a God who speaks through these people and texts or sayings. Trust is a personal relationship, not, primarily at least, a commitment to a set of doctrines. The Jew or Christian who deeply trusts God, but doesn't understand or dissents from this or that doctrine about God, is often thought to be beloved by God despite his creedal failings; the Jew or Christian who understands and fully accepts a traditional creed, but cannot bring himself to care much about the God that the creed describes, is not generally thought to be so beloved.

But it is important not to exaggerate the distinction between trust in persons and trust in propositions. Trust in persons corresponds closely to what some philosophical theologians call "faith in," contrasting it with a propositional attitude they call "faith that" and arguing that the former rather than the latter is central to religious commitment.[1] I like this proposal, but the two kinds of faith are not easily separable. Suppose we do put our religious trust primarily in teachers, rather than teachings—if we are theists, in a God and people who lead us towards Him; if not, in people who have attained a higher level of enlightenment than we have. Even then, propositions of various sorts help us figure out what to *count* as God, or an enlightened teacher, and why we might want to maintain a faith in such a God or teacher. A "faith that" certain sentences are true can also be an intrinsic element of "faith in" a person. In one sense this is obvious. I trust certain sentences because I trust their speakers. I may trust certain sentences passed down in the Buddhist tradition because I believe that the Buddha spoke them, or trust sentences in the Bible because I believe that they come from God. A "faith in" can thereby lead to a "faith that." But a "faith that" can also be a way to enhance a "faith in." I may maintain a faith that a proposition you affirm is true because I want to maintain my relationship with you. You say, "This is the fastest way to John's house," and I accept what you say because I want to demonstrate or increase my trust in you. And my trusting you, and your seeing that I trust you, may indeed enrich our relationship whether or not this is, in fact, the fastest way to John's house.

I may also rely on your words as part of my interest in building or retaining a relationship with you even when you are not there to witness my trust. You write me a letter from far away, recommending that I check out a certain bar or bookstore, and I take up your recommendation in order to maintain a feeling of connection with you. Or I rely on the words of a loved one who has died in order to feel that I still have some relationship to her. Or, again, I follow the advice of an ancient sage because I want to emulate his character. A Buddhist friend of mine who had for a while been willing to drink wine told me, after renouncing alcohol again, "If it was good enough for the Buddha, I figure it must be good enough for me." He *trusted* the Buddha, and was willing to set aside his own inclination to regard wine-drinking as harmless in order to be led by the Buddha. The trust here is part of a love for and emulation of the Buddha. People similarly take to heart admonitions of a saint or guru or rebbe as part of their admiration for and desire to emulate the speakers of those admonitions. In my personal observance of *kiddush*—the Jewish ritual that inaugurates the sabbath— I follow one practice recommended by Maimonides and one practice recommended by Joseph Soloveitchik, largely out of admiration for them and their view of Judaism.

All this can apply to what for theists is the ultimate personal relationship. I might follow words that I take to come from God because I want to feel close to God or to learn from or emulate Him. I might, indeed, take certain words *as* coming from God because I hope that putting that sort of trust in them can bring me into closer relationship with Him. Creedal faith may thereby be a product of faith in God, rather than a means to it.

But it is faith or trust in God—or in a supernaturally enlightened teacher—that is primary. It is that sort of faith or trust that has moral value, and can take us to a highest good we would not otherwise have seen. When religions praise the faithful and criticize the faithless, they have in mind primarily a faith in persons, not in propositions. It is personal trust, not faith in propositions, for which people can be praised and blamed; it is personal trust that has ethical significance. We value personal trust even in ordinary human relationships, and can readily imagine that it also has value in our relationship to God.

2. What is so valuable about personal trust?

There's a children's game called "trust." One person falls back into the arms of another, to show that she trusts the latter to catch her. The point is to teach the falling person the connection between friendship and trust. It's important to the game that one never *knows* that one's friend will catch one; giving up the demand to know that, being willing to live with something less than knowledge, is essential to what the game teaches. One learns, if the game works, that there will be moments in life when one can and should trust other people even though one will not know they are reliable.

And a familiar example of that sort of moment might be the following:

I am lost in a strange city and a passerby offers to help me back to my hotel. He seems kind and honest, so I decide to put my trust in him. I follow his lead fairly blindly, taking certain roads and turns against my own judgment about how to go—although I may also feel the need gently to explain some of the time-pressures I am under if the route seems to be a more scenic one than necessary. My trust in my guide is not entirely blind: I wouldn't have chosen to follow him if he hadn't seemed kind and honest, and I will no longer follow him if, along the way, I pick up evidence that he is not so kind or not so honest, or that he is unable to find his way around or understand where I want to go. So my trust is conditioned by certain rational criteria. But if we get back to the hotel successfully, I will feel that it is trust in my guide, and not the rational conditions on that trust, that did the real work in getting me back. And I will feel correspondingly grateful to my guide.

One consequence of these sorts of experiences is that we are brought sharply to recognize our dependency on other human beings, and have an opportunity to enjoy being part of a mutually supportive species. Once in Fez, notorious for the sleazy professional guides who take advantage of the tourists lost in the maze of its old city, a local man with no financial interest in me took an hour out of his day to lead me back to my hotel. I have had similar experiences in many other places, and they have consistently been among the highlights of my travels. This is obviously *not* because I was able to get to my destinations efficiently, but because they demonstrated vividly to me that there were human beings I could trust all over the world. They assured me of the existence of some sort of universal human community, and of the universality of certain human virtues. Without that assurance, it is hard to have respect for humanity, or to enjoy being a part of it.

So trust in a guide has value even where the guidance serves a relatively minor purpose. But a guidance relationship can do more than get us to a hotel or train station. Let us ring a change on my Fez story, to bring out how a guide might provide us with ends, rather than means to an end we already hold. Suppose a guide offers to lead me, not to my chosen destination, but to some other place that he promises I will enjoy. Of course, if I am a seasoned traveler, such an offer is likely to set off alarm bells, and I will look for more signs that I can trust this person than if he were offering to lead me to a place I had named. The vagueness and open-endedness of the promise leaves more room for trickery, and therefore raises the threshold of credibility I require. But, in some cases, this threshold will be met—perhaps his manner is so frank that I feel he

would have to be an extraordinarily good actor to be deceiving me, or perhaps his age
or status assures me that he could have no motive for deceiving me. I then follow the
guide, trusting him again as long as I do not come across strong evidence to override
my initial reasons for doing so. This time I may wind up not just following his lead
physically, however, but also learning from him about how to enjoy the experience to
which he takes me. Suppose he had in mind a local dance or religious event. Then
I might at first find it merely baffling, and he will have to tell me what to look or listen
for, and how to understand elements of it. Or he may tell me I will enjoy the event
more if I shut my eyes, or participate in it in some way—join the dance, perhaps.
Of course, some of these suggestions may reawaken my suspicions. But if he is not
misleading me and I continue to trust him, I may have a wonderful experience of a sort
I have never had before, enjoyable or illuminating in ways I could not have foreseen.
And the fact that I had a guide and trusted him may then be essential to the joy or
illumination I achieve: I might not have arrived there by the lights of my own reason,
including the reasons I used when deciding to trust my guide. It may be that only
humbling my pretensions to know, setting aside my confidence in my own reason,
enables me to achieve the joy or understanding that an experience like this has to offer.
Certainly, I will be able to come into a rewarding relationship with my guide only if
I humble myself in this way. By humbling myself to his guidance, I show him respect
and invite him to respect me in turn. I also open myself to sharing his way of
experiencing the world; in relationships of trust, we break out of our egocentricity.

   Now if there is a God, some of these virtues should transfer over to a trusting
relationship with God. Putting trust in God similarly means humbling my arrogance,
restraining selfish desires and overly confident claims to knowledge. It means attending
to what God does or wants, to the extent I can discern that, and it thereby allows me, to
the extent this is possible for a human being, to share God's view of the world, and to
learn new ways of doing things, and of attending to the world, from Him. I also show,
and develop, my respect for God when I take on projects I regard as His. I do not
expect or aim for a relationship of *equality* with God, of course, so my respect for Him is
quite different from my respect for other human beings.[2] But even the idea of respect
as a two-way street need not be entirely absent from a trusting relationship to God.
It is a long-standing theological idea that God wants above all to be worshipped by us as
thinking, free-willing, beings, not automatons or slaves. Consider Abraham's challenge
to God about Sodom and Gomorrah, and the respectful way in which God is presented
as receiving that challenge, or God's preference for Job's anger over the apologetics
of Job's friends.[3] Respecting God involves a thoughtful and courageous, rather than
a blind or fearful, willingness to take on God's aims, and it thus opens us to a certain sort
of respect *from* God, albeit not as His equals.

   This brings us to the role of independent thought in a trusting relationship. We
might be tempted to think that the most trusting relationship is one in which the
trustee does all the thinking while the truster follows the trustee around in blind
devotion. And I don't want to deny that unquestioning commitment does figure in

trusting relationships. But surely, the most respectful sort of trust, the one that does most honor to the trustee, most allows trustee and truster to share experiences, and most enables the latter to learn from the former, is one in which the person doing the trusting is capable of a high level of independent thought, has made use of that capacity to understand, as best she can, the terrain through which she is being led, and nevertheless makes choices that take her against what she would do on the basis of her own judgment alone. Rather than merely following along without judgment, she *suspends* her judgment out of respect for the person she is trusting. This is a very deliberate respect, reflective of a deep appreciation of the person she is trusting, and capable of bringing her into the other's ways of seeing and acting with her own intelligence intact, and on the alert for what she can learn.[4]

3. Our model of trust has at least the following six features:

(1) It is likely that I will not achieve most of the goods of guidance relationships, and certain that I will not achieve some of them, if I insist on substituting verification for trust throughout the relationship. The Cold War slogan about arms agreements, "trust, but verify," essentially means "do *not* trust," and if I insist on asking everyone who offers to help me for proof that he is not out to get me, guides of the sort I have been describing are likely simply to walk away—even, in some cases, to turn into the manipulative cheat I am implying they may be. (Giving up on the pleasure of simply helping a fellow human being, or making a new friend, a potential guide decides he may as well get what he can from me.) This will not always be the case. Some people are phlegmatic enough to put up with suspicion of their bona fides, or feel an obligation to help even unpleasant strangers, and will therefore lead me safely to my hotel even if I keep asking suspicious questions. It is harder to imagine that they will bother trying to introduce me to exciting new experiences, however, and virtually inconceivable that I could achieve the goods of honest friendship or mutual respect. And it is logically impossible for me, in that case, to achieve the goods that may be found by humbling my reason. Trust is essential, not accidental, to some of the most valuable features of guidance relationships.

(2) The trust I have described is, however, not blind. Instead, it is conditioned throughout by criteria for what sort of people count as trustworthy, and what sorts of situations call for trust. I employ those criteria when I enter into trusting relationships, and they remain in the background as the relationship proceeds. But the criteria that underwrite my trust, and the rational capacities that enable me to come up with such criteria, will not themselves get me to my hotel or train station, much less bring me into a dignified and warm relationship with my guides, or to an unexpected joy or illumination. Reason and trust work together here.

(3) Rational trust of this sort is appropriate only in certain circumstances—where, above all, I cannot figure out what I want to know on my own. Not only would

it normally make better sense for me to find my way to my hotel or train station on my own if I know it perfectly well, but I will then not really be *trusting* my guide. Trust is a fraud where I could rely perfectly well on my own information and cognitive capacities to reach my object. And if we now replace "trust" with "faith," we arrive at Kant's view of rational faith: that it is appropriate only where knowledge is insufficient to guide us, that one needs to draw limits to knowledge in order to make room for faith.

(4) A fourth feature of the kind of trust I have described is that it has moral virtues. We come to recognize our dependency on others and their willingness to help us, and to achieve, therefore, some measure of friendship and some measure of humility, when we put trust in a guide. Of course, we don't put trust in guides *in order* to achieve these virtues—they come along by the way, as it were, while we pursue other ends—but it is not easy to achieve them without trusting relationships. For these are virtues that cannot easily be aimed at directly. Humility especially, but also the kind of respect for others that comes with gratitude for the help they give us, may come about *only* when we have to depend on other people. Only the experience of being helped by others gives us *reason* for humbling ourselves to others, or being grateful to them.

(5) Trust in a guide may also enable us to achieve certain cognitive goals. We may grasp the meaning of the dance or ritual to which a guide leads us only by attending to his teaching, and restraining our impulse to employ our own usual cognitive strategies. But we can never be given any proof in advance that there will be something of this sort to grasp: the possibility of such proof would undercut the claim that we need a guide to grasp it.

(6) Finally, in most of the cases I have described, trust in our guides serves as a principle of orientation, something that relieves us of the vertigo we feel when we are lost and puts us in position to find our way around an area or attend appropriately to an event. Puts us in *position* to find our way: trusting a guide does not of itself yield a set of directions leading us to our goal. Trust consists not so much in explicit beliefs, either about our guide or about our way, as in a state of mind, an attitude or mood, that precedes belief, a condition enabling us to *acquire* beliefs. It is largely an affective and precognitive state, although it may be made possible by certain cognitions, undermined by other cognitions, and lead to new cognitions. This brings it very close to a characterization of faith at the heart of a great eighteenth-century debate on the subject: as a mode of orientation, that precedes and guides our reason.

4. In his *Morgenstunden*, Moses Mendelssohn argued that reason sometimes needs to be oriented by common sense. He was responding to F. H. Jacobi's insistence that reason fails to bring us to God, and should be replaced with faith. Jacobi reported that Lessing, at the end of his life, had declared that "there is no philosophy other

than Spinoza's." To Jacobi, this showed that rationalism inevitably led to atheism (Spinozism and atheism being equivalent, for Jacobi). By dabbling in rational theology, even someone as wise as Lessing had been led to atheism.

Mendelssohn tried to save rational theology from this attack by conceding to Jacobi that reason alone cannot always lead us to God, while insisting that a properly guided reason was up to the task. Sometimes common sense comes into conflict with the results of speculative reason, and then reason as a whole needs an orienting principle to decide which of the two to heed. Mendelssohn claims he dreamt that he was traveling through the Alps with two guides.[5] One was "a coarse young Swiss, strong of limb, but not of the finest understanding"; the other was "tall and thin, earnest, with sunken eyes," of "fanatical" (*schwärmerisch*), and other-worldly appearance, and with something like wings behind her head. Suddenly, at a crossroads, one guide went off in one direction and the other in the opposite direction. Mendelssohn stood there, not knowing which way to go, until an elderly matron came by and told him, first, that the rustic's name was "Common Sense" (of course), while the dour angel was called "Contemplation," and, second, that eventually they would come back to the crossroads to have her settle their disagreement. They always do that when they disagree, she says; she usually decides for Common Sense, and Contemplation normally goes along with that decision. Common Sense, by contrast, laughs at her in his "rustic way" and ignores what she says. But travelers who trust her will learn whom to follow from her decision. And what is her name? On earth she is known as "Reason," she says, but just as she is about to tell Mendelssohn her heavenly name, they are interrupted by a fanatical horde that has returned under the leadership of Contemplation and is about to attack both Common Sense and Reason. Mendelssohn wakes up in terror.

Now "common sense," as Mendelssohn uses the phrase, is very much a sort of faith. It is a confidence in the ordinary way of life around us, and in the moral, religious, and pragmatic beliefs invoked in the course of that way of life. If it is a type of reasoning—and for the most part Mendelssohn assumes that it is—it is "a subconscious and intuitive form of reason," as Frederick Beiser says, not a conscious and discursive one.[6] The main lesson Mendelssohn intends to teach is that reason as a whole contains this sub-conscious and intuitive form, as well as the process that leads to the construction of abstract philosophical systems. It therefore can be reasonable for us to reorient our abstract thinking so that it is closer to common sense. Of course, the idea of reason as a mediator between common sense and contemplation also suggests that our thought may need to be reoriented in the contemplative direction on occasion. Beiser says that Mendelssohnian reason "recognizes that there are times when common sense will err because it is too hasty or careless in its judgment."[7] But Mendelssohn seems to believe there is a greater danger of letting our philosophical speculations run wild in the absence of common sense, and he urges philosophers, when they find themselves at odds with common sense, to retrace their steps to a "crossroads" where they can re-orient themselves.

For all its creaky unsubtlety, the symbolism of Mendelssohn's dream is surprisingly flexible, and it lends itself to a number of other readings besides the one Mendelssohn himself drew from it. Beiser points out "Mendelssohn's deep anxiety about the powerlessness of reason" in the dream, the way it suggests that reason might *not* be able to settle all conflicts between philosophy and common sense.[8] I would draw attention to two other features. First, it is speculative philosophy, not the religious beliefs embedded in common sense, that seems for Mendelssohn to pose the greatest danger of fanaticism or "enthusiasm" (*Schwärmerei*). This goes against the grain of standard Enlightenment views about how enthusiasm arises. Hume described enthusiasm as the product of a rejection of reason, and saw metaphysical error as a set of "intangling brambles" that "popular superstitions" set up to protect themselves against critical scrutiny.[9] Adam Smith also worried about the dangers of "popular superstition and enthusiasm," and hoped philosophy could serve as an antidote to these dangers.[10] So it is surprising to find Mendelssohn—an admirer of the Scots—telling us that philosophical speculation is the source of enthusiasm, rather than its cure.

Second, the suggestion that the matron has two names, and that her truer (heavenly) name is *not* "Reason," is very intriguing—especially since the interruption of the dream prevents us from finding out her true name. Why might Mendelssohn have disguised her true name, or suggested that we don't know it? Perhaps because he himself, and we, don't know whether what we call "reason" is properly such? Do we then, even when reasoning, not know what reason is? That would be unnerving, especially for an Enlightenment thinker.

This brings us to the aspect of Mendelssohn's response to Jacobi that disturbed Kant. The idea of orientation appealed to Kant, but he was unhappy with the characterization of reason in Mendelssohn's parable. How can reason mediate between common sense and philosophy unless both common sense and philosophy are rational? But in that case, there is no need for a three-way relationship: common sense and philosophy should already be reconciled, by virtue of their shared rational nature. It would seem that either reason is identical with one of the faculties whose disputes it is supposed to settle,[11] or they are close enough to each other that they need no mediation. Alternatively, one or both is not properly rational—but then reason should always side with the other one. In fact, Mendelssohn's "common sense," as we have seen, is more or less equivalent to faith. But in that case, for reason ever to side with common sense over philosophy will be for reason to oppose itself—to side, in Jacobi-like manner, with the non-rational over the rational. Kant considered this a betrayal of the Enlightenment commitment to reason.

In response to Mendelssohn, Kant argued that common sense could be left out of the issue about orientation.[12] Either it is otiose, since it is just another term for reason, or it is inappropriate, since reason must never be guided by a principle outside of itself. Philosophical reason does need to be "oriented" when it gets lost in speculation over matters, like the existence of God, where it can find no proofs, but the proper faculty to do the orienting is *reason itself*: "practical reason," the reason that pertains to practice or morality. This position fits beautifully with Kant's larger philosophical project. For Kant, practical reason takes priority over speculative reason, and itself requires a certain faith—in freewill, at least, and perhaps also in God and an afterlife.[13] A major effort of the entire Critical project, indeed, is to prove by reason's own means that reason cannot prove the existence of free will, God, or an afterlife, but we may believe in them anyway. So there is nothing wrong with reason using itself as a principle of orientation—it remains autonomous that way—and there is something appropriate about calling that orienting function of reason a "faith."

5. Let me add two more elements of Kant's response to the Jacobi/Mendelssohn debate, before drawing some consequences from this passage in the history of ideas. First, in WO? Kant complains about people of "genius" who abandon reason in favor of "daring flights" of fancy, and thereby encourage enthusiasm (*Schwärmerei*). Kant regards the latter as a source not just of nonsense, but of violent or oppressive politics. It is worth bearing this admonition in mind when we come to the *Critique of Judgment* (CJ), in which "genius" is given a more positive role.[14] But in CJ, genius is the faculty by which we create *art*, not a source of advice on morality or politics or theology. Genius consists, Kant says there, in a balance of "originality," an overflow of imaginative richness, with "exemplarity," an ability to channel one's imaginative insights into a form that others can grasp. This two-sidedness of genius in turn reflects the two-sidedness of the experience of the beautiful, which for Kant consists in an imaginative richness that exceeds our conceptual grasp, while at the same time giving us the feeling that our understanding, our source of concepts, could in principle come to grips with it. Finally, genius for Kant is something that the person who has it feels he himself does not control, or even understand: "the author of a product that he owes to his genius does not know himself how the ideas for it come to him, and also does not have it in his power to think up such things at will or according to plan" (CJ §46, Ak 308). It flows through a person, like an outside force, and cannot be controlled, or defined scientifically, without losing its essential ability to break through and challenge our conceptual repertory.

All of this sounds very much like the way prophets have been described in religious traditions,[15] and like a quality one might well take, if one had it, for a voice of God. I suggest that the artistic genius of CJ is much the same as the religious genius of WO?, and that Kant's point is precisely that this super- or sub-rational faculty is indispensable for the production of beauty, but dangerous, and fully dispensable, for the conveyance of moral or religious truths. Kant is extending his contribution to the Jacobi/Mendelssohn debate in CJ, trying to show a proper respect for the great poetic renaissance in German letters that the *Sturm und Drang* movement had released while restraining its political and philosophical pretensions. More generally, he is trying to give a place to the non-rational aspects of human thought that contribute so much to what makes us find life beautiful while keeping them out of science, politics, and religion. What Kant failed to understand, I think, is the significance of the aesthetic *for* religion. Artistic genius came in the nineteenth century to play the role that prophecy had once played because prophecy was always in good part directed towards filling our imaginations with the love of God—always in good part a matter of breaking us from what can feel like the cage of reason and leading us, by way of our affective natures, on a path that we hope will allow us to experience God's presence. The ancient prophets were literally poets, and at their best showed artistic genius. And in modern times artists have aspired to be prophets.

6. The second point to add about Kant and the Jacobi/Mendelssohn debate concerns his treatment of common sense in CJ. In CJ § 40, Kant distinguishes between two kinds of common sense: one by which it means, as it usually does, the opinions that circulate in everyday conversation, and one by which it is identical with the "sense," the feeling, by which we make aesthetic judgments—the process that Kant characterizes earlier in the book as the harmony of the faculties. The former, which Kant prefers to call "common human understanding" (*gemeiner Menschenverstand*), is an incipient but poorly developed form of reasoning, and Kant regards it as a rather unimpressive cognitive achievement. We may hear in this an echo of his response to Mendelssohn: that common sense, as usually understood, either does not stand enough outside reason to orient it or stands outside it in a way that should lead us to reject it.

On the other hand, Kant's new meaning for "common sense"—the only meaning, he insists, that allows it properly to be called a *sense* (*Sinn*)—is a non-rational process that deserves full respect from reason. It is a process of reflection by which one tries to bring one's feelings about a particular representation into accordance with the feelings that anyone with the same representational faculties might have—the feelings characteristic of human knowers, as opposed to both divine and non-rational knowers—and thereby to *feel* in common with all other human beings. It is thus quite literally a "communal sense" (*gemeinschaftlicher Sinn*), a sense that enables us to come into community with our fellow human beings. Kant, indeed, hints that it is connected to the state of mind that allows us to break out of our private viewpoint on political matters, to see other people's points-of-view: to become "broad-minded," as he says (CJ 295).[16] Our ability to feel together with others, to share aesthetic tastes, becomes the source or model for our ability to think together with others: "common sense," in its ordinary meaning, derives at its best from the "communal sense" we experience in aesthetic contexts. The opinions that circulate casually among us may reflect just our failure to think deeply enough about certain issues. We share platitudes and prejudices and superstitions because we have not thought things through enough on our own, and we need to correct that sort of common sense by reason. But reason may rightly be guided by a feeling of commonness with all other human beings. And that feeling is properly located, not in any of our raw biological impulses, which have no rational content, but in the pleasure we get out of bringing our cognitive faculties into harmonious play with one another: the pleasure we get from reflection. Reflective feeling is a precognitive point of orientation for human beings—because it is a point that exemplifies what it is to *be* human.

7. What should we make of this debate over orientation and faith?

On one point, I agree entirely with Kant: it makes no sense to say that we can have reason to oppose reason, reason to adopt irrational beliefs. Jacobi's project of showing that we should adopt faith as *against* reason is incoherent. But the idea that reason needs orientation by something *outside* itself is not so clearly unacceptable. And a precognitive, largely felt state, which involves reflection and inspires cognition, might be just the sort of thing to fit this description. It is *non*-rational, but not *ir*rational. Indeed, in its reliance on reflection and tendency to inspire cognition, it is suited to rationality.

At the same time, Kant's response to Mendelssohn may miss Mendelssohn's main concern. Mendelssohn worries about whether reason, at least in the developed form it takes in speculative philosophy, is self-guiding. Kant says "yes," shows that reason can guide itself, and argues, largely on political grounds, that it must guide itself. But what most deeply worries Mendelssohn, what motivates his intriguing hint that we do not know what reason properly is, may well be a concern about whether reason betrays its own fundamental imperative when it tries to justify itself. It is essential to reason that we provide grounds for what we believe, where a ground is, minimally, a claim independent of whatever it is supposed to ground. If you ask me why I believe P, and I say, "Well, because P," I am begging the question. But this puts me in a difficult situation if I am asked to defend the very claim that I ought to find reasons for what I believe. To offer reasons in defense of that claim would seem to be begging the question. *Not* to offer reasons in defense of it would seem, on the other hand, to defy the imperative that I give grounds for what I believe. I fail both if I do and if I don't give grounds for the need to give grounds. So it seems that reason cannot defend itself. At the most fundamental level, if we accept reason as the proper basis for everything we believe, we have a sort of non-rational faith in reason itself.

Arguably, this conundrum has shown up in one guise or another throughout the history of modern philosophy: in the so-called "Cartesian circle," in Hume's willingness to let nature lead us when reason cannot, and in Kant's antinomies, among other places. On some readings at least, Descartes did not believe that reason could be ultimately vindicated—believed that, from God's perspective, the world might indeed be irrational—but thought we must still proceed as if reason were a reliable guide.[17] On any reading, Hume argues that we must follow the lead of our instincts and habits, rather than of reason, in coming to our basic beliefs about the world. And while Kant agrees with Descartes that there is no choice but to follow the lead of reason, he comes close to acknowledging the impossibility of vindicating reason from the outside in his antinomies. What gives rise to all the antinomies is supposed to be the fact that reason seeks a completeness in the series of grounds for our beliefs that it knows we can never properly grasp. In Kant's language, we are torn between a finite series of grounds that our understanding can grasp, but is too "small" for our rational ideas, and an infinite series of grounds that would satisfy the ideas of reason, but is too "large" for our understanding (CPR A 486–487=B 514–515). But this is very close to the problem I have described. The grounds for the need to give grounds extend infinitely, such that every time we think we have defended it we need also to defend that defense, while our actual capacity to grasp a series of grounds demands that we have a finite such series. The problem about giving grounds for giving grounds—about reason's defense of itself—is an additional antinomy, or a way of describing the structure of all the antinomies.[18]

Now there are many ways of responding to this problem. We might maintain that it is a pseudo-problem, arising from an unsatisfactorily formulated question, or that the skeptic of reason cannot make his position intelligible, or that the problem can be solved by a holistic, non-foundationalist rationalism of the sort to be found in Spinoza and Hegel. All these responses have defenders in the contemporary philosophical world. But the most direct way of resolving the issue would be to find an external defense of reason, a ground for employing reason that can be regarded as not itself a product of reason. This is where we re-join the Jacobi/Mendelssohn debate. What Jacobi denied, and Mendelssohn tried to find, was a principle somehow outside reason (reason in its fully-developed philosophical sense, at least) that could "orient" us back towards reason. If reason isn't self-sufficient, perhaps something else can prop it up. And if nothing can do that, then perhaps we really do face the choice between abandoning reason for a non-rational faith and holding a non-rational faith in reason itself.

Of course, there is a deep problem in the very notion of providing external grounds for the use of reason. Any ground, after all, if it is a ground at all, will be a reason of some sort. Anything that vindicates reason, anything that leads us to follow reason because we come to believe we *should* do that—rather than because we are forced or manipulated into doing that—will by that fact become part of reason. The antinomy we have encountered is built into reason: it arises because anything that could possibly count as a reason for using reason would seem by that token to violate the prohibition against argument in a circle. So it seems impossible that we could resolve the antinomy by appeal to non-rational factors.

8. Let's step back a bit now. Our discussion of this issue may be misconceived—albeit in a way shared by Kant's response to Mendelssohn. If the problem about orientation is thought to arise at the grounding—the foundation or "beginning"—of reason, as we have supposed thus far, then it may well be perilous to employ any method of orientation other than one prescribed by reason itself. If reason is guided at its root by something outside itself, then it loses its autonomy and is in danger at every point of licensing superstition and nonsense. Once we admit a non-rational principle into the groundwork of our thought, we open up the possibility that reason can at any point be trumped by this non-rational principle—that whenever we don't like a conclusion we can say, "Well, we don't need to listen to reason: our faith allows us to proclaim a conclusion true even when reason tells us otherwise." Reason would then be corrupted at its root, would indeed cease to *be* reason. Reason must have jurisdiction over all our conclusions if we are to be rational at all. Only where reason is silent, or unable to reach a conclusion, can it allow itself to be supplemented by something like faith.

But if we read Mendelssohn's dream aright, the question of orientation arises only in cases of the latter sort, not at the outset or foundation of our thought. We do not find ourselves disoriented when we first set out on a path. That happens rather at a *crossroads*, when we have been proceeding awhile, but discover that our guides are less helpful than we had initially supposed. So it is perfectly compatible with our hiking metaphor that all thought starts out from reason, and that reason remains in charge of how we think throughout. It is just that there are points at which reason herself permits the decision about how to proceed to fall into other hands. (That is exactly what the matron does in the dream.) Reason, that is, guides us even when we turn to faith, although faith is different from reason: reason *allows us* to follow the guidance of another principle. This is "rational faith," if not quite in the sense that Kant uses that phrase. It is not a faith *in* reason, as Kant would have it—in a proposition that reason holds out to us as necessary in its practical capacity, but cannot prove in its speculative capacity. Rather, it is a faith *approved by* reason.

More precisely, it is a feeling or attitude, and concomitant set of commitments, that reason permits us to have. It is not a feeling we merely happen to have, a gut sense or instinct. Instead, we check the feeling against the requirements of reason, making sure that it is not ill-formed (formed under manipulation, or out of fear or weakness), that it is morally acceptable, and that the beliefs to which it leads us are ones on which reason is silent or torn, as opposed to beliefs that we have good reason to reject. The feeling may change as we go through this checking process, and what we count as reasons may also change. The feeling may lead us to revise our imaginations such that we pursue ends, for instance, that we had not seen as worth pursuing before. So we really go through a sort of play of the faculties, and what results, if we reach harmony in our play, deserves to be considered a *reflective* feeling.

A comparison: Reason tells us to rely on perception, in order to figure out many things, although perception is not itself a form of reasoning. We are licensed by reason to rely on perception, we might say, and reason maintains a sort of scrutiny over how we do so: we withdraw our reliance when we discover that our eyes or ears are in bad shape, or that we are in circumstances likely to produce a sensory illusion, or that what our senses seem to tell us conflicts with well-established conclusions drawn from other evidence. Perception is therefore governed by reason. To perceive is not precisely to reason, but reason nevertheless recognizes perception as essential to its own work.

A further comparison, this one inspired by Heidegger:[19]

Reading Kant's first *Critique* against the views of Kant himself, Heidegger points out that for us to achieve objectivity, we need both to control the sensory material we take in—apply concepts and laws to it—and to restrain our very tendency to take such control: to *allow ourselves to receive* information. We need, that is, not just active ("spontaneous") faculties of understanding and reason, but an active faculty of imagination as well. For Kant, however, imagination is by definition something passive.[20] So Heidegger is essentially calling for a sort of active passivity, a spontaneous holding back of our spontaneity. He calls this, variously, "spontaneous receptivity," a "free binding"

296 I. MODELS OF FAITH

of ourselves to acknowledge what appears to us as having so appeared, and a stance that allows "the intuitive offer" to be made to us, that enables us to accept the gift of intuition. We have to let things resist us, or let ourselves resist them—"the peculiar character of resistance" that marks objectivity, says Heidegger, is something "the subject gives to itself"[21]—if they are to appear to us as other than us, as given. Givenness, he says, depends on a prior "letting-givenness-occur."[22] Nothing can "stand over against us" (*Gegenstehen*, the verb from which *Gegenstand* ["object"] derives) unless we prepare a dimension within which such an encounter can take place—unless we distinguish ourselves from what appears to us so that we can see it *as* appearing.

The idea of a free "allowing for reception" slices neatly across the activity/passivity divide that usually characterizes Kantian epistemology. It is a marvelous way of accounting for the failure to achieve objectivity of certain kinds of paranoiacs—people colloquially so described, as well as clinical ones. The Trotskyites and followers of Lyndon LaRouche who sometimes set up tables on college campuses are precisely people who do not let reality break in upon their fantasies, who prepare a thick screen through which to filter every bit of political information they encounter, so that it cannot appear as other than what they expect it to be. Every reported event is either interpreted to fit their scheme for understanding the world or rejected as false; they reject, *ab initio*, the possibility of something appearing to them that might challenge their beliefs.

I expect that anyone inclined to read this book will readily agree that Trotskyites and LaRouchies do not allow the world to be given to them, but we might disagree about whether that was going on in many other cases, and it is in general not an easy task to be open to givenness, to let things stand against us—even to know whether we are doing that or not. Notoriously, Heidegger himself did not manage the task as regards the evil of Nazism (or, later, as regards his responsibility for collaborating with the Nazis). We are often all too ready to fit everything we encounter into concepts and types of explanation that grind them into a confirmation of what we already believe, by which they do not stand over against us, but are assumed from the beginning to fit neatly into our worldviews. Letting givenness occur, pushing back our own sub-jectivities so as to make room for objectivity, takes a real effort. And success in that effort amounts to an active, free embrace of a non-solipsistic, non-idealistic stance toward the world, a recognition of our finitude, of the fact that we share a world with things radically different from ourselves.

But if this is right, reason again makes room for something other than itself to do a significant part of our cognitive work. Reason requires us *not* just to reason, but to step back from our reasoning and allow things to appear to us. Indeed, it is clearer in the case of "spontaneous receptivity" than in the case of perception (although the two are related) that the faculty or process making room for such appearances must *not* be reason. Spontaneous receptivity, "letting-givenness-occur," is precisely a matter of holding back the use of our concepts, and the modes of argument that employ those concepts: of letting the thing before us stand over against our concepts before we try to fit it into them. Trotskyites and LaRouchies are not unskilled *reasoners*. On the contrary, they rely too *much* on reason. They "have an answer to everything"; they bring their interpretive scheme to bear on everything before making any serious attempt to absorb it; they sift the data appearing to them so quickly into the "useful" and the "irrelevant" or "false" that they don't take the time to attend properly to what they are discarding. One who truly opens him or herself to the intuitive offer lets the given stand there *as* offered, lets it *be given*, before making any attempt to absorb it into rational patterns.

Trotskyites and LaRouchies are merely extreme, and therefore clear, examples of a kind of breakdown that can occur in anyone's cognitive faculties; they stand in for a failure, which we all experience on occasion, in the use of capacities that our reasoning presupposes, but does not include. Of course, in saying that these capacities are prerational, rather than irrational, I mean to imply that their deliverances must be somehow taken up into our reasoning, that what they accomplish is directed toward reasoning. That is not enough to assimilate spontaneous receptivity to reasoning, however, and if religious faith is comparable to spontaneous receptivity, it too will be prerational, rather than rational.

In fact, religious faith is not just comparable to spontaneous reception; they are connected. Faith, the reflective feeling by which we commit ourselves to a telic vision, depends crucially on our willingness to restrain our restless urge to impose our categories on the world.[23] Perhaps, since faith is a form of commitment, a love that shows itself in actions as well as feelings, it cannot quite be identified with spontaneous receptivity, but an active letting–givenness-occur is essential to it. Insofar as faith orients us toward something our reason alone is unable to teach us, it is impossible without spontaneous receptivity. Only then can we be ready to accept a vision as reliably presenting, and leading us toward, the highest good. Spontaneous receptivity plays an important role in all knowledge. No good scientist rushes to fit every incoming piece of information into a pre-given scheme or theory. But spontaneous receptivity is yet more essential to the perception of God's presence in an event or text: without it, there will be nothing to see. And in that capacity, it represents a radical holding back of all other knowledge, a radical waiting, a trust of exactly the sort we have been describing in this chapter.

"Do not stir up, do not rouse love until it please." (Song of Songs 8: 4). When does it please? When we are ready to accept it, when we stand in spontaneous receptivity.

And the love here, according to the rabbis, is the love of Torah. "Till Solomon arose no one was able to understand properly the words of the Torah," runs a midrash on the Song of Songs, which the rabbis attribute to Solomon. That book, they claim, made it possible for everyone to comprehend the Torah.[24]

But how can that be? The Song of Songs is more obscure than the Torah, not less.

The point of the midrash seems to be that the Song of Songs forces its readers to interpret texts metaphorically—"till Solomon came there was no parable," it goes on—which is the key to understanding the deeper wisdom hidden beneath the surface of the Torah. And it is that deeper wisdom that inspires love in us. The eros on the surface of the Song of Songs leads us to a deeper eros whereby we can embrace it, and the Torah, as God's word. And that transformed eros, that active reworking of the quintessential passion, is spontaneous receptivity.

9. Back, now, to orientation. What is it, exactly? It's neither a belief nor an action. It's not finding one's way; it occurs before that, *enabling* one to find one's way. "Ah, there's the tree we saw on our way up: now I know where we are." Or: "The sun's to our left: we must be heading south." Once I see the tree, or the sun, I can figure out which way I should be going. I don't yet know which way I should be going, but I can figure it out. Orientation involves a certain confidence, and reflects an awareness of one's surroundings and direction. It isn't yet the embarkation on a path, however, or the adoption of a belief about the right path. For Kant, physical orientation is what connects the subject to the realm of space—what places us within space—and intellectual orientation is, similarly, what connects us to, places us within, the space of concepts.[25] It is always something subjective, for Kant, although it enables us to locate ourselves within an objective arena.

But can faith then be *just* orientation? Doesn't faith involve beliefs of some sort, or at least commitments to a certain guide or path?

Imagine being on a path in which feelings about the path itself serve as a good means of orientation. Suppose the path is extremely dark and you need to be guided by temperature. Feeling cold or hot, or progressively colder or hotter, might then be a good way of orienting yourself. ("Yes, this must be right: it got progressively colder as we went up, so it should get progressively warmer as we go down.") Or perhaps a feeling of comfort or discomfort, even though you don't know its source, will be a good indicator that you are on the right path.

From the latter possibility, especially, we can explain how faith may be a principle of orientation. I feel, let us say, a certain reflective pleasure in response to some experience, or vision of the world. I feel that the world is wholly beautiful, and that its beauty marks something about it that I will never wholly grasp. I feel joyful about the world I live in, and joyful about that world in good part because it seems to me a mystery: because of what I do not understand, cannot put into my usual concepts, about it. An experience like this could be an excellent indicator that I am on the right path to experiencing the presence of God. The path itself, then, is marked by moments that contain something of its destination, and those moments help orient me, help get me back to the path if I have strayed from it, or find clues as to how to continue along it (I go in the direction of greater mystery, say). So the feeling that orients me is a crucial element of my faith; my faith consists to a large degree in the sense that I have a right direction, or know how to find one. Of course it also consists in *proceeding in* that right direction, and that may involve taking certain actions, or maintaining certain cognitive commitments. But the sense of orientation is primary. It is a non-rational, subjective, action-directed but not yet active condition that makes possible my religious actions and commitments. It may rightly be considered, therefore, the core of faith. It disposes to action, and to belief, but is not itself yet an action, nor a belief.

10. I have come close to suggesting that the feeling arising from the harmonious play of the faculties, which Kant identifies with aesthetic response, is equivalent to religious faith. That can't be quite right: surely the feeling that a work of art or natural scene is beautiful is not the same as faith in God. Still, there are strong connections between these conditions.[26] The feeling that the world contains more than I can ever capture in my concepts, that I am in the presence of one of its mysteries, that I am being pulled forward to wonder at, probe and learn more from this mystery, and that that mystery and the way it entices me is a source of great, unselfish joy, is very much the sort of thing that I am likely to hope lies at the end of a path of faith. It can therefore be taken as some confirmation that I am on the right path: as, quite literally, a means of orientation, if I take my path to be one in which intimations of the destination serve as signposts. (And it is reasonable to suppose that that is the sort of path an all-good but essentially mysterious being would lay out for me.) What needs to be added to the feeling in order to arrive at faith is the *taking of* this feeling as a sign that one ought to proceed in a certain way, the trust that the feeling is a sign to one from God and that it points in a certain direction. To be prompted to this trust we need, not just experiences of the beautiful, but moral promises—signs that the path before us promotes the dignity and welfare of all humanity. The beautiful must be integrated with the moral to yield our highest good, and any path we take an all-good Being to have laid out for us must be morally good. So religious visions must bring moral promise together with beauty, and religious faith is a commitment oriented by a combination of moral beliefs and aesthetic joy.

Even this is a bit too simple. The feeling that sparks religious faith is not an unmixed joy, but a combination of joy with uncertainty and unease.[27] We are putting our faith, after all, in a Being whose existence cannot be scientifically or logically proven, who lies beyond the limits of everything we can know, and whose signature, *ex hypothesi*, is an experience of mystery, of what we have not grasped. But insofar as the world is mysterious to us, it may *defeat* our hopes and expectations, rather than fulfill them. Hidden in the mystery that entices us could be no God, or a God who demands that we give up many things we care about.[28] The challenge to the concepts we normally have, at moments that set our faculties into free play, may threaten our dreams, rather than endorsing them. Kant describes something like this threat, and the way it can be simultaneously terrifying and joyful, in his account of the sublime, and I take the high moments of aesthetic experience to combine the beautiful with the sublime. But that is to say that faith, or the orienting experience that leads to and affirms faith, is simultaneously terrifying and joyous. There is terror in not knowing that one is taking a sensible path, in the thought that one is committed to an illusion. There is joy in being aware of the courage it takes to proceed despite these doubts, in aspects of the path itself, and in the relationship of trust we take ourselves to be building with the God who has laid out the path. But the terror and the joy are so mingled, belong so intimately to the same experience, that it would be a mistake to identify faith with the latter to the exclusion of the former.

Indeed, a religious faith without terror is an inadequate faith, a faith that does not recognize what it is truly committed to—a blind faith and possibly an idolatrous one. A person confident that the world around her is a good place cannot have fully appreciated the intensity and pervasiveness of the evils in it. And a person confident that God guarantees satisfaction for us in spite of those evils is someone who supposes she can *know*, rather than merely have faith, that there is such a God, who doesn't understand that God is shrouded in mystery. These are people with blind faith: uninformed, thoughtless faith, a faith kept away from their cognitive faculties rather than scrutinized by those faculties. And this kind of faith will be drawn to the wrong sort of object. A god whose existence can be empirically proven, and whom we know will satisfy our desires, is a sort of super-hero—the Spiderman or Dumbledore god we mentioned in Part I (§ 3)—a being locatable within the known universe, whose nature and achievements are fully capturable within our concepts. To worship such a being is idolatry, worship of what the Biblical psalmists and prophets call "the work of human hands."[29] To worship a Being who transcends our concepts, by contrast, induces terror as well as joy.

11. Some implications of the relationship among orientation, faith, and the harmony of the faculties that I have been exploring:

First, even if artistic geniuses are not prophets,[30] it may be useful to regard prophets as artistic geniuses. Then we can see the point of prophecy as to inspire the feelings that provide religious orientation, rather than to tell the future or come up with moral codes. It seems to me this is closer to what Biblical prophets actually do.

Second, on my account religious faith is something largely non-cognitive, but not in a way that resists correction by new information or insight. Religious faith will be a feeling, but a feeling responsive to moral and other ideas, as our aesthetic responses are. It will be an imaginative commitment, a commitment of and to the imagination, but a commitment to the reflective use of our imaginations, in which we try to harmonize them with our understanding and our reason.

Third, the feeling that orients us religiously may also be, or be closely related to, the feeling of common humanity that Kant identifies as our "communal sense"—our "common sense," in one meaning of that phrase. That would help explain why true religious commitment is thought to go along with a commitment to the well-being of all humanity.

Finally, if the harmony of the faculties helps inspire or constitute faith, that would help explain why it seems so very important: why the experience of great art, and natural beauty, has so often appeared—even, on occasion, to avowed agnostics and atheists—to be a religious one.[31] And appreciating the religious quality of aesthetic experience may in turn help us appreciate the aesthetic quality of religious experience: the fact that the experience of revelation is much like the experience of great art, or natural beauty.

2

Revelation

12. Revelation arouses faith. So if faith is, first and foremost, a state of our imaginations, revelation must speak to our capacity to imagine. It is no wonder, then, that the texts regarded as religious revelations—the Torah, the Quran, the Vedas, the Guru Granth Sahib, the Tao Te Ching—all take the form of poems, not of philosophical treatises, and are read like poems even by the legal traditions drawn from them.

More precisely, there are two moments to revelation. One is the moment that imposes itself upon us—by which we accept in spontaneous receptivity a vision that comes, we believe, from something radically beyond us. This is the moment that must be couched in poetry, and it has authority over us, like a mountain hanging above our heads.

The second moment is the moment of interpretation, implicit even in our reception of the poetic vision (we cannot truly accept anything without trying to understand it) and necessary if that vision is to have consequences for our practice. This is the prosaic aspect of revelation, the moment expressed in philosophical and legal and literary interpretations of the poetic vision. In it we are partners in the establishment of the truth revealed to us, as if we had entered into a contract with the source of revelation, and He/She/It had given us the right to adjudicate the terms of that contract.[1]

These two moments interact much as the imagination does with the understanding in Kant's account of aesthetic experience, or as the aesthetic moment of faith does with the moral one. For moral purposes, the understanding dominates—it governs how we relate to our fellow human beings, so must determine how revelation informs that relationship—but for telic purposes, the imagination dominates, as it does in aesthetic experience. Literary interpretation does not rewrite poems, merely tries to grasp them, in the awareness that it will never fully succeed. Religious interpretation similarly does not rewrite divine teaching, merely tries to grasp it, with even less hope of full success.

The following chapters develop an account of revelation by way of these two moments. On the whole, the first, poetic and elusive aspect will dominate through

Chapter 5 while the second, prosaic and rational aspect of revelation will come to the fore in Chapters 6 and 7. But the two moments interact throughout, to a considerable extent.

13. If we regard revelation as something purely beyond us—purely a mountain held over our heads—we may feel relieved of the fear that what we take to be God's word has actually been made up by us, is a projection of our desires and fantasies. As a child, I was sure that whatever revelation precisely was, it had to be something that human beings could not themselves have invented. A revealed text had to be clear of human input. Otherwise, it might represent just what human beings *think* God would say.

This is a fairly common view of revelation among so-called "fundamentalists" in Judaism, Christianity, and Islam today (and among many unbelievers, who use it to show that the conditions for revelation are never met). That is the reason for the emphasis laid on the miracles that supposedly accompanied the events on Sinai or that Jesus is supposed to have performed, and on the supposed superiority of the content of the Torah or Gospels or Quran to anything found in other writings. We are supposed to see that human beings could not possibly have come up with the teachings of revelation on their own. One consequence of this view is that the supposedly divine teachings get treated as a surd: something that must be accepted with a minimum of interpretation, so as not to be corrupted by the merely human values that they correct. A rigid, anti-humanistic conception of religious law is the result. If God's text declares that Jews or homosexuals are damned, then Jews or homosexuals are damned. If God's text puts men in charge of women, then men should be in charge of women. Even those with a view of this sort admit that *some* interpretation is necessary when it comes to ambiguous words or metaphors, but on the whole they are driven to see the text as maximally clear and unambiguous. Too much interpretation will simply put the human back in a message that is meant to trump, to override and humble, all human beliefs and desires.

Call this "the child's view of revelation." The most obvious of the many problems with it is that if a text or speech really was such that no human being could possibly have composed it, no human being could understand it either (or, therefore, recognize its truth). If we are capable of understanding something, then we are also capable of composing it. I think when I held my own child's view of revelation, I tried to distinguish between coming up with an idea and understanding it. But, while some distinction along these lines makes good sense and will indeed be part of the view developed here, there is no reason to suppose that we could understand and recognize the truth of an idea that we could not *possibly* have invented.

In addition, the child's view of revelation contains an internal contradiction: it implicitly sets humanistic standards for revelation even while explicitly rejecting them. The very idea that revelation should be clear of human content is, after all, a demand *we* put on what we are willing to count as revelation. We think human beings are too confused or petty or materialistic to come up with a proper conception of the good on their own, or we think that, however good people might be, they are finite and therefore cannot come up with the idea of the infinitely good. But that is to say that an eminently human view of ourselves, or of the good, stands behind our desire for a purely non-human revelation. An insistence that God speak to us in terms that trump or humble our humanity is just as much a human condition on revelation as an insistence that God speak only in terms that our reason could itself produce, or that jell with our pre-existing customs and traditions. To say that we will count as revelation only something utterly different from our humanistic views of the good is no less an imposition on what God tells us than to say that we will count as revelation only something identical with our humanistic views. And the second view at least admits what it is doing—is, therefore, consistent with itself—while the first does not.

Nevertheless, there is something to the child's view of revelation. To call something "revealed" is to say that one did not know it before it was revealed. The whole point of saying that something was "a revelation to me" is precisely that it did not come *from* me, that I did not produce it or already contain it. In revelation, I stand back and a truth appears to me. I find it when I withhold myself; I am passive in regard to it. I make space for it to come before me and then receive it; I don't get in its way.

But if this is the language appropriate to revelation, it would seem obvious that those, like Lessing and Kant and Hermann Cohen, who have tried to read revelation as an expression of our reason must be missing the point of the idea. I do think that is true in the end, but there are ways in which the demand that revelation come from "outside" me can be met with surprising ease. We might, for instance, identify the "me" from whom revelation cannot come, on pain of ceasing to be revelation, with a certain subset of my psychological states, and leave room for revelation to come from some other, more truth-tracking condition of myself. Consider, for example, the common eighteenth-century distinction between an impassioned and therefore confused or blinded self, and a calmer self that we should draw on for proper cognition and moral deliberation. Joseph Butler contrasts the self in a "cool hour" with the self of passion.[2] Adam Smith says that when I examine my own conduct, "I divide myself, as it were, into two persons; and that I, the examiner and judge, represent a different character from that other I, the person whose conduct is examined into and judged of" (TMS 113). Kant distinguishes between an empirical and a transcendental self, maintaining that the latter properly has authority over the former. In each of these cases, a truth that the cool, judging self displays to the passionate, judged self might count, from the latter's perspective, as a revelation.

But this is not enough, I think, for what most religious people expect from a revelation.[3] To make room for revelation, we need to make sense of what it might mean for a truth to come from something more radically outside ourselves, more radically different from any aspect of who we are: "Other" to us, in contemporary jargon. At the same time, a revealed truth cannot be wholly Other to us; if it is true, it must somehow mesh with the views we already hold. So the question cannot be, "*Is* there some human contribution to the process of revelation?," but rather, "How *much* can that process be shaped by our desires and beliefs and still count as revelation?" To what *degree* is revelation shaped by its interpreters, by the people to whom it is revealed? There is room for a balance between divine and human contributions to revelation, between what is given and what the receiver must do to accept what is given. We do not need to accept the Kantian idea, at the other end of the spectrum from the child's view of revelation—we might call it the "too-knowing adult's view"—that our own reason must supply the whole content of religious truth.

And this reinforces the point that the function of revelation is not primarily a moral one. We have seen that we don't need revelation to develop moral systems, or be motivated to follow them—that, on the contrary, we need to bring an independent moral view to the interpretation of revealed texts if we are to see them as representing the will of a good God. Purportedly revelatory texts tend in fact not to present themselves as inventing morality. There is usually supposed to be *something* morally new in a revelation—we are supposed to gain from it morally—but revelation is supposed to transcend morality, to display something to us that, as Kierkegaard put it, raises the possibility of a "teleological suspension" of the moral. Revelation shows us a telos that transcends morality, a picture of what makes life worth living: of how we could love our lives, reconcile ourselves to the world.

To put this in more explicitly religious terms, let's use the term "holy world" for a world we could love, a maximally good world in which people are both virtuous and have their telic yearnings satisfied. A holy world will be such as to inspire, and merit, unmitigated reflective love. And let's call a glimpse of such a world, or of how our world could be or already is like that, a moment of holiness, a holy experience, for some person or people. Then a revelation will be a moment of holiness that promises that the whole world can be holy. And it maintains that promise in part by offering us a discipline by which we can experience further moments of holiness, and feel, reasonably, that we are getting closer, and bringing our fellow human beings closer, to a time in which those moments are continuous, an era of everlasting holiness. A revelation offers us a trustworthy path to holiness.

14. What texts might be trustworthy in this way—might be holy, or offer us a glimpse of holiness? On what basis might a reasonable person ever regard a text as recording or occasioning revelation? Any answer to that—other than that it is never reasonable—will be difficult and complex, especially if the very idea that our lives have a telos eludes rational explanation. I don't think it is possible to *prove* so much as that revelation is possible, much less that it has occurred in any particular case. Nevertheless, I will try to sketch the marks that draw reasonable believers to purported revelations. The goal is to provide more a phenomenology of commitment to revealed religion than an argument for it.

Two general criteria guide this attempt to fill out the content of revelation. On the one hand, a revelation will have to be something to which it is appropriate to respond with spontaneous receptivity and imaginative commitment, and that can orient us in our pursuit of the highest good, in part by giving us a glimpse of it. On the other hand, a revelation will have to look something like the texts that have in fact been taken to be revelations: like the Torah or Vedas or Tao te Ching. The importance of the first criterion is obvious, if my argument thus far is correct, but why need a philosopher heed the second one? If our philosophical position leads us to think a certain kind of text would be revelatory, but no such text exists, can we not say, "So much the worse for the actual claimants to revelation"?

In principle we could say that, but to do so would undermine the project I have set myself in this book. I am trying to show why actual revealed religions are appealing, what it is about them that draws people away from purely secular moral philosophies and ways of living. Defending a purely notional revealed religion would do nothing to further that project. In addition, one main point of submitting to revelation, as I understand it, is to humble our thinking about how to live, including our philosophical thinking on that subject. We would begin badly on that route by transforming revelation into just another philosophical conception, and refusing, on the basis of that conception, to respect any actual claimant to revelation.

One caveat, however, about looking around at actual revelations. The word "revelation" is to some extent a term of art, not common in the premodern histories of many religious traditions. Even Judaism and Christianity, while studied for centuries by philosophers in terms of their doctrines of Creation, Revelation, and Redemption, did not necessarily see themselves in those terms until fairly late in their history. There is no good Hebrew word for revelation—the event at Sinai is traditionally called "the giving of the Torah" or "the standing at Sinai," not "revelation"—and the Christian Bible uses the word for its concluding, weird prophecy of the end of days, rather than for the Gospels and the teaching of Jesus. Once we look beyond the Abrahamic traditions, moreover, the idea of a revelatory speech or text—a moment in history at which God explained His will for human beings—can seem very out of place. For Buddhists and Taoists, whose understanding of the ultimate stratum of reality is non-theistic, the idea of divine revelation is at best irrelevant to their central teachings, at worst incoherent. For Hindus, for whom divinity is an eternal element of the universe rather than a person-like being, the ultimate spiritual truths, including the truth about how we should live, have in some sense always been out there; they were not specially revealed to a particular person or group of people at a particular moment in time.

With that caveat in mind, there are strong similarities in function among the Torah, Gospels, and Quran, on the one hand, and the sayings of the Buddha, the Vedas and Upanishads, and the Tao te Ching, on the other, and it is to these similarities that I want to draw attention by using the word "revelation" for all of them. Above all, in each case the text is seen as *grounding* an entire way of life, and is accordingly treated reverentially, as the foundation of the tradition's thinking about how to live, not analyzed or criticized in the light of other, more fundamental ethical views. Since it is foundational to the tradition's ethical reflections, it cannot be judged as faulty by any other standard for those reflections.[4] But precisely this reverential attitude towards the text is what leads people of a more rationalistic bent to scorn such texts, to argue that they are a baleful obstruction to the proper use of our practical reason rather than an admirable complement to it. And since that is the view this book is trying to rebut, since what I am out to defend is precisely the faithful, reverential humbling of one's reason, in the orientation of one's practical life, to certain texts and traditions, it makes sense to lump all the religions that call for such humbling together in the course of that defense. Enlightenment philosophers of religion spoke interchangeably of "historical," "positive" and "revealed" religion, which they contrasted unfavorably with "rational" or "natural" religion. A revelation, for them, was just a revered historical teaching, a "positive" teaching given authority, in certain ethical contexts, over the conclusions we might come to by way of individual reasoning. That was what was wrong with revelation for the Enlightenment, and that is what I want to say is right with it.

Kierkegaard argues that the mark of revelation is authority: the speaker of revelation, he says, by definition has authority over us.[5] He adds that the authority he has in mind is absolute and unquestionable, suitable to the "qualitative difference" between us and God, not the provisional authority we grant one another in our human "political, social, civic, household, or disciplinary relationships." The latter must in the end be "only . . . transient, vanishing," since the relationship between one human being and another is essentially equal. The former is a relationship between persons essentially unequal. It is *defined* by the fact that the superior Person has authority over us.

But it would seem that we could not possibly understand a qualitatively different Being. Equality is a condition for communication. How then could a qualitatively different Being exercise authority over us? To command us, surely It would have to be understood by us.

There is something paradoxical, then, about the very notion of absolute authority— as there is something paradoxical, for Kierkegaard, about the very notion of revelation, of a God coming into relationship with human beings.[6] And Kierkegaard is right. There is revelation only if there is a source of ethical teaching that has absolute authority over us and there can be such a source only if there is something qualitatively different from us, supremely and unquestionably good, to which we at the same time have access. But the idea that anything can be both qualitatively superior to us and accessible to us is deeply paradoxical.[7]

Setting the paradox aside for a moment—we will encounter it in numerous forms as we proceed—I want to suggest that the relationship between revelation and authority goes also in the opposite direction. Not only is revelation absolutely authoritative for us, but anything absolutely authoritative for us is revelation. What we *mean* by revelation in the course of a religious life is a text or saying that we see as qualitatively beyond our own understandings, something that corrects us, but that we do not correct, something that teaches us from a position beyond us, rather than from a position to which we have access. In this sense, the sayings of the Buddha or Confucius function as revelation in their respective religious communities just as the Torah and Quran do in Jewish and Muslim communities. This remains true even if, in the case of the Buddha, a hope is held out that believers may someday, at a point of supreme development, be able to achieve the historical Buddha's condition and, from that position, set his words aside. From the position we are in now, for a Buddhist, the enlightenment of Siddhartha Gautama is qualitatively different from the state that the rest of us occupy, and his words therefore appear to us as absolutely authoritative: as revelatory.[8]

15. What general characteristics do we find, when we look at the authoritative texts in the religions around us?

(1) As noted at the beginning of this chapter, they take a poetic form. The Vedas and the Quran consist entirely of poetry, the Torah is largely an epic poem, and even its legal and narrative sections are compressed, enigmatic, and suffused with metaphor and allusion, and Jesus, Confucius, and the Buddha talk in parables and gnomic sayings. The Vedas, Quran, and Torah are indeed traditionally sung. This serves a mnemonic purpose, of course, but that does not preclude a deeper connection between revelation and song. Perhaps the telos of our lives can only be presented to us musically.

(2) They take the form largely of a rejection, or deep criticism, of the dominant morality and/or religious practices of the cultures in which they are supposed to have been written. What is revealed in them, in the most literal sense of that word, is supposed to be a hitherto hidden deep flaw in the way the people of ancient Egypt in the time of Moses, or Arabia in the time of Mohammed, or India in the time of Siddhartha Gautama, were conducting their lives.

(3) They are accompanied by a path, a combination of ritual and moral practices, that is supposed to lead those who revere the text to the good it helps them envision. Sometimes the path is largely inscribed in the text itself, as with the Torah. Sometimes there are hints in the text that are later used to develop the path, as with the Gospels and Quran. And sometimes the path is wholly a later development, but attached to the text, in various ways, by the community that receives the text. Even when the path is a wholly later development, however, the reverential place given to the text has a lot to do with the way it justifies or illuminates that path.

(4) They are comprehensive, offering a key to the entire course of human life. The Jewish and Christian Bibles are unusual in explicitly including an interpretation of all human history, but the *Analects*, the sayings of the Buddha, and the *Tao te Ching* are also comprehensive in their aspiration to resolve all the problems that plague humanity.

(5) They are supposed to be read in a specific language, which is regarded as holy and is generally the language of the nation or ethnic group that regards itself as the primary keeper of the religious tradition. This is especially true of the Quran and Torah, but holds also to some extent of the Vedas and Guru Granth Sahib as well. Nor are the Christian Scriptures wholly an exception to this generaliza-

tion. For over a thousand years the largest Christian church required that they be read in Latin, the language of the Empire in which that church was founded, and later many Protestant churches associated themselves with a particular nation and treated a translation into that nation's language as especially inspired. In general, revelations establish and help shape historical communities, which in turn preserve and interpret them. Even when their message is supposed to go out to all humankind, it is not received just by individuals, scattered randomly throughout the world.

All these features inform the account I shall give of revelation. I will de-emphasize some, in light of the general philosophical considerations that also shape my account, and give others greater stress than they receive within most actual religious communities. But I cannot afford to let any of the features go entirely unexplained without losing touch with the idea of revelation, in its ordinary sense.

16. So how do people come to regard a text as revealed? What features arouse our imaginations such that we come to trust a text as a guide to the holy, and orient our lives by it?

Well, let's start with a concrete example.

In the Torah, God is represented as speaking to a people after they have come out from slavery; the fact that God has taken them out of slavery is indeed the first thing He mentions in the revelation at Sinai. How do we understand the significance of this narrative detail? That is: how do we imagine the importance it would have for us if we were *in* the story recounted by the Torah?

Here's how I imagine it: I picture myself growing up in a slave house in Egypt, knowing only brutal work and punishment. I picture also seeing all around me, from childhood, evidence that the regime inflicting this oppression on me and my people is invincible, militarily superior to every other country in the region and capable of crushing any internal rebellion. And I imagine growing up with a sense of the moral hegemony of this regime as well, with a sense that even the oppression of me and my people must be somehow deserved, that our oppressors' view of the right and the good must be correct. The gods must want them to rule us, else they wouldn't be able to. And we must be so evil or incompetent that we deserve to be enslaved.

Then one day a charismatic person, tied to the royal house, but born among us, tells us that the moral propaganda we have been accepting is wrong and that our slavery will soon end—despite the seemingly absolute power, over bodies and over minds, of our oppressors. We don't really believe him, but what he says comes true, by way of a series of bizarre and unexpected events. We flee to a barren desert, our oppressors are annihilated when they pursue us, and we come to a small, bare, remote mountain. There, with no other human beings around us—no kings or warriors or slave-drivers, and none of the priests who justified the oppression in Egypt—we are told, in the name of a single God who supposedly stands beyond all oppressive powers, that we should never ourselves worship projections of human might, never endorse the desires and fantasies that make for oppression. We are also given a code of conduct to help wean us from our habit of worshipping human projections and to steer the feelings that sustain that habit into an attachment to the one, transcendent God of freedom. The code meshes well, on the whole, with what we already intuitively take to be morally good (insofar as we can separate that from the propaganda that was foisted upon us), and repeatedly denounces many of the sources of our suffering—oppressing strangers, worshipping the projections of human lust, establishing grand royal houses. Given our history, the idea that the path to holiness centrally involves freedom from oppression, and that human self-worshippers stand most in the way of both freedom and holiness, makes perfect sense to us. So why should we not believe that the message and code we are being given comes from God? The miracles in Egypt, and the sound and light show on Mount Sinai, are not what convinces us. What convinces us is *ethical* evidence, the sort of evidence appropriate for a claim that a certain path leads to the maximal human good: a sense that the world we have been released into, in our new-found freedom, is capable of overcoming its sources of evil and is in addition deeply beautiful.[9]

So the story in the Torah, whether historically true or not, and independently of its miracles, makes good sense of why the people in that story would take the words they receive on Sinai to come from God.

But why do *I*, now—Sam Fleischacker in the early 21st century, not the imagined me who came out of Egypt three millennia ago—believe that the Torah is the word of God, especially if I have reason to doubt the historical veracity of the story it tells? The simplest answer to that, and an answer in line with an ancient Jewish tradition, is that I feel I have stood at my own Sinai, which is to say that the story rings true to me ethically, that it provides a believable explanation of my own ethical experience: of how I imagine my telos and its relationship to a moral life. My imagination's telic yearnings—disappointed by every account of the highest good I have encountered in the secular world, and in religions other than Judaism—have been satisfied by the story of the Torah and the path it offers. I feel therefore that I have been given an answer to my greatest ethical question by the Torah. And I do mean "given": I feel that it has been offered to me, to accept in spontaneous receptivity, rather than being something I have developed out of my own rational and imaginative resources.

17. When have I stood at Sinai? When have I received ethical insight that seemed to come from radically beyond my horizon?

There are a number of moments in my life I interpret that way. Here is one I remember particularly clearly.

At the end of my first serious romantic relationship, I was a wreck. We had told each other we would be together forever, and I could not envision a life without her. Nor was I willing to recognize that my emotional state was fairly typical for people in such situations. I insisted (to myself and to anyone else who would listen) that my situation was unique, focusing my attention on features of our relationship that differentiated it from other relationships I knew, and on unusual features of our personalities that, I thought, would make no future relationship nearly as satisfying to either of us. I didn't realize, or refused to acknowledge, that this sort of insistence that one's lost relationship was unique and irreplaceable is also a typical feature of break-ups, especially first breakups. And I certainly didn't realize, or refused to acknowledge, that there had been something unhealthy in my attachment to this young woman, that I had been obsessed with her, overjoyed by her good moods and made desperate by her bad ones in a way that deprived me of rational control over much of my life.

At the time the relationship ended, I was in Israel studying traditional Jewish texts for the first time, and my despair initially held me in a tight enough grip that I couldn't concentrate much on what I was supposed to be learning. I was also absorbed in plans and fantasies for restoring my relationship, which found their way far more than they should have done into whatever religious moments I was having. But after a few weeks, I began to be aware, dimly and without yet being able to articulate this to myself, both that the relationship was permanently over and that that was not altogether a bad thing. Then one day I was at morning prayers for the beginning of a Jewish month when I was struck, sharply, by the verse "In distress I called unto You, Lord; You answered me by setting me free" (Psalm, 118: 5), which is recited in the course of that service. The beginning of the verse seemed to fit my situation perfectly—I had been in great distress and had called on God for help—while the rest of it helped me see clearly, for the first time, what I had begun to sense dimly: that the solution to my situation was not to have my erstwhile relationship restored, but to become free of the need for it. I felt suddenly that I had been answered by God, but in a way that surprised me. Instead of the satisfaction of my fervent desires, I had begun to be free from those desires. Further down, the psalm assures its readers that "It is better to trust in the Lord than to trust in human beings," and to exhort them not to be entranced, or frightened, by the swarm of "heathens" around them. I understood all this as a warning against the idolatry of erotic love so common in the secular society of both the US and Israel. And the psalm concludes with a promise that God's punishment doesn't last forever, and a call for the "gates of righteousness" to be opened so that the believer can enter and praise God. Again, I read this in light of my own situation, taking it to mean that the pain that had come with the end of my love affair was deserved, but would eventually pass to make room for the "opening" of a higher realm of value, which I could rejoice in and be thankful for.

It didn't hurt that the word for "distress" here literally means "narrow or confined place," while the word for "freedom" literally means "expansion" or "broadening," and is related to *rechov*, the word for "public road," which is used in modern Hebrew as the everyday term for "street." I liked the idea that I had moved from the narrow, cramped, private place of my love affair—private in the intensity with which we had been absorbed in one another, and yet more private, yet narrower, in my solipsistic obsession with her—to a "public street" in which I was beginning to share a community with other observant Jews. I also found fascinating the geological image of being released from a narrow place, perhaps a gorge somewhere, to an expanse in which one can move about freely.

So the line from the psalm confirmed for me that I was proceeding in more or less the right way to get out of my situation, as well as the unexpected (to me) moral teaching that it is freedom *from* dearly held desires,[10] not satisfaction of them, that best resolves many tragic impasses. And it did so in a way that was itself beautiful, enticing, that enriched my understanding of the new-found freedom in which I was beginning to find myself and helped me detach my desires from my relationship and attach them instead to the process of self-understanding. I looked at the line, and felt as though it had been written, for me, at that moment: as if God was speaking it, right then as I was praying, to me. Of course, it was actually written a long time ago, by human beings who intended something quite different by it, and for people quite other than me. But insofar as I regarded the text as coming from God, there was no problem in seeing its human authors, and the entire chain of tradition that brought it in front of me, as mere instruments by which God could speak to me now. God, existent everywhere and everywhen, need not write a text at one time, like a human being, for one limited audience. Rather, a text authored by God can be a means of communication with an infinite number of people at an infinite number of times, conveying, perhaps, very different messages to each of its readers or hearers. (So it is necessary, not accidental, to revelation that its language be capable of shifting, in the way we discussed in Part I, §§ 27–29.)

That is: I had every reason to believe that if God has ever "written" anything, He had written that psalm—and *just* written it, *for* me, on that day in 1982. I had reason to take my encounter with the psalm to be a revelation.

18. This may seem a disappointing example. After all, the truths revealed to me were fairly obvious to anyone outside the kind of passion in which I was immersed. What need is there here of revelation? Surely the word of a good friend or therapist could have led me out of my obsession just as successfully.

But this seeming drawback of my example is in fact an advantage, and a key to what goes on in more dramatic cases. For revelation, on my view, need not bring us an insight that human reason could not possibly reach on its own. Rather, revelation shows a certain person or people what *she* or *they* could not then see, but recognize, once they do see it, as true or likely to be true. And yes, it is important that the recipient of the revelation feels he or she would not have learned the same lesson from an ordinary human interaction—I would not have listened to a friend or therapist at that time: it took the sense that *God* was speaking to get me to listen—but it needn't follow that other people, in other situations, couldn't have grasped the lesson in a more ordinary way. Revelation is always relative in this way, always responsive to the needs of particular people in particular situations and always offering something that those people need to hear, and can't figure out on their own, rather than something to all human beings everywhere. Even a revelation supposedly intended for everyone and all time, like the Gospels or Quran, functions in that universalistic way only by acquiring different meanings in different places and times.

19. One thing my example does lack is comprehensiveness. I took it as revelation because it came from a tradition that I already regarded as revelatory: where I already expected to find revelation and from which I was already willing to accept it. Once we have the notion that God can communicate at all, then we may find signs of His guidance everywhere. But nothing like my encounter with the verse from the Psalms could play the role of the Torah in opening up revelation altogether. The verse from the Psalms was not, could not be, what we might call a *foundational* revelation, if only because it told me so little. We need to understand a text as addressing our whole lives, giving us a comprehensive telos, before we can take moments of the sort I have described as revelatory.

So let's try a more comprehensive version of my story. Suppose I were to go through a period of feeling that my life as a whole is empty, filled with evil or shallow goals or otherwise misdirected, without being able to figure out why that might be. Perhaps I sense something wrong about my life, but it seems perfectly OK in terms of the moral standards I am used to (I am a decent employee, husband, father). Or perhaps I can see that I am regularly doing wrong (I am a gambler, drug-dealer, swindler), but somehow can't find a way to stop myself, to pull myself back from the behavior that brings me shame and self-revulsion.[11] Then suddenly, after I happen to go to synagogue, or spend a long bus ride talking to a religious Jew, it strikes me that what my life lacks is a sense of what the Torah calls "holiness," or that what regularly leads me off course is a version of what the Torah calls "idolatry." I may even imagine myself into the shoes of the misguided people in classical Jewish stories—my drab role-following as the conformist idolatry attributed by the Midrash to Abraham's father Terah, or my petty vices as a version of Pharaoh's evils—and imagine sloughing off my contemptible character as my own personal leaving of Ur for Canaan, or Egypt for the Sinai.

In that case, verses from the Torah might strike me as revelatory in the way the verse from the Psalms did in my earlier example. Perhaps that is how I would feel about "I am the Lord your God, who brought you out of the land of Egypt, out of the house of bondage" (Exodus 20: 2). Or: "Become holy, for I the LORD your God am holy." (Leviticus 19: 2). But now the single lines will gain their significance from my sense that the Torah as a whole is revelatory, and that what it reveals is not just a way out of a particular problem, but a comprehensive solution to what gnaws at my life as a whole. The individual verses will simply be paradigms of how the Torah speaks to my situation, shows me a comprehensive telos that, in my situation, I thought I would never see.

It is characteristic of revelatory texts that they seem to speak directly to individuals in this way, addressing their concrete circumstances and concerns. Eknath Easwaran, a professor of English literature turned teacher and translator of the Upanishads, recounts how he returned to the wisdom of the Hindu tradition in which he had been raised after a midlife crisis in which all the pleasures he had been enjoying seemed meaningless to him:

About this time . . . I came across a copy of the Upanishads. I had known they existed, of course, but it had never even occurred to me to look into them. My field was Victorian literature: I expected no more relevance from four-thousand-year-old texts than from *Alice in Wonderland*.

"Take the example of the man who has everything," I read with a start of recognition: "young, healthy, strong, good, and cultured, with all the wealth that earth can offer; let us take this as the measure of joy." The comparison was right from my life. "One hundred times that joy is the joy of the gandharvas; but no less joy have those who are illumined."

Gandharvas were pure mythology to me, and what illumination meant I had no idea. But the sublime confidence of this voice, the certitude of something vastly greater than the world offers, poured like sunlight into a long-dark room. . . . I read on. Image after image arrested me: awe-inspiring images, scarcely understood but pregnant with promised meaning, which caught at my heart as a familiar voice tugs at the edge of awareness when you are struggling to wake up.[12]

Eboo Patel describes his re-discovery of Islam, after many years of exploring other kinds of spirituality, in similar terms:

Who has not felt the heat and thunder of anger rise up in him or her? Who has not known the total release of fury bursting forth?

I still remember the time I got burned on a fly pattern during a pickup football game in junior high school. David caught the ball . . . over his left shoulder, did a dance in the end zone, said a few choice words to me, and trotted across the field. Five minutes went by. . . . The sting remained. David was about ten feet away. He had his back turned, talking and laughing with his teammate. Were they mocking me? I felt the rage rush up, and it was almost as if I couldn't help myself. I got a running start, aimed my shoulder into the small of his back, and rammed into him with all the force I could muster. His body crumpled under the weight of mine, and I felt a sense of total resolution. . . .

[Later, wanting to overcome my own temptation to violence] was precisely the reason I was drawn to religion . . . I wanted to overcome those parts of me that would tackle somebody from behind. . . .

It was in Islam that I found the clearest articulation of this inner struggle. The story goes like this: As a victorious Muslim army was celebrating its triumph in battle, the Prophet Muhammad told the men they had won only the "lesser jihad." Now, he said, they had to move on to the "greater jihad"—the *jihad al-nafs*, the struggle against their lower selves. The first time I read that, I felt as if the Prophet was speaking directly to me, as if he could see the thousands of times in my life that my lower self had won, as if he was personally returning Islam to my consciousness.[13]

Or consider a fictional, but very realistic account of how a modern Jain, feeling trapped in his conventional roles as husband, father, and heir to a large fortune, returns to the teachings of his ancestral religion:

I sneered [at the Jain monk passing on to me teachings of the Jain founder, Mahavira] but at the same time I found myself intrigued by the possibility that this old monk, with his limited knowledge of the world, might know some secret of the heart that could shatter the shell of numbness that enclosed me.

As if reading my mind, the monk said slyly, "What do you lose by hearing Mahavira's description of the skepticism and nihilism that disturb a man when he finds he is not free, although he continues to perform the role that society requires of him?"

I was taken aback. "Mahavira spoke about these things?"

The monk was amused by my reaction and offered to instruct me further.

Over the months the monk's teachings continued to surprise me. He was able to predict how I would feel long before I arrived at the emotion myself, describing to me the states of my despair with greater accuracy than I seemed able to experience them.[14]

In each case, the religious text seems able to address the reader or hearer's particular circumstances, which philosophical texts, even on ethical issues, almost never do. The religious texts are also able to bring out difficulties that the reader or hearer has not yet been able clearly to see as such—problems, like a mild nausea, that can be covered over by what seems like a happy and generally virtuous life. The very nature of the problem, let alone a possible solution to it, is hidden from the sufferer, and a text that uncovers the problem realistically is already for that reason something of a revelation. The honesty with which it describes the problem lends credibility to the solution it proffers.

Interestingly, in several of these cases, including my own, the passage that seemed revelatory to the particular reader or hearer might have appeared fairly obvious to its original readers, and is not the text's own paradigm of a revelation. This again brings out the fact that a text may function to uncover wisdom primarily to later readers, rather than to the generation for which it was written. But that does not make it any less revelatory, nor does it tell against using the tension between a text and its readers' way of life as a mark of revelation. It may happen only long after a text has been produced that some community of its readers take it to show deep failings in a way of life that had hitherto seemed, to them and most of the people they knew, natural or obviously reasonable. But it is precisely at *that* point that they begin to see the text as "sacred"—even from the theological standpoint, it may well be only then that it *becomes* sacred for them (see § 79, below). Thus, it may have taken Shankara, in the eighth century CE, to rework Hinduism such that the Upanishads could become holy; several generations of rabbis, long after the Torah was written, to establish its sanctity; and a generation of Muhammad's followers to bring the Quran into the space of holiness. That does not diminish the sacredness of these books.

It is also an interesting fact, not to be overlooked, that in all the cases I have described people return to a religious tradition in which they themselves were raised. Too much coincidence, that the wisdom they find should happen to be located in their own tradition, rather than in the sacred texts of some other religion? Not at all: why should God not speak to each of us through our upbringings? Or why should the truth about how human life can be worthwhile not in part be a truth about how our particular lives, with their particular upbringings, can be worthwhile?

20. We'll return to the connection between revelation and upbringing later (§ 80). For now I'd like to ask whether the individualistic examples we have been considering can be used to illuminate how an entire community comes to regard a text or event as revelatory.

Well, there is an analogy on the communal level to the way revelation seems to address an individual's concrete circumstances, and to address them in an unexpected way. What are taken to be revelations tend to come in response to a particular moral problem in a particular historical era. They also tend to reject a dominant moral outlook. These points are related. The sort of problem that opens one to a revelation is generally made difficult *by* the dominant moral outlook around one, and a solution to it can therefore exemplify a wholesale overthrowing of the dominant morality.

Thus in the ancient Near East, as in much of the ancient world, there seemed no way of escaping the worship of kings, and gods who were fairly obvious projections of kings. Moses, the humble shepherd who defeated Pharaoh, and then stood on Sinai to pronounce a law that is wary of kingly power—and in any case never made him a king—showed ancient Israelites a way out of that (indeed, even if there never was a real Moses, the *story* about this Moses helped ancient Israelites see the human provenance, and limitations, of kings). In ancient India, an erstwhile Hindu prince showed the people around him a sensible middle way between the extreme asceticism and extreme indulgence in luxury that marked the society around them, while offering simultaneously a plausible understanding of human experience that justified this middle way (and again, the *story* of this prince helped a community find this understanding and middle way, whether or not it is historically accurate). A few centuries later, in the Near East again, the Jewish community seemed to some of its members arrogant and hypocritical, proclaiming its supposed moral superiority over others, while treating the poor and weak contemptuously. Jesus, born into this community, proclaimed a God Who suffers with the poor and cares for inner humility rather than outward observance. And yet again in the Near East, after yet a few more centuries, the leaders of a society that seemed brutal and sharply inegalitarian to many of its members used a set of myths about a mysterious black stone to maintain their power. The courageous merchant Mohammed, born into this society, proclaimed to it a fairer, more decent way of life, and more inspiring conception of God, and led them to reinterpret the symbolism of the black stone in that light.

Four features of these cases.

First, in each the message is directed to the specific problems worrying people in a specific society; there is no way for it to retain its power if it is separated from the historical context in which it was received. This is just how revealed texts speak to individuals in their concrete situations. Revelations are, I would like to say, angled: they address their recipients from a particular angle rather than appearing to represent a view from nowhere.

Second, the message in each case is a revelation to its hearers in that it is *news* to them—it is unexpected—and it is a superhuman (supernatural) revelation in that they cannot see how any human source in their environment could have come up with it. It comes from beyond the limits of the entire worldview with which they have been raised.[15]

Third, in each case the central message offers a comprehensive telos for human life, but does so in a way that interweaves the telos with moral commitment. Indeed, what is revealed in each case concerns the relationship between the telic and the moral aspects of the ethical life. The telos held up in the daily life of a particular people seems unappealing or implausible, or a tool used by cruel or unjust ruling powers to win submission from their subjects, and the revelation presents a new, more attractive telos, as well as a new, more attractive conception of how the telos can be related to moral concerns. There is also some suggestion that the new telos will transform how people carry out their moral actions in the future—how, indeed, they carry out all actions. A new way of living, a new set of practices, tends either to be contained in or gestured at by the new way of looking at the world.

And finally, the story is in each case a gripping one, full of heroic characters who face temptations and dangers and moral quandaries, and told in an intriguing way that cries out for literary interpretation. That feature of the stories is inseparable, I believe, from their ability to present a community with a vision of their telos. The community *loves* its story, and they hearken to its message—they let it give them a telos—because they love it. The poetic quality of revealed texts enables them to win the allegiance of individuals and communities, who are then inspired to work on making moral sense of them. The aesthetic and moral aspects of faith belong together, and revelation arouses them simultaneously.

21. From the various case studies we have considered, we may cull some criteria for revelation, some general marks that would-be believers look for in a text before they allow it to command their faith:

(1) It claims to solve a difficult moral problem, showing or suggesting how all moral problems might be solved as it does.
(2) It is beautiful, in the way an artwork is: gripping, elusive, and suggestive of inexhaustible material for interpretation.
(3) It suggests or lays out a path to a clear and permanent vision of the highest good, a set of practices by which the believer might come to see the world as holy: as combining beauty and moral goodness so as to inspire unending reflective love.

I will elaborate my account of revelation by devoting a chapter to each of these marks of it. A fourth feature, the unexpectedness that I have stressed at various points, runs through all three. Although it is perhaps the main thing that leads believers to see a revelation as coming from beyond them, it gains its significance from the way it shapes the other three features and cannot be made clear sense of on its own. Accordingly, I will explicate it as it appears, somewhat differently, within each of them.

3

Aspects of Revelation (I)
Moral Teaching

22. When asked why they consider their text sacred, believers tend to point first to its moral content. For all that I have said about the independence of religion from morality, religious people generally believe that their revelation offers them moral guidance that they could not get elsewhere. Moses is regarded by believing Jews as the most virtuous person who ever lived, and the law of Moses seems morally better to them than all other laws. Jesus is the paradigm of virtue to faithful Christians. Mohammed's moral teachings, and way of creating a community, seem so strikingly good to Muslims that they view him as the last and greatest of the prophets. And Confucius and the Buddha and Mahavira and the Baha'u'llah all seem, to their followers, the most profound source of moral wisdom.

At the same time, few religious believers take their revelations solely to offer moral teaching. For mainstream Christians of all denominations, Jesus came primarily to provide us with a mode of salvation that transcends the moral sphere. The Buddha's teaching is primarily a metaphysical one, and is supposed only secondarily to help improve us morally. Something similar can be said of all revealed or historical religions. The central teachings of revealed religions are not moral ones, although they may have moral consequences. Indeed, the moral content of revelatory texts serves mainly to help confirm that they are revealed, which it could not do if it were itself being revealed. The would-be religious Jew feels that the Torah might, indeed, be the word of God when he reads the command about not entering the poor person's house to collect a debt, or about loving the stranger (Deuteronomy 24: 10–11). The would-be convert to Christianity is filled with love for the religion when she reads about Jesus taking care of the poor and despised, or admires Jesus's compassion in forgiving those who have crucified him. Both affirm the revelatory text against the background of a morality they already accept, rather than learning a new morality from the text.

So what is the role of morality in a revealed text? We'll try to understand that in this chapter, setting aside the other features of revelation for the moment.

23. The Buddha, sitting under a tree, suddenly sees how all moral problems might be solved. As against the life of both the voluptuary and the Hindu ascetic, he proposes a middle way, something like Aristotelian virtue, involving restraint of the passions, and the cultivation of compassion, rather than selfishness, but at the same time an acceptance of ordinary pleasures rather than an attempt to eradicate them. His main point is not this moral way itself, but the justification for it—that only a true understanding of the illusion of selfhood, not ascetic discipline, will enable us to overcome our desires. Still, he gains followers at first because the practices he recommends are morally attractive.

In the midst of a community that pays great attention to ritual, while attending little to the needs of those who suffer, a person appears who claims that caring for those who suffer is what counts, and a truer sign of devotion to God than any ritual. His main point is not this moral way itself, but that a deep humbling of ourselves to God—exemplified, ultimately, by his own acceptance of an ignominious death—will lead us to our highest good. Still, he has a following, at first, primarily because of his moral teachings.

In the midst of a stifling commercial world where powerful clans justify their cruelties and injustices by claiming special access to equally amoral gods and goddesses, a man of great integrity appears, with a code of conduct that promises equity and compassion for the poor. His main point is not this moral way itself, but that the worship of amoral supernatural powers needs to be replaced by submission to a single God who cannot be manipulated. Still, he first wins people to this teaching primarily by its moral implications.

And the Torah, viewed this way, is a story about how monotheism lifts a people out of the orgies and child sacrifices characteristic of ancient pagan cults—about how the revelation at Mount Sinai taught the Jews the nature and importance of justice, respect for parents, and faithfulness in marriage.

24. But is this what the Torah actually says? Are the Israelites supposed to have learned at Sinai for the first time that they should not kill, steal, or commit adultery? Surely they knew that already—they are supposed to descend from people who had known that long ago. And they are explicitly taught one of the Ten Commandments—the keeping of the sabbath—before they come to Sinai (Exodus 16: 23–26).

I think the central point of the story of Sinai is that the laws announced there come from a God beyond any human being—that they are not a merely human product and their goal is not merely the satisfaction of human needs and desires. "I am the Lord your God Who brought you out of the land of Egypt," the revelation begins. Until now, perhaps the Israelites attributed the redemption from Egypt to Moses, who was able to work feats of magic. Before the redemption, they lived in a world in which rulers were supposedly divine. The plagues, and the freeing of the slaves, undermine Pharaoh's claim to divinity, but one might have been forgiven for thinking that Moses was to replace Pharaoh as the proper object of worship: that one human god would take the place of another. Not so, say the opening words of the Sinaitic story:[1] *no human being, but a God beyond us all defeated the would-be divine ruler of Egypt and brought you out of enslavement to human self-worship of any kind. Never again shall you worship a human being, or anything less than the source of the entire natural order:* "You shall have no other gods before Me." And if you restrain from doing *that,* you will see the reason for, and be better able to keep, the moral demands that human beings everywhere make of one another: not to kill, not to steal, etc. The attack on idolatry, which is essentially self-worship,[2] is the clue to all morality for Jews.[3]

This is a revelation to the Israelites at Sinai in that the entire world around them believed otherwise. Idolatry was practiced and approved of in Egypt, whence they supposedly came, in Canaan, where they were going, and in Babylonia, from which their ancestors came. The teaching thus runs up against the going morality of their day in much the way that the Buddha's does. And it remains a moral revelation today if one thinks that idolatry in some form (worship of money or art or erotic love) remains an overwhelming temptation, and that we need a path out of it to find virtue. But that virtue itself need not be substantially different from the virtue of which Christians and Muslims and Buddhists would approve. The *solution* to immorality is different from theirs (not so different from the Muslim one), but the *problem* is the same and the result, when the problem is solved, should be more or less the same as well.

This view of what happened on Sinai—or in the hills of Galilee or under the bodhi tree—fits the ordinary use of the word "revelation" nicely. We say, "That was a revelation to me," when what we learn is both newly manifest to us and something that had hitherto been hidden in or behind the manifest. And that is exactly what is supposed to happen in moral revelation. One who thinks it has been revealed to him that idolatry is the ultimate cause of all human evil is saying that what is wrong with idolatry had in some way been before him all the time. The uncovering of something hidden in plain view, like Poe's purloined letter, is a revelation. To reveal is to peal back layers that have covered over an important object or truth, to offer something like a Freudian diagnosis, which the patient accepts, if he does, because on some level he has already been aware that it is true. A divine or sacred revelation, when understood from the moral perspective, is just a more comprehensive diagnosis than the one to which the successful therapist leads his patient. A sacred diagnosis brings out a deep flaw in the unconscious of all human beings, and shows us a way to overcome it.

25. It is essential, not accidental, to what the Torah and its ilk have to teach that their revelations are portrayed as coming amid concrete historical circumstances. Simply to be told, as an abstract principle, that idolatry is the root of all evil would be neither interesting nor convincing. It is far more interesting, and far more convincing, first to be shown the arrogance of Pharaoh—displayed in everything from the cruelty of his slave system to the duplicity and stupidity with which he responds to the plagues—and then have the lesson about idolatry fall out of that. This concrete image of idolatry

corrupting a person and political system does far more than any abstract theory would do to illuminate other concrete cases in our own lives. I can map a politician or businessperson I know onto Pharaoh, and the people he oppresses onto the Israelites, and thereby see the evil at work, and its latent source in idolatry, much more clearly than I would be able to do if I knew just that people shouldn't overrate themselves. I can also map *myself* onto Pharaoh, and use the details in the story about his psychology to see more clearly the workings of my own tendency to idolatry. The details of the story may jump out at me when I behave badly, and thereby awaken realizations, and an inclination for repentance, that I have kept at bay with years of self-deceit.[4] The story arouses my imagination as no mere argument could do.

Moreover, the fact that the evil events in the Torah are depicted so realistically, that we can imagine ourselves into the shoes of its characters, means that the solution to evil it offers is not, as it were, developed on high and then plunked down any which way on the world in which we live. The solution arises, instead, from *within* the texture of the evil it resolves. Like a good novel, the Torah presents evil and suffering as something that needs to be fully explored, waded into, before it can be cured. Philosophies that present a sweet, unexceptionable slogan to take around in life can easily be forgotten, or upheld in name only, because they don't say enough to give us guidance when we have to work our way out of evil. Novels and plays that find too easy a solution to the problems they describe, or present their good and bad characters in too flat and simple-minded a way, evoke scorn or disgust. We feel that a solution to human evil must be somehow *wrested from* that evil, that the powerful, often apparently good forces that make evil possible must first be presented realistically, understood, even accepted to some degree, before a proposed way out of those forces can be convincing. The cure for evil, if there is one, is in good part homeopathic: we need to make use *of* some of the forces causing it in order to nullify those forces, or purge them from ourselves. And the Torah's recognition of this hard truth helps greatly to make it morally useful.

Concrete historical detail is similarly crucial to the moral effectiveness of other purportedly revealed texts. Revelations of a new moral way generally come in response to concrete historical events. But only certain kinds of historical events will do. The event must so impress its original hearers that they can take a response to it as revelatory of a truth about morality in general, and it must be something that can also be taken as exemplary by people in later generations. The later followers must be able to read themselves into the original event; the event must therefore be readable as a paradigm of human suffering.

But this characterization of the event has something paradoxical about it. Revelation seems always to be angled, always to come from a particular perspective, yet it lays claim to being a view of the whole human condition, from no particular angle. Revelation shows one how to see the world as if it ultimately contains no evil—as if all evil could be overcome or compensated for—but precisely what leads one to see the world this way is that one comes across a solution to a seemingly intractable evil about which one had been worrying. One sees how the world could be completely good, how it could compensate for or overcome all evil, when one comes safely through a terrible threat of death or suffering, or recovers from a great betrayal, or when an oppressive system collapses and the people who had been persecuted by it are able to breathe freely again. But this means that one has in hand precisely the evidence that the world *does* contain evil, just as one wants to proclaim that it does not.

This paradox may be ineliminable from the moral power of revelation. Suppose there were a revelation of perfect morality—the sort of revelation a moral philosopher might expect, something that contained nothing but a description of the morally ideal person or society, or a set of rules or virtues that could lead us to such an ideal. It would have to consist just of general platitudes, perhaps just "Do good" or "Love one another."[5] But it's hard to imagine why we would need revelation for this, and how it could offer guidance to anyone trying to make a difficult moral decision. It would not show Albee's George and Martha a way out of the quagmire of their marriage or help Alyosha Karamazov improve his brothers or tell Hamlet whether he should kill Claudius—it could not do that without describing specific cases and taking sides in them, without allying itself with one human being or group against others, in struggles that can serve as paradigms for moral decision-making because good can be found on both sides. If a text is to shed light on our concrete moral decisions, it must be angled, must take up a specific point of view on good and evil—even as it also claims to represent the ultimate good beyond all points of view. Perhaps that is why revelations are always of a condition that *could be* rather than a condition that *is*—always of a future or possible state of the world, in which the good might be whole and everlasting, rather than of the actual one.

But what goes along with this angling, this perspectival feature of revelation, is that each revelation's presentation of a comprehensive cure to human evil comes at the expense of some alternative view of the human good. Revealed religions take sides. Revealed teachings always reject some prior view or way of living, deny a view of how to live that some earlier group of human beings had upheld. That is what makes the new teaching a revelation, an uncovering of something hidden. If the teaching was transparent, out there in plain view, there would be nothing to reveal. And if it were simply a discovery, a presentation of something no-one had hitherto known, but no-one had denied either, it would not resonate with the hearer as a revelation does, not appear to have been hidden in the manifest. We think we have experienced a revelation when someone shows us that and how a way of life around us is wrong, when he or she brings into clear light a systematic problem of which we have long been dimly aware. That is what enables us to greet the revelation as both unexpected and true.

Which is to say that what makes this sort of truth seem revealed is inseparable from its perspectival limitations. Revelatory texts strike our imaginations, and allow us to imagine ourselves into them, only because we take sides, with them, for one versus another view of the human good. Revelations focus on a particular, seemingly irremediable kind of evil, which stands in for or is the source of all other evil, and show us how it can be overcome. They project us, imaginatively, into the heart of this most powerful or original evil and lead us, from there, out of it. But it is inevitable, then, that the backdrop against which the revelation appears be portrayed as wholly unacceptable, that there be no room for a follower of the new vision to be tempted back into it. Pharaoh and the ancient Canaanites, Jesus's Jewish opponents, the powerful clans in Mecca—these must all be demonized if the power of the new vision of goodness is to come out clearly. Even when the revelation invites us to enter sympathetically into the motives of these characters, it must urge us to reject their way of life if it is to make the case for the transformative nature of the alternative it offers. We need blinders to the possible goodness in the paradigm of evil we are leaving behind in order to embark wholeheartedly on a way out of that evil.

At the same time, this teaching by means of rejection sits ill with the claim to absolute goodness of a revelation. If each revelation denies the goodness of an earlier worldview, it is hard to see how it can show proper respect for all human beings. One would expect a comprehensive view of the human good to incorporate the core of what is right in all human ways of living, not to reject some of them as wholly erroneous. Certainly, the idea that the Jews are thoroughly misguided, as the Gospels suggest, that both Jews and Christians have a distorted way of life, as the Quran seems to hold, or that Hinduism is deeply confused, as Buddhism maintains, is disturbing, even to many who have faith in these texts. It is implausible that just one group out of all humanity has stumbled on moral truth. If there is a good God, certainly, it is hard to imagine that He would allow just some of his human creatures to know that truth. The historical specificity of revelations thus stands in tension with their claim to universal moral insight.

That tension is reflected in the internal workings of religious communities. Revelations are addressed to and taken up by communities. The experience of their founding events is a communal one, if only in that the individuals who embrace that event as revelatory—the initial followers of Jesus or Mohammed or the Buddha—find that they need to interpret the significance of the event in conversation with others. But once they start to do that, they and their children gradually come to interpret more and more of what happens in their lives in terms of the revelatory event. There is a feedback mechanism by which people drawn to the revelatory experience are thereby also drawn to one another, while their lives in companionship with one another also help them build stronger bonds of attachment to the revelation. Recall that the original event only works as revelatory because it can be taken as exemplary: individuals identify with the event, in later years and later generations, and thereby find it revelatory in circumstances very different from the ones described in the founding texts. But that means that they want to replay it in various ways, to recall it and discuss it and celebrate it. Of course, there is also a self-selection process, by which those who cease to find the original experience revealing fall away from the group, moving to other communities, forming new, "heretical" communities, or staying on amid the others as lax, unenthusiastic participants. But to the extent that the community retains its religious identity, it will come to consist heavily of people who use one historical event or story to define their lives, and resist imbuing other events and stories with equal significance. This core of the community will therefore tend to disparage outsiders, and exclude the heretics and the unenthusiastic from full participation in its activities. That creates tension within the community, and the practical tension reflects a difficulty within revelation itself, construed morally: How can one claim to have a key, in a particular event, to the way to virtue for all human beings while simultaneously excluding people who focus on other events—even when those people draw, from their own favored events, much the same moral lessons?

There is thus a paradox at the heart of revelation when it is seen as a source of moral teaching. We can respond to that paradox by drawing something other than morality from revelation. But we can also respond by allowing that there is something paradoxical about revelation however it is seen—as we noted earlier, paradox may be the mark of revelation[6]—and asking whether we can learn something of moral value from that fact itself.

I think we can. In the first place, as I suggested earlier, we might stress that the ideal human condition to which revelations point is always posited as something that will be actual in the future, towards which we need to work, rather than something we can find around us now. That makes room for the possibility that the people whose worldviews we regard, within our revelatory traditions, as blocking the realization of that ideal—Canaanites (for Jews), Jews (for Christians and Muslims), Hindus (for Buddhists)—may yet come to a different view (perhaps our own, or perhaps just something not opposed to our own), or that our movement out of the evils in which we feel immersed will lead us to a position in which we can afford to have a gentler attitude towards them.

In the second place, we can learn the importance of carefully interpreting our revelations. The angled quality of revelation leaves a task for future interpreters: to overcome its blind spots, its historical limitations, and transform it into the truly comprehensive vision it aspires to be. Revelatory texts are pockmarked by history, and it is the job of the interpretative traditions to which they are thrown to heal those pockmarks, to give the texts the perfect, radiant sheen they seem, to those who fall in love with them, always to have had.

26. Heidegger's "Origin of the Work of Art" (OWA)—from which much that I have been saying is derived—gives us further insight into the paradox we have been considering.[7] At each moment, the things around us conceal themselves from us in two senses: we don't know exactly what they are (they "refuse themselves to us," says Heidegger) or they mislead us (we take one thing for another, or think of a thing in one way while it is really quite different). Moreover, these two forms of concealment conceal one another: when we are puzzled about a thing, or thwarted by it, we don't know whether the source of our puzzlement is refusal or illusion. Heidegger adds

that one main source of all these forms of concealment is familiarity. The ordinary is precisely what we don't investigate enough to grasp fully, and in which, therefore, any obscurity, and anything misleading, is likely to remain unquestioned.

Heidegger thinks that the forms of concealment he describes are ineliminable from all human knowledge. The "clearing" in which we achieve knowledge, and see our way to what to do, "is pervaded by a constant concealment." Indeed, concealment provides a "constant source to all clearing": the concealment holds open what has been cleared, as shadows allow us to see where a light falls. In literal terms: without familiar presuppositions, and familiar ways of doing things, neither theoretical nor practical reasoning about the unfamiliar would be possible. An unquestioned familiar background is necessary if we are to question the unfamiliar, or deliberate about situations we have hitherto not encountered.[8]

But if this is so, we will be particularly struck when one of the concealed elements of our familiar paths is suddenly uncovered—unconcealed—for us. There can be no systematic way of bringing this about: systematic ways of proceeding will be too beholden to the familiar to be able to probe it deeply. But occasionally an event or artwork or philosophical speculation may bring us face to face with a piece of our presuppositions we had been unable to recognize before. This is what Heidegger calls "truth."

He also says that this truth is always "un-truth." That means: (1) it occurs as an undoing of what had been regarded as true up until that point, and (2) it throws a new set of things into the shadows—creates, even as it brings some things out of the presupposed and overly familiar, a new set of presuppositions that will come to be overly familiar, and therefore a source of concealment. "The nature of truth . . . [as] unconcealedness," says Heidegger, "is dominated throughout by a denial" (OWA 53). We deny what has hitherto been taken to be obvious, ordinary, familiar, in order to show what is questionable in it, to show what it conceals, but that can be done only if at the same time we create a new set of norms and presuppositions by which to preserve and explore what we have now discovered. Denying the truth of one set of beliefs is "not a defect or fault" in truth, "as though truth were an unalloyed unconcealedness that has rid itself of everything concealed." Rather, unconcealment always takes place by denying the truth of a hitherto accepted worldview—by throwing it, with its wisdom and unwisdom alike, into a new concealment. We cannot achieve a comprehensive unconcealment. Rather, we move from one clearing to another, seeing now this, now that, in the light, but always surrounded by some things in shadows. In full light, we would not see anything. The sort of truth Heidegger discusses is always *particular* (OWA 59), always about some particular thing or belief, but therefore always also such as to throw other particular things into darkness. It can never encompass everything there is to know.

We can therefore never attain any final and complete truth of this sort. If this is the sort of moral truth that revelation has to offer, it will be a mistake to regard any revelation as containing the full truth about morality. Indeed, a revelation will best mark itself as morally true if it wears its limitations on its surface, if it displays its historical pockmarks proudly. Heidegger gives artworks priority over science and philosophical theories, in the uncovering of truth, precisely because we never feel we understand the former fully, because they wear their impenetrable materiality and historicity proudly. Each artwork is unrepentantly one particular thing, offering a particular, angled, view, not, even in aspiration, a comprehensive, fully correct picture of the universe. And each revelation, if it is in this respect like an artwork (I think revelations are in many respects like artworks), will be a particular, historically-located view of how human beings should live, obscuring some sources of goodness even as it opens up others. This feature of the revelation will inevitably conflict with its aspirations to provide a comprehensive vision of the good, but also give it power over our imaginations. What is crucial, if it is to guide us morally, is that it not hide its historicity. Even to allow later interpreters to release the comprehensive truth that it may contain, it will have to display its historicity openly, to make clear, rather than to disguise, how much it is indebted to its origins at a particular moment in history, in the context of a particular struggle among human beings with different moral worldviews.

27. With this in mind, we can explain, even embrace, the hard passages in the Torah, the passages that seem mere products of its historical origins: what I call its "historical pockmarks." Artworks, says Heidegger, display their submission to the concealed by their stubborn refusal to allow the mute colors, the specific sounds, the wood or rock out of which they are made to fade from view (OWA 44–46), by their insistence on making these "earthy," non-verbal elements of themselves essential to what they have to say. This is especially true in the non-verbal arts, but even poems have a mute, earthy quality when they celebrate sounds and rhythms normally irrelevant to meaning, or delight in rather than suppressing the fact that our words have all sorts of ambiguities and obscurities. And by taking poetic form, revealed texts share in this submission to the concealed. But their historical pockmarks, the moments in which the ideal goodness to which they lay claim conflicts with their perspectival origins, display this earthiness yet more dramatically.

The bizarre ritual to allay the fears of jealous husbands in *Numbers*, the command to wipe out the Amalekites and the nations of Canaan, the permission to kill stubborn and rebellious sons—these are the "earth" of the Torah. They are its historical pockmarks, provoking generations of interpreters to try to minimize their literal meaning or force it into a mold compatible with morality. They are reminders that the text *needs* interpretation, that it does not limpidly reflect a moral ideal, as the visions of a Kant or a Rawls seem meant to do. They are the grains of sand in the oyster of the Jewish community, irritating it into producing the pearl of the Jewish interpretive tradition. They are obstacles to any cheerful complacency about reading morality straightforwardly off of the Jewish sacred text; they keep Jews from literalism and fundamentalism. They also keep Jews from supposing that they can simply identify themselves with humanity as a whole, see themselves, straightforwardly, as possessors of a worldview they could share with everyone. Cosmopolitanism is hard work, something no-one wholly achieves.[9] Those who do work toward it should therefore see it, at each moment, as an ideal they can only approximate. And the discomfort Jews feel, when they run up against the thorny bits of the Torah, reminds them that they are far from the cosmopolitan ideal that they are trying to reach. In this way, the tension between the effort of the Jewish hermeneutical tradition to bring its teachings into line with comprehensive moral ideals, and the historically located Torah out of which those ideals must be read, is itself morally valuable, a humbling reminder of how difficult it is to bring the notion of a completely adequate moral system into historical reality. The hermeneutical struggle to make moral sense of one's revealed text *enacts* the homeopathic process, represented in the Torah as in other revealed texts, of curing human failings by methods that require us first to face, and sympathize with, those failings.

28. Struggling with the historical pockmarks of a text does not mean explaining them away historically. To say, "This was written by people in a more sexist or xenophobic or violent time" pushes the difficult passages away from oneself, allows one to cease working through its difficulties to a comprehensive vision of the good. Historical explanations of a text—"it reflects what people thought then; now we know better"—place the reader in a position of superiority over it, from which to analyze and judge its errors: precisely the opposite of the position in which one can take it as revealing truth to one, in which one can learn from it.[10] If we write off certain passages in our revealed texts as not belonging to their unveiling of the good, we avoid the kind of imaginative exercise from which we might learn how to work through our own points of moral blindness. Only if we say, "This too is part of the revealed truth, and I must learn from it" do we allow it to give us imaginative insight into our own sexism and xenophobia and tendencies to violence: and, therefore, into how we might find our way out of those evils. Only thus are we forced to confront the possibility that we ourselves may share some of the ugly moral qualities that we see in the text. If we accept the sexist or violent passages in the Torah as belonging to its revealed content, we accept sexism and violence as parts of ourselves; the process of interpretation then contributes to the process of overcoming those aspects of ourselves. If we write off the passages as belonging to the limitations of a more primitive age, we distance their disturbing aspects from ourselves, and pretend, prematurely, that we have overcome such failings.

For this reason, modern historical scholarship on sacred texts has little to contribute to their religious meaning. What sacred texts mean when viewed *as* sacred is radically different from what their human authors may have meant, or initial readers took them to mean, and only the former way of looking at them allows them to unveil our telos to us.[11]

29. The central text of Christianity has fewer and less obvious pockmarks than the Torah. Christians have often argued that this shows the moral superiority of their religion to Judaism: shows that theirs is a kinder, gentler sort of religion. The history of the two faiths makes this claim look absurd, but is it perhaps true in principle that it is better for a revealed text to be minimally pockmarked, to show as few signs as possible of its origin in an age with long-discarded moral standards?

I think not. Indeed, the relative absence of moral pockmarks in the Gospels may be a source of some of Christianity's characteristic moral problems. The Jewish tradition has a tendency to foster insular attitudes, to permit, even encourage, an indifference towards non-Jews; Jews alert to the evils of this indifference need to work hard to keep their community from lapsing into it. But certainty that one's own way is the only right one, and a concomitant intolerance of others, are not characteristic of Judaism. They are characteristic of Christianity—Christians concerned about the evils of this attitude need to work hard to keep their communities from lapsing into it—and they may spring partly from the relative *absence* of obvious pockmarks in the Christian sacred text.

Jesus is presented in the Gospels as so thoroughly gentle and sweet that the few moments when he does do something morally disturbing—refusing to see his parents, shriveling a fig tree, hurling curses at Pharisees or calling Jews who question him children of the devil[12]— can be read as a correction of what ordinary morality tells us, rather than a hint that the reader should seek a deeper, non-literal interpretation of the text. And Christians have in fact often read the Jews in their text as truly evil figures: *literally* children of the devil. Similarly, the passages in which Jesus condemns divorce, or Paul urges slaves to submit to their masters and women to their husbands,[13] have seemed to generations of Christians close enough to what an independent morality might teach that they have read them as proof that one *should* condemn divorce, and permit slavery and sexual hierarchy. Christians have not necessarily seen these moments as pockmarks, that is, in need of energetic human interpretation if they are truly to reveal God's will. Some passages in the Gospels and Paul's epistles might raise a moral eyebrow here or there but they are not as glaringly shocking as the command to wipe out the Amalekites, or kill stubborn and rebellious sons. They have therefore not inspired quite the effort at moral reinterpretation that the Jewish tradition has bestowed on its text.

As a result, Christians have been able unworriedly to see themselves as representatives of a fully humane, universal religion, to hide from themselves the degree to which their tradition arises out of historical struggles with other traditions and reflects a partly blinded denial of what is good in those traditions. This premature universalism is easily accompanied by a demonization of everyone outside their religious community.[14] If one thinks one is holding on to the comprehensive truth about goodness, rather than a partial, angled view that needs to be transformed into such a comprehensive truth, then those who don't share one's beliefs must be wrong, even opposed to goodness.

Christians often see themselves as having arrived at a true concern for all humanity, rather than being merely on the way to such a state, and accordingly fail to see the tribalism, the historical limitations, of their community and tradition. They might be less complacent, more sensitive to their own limitations and the good features of other traditions, if they paid more attention to the pockmarks in their sacred text.

30. I don't mean by anything I have said to disparage the moral aspect of revelation. There is great moral wisdom in sacred texts, and religious believers rightly love these texts in part because they gain such wisdom from them. I have found the Torah calling me to a higher level of concern for the poor and the weak than the secular morality around me demands. It also seems to me to require a higher level of willingness to dissent, to stand up against the drift of one's society, than does conventional morality in America: I think of the verse commanding Jews not to join a majority to do evil (Exodus 23: 2) whenever I am tempted to go along with a politically correct line on an issue. And I know that faithful Christians and Muslims similarly draw important moral insights from their sacred texts. Eboo Patel's story, cited earlier (§ 19), about how the Quran helped him struggle against impulsive anger is a case in point.

So we can certainly get moral guidance from our revelations, and we are often inspired to a more fervent or thoroughgoing commitment to morality by them. It is just that we cannot take our revealed texts to be wholly moral on their face—passages in almost every such text must be reinterpreted in accordance with independent moral standards—nor can we get the whole of our moral systems from them. The moral function of these texts, while real enough, thus presents something of a puzzle. How do they acquire moral value if moral teaching is not all they do, and if they need correction by independent sources of moral guidance?

Well, one answer to that is precisely that the texts inspire us to *interpret* them morally. Their nuggets of profound moral insight lead us to become convinced that they must latently contain a complete, ideal system of morality and we labor to bring that system out of them. If God is the author of these texts, perhaps that's exactly what He wants us to do with them. An all-good God might well want a free, dignified trust out of us, a trust by which we are willing, like Abraham, to argue with Him, and perhaps the fact that He draws us to Him by way of these powerful but flawed texts is a sign that we should use them to develop our own moral resources. The point of revelation may be as much to spark a human tradition of interpretation as anything else.

Alternatively, perhaps the moral teaching of these texts cannot properly be understood apart from their other, more central function: to give us a vision of our telos. As we will see in the next chapter, this function is bound up with the beauty or sublimity of the texts. Even while considering them as sources of moral teaching, I have described them as "powerful," "inspiring," etc. These are aesthetic terms, and I have also made use of Heidegger's account of art to explain how we may regard them as disclosing moral truth. We may say that revelatory texts beautify morality, invest it with an aesthetic appeal it does not always have when presented by parents and school teachers and philosophers. But that is just a rough way of expressing their ability to set morality into a wider telic context, to locate our moral practices within a vision in which we can see human life as intrinsically worth living.

Now part of what enables them to provide such a telic vision is their moral power—we suppose that a text with such moral insight must also be onto something when it tells us what our lives are for—but on the whole, the relationship between the moral and the telic aspects of revelation goes in the opposite direction: revelatory texts gain moral power because and insofar as they offer a telos for our lives. The Israelites come to Sinai and are vouchsafed a vision of God, or of what it is like to stand in God's presence. Later they are told that by following a path that goes along with this vision, they can "become holy": become close to God, or capable of seeing, as God does, how the world as a whole is beautiful.[15] In this light, their moral laws have a new importance, and they are more willing to follow them. In this light, morality has a *point*: it serves our deepest needs, rather than merely helping us co-ordinate our actions, or keeping us from interfering with one another's freedom and pleasures. And seeing morality this way can help us overcome evil. For the fear that our lives are pointless is the most dreadful of fears, leading some to a despair or anger they express in cruelty, others to an irresponsible indulgence in momentary pleasures. So if we can find a way to see our lives as very much *not* pointless—and to see being moral as part of achieving that point—we will be relieved of a profound source of our temptation to evil.

Note that the fear of pointlessness is not a purely selfish emotion. In fearing that *my* life is pointless, I also fear that yours is. That threatens my ability to maintain a sense of the importance of my moral duties to you. If your life is not worth living, how can it matter whether or not I help protect you from danger or improve your material condition? Unless your life is worth protecting, and the material improvement goes towards something worthwhile, why bother? The revelation of a point, a telos, to human life is thus good for all of us and can lift us all, together, out of our egocentricity. So if the main function of revelatory texts is to provide us with a vision of worth, that is itself a great, if indirect, contribution to morality. We do not really leave the moral aspect of revelation behind, therefore, when we turn to its telic aspect. We saw earlier that the highest good must be structured so that our telos, while separate from virtue, is built onto it. By appearing to us initially in a moral light, and demanding a strenuous commitment to morality of us, revelatory texts mirror this structure. But by doing so, they point towards an end that transcends morality, and that we will not see properly if we insist on viewing them in a moral light alone.

4

Aspects of Revelation (II)
Beauty

31. Essential to how a revelation can satisfy our telic yearnings is its beauty. A vision of our lives that makes them seem worth living must render them, or the world in which they are lived, beautiful, and to do that, the vision must itself be beautiful.

But how is beauty related to the telic? What is beauty, that it can help constitute an adequate vision of our telos?

Here are a few possibilities:

(1) We call something "beautiful" in which we take a reflective pleasure. But the subjective criterion for the highest good is supposed to be something similar: that it evokes reflective love. The pleasure we feel in the presence of the beautiful also seems inexhaustible—seems as if it could be forever renewed— and the pleasure inspired by the highest good must be just as inexhaustible. That is how it can relieve us of the fear that eventually we will find our lives unutterably boring.

(2) The highest good must be in significant part obscure, mysterious to us. It must engage with the concepts we use in our other, more limited projects, but it must also transcend them: it must serve as an end for them to aim at, a point of orientation that guides them. But what makes things beautiful—what makes artworks beautiful, at least—is a certain mystery about them, the fact that we are unable, fully, to grasp them. The beautiful tantalizes our conceptual frameworks, seems suited to conceptual grasp, but always eludes it. It is always somewhat unexpected, never captured fully by the intellectual frameworks we have in place when we encounter it. But a revelation, too, must be elusive and unexpected. The unexpectedness of revelation, its transcendence of our own mental resources, is what leads us to humble ourselves to it, to see it as coming from a source beyond ourselves.

(3) Aesthetic appreciation consists in a rapt attention to the particular. The word "beautiful" is wrung from us when we are absorbed in a moment, a particular,

to the exclusion of the rest of the world. But a state in which we could be utterly satisfied with the particulars before us, in which we could love each moment of our existence as it happened, would be a state in which we would no longer worry about what our lives as a whole amount to. Our absorption in the particular would remove the threat of boredom that makes that question seem pressing. Goethe did well when he had Faust wager everything on the possibility of saying to the passing moment, "Stay a while: you are so beautiful." (Although he did even better to suggest, at the end of the two plays, that no individual moment could meet that condition.)[1]

(4) The beautiful—again, in art at least—is supposed to be produced by a source that transcends normal human capacities: by "genius." But this trans-human authorship is also what we attribute to revelation, and what allows us to hope that there is some intelligent, and good, author of the entire world in which we live. Correspondingly, we give beautiful art something like the same authority over us that we give revelation: we submit to its terms, try to learn from it, rather than scrutinizing it for imperfections, or assuming that we already know what it has to teach us.

I will go through each of these possibilities in this chapter; each contributes a great deal to our understanding of the telic function of revelation. But the second is by far the most important, and the most complicated. After considering (1), I will spend about half the chapter on (2), and come only briefly to (3) and (4) at the end.

32. To begin with (1), our subjective response to beauty:

Plato argues that love ultimately aims at the form of beauty, which is for him a synonym for the form of the good. Later Platonists, from the medieval Christians, Muslims, and Jews who used erotic imagery to describe the soul's union with God through modern secular ethical and aesthetic theorists like Lord Shaftesbury, maintained a tight connection between beauty and love. Love, for all of them, was the criterial response to beauty, whether in a human being, a work of art, or a natural landscape. So the Platonic tradition would seem to be a good place to look, if we want to identify our telos by its beauty, and its beauty by our love for it.

One might think that this passionate aspect of the response to beauty is lost in Kant. Kant uses the phrase "disinterested satisfaction" for the criterial response to beauty, meaning by it to describe a feeling of pleasure in an object that does not come from consumption or possession of it, that is content to let the object be and admire it from afar.[2] Love is the epitome of a hot passion, it would seem, and disinterested satisfaction of a cool one: at first glance, the two could not be further apart. Yet Kant and Plato turn out not to be all that far apart. Plato begins his account of aesthetic appreciation with straightforward erotic love, where a hot, uncontrolled yearning is definitive of our relationship to the objects of our desires. This, however, is just the lowest version of the pursuit of beauty for Plato. We do call our beloveds "beautiful," but we learn, or can learn, that what is beautiful about them is realized more fully in natural objects and works of art, yet more so in the objects of philosophy, and most fully in the form of beauty itself. As we ascend this ladder, the kind of love we feel gets cooler. Indeed, it is the experience of cooler, more reflective kinds of love that helps teach us that the more abstract and universal kinds of beauty are higher than the beauty of the naked young person we first desired. How, after all, could we so much as understand the Platonic argument that particulars derive both their reality and their cognitive accessibility from their participation in general forms, unless our ardor for particular bodies has cooled enough that we can appreciate philosophical abstraction? And the structure of Plato's *Symposium*, which moves from an initial feverish, sexually charged monologue to the measured dialogue-speech of Socrates, seems designed to educate our sentiments in just this way.

Which is not to say that Eros, in its usual sense, is entirely lacking at Plato's higher levels of the appreciation of beauty. On the contrary, the whole point of the *Symposium* is that Eros unites the spectrum of our pursuit of beauty: that hidden even in our sexual desires is a deeper desire for truth and goodness, on the one hand, and that our yearning for truth and goodness is ultimately as intense as our sexual desires, on the other. But our yearning for truth and goodness is a *reflective* yearning, a yearning for reflection and a yearning informed by reflection, which is content to contemplate its objects without possessing or consuming them. (Anyone who thinks they could possess or consume the Forms does not yet understand what they are.)[3] There is little difference between this sort of love and Kant's disinterested satisfaction, and both resemble what I have called reflective love.

Part of the point of Kant's emphasis on disinterestedness is that a disinterested pleasure will be *free*—it will not depend on desires determined by our biology or socialization. Because it is free in this way, aesthetic pleasure can reasonably be seen as expressing our subjective natures; that gives us reason to expect all subjects like ourselves to share it. But Kant's emphasis on disinterestedness is also meant to capture the distinction between being in the throes of a passion and reflecting on our lives at a greater distance, and the intuition that the feelings we have in the latter position are more likely to express our considered judgments. Kant's disinterested satisfaction echoes the criterial response to morality among the British sentimentalists who preceded him. Joseph Butler and Adam Smith both thought that it is only the approval and disapproval we feel in our cooler, more reflective moments that can properly be identified with moral judgment. Kant takes moral judgment out of the realm of feeling, but allows aesthetic judgment to be identified with our cool, disinterested feelings.

For Kant's predecessors, the distinction between the moral and the aesthetic was not a sharp one. Smith, like his teacher Hutcheson and friend Hume, speaks of "moral beauty" and characterizes the highest kind of moral evaluation as "admiration."[4] I think we can bring Kant together with his predecessors by recalling the relationship we laid out earlier between morality and ethics. When we consider moral actions under the wider rubric of ethics, we open up the sphere of evaluation as a whole, and therefore need to be able to commensurate aesthetic and moral properties, to weigh aesthetic properties in moral terms and moral properties in aesthetic terms. But it is from this perspective that we must consider the central question of ethics: whether our lives as a whole are worthwhile. It follows that in the consideration of this question, we cannot usefully distinguish between moral and aesthetic value. The freedom necessary to telic value must be both a moral and an aesthetic one; indeed, telic evaluation seems, if anything, closer to aesthetics. If we can take a disinterested satisfaction in our lives—a thoughtful, free satisfaction, informed by reflection and independent of our immediate interests and passions—that seems equivalent to finding them worthwhile.

Of course, the satisfaction would have to *last*. But for Kant, as for most philosophers before him, aesthetic satisfaction is the pleasurable feeling most likely to last. Our joy in beauty builds on itself, rather than fading. The longer we spend with a great Rothko, the more we find to enjoy in it, and the more we can enjoy other paintings (by Rothko and by others). "We *linger* over the consideration of the beautiful," says Kant, "because this consideration strengthens and reproduces itself." The beautiful "is always new for us, and we are never tired of looking at it" (CJ 222, 243). This is definitive of beauty: we do not apply the term except where we experience something that promises "always [to be] new for us." So aesthetic pleasure accumulates over time—each moment of it adds to the preceding one—and seems at least capable of continuing eternally. It is, therefore, unlike other pleasures, commensurate with the temporal shape of our consciousness.[5] That doesn't mean that a collection of pleasures in beauty will add up to a worthwhile life—we saw the problems with that idea earlier (Part III, §18)—but it gives us reason to think that the aesthetic stance is the appropriate one from which to judge *whether* our lives are worthwhile. To find our lives, or the world in which they take place, beautiful, to find that they yield us disinterested satisfaction, just is to approve ethically of those lives.

33. For Kant disinterested satisfaction is a response to what he calls the "purposive-ness without purpose" of an object. He means by this just what he calls its subjective purposiveness, not any purpose it may have objectively, but the idea that beauty somehow represents what it is for something to be an end resonates intriguingly with Plato's indication that the beautiful is but one face of the good. (Kant differenti-ates the beautiful from the good, but sees the former as a symbol of the latter—CJ §§ 4–5, 59.) Plato also hinted that our ultimate good may have to be somewhat obscure to us—and obscurity, I have suggested, is also a feature of beauty (§ 31, point (2)). Indeed, it is the feature of greatest importance to our concerns here, and without relying too heavily on the exact views of either Plato or Kant, I would like now to explore the possibility that there is something about the very notion of purposiveness that requires our ultimate purpose to be beautiful. If so, there would be deeper reasons than we have yet seen for a vision of that purpose—a revelation—to be beautiful: and, in that capacity, obscure. Only that beauty and that obscurity, I'll suggest, allows the vision adequately to represent its object.[6]

The connections between purposiveness and beauty, beauty and obscurity, and obscurity and particularity are complex; the Kantian and Platonic materials that illuminate these connections are also complicated. I will therefore take some time trying to explain all this. In the course of that explanation, I will also suggest, tentatively, that an obscurity inherent to the highest good explains why we had such difficulty finding an adequate candidate for it in Part III of this book. Our ultimate telos cannot be found in any purely rational way.

I am tentative about this suggestion for two reasons. First, as will become obvious, it cannot be proven (it is suited to faith rather than knowledge), and I am not sure that I have been able even to articulate it properly. Second, there are revealed religions that account for the mystery about our highest telos quite differently—maintaining that our sinfulness, say, or the confusions engendered by our bodies, make it difficult for us to see our proper end—and I am trying in this book to provide a defense for revelation that can be used by as many different traditions as possible. If my points about beauty and obscurity seem unsatisfactory, moreover, the claim that beauty is important to revelation can rest on the other grounds I offered for it in § 31. But the points about beauty and obscurity make richer sense of the connection between beauty and our telos than any other explanation I know.

34. At one point in the *Republic,* Plato indicates that the idea of an ultimate telos may be inherently obscure, inherently resistant to capture in conceptual terms. The form of the good, he says, lies beyond truth: the good is "the cause of knowledge and truth, ... different from, and still more beautiful than," they are (Rep 508e–509a). A bit later he tells us that the form of the good is "the thing seen last" in the intelligible realm, and that it produces truth and reason (Rep 517b). What can this mean? Don't we want to say it is *true* that this ultimate good exists, that we *know* that to be so? But if we say that, we implicitly give truth and knowledge priority over the good.

Part of what Plato means, almost certainly, is that without the form of the good, nothing would come to be at all, that things need a goal, a telos, to develop and that the good, as the telos of the universe, is therefore the source of all reality. The reality to which thought responds would therefore not exist without the good. Then the correspondence between thought and reality—truth—would also not be possible. So the good is the "cause" of truth.

Another part of what Plato may mean is that if we are to choose to *aim* at truth, to seek knowledge, we need first to believe that it is good to have true beliefs. More strongly, he may hold that our decision to hold any claim true depends on its fitting into a system of beliefs that, we think, leads us to a good way of life. Particular claims are validated by more general principles and procedures, which are in turn validated by a general theory about how to pursue truth, and this theory needs itself to be validated by something that does not simply, in circular fashion, appeal once more to truth. Rather, we consider how the theory fits into our lives as a whole, what sort of a life it promotes. So the ultimate criterion that enables us to choose which theory of truth to accept is the good. We seek the *best* theory of truth.

But if so, we will not be in any position to evaluate our understanding of the ultimate good in terms of other principles, and Plato for that reason has Socrates insist that he can speak of the ultimate good only by way of metaphors—the sun, the divided line, and the cave—and that his hearers will ultimately perceive that good only if they are "turned around," converted, from a framework for thought blinded to it to one on which it is visible (Rep 518 c–d). The goal that makes all our activities, including all argument, worthwhile cannot itself be shown by argument, cannot be proven to be "truly" that goal. What makes our lives worthwhile is therefore necessarily, not accidentally, beyond rational investigation. We can tell parables about it, but we cannot define or analyze it in other terms, let alone demonstrate its existence.

35. Rational investigation is discursive investigation, an attempt to grasp the world by way of concepts, and the argument I have just sketched turns on features of conceptualization. We can retain these features even while discarding Plato's view of concepts as more real than concrete objects. Suppose concepts are instead, as most people today believe, our constructions, ways of splitting up the world that we come up with for various purposes. A question then arises about what purpose should guide the process of construction itself. To answer that we may, initially, point to various purposes we happen to have—things we want to do, or that our society represents as good—but we eventually need to evaluate these purposes themselves, ask whether we should be pursuing them. We need to sort our purposes themselves into categories, some of which we'll be inclined to judge worthwhile and others not. We want, then, some guide, some criterion, for how to do this, and the natural candidate, given the way that purposes come nested in one another (I go to the store to get coffee, I drink coffee to wake myself up, I wake myself up to get some work done, ...), is our *ultimate* purpose: our highest good.[7] So an ultimate purpose may be necessary to guide the very process by which we evaluate purposes—and to guide in turn, therefore, the process by which we construct concepts. If so, however, that ultimate purpose will need itself to stand beyond the process of construction, not be one of the concepts we construct. The ultimate purpose of all our activities, including our cognitive activities, cannot, on this view, be conceptualized. As Plato says, it will be "the *cause* of knowledge and truth, ... different from, and ... more beautiful than," they are. It will lie beyond, not within, the sphere of what we know.

There are other modern ways of arriving at a similar conclusion. For instance: concepts are general rubrics, by which we classify the bits of the world we encounter and which we can then use to make predictions about these bits, explain connections among them, and design new bits. They are also essential to the ends we set for ourselves—we aim normally at a *type* of thing, not a particular one, since we can't know what particular outcome would satisfy our strivings until we have achieved it— and to the way we evaluate and revise those ends. We can't be pure particularists, immersed in all the details around us without worrying about how they might be grouped into types. The universe is never exactly the same at two different moments,[8] so our only hope, now, of guessing what it will be like and how to get around it in the future is to pick out types of things and hope that the future will contain particulars similar enough to the ones around us that they can be placed under the same types. So we split up the world conceptually: into male and female, Democrat and Republican, animal, vegetable, and mineral. We need to do that, to get things done. Which is to say that concepts, and the words that express them, are tools that lose their point if stripped of all our purposes and projects. They are suited for a being outfitted with something definite to do, a bit of the world to experience or alter, not for one that can rest satisfied with bare contemplation of all the bits, or of the scene as a whole.

But in order to see our lives as valuable, we may need precisely to take such a step back and contemplate the world as a whole, not to pursue one end among others within the world, or favor some things and disfavor others in the course of that pursuit. What enables us to do this rather than that gets in the way of our loving the whole world. We have to turn our approving attention away from some things and toward others in order to pursue a particular course of action, but this sort of partial, blinkered attention necessarily obscures the value of some things even as it makes others light up.[9] If so, however, our concepts will be useless to us when we try to contemplate or love the world as a whole: they draw precisely the sorts of distinctions we need to avoid. Here, we need a state of satisfaction, not with this or that state of the world, but with the *entire* world. We need a type of satisfaction utterly different from the one we feel when a particular project of ours works out successfully, or a particular expectation is met. The ultimate value of our universe, or of our existence in it, cannot, on this view, hang on the sorts of things that could be demonstrated by means of the concepts we use to find our way around *within* it.[10] We cannot affirm the whole universe as long as we are attached to some parts or moments of it and not to others. Knowledge helps us do things, predict and control the universe. But perhaps the point of our lives is *not* to do things—to step back, instead, and contemplate.

Of course, this is quite a stoic view of what it means to find the world a good one; it urges on us a kind of reconciliation with the universe that may be impossible for us. But even if we don't go the whole way with the stoics, it seems right to say that our concepts fit into our various projects and that what gives these projects value, if they have that, may be visible only to one who steps out of the projects and evaluates them *sub specie aeternitatis*: from the perspective of the world as a whole.

Both of the arguments I have offered eschew Plato's picture of concepts as real entities, in an abstract world of their own, in favor of a more subjective and instrumentalist account of them. On Plato's own picture, the argument for the highest good goes through straightforwardly. My point is that it may go through even on a subjective and instrumentalist account of concepts.

On the seventh day God created holiness (the word "holy" appears for the first time when God sanctifies the sabbath in Gen. 2:3): the purpose, end, telos (tachlit) of the universe. Holiness is, or depends essentially upon, shabbat—"ceasing," "refraining," "holding back," "spontaneously receiving." Only this completes the universe (Genesis 2:1: vayekhal): makes it possible for the universe to be something complete, to be a whole (Genesis 2:1: kol melachto). But wholeness is beauty, or a condition for beauty: even God cannot properly admire the universe until it is a whole, until He can stand back from it and (as it were) consider it reflectively: until He can gaze at it. So the universe is "very good" on the sixth day, but it is more than that when a separation comes between it and God on the seventh. Or perhaps its "very goodness" can only then be seen by beings other than God. Perhaps shabbat—restraint—constitutes the bridge between God and His creatures, the link that enables them to share His way of seeing what is good about the universe. In any case, the seventh day takes a step beyond all particular good things and actions, contains the empty space that makes it possible for everything good to shine forth as such, to shine as a glowing whole from a distance. Without shabbat, there would be nothing holy. After the creation of shabbat, we live forever in the space of that shabbat—or can so live, in a future, more ideal world: yom sheculo shabbat ("the day that will be all shabbat").

36. Sacred texts from all over the world contain passages suggesting that the holy cannot be conceptualized, that one needs to step beyond concepts—beyond words— to experience the presence of the divine:

> There is a thing chaotic yet formed,
> It was born before Heaven and Earth.
> Silent. Empty.
> ... It could be considered the mother of all creation.
> *I do not know its name*; I call it Tao.
> If forced to name it, I would call it Great.[11]

> The Self in man and in the sun are one.
> Those who understand this see through the world
> And go beyond the various sheaths of being
> To realize the unity of life.
> *Realizing That from which all words turn back*
> *And thoughts can never reach*, they know
> The bliss of Brahman and fear no more.[12]

> Action and misery having ceased, there is nirvana.
> *Action and misery come from conceptual thought.*
> *... What language expresses is nonexistent.*
> *The sphere of thought is nonexistent.*
> Unarisen and unceased, like nirvana
> Is the nature of things.[13]

> The heavens tell the glory of God; and the firmament proclaims his handiwork.
> Day to day pours forth speech, and night to night declares knowledge.
> *There is no speech, nor are there words*; their voice is not heard;
> Yet their voice goes out through all the earth,
> And their words to the end of the world.[14]

Each of these passages presents a metaphysical source of the universe, or goal for our lives, as lying beyond language, beyond concepts. And for each, our relationship to that source would seem to consist, ideally, just of being aware that it is there, of contemplating it; the stillness we would thereby achieve might end the misery that goes along with restlessly trying to *do* things. Doing things—trying to control the universe—gets in the way of our ideal condition. That is exactly what the second of our modern versions of the Platonic thesis suggested. What makes our lives worth living, that for which we do everything else, may have to be a condition in which we do nothing. We may need somehow to set aside all our doings, and the concepts that enable those doings. Our telos may appear to us, or consist, in a mystical vision that lies beyond all our practices and concepts.

37. But if our telos lies beyond our concepts, beyond anything we could prove or analyze, how can we get any sense of what it is? Why, indeed, should we believe that it exists? Well, if we continue to draw on Platonic insights, we might note that in the *Symposium* Plato presents Eros as leading us, via our love for concrete beautiful things, to a loving union with the highest form. A long medieval tradition of neo-Platonic mystics used this idea to suggest that there is a sort of non-conceptual, direct mode of knowing, rooted in love, by which we can grasp our highest good (the vision of God, for them). The early Wittgenstein, too—possibly influenced by medieval neo-Platonism[15]—identified value with "what is mystical," and explicitly brought the aesthetic and the ethical together under this heading.[16] And Kant, while eschewing any direct relationship between the beautiful and the good, or between the beautiful and the object of our religious hopes, repeatedly returns to the suggestion that the beautiful symbolizes both the good and the transcendent. Indeed, according to some commentators, what is most important about the beautiful for Kant is that it gestures at how the transcendent substratum we posit in ourselves could be united with the transcendent substratum of the universe.[17] So perhaps mystical love can replace discursive knowledge, when we try to grasp the highest good. That would simultaneously make sense of our difficulties in pinning down the highest good and fit nicely with the aesthetic aspect of revelation. There are certainly long precedents in philosophical theology for the idea that the beautiful is the mystical, or that the mystical is one variety of the beautiful. And, of course, that would seem to make it obvious that revelation must be beautiful.

The problem with this move is that "the mystical" is a black box. No-one knows exactly what it means—it seems to mean very different things in different cultural contexts—and there is a danger that it is simply identical with the unknowable. But then we will have made no progress. If "mystical" is simply another term for "unknowable," the idea of *knowing* something in a mystical manner will be unintelligible. So will the idea of mystical experience, as long as experience is understood as a kind of knowledge.

Indeed, mystical experience, if it is supposed to occur without concepts, may be unintelligible even if we withdraw the demand that experience amount to knowledge. Concepts are our tools for coming to grips with the world and mystical experience is supposed to break through those tools. But there is good reason to argue, as Kant did, that we cannot have any experience without concepts. Without concepts, we cannot have objects. An object is a relatively enduring presence, against which we define our own existence as subjects. We would be unable to think at all, we could not even distinguish ourselves from the flow of sensations in which we are immersed, if some things did not stand relatively fast before us while our thoughts change. So we need objects if we are to be subjects. But we need concepts if we are to have objects. Concepts, literally, bring things together (con-cept: to take together): they collect different things under the heading of "red" or "round" or "hedgehog." They also bring the "same" thing together over time and space. The similarities between our perception at t_1 and our perception at t_2 lead us to infer that they are perceptions *of* the same thing, and we also use notions of what sorts of general qualities belong together to determine where one object ends and another begins. We pick out the fire hydrant before us as a single object because we know it belongs together with other fire hydrants, and not with the sidewalk on which it rests or the air moving past it, as well as because some of its general properties (a dirt smudge here, a crack in the paint there) are *not* shared with other fire hydrants. We locate the particular object by way of its general properties, by way of the many "takings together" that relate it to other objects. It is this strong tie between concepts and objecthood that makes the idea of a non-conceptual experience, along the lines touted by mystics, virtually unintelligible. A blur of uninterpreted sounds and colors—"less, even, than a dream," as Kant calls it (CPR A 112)—can hardly be the highest experience of God, or of beauty.

So even if there is something beyond all our concepts, we can get a glimpse of it only while using our concepts. With this in mind, I will try in the next few sections to develop a different interpretation of the mystical, one which uses Kant's theory of aesthetic experience to get at something like the Platonic vision of the good. On this interpretation, the mystical is a mode of experience that occurs in the interstices of our systems of concepts, rather than doing without concepts altogether. The mystical vision of our telos, if we have one, occurs as an *inter*-conceptual rather than a *pre*-conceptual moment in our cognitive practices. Words, concepts, inform it even if they are also inadequate to it. That explains why it occurs paradigmatically as a poetic *text* or *saying* that ignites or inflames our religious fervor, rather than a moment of silence. By way of some Kantian materials, I will suggest that the beautiful aspect of revelation consists in a rupture but not an abandonment of our normal ways of using concepts— in something that shakes up, but thereby also anchors, the structures we build for organizing our thoughts and practices. What is most significant about revelation—the way it orients our practices as a whole—cannot be captured by our concepts, but nevertheless works among them.

38. Kant refers the pleasure behind any judgment of beauty to what he calls the "free play of the imagination and the understanding" (CJ §9).[18] What exactly is this, and why is it pleasurable? The understanding is the faculty of rules or concepts; the imagination is that which gathers, and places into space and time, the manifold of intuition. According to Kant, the state of mind that leads one to make judgments of beauty is one in which these "cognitive powers... are ... in free play, because no definite concept limits them to a definite rule of cognition." It is a precognitive state, a state that makes use of our cognitive powers, and in which a condition for knowledge is met, without our achieving knowledge itself. We expect others to share our pleasure in beauty because beauty satisfies a need that any creature with cognitive faculties like ours must have: the need for the material we gather from our world to be orderable by the concepts we try to apply to that material.

Now these claims have been understood to mean that the intellectual state that responds to beauty is a pre-conceptual one, a state that does without concepts. The clause, "no definite concept limits them to a definite rule of cognition" has been read to elide the word "definite," as if it said that "no concept" limits the cognitive powers. The play/harmony of the faculties,[19] on this reading, is precognitive because it is pre-conceptual. In my *Third Concept of Liberty*, I argued that this reading is mistaken, both on textual grounds and on grounds of intelligibility. Kant's play of the faculties is instead an *inter*-conceptual state, I maintained, making use of many concepts without being limited by any single one.[20] It is a play not *of* the imagination, but *between* the imagination and the understanding.[21] I am now persuaded that there are good textual grounds for the pre-conceptual reading of Kant as well as the inter-conceptual one (Kant himself was torn, I think, between two different views),[22] but continue to believe that the inter-conceptual reading makes for a more intelligible view. As we saw above, it makes little sense to suppose that we have experience of any kind without concepts.

So Kant's play/harmony of the faculties can give us a hint as to what a state that uses concepts, but is not bound by them, might be like. On the inter-conceptual reading of Kant, the understanding, the faculty of concepts, is not absent in judgments of beauty. It just interacts with the imagination differently from the way it does in an attempt to know something. Concepts have a role in the free play of the faculties, just not the one they ordinarily do in cognition: they don't *govern* our reflections, don't pin them down to a particular conclusion. I stress, rather than eliding, the word "definite" when Kant says that in free play "no definite concept limits [the faculties] to a definite rule of cognition."[23] To think without a "definite" or "determinate" concept is to use concepts without defining or determining precisely *which* concept:[24] to allow an array of concepts to play with the contents of one's imagination instead of fixing one of them determinately to that content.

What might that mean? Well, imagine you are trying to show a friend the beauty in a Jackson Pollock or Anselm Kiefer painting. The sensory material is confusing, but you feel it has some kind of order, and you point out to your friend Pollock's ways of questioning the distinction between line and color, or Kiefer's ironic use of myth. These concepts—these organizational tools—help give some coherence to the sensory intuitions, and there is a pleasure in using them to bring erstwhile confusion into focus. But your friend, if she is aesthetically sensitive, will not long be satisfied by your remarks, will complain that there is much more in the paintings, that your conceptual tools are inadequate. The randomness of Pollock's way of distributing paint, she might say, defeats any thematic reading of his work, or the thickness of the painting's texture is left out by a bald contrast between line and color. And there is a pleasure, too, in being able to knock down the conceptual tools of aesthetic criticism, in showing how the sensory manifold overflows the concepts that are supposed to contain it. All the same, having had one interpretation knocked down, you will come back with others— well aware that, if the work is richly interesting, these tools will also prove to be inadequate. This is the free play of the faculties. And your friend will find the work beautiful not if one of the interpretations is finally unanswerable, but if she feels able to continue the play indefinitely.

39. I think we have here an accurate and reasonably familiar description of aesthetic pleasure. We also have a description of what it might be like to become aware of something that transcends our conceptual systems. Why we might want to think of this sort of experience as having anything mystical about it is still unclear, however. We can begin to clarify that connection with a fuller account of concepts. I will give an account that I think is close to Kant's, but for simplicity's sake (and so that I can revise Kant where I think necessary), I will develop it without explicitly referring to his writings.[25]

To have a concept is to have a set of skills.[26] Concepts are modes of what Wittgenstein called "seeing what is common"[27]—being able to associate things with one another and distinguish them from other things. And we can do that only if we can recognize the things to which the concept applies, know their uses or characteristic marks or activities, and relate these things, and their uses, to other types of things and their uses.

To have the concept "beer mug," for instance, is to be able to associate different beer mugs with one another; distinguish them from coffee cups and shot glasses; recognize at the same time that beer mugs belong, together with coffee cups and shot glasses, under some more general category like "drinking utensils"; know what substance characteristically goes into a beer mug; know, normally, something of the customs surrounding the drinking of beer; and have, therefore, some idea of when and where beer mugs tend to be brought out, why they have the sizes and shapes that they do, and why they are made of certain materials, rather than others. To have the concept "beer mug" is to be able to *locate* beer mugs among the other things in the world, both spatiotemporally and causally. There is no sharp line establishing how much of this information one needs to know in order to have the concept at all—we might say a young child, or someone who has just come into our culture, has the concept when he is barely able to distinguish beer mugs from coffee cups (there are degrees of having concepts, however, and this is a pretty low one)—but possession of a concept is always tied to the ability to relate it to and distinguish it from other concepts, and to integrate it, thereby, into one's explanations and practices as a whole. Each concept is linked with a whole network of other concepts; no-one could have just one concept, any more than one could be able to locate just one point in space.[28]

We should note that things are a little different if the concept is of a natural kind, rather than an artificial one. But not very different. Both types of concept figure into explanations and practices, and possessing either type of concept entails recognizing the things covered by that concept, grouping them together and distinguishing them from other things, and knowing something about the causal relations that things of that kind have with other things. The most obvious difference between artificial and natural things is that we group the former but not the latter by way of the purposes they serve. This may lead us to think that concepts of the artificial are under human control in a way that natural kinds are not. But that impression is misleading. Indeed, the very contrast between the artificial and the natural by way of purposes is misleading. To determine whether a thing counts as a thornbush or not, we do not appeal to the purpose of thornbushes, but we do appeal, implicitly at least, to the purpose of the *concept* "thornbush." Something may count as a thornbush for people who simply want to avoid sitting on prickly things that would not count as such for a botanist. So human purposes play a role in the formation of both natural and artificial concepts. It is for that reason that we often regard our concepts as something we impose on the world, rather than something given to us. We group and split up the things around us in accordance with our purposes, and that gives us reason to fear that our groupings are arbitrary, unguided by the world's own structure.

This fear is based on a confusion, as a Wittgensteinian argument, recently elaborated by John McDowell, shows.[29] We would not be able to use concepts—we would not be able to formulate the very worry that concepts could fail to fit the world—if there were no non-arbitrary way of using concepts. The very idea of an arbitrary as opposed to a world-guided use of concepts depends on it being intelligible to speak of world-guidedness, which in turn depends on some concepts *being* world-guided: indeed, on most concepts being world-guided most of the time. That leaves us plenty of room to worry about whether a particular concept is arbitrary, or seems to be world-guided, while really arising from a human projection onto the world. But we can make sense of such worries only against a background in which most concepts are world-guided rather than arbitrary.

So what does a worry about the world-guidedness of a particular concept look like? Well, if concepts are as tightly linked as I have suggested, and if they at least indirectly serve human purposes, then a widely-used concept or set of concepts may be driven more by a certain human project than by facts about our world. Moreover, that concept or set of concepts may help to maintain, unquestioned, the project it serves; our concepts shape our purposes, as much as the other way around. A network of concepts and purposes may therefore propel itself along independently of any reflection on whether it is a good or even useful set of concepts and purposes for us to have. Concepts of "slave" and "witch" both provided support for and were kept in place by practices of slavery and witch-hunting. Eventually, a worry arose about whether "witch" belonged among our scientific concepts and whether a decent moral system should make use of either concept. But such doubts were not dispelled by abandoning the individual concepts alone. That was not possible until the entire network of concepts to which they belonged had been shaken up. Only when explanations of the world in terms of magic faded from the scene did the concept "witch" fall from use. Nor would it be possible to revive it without reviving a whole system of magical concepts and practices. Similarly, to use racial categories today— "Negroid," "Caucasoid," etc.—is both to presuppose and to promote the idea that there is a coherent, scientifically useful concept of race, and to speak of "jewing someone down," or "a woman's way" of getting things done, is to presuppose and promote a network of anti-semitic or sexist categories and modes of explanation.

We can see the mutual reinforcement of concepts and practices even in the small-bore examples I gave earlier. People who use beer mugs tend to drink beer (a fondness for the mug may even be part of what a person enjoys about the beverage), and people who produce beer mugs help foster a market for beer. People who use beer mugs also tend to drink a not insubstantial *amount* of beer at one go. So a move to cut that amount down to, say, the serving of espresso that people tend to consume at one go would have to contend with the entire way we drink beer in our culture, and the concepts involved in that way of behaving.

Of course, in this case the notion of "beer" drives the notion of "beer mug" far more than the other way around, but I hope I have said enough to indicate that even here each concept in the relevant network plays some role in encouraging the use of the others, and that a practice, and mode of discussing that practice, is driven by an entire set of concepts.

To some extent, if not entirely, we can correct a network of concepts, and its associated practices and modes of discourse, by way of what we might call meta-concepts and meta-purposes. If a scientific theory comes regularly to make bad predictions, or to be able to explain observations only by way of *ad hoc* epicycles, we have canons of simplicity and predictive success that will lead us to look for another theory. That is how concepts like phlogiston disappear. And if a set of moral or pragmatic propositions appears regularly to lead us into acts of cruelty or unfairness, we have canons of basic decency that may lead us to look for an alternative moral view. This is a slower and less reliable process than change in science, but it can and has brought on reform in such areas as penal discipline and attitudes towards poverty.

Now, both when we unworriedly apply a going concept to a new object and when we radically revise a concept or network of concepts, we normally feel that what we are doing is somehow forced on us. We have no choice: the concept fits or doesn't fit, or is given to us or taken from us by our meta-concepts and purposes. But what happens when we come across something that doesn't *quite* fit our ordinary categories? Perhaps it resembles a beer mug more than any other container we know, but is used for a different drink in a different culture and differs from a beer mug, therefore, in small, but important ways. Perhaps, like a sponge, it is something we are told to consider an animal, but that defies most of what we otherwise know about animals. Or perhaps it is a curious act of seeming unkindness, like the gruff pronouncements of David Copperfield's Aunt Betsey, beneath which we suspect there lurks a deeper kindness than most people ever achieve.

Well, one thing we may do in these cases is *play*, in precisely the sense Kant has in mind when he talks of the "free play of the faculties." As long as we don't need to decide how to categorize the thing we are experiencing—we aren't building a scientific theory or making moral decisions, so don't need to slot the quasi-animal under a scientifically useful concept or the quasi-kind act into a category we might use for thanking or praising or forgiving—we can try out different concepts on the thing, seeing how now one, now another classification brings out interesting features in it. We suspend the whole project of conceptualization for a bit, and watch how the phenomenon draws our attention to problems in some of our concepts, and confirms the reasonableness of others.

Suppose now that someone *deliberately* sets out to challenge our conceptual frameworks and lead us into this sort of play. He places a beer mug, let us say, on a church altar. Or he creates a beer mug that liquids pour out of as soon as they are poured in, or the handle of which gives its holder an electric shock. Here, the usual setting or purposes of the beer mug are defeated, and we are brought to question our entire ordinary use of the concept. Perhaps the beer mug on the altar is meant to suggest that people worship beer; perhaps the leaky or shocking mug is meant to raise questions about what it is to contain something or why grasping a handle is normally so pleasing. In any case, what we have here is an example of conceptual art (a poor one, admittedly!) and it will help us get a grip on the function of art more generally.

A beer mug that is not quite a beer mug, whether because it serves slightly different purposes or because it is presented as a piece of conceptual art, is very different from an object that simply doesn't fall under the concept "beer mug" at all. Coffee cups do not challenge our concept of beer mugs, nor do plates or elephants or blades of grass. Knowing how to use the concept "beer mug" is just as much a matter of knowing what unproblematically does not fit under it as of knowing what unproblematically does. The difficulty comes when something seems both to fit and not to fit, when some important elements of the scheme in which "beer mug" is enmeshed incline us to bring an object under it, while other important elements incline us to keep it out. It is these intersticial cases that properly challenge our concepts—and it is this intersticial, challenging position that great art, I want to suggest, normally occupies. Vermeer's transformation of quiet domestic scenes into sacred moments; the jarring shock one receives, on reading Dostoevsky, to one's ordinary concepts of moral responsibility, or saintliness, or liberalism; Mussorgsky's, Janacek's, and Steve Reich's various ways of erasing the normal lines between speech and song—at the heart of what fascinates us in the work of all these artists is a challenge to our standard conceptual systems.

The effect of such a challenge is twofold. On the one hand, we are confronted with a case that does not fit a classification—and, implicitly, a classificatory and explanatory system—which had hitherto seemed to work well. On the other hand, the very fact that this case does not fit is reason to believe that other cases did. The failure of fit in this case is some confirmation that our earlier uses of this concept were not mere blind impositions of a human construct onto the world. When I am confronted by an object that challenges the way I use the concept of a beer mug, I am given reason to think that I have not in the past used that concept in a wholly arbitrary way. Otherwise I could simply impose the concept on, or withhold it from, this case as well. If the world were pliant cookie dough to my conceptual cookie-cutter, if I could impose any concepts I liked on everything that came before me, then I would never run into cases that buck my concepts. The very idea that things could resist my attempts to classify and explain them would be unintelligible. So the failure of fit, in the challenging cases, is evidence that there is such a thing as fit: that the concept of fit, between concepts and their objects, makes sense. Ironically, a challenge to the validity of a particular concept, or network of concepts, is thus reason to affirm the validity of our attempts to conceptualize the world in general. The challenge helps us see that when our concepts go *un*challenged, they probably do fit the phenomena to which they are applied, and our purposes in applying them.

And there is no other, more direct way to establish the validity of most of our concepts. Transcendental arguments, of the sort Kant gives in his first *Critique*, establish at most that we need certain very general concepts in order to have experience— concepts that articulate the very notion of experience itself: the concept of "concept" itself, for instance, and of "object," perhaps also of causality and of a knowing subject. No empirical concept could be justified this way, else it would arise from the nature of all experience, rather than from the specific experiences it is supposed to help classify and explain. As regards empirical concepts, we might idly wish we could get some re-assurance from the trees and bushes in the world themselves that we are right to distinguish them by different concepts. But, of course, they can't speak to us (and if they could, they too would have to use concepts, general terms, not address us out of the very particularity we want them to express). So we can justify the fit between concepts and their particular instances only by way of the fact that we are sometimes aware of a *failure* of fit; the possibility of such failure shows us that, absent failure, there is a true relationship here and not a mere imposition of one thing on another. This is one of the main sources of the satisfaction we take in coming across phenomena— in nature or in art—that challenge our classificatory systems. We are relieved, if only for a moment, of the anxiety that our concepts generally are a mere arbitrary imposition on the world.

That satisfaction goes together with another one: we are delighted to find that there is more wiggle-room in our conceptual frameworks than we had expected, that we are free to use a somewhat different set of concepts. The fact that we can't suspend any single concept without shaking up whole systems of understanding can seem stifling. Concepts are networked with one another, so if we want to suspend a particular one— e.g. again, "witch" or "Negroid"—we will have to suspend quite a few. How then can *radical* change in the way we see our world be possible? How might we get enough distance from our networks of concepts to evaluate them properly, assess whether they are really well-suited to our world, or our purposes? We seem forced to place everything we experience into the conceptual networks we already have, and that demand can feel like a burden, something that makes it impossible to encounter the world afresh, free of categories and purposes that may be misleading or harmful. Aesthetic experience responds to this worry. We encounter something that doesn't quite fit our going frameworks, and that therefore allows us to play with those frameworks rather than simply deploying them. We break space open for questioning our frameworks from within, even if we don't break free of them altogether. We use them enough to make our experience intelligible, but find we are nonetheless able to probe and alter them. This gives us a feeling, if not precisely of encountering the world "as it is," independent of human imposition, at least of an encounter in which we have some freedom to choose the prisms we impose. And if we can keep interpreting and re-interpreting the atypical object, we have reason to think that our feeling of freedom is responding to something in reality, that it reflects a real opening in our conceptual frameworks.

In art, it is such atypical, mentally stimulating objects that we honor with the word "beautiful," and we should now be able to understand better how the pleasure we take in them comes from the satisfaction of an intellectual need. Both the reassurance we feel when we find that our concepts generally fit the world, and the delight we feel when we find that they can be shaken up, explain the pleasure we take in the play of our faculties, by which we try out here one, there another way of making sense of an anomalous phenomenon. The freedom in this play helps confirm and enrich our moral freedom—we have more latitude in our decision-making if we can reinterpret cases rather than having to take the facts of those cases as given—and it opens up the possibility that we can continually rethink the purposes we set for ourselves, that we will always be able to revise them or find new ones.

This last point is especially important. One of the things we organize under concepts is our ends. "Love," "freedom," "a nice house in the suburbs," "a just peace in the Middle East"—these are all concepts, ways of organizing the things or moments we might experience. They take specific forms, are nested, along with concepts of empirical facts, in complex systems, and can be altered if there is a lack of fit between them and either the phenomena to which they are supposed to apply or the meta-concepts guiding them. Even those who insist that everything we do is aimed at pleasure—a simple end given to us by nature—may grant that what we consider pleasurable varies in accordance with our experience. We set ourselves "swimming in the Mediterranean" as a goal one day, "going out with the person we met on the beach" the next, "having a fine meal" the day after that. But each of these remains a goal for us only so long as we understand the relevant facts in a certain way—if the Mediterranean is covered with an oil slick, or the person we met turns out to be a jerk, we will take a different goal—and as long as the goal seems suited to our conception of pleasure. Changes in any part of our network of concepts may thus lead us to specify our goals very differently. Even if my end is just pleasure, I will have occasion to re-interpret what pleasure means for me, and if I have a more complex end or set of ends, the process of reinterpretation may lead me to a new end altogether—a new concep-tion of my end, at least, but that amounts to a new end.

So the fact that our conceptual frameworks can be shaken up entails that our purposive frameworks can be shaken up; the freedom of our concepts is a freedom of our purposes as well. Our purposes are not simply given to us, or fixed. Rather, we can always discover or invent new purposes for ourselves, just as we can discover or invent new concepts. The play in our conceptual framework makes room for newness in our lives, for us constantly to see the world differently and look for different things in it.

40. And *that* can relieve us of the fear that our existence might necessarily become, at some point, unutterably boring. The fear of boredom consists in the thought that eventually I should be able to classify and explain every thing I come across, and determine and fulfill all my purposes. Under such circumstances, an eternal existence would be a recipe for eternal boredom. After a while, nothing could possibly be unexpected anymore, and I would have no further purposes to fulfill. And a finite existence would be interesting only because I happen to be ignorant of some things that, in eternity, I would come to know; to the extent that my life on earth approxi-mated eternal existence, it too would be unutterably boring. So eternal existence would amount to a Platonic Form of the completely worthless life, and our finite lives on earth would be worthless to the extent that they approximated that Form. The idea that conceptual frameworks are in principle incapable of fully grasping everything we might want to know, and of setting purposes we would never have further reason to alter, the idea that there is more in the world than could be contained in anyone's philosophy, is therefore a great relief, an exciting, invigorating thought.

Of course, we can never prove that it is true. Nor can we prove that any particular moment is one that challenges our conceptual frameworks—that is the point of Kant's thesis that claims about the beautiful, while calling for universal agreement, are inherently unprovable. We "woo" others to agree with us about the beautiful, he says in one of his own most beautiful phrases,[30] but cannot offer them arguments that would rationally compel such agreement. Proof requires bringing things under con-cepts. When deductive, it works among concepts, and, when inductive, it projects a conceptual relationship, a generalization, into the future. The best we can do therefore is *feel* that a particular experience opens up our conceptual frameworks to reinterpretation, or displays a variety that cannot be adequately conceptualized, and play out that feeling in ongoing discussion of the experience with others who have a similar reaction to it. But the feeling, in itself and as it works its way into our conversations, is a tremendously reassuring one. And we cannot disprove its promise of newness any more than we can prove it. Disproof, too, requires concepts.

> *Faith that the world will always be new to us is basic to religious commitment. Hence the oft-used prayer, in the Jewish tradition, that thanks God for bringing us to new experiences, and the prayer in the Jewish morning service that thanks God for renewing the world. That is indeed one meaning of "creation": God creates the world, every day anew, by renewing it (m'chadesh b'tuvo b'chol yom tamid ma'aseh vereishit—which is followed by a verse from the Psalms declaring that God makes [rather than made] the great lights: as if He continues to make them every day). God is what Hermann Cohen calls the "originative principle,"[31] a source of the universe that ensures that it will always be an origin, always be original, always be something from which we can take a new beginning.*

41. It is this sense of newness, freshness, freedom from the processes that bind us to a fixed way of living, that I think most gives us hope that poems like the Torah or Quran may reveal our highest end. Moments that seem to reveal a perpetually renewable source of interpretation and reinterpretation, of rupture and repair, in our conceptual frameworks, that hint at a potentially inexhaustible source of freshness behind our ways of grasping the world—*those* are moments to which we can imagine saying, with Faust, "Stay a while: you are so beautiful." And a world that continually threw up such moments before us, that was eternally renewed for us in this way—eternally unexpected—would be a beautiful world, a world we could wholly love. When I imagine an eternity constantly renewed by conceptual rupture, an eternity in which I might always enjoy the pleasures of interpretation and reinterpretation, and in that light renew and alter my purposes, I can imagine wholeheartedly embracing my existence. This is an existence that I imagine would never bore me. It is also an existence in a world that would remain always and essentially *beyond* me, a world of mystery, a world that transcends me. I can love the eternal play of my faculties because it connects me to something beyond me. Reflective play seeks an outside to our concepts: the drive to push our conceptual framework to the breaking point is the drive that Kierkegaard described as that of thought to the unthought.[32] So the love of a world that constantly breaks in on our conceptual frameworks is a love of objectivity, of what is outside us. And if God is what is ultimately outside us (radically different from us), this can be called a love of God. Boredom will then be a disgust with remaining enclosed within ourselves, an unwillingness to exist solipsistically.

A love for a world in which our conceptual frameworks are constantly renewed and enriched is also a love that fits with our desire for eternity. The sort of existence I have described is one whose joys could increase over time, and need never be exhausted. If the play of the faculties constitutes worth, or opens it up for us, our yearning to live forever begins to make sense. It's not hard to see why, if the inexhaustibility of the world is what one most wants, one might want to be inexhaustible oneself.

42. The play of the faculties is at least the right intellectual state for *perceiving* ultimate worth. In it—and not in the state in which we pursue science or morality—mystery is welcome and fixed concepts and purposes are suspended. What doomed our earlier attempts to pin down ultimate worth was in good part that we kept trying to tie it to the concepts and purposes we already have. We cannot hold any purpose fixed without understanding it as part of a network of purposes we already endorse, and we endorse such networks only because and insofar as they mesh with the desires and interests we already have. Accordingly, we justify any concept of our ultimate end, too, only by tying it to our going conceptual and purposive networks: which is to say that it cannot function as a truly *objective* end for us, an end that stands over against our going desires and interests and can correct them. A truly objective end would seem, then, uncon-ceptualizable, in principle out of reach of the concepts and purposes we already endorse. How then can we make any sense of it? Well, perhaps it can appear to us, as great art does, in and through the *breaks*, the fissures, in our conceptual systems. We glimpse our highest good—Plato's highest good, which precedes truth and knowledge—in the cracks between our concepts, the holes in what otherwise seems our fixed conceptual frameworks. It is a sun that peeps through the openings in our built environment, reveals itself in shadows and flashes of unexpected light, not a sun at which we can gaze directly, rising over an open sea.

43. But in that case we need a built environment through which the sun can shine; we need conceptual networks that can be opened up by what lies beyond them. Beauty as a normative concept—beauty in the sense that we think everyone ought to enjoy it—is to be found paradigmatically in works of art, since only works of art explicitly address themselves to our faculty of concepts, and thereby allow for those concepts to be challenged.[33] Only works of art can put our going concepts in question, because only they are themselves designed by and for concept-using beings. Of course, if they simply "send a message," if they do nothing but convey an explicit claim that the artist wants to teach us, then they will confirm the concepts we already use; they will not allow for a play between the understanding and the imagination. Didactic works like this generally strike us as shallow and boring, not beautiful. When a work strikes us as beautiful, what makes it exciting is precisely that a concept-user like ourselves has submitted his ways of ordering the world deeply enough *to* the world that an array of new ways of seeing sensory particulars, and new connections between them, pops out. What is striking is that the artist has humbled his own conceptual faculties, as well as ours, to the sensory richness they sometimes occlude. We see the world that lies beyond our control more clearly precisely because a human being has intervened in it, and allowed his intervention to be captured by elements that he cannot control. A temple, "standing there," as Heidegger says, "makes visible the invisible space of air"; its "steadfastness ... contrasts with the surge of the surf, and its own repose brings out the raging of the sea" (OWA 41). A van Gogh painting brings out the dirt over which a pair of shoes may tread far more vividly than the shoes themselves, or the dirt, can do. Only the deliberate use of human representation,

attempting to capture what the representer himself finds difficult to capture, arouses our faculties of representation to recognize a mystery beyond their grasp. Only something conceptual can challenge our conceptual networks.

As applied to revelation, this means: only in speech can the transcendent be revealed. Only when we have a *text* that purports to represent the will of God can we so much as reflect on what God might will. Only when God takes on human language (*lashon b'nei Adam*) can He engage with our conceptual frameworks enough to shake them up, to open them to His presence.

Which is to say: the mystical, and the new, if it is to be found at all, is to be found in the midst of our ordinary thought, not beyond it or by way of a renunciation of thought. Recall the passages from revelatory texts that I cited earlier, in support of the notion that the mystical might do without concepts:

> The Self in man and in the sun are one.
> Those who understand this see through the world
> And go beyond the various sheaths of being
> To realize the unity of life.
> Realizing That from which all words turn back
> And thoughts can never reach, they know
> The bliss of Brahman and fear no more.

> The heavens tell the glory of God; and the firmament proclaims his handiwork.
> Day to day pours forth speech, and night to night declares knowledge.
> There is no speech, nor are there words; their voice is not heard;
> Yet their voice goes out through all the earth, and their words to the end of the world.

I would now stress the fact that these passages use words (concepts) to point to the supposedly wordless (non-conceptual) moments we are supposed to reach, and indeed that those moments are presented as having a certain relationship to words. The bliss of Brahman *turns back* words, and the heavens and firmament, although speechless and wordless, "pour forth speech" and send their words "to the end of the world." (Similarly: "I do not know its name", but "I call it Tao.")[34] The *paradox* of a moment that eludes concepts is highlighted here; the source of goodness being portrayed must work by way of words even if it lies beyond them. Moreover, the teachings that present this source take hold of our imaginations only by way of the poems in which they are embedded. So even if the teachings want us to recognize silence, or the unworded, as the highest point of consciousness, they nevertheless need to bring us to that recognition by way of words: albeit words that stretch and challenge our ordinary vocabularies rather than employing them in an ordinary way. And just as the silences in musical compositions have very different characters depending upon the contexts in which they are set (a single Beethoven quartet may contain tense, joyful, meditative, and gloomy silences), so the different sorts of poetic revelations bring us to different sorts of silences, give us different reasons for moving beyond concepts, and different ways of doing so.

Why did God create the world? Well, by creating the world, He made human beings possible. And by making space for human beings, He made language possible. And we human beings, in creating language, make revelation possible: create the space in which God can appear. Language is necessarily human; God can't create it without our help. So God creates us so that we can enable Him to appear. But if God couldn't appear, He wouldn't fully be God. So God creates us in order to be His full self.

Why can't God create language without us? Imagine God creating a language for His own use. That would be a private language, a language without multiple users, which, as Wittgenstein showed, is not a language at all. A language exists only where speakers can correct each other's uses of words: where there are rules, and a community whose judgments establish those rules. Who would correct God? And why would He, and how could He, correct Himself? The wonderful theological consequence is that the necessarily fallible realm of language, in which meaning comes about through a process of different speakers interacting with one another, is the means for God's appearance, even for God's full self-realization. We make God's full expression possible. ("In that day God shall be one and His Name one.")

44. The differences among poetic revelations bring us to the third feature of beauty I mentioned at the beginning of this chapter (§ 31, point (3)): that it arises always from attention to some *particular* thing, not from a general quality or idea. The disclosure of our world and its limits, says Heidegger, takes place "always in some particular way," always as "*this* openness." Only when "some [particular] being" breaks through our concepts and projects—challenges our ordinary ways of living and thinking—can that breach "take its stand and attain its constancy" (OWA 59). The poet Hugo von Hofmannsthal had similarly emphasized the way particulars elude our conceptual grasp, and the fascination they thereby have for us, in his "Letter to Lord Chandos." And a contemporary of Heidegger's, Marcel Proust, returned again and again to the power of the particular:

[S]uddenly a roof, a gleam of sunlight reflected from a stone, the smell of a road would make me stop still, to enjoy the special pleasure that each of them gave me, and also because they appeared to be concealing, beneath what my eyes could see, something which they invited me to approach and seize from them, but which, despite all my efforts, I never managed to discover.[35]

The particular, as particular, necessarily resists our understanding's attempts to grasp it, necessarily presents itself as a locus of mystery. We understand things by placing them in general categories, so that they can be linked with other things and placed under the rubric of general laws or types of explanation. So the more we try to grasp what is unique about a particular thing, the more we run up against the limits of language, reduced eventually either to saying, simply, "Look at this!" or twisting language out of its ordinary shape, stretching the meaning of words or clumping them oddly together so that they achieve a uniqueness suited to the uniqueness of our experience: "The sea, tasted, drunk away, dreamed away."[36] Or we can turn from language altogether, and try to convey the uniqueness of things in painting or music, twisting and reshaping their conventional forms, too. We need poems or other artworks to see particulars in their particularity. Unlike scientific or philosophical treatises, a painting or piece of music or poem can present an object or moment of experience in its particularity—its haecceity, to use the term of Duns Scotus, the philosopher who first emphasized the importance of particularity—because it invites us to contemplate what cannot be captured in rational terms, what gets lost when we try to fit things into general explanations or laws.

And that uniqueness is important to us in part because it reminds us of our own uniqueness, our unwillingness to be reduced to what we have in common with other human beings. As a unique individual, what matters most to me are the particular experiences *I* have at each moment, the particular things around me or thoughts that occur to me—not what happens to human beings as a whole. Ironically, in thus attending to the particular, I can lose some of my obsession with myself. The joy and relief in finding myself simply present, here and now, together with this other thing here and now before me, allows me to be absorbed in it, unworried about my future. Thomas Nagel talks of an "attitude of non-egocentric respect for the particular" (VN 222): an attitude in which one attends wholly to the things around one, without regard to self. "Particular things can have a non-competitive completeness which is transparent to all aspects of the self," says Nagel. I suggest that the completeness is non-competitive because it satisfies our fundamental interest in being here now—in exist-ing—rather than serving one of our projects merely to preserve our existence. *We* feel complete as long as we can be absorbed in this complete object; *it* is complete because it includes our absorption in it. Completeness is of course a traditional mark of beauty, and Nagel rightly says that the attitude he is describing is "conspicuous as an element of aesthetic response." "The experience of great beauty tends to unify the self," he says, since it engages us so fully that the conflicts that otherwise take place within us fall away, or are at least stilled, for a moment.[37]

But if this unifying, deeply satisfying experience occurs only when we are absorbed in particulars, then what we require is an existence in which we are brought ever anew into the presence of such particulars.[38] No eternal truth we could discover, no general fact about the universe, could on this view suffice to give us the sense that our lives are worth living. If anything does that, it will have to be particular experiences, of particular things, even if those experiences share some general qualities. But it makes eminent sense, in that case, for the founding revelations of different individuals and peoples to be essentially tied to particular stories or events, with all the details that mark such stories and events off from similar ones at other places and times. Revelation for a Jew may have to stem from the storied moment at Sinai, with its strange thunderings and its sexually purified audience, while revelation for a Hindu may be impossible without the erotic tenderness of Krishna, and for a Buddhist may be inseparable from the life of Siddhartha Gautama. It is not that any of these events have to have *happened*, as the traditions centered on them say that they did: it is just that our imaginations cannot be set into play without the detail of these events.[39] We need particulars to grapple with, in our revelations, if they are to help us attend to the particulars around us. We will not be aroused into free play otherwise, and we will not otherwise keep the mystery in the object of our attentions constantly before us. So our revelations have to take their stand, attain their constancy, by presenting some particular event or person as their source, and by being handed down in some particular historical tradition, with all the quirky details such traditions acquire over the generations. It will be a mistake to seek a general essence that all such traditions share: that will remove precisely what enables them to guide us toward a telos we can reflectively love. It is the particular shape of each tradition that awakens us to the joy of conceptual rupture, by which we may glimpse a mystery beyond our concepts. Remove the particularity of each tradition, and you also remove its telic power.

45. With this in mind, we may revisit what we called the "pockmarks" of revelatory texts in the previous chapter. There we saw such pockmarks as a reason for bringing an independent standard of morality to the texts when we interpret them—as God's own indication to us, perhaps, that we need to exert our autonomy, and transform the texts into a proper source of moral teaching. Now we may see the pockmarks, in addition, as a sign of the particularity of each text's vision, and as prompting the play of our faculties. The pockmarks, the disturbing features of the text that resist easy rational explication, again incite us to interpretation, but now the process of interpretation is itself what we hope for from the texts. It is that process that marks the texts as beautiful, that indicates that we are in the presence of the sort of conceptual rupture through which God might appear.

46. I am taking the play of the faculties in a direction of which Kant himself would probably disapprove. For Kant, the play of the faculties yields nothing but pleasure, albeit pleasure of a universalizable kind, and of a kind that may symbolize moral freedom and/or a transcendental substratum of the universe. No belief, no claim, is supposed to follow from this state of the mind. I have been suggesting, by contrast, that the play of the faculties in response to certain sorts of texts may reasonably increase our confidence that those texts offer us an adequate telic vision. The play contributes to faith, understood as trust in a vision that helps orient our practices. Perhaps this is not quite a belief in the sense that Kant has in mind when he insists that beauty involves no beliefs—faith, as I understand it, functions more as a pre-cognitive than a cognitive state (see § 9 above). Certainly, it is not a belief aiming at *knowledge*: I know, even as I maintain the faith, that there is no hope of justifying it properly, of transforming it into a justified true belief or set of such beliefs. So if beliefs are, inherently, aimed at knowledge, the faith I am describing is not a belief. Still, on my view the feeling inspired by the beauty of a revealed text is more than just a pleasure, even a universalizable pleasure: it is a source, and an appropriate source, of my trust in a way of life guided by that text. It helps orient the most fundamental of my practical commitments. That is not a role Kant would allow us to attribute to beauty.

47. I said earlier that I offered my central explanation of the importance of beauty to revelation tentatively, both because it cannot be proven and because some of the revelations I want to defend might not themselves regard the vision of something beyond concepts as their ultimate goal, or might understand such a vision differently from the way I do. (I am aware that my account, with its emphasis on an endless process of interpretation and re-interpretation, fits the talky Jewish tradition better than it does many others.) So what should I say about religions that, for instance, place a higher premium on silent meditation than on the interpretation of texts, or maintain that we don't properly perceive our highest telos in this life because we are too attached to our bodies, rather than because of anything about how concepts work?

Well, even these traditions can readily grant that the teaching they want to convey must be couched in poetic—beautiful—language (the form that their foundational texts take suggests that they do grant this). It may be that they emphasize a different feature of beauty from the one I have stressed. Buddhists, for instance, may find the idea that beauty fosters in us an absorptive attention to particulars more significant than the idea that it ruptures our conceptual networks. Other traditions may see no intrinsic value in either of those ideas, but agree that we can reach, or accept, an adequate view of our telos only from a stance in which we feel the calm love—disinterested satisfaction—that beauty evokes.

There is in any case good reason to suppose that any telic hypothesis will be made most convincing if it can be put in a beautiful form: a form that inspires disinterested satisfaction in us, and appeals to the play of our faculties. If you want to persuade me that I will understand ultimate worth in an afterlife, or that a path combining philosophy, bodily discipline, and meditation will lead me to overcome the confusions that lead me to seek vainly for an intelligible notion of ultimate worth, then you would do well to start by giving me a glimpse of a state in which I might be able to accept your view. In the play of the faculties I can both feel how I might be reconciled to the world and see how the conceptual framework that leads me to my current view of ultimate worth could be opened up, shifted, or otherwise altered so that I could come to a different view. The play of the faculties is thus a good means to the acceptability of any story about worth whether or not it also constitutes a part of that story.

48. How are the moral and the beautiful aspects of revelation supposed to interact? If our telos is supposed to be conditioned on morality, and if beauty is the appropriate mode of appearance for the telic, then it makes sense that a revelation of that telos would have both moral and beautiful aspects. But they should not simply coexist in the revelation, side by side as it were: the latter should be conditioned on the former. How is that supposed to happen? Why should morality be a condition for seeing the world as beautiful?

Well, perhaps developing a moral character, in addition to helping others, enables me to restrain my excessive passions and desires so that I can properly see the beauty in, or opened up to me by, a revealed text. Aristotle thought that virtue could be a condition for certain sorts of perception, including the perception of what is valuable in contemplation—our highest good, for him—and an analogous thought runs through the Buddhist tradition: only the virtuous person has the emotional capacity to grasp the truths that end suffering.

Alternatively, perhaps the beauteous vision that satisfies our telic yearnings is meant to go out to human beings in community, and virtue is a condition for building communities that can accept such a revelation.[40] Perhaps God wants us to help each other reach a position in which we are free enough of oppression and material want that we can turn our attention to telic questions and their solution. Perhaps God withholds the vision of His good for us until we first recognize, and honor, the image of divinity in each other.

Yet another possibility is that the telic aids the moral. Perhaps moral evil springs above all from the fear that our lives are pointless, and an answer to our telic worries is therefore an answer to our moral problems as well. It is not implausible that many people indulge in violence and cruelty, greed and betrayal, out of a fear of boredom and death, that this is how they distract themselves from a conviction that their lives are meaningless. A vision that inspires them with a sense of the intrinsic value of their lives, or that is itself endlessly fascinating or that helps them achieve a fascinated attention at each moment, to the particulars around them, may then take them out of the psychological conditions leading them to evil. The beauty of revelation would then help solve moral problems. Revelation may beautify morality: make it interesting, exciting, moving, in a way that it is not when we see it as merely enabling society to survive, maximizing happiness, and the like. If kindness to the poor becomes an aid to seeing God, as well as a proper mark of respect for and solidarity with our fellow human beings, it gains a fascination it would not otherwise have.

There are, that is, a number of different ways one might connect the moral and the beautiful aspect of revelatory texts. I don't know how one could determine which is the best way to do that in advance of a commitment to a particular revelation, giving morality a particular place in an overall picture of human life.

"And the whole community, and the stranger among them, shall be forgiven, since the whole community acted unintentionally." (Numbers 15: 26). The rabbis bring this verse together with Numbers 15: 22, which talks of failing to observe "all these commandments," to suggest that the "unintentional" act in question involves a violation of the entire system of law commanded by the Torah. But how can anyone violate the entire system of Torah law? By committing idolatry, which the whole system is designed to eradicate. So Numbers 15: 26 tells us that even idolatry—seemingly the paradigm of an intentional action—may be committed unintentionally, and, therefore, be forgiven. God, say the rabbis, interpreting our actions with the maximum of charity, will construe even our worst betrayal of Him as unintentional and therefore forgive us, where a human judge would not. Thus construed, the verse is incorporated into the liturgy for Yom Kippur, as a promise of the forgiveness of all sin, at least to those who truly repent. Repentance itself is then understood as a process of transforming intentional sins into unintentional ones.[41]

Why might idolatry be the paradigm of all sin? Well, any violation of a system of law one sees as God-given is tantamount to setting up an object of one's desires as an alternative god and worshipping that. Anyone who believes that God wants him to keep shabbat, be faithful to his spouse, not oppress his neighbor, etc. would hardly violate these commands unless he places greater value on some object of his own choosing than on God. But the person who pursues money or fame or sexual satisfaction at the cost of violating what he takes to be God's will may not see his action in that light. Instead, he may represent himself to himself as pursuing a real good. ("I can make better use of this fund than the people I'm defrauding.") A charitable interpretation of his action is therefore that he doesn't really know what he is doing: doesn't see it clearly. And it seems reasonable to say that while we fellow human beings must hold each other responsible for having a clearer understanding of what we do than this sleazy egoist does, a supremely merciful God might be willing to regard him as acting unintentionally. Perhaps, moreover, the process of repentance we are supposed to go through on Yom Kippur might allow us to penetrate our self-deceit further than we usually do, and thereby root out some of the idolatrous source of our sins. We reinterpret our selves, and thereby change them.

A single verse brought into midrash and liturgy thus comes to express the beautiful moral teaching that even the worst of human beings can be transformed. This thought allows us relief from the paralyzing worry that we are so evil that we cannot improve ourselves or compensate for the harm we have done. The idea of radical forgiveness by God, and the concomitant idea that God enables us to re-read and rewrite the structure of our intentions, offers us a hope that we can come out of any cycle of vicious habits. That hope itself is inspiring: it is a paradigm of the kind of thought that Kant believed religion could offer morality.

And the moral value of this thought is inseparable from its beauty. We find the verse beautiful in large part because it is enigmatic, and we need to work to pull out its morally useful meaning. And we find it morally valuable in part because the process of interpreting it—the process by which it acquires beauty for us—pushes us to a deeper understanding of sin and forgiveness. So the moral and the beautiful aspects of revelation come together: the verse, when reflectively received, beautifies morality and moralizes beauty. The process of moral deliberation becomes exciting and joyful, while the process of interpreting poetry, drawing rich meaning from a terse and obscure utterance, acquires a moral dimension.

49. One might object that my view of revelation dissolves the distinction between religion and aesthetics, comes too close to making any work of art into a revelation, and reducing revelation to art. Of course, I have said that a revelatory text must have a moral component as well as an aesthetic one, but many artworks meet that criterion, and in any case, the moral component of revelation, as I have described it, comes as much from the way we interpret our sacred texts as from anything in those texts themselves.

I do not think that revelations are reducible to artworks, but my initial response to this objection is to ask why, even from a religious perspective, we should resist the possibility that artworks are revelatory. At the end of Mozart's *Marriage of Figaro*, the Count falls before the Countess to beg forgiveness for his unjustified jealousy, and his many infidelities. She in turn, with great dignity, but also every sign of love, restrains her justifiable anger at him and forgives him. The music turns from light-hearted patter to something that could fit into a Mass; the Countess is transformed by it, for a moment, into Christ or the Virgin Mary, a figure who can work near-divine reconciliation.[42] And Mozart thereby reveals to us how troubled marriages can sometimes be saved, or at least maintained.[43] The opera had mostly engaged until this point in the amusing trickery typical of eighteenth-century comedy, but here it suggests that such trickery cannot resolve deep emotional struggles between people, that one needs an honest request for forgiveness, and a dignified acceptance of that request, to accomplish that. I have often been guided by memories of this moment when I have encountered tensions in my own personal relationships. So it is not hyperbolic to say that *The Marriage of Figaro* has functioned for me as a partial revelation of God's will.

Moreover, to come finally to the fourth feature of beauty mentioned in the beginning of this chapter (§ 31, point (4)), there is a long-standing tradition in philosophical aesthetics comparing the genius who creates art with a prophet. Genius is supposed to arise from a condition in which one's imagination can somehow reach beyond the conceptual networks of one's society and point to something new. And only divinity, it was once thought, can inspire such radical creativity; artistic geniuses have in any case often said that they do not know the source of their creativity, and cannot wholly control it. The genius is thus quite like a prophet, responding to possibilities that seem to him built into the words or stone or sounds with which he works, and giving birth, thereby, to a new vision that can inspire his whole society: "forg[ing] in the smithy of [his] soul the uncreated conscience of [his] race," as Joyce has Stephen Dedalus say in the closing lines of *Portrait of the Artist as a Young Man*.

The idea of genius can also help us integrate revelations into our account of faith as a trust in persons. When we see a work of art as arising from genius, we come into relationship with it as the product of a certain *person*, and not just as a material thing: we see it by way of its author, and feel a connection with that author, with the mind that created the work.[44] But genius also points us beyond any ordinarily human type of person, and of course prophecy does that only more explicitly. So when we see a text as prophecy, we are admiring or loving or being awed by a superhuman person of some sort: by God, perhaps, as an author. We are admiring or loving God's mind in the way we can admire or love the mind of a human being—not just generally, as the mind that, because It is all-good, *ought* to be loved, but in some specificity, as a mind that, through its beautiful product, we have come to know in some detail, a mind that can fascinate and awe us, perhaps even amuse, us, that can in any case communicate with us, as one person to another. And when we trust the text that has inspired this love, while seeing it as God's word, we are, quite literally, trusting God as a person.

For these reasons, I am unsympathetic to the fuss often made to distinguish the prophet from the poet.[45] Struggling to make a case for the distinctiveness of Torah, Robert Gordis writes that there is a qualitative difference between the sort of "inspiration" one might want to attribute to a Shakespeare or a Mozart and the "revelation" that religious believers attribute to prophets:

The superlative endowment that causes a Shakespeare to issue from some ordinary English farmers, and a Mozart from some moderately talented musicians, we call "inspiration." [But we restrict] the term "revelation" to the sphere of religious and ethical truth ... There is a qualitative difference between the two phenomena not to be ignored. God's creative power enters man's spirit in countless areas, such as science, art, music, literature . . . All those whom He singles out for greatness in one area or another have been granted His authentic inspiration. But when God reveals a glimpse of His truth, not on one limited aspect of life, but rather on man's total relationship to the universe, when He grants insight into the character of man's nature and duty, the human being that God has chosen as His spokesman has experienced Revelation.[46]

Abraham Joshua Heschel wrestles with the same problem by saying that "the inspiration of the poet . . . breaks forth suddenly, unexpectedly, from an unknown source" while the inspiration of "the prophet is distinguished . . . by an awareness of its source [and] . . . by the coherence of the inspired messages" with one another and with the messages of earlier prophets.[47]

Well, I don't know. Gordis's description of a prophet seems to me to *fit* Shakespeare and Mozart—and certainly to fit Dante and Goethe and Tolstoy and Joyce. They give us considerable insight into "man's total relationship to the universe" and the character of our "nature and duty." They give us a far more comprehensive view of human life, in fact, than, say, Amos or Obadiah or Jonah, who focus sharply on "one limited aspect of life." As for Heschel's concerns: Bach and Bruckner and Scriabin thought they were inspired directly by God (they were "aware of [the] source" of their inspiration), as did many ancient bards;[48] and practically no major artist, in any medium, has seen his works as coming to him in a series of arbitrary, incoherent bursts. Anyone who has looked at a few Vermeer paintings, read more than one Dickens novel, or heard more than one Verdi opera, knows how deeply each work is tied to the others—and to the works of many painters or novelists or composers who came before them. Heschel says that prophets, as distinct from artists, are aware of "being a link in the chain of prophets who preceded them," but that's *exactly* how a van Gogh, painting self-portraits that echo Rembrandt's while deliberately flattening them, or a Joyce or Beethoven or Schoenberg, also see themselves.

The fear of the comparison between artistic inspiration and prophecy has most to do, I expect, with the thought that if revelation is like art, then it is supposed to serve our pleasures, and we need not pay attention to it if we don't feel like it. But this idea depends on a peculiarly modern and anemic conception of art. In many places and times, including the West in the Renaissance and nineteenth and early twentieth centuries, artists have been seen and have seen themselves as mouthpieces for God, and the primary point of their work was to raise people to a higher level of experience, not to give pleasure. An ancient bard was seen as inheriting an oracular tradition and as needing to allow a non-natural, wise and sublime, force from beyond infuse his works. Works of art have also often called on us to rethink our nature or moral practices, or renew our sense of love and commitment to a religious way of life, and that is as much as many prophets do. Nor is the kind of thing we need revelation to teach us different in principle from the kind of thing we can be taught by art. On the contrary, poetry and prophecy both teach far more by way of form than content, and both contrast more sharply with literalist modes of discourse, whether scientific or moral, than they do with one another.

Finally, if the point of artworks is not primarily to give pleasure, heeding what they say need not be optional. If the point of art is instead, say, to challenge our conceptual frameworks, or otherwise to bring out something that is essentially obscured by our ordinary ways of thinking, then we may miss that point entirely if we treat artworks as if their importance depends on whether we're pleased by them. Heidegger, who regarded art as unveiling truth, as we have seen, rather than giving pleasure, talks about the need to "stay within the truth that is happening in" an artwork, the need, if we truly want to preserve that truth, to "submit" to the artwork's terms and "transform our accustomed ties to world and earth" accordingly (OWA 64). This sounds just like the way a traditional Jew speaks about the Torah (and a traditional Christian or Muslim about the Gospels or Quran): we preserve the truth in it only by submitting ourselves to its terms, and letting those terms transform our customary ways of living, rather than submitting it to our terms, correcting or reshaping it in accordance with our desires or political programs.[49] There is a close analogy between the resistance a lover of Shakespeare or Mozart might put up to historicist or political programs of interpretation that reduce the works she loves to the value they have for some political cause, and the resistance a lover of a revealed text puts up to hermeneutical programs that take away from the value that the text has when one remains within its own terms, stays within the vision it unveils. As when we stand before a work of artistic genius, we feel at a moment of revelation that the vision we are being given transcends the possibilities of any merely human understanding. We stand before a prophecy as before a great poem, wanting to listen rather than to talk back. And great poets stand before their own creative process, as it were, wanting to listen—great poets see themselves, in Heidegger's words, as listening to language rather than speaking it[50]—not as self-conscious masters of language, reaching for words they have confidently at their disposal.

50. Nevertheless, I do not mean to suggest that all artworks are revelations, or that revelations can be reduced to their aesthetic component. Moments in art can be revelatory, as the penultimate five minutes of *Figaro* have been for me. But what *Figaro* lacks, as compared with the Vedas and Torah and Gospels and Quran, is a comprehensive path for their lovers to follow. *Figaro* cannot serve as the foundation of a religion because there is only a limited amount of practical teaching we can derive from it. The moments of beauty it provides do not add up to a vision of an ultimate telos for our lives: do not amount to a picture of an existence in which we can imagine dwelling eternally, or for the sake of which we can imagine dedicating everything else we do. Maimonides described most prophets as experiencing but a moment of divine insight over a lifetime, like a flash of light on a dark night. Only Moses, he said, had the darkness in which we normally grope for God's presence thoroughly illumined for him; only Moses's teachings, consequently, can serve as a foundational revelation.[51]

On this characterization, Mozart may count as a limited prophet of sorts (not unlike Amos or Hosea), who communicated flashes of divine insight, but could not provide the founding vision, the comprehensive story, by which those flashes might orient a whole life. For that one needs a poem with a vision of how a whole life can be worth living, and a way to realize that vision.

Which brings us to the third mark of revelation I mentioned at the end of Chapter 2 of this Part. Purported revelations are regarded as such not only because they endorse and illuminate our moral beliefs, and not only because they are beautiful, but because they lay out a practical path for their adherents to follow, a distinctive mode of action that can shape an entire life. They come with a discipline, a set of practices, including but not limited to moral practices, by which we may transform ourselves into people adequate to the vision they hold out for us: by which the vision we glimpsed when we first came to the text can wholly infuse our lives. We turn to this aspect of revelation in the next chapter.

5

Aspects of Revelation (III)
A Path

51. Every revealed religion comes with a practical path. In some religions following a distinctive "way" (a *tao* or *halacha*) is practically the entirety of the religion. In others, a set of practices is said to be essential for reaching the stage at which one can properly grasp the religion's teachings. In still others, belief in the doctrines is supposed to lead to a willingness to follow the practices; the path *expresses* the beliefs. But there is no revealed religion without a path. In many the path is more important, and more widely shared in the religion's community, than any doctrine. And the fact that one's beliefs issue in or from a path is something that brings religions together, and distinguishes them from philosophical or moral teachings. Recall the story about Aloysius, in Part I, which gave us our model for religious truth-telling. The person who heeds the advice of Aloysius must act before he can understand what Aloysius really means. When we attribute truth to a sacred text or teaching, practice must similarly to a large extent precede understanding (as Jews like to say, echoing the response of the Israelites to Moses in Exodus 24: 7: "We will do and [then] we will understand").[1]

For many theories of religion, this is an embarrassment, something that needs explaining away. The practices of revealed religions are seen as mere symbols of a truth that could be expressed in other ways. On my account, the practical component of religion is not an embarrassment: it is, instead, essential to what revealed religions have to teach. Both the moral and the telic aspects of revelation require that it yield up a path.

From the moral point of view, a revelation needs a path because it is supposed to orient us toward our highest good. Since the highest good presupposes complete virtue, any attempt to achieve it must include practices that can help us enhance our virtues. In addition, what is moral about revelation fully comes out only when the revelation is taken up into an ongoing way of life by a community. Moral revelation consists in a tension between an angled, powerful insight into how a particular problem of a particular person or people might be solved and a comprehensive picture of how everyone ought to live. And the struggle to draw the latter from the former, to develop an equitable and universalist moral vision out of a powerful but skewed local moral insight, requires a path, an institutionalized set of practices, that holds on to the excitement of the original insight while accommodating it to the moral way of the world.

From the telic point of view, a revelation needs a path because the vision it presents cannot be grasped in a purely rational way. Grasping it is, rather, an affair of the imagination, of our ability to project ourselves into a certain vision, and to see ourselves, in that projection, as reconciled to the world. To grasp the vision, then, we need certain feelings and attitudes. And since the revelation, *as* revelation, is conceived as coming from beyond ourselves, outside our normal way of looking at the world, these will not be our normal feelings and attitudes. But feelings and attitudes are aroused by actions, and we need an unusual course of actions to develop or arouse unusual feelings and attitudes. So to have the appropriate kind of emotional capacity, which is to say the appropriate kind of perceptive capacity, we must engage in out-of-the-ordinary practices. We need to bring ourselves to the point at which we can see a truth about our lives that defies our ordinary ways of looking at them. We need, in particular, to cultivate the state of spontaneous receptivity, by which we are willing to stand back patiently from our revealed vision and learn from it rather than rushing to impose our conceptual systems on it. A path of action, fostering spontaneous receptivity and the feelings suited to an extraordinary vision, circles out from the revelatory moment and back to it, drawing on elements of the revelatory text, or what it depicts, so that we can project ourselves in imagination back into the moment of revelation, and keeping awake or reawakening what it was about that moment that we took to represent ultimate worth. Perception takes the place of argument, to a large extent, in a commitment to a revealed tradition, and perception is aroused and shaped by courses of action. And since the perception integral to a faith in revelation is of an extraordinary kind, different from the sort of perception we employ in common sense or science, the kinds of actions that cultivate this perception must also be out of the ordinary: must be, to some extent, absurd from a common sense or scientific stand-point. Hence the large role for ritual in revealed religion.

> Jewish practice directs my attention to many details of ordinary life that I would not otherwise notice. By so directing my attention, it transfigures them, makes them extra-ordinary: sanctifies them. Any observant Jew who has checked the calendar to see when shabbat arrives in an unfamiliar place, or gone outside on Saturday night to see whether three stars are yet visible (and shabbat, therefore, over) will know what I mean. Dusk and nightfall, and the difference between them, and the way they change over the seasons, acquire a significance from Jewish ritual that they otherwise have only for sailors.
>
> Similarly, I am never as conscious of what shelter means, and how it functions in human life, as when I sit in the light, spare, raised-roof sukkah my wife designed for us, where the difference between being sheltered and being out in the open is gossamer-thin, as fragile as it can be without disappearing.
>
> Halacha serves as a practical training in phenomenological attention. It imposes a grid on reality forcing us to attend to distinctions, to what Rabbi Soloveitchik called the "fine and detailed particulars" around us:

Halakhic man examines the sunrise and the sunset, the dawn and the appearance of the stars; he gazes into the horizon—Is the upper horizon pale and the same as the lower?—and looks at the sun's shadows—has afternoon already arrived? When he goes out on a clear, moonlit night . . . , he makes a blessing upon it. . . . When a fruit is growing, halakhic man measures the fruit with the standards of growth and ripening that he possesses: budding stages, early stage of ripening, formation of fruits and leaves, and reaching one-third of complete ripeness. He gazes at colors and determines their quality: distinguishes between green and yellow, blue and white, etc., etc. 'between blood and blood, between affection and affection' (Deuteronomy 17: 8).[2]

Halacha is a living phenomenology, a mode of separating ourselves from a mere immersion in our ordinary way of moving through the particulars around us, so that we can be aware of those particulars. And this separation (holiness, for Jews, is essentially separation) allows the universe, and our lives in it, to stand enough at a distance from us that we can love them.

52. Rituals do not merely break us from our ordinary ways of feeling and seeing. Rather, they have their own internal logic, in accordance with the sacred text and central doctrines of the religious tradition that maintains them. Jains engage in extreme practices of asceticism and penance in order to be redeemed from suffering, which they see as arising from the mind's attachment to material things. Buddhists see such practices as pointless. Given a Buddhist understanding of suffering, the idea that mind has any more content than matter is itself an error, and a distraction from the deconstruction of concepts that can alone bring relief from the wheel of desire. Christians and Jews construe their rituals in an entirely different way, giving them more historical resonance—ceremonies are performed to recall events in the life of Jesus, or of the Jewish people—and directing them towards the acceptance of grace, or the eradication of idolatry, rather than the overcoming of suffering. There is also debate within each tradition over the meaning of rituals. Some Jews, for instance, like the Jains, see their practices as a way of freeing themselves from matter, while others see those practices as a way of *embracing* the material world. But for all the importance of these explanations of ritual, it is crucial to the ability of any set of religious practices to foster spontaneous receptivity, to help us restrain our rational structures and let our imaginations roam free, that they have an ineliminably non-rational—"absurd"— component. Pace the progressive Jews and Christians who have tried to interpret all religious practices as metaphors for or aids to moral action, ritual cannot be reduced to what reason might demand of us without revelation. The point of ritual is to take us beyond the rational: beyond, therefore, the moral. Ritual opens us up, or keeps us open, to a non-natural telos; it helps unite morality with a religious telos. But to do that it cannot consist simply in morality.

53. The most important virtue, in following a religious path, is humility.

We need a path, a discipline or regimen, to learn any sort of virtue. The fact that revelations offer us a path is in part a recognition of the Aristotelian point that morality is achieved more by the development of habits than by theoretical lessons. Virtues are dispositions to right feeling, which give the proper starting points to deliberation.

A person steeped in vice literally doesn't see the occasions for action in the right light—sees situations as opportunities for greedy accumulation, or fails to see the need for courage or kindness in other situations—and therefore doesn't have the right premises for deliberation.[3] But feelings are developed by courses of action. A small child doesn't enjoy being fair, if that comes at the cost of the amount of candy he would otherwise get. With suitable training, however, he can eventually come to take a certain pleasure in being fair. Only then will he see the point of fairness, grasp the fact that it is a virtue.

So we need certain habits even to think correctly about morality: moral theory itself is not possible without a great deal of prior moral practice. But thus far this point urges us just to be good Aristotelians, developing the habits that a reasonable account of virtue might require. The difference between the path of a revelatory text and the path of a rational moral theory is that the former requires us to *humble* our reason. For Aristotle, this would make little sense. No form of humility can be found among his virtues, but it would be virtually unintelligible, even if one remedied that defect, that there could be an Aristotelian value to humbling one's reason. Followers of revealed religions need to take their leave from Aristotle here. For them a humbling of reason is essential.

Humility in general has moral advantages. Arrogance and self-absorption are common sources of wrong-doing. Arrogance breeds anger, impatience, and contempt for others, which in turn can lead to quick and inadequate deliberation, indifference to other people's suffering, and a thoughtless dismissal of their complaints about one's behavior. Self-absorption facilitates greed and vengefulness, the source of some of the worst evils human beings inflict on one another. Humility serves as a healthy corrective to these evils. It restrains some of our worst selfish passions and makes it possible for us to reason together with others.

But the humility that makes these moral goods possible—even the good of reasoning with others—may include a humbling of our very faculty of moral reasoning. People frequently enlist their skills in argument to rationalize arrogance and self-serving behavior, and disguise from themselves that that is what they are doing. The correction for this is to suspend our judgments about how to act until we first listen carefully to others who might be affected by our action or who can view it more impartially. Quite often this means that a highly intelligent and articulate person needs to listen to, and can learn from, someone much less intelligent or articulate, less capable of fitting his thoughts into a clear rational pattern. A humbling of reason may thus be necessary *for* some kinds of reasoning. We may each have to hold our reason back a bit if reasoning together, communal deliberation, is to be possible. And the paths of revealed religions characteristically require precisely this kind of humbling: the submission of all to a communal set of practices, passed down from generation to generation in such a way that not even the leaders of the community, at any given time, can control those practices. *Everyone* submits to modes of action that *no-one* determines for him or herself. This establishes a certain equality in the community, which keeps down the arrogance and self-absorption of its individual members.

Humbling our reason also has other, epistemic advantages. It is, as we saw earlier, a condition for the reception of any truth, and for a proper aesthetic attention to particulars. We cannot so much as see the details of things aright if we suppose immediately that we know what they are, and everything that can be said about them. Holding ourselves back, letting our minds play with the objects before us—perhaps also take in, in the course of that play, what others say to us about them—can thus be a condition for proper perception. Spontaneous receptivity requires humility.

By imposing practices on us that do not seem particularly reasonable, a revealed path can thus effect a condition that helps us see things we did not see before. Both the moral and the epistemic aspects of humility accomplish this. Virtue is a way of seeing,[4] and the specific virtues that involve calming our arrogance and self-absorption, and listening respectfully to others, are especially helpful to seeing moral premises we might otherwise overlook or dismiss. At the same time, humility as spontaneous receptivity leads us to attend to details, and perceive rifts in our conceptual networks, that we hadn't noticed before. So by humbling us, the non-rational practices imposed on us by a revealed religion can help us grasp more fully the vision that the revelation offers us. Certainly, that is what religions tend to say about their paths. We can't accept revelation as a given, allow it to set terms for our thought and practice, without humility.[5]

54. Another way to put the importance of humility: Worrying about whether our lives are worthwhile can seem very selfish. These worries take an essentially first-personal form—"Does *my* life seem worthwhile to *me*?"—and the answers that that question can take seem, at first glance at any rate, not to require any reference to the good of others. If I find an activity or experience or attitude that leads me to be fully satisfied with my life, fully reconciled to the world in which I live, I will answer the question positively, even if others are suffering. And if I cannot feel that way, I will answer it negatively, no matter how much good others are experiencing. Now it may turn out that I refuse to be satisfied with my life unless everyone else is satisfied as well, but I need not be so altruistically constructed. Earlier I argued that no-one should take a condition as making his or her life worthwhile unless it can make everyone's life worthwhile (Part III, § 16). But that argument was too complicated to be fully convincing, and in any case does not represent how many people actually think about worth. The question about the worth of human life is often asked from a self-centered perspective, and not uncommonly answered in a selfish way as well.

That is not supposed to be true when the answer is a religious one, yet the language of religious people can also seem very selfish. Noble as Kierkegaard's anguish over the relation between religion and morality may be, there is something disturbingly self-centered about the fact that he frames the central religious question as a matter of what can secure the believer's "eternal happiness."[6] Similarly, the Jain seeker in the story I quoted in Chapter 2 talks about how he hoped the monk he encountered might be able to "shatter the shell of numbness that enclosed me." And Eknath Easwaran describes the quest that led him to the Upanishads as a search for something that would "appease[...] the hunger in my heart." These are typical expressions of the motivations impelling people towards a religious life, and secular people often react to them by exclaiming, "How selfish! Who cares about your 'eternal happiness' or the 'numbness' or 'hunger' in your heart? Shouldn't you be more concerned about those who don't even get temporal happiness, who are *literally* numb or hungry, or who suffer from oppression or terrible illnesses?" These reactions are often justified. Spiritual seekers can be very selfish people, absorbed in their existential angst to the exclusion of social, political, and even ordinary moral commitments.

But it is central to religious visions of what should *still* our existential angst that achieving the vision entails transforming ourselves into people who care deeply for others. The petty empirical ego must yield itself up to the transcendent Self that is present in all life, for the Hindu adept: "the wise," who see this greater Self in all creatures, "forget [their petty selves] in the service of all."[7] Kierkegaard knows that his eternal happiness consists in participating in Christ's love for all humanity. And for a Jew the highest state of holiness can be experienced only communally, and each of us can be redeemed only insofar as we participate in the repair of the entire universe (*tikkun olam*).

Moreover, in each case I just described the idea is not so much that God rewards us, privately, for helping others, as that a condition in which we *want* to help others, in which an end to the suffering of others relieves our own deepest yearnings, is part of the redemption we seek. It is not wrong to see the religious seeker as, often, initially a "selfish" person, in the literal and derogatory sense of that term. But if the ultimate worth such a person seeks is something that must give worth to all human lives, what one hopes for when one hopes for a vision of such worth must be in part to become a person who is no longer purely selfish, who can enjoy a good that is shared by all. The irony in religious yearning is that one selfishly hopes to become unselfish. The suffering or numbness or emptiness in one's life is partly due to a feeling that one cannot come out from under the oppression of purely selfish desires, and one wants a more expansive self that would directly take joy in something that matters to people aside from oneself. The Upanishads express this yearning well:

> Like two golden birds perched on the selfsame tree,
> Intimate friends, the ego and the Self
> Dwell in the same body. The former eats
> The sweet and sour fruits of the tree of life
>
> As long as we think we are the ego,
> We feel attached and fall into sorrow.
> But realize that you are the Self, the Lord
> of life, and you will be freed from sorrow.[8]

We begin with one self, but feel a need—*as* that self—to achieve a different one. The other self doesn't look like a self at all, since it belongs to the entire universe. But in the end it is not alien to our ordinary selves: there is an element even in our most selfish desires that is part of, and yearns to be more fully part of, a larger, less individuated unit.

Selfishness is a source of sorrow, of the misery that comes of seeking things we desire for our particular selves alone, and must compete with others to get. For selfish reasons, therefore, we yearn not to be selfish. This is a paradox not unlike our Kierkegaardian ones, earlier, about how an eternal and universal good can speak to a particular person, in particular spatial and temporal circumstances.[9]

Of course, the Upanishads offer a solution to this paradox tailored to the metaphysical views characteristic of the Hindu tradition. For a Buddhist, the solution to the problem of attachment to our selfish desires lies in giving up on the notion of self, not in uniting with a more universal one. For most Jews, Christians, and Muslims, one retains one's particular self even as one transforms oneself into an unselfish enough creature to appreciate the vision of God. But there are structural similarities running through these cases:

(1) A set of desires oriented toward private satisfaction is seen as a barrier to perceiving or participating in ultimate worth.
(2) The desire to have a higher, better self is understood to be itself one of these purely selfish desires, or intimately interwoven with all of them.
(3) Even though one cannot arrive at the higher or better self without ridding oneself of this latter desire too, one can only move toward the higher self by making use of the selfish desire to get there: that selfish desire must be carried along until one is transformed enough to let go of it.

In all these cases, the self is transformed into a being with a different set of desires as it approaches whatever is supposed to shed ultimate worth on its life (or remove the temptation to look for such a thing). It thereby simultaneously *sheds* its selfish yearnings and *satisfies* one of the most basic of those yearnings.

The self, that is, must burn off selfishness to realize the vision of ultimate worth held out to it. The self must become cooler, more removed from the appetites and lusts that direct it to objects it can only enjoy privately; it must strip itself of everything we commonly call "selfish." And to achieve that, to strip the self of its privacy, we need a course of action directed against the sorts of aims we naturally have and with which we most commonly identify: against the desires to which we are most strongly attached, and which we regard as most properly our own. What is this, but a course of action directed towards humbling ourselves? The rituals of religious traditions are aimed in large part at suppressing or eliminating selfish appetites and lusts, and passions that cloud our judgment. Their "absurd" component serves in addition to suppress or eliminate our private, selfish attachment to our individual faculties of judgment, our pride in our skill at always coming up with the right way to act on our own.

Of course, there will be different ways of burning off selfishness in different traditions, in accordance with different visions of ultimate worth, different ideas about what is to be seen once the private self evaporates.

55. Humility is not the only virtue taught by religious paths. Typical religious practices include abstaining from alcohol, and from certain foods and kinds of or occasions for sexual intercourse. The purpose of the practices—in Judaism, Islam, Buddhism and Hinduism, certainly—is understood, often, to be a way of developing temperance. Other practices impose a stricter discipline of truth-telling, or of refraining from slander, than most secular moral theories would require. These practices may be understood, in a secular Aristotelian light, as aiming at one extreme in order to correct for our natural tendency to veer towards the opposite extreme. Still other practices— public prayer, sabbaths and festivals, pilgrimages to sacred shrines—directly build community and indirectly encourage the virtues necessary to be a good citizen in a community: a disposition essential to virtue in general, for an Aristotelian.

All of these virtues, as virtues, are modes of seeing, and all, as religious virtues, are modes of seeing the details of a particular conception of our telos. Again, the first point is an Aristotelian one, but on its own would lead us to pursue just the virtues we could come up with rationally, while the second point requires the rationally irritating type of mandate "from above" that comes with revealed religion. A secular Aristotelian will urge temperance because it helps keep us from anti-social behavior and aim at modest enough pleasures that we can reasonably hope to satisfy them. An Aristotelian Jew will urge temperance for similar reasons, but also because the immoderate person sees excessive value in his own pleasure and not enough value in the worship of God. A secular Aristotelian will praise justice as a virtue that enables citizens to share a polis. A Christian or Jewish or Muslim Aristotelian will see the civic value of justice as also serving a higher goal: enabling us to appreciate how God wants human relations to be structured.

Even virtues that religious and secular people share, that is, will have telic aspects when incorporated into a religious view that have no counterpart on a secular view. Correspondingly, there will be non-rational—ritual—elements to the practices cultivating even these virtues when they are understood in a religious light. Hence the divine-command structure even of practices aimed at temperance and justice when they are part of a religious path. It cannot be up to the individual to foster in herself just the temperance or justice that seems reasonable to her if those virtues are supposed to help her perceive or grasp a telos that lies beyond her rational capacities.[10] Humility, we might say, is at the center of all virtues from the religious perspective. The virtues of revealed religions are shaped and unified by humility. They require submission to a divine teaching even if they also foster qualities we could have come up with by looking to the way of the world alone.

56. Partly because a religious path must foster humility, partly because it needs to integrate a telic vision with ordinary morality, and partly for other reasons, it needs to be communally shared, rather than developed by each of us as we individually see fit. It is when I submit to the guidance of others, when I am willing to follow a communal path rather than act always on my own judgment that I begin to develop real humility.

And it is when a community has to figure out how to make sure that all its members can, say, implement a command like "rest on the sabbath," or how such ritual commands can be integrated with people's needs for food, a loving family, or peace, that it comes to grips with the tensions between the moral and the telic aspects of its revelation. The practice of an ongoing religious community tends to soften the harsher and more outlandish demands of its revealed text, to bring the rituals it finds in those texts into line with a broader human morality that it shares with people outside its religious limits. (For which reason, believers who demand a "return to the text," as opposed to the oral tradition that has interpreted those texts, are often very dangerous.)

The path of a religion therefore consists in communally-shared practices. Indeed, in many cases, the religion would not have a path, if a community had not developed that path. I've said that a path must "accompany" a revealed text; it will often not be expressly laid out in that text, and arguably is never laid out entirely there. Not every revealed text explicitly prescribes a set of actions for its adherents to follow. The Torah consists largely in a code, with laws touching every domain of human life, but the New Testament largely inveighs against such a practice-oriented conception of the religious life, containing just a few scattered remarks that might be construed as regulating practice. And the *Tao te Ching* is written in an ethereal manner that disdains practical prescriptions. But the religions associated with all three of these texts have rituals that are taken very seriously by their adherents. Christians take certain of Jesus's acts, as described in the Gospels, to gesture towards a path they should follow. He ate bread and drank wine at the Last Supper, so a stylized eating of bread and drinking of wine became a central act for subsequent Christian communities. A form of prayer he recommended has become integral to Christian liturgy, and his birth and death are of course commemorated in major holidays. Specifically Christian modes of marriage and burial have also been developed, as well as ceremonies to mark birth and entrance into the Christian community. The New Testament itself does not prescribe any of these things (although it hints at something like communion), but if one is to develop specifically Christian ways of praying, affirming community with one's fellow believers, and marking life-cycle events, these seem as reasonable as any. They recall details of the founding events of the religion and thereby integrate what those events are thought to have revealed about coming to God into both the ordinary routine and the major turning points in the life of its followers.

Moreover, this process is not very different from the way *halacha*, the Jewish path, has developed in relation to the Torah. To be sure, explicit ritual commands take up far more space in the Torah than in the Gospels, but the practices Jews derive from the Torah often differ considerably from what it seems, literally, to say, and include rituals that recall elements of it, but are nowhere to be found in it. Thus, the Torah mandates some sort of abstention from work on the seventh day of the week, but what exactly that means has been a matter that Jewish interpreters debated over many generations. Thus, on the other hand, the Torah nowhere says anything about how one ought to conduct a marriage ceremony, but Jewish tradition—judging, reasonably, that a religious path ought to mark events like this—has constructed such a ceremony, incorporating allusions to both the Torah and other parts of Scripture. And Jewish liturgy, like Christian liturgy, draws heavily on elements in Scripture, but doesn't restrict itself to the explicit prayers to be found there.

So the connection between a revelation and a practical path needn't be made *by* the revealed text itself; it may instead develop as that text comes to guide a particular community's way of life. As we shall see in the next chapter, this is but one respect in which a text may essentially become a revelation only insofar as it is regarded as such by a religious community. That erodes, to some extent, the usefulness of calling the demand for a path a criterion for revelation: texts that do not explicitly demand such a thing may yet come to acquire one. In principle, Mozart's *Marriage of Figaro* or Plato's *Republic* could yet become revelations: some community would just have to take them as such and develop a path that preserves their insights. Of course, this is a bit unlikely, since neither of these texts says enough about how one ought to live that one can imagine how a comprehensive set of practices might be attached to them: any such attachment would have to be quite arbitrary. A revelatory text needs to be somehow *open* to a path, *suited* to inspire a comprehensive mode of living. That is true of the Torah, Gospels, and Tao te Ching, if only because they inserted themselves into ongoing discussions of ritual and morality in their time (all three comment on or refer to contemporary practices) and offer a perspective from which to rethink those practices.

57. My emphasis on practice rather than doctrine is probably the most Jewish aspect of my account of revealed religions. At least, it seems the most un-Christian: the central teaching of Christianity would seem to be that an internal faith is immeasurably more important than performing any actions, especially ritual actions. Nevertheless, even Christianity emphasizes a path as well as a doctrine. For one thing, Christian faith, in almost all churches, is supposed to be manifest in a set of sacraments, from baptism to communion to proper marital and funeral rites. For another thing, Christian faith itself amounts to a sort of ritual practice. Kant already pointed this out. Churches tend to make "belief in [Christian] revelation, as the sacred history recounts it to us" into a required religious action of exactly the same kind as the rituals of other religions. The traditional Christian, Kant says, "make[s] for himself . . . a divine service out of the belief, of the acceptance, the profession, and the glorification of all that is revealed."[11] Indeed, for Kant, this service, when thought of as requisite to be "well-pleasing to God" rather than a symbolic vehicle for a moral teaching, is more onerous than any other sort of ritual: "for in all other compulsory works [a person] would only be doing something superfluous at most, whereas here, by making a declaration of whose truth he is not convinced, [he is doing] something contrary to his conscience."[12]

Part of Kant's point turns on reading the sort of belief churches require as outward expression of something one may not inwardly believe, but we can locate a ritual aspect in Christian faith even if we give a more sympathetic reading of it. The notion that God, the eternal Being beyond all space and time, has become a particular human being, and the notion that God is simultaneously three in one, are not easy to grasp. So in order to come to grasp them, it may be necessary to suspend one's normal conceptual structures and modes of reasoning, and work instead through one's imagination and modes of affection. The process of coming to faith will then necessarily involve activities like repeating certain formulations, discussing them with a community of like-minded people, incorporating them into song and prayer, representing them symbolically in the design of sacred spaces and symbolic objects, and having the importance of believing them urged on one by respected leaders. The process of coming to Christian faith may necessarily have, that is, significant practical and communal components. But if so, even Christianity, for all its emphasis on an internal state as the ultimate goal of religion, will need to give great importance to a path of action, a discipline.

58.   This is a good place to say something about the place for doctrine in my view of revelation more generally. It would be folly to deny that doctrine plays a central role in the self-conception of almost every religion. What is Islam without the belief in one God, or in Muhammad as the greatest prophet? What is Hinduism without the belief that a spirit of some sort animates the universe, or Buddhism without the idea of no-self? One can't capture the point of these religions by translating their revelations into a set of actions and imaginative presentations while entirely ignoring their doctrines.

But doctrine, it seems to me, is an interpretation of what is latent in a vision of the highest good rather than something explicit in such a vision. Moreover, one grasps the doctrines of almost every religion by way of a set of images and practices: the importance of the belief becomes clear when one sees the world in a certain way, or loves it, and one gets to that point by habits of the imagination and affection. Doctrines, in revealed religions, play the role of "faith that" in the course of a "faith in" a human guide (compare § 1 of this Part). They clarify where we are heading, but are secondary to a more primitive, personal commitment. Ultimately, we have faith in a person in the Abrahamic religions—a personal God—and we employ faith in persons on our way to enlightenment in many Eastern traditions. The doctrines are merely an aid to this faith, or an imperfect expression of it. What would most lead a believer to feel misled by his religion? That he finds out, at some point in a later, clearer life or at some peak of enlightenment, that God was *not* incarnate in Jesus after all, or did not give the Torah? Or that his path leads to no point at which his life seems worth living? Suppose that by following a particular religious path we reach a point, in this life or another one, in which we can wholly love our existence, wholly rejoice in it, but realize that the doctrines about the nature of God, sin, the self, etc. that went with our path were incorrect. Would we accuse God, or our religious teachers, of having deceived us? Now suppose that the doctrines we are taught about God's nature and will, etc., are quite correct, but the path that goes with them leads nowhere or to despair. *Then*, surely, we would convict whoever led us on this path of being a deceiver, or at least a cruel and rigid dogmatist, concerned with getting human minds into a correct cognitive state to the exclusion of all else. God is not supposed to be like that, nor are the teachers in whom non-theistic religious believers put their trust.

Finally, it follows from this view of religious doctrine that a defense of such doctrines is likely to be persuasive only if carried out from within the perspective of each religion, not by a philosophy attempting to justify revealed religions in general. That is why I am not spending much time on them in this book. If doctrines are articulations of views we are initially inclined toward on the basis of an imaginative commitment to a certain text and set of practices, then defending them will require that we start from a position that already affirms that text and set of practices. The central doctrines of Christianity, Judaism, Islam, and Buddhism can all be made out to look rational from a purely philosophical standpoint, but also to look ridiculous, and I don't think the doctrines of any one of them have much of an advantage, in this regard, over the doctrines of the others. A rational defense of revealed religions can justify the faith required for each of them, the fact that certain kinds of poetic texts—revelations—arouse that faith, and the fact that faith is fostered by practice, but not the doctrines that come with these texts and practices. We can rationally justify the non-conceptual form of revealed religions, but not the content that they take to be conveyed by that form.

59. The word "truth," we said many chapters ago, is first and foremost applied in religion to people who guide us along a path, or course of action. And what people mean when they call a revelation "true" is above all, I think, that the path it holds out to them is a trustworthy one, that they can trust it to bring them to a position in which their telic expectations will be met. The truth of a revelation rests, not on the truth of its historical or moral claims (we *bring* a morality to it), but on its reliability as a guide to our highest good. Which is to say that, when we apply truth to revelations, we use "true" in the way we do when we trust Aloysius (Part I, § 29). We use it to mark our commitment to a path that we expect will guide us to a different way of looking at things, or to the guide (God, or a prophet or guru) who offers such a path. We hope to be transformed by a revelation so that we can see our telos properly, and, therefore, begin to achieve it, not to receive from it means to ends—whether prudential or moral—that we already have. But that means that we cannot wholly judge it against the ends we already have, or use the established methods of testing truth-claims that go with those ends. We can't test it simply by our own senses and reason, or by its accordance with a regime of experts who are supposed to extend our sensory and rational skills.

By the same token, we must accept the ever-present possibility that the meaning of the revelation we accept may shift as we, or our community, continue down its path. We may be able to see what it really has to tell us only over time, as we follow its guidance (cf. Part I, § 29–30). It is essential to a text regarded as revelatory, that is, that what seems to be the literal meaning of any of its verses may shift into another key, or that the cast of the whole may at one point seem designed to shape a nation, at another to be an allegory for Platonic philosophy, at yet a third to accomplish a Heideggerian disclosure of a truth beyond reason. The process by which the etiological legends of the ancient Israelites became transformed into the Jewish Bible and the Christian Old Testament,[13] and were later transformed again, on the one hand by the readings of the Talmudic rabbis and Maimonides and the Kabbalists, and on the other by the Church Fathers and Aquinas and Luther and John Wesley, is thus perfectly suited to the kind of truth that a revelation has to offer. Telic truth must be suited to the moral views and imaginative shape of a particular recipient or community of recipients at a particular time, and must change—must offer different kinds of guidance—as those recipients follow a path that transforms their feelings and modes of perception.

Which is to say that interpretation—the active reception of revelation—is intrinsic to what revelation has to offer. In the next chapter, we take up that process.

6

Receiving Revelation

60. Some parts of a revealed text become well-known among its adherents while others languish in obscurity. Jews use the exodus from Egypt as a metaphor for all sorts of events and stages they go through in their lives, while paying far less attention to the plague of poisonous snakes in the book of Numbers, or any part of the book of Job; Christians play up the aspects of Jesus's teachings that move away from traditional Jewish rituals and pay less attention to passages in which his life was marked by such rituals (e.g. Luke 2: 21–24). Jews and Christians, who nominally share a sacred text, often emphasize different parts of it. Christians do read Job, for instance, while Jews read Leviticus and Numbers, which many Christians barely know.

A single religious community may also have a very different moral understanding of its text at different times. Pacifism was central to early Christianity, but virtually disappeared from Christian practice after the conversion of Constantine. At different times, Jewish, Christian, and Muslim communities have held widely different attitudes towards the study of "pagan" philosophy, and towards followers of other religions. A defining mark of traditional Jews, Christians, and Muslims in many places today is their hostility to homosexuality, but some leading religious figures in all three traditions wrote homoerotic poetry in the Middle Ages.[1]

Again, a religion may be understood wholly differently, even at the same time, by different sub-communities. One group of adherents may translate the text primarily into a set of ceremonies, another into an allegory for philosophical or mystical doctrines, a third into a call for political or social action. Quakers and Catholics, Hasidim and Reform Jews, Sufi liberals and Wahhabi sympathizers of al-Qaeda look like they must belong to entirely different religions, even though they regard the same text as sacred.

All these phenomena fall under the heading of how we receive revelation. No text is self-interpreting, and the gnomic, poetic texts that are constitutive of revelation are harder to interpret than most. No moral code is self-applying, and the moral codes embedded in religious teachings—interwoven as they are with telic concerns, and marked by historical features even while being held relevant to all times and places—can be more difficult to apply than most. A community must therefore have a theory of interpretation (in combination, usually, with a moral theory and a theology) if it is to be capable of receiving a revelation. Some religious believers deny this. Fundamentalists, as they are often called,[2] claim that their sacred texts wear their meaning on their face, and that any theory about how they should be read is an illegitimate interposition between God's word and the faithful. But even this is already a theory about how the texts should be read, a theology and hermeneutics that is as much a human product as the ones that understand sacred texts in Aristotelian or mystical fashion; even this is a human constraint on what the text means. A human mode of reception is not an option, in response to revelation. It is inevitable.

It is also a good thing, religiously. Pace the fundamentalists, the fact that human beings must make decisions about how they are going to understand and implement the teachings of their revealed texts is not a regrettable necessity, but something integral to what revelation is—something that God Himself, if He gave these texts, must have intended. Revelation and its reception need each other.

In one sense, this is obvious. If revelation is given rather than found within ourselves, we need to receive it, while if we are engaged in reception, there must be something to receive. Giving and receiving need each other, and in that sense it is tautologous that revelation needs a reception and vice versa.

But I don't mean just this. I mean that revelation needs a certain *kind* of reception to be fully what it aims to be. Revelation, as I have characterized it, is angled and obscure and edgy—endlessly interesting, somewhat out of reach and addressed to us paradigmatically in a particular situation: thus not well suited to the needs and aspirations of human beings in every and any situation. But revelation also purports to be a holistic vision of how all human life can be worthwhile, and in that capacity its obscurity and edginess are problematic. The reception of revelation aims to resolve that problem, or reduce it, to transform the angled vision of the original text into something that can be recognized as at least in principle a good one by all humanity.[3] The reception of revelation cannot offer what revelation itself provides—it is not conceptually challenging enough, not exciting enough, not obscure enough to provide a satisfying vision of our ultimate telos—but revelation also cannot give us the virtues of its reception. They need each other roughly as the beautiful and the moral do in order to compose the highest good. But revelation is supposed to lead us to this highest good. If my account thus far is correct, it can do that only if the path it yields is shaped both by a foundational text and by a process in which we actively receive that text.

We need to keep these moments separate. Revelation is received by a process quite different from itself. We might say that it is given in poetry, but received in prose. It is given in poetry because it is essentially mysterious, and poetry preserves mystery. But something we cannot grasp at all is not even a mystery—it is merely unknown—and certainly not a mystery in the light of which we can live. So the poetry of revelation must be translated into prose: an attempt, perhaps always an inadequate attempt, to make clear sense of what it says. Only thus can the poetry yield a path. To engage deliberately in practices, to choose them and plan our participation in them, we need to know their shape in advance, and to do this effectively, and in accordance with morality, the practices need to be integrated into a socially-shared way of life. The reception of revelation makes this possible. It fits a vision of what makes life worth living onto a path that can be shared by a community, and that promotes decency and justice. But it remains reception, rather than the construction of a purely human code of conduct, only as long as it recognizes the asymmetry between its own workings and the revelation to which it responds. What ruptures our ordinary frameworks of thought, breaks through the modes of reasoning that reduce candidates for ultimate worth to something that does not seem worthwhile, can only appear as such if it contrasts with our ordinary frameworks. At the same time, what is radically new, what ruptures our normal frameworks, also confirms those frameworks *as* normal, and as ours, helps us see how important they are to us, how much they define us or set limits on what we can take to be true. By being so different from us, revelation helps us know who we are, and we help it be what it is by accepting it while maintaining our difference from it: by giving it room to teach us. So revelation and its reception belong together by contrast.[4] This is a deep belonging together, but the relationship is lost if they are reduced to the same kind of thing, if the contrast between them is lost. That is the mistake of Enlightenment theories of revelation, from Lessing and Kant to Hermann Cohen.

61. James Kugel says that the canonization of the texts that became the Hebrew Bible was inseparable from a certain way of reading those texts. Had they not been interpreted in this way, the texts would not have been canonized. Had they been understood as the "etiological tales and priestly polemics and political speeches" they seem to have been when originally written, no-one would have sought divine teaching in them.[5] Kugel identifies three crucial assumptions behind the mode of interpretation that all ancient Jewish and Christian interpreters shared, when approaching the Bible:

(1) It is cryptic: its meaning is not apparent on the surface.
(2) It is inerrant: all contradictions and mistakes it seems to contain are resolvable if one penetrates beyond the cryptic surface. One thing this means is that nothing in it is irrelevant or repetitious. It is an organic whole, to which each verse is necessary, and can be read in the light of any of the others.
(3) When properly interpreted, it has something ethically valuable to teach each reader, in every generation.

These assumptions, Kugel says, were preconditions for regarding the Bible as divinely authored.[6] I think this is quite right, and agree with Kugel, too, that it is nicely expressed in the traditional Jewish idea that an "oral Torah"—a tradition of oral interpretation—goes along with the written Torah (more about this in a moment).[7] Sometimes Kugel writes as though *particular* readings of the ancient interpreters, such as the transformation of Biblical characters into all-good or all-evil types, are also essential to the oral Torah that canonized the written one.[8] That seems wrong to me. The oral Torah is a process, not a fixed set of readings, which can go in many different directions and which in fact often contains radically different, even contradictory, ways of handling the same passage. No particular such reading is demanded by the assumptions that Kugel lists, nor does it follow from them that characters in the sacred text must be regarded as all-good or all-bad. Moral ambiguity might be one of the ethical teachings that a cryptic and inerrant text has to offer its readers.

With that caveat, I think Kugel has identified necessary conditions for the reading of any sacred text, not just the Bible. More precisely: he has identified conditions necessary for *regarding* any text *as* sacred, for receiving it as revelation. To regard it as revelatory simply is to regard it as ethically authoritative: as our supreme guide to our telos. But to take a text as authoritative is to set it up as superior to one's own judgment; one cannot simultaneously regard it as authoritative and find fault with it. Finding fault allows one to reject it whenever it conflicts with one's views or inclinations, in which case it cannot serve as a guide.[9] Hence, insofar as we regard the text as authoritative, we can dismiss no part of it as unnecessary or mistaken. But this approach to the text, when conjoined with the way-of-the-world beliefs about truth and morality that, I argued earlier, must also be brought to the interpretation of any text we see as ethically valuable, will entail that all known candidates for revelation must be at least in part cryptic, unavailable to simple, literal interpretation. There are no purportedly revealed texts whose surface meaning coincides at all points with what the people following it have, over time, believed to be true scientifically and morally. It is hard to imagine how a text written or accepted at one point in history, and therefore speaking to the beliefs and values accepted at that place and time, could continue to seem unproblematically true across many later generations. So the idea that a text is cryptic follows readily from the idea that it is sacred, and an intricate, non-obvious way of interpreting such texts—of unlocking their hidden secrets—is therefore inseparable from their canonization.

Is canonization essential to sacredness? I think so. It's hard to see how one could have an authoritative text otherwise. One might imagine a body of texts whose sacredness is constantly in flux, each text being regarded by some individuals, but not others, as sources of revelation, or all of the texts being regarded by individuals as a source of revelation at some times, but not others. This would not really be sacredness, however. In the first case, the texts would lose their ability to focus the practices of a *community* of believers, and in the second, they would lose authority over the lives, as a whole, even of individual believers. A community needs to canonize certain texts, fix them as sacred for all believers, if it is to see them as authoritative. It is not essential that those texts be written. By "text" I just mean a teaching passed down so as to preserve, more or less strictly, the same wording from generation to generation, and some cultures accomplish this by developing elaborate modes of memorization to pass on the teaching orally, rather than by writing it down. But there must be some separation between a given, relatively stable teaching and its receivers for the process of interpretation to get underway. This is true even if the canonized text contains, as the Hebrew Bible does, passages that themselves reinterpret other passages in it.[10] What matters is that at some point a teaching or set of teachings is marked off as an authoritative whole, standing over and above its receivers,[11] so that they can take it as complete, consistent, cryptic, etc.—as something from which they can learn. As long as the text is fixed, the process of reception can afford to be open and flexible, even contain contradictory theories and modes of practice. Speculative readings can be tried out; readers who differ can yet respect each other's views as responses to the same source of teaching; moral or spiritual mistakes in the community can be corrected by returning to the fixed text and finding other ways of understanding it. The fixity of the text holds open possibilities for variety and change in the mode of reception, holds these flexible readings and practices together *as* modes of receiving a single revelation. Without a fixed text, the difference between the source of revelation and the response to it disappears. Readers get to choose which text they will interpret as well as how to interpret it. So there is no "given," no reason to invest the texts being read with any greater ethical authority than the readings offered of them, and eventually the idea of a revealed teaching will be replaced by a philosophical argument about the good among rational peers. The distinction between the giving and the receiving of revelation will disappear. The idea of spontaneous reception, as a distinctive mode of thought, of the imagination playing with something that stands beyond it, will disappear. Faith will disappear.

But faith will also disappear, to be replaced by rigid dogmatism, if canonization does not go along with a fluid process of interpreting the canonized texts. At its best, canonization serves, not to entrench a certain set of religious authorities, but precisely to open up debate over the true meaning and import of a revealed text. Canonization sets the terms for an ongoing process of reception, an ongoing attempt by a community of religious believers to grapple with their shared religious vision. If we hold on to a fixed text, but reject the idea of an active process of reception, we get communities who hide from themselves the fact that they are engaging in interpretation, and seek in their sacred text either the simplest, most literal meaning they can find or a meaning that coheres with dogmas their religious leaders have told them to accept. Neither of these attitudes is compatible with revelation as a source of ethical teaching: as a provocation to *reflective* love of the good, or something that can be *spontaneously* received. Revelation must be given, which requires that it be fixed, canonical, but it must also be received, which requires that it be adapted to the way of the world it is supposed to illuminate.

In speaking of two Torahs, an oral as well as a written one, traditional Judaism recognizes the distinction between the giving and the receiving of revelation very well. Partly for that reason, and partly because the receiving of revelation occurs to a great degree in informal, intimate settings —at home, at school, at church or synagogue— and I know only the Jewish community in this intimate way, I shall illustrate the process of reception largely through Jewish sources. But I have encountered or read about parallels to the features of the process I will describe in Christian, Muslim, Hindu, and Buddhist communities, and there are general reasons, to which I will turn at the end of the chapter, to expect a process with roughly these features to spring up in every revealed religion.

> *I see the Jewish hermeneutical tradition as a sort of tent for God's word, a way of welcoming it into our world and giving it a home among us. The Torah says: "Let them make Me a sanctuary that I may dwell among them." (Exodus 25: 8), and commentators have for centuries stressed the fact that this verse says "among them," rather than "in it." But what is a sanctuary that allows God to dwell among the people? Well, it might be a project of some kind, involving the whole community. The tabernacle in Exodus may be a metaphor for a process—perhaps the very process by which it came to be built. And indeed, traditional Jewish commentary has taken the process of building the tabernacle to be the Torah's model for all work: for what needs to stop on the sabbath, but at other times is the sort of human effort that serves God. (Even ideal work ceases on the sabbath; God's own work ceased on the first sabbath.) God's sanctuary would then be a communal, ideally-motivated activity: a project undertaken by the people for the sake of receiving God's presence.*
>
> *And in that case, there could still be a sanctuary for God among the people of Israel now that its physical sanctuary has been destroyed. Perhaps the Temple was replaced by the writings of the rabbis— the process of interpreting the Torah that has preserved Jewish communities for 2000 years. The oral Torah—the rabbinic process—may indeed be the true, the ideal sanctuary. God can dwell among human beings only where they make a living place for His presence, only where they are wrestling with His word and its implications. Only then can God's word come alive for them, and not fade into superstition. We must create living, interpretive sanctuaries to catch and preserve our divine teachings, else God cannot dwell among us. God cannot build these sanctuaries Himself. It is logically impossible for Him to be received by us unless we do the receiving (hence: "Let them make Me a sanctuary . . .") God knows that His word goes out to human beings; God knows that human beings cannot receive any teaching unless they interpret it, adapt it, fit it into what else they believe and do. So God must have intended the process of reception to go along with any and all revelation. God Himself must have commanded that we take on His commands autonomously.*
>
> *And autonomy requires that each community, in each era, continue the process of interpretation: adapt the revealed text to its historical situation, integrate the text with its moral beliefs, draw out implications from the text that it finds inspiring and beautiful. Each community, in each era, must expand and enrich the ability of the interpretive process to bring down God's Presence: "Enlarge the place of your tent. Let the cloths of your dwelling extend." (Isaiah 54: 2, 7.)*

62. The Torah contains the following notorious passage:

If a man has a stubborn and rebellious son, who will not heed the voice of his father or the voice of his mother . . . , then his father and mother shall take hold of him and bring him to the elders of his city and the gates of his place, and say to the elders of his city, "This son of ours is stubborn and rebellious; he does not heed our voice; he is a glutton and a drunkard." And all the people of his city shall stone him with stones and he shall die, and you will destroy the evil from your midst, and all Israel shall heed, and fear. (Deuteronomy 21: 18–21.)

How can a text supposedly authored by God contain a law as horrible as this one? Or how can we possibly consider a text with a passage like this one to be authored by God?

The rabbis of the Talmud respond to this passage by demonstrating what happens if one tries to take it extremely literally, and incorporate it into a working law code.[12] They start by pointing out that the son in question, if he is still required to listen to his parents (and "rebellious" presupposes that), has got to be less than a mature adult, but at the same time cannot be too young if he can be held responsible for his sins. This leads them to narrow the age at which the law might apply to some months around the time of puberty. They also add other conditions—the child can't be deaf, else he wouldn't be able to heed the "voice" of his parents; the parents can't be lame, else they couldn't "bring" him to the elders of the city—until eventually one rabbi, leaning on the fact that the father and mother are supposed to say that their son does not listen to "our" voice, declares that the father and mother must speak, literally, with the same voice. But that is impossible: men and women have different voices. So the law cannot be carried out. The Talmud backs up this view with an anonymous quotation from an earlier rabbinic generation: "The stubborn and rebellious son never was and never will be. Why was it written then? Interpret [it] and receive reward."

And that view has carried the day in Jewish practice. Nevertheless—the Talmud being the book of argument that it is—one participant in these debates, a Rabbi Jonathan, dissents: "I have seen [a stubborn and rebellious son]," he says, "and I sat on his grave."[13]

63. Another difficult passage in the Torah calls on the nation of Israel to destroy any city in its midst that has gone astray:

> If you hear it said, about one of your cities that your Lord has given you to dwell in, that some sons of Belial have gone out from your midst and led astray the inhabitants of the city saying, "Come, let us worship other gods, whom you have not known," then you shall investigate and inquire and question thoroughly, and behold, if the thing is true and definite—this abomination has been done in your midst—you shall surely strike the inhabitants of that town with the sword, destroy it utterly, and [kill] everything in it and the cattle. You shall also gather all the spoil of it in the middle of the public square in the city and burn with fire every bit of the city and the spoil of it to the Lord your God. And it shall be a ruin forever. It shall not be built again. (Deuteronomy 13: 13–17)

Again, the rabbis use the words of the passage itself—along with other passages in the Torah—to narrow the scope of this law. One view, relying on the demand that the spoil of the city be burnt in its public square, holds that no city can be condemned if it lacks a public square.[14] Other rabbis use a verse that calls for an individual idolater to be executed at the gates of his or her city (Deuteronomy 17: 5) to derive the conclusion that only individuals can be condemned by their own city: an entire city must be tried and convicted by the entire Sanhedrin—the national court—if it is to be condemned.[15] Rabbi Eliezer this time plays the trump card:[16] a city with a single mezuzah on a single one of its doors (practically every Jewish home has a mezuzah on its front door) cannot be destroyed, since the mezuzah would then also have to be destroyed and we know from elsewhere that we are not to destroy objects dedicated to God.[17]

Again, the Talmud supports Rabbi Eliezer's argument with an anonymous quotation: "The condemned city never was and never will be. Why was it written then? Interpret [it] and receive reward."

And again we hear the dissenting voice of Rabbi Jonathan: "I saw [the condemned city] and sat on its ruin."

64. A word on Rabbi Jonathan. He got around! Imagine seeing both a stubborn and rebellious son and a condemned city while your peers are under the impression that neither of these things ever happened . . .

But surely if either of them did happen, that would have been big news. If there was so much as a widely-shared impression that the law about stubborn and rebellious sons was non-justiciable, a case in which it was carried out would have been bound to arouse much discussion. And the destruction of an entire Jewish city could hardly go unnoticed, nor was it permitted without a trial in the center of the country. Yet, aside from Rabbi Jonathan's testimony, there is no indication anywhere in rabbinic literature that anyone was ever stoned as a stubborn and rebellious son, or that any Jewish city was ever condemned as idolatrous by fellow Jews.

So Rabbi Jonathan's interventions are almost certainly hyperbolic, a way of insisting that the literal application of God's law cannot be reduced to the vanishing point. We can't take seriously his claim that he literally saw these events, nor should we suppose that he expected anyone to take him literally. But then the literalist in this discussion himself speaks non-literally. And the function of what he says is to enrich the debate over how to interpret Biblical verses, to help fulfill the admonition that the mainstream view applies to the verses they are considering: "interpret [them] and receive [the] reward [of interpretation]." The voice that calls for a real destruction of wicked children and cities thus becomes just one element of a discussion among those who would translate those commands into a demand simply to struggle with what it means for God to speak to us. Rabbi Jonathan is a pupil of Rabbi Ishmael, who was known for his insistence on understanding the Torah in a straightforward way. Rabbi Ishmael had earlier wrangled with his contemporary Rabbi Akiva, known for his delight in subtle, non-straightforward interpretations, over the question of the condemned city and for once the latter agreed that in this case the Torah should be understood "as it was written"[18]— whatever exactly that means. So the discussion of these difficult passages is haunted by an anxiety about whether the literal meaning of these difficult passages might get lost, as a result of the rabbis' fervent attempts to read their apparent commands out of actual Jewish practice.

65. It may seem that the rabbis are cheating when they read the Torah in this way, that they are seeking excuses to purge it of commands they found troubling for independent moral reasons. But why should they not understand it in accordance with their independent moral beliefs? If the Torah comes from God, and not from human beings stuck in the cultural norms of their time and place, then its meaning

should harmonize with what we would expect an all-wise and all-good being to demand of us. A God who created us presumably instilled in us our moral feelings and capacity for moral reasoning (our sources for the very idea of an all-good being). Why would He want us to let these aspects of ourselves fall by the wayside when we try to interpret His word? An all-wise being must also be capable of intending whatever a clever human being could intend, so if a clever human being can write a book with the hidden or indirect or implicit meanings that the rabbis find in the Torah, then God can too. Anything we can plausibly see as an interpretation of the text, God could have intended by giving us the text; any meaning we find in it is a meaning God could have put in it. God's word need not take the form of a simple narrative or law code. It can demand as sophisticated a hermeneutic as the most sophisticated of human writings.

Moreover, the rabbis use some pretty good clues to suggest that the morally troubling commands about the son and the city are not as straightforward as they seem. There are also nice literary and moral resonances to their readings. Consider the fact that the passage about the city led astray uses a form of the word *darash* when it tells the nation to "investigate" whether the reports of such a city are true, and that the rabbis use a form of the same word when they translate the passage into a command that the nation "interpret" (*darush*) these verses and draw a spiritually valuable lesson from them. Or consider the fact that the two passages describe people who are rebelling against the entire idea of goodness, as it is understood in the framework of the Torah: are rejecting the very source of the Torah's vision of the good life, in the city's case, and of its ability to pass down that vision, in the son's case. So these are cases of what philosophers call "radical evil," evil that results not merely from ignorance or self-deceit or weakness of the will, but from an attack on the very existence of goodness. But philosophers from Plato to Kant have argued that we can barely make sense of the idea that a human being might act for the sake of radical evil. Radical evil, they say, makes sense only as a sort of thought experiment, an element of our theoretical models of morality rather than of actual practice. In actual practice, it is far more likely that we can explain any apparent wicked son or city as acting out of blindness, or irresistible impulses, or reaction to a terrible injury inflicted on him or them (child abuse, perhaps, in the son's case; famine or civil war, perhaps, in the city's case), than as freely choosing to promote evil. It makes good sense, therefore, to treat the irredeemably evil son and city as elements of moral or spiritual discussion rather than real cases: to seek in the very description of the cases evidence that we should regard radical evil as an element of our theoretical models, rather than something to be found in the world. And it makes excellent sense that an all-good being might include such cases in His law only in order to teach us something of this sort. The rabbis say that both passages were included in the Torah so what we should "interpret them and receive [the] reward of interpretation." This is tantamount to saying that God put them there to spark precisely the sort of complex hermeneutical and philosophical discussion in which we have just been engaged, to force us to struggle with the question of how, morally, to read sacred texts.

Perhaps it enriches the discussion of such cases to retain a nagging sense that discussion is an inadequate response to great evil, or perhaps a nagging anxiety over whether we are letting our cleverness in interpretation run away with us helps stimulate such a discussion, or keep it honestly attentive to the text—Rabbi Jonathan's voice may be one we need always to hear. But in the end surely we can agree that *talking* about radical evil, and trying to understand where and how it might seem to occur, is preferable to supposing one has actually spotted it, and rushing to eliminate it. The rabbis' handling of these passages strikes me as brilliant, a model for reading a sacred text. This is casuistry at its best.

66. A moral compass of some sort, an independent source of moral principles, seems to guide the rabbis into eliminating the laws calling for the destruction of the wicked son and wicked city from Jewish practice. They do something similar elsewhere. The "eye for an eye" passages in the Torah are translated into a tool for determining the appropriate financial compensation for each kind of wound.[19] Capital punishment gets so hedged about with pre-conditions that Rabbi Eliezer ben Azariah could describe a Sanhedrin who condemned one person to death in seventy years as a bloody Sanhedrin.[20] The rabbis also found ways to ensure that women consented to marriage and had a right to divorce, without any textual basis for such requirements in the Torah. In these and many other respects, the rabbinic reception of the Torah softens the harsh demands that the text seems to make, and molds its laws into something more respectful of the dignity of each individual—a norm that the text may well contain implicitly[21] but does not explicitly emphasize. The rabbis bring the Torah into line with justice and mercy; they don't simply find those virtues jumping off the page at them.[22]

> And one point of the giving of the Torah, from a theological perspective, may be precisely that it has prodded Jews to bring it in line with justice and mercy: that, by inspiring centuries of moral interpretation, it has taught us that justice and mercy are hard to find, that they need to be wrested from texts and situations and are often not to be found in what seem superficially to be "the obvious places." We realize our freedom, our autonomy, in the struggle to bring out these moral qualities, and it is not unreasonable to suppose that God gave us an obscure text in part to prod us into realizing our freedom. In any case, the joy—the experience of holiness—that we take in the process of interpreting our sacred text comes as much as anything from the relief of discovering how goodness can be found in the most unlikely places.

67. But the rabbis do not *say* they are guided by a moral compass, and there are problems in attributing such a mode of interpretation to them. In the first place, they make no effort to develop an explicit moral theory. There is no natural law theory in the Talmud, nor any sustained reflections on the nature of virtue in the mainstream Jewish tradition until the time of Maimonides.[23] And there is reason to think the absence of moral philosophy in the formative rabbinic period was no accident. For the rabbis not infrequently express reservations about philosophy. In one remarkable passage, which includes anecdotes suggesting that the study of Greek philosophy

was a partial cause of some national disasters, they consider a prohibition on learning Greek, and conclude that learning the Greek language is permitted, but learning "Greek wisdom" is forbidden.[24] Elsewhere, a tale is told of four rabbis who "went into paradise"—widely interpreted as a metaphor for philosophical study—three of whom were thereby led to death, madness, or apostasy.[25] Then there is the midrash that says the Torah begins with the letter *bet*—a letter closed on all sides except the one that faces forward—in order to teach people that they should not inquire into what is "above" and "below," or into what comes "before" creation.[26] And in *Pirkei Avot*, Rabbi Elazar Hisma declares that the precepts about "the sacrifice of birds and the beginning of menstruation are central laws," while "astronomy and geometry are on the periphery [*parparot*] of wisdom" (3: 23). Astronomy and geometry were two of the great sciences in ancient Greece and Rome, regarded by Plato as preparation for philosophical dialectic. Here they are banished to the sidelines while the most absurd of Jewish laws—even within the rabbinic way of looking at these things—are said to be of great importance.[27]

So there is ample reason to see the rabbis as suspicious of philosophy, in stark contrast with the literati of most of the ancient Mediterranean world. But the main function of philosophy in this era was to help human beings develop an independent moral compass. Most ancient schools of philosophy, and certainly the Stoic and Epicurean schools that the early rabbis were likely to have known, saw their skills and doctrines as dedicated to helping human beings achieve a virtuous life. To be skeptical about the value of philosophy, then, was to be skeptical about whether reason alone can lead human beings to virtue. The rabbis' doubts about philosophy make best sense as reflecting a fear that a reliance on reason alone will undermine the authority of the Torah.[28] And while that fear was directed against all modes of purely rational thinking, even astronomy and geometry, it was particularly aroused by the idea of conducting one's moral investigations in this way.[29] For if there can be an adequate account of morality based on reason alone, of what point are the moral laws to be found in the Torah? And if reason can spin out a complete account of how we should live, if it can show us our ultimate goal and everything we need to do to attain it—as Plato, Aristotle, and the Stoics suggested it could—then what need do we have for any of the laws in the Torah? Surely everything in the Torah will then be either wrong or unnecessary: wrong if it contradicts what reason alone would tell us, and unnecessary if it could be derived from reason alone.

Nevertheless, the cases we have considered provide evidence that some independent idea of right and wrong guides rabbinic interpretation of the Torah, and at times the rabbis come close to admitting that. In the medieval period, one major commentator uses Deuteronomy 6: 18—"You shall do the right and the good"—to suggest that Jewish courts must seek compromises that go beyond the letter of the law of the Torah, and another both endorses that position and takes a verse in the middle of the Torah—"Be holy, for I the Lord your God am holy" (Leviticus 19: 2)—to suggest that Jewish law aims, at its core, to lead us to a higher level of virtue than anything that can be explicitly commanded.[30] Both gesture towards a mode of moral thinking independent of the Torah. I suggest that this is at work behind the scenes in the Talmudic passages we have considered. Perhaps, for the rabbis, such independent moral thinking is inadequate to guide us to all value, but they seem to acknowledge that it can in certain cases provide a clear, undeniable guide to what we may and may not do. Killing our children, destroying entire cities, carrying out the death penalty without adequate safeguards, and forcing women into unwanted marriages, may be so clearly wrong that we could not accept a text as divine if it ordered us to do such things. If it seems to us that the text we regard as divine violates these basic standards, we must have misunderstood it.

68. The cases I've discussed show how the rabbis deal with what I earlier called the pockmarks of the Torah, bringing out the morally smooth skin that they believe lies beneath the blemishes. But a reader for this book complained, reasonably enough, that revealed texts are often far more problematic, morally, than any talk of "pockmarks" would imply. There are not merely a few unsightly blemishes on the Torah, Quran, Gospels, etc., said this reader, but for instance a pervasive sexism in the Torah, detailing what he meant with a three-page list of the many passages and commands that seem to presuppose the inferiority of women.[31] (He could just as easily have compiled a list of passages that seem xenophobic, or reflective of a crude, vengeful conception of divine justice.) How can texts that systematically reflect morally obnoxious views be regarded as revelations from a supremely good being?

The key to answering that question turns out to lie, after all, in how traditions of reception respond to the pockmarks on these texts. Modes of receiving revelation that re-read the pockmarks of a sacred text inspire and make possible more substantial reinterpretations of them. Maimonides devoted a large part of his *Guide for the Perplexed* to showing how the pervasively anthropomorphic language about God, in the Jewish Bible, can be re-read so that every bit of it is metaphorical for a non-anthropomorphic conception of God. And while Maimonides's views on this topic were rejected by much of the subsequent Jewish tradition, his most fervent opponents—the Kabbalists—located their own baroque theosophy in the Torah by way of an analogous reading of the text against its literal grain.[32] The methods are analogous because both varieties of Judaism were made possible by the rabbinic techniques discussed above, where the literal level of the text is pressed in such a way as to radically revise its straightforward meaning.

So there is no reason why even global moral problems with a sacred text, like pervasive sexism, cannot be handled by a mode of interpretation premised on the notion that the text must contain a morally admirable view. If Maimonides can find a non-anthropomorphic God in the Torah, we should have no trouble finding a non-sexist God there as well. And in fact even the Orthodox Jewish community has worked quite hard to minimize, in practice, the sexist implications of its sacred text. More needs to be done—the issue is indeed one of the most discussed in the contemporary Jewish community—but sexism is a moral flaw to which the community receiving the Torah as revelation is certainly alert. It has done far less to minimize the xenophobia of the Torah. Still, there are many Jewish teachers and religious leaders today whose readings transform passages that seem hostile to non-Israelite peoples into something cosmopolitan and respectful of religious difference.

I don't know nearly enough about how the process of reception works within Christian and Muslim communities to bring out detailed parallels with rabbinic thought there. But it seems clear that neither the Aristotelianism of many medieval Muslims nor the generous mysticism of the Sufis would be possible without a similarly thorough re-reading of the Quran. Nor would the pluralism of many modern Christians, according to which people can be saved without explicitly embracing Christ, be possible without an analogous upending of a central theme of the Gospels and Pauline epistles, when taken literally.[33]

It's worth stressing that the search for a morally admirable reading of one's sacred text is not a desperate maneuver to save the text in the face of external moral challenges, nor a mere projection of the beliefs of the reader into the text. Rather, it is *required* by the very act of faith by which one takes a text to be revealed. To regard a text as a communication from an ideally good being, or as expressing an ideally good way of life, just is to see it as containing the highest standard of morality—to see any moral flaws it may seem to have as a reflection of one's own blindness or corruption rather than a fault in its Author, and to seek, therefore, a way of understanding it that corrects for those flaws. To see a text as such an ideal is to remove it from its historical context and place it instead in a Platonic space. So the normal constraints on how to read historical texts fall away. Perhaps one is wrong to regard the text as revealed, but *if* it is revealed, it must represent the highest possible moral standards.

Which leaves us with the question of whether a text, once regarded as revealed, might turn into nothing more than a blank slate for the readings of its receivers. What's left of the text if one can read even its obviously sexist or anthropomorphic language so against the grain that it comes to teach the opposite of what it seems to teach? Why regard *that* text as revealed, if one is going to re-read it so strenuously? Does it matter, anymore, if one regards the Torah rather than the Gospels or Quran or Vedas as revealed? And does anything go—is anything one wants to find in the text already there?

This is, I think, the truly difficult question that springs from my reader's complaint. It is not that the pockmarks approach to moral problems in revelation has nothing to say about problems like pervasive sexism in the text. Rather, it has too much to say—it seems to reduce the revealed text to nothing more than an excuse for morally inspirational readings. I don't think that is in fact what happens, however. Even fervently Maimonidean or Kabbalistic Jews try valiantly to link their worldview back to specific elements of the Torah. But there certainly is a danger that the readings will substitute for the text, and rival groups within each religious tradition often accuse one another of having succumbed to that danger.

Are there limits to what the text can mean? Of course there are, but it is hard to draw any sharp line showing where they lie. It is hard to do that with any text. A widely-shared view in the philosophy of interpretation is that there can be no rule, independent of the process of interpretation itself, determining which interpretations are legitimate and which illegitimate. Any such rule, after all, would in turn have to be interpreted—applied to specific cases—and would then be subject to precisely the indeterminacy that it was formulated to rule out. Even rules intended to delineate the sphere of literal meaning fall prey to this limitation. The project of establishing a firm test, in advance of the process of interpretation, to determine what counts as genuine and what as spurious interpretation is an unfulfillable dream.

We solve this problem, according to many hermeneutical theorists, by looking within practices of interpretation for the limits they determine for themselves. Interpretation is a practice that works out its own boundaries as it goes along. Interpretation moves between a text or theory and the attempt of particular listeners or readers to draw out implications of that text or theory at a particular moment, and it must somehow be responsible both to the text or theory and to the situation and purposes of the particular readers. The relevant notion of "responsibility" itself, moreover, comes out when we put each particular interpretation into the context of the practice as a whole, so that it can be assessed against prior, similar interpretations, much as legal decisions, in common law systems, are assessed against precedents. "We use judgments [particular applications of rules to cases—particular interpretations] as principles of judgment," says Wittgenstein. He also says: "My judgments [interpretations] themselves characterize the way I judge, characterize the nature of judgment."[34] There *are* good and bad interpretations—there must be, if there is to be interpretation at all—but the line between them is determined variously, in the course of interpretation, by the specific norms of the kind of interpretation being employed, and by the purposes both of that practice of interpretation and of the wider network of practices into which it is supposed to fit. Hence, *within* a Kabbalistic or Maimonidean framework—within a sub-community of Jews that orders itself in accordance with one of these views—particular interpretations will be judged more or less good and bad, more or less "legitimate" and "genuine" or "illegitimate" and "spurious," in accordance with how well they fit with the norms of this framework, and with Jewish practice and thought more generally, as well as with how well they seem to fit the text. "Fitting the text" will itself be judged, moreover, by reference to prior instances of the going mode of interpretation, precedents for each reading in the ongoing practice of which it is a part. There is no neutral framework, on this view, for determining correct and incorrect ways of reading the text. Even the supposedly literal readings insisted upon by fundamentalist religious communities have norms and precedents to guide what counts as a "literal" reading of their text.[35] No Christian community of that kind will for instance accept a unitarian reading of their Scripture, despite the fact that the doctrine of the Trinity never appears explicitly there.

Nothing about this account of interpretation conflicts with the idea that God is the Author of one or more sacred texts. God's own purpose in giving us Scriptures, as I indicated earlier, may well be in large part to make us conscious of the openness of interpretation, and the joy and freedom that can be found in making rich use of our interpretive faculties.[36] No text will call as much on us to use such resources as a text that purports to guide our entire lives—nor can a text with full-throttled telic aspirations like that help but be reinterpreted drastically in different places and times—and those of us who believe that there is at least one such text therefore have good reason also to believe that we are expected, by God or whoever/whatever else has given us a telos, to embrace our capacity for creative interpretation.

And nothing about the view I'm endorsing implies that "anything goes," that interpretation is a matter of saying whatever occurs to one and attributing it to the text. Any framework of interpretation, to be a framework of interpretation at all, must see itself as trying somehow to bring out what is already in the text rather than just projecting things into it. But any framework of interpretation also has to meet norms for what counts as being "in" the text that cannot themselves be found in the text alone, or given in advance of a practice that actually yields up interpretations. People have every right to reject particular interpretations as mere projections of the interpreter, but the criteria for such a rejection will always come from a practice of interpretation that has developed norms for itself out of its prior cases.

So I do not want to let go of the distinction between legitimate and illegitimate readings of a sacred text, just the idea that there is any sharp way of drawing that distinction, in advance of actual practices of interpretation. The best we can say is that there is a line to be observed, by people of faith, between attempting to hearken scrupulously to the words of one's Scripture and recognizing that the Author of a sacred Scripture must expect us to bring to it the full range of our moral understanding and aesthetic imagination. Liberal theologians tend to play down the former—the givenness of Scripture—while conservative theologians tend to play down the latter, the fact that a Scripture is given *to* autonomous beings, who need to receive it autonomously. But both are necessary if revelation is truly to orient a human life.

69. The rabbis adjust the law of the Torah to non-moral as well as moral conditions. Indeed, the main point of the dense, enormously long Talmud is to iron out the apparently incomprehensible or pragmatically unworkable aspects of the Torah so that it can be used as a real code of law. The rabbis iron out apparent contradictions in the text (why does it require eating matza for eight days in one place and seven in another?), clarify what is obscure or vague in it (what does it mean to "write" certain passages of the text on one's hands and between one's eyes?), and offer explanations for its apparent redundancies (why does the command not to boil a kid in its mother's milk appear three times?). They find a variety of connections between widely separated sections of the text, and of symbolic meanings for the commandments. They also try to ensure that the Torah's demands do not burden ordinary people's lives to a degree that

might lead them to reject it,[37] and they develop practices and legal codes to cover areas on which the Torah has little to say—marriage and divorce, civil disputes, prayer. To do the latter, they draw on established practices in their community and general notions of law as well as bits of revealed text, acknowledging sometimes that they are draping their precepts quite loosely onto the text: "The laws concerning shabbat, festival offerings, and the misappropriation of sacred objects are as mountains hanging by a hair, for they have little Biblical basis, but many laws."[38]

The rabbis may feel uncomfortable about using independent moral principles to interpret their sacred text, but they positively revel in the transformative effect of their interpretations more generally. A passionate argument over whether the Torah should be construed narrowly, in accordance with the strict meaning of the text, or more broadly, in accordance with the understanding that living teachers and communities bring to it, lies behind the very project of the Talmud, and the victors in that debate are emphatically those who think that the written Torah must be construed in the light of a living, oral tradition.

Two striking passages will have to do, as illustrations of how the need for the oral Torah was defended:

> The story is told of a non-Jew who came before Shammai[39] [and] said to him, "How many Torahs do you have?" He replied, "Two: a written Torah and an oral Torah." Said the non-Jew: "The written Torah I believe in, but the oral Torah I do not believe in. Convert me, on condition that you teach me [just] the written Torah." Shammai rebuked him and drove him away in anger. He [then] came before Hillel[40] who converted him. One day Hillel began [teaching him] by saying, "*aleph, bet, gimmel*...[A, B, C ...]"; the next day he taught him the reverse ["*gimmel, bet, aleph*...[C, B, A...]"]. The man said to him, "But this isn't what you taught me yesterday." Hillel said to him, "If you rely on me for this, you need to rely on me for the oral Torah as well."[41]

Here, the point seems to be, not that there is a *specific* oral teaching that must accompany the written Torah, but that *some* oral teaching must accompany a written text if its meaning is to be passed down over generations. Hillel illustrates this with the need for a would-be reader to learn the alphabet orally, which nicely shows, to a literalist about reading, how the act of reading itself literally begins with something not read, but he could also have appealed to the need to learn the grammar of the language in which a text is written, the rules of inference that the text follows (what kinds of evidence or argument it takes as sufficient to establish a point), or how it signals irony and other non-literal language.

A more radical passage uses language from the Torah itself as a prooftext that God has given power over what the Torah means into the hands of human beings:

> [On one occasion,] Rabbi Eliezer replied [to the other rabbis on a matter of ritual purity] with all the responses in the world, but they did not accept them from him. [Then] he said to them, "If the law is in accordance with my view, let this carob tree prove it." The carob tree was uprooted from its place one hundred cubits... They said to him: "One does not bring proof

from a carob tree." He then said to them: "If the law is in accordance with my view, let the channel of water prove it." The channel of water turned backward. They said to him: "One does not bring proof from a channel of water." . . . He then said to them: "If the law is in accordance with my view, let it be proved from heaven." A heavenly voice went forth and said: "What do you have against Rabbi Eliezer, for the law is always in accordance with his view?" Rabbi Joshua rose to his feet and said: "'It is not in heaven.'" (Deuteronomy 30: 12) . . . Rabbi Jeremiah said, " . . . The Torah was already given on Mount Sinai, and we do not pay attention to a heavenly voice, for You already wrote in the Torah at Mount Sinai, 'Incline after the majority.'" (Exodus 23: 2)[42]

The verse that Rabbi Joshua quotes comes from a passage in Deuteronomy that talks about repentance, and one could easily read it as saying that repentance, not the entire Torah, is "not in the heavens." But one can also read it in the way Rabbi Joshua does. The pronoun "it," in the verse, is ambiguous. In context, it could refer either to the commandments of the Torah as a whole or to repentance.

So the rabbis hang one of their most important defenses of their right to interpret the Torah on a pronoun of ambiguous reference. That can be unnerving—what a weak reed on which to hang a claim of such moment!—but it is also fitting: the need for interpretation is made especially obvious when one comes across an ambiguous pronoun in a text. We can even see the presence of such a pronoun as God's way of signaling to us that we must engage in the process of interpretation.

And the rabbis sometimes make exactly this point, saying that God gave the Torah "as wheat from which to make flour and flax from which to make clothing, through the rules of interpretation."[43] Those who think the wheat should be kept as wheat, and the flax as flax, do not understand what they have been given.

70. Essentially, the rabbis recognize what the philosopher Donald Davidson made known as "the principle of charity."[44] In order to interpret any bit of language, we must read into it much that we already take to be true. Otherwise we cannot recognize it as so much as a bit of language, as opposed to a meaningless noise or mark. Working out from a radical rejection of foundationalism, Davidson holds that we cannot begin to interpret other people unless we start with the assumption that they are saying something much like what we would say in their shoes. If there are no special, foundational sentences, then we can establish a basis of translation with speakers of another language only by assuming that *all* our beliefs bear some similarity to theirs. "Charity is not an option," Davidson says, "but a condition of having a workable theory" of what others mean. It is therefore "meaningless to suggest that we might fall into massive error by endorsing it . . . Charity is forced on us; whether we like it or not, if we want to understand others, we must count them right in most matters."[45] Even an "omniscient interpreter" would have to use charity to figure out what we mean.[46] The principle of charity is indeed constitutive of meaning; meanings exist, not in our heads, but in a space of interpretation that would not exist without that principle.

But if charity is constitutive of meaning, then it must apply, *inter alia*, even to what God means. So if God has given us a text, the interpretation of it *cannot* be "in heaven." The very attempt to communicate linguistically presupposes that we share a space of interpretation with God, that God has entered the space in which we talk. By speaking to us, God presupposes that we will use our own beliefs and values to understand Him: God consents to our interpreting Him with the principle of charity. Of course, insofar as we regard a text as coming from God, rather than just recording what some human community *thought* that God said, we cannot at any point regard it as mistaken. Davidson allows for us to relax the principle of charity in accordance with our awareness that some of the beliefs other people have may be the product of "social conditioning," and "our common-sense, or scientific, knowledge of explicable error."[47] But God, if He exists, is not subject to social conditioning or any sort of error. So if we interpret a text that we take to be authored by God, we cannot at any point relax the principle of charity. That said, to use the principle of charity is to assimilate God's words to what we can understand, to assume that God speaks to us in our own terms—terms that accord, *inter alia*, with the moral views we uphold independently of religious commitment—and expects us to understand Him accordingly. God speaks in human language, says Rabbi Ishmael.[48] This is a way of entering the human community not significantly different from what Christians call Incarnation.

And for Jews as for Christians—for all followers of a revealed text, I suspect—it is in responding to this divine gesture of humanity that we experience God's love. For God to speak in our language is for God to invite us into conversation with Him. There could be no greater miracle, no greater promise of the possibility that we can reconcile ourselves with our universe. But conversations are two-way affairs. So we need to speak back. Interpretation of God's word is thus a central religious act.

> "Spirit . . . dwells in His community, dies in it every day, and is daily resurrected," says Hegel;[49] his point is that the Christian community, by enacting and interpreting Christian doctrine over the course of history, makes for a truer and more deeply internalized Christianity than one could find by reading the Gospels alone. That's exactly what I want to say about how the Jewish community appropriates and transforms its grounding text. But of course I would put the point somewhat differently: "Spirit dwells in His community, speaks in it every day, and is daily taken up into the oral Torah." Jews don't need God to die and resurrect, as Hegel does, because we don't need to deny full reality to the material world. What we need to know is just that God can speak to us even from **within** the material world that seems so disenchanted—that He can animate it with a voice—and that we can hear that voice, and understand it, and bring its words into our lives..
>
> And the fact that the Jewish version is so much less dramatic than the Christian one speaks in favor of the Jewish one, by my lights. I don't need a dramatic God. The God with the still, small voice will do.

71. Davidsonian interpretation does not give an especially good account of how we grapple with poetry.[50] It tends to press us toward a single meaning for every utterance, and a theory that will yield a definitive function for each element of a language we are

trying to understand. It has little room, therefore, for the ambiguity of poetry. Revelation, which is not only poetry, but an especially mysterious kind of poetry, will fit poorly into such a grid.

One solution to that problem is to recognize that every attempt at a charitable interpretation of a revealed text must be inadequate, that the process must be revised and renewed constantly, drawing different meanings from the text on different occasions and in different generations. The process of interpretation—of receiving revelation—will then always be a matter of approximation, of drawing something fixed from the text for moral and ritual purposes while knowing that one will need to return to it endlessly, to draw out something more and different. Revelation is given once, but received over an eternity. Or: It is given over the span of all the generations in which it is interpreted, given *to* a community that will interpret it over generations and regard it as something to be endlessly interpreted. This sort of giving would fit its telic function nicely. It is in the process of interpreting the divine word that we see its holiness—that it *becomes* the unveiling of a telos that can endlessly interest us, endlessly be new for us.

The rabbis recognize the approximate quality, and endlessness, of receiving revelation quite explicitly. It comes out when they compare the Torah to a deep well or describe each of its verses as having seventy different meanings.[51] It also comes out in a commitment they had for a long time to not writing down the oral Torah. The flexibility of oral discourse, they seem to have felt, was as essential to the reception of revelation as the fixed, definite aspect of the written teaching thus received. There is a lot to this insight, but eventually the oral Torah was recorded, first as the code of oral law called the "Mishnah," and then as a sort of transcript of the debates that ensued over the proper meaning of and sources for the Mishnah. The latter is called the "Gemara"; together, the two make up the Talmud. To some extent the debate over writing down the oral Torah was made moot by the form that the Talmud ultimately took. As a record of conversations, it includes dissenting views alongside mainstream ones, leaves many issues open, and steers the reader to further discourse, rather than to an authoritative decision.[52] Moreover, the terse, obscure language of the Talmud, and the odd if often brilliant modes of interpreting text that it contains, makes it all but impossible to read without an oral teacher.

So the oral Torah was written down, but written down in a form that promotes and approximates oral discourse, and it retains much of the open-endedness, indefiniteness, and diversity of views that marks the oral as opposed to the written.

72. Of course the rabbis never describe themselves as following the principle of charity, or as adapting revelation to a humanly usable form: that is merely one way of reconstructing what they appear to be doing, in the Talmud and the codes and commentaries to which it gave rise. A different reconstruction is prevalent among strict followers of the rabbinic tradition today; the Talmud tends to be described as passing down a precise oral revelation that accompanied the written one, exactly like the latter in every way except its mode of transmission. God is said to have dictated

both the written and the oral Torah to Moses, and the enterprise of the Talmud is understood as an attempt to reconstruct the oral teaching as originally given, with disagreements among the various rabbis reflecting nothing more than differences in historical memory. Anything transmitted orally undergoes corruption over time, and the rabbis of the Talmud, on this view, are arguing about nothing more than which school of transmission correctly preserves the original teaching.

This understanding of oral Torah would erase the distinction I have been trying to draw between revelation and its reception. Fortunately, there is no good reason to believe that the Talmudic rabbis saw the oral Torah in this way. It is indeed more anachronistic than the Davidsonian construal of their method that I have offered. In the first place, on the assumption that the oral Torah is just like the written Torah, and that both were dictated word for word to Moses, it is hard to understand why Moses didn't bother to write them both down.[53] It is even harder to understand why the rabbis should have refused to write down the oral law for so long. Given the risk that anything transmitted orally is likely to be corrupted—a risk with which the rabbis were well acquainted[54]—how could they possibly justify *not* writing down something so important? If the oral teaching was a complete body of law and doctrine like the written one, a fixed text that just happened to be unwritten, there can be no good answer to that question. Only if oral teaching is of a different *kind* than written teaching, and if there is something intrinsic to oral teaching that resists written form, does the traditional prohibition against writing it down make good sense.

In the second place, Talmudic argument rarely fits the theory that the rabbis were trying to recover an oral teaching corrupted in transmission.[55] The rabbis rarely rest their arguments on the superiority of one line of transmission over another. Their disputes turn instead on different methods of interpreting verses in the written Torah,[56] different inclinations towards leniency and strictness, different views of what the community can live with and how much that matters, and, sometimes, different moral attitudes. Studying the Talmud, one feels in the presence of different schools of interpretation, not different schools of historical preservation. Famously, the rabbis say that their different views, even when they contradict one another, "are all words of the living God."[57] That makes sense if these are views based on different, but equally plausible and thoughtful, philosophies of law or interpretation. It makes no sense if they are based on different historical traditions. In that case, one party must in the end just be right and the other wrong.

Finally, most of the passages in which the Talmudic rabbis defend the importance of the oral Torah don't fit the "unwritten text" view of it. The Hillel/Shammai story discussed above, as we saw, gives an argument for some oral teaching to accompany any written text, not for a specific oral teaching to be regarded as just like the written Torah. The "not in heaven" story, similarly, is supposed to show that the meaning of the written text has been placed in the hands of a living community of interpreters, not to show that another text, like the written one but unwritten, *is* "in heaven" and can be used to trump the written one. I think practically every place in which the Talmudic rabbis describe or defend the oral Torah can best be understood as characterizing a *process* of interpretation rather than a *body* of interpretations. Sometimes, indeed, the rabbis suggest that what they see in the Torah would have been foreign to Moses himself.[58] Here, and throughout, they present the oral Torah as a different kind of thing from the written one—a process, a way of reading and of coming to communal decisions, rather than a set of prescriptions analogous to the revelation that it receives.

73. Which brings me to the point of this excursus on the rabbinic tradition: that a well-developed hermeneutic and way of thinking about ethical matters, not itself revealed, needs to be present in a community for that community to experience revelation. The rabbis' discussion of oral Torah provides an excellent model of this sort of practice, and of how it can be seen as both different from and necessary for revelation. What the rabbis essentially recognized is that God's words must meet certain conditions if we are to hear them *as* God's words. There are transcendental conditions for the possibility of revelation, we might say, without which we could not recognize any experience as revelatory, could not make sense of a belief that we had "seen" or "heard" God.[59] Kant points out that "if God should really speak to human beings, they could still never *know* that it was God who spoke to them," since the infinite cannot be grasped by our senses, and draws from this the conclusion that compatibility with the morality we find in our reason must be a condition for taking anything to be the word of God.[60] Without going as far in this direction as Kant—without, especially, reducing the content of revelation to a rational morality—we may agree that having an independent idea of the right and the good is a necessary condition for us to recognize any word as God's. And, precisely if we do not want to reduce revelation to morality, we may presume that there are other ideas we will have to maintain independently of any word from God, in order to receive such a word.

With this in mind, let's try to generalize the model of receiving revelation we found in the rabbinic tradition. We may describe the rabbinic method as an attempt to develop a reading of their sacred text that renders it (1) cogent, (2) usable by a community, (3) morally admirable, (4) moving and intellectually interesting, and that is at the same time (5) attentive to the details of the text—that tries truly to *listen* to what it has to say. These five features of their reading can readily be seen as minimal conditions for recognizing any text as revealed, on the model of revelation I have developed. To give us a vision of the highest good, a revealed text must express the highest morality (3), but also arouse our cognitive and affective faculties so that we can achieve a reflective love for our world (4), and must be cogent and practicable enough (1 and 2) that a community can develop a discipline out of it by which its members can increase both their virtue and their reflective love for the telos it presents. Finally, if the text is truly to *reveal* the vision and path its community finds in it, rather than to have that vision and path projected into it by the community's members or leaders, all four of its other features must be found by way of an attentive listening to its details (5).

I'll close this chapter by elaborating each of these features. As a whole they capture, I think, what it is to stand ready for revelation, and be capable of receiving it as such.

74. **Cogency**: A revelation needs to issue in a path. But a path needs to be something that can be followed, something with enough guideposts and signs of direction that we can intelligibly say there is such a thing as following and not following it. Not everything that can reasonably be called a path has strict borders or markings setting it off from the terrain around it, but even the vaguest of footpaths across a field must be somehow distinguishable from the rest of the field. Perhaps I don't need to be told to make ablutions at 4:35 a.m. every Thursday if I am to say that a discipline of bathing is part of my path, but it will not make sense to say that unless I am given *some* idea of better and worse times for or types of bathing. The same goes for every other activity that might be included in my path.

But to favor some ways of carrying out activities over others, we need some clarity about the norms for our path, and some clarity, therefore, about how to draw such norms from our revelation. A wholly obscure or openly contradictory text, however much thought it may provoke and however interesting it may be to discuss, cannot issue in a path. So apparent contradictions and hard-to-understand prescriptive passages have to be ironed out, just as they are in the rabbinic reading of the Torah.

75. **Communal usability**: A path can hardly have norms if there is no way for one person to correct another about how to follow the norm. Nor can it achieve the humbling effect crucial to revelation unless such correction is allowed for. If I see a path as given to me by an authority beyond me—by God, or a supremely enlightened human being—then I cannot believe I have incorrigible access to the contours of that path. I must instead be willing to be corrected by others, to recognize that the limitations of my understanding or will may get in the way of my following the path rightly.

A practical path will also require social support for the same reasons that human activity in general requires social support. We need others to help us avoid dangers, get food and drink, and raise children. None of that changes if what we do with our lives is supposed to be informed by a revelation. It is therefore hard to imagine how an all-good Being, or an authority on the good for all humanity, could possibly give us a way of living that does not fit into a society. How, for one thing, could such a way of living possibly be *passed down*, from generation to generation? But if it cannot be passed down, then how can it possibly represent a good for all humanity, across all time?

So the path of a revelation must be shared by a social group of some kind rather than given to individuals privately. The social nature of humanity may not provide a sufficient telos for our lives—I rejected that Aristotelian thesis earlier (Part III, § 17)—but it is certainly a necessary element of anything that can count as our telos. Here, as in other respects, a vision of the ultimate good must incorporate our understanding of our ordinary goods.

And this social aspect of a path has clear consequences. If a path is to be passed down by a society, then it must, in the first place, accord with the overlapping moral consensus that enables societies to survive. It also cannot make other demands incompatible with the survival of a society. It cannot mandate universal celibacy of its followers (unless, as the Shakers did, it works out a symbiotic relationship with another society by which to gain new members), nor require enormous amounts of fasting, or other extreme ascetic practices that jeopardize the lives or livelihoods of most human beings.[61] Again, it will need to be careful about radically overhauling the conventions and traditions of the societies in which it is to be implemented, and cannot itself take the form of a never-ending stream of radical changes. People need stability and predictability in their way of life if they are to make commitments over time and co-ordinate their actions with others. These requirements support the respect that the rabbis accord to actual practice, their resistance to quick or radical change, and their attempt to interpret some of the more demanding Jewish practices in a mild enough way that ordinary people can be expected to keep them.

A society is something that continues over generations, and the social aspects of a path make clear why revealed religions are inevitably traditional religions. A revealed path is, necessarily, given to an ongoing community, a group of people who for the most part come to it by way of the teaching of their parents and try to pass it down to their children. And the need to pass down the path leads its interpreters to accommodate it to basic morality, and ensures that each generation comes to it with humility. But that is to say that the deference to the past that has so irked would-be reformers of revealed religions since the Enlightenment is actually intrinsic to the very moral qualities of religion that the reformers like to stress. The distinction between a revealed religion and a cult lies in the antiquity of the former. A revealed religion has proven its ability to get passed down over generations—and has changed itself as a result—while a cult depends on manipulative or violent practices that will lead it eventually to self-destruct. Cults that do manage to keep the attachment of an ongoing community will have to abandon manipulation and violence, and in other ways change. If they succeed in doing this, they eventually turn into revealed religions.

76. **Morality**: It is essential that a vision of the ultimate good fit in with what we take to be morally good and right independently of that vision. There are obvious connections between this aspect of reception and its social aspects, but the two are not identical. There can be and have been evil and insufficiently good societies, societies that oppress their weaker members or act abominably towards outsiders. That may indeed be more the norm than otherwise. But a path that is supposed to lead us to the highest good must express our highest moral ideals, not just the minimal morality that allows societies to survive. The interpretive traditions that translate revelations into a communal path for a community do, and should, expect that path to express an ideal, not a minimal, justice and kindness towards all humanity, even if no-one has yet figured out exactly what ideal justice and kindness looks like. It is a task for interpretive

traditions to refine their understanding of morality over time, and to hold the text they are interpreting up to what they understand, at any given time, to be the highest moral norms. To the extent that the revealed text itself may appear to fail to do that, let alone to offend against more minimal moral standards, the interpreters rightly see their task as re-reading it. Again, the rabbinic method, when it takes up topics like the wicked son and wicked city, is a model of this process. Which is not to say that the rabbis always live up to the model they represent in this respect, or that Jewish communities have yet come close to completing the task of moralizing their tradition. No religious community I know has done that. The task is probably an endless one, and needs to be revisited constantly.

77. **Aesthetic criteria**: The three features we have considered thus far bring the shocking or exalting conceptual rift that is revelation closer to the way of the world. They tame revelation, make it more accessible to a human community. But that can't be all that the reception of revelation accomplishes. If revelation presents us with a vision of the ultimate good that we could not attain on our own, any process of interpretation that reduces it to what we *can* figure out on our own will betray it. So the process of interpretation must preserve a space for what is radical in the revealed text, for ways in which it challenges how we might otherwise expect to live.

Receivers preserve that space, in good part, as sensitive lovers of art preserve the beauty in what they see and hear: by ensuring that they understand it in a way that is always deeply moving and intellectually interesting. Together these responses constitute how we receive the beauty of revelation. I don't know whether the beautiful should be defined as arousing a primarily affective or a primarily intellectual condition—probably it should be defined as arousing affective conditions *by way* of an intellectual condition ("the play of the faculties"), or arousing each by way of the other—but it surely does both. And the lives we lead if we follow the revelation's path must appear to us as beautiful in this sense. An all-good Being could hardly want us to lead a dull or apathetic life anymore than It could want us to lead an immoral one. The rabbis' attempt to link Jewish practice to an endless, joyous, study of the Torah reflects this aesthetic condition for revelation, and the strangeness of Jewish ritual also keeps the path from becoming dull, rendering it instead a constant challenge to a Jew's ordinary moral and prudential life, to her participation in the way of the world. The hermeneutics and ritual practices of all traditional religions are similarly moving and intellectually engaging to their followers—that's what commands their adherence—and challenging to what those followers otherwise see as the most rational way of engaging with their environment.

It's worth stressing here that ritual has far more to do with the aesthetic than the moral aspects of revelation. Medieval rationalists like Maimonides tried to find a moral meaning in all ritual practice, and religious reformers since the Enlightenment have often held that rituals should be maintained only insofar as they foster virtue. But this misses the point of ritual. Rituals spark the imagination, give us ways to see our world as moving or fascinating, and provide a discipline by which we restrain our impulse to think we always know how to impose our conceptual networks on the world. They thereby help us see the world as holy, not just morally good: transforming moments in our lives so that we can find an elusive beauty in them, or attend to an elusive beauty around us, or recall how an otherwise ordinary activity fits into the telic vision to which we are attached. And they achieve this precisely because they are *given* to us by our tradition, because we do not choose, individually, how to perform them. By the very fact that, in performing them, we humble ourselves to a tradition outside of ourselves, they call us back from the arrogance by which we might think we can make up our ethical views on our own, back to the attitude of trust that defines commitment to a revelation.

78. **Attentiveness**: The quality of being attentive to the text, of humbling oneself to it, might seem on its own to constitute what it is to receive revelation. This quality cannot stand alone, however. It is not even possible unless we also see the text as making sense, which requires that it meet the condition of cogency, and as expressing a superhuman wisdom about the good, which requires that it meet our other three conditions. But we can't honestly regard ourselves as receiving a text, rather than projecting what we want to see onto it, unless we can prescind to some extent from all the frameworks we use to understand it, including the four conditions listed thus far, and still find something in it that speaks to us: unless there is what hermeneuts like to call a "surplus" of meaning in the text, beyond what would be generated by our expectations of it. We need to stand in spontaneous receptivity towards the text; we need actively to turn away from our temptation to project our views into it, actively to withhold the imperial aspirations of our conceptual frameworks, to hold ourselves back from speaking so that we can listen.

There is, however, no way of prescribing exactly what it is to listen to a text. It is impossible to set down rules for good interpretation—interpretation is always *of* rules, *inter alia*, so any rule for interpretation would in turn need to be interpreted—and the only test of good interpretation, therefore, must come through further interpretation. The problem here becomes more acute when the text to be interpreted is supposed to teach us something radically new, radically outside our established conceptual frameworks, as is the case by definition with a revealed text. If the text has something to teach that cannot be drawn out from what else we believe, then no preconditions can tell us what that something is. It follows that we cannot lay out firm criteria to establish when a tradition is and when it is not truly listening to its sacred texts. Nevertheless, in the course of interpretation, we may be able to judge each other's readings as attentive or not. People often agree strongly about the quality of a particular reading, whether or not they agree with the reading itself. This is especially so within specific traditions of interpretation. People who share the same faith expect each other to engage in a certain style of listening to their shared sacred text, and pull each other back into an attentive stance when a reading threatens to turn into a mere projection of the reader.

In this respect, the Talmud provides an outstanding model of reception. What makes the project of the Talmud so difficult is that the rabbis retain a strong sense of the need to attend closely to the written Torah even as they struggle to fit its apparent prescriptions in with what else they take to be true. Even in the cases of the wicked son and wicked city, the rabbis use ingenious readings of details in the text to reach the conclusion that their moral common sense points out to them, and in most cases they are far more respectful of the text than that. In general, moreover, they do their best to find significance in every element of the text—every story, every verse, every cross-reference and echo. Sometimes they will even find meaning in an oddly transcribed letter or mark of punctuation. All this takes place within the prism of their favored theories of interpretation, of course, but that much must be conceded to any reading.

These practices of reading capture the main import of the idea that a text is God's word. Attributing a text to God's authorship cannot be a claim about the *production* of the text. The idea that God, like a human being, literally took up a pen and wrote something down, or dictated it to someone, is theologically untenable. That a text comes from God must rather be a claim about its content: about the authority of that content over its readers and the way, consequently, it needs to be read. And that claim is just what is expressed by the interpretive practices of the Talmud: that every word of the text, every turn of phrase, every variation in spelling or expressive connotation, contains a profound moral or telic teaching. What the rabbis of the Talmud never do is ask, like many readers today, "What might a person who lived when the Torah was written intend by these words?" and then proceed to alter or ignore the demands of the text on the grounds that what people intended then need no longer hold now. The rabbis of the Talmud never take up this stance of superiority towards the text, never take their own moral or spiritual values to be higher than the ones informing the text. They assume, rather, that the text, however and whenever it may have been written, can be read even in their own day as speaking to their values, if only they allow it to contain the same levels of wordplay, irony, indirect communication, etc. with which they themselves might compose a text. They see themselves, in accordance with a suggestion in the Torah itself (Deuteronomy 29: 13–14), as standing at Sinai alongside the generation that supposedly did that historically. They see themselves as receiving revelation in the present moment, even as that original generation did, and as having, therefore, as much right to interpret that revelation as any earlier generation. They see the Torah as containing all wisdom (compare Part I, §§ 1–2), and treat the claim "It is written," when applied to the Torah, with great reverence, but at the same time they always bear in mind that wisdom is hard to interpret, and that *what* is written in a sacred text cannot be straightforwardly determined. (In one sense killing stubborn and rebellious sons is written in the Torah, and in another sense it is not.)

This is what it is like to see a text as composed by God and addressed to oneself. One sees it as already containing the best possible meanings one can find in it, and as capable of having different meanings for different people, in different generations.

79. It thus turns out to be essential, *pace* the child's view of revelation (§ 13 of this Part), that revelation be *un*clear, that what it means not be fully and readily available on its surface. If what is revealed is something essentially mysterious, what does the revealing must also be in part mysterious. One thing that means is that no moment of reception will ever be wholly adequate to the revelation it is trying to receive, and that the process of reception goes on indefinitely. But that is as it should be. If the promise of holiness is precisely that we will be able forever to find the world fascinating—new, unexpected, mysterious—then it is essential to revelation that it never be comprehensive, never show on its surface the whole of the goodness it promises. There is a tension between the completeness of the good that is supposed to be revealed and the need for that good to promise a recurrence of the unexpected or new, but that tension can be alleviated if we see the text of the revelation as offering us a full good only over time, as unfolding its true meaning, not at a single moment, but over the entire time, perhaps an infinite one, in which we regard it as our primary guide.[62] The initial moment of revelation is one in which we perceive just a hint or glimpse of the ultimate goodness and beauty of the world—a moment of holiness. That is enough to get us to embark on a path that returns us continually to holiness. We might say: the revelation itself needs continually to be revealed. Or, less paradoxically: the revelatory text, the source of revelation, becomes full revelation only in the never-ending, always inadequate process of reception.

7

Multiple Revelations

80. On the account I have given, revealed texts can be true in the way that Aloysius's claim about a treasure in the next village could be true (Part I, § 29): they can be reliable guides to how we should act, how we can attain an end of great importance to us. But this opens up the possibility that there may be different, equally true revelations—equally reliable paths, for different people in different situations, to their ultimate telos. Aloysius's advice is true only relative to the attitudes, needs, and situation of his particular advisee. It might not provide reliable guidance for someone with a different character. Similarly, a particular text may accomplish the job of revelation—may *be* a revelation—for some people, but not for others. There will be general criteria by which all of us test a purportedly revealed text or tradition, but we will also use criteria that are peculiar to our individual telic worries. We judge a claimant to our religious attention by the mesh between its moral and its aesthetic features, by the plausibility and insight of its moral claims, and by whether it moves us. These features will vary according to our individual personalities and circumstances. Do we, upon starting to follow it, experience a relief from our addictions or anxieties, or from our self-deception? Can we say, with Paul, that in coming to Christ we have been delivered from the internal war that the law inflicted on our souls, or, with certain Jewish mystics, that we find studying Torah to be like a great erotic love?[1] The features of a text or tradition that capture our imaginations depend primarily on our telic worries rather than our moral ones, and they speak to obstacles to a reflective love of our lives that we face as individuals, with histories that differ from those of other individuals, not merely to the capacities we share with every human being.

But if religious visions speak in significant part to factors that differentiate us from one another, then it would seem that different religious visions might be true *for*—suited for—different people. This seems to some a problem. Surely if God speaks, He should speak with one voice to all. In addition, a number of religious traditions, both theistic and non-theistic, insist that they hold the one right path, and religious vision, for everybody. Does my view of revelation demand that they give up such claims, that they embrace pluralism? I don't think so, but I also think pluralism is less threatening to religious commitment than it may appear.

A story can help answer the apparent theological problem with pluralism. The four main characters in L. Frank Baum's *Wizard of Oz* are granted separate audiences with the wizard, and he appears in a completely different guise to each one: as a large head to Dorothy, a beautiful woman to the Scarecrow, a terrible beast to the Tin Woodman, and a ball of fire to the Cowardly Lion. For my purposes, it would have been better if these appearances were more closely suited to the yearnings that led each of these characters to the wizard—if the large head, say, had appeared to the Scarecrow, seeking a brain, the beautiful woman to the Tin Woodman, seeking the ability to love, and the beast to the Lion, seeking courage. Baum does not do this, and he also, of course, eventually has the characters find out that one unimpressive little man is behind all the appearances. That makes them clearly *illusions*. But imagine a series of wizard-of-Oz-like encounters in which the appearances do fit the character encountered and in which "the man behind the curtain" cannot, even in principle, be seen. Then we might have a model for religious pluralism. God appears differently to different people in accordance with the yearnings with which they approach Him. Even if there is some unified Being behind these different appearances, we don't know what He or She or It is like: we know only the appearances, which are then not mere illusions, but our only access to what God is in reality. Perhaps we will someday find out more about that Being, and about what It might want of all humanity, but for the moment the different appearances are all we have to go on, and they lead us to different ideas about both God's nature and God's will: God's will *for* each of us, at least. Even the idea that there is one right vision of God, or way of fulfilling God's will, may here be just part of the way God appears to some people, in accordance with their peculiar yearnings. Perhaps people drawn to mainstream Christianity or Islam are so constituted that they cannot easily embrace a way of living as God's path for them unless they are convinced that it is also God's path for everyone. God may, that is, want us just to embrace *a* revelation, regardless which one it is, but nevertheless allow some of these revelations to give their followers the impression that they are the one right way for everyone—disabusing us all of that impression, perhaps, at the end of days.

This theological story may not be correct, but it is coherent. That shows us that even a single God who wants all humanity to do His will could yet allow for a plurality of equally good religions. Here's another version of the story, this time with a more sophisticated literary source and a correspondingly deeper philosophical point. In the middle of Gotthold Lessing's play *Nathan the Wise*, Nathan offers a parable to account for the differences among Judaism, Christianity, and Islam. A man once had a ring, he says, that could make its wearer beloved to God and man. This he passed down to his favorite son, who passed it down to his favorite son, and so forth. Eventually, one heir had three sons whom he loved equally. So he had two exact copies of the ring made and told each child that that child had received the true ring. After he died, the three brothers went to court, squabbling over which of them truly had the ring. In court, the judge notes that the fact that the brothers are in court suggests there may be something wrong with all their rings:

I hear the genuine ring enjoys the magic power to make its wearer . . . beloved of God and man. That must decide! For spurious rings can surely not do that. Whom then do two of you love most? Quick, speak! You're mute? The ring's effect is only backward, not outward? Each one loves himself the most?—O then you are, all three, deceived deceivers! Your rings are false, all three. The genuine ring no doubt got lost.[2]

But he follows up this barb by giving them some advice:

My counsel is: Accept the matter wholly as it stands. If each one from his father has his ring, then let each one believe his ring to be the true one.—Possibly the father wished to tolerate no longer in his house the tyranny of just one ring. And know: that he loved all three of you, and loved you all alike; since two of you he'd not humiliate to favor one. Well then! Let each aspire to emulate his father's . . . unprejudiced affection! Let each strive to match the rest in bringing to the fore the magic of . . . his ring! Assist that power with all humility, hearty peacefulness, and with profound submission to God's will.[3]

On this model, there may in fact be one true religion, but we don't know which it is, and the appropriate way of testifying to its truth—witnessing to it, as Christians say—is to be the best person one can be: to be, above all, kind, peace-loving, and humble. Pushing people to accept one's own religion as the right one, when they resist, will be a way of witnessing *against* its truth or greatness, and a pluralistic attitude, of respect and warmth towards other people in spite of theological differences, will be the right one to take up even if monism about religion is correct. From the theological point-of-view, moreover, we may explain why God has given us many different religions: as a supremely loving father, it is more important to Him that we compete with one another in developing traits of kindness and decency than that we possess the full truth about Him. Lessing suggests—here, and in many other places—that how we act is more important than what we think, and that a decent and earnest *pursuit* of truth, especially in religious matters, is more properly the human task than the attainment of truth. It is compatible with the story of the three rings that there is in the end one correct religion, but it is also compatible with that story that there is no correct religion: that the point of religious visions is just to spur us to morally good action. Lessing thinks we don't need to worry about this issue. Perhaps we will be most effectively motivated to moral action if we each "believe [our] ring to be the true one." But it doesn't matter whether or not there is in fact a true ring—the promise of the ring can be fulfilled by human virtue alone.

I like the elegance of Lessing's story and its openness to a variety of theological interpretations. I also like the suggestion, played out richly in the rest of *Nathan*, that religious differences are rooted in family differences—that loving a particular religious tradition is tied to loving the parents from whom one received that tradition. "Whose faith are we least like to doubt?" asks Nathan. "Our people's surely? . . . the ones who from our childhood gave us proofs of love? . . . How can I trust my fathers less than you trust yours?"[4] But I don't accept Lessing's reduction of religious truth to strictly *moral* teachings, and I am uncomfortable with the fact that the most straightforward reading of his story would have it that ultimately either one religion is correct or all religions are incorrect. An intermediate position according to which each religion might be correct for some people but not for others is hard to square with the story. I began with a variation on the wizard of Oz instead of Lessing's three rings for that reason. In my version of the Oz story, there is no correct view of the wizard, and it is clear that the differences in the visions reflect the differences in the temperaments and interests of the viewer, not a difference in the accuracy of their perceptions.

Setting aside both Lessing and the wizard, now, here is the view of religious pluralism I myself favor, as a religious believer. We come, if we do, to a vision of the end God has set for us, and the path to that end, by way of an imaginative—hence affective—commitment. One of the religious visions in the world speaks to us: which is to say it arouses love in us, offers satisfaction to our telic yearnings. But the yearnings that we each have, and the love that satisfies them, will depend on the circumstances in which we were raised and in which our affective dispositions were shaped: including, prominently, our relationship to our parents. It is therefore no surprise that the vision that generally speaks most profoundly to each of us is a vision presented in our families, and that the love we feel for it is, initially, an extension of our love for our parents. (And when that does not happen—when people convert to new religions, or give up on all religion—it is usually because their parents either did not present any religious teaching, or because they had a troubled relationship with their parents.) Nor should it be a surprise that, to the extent that our religious commitments go beyond what our families teach us, they are shaped, generally, by a larger culture to which our family belongs. It is in the context of that culture, after all, that we normally both have the traumas and joys out of which we develop a yearning for some vision that would make our lives worth living, and find the language in which to express those traumas and joys. The answer to the telic questions we are likely to ask will make best sense to us if couched in the vocabulary of the culture in which we asked those questions, and our love for that answer—the basis on which we accept it—will again be in part an extension of our love for our community.[5]

Nor, again, should it be surprising that a loving God might allow us to develop our religious commitments in this way. If God must speak in human language in order to express His will to us, then why should God not also have to work through the normal patterns of human love in order to express His love for us? Indeed, these are just intellectual and emotional versions of the same point. We can grasp the ultimate end God holds out to us intellectually only through parables and prescriptions couched in ordinary human language, and we can grasp that end emotionally only through the modes of affection by which we commit ourselves to ordinary human relationships. God must speak through human emotional formations, through the patterns of love and commitment we develop in our families and cultures, just as He must speak through human linguistic formations. They are not, indeed, sharply separable. And the God I personally believe in—the God who places honoring parents in the first tablet of the Ten Commandments,[6] who repeatedly emphasizes the need for parents to teach the Torah to their children, and who makes remembering the history of one's people essential to religious commitment—seems expressly to recognize, and to want us to recognize, that faith is not primarily an exercise of either individual reason or individual feeling, but a response to and development of the modes of love taught in a family and a culture.[7] It would follow, as most of the Jewish tradition has held, that this same God relates to people in different cultures through teachings other than the Torah, that His vision for them is different from His vision for the Jews. Even in the Messianic era, says Maimonides—and he is far from the most pluralistic of Jewish thinkers—the peoples of the world, aside from observing a few basic, universal rules, should "stand in their own teaching," rather than converting to Judaism.[8]

There is room in this picture for some revealed religions to be better than others, and for them to perform different sorts of tasks for humanity as a whole. A loving God could want us to refine each other's teachings by way of the friction between traditions. Other traditions may teach us things, of value for interpreting our own, that we would not otherwise have seen. Or a moral and spiritual competition among religions may lead us to pursue our traditions in a more virtuous or spiritually deeper way. I have been inspired by Gandhi to incorporate a great respect for non-violence into my understanding of Judaism, seeking parallels to Gandhi's teachings in rabbinic thought (if not exact parallels: virtually all forms of Judaism reject complete non-violence, as I think they should), and I have learned a lot about prayer from the moving spontaneous benedictions I have heard Christian friends offer. On a communal level, it is clear that Jews and Christians learned from the merger of Aristotle and revealed religion first carried out by Muslims, that in a later day Kant profoundly shaped how Jews of all denominations came to understand their tradition, and that elements of Hindu and Buddhist practice have in recent years had an impact on virtually all liberal religious communities in America. These phenomena can lead one to think that eventually all religions will converge, but the religions could also remain distinct even while learning from one another. Or we could all someday join just one religion, but it might by that time have been altered and improved by going through a history of learning from and competing spiritually with the other traditions. I am inclined to hope for something along the lines of the second of these possibilities: that, in the end of days, everyone will "stand in" his or her own religion, as Maimonides says, but that all religions, including Judaism, will by that point have been refined, and brought to agreement on most important issues, by their interactions with one another.

This is, however, just my *religious* view of religious pluralism. The philosophical framework I have been developing here does not entail that view. For all that that framework has to say, there could be just one correct form of imaginative commitment: although, of course, if such commitments are more an emotional than a rational matter, witnessing to the correct one will still take the form of displaying kindness and respect to the would-be convert, not bullying him by argumentative cleverness, let alone forcing him into one's own path. Kindness and respect for other people inevitably requires some respect for their beliefs and practices, moreover, so a monism about religion that goes along with the belief that religious conviction is a matter of imaginative commitment probably requires a stronger attempt to understand other people's religions sympathetically than a more rationalistic monism might require. But the notion of religion as imaginative commitment does not mandate either monism or pluralism. Whether one is a monist or a pluralist about religion will depend on the particular content of the tradition to which one commits oneself, not on the considerations that lead one to take up such a commitment at all.

81. The room my view makes for pluralism has its attractions, but one may worry that it goes too far. Must every bizarre cult that holds up a text containing a telic vision stand next to rich, old traditions like Taoism and Islam as a worthy candidate for imaginative commitment?

There are some easy ways of answering "no" to this question. I have argued that a revealed religion must show itself to be compatible with widely accepted moral standards, and received by a society that continues over time, so merely holding up a text that contains a telic vision will not be enough to enter one's group into this category. But there is admittedly something a bit arbitrary about which texts count as revelations on my account. Any text that can be construed as offering an attractive telic view coupled with new insight into moral problems, and that has a path associated with it, would seem to be a candidate for revelation. Plato's *Republic* may fail to be a revelation today only because no community regards it as such, and tries to follow a path derived from it. And Joyce's *Ulysses* or a collection of Gandhi's sayings could be a revelation, if some community interpreted them so as to yield a comprehensive vision of the point of our lives, and a path to express or pursue that vision.

I think this is again an advantage, not a disadvantage, of my view. Plato was in fact once regarded by some people as divine,[9] and I don't see a problem in saying that his writings may at one time have been a revelation but are no longer so, or that other texts may once not have been a revelation, but later became so.[10] It is at least as reasonable to suppose that a God could allow hitherto non-revelatory texts to be transformed into revelations, once a community takes them up as such, as that He has designated certain texts to serve as revelations from the moment they were written. Indeed, it makes eminently good sense that God might allow texts to be transformed into revelations if and only if communities take them up as such: since "taking them up as such" is a process that requires interpreting them so as to yield a morally admirable way of life, and a vision of ultimate worth that is at least intelligible to all human beings. The process of reception inevitably transforms what it receives. So it is not impossible that an all-good source of the universe might allow people to take any text they like as the authoritative basis for their way of life as long as they interpret it in a beautiful and morally admirable way.

Of course, this requirement might itself limit the texts that would be suitable for such uses. For different sorts of reasons, I can't imagine Casanova's memoirs, an Agatha Christie novel, or the diagnostic manuals of the American Psychiatric Association ever being transformed into a revelation. But, even in cases like these, who knows what miracles the power of interpretation might work? Certainly, an Agatha Christie novel that was received by a community in such a way that it enabled them to solve difficult moral problems, find an attractive vision of the highest good in it, and forge a path to bring them back, recurrently, to that vision, would come to mean something very different from what its literal surface would suggest. Nonetheless, some texts are undoubtedly better suited to being received as revelations than others, and it is no accident that the authoritative texts of most prominent religious traditions seem like plausible candidates for revelation to believers in other traditions.

82. I don't mean to suggest that what counts as a revelation, or what leads believers to one revealed religion rather than another, is purely a matter of happenstance. The affective aspects of religious commitment may have a contingent basis, but we nevertheless decide, as adults, which of our affections to trust. We also judge religious traditions by more than their appeal to our imaginations. As I have stressed repeatedly, the love that constitutes faith is a *reflective* love, and that requires that it cohere with what our reason tells us about morality and metaphysics. So our attachments to our particular revealed traditions are not merely a function of our relationships to our family and culture. In my own religious life, I certainly do not take it to be a matter of mere contingency that I continue to be Jewish. Nor do I regard my particular religious tradition as an uninteresting accident overlaid on a more fundamental commitment, simply, to God. I am not inclined to feel I might just as well be a Christian or Muslim or Buddhist. Instead, I am inclined to find Judaism deeper and wiser than other religions, to think that, if there is any single right religion for all human beings, Judaism is the best candidate for that role.[11] I find the Jewish conception of God, in its most thoughtful forms, more noble and more philosophically acceptable than others I know, the Jewish code of law a more sensible blend of morality and ritual than other religious paths, and the Jewish way of reading sacred texts superior, morally and intellectually, to any other practice of sacred interpretation. I also find the Torah inspiring, its insights into human psychology nuanced and astute, and its central narrative extremely moving. By contrast, I'm rather put off by the Gospels, which seem overly sentimental to me—the idea of a God-man also strikes me as a falling away from the sublime humbling of all human beings before a transcendent God in the Torah—and by the Quran, which seems harsh to me, and lacking in the nuance of the Torah. I'm not particularly awed or inspired by what I've read of the Vedas either (I *am* impressed by the Upanishads), and the teachings of the Buddha strike me, mostly, as unconvincing.[12]

But I have no idea how much of all this is due to my imagination's having been shaped *by* the Torah, rather than the Gospels, Quran, Vedas, etc. Our revelatory texts speak to our imaginations, but they also shape the ways in which we imagine. We are therefore not accidentally drawn to the text of the particular tradition in which we were raised more than to other sources, when we seek a telic vision we can love. It's rather like how we fall in love with a person. An initial spark we could have had with many people draws us into a relationship, but then the love we share enables us to be moved more by this person than by others. And if that's how each community feels about its particular text, it's easy to see how it can fall under the illusion that an impartial observer would agree that its text is better than the others.

In addition, I can't imagine how I could argue for the superiority of the Torah over other revealed texts to someone who does not already share my affection for Judaism. The idea that a good God would enable just this one people to have a good account of His will seems preposterous to me. The idea that Jews have a better way of life, in all respects, than all other communities, seems no less preposterous. And I am aware that I, like most people, don't know enough about religious ways of life other than my own to say what exactly their sacred scriptures mean when interpreted within those ways of life. So it seems more sensible to say that my attachment to Jewish revelation reflects the shape of my particular imagination, that others reasonably make imaginative commitments to different traditions, and that God, understanding how we function, and loving us with all the quirks of our imaginations, has chosen to speak to us in different ways, and to allow us to come to different sorts of reflective love.

Finally, I can quite easily imagine that God might one day show me how Christianity or Islam or Hinduism represents just as good a way of worshipping Him as Judaism, or even that one or more of them are better. I am well aware how often my beliefs and attitudes on all sorts of subjects are mistaken, and I would not be shocked to find that that includes many of the ones grounding my commitment to Judaism. What *would* shock me, and what is incompatible with my belief in God, is that I would be condemned by Him for making a mistake about these matters, or for honestly following my conscience about what religious doctrines to believe. I regard the "faith that" I have in various propositions about Judaism vis-a-vis its religious rivals primarily as ways of focusing my "faith in" God: I follow God, as a personal guide. *through* the Jewish tradition as opposed to the Christian or Muslim or some other tradition. But my faith is fundamentally in *God*, not in Judaism. I have a *Jewish* faith in God, a faith in God shaped by Jewish beliefs and practices, but whose ultimate object is God, not the Jewish beliefs and practices themselves. A worship of Jewish beliefs and practices themselves, a placing of them above God, would be idolatry, which Judaism itself forbids.

My personal stance, in this respect, may or may not be widely shared, but it demonstrates how religious believers can hold together a firm commitment to a particular tradition with a certain pluralism about other religions. We may have, not just an emotional attachment to our own religion, but plausible reasons for preferring it to others, while still recognizing that the force of those reasons is likely to diminish when addressed to people who do not share our faith. An awareness of the importance of affection to faith, and of the fact that most people stick with one religion rather than another primarily out of love for the friends and family with whom they share it, induces a certain cautiousness about the degree to which our religious beliefs will legitimately capture the allegiance of people outside our community. It is also quite easy to understand why a good God might suit other beliefs and practices to people with a different circle of friends and family. So the believer can *both* have reasons to prefer her own set of beliefs and practices over the alternatives she knows *and* recognize that she may be wrong to do so, that other forms of worship could in the end be equally good.

83. One question raised by this last point is how, in practice, believers in one religion can and should interact with believers in other religions, and with non-believers. Does my model of religious faith as imaginative commitment have anything distinctive to say about the hoary problems of how religious and non-religious people, and people of different religions, can live together in one political community? That's a concern to which I will devote much of the final section of this book.

Meanwhile, we might consider the religious advantages of seeing oneself as committed to a particular religious vision primarily by way of affective ties, shaped heavily by one's family. I see myself as a child of Jacob (Israel), perhaps, or of Abraham and Sarah, and know that insofar as I belong to that particular family, and bring my children into it, I am not simply a human being in general, and need to work toward respectful and just relations with members of other families just as Jacob and Abraham and Sarah did. I know that God has other relations with other families—if I don't remember that, the prophet Amos reminds me: "Are ye not as the children of the Ethiopians unto Me, O children of Israel? saith the Lord. Have not I brought up . . . the Philistines from Caphtor, and Aram from Kir?" (Amos 9:7)—and that, while we are ultimately all members of the great family of Adam and Eve, we have long been dispersed, scattered into nations with different assumptions, attitudes, and ways of life (Gen. 9:6–11). Perhaps I see myself as some Lurianic Kabbalists do: as redeeming, simply by following my family's/nation's religious path, and showing kindness and justice to members of other families/nations, the scattered sparks of God in all humanity. Or, if I were not Jewish, I might see myself as carrying out Jesus's injunction, "Judge not that ye be not judged," or following the Jain path of absolute non-violence that Gandhi equated with the proper way to cling to truth and lead others to it, or respecting the Quran's declaration that God fashioned us into different peoples "that we may know one another." In any of these ways, I can take it to be my primary task to pursue my own path with integrity rather than condemning others for following a different path. I may of course hope that an honest and decent pursuit of my path will win others over to it as well: I may hope that they will enter my family. But I will do well to recognize that the expansion of my family is God's work, not mine, something that should happen, if it should, because those joining the family see its telic vision as representing God's will for themselves, feel that God Himself has called them to it. It is a messianic hope, not something any of us can deliberately bring about, that human beings will eventually come together as one. Our role, as religious believers, is to carry out the tasks assigned to us, to appreciate joyfully whatever God might do to bring the messianic age closer, and to trust, when He doesn't seem to do anything of that sort, that He will do so in His own good time. That, at least, is one understanding of what it means to "do justice, and love mercy, and walk humbly with your God" (Micah 6: 8).

PART V

Divine Teaching and the Way of the World

While [a] jesting phrase winds its way drolly through ... [a] conversation, the speaker may privately have a rendezvous with the Deity, who is present as soon as the uncertainty of all things is thought infinitely. For this reason one who really has an eye for the Deity can see Him everywhere ... It would sound like jesting, if a prospective guest were to say on receiving the invitation, "You can count on me, I shall certainly come; but I must make an exception for the contingency that a tile happens to blow down from a roof, and kills me; for in that case I cannot come." But it might at the same time also be the highest earnestness, and the speaker, though jesting with men, might exist before God.

Kierkegaard, *Concluding Unscientific Postscript*

What remains is to show how the "way of the world" and "divine teaching" parts of my story hang together. How, if at all, does a telic commitment affect one's view of truth? How do the telic aspects of ethics affect the moral aspects: what difference does a religious telic commitment make to one's moral practice? Above all, how, and to what extent, should believers in revealed religions try to bring their views into the broader discussions of the multi-religious and non-religious publics in which they live? How, and to what extent, on the other hand, should they try to incorporate the discussions of the secular public around them into the way their traditions receive their respective revelations?

These questions take us to some of the topics with which this book opened, but now from the perspective of a person who has decided to make an imaginative commitment to a revealed tradition. At the same time they open up a political question of great importance in the modern day: about whether a common public realm can be composed of people attached to different revealed religions, and to no religion. I will end this book with a sketch of how one might answer this question positively—of how people committed to divine teachings can integrate themselves harmoniously into a secular way of the world.

1

Truth Again

1. Nothing I have said since the first section of this book changes the main conclusion of that section: that religious people have every reason to affirm exactly the same notion of truth as secular people, and to endorse the same truth regimes, on scientific matters, that their secular peers do. It is just that religious people exploit a rather special use of the common notion of truth—the one identified with our Aloysius story—and apply that to the revelation that orients their activities. Secular people may prefer to avoid that use of truth, or they may apply it to secular telic visions, but refuse it to religious ones.[1] But on my understanding of religion the differences between religious and secular people will not be over the notion of truth—or over the truths of science, or how one should pursue scientific truths.

Is there then anything distinctive, on my view, about the religious believer's attitude toward truth? Yes, in a couple of senses there is. First, the religious believer has reason to care rather *more* for the open, honest, largely secular pursuit of scientific and philosophical truth than other people do. If one thinks one's entire life depends upon whether one is committing oneself wisely rather than blindly to a particular telic vision, then one wants as much information as one can possibly have about the world, and about the nature of information, in order to make sure one is not making a mistake. The reflective component of reflective love can demand a wider base of knowledge, and a more rigorous, skeptical scrutiny of claims to knowledge, than even dedicated secular intellectuals think necessary.

Second, the religious believer needs to be extremely careful about differentiating the use of "truth" he applies to revelation, and the faith-based project of which that use is a part, from the truth claims he makes, alongside his secular neighbors, about science and other ordinary factual matters. Otherwise he cannot either pursue the interest he has in a wide range of knowledge or preserve the peculiar qualities of the trust he places in God or his religious authorities. Trying to test God's word scientifically would be a betrayal of trust in God. And *refusing* to test the word of ordinary human beings— including one's religious leaders—when they make scientific or other factual claims would also be a betrayal of trust in God: it would impute divinity to beings who are less than that. The religious believer needs a distinction between what I will call, adapting a Kantian phrase, "public" and "private" reason, and a constant awareness of which of his beliefs belong in which category.

I will devote the rest of this chapter to these two aspects of a religious attitude to truth.

2. Religious commitments can strengthen our reasons for wanting to find and tell truths. The state of nature account I gave in Part I for the importance of truth had its origin in a book by Bernard Williams, but Williams worries, justifiably, that that account gives us no intrinsic reason to tell the truth. The state of nature account, he says, represents "the values of Accuracy and Sincerity . . . [as] *instrumental*: they are entirely explained in terms of other goods, and in particular of getting what one wants, avoiding danger, mastering the environment, and so on." But such an instrumental approach to truth is unstable: there is too great a danger that people will free-ride when they can. Williams says that "no society can get by . . . with a purely instrumental conception of the values of truth" (TT 58–9), and that cultures have consequently evolved norms attributing an inherent value to truth-telling. Sometimes truth-telling is connected to "ideas of honor or nobility" (TT 115). Sometimes it is understood as a foundation for friendship. Sometimes, as in Kant, it is considered a precondition for mutual respect among people (TT 121–2). Williams does not regard the arguments traditionally given for these cultural norms as particularly strong, but he thinks the ideas themselves are necessary, if we are to maintain a stable societal structure of truth-telling. Here as elsewhere Williams is dismissive of the arguments given for moral notions while endorsing the notions themselves. He agrees with Kantians that truth-telling is important to freedom and trust among people, and he approves of freedom and trust, and the liberal type of society they sustain (TT 118–122). Others who feel the same way, he thinks, will likewise see a more than instrumental value in truth-telling. We can all share the feeling that it is "an unlovely idea to turn into a liar" (TT 120), and that will be enough to give truth-telling an intrinsic value.

Williams's question is an excellent one, but his answer to it is unsatisfying. Why should others share Williams's fondness for freedom and trust, or for the type of society they sustain? Why, in particular, would the free-rider who had been prepared to defect from his society's practices of truth-telling when they were grounded in an instrumentalist way be persuaded by Williams's account? Telling the would-be defector that it is "an unlovely idea to turn into a liar" might pull him into the fold if he shares Williams's emotional configuration and has no strong motive to lie, but not if he has a great stake in the lie, or if the mischievous pleasure one can gain by lying outweighs its unloveliness for him. The fundamental problem here is that Williams gives us instrumental grounds for wanting a non-instrumental account of truth-telling. "No society can get by," he tells us, without a non-instrumental account of the virtues of truth-telling— but then the real justification for the cultural resources that portray truth-telling as intrinsically good is an instrumental one, and anyone aware of that fact is bound to see them as hollow or hypocritical. No story that purports to give us reasons for truth-telling independent of its value to society will be convincing if it rests in the end on that value.

What's the alternative? We could revert to Kant's defense of truth-telling. Most people in most societies will not be convinced of the intrinsic value of truth on Kantian grounds alone, however. A more promising strategy would be to broaden our instru-mentalist grounds for truth-telling. We can show individuals who are tempted to defect that truth-telling is more useful to them, as individuals, than they may have thought. We can note that the consequences of lying are likely to be far worse than they suppose. We can stress the likelihood of being exposed, for instance, and point out the effects that exposure will have on the defector's relationships with people other than the one to whom he is lying, the internal anxiety and self-contempt that the defector is likely to feel, etc. We can, that is, make the same sort of case for truth-telling that we would to a "sensible knave" contemplating any vicious act.[2] And the fact that society as a whole has strong reasons to value truth-telling means that would-be defectors will normally be raised with an emotional disposition that makes lying disruptive to their psychic economy, and will normally be made to pay in other ways if their internal incentives for honesty are not strong enough. We impose a cost, as a society, on virtually all lying, and this makes truth-telling a relatively stable virtue even if we value it for purely instrumental reasons.

Not good enough? Well, this is certainly not an *attractive* basis for truth-telling and it could, under the right circumstances, unravel enough that truth-telling ceases to be stable. In any case, an individual unconvinced by Kantianism may yet want a reason to value truth-telling intrinsically, not just out of a realization that society, and the psychological structure he possesses as a result of being socialized, will punish him if he becomes a liar.

Here is one place where divine teaching can help the way of the world. Divine teaching can give one intrinsic reasons to value truth and will in any case vastly expand one's instrumental reasons for doing so. To begin with the latter: one who seeks assurance that he is right to take a particular text as his source of divine revelation, or to interpret it in one way rather than another, has reasons for valuing truth independently of the material needs that everyday truth-telling serves. The content of his revelation, too, is likely to make truth-telling a condition for achieving whatever it sets up as the highest good for humanity. Liars and self-deceivers cannot grasp what one needs to grasp to achieve nirvana, nor are they in the proper state to accept Christ, or participate in what the Torah calls *kedushah*. And if these ends are indeed our *ultimate* ones, there cannot be a serious question about whether or not to put them above our more limited, material ends. If achieving enlightenment or standing before God conflicts with a material end,[3] surely the former must come first. Indeed, an orientation towards the former may well change one's estimation of material goods—remove the sources of temptation one would otherwise have to tell lies. So the role of divine teaching in one's life can add instrumental reasons for valuing truth that support a norm of truth-telling almost as exceptionless as the Kantian one.

In addition, truth can gain intrinsic value from the content of a revelation. According to a number of religious traditions, our ultimate end includes or even consists in grasping truth for its own sake. Grasping truth, if we live in a universe structured by an all-good Being, is equivalent to getting to know more about that Being, and that may in itself be a joy, and a mode, perhaps the definitive mode, of loving Him. (Maimonides held such a view.) Alternatively, seeking truth may be understood as another term for always being ready to see the universe anew, standing in a permanent condition of wonder or fascination. These are views on which truth gains a powerful intrinsic value, and a believer in such views has reason to tell the truth, and seek the truth, regardless of what material goods he may gain or lose therefrom.

That said, religious believers do not in fact tend to be outstanding truth-seekers, especially in the contemporary world. They are frequently inclined, instead, to use their faith to *block* the search for truth. But this arises, I argued in Part I, from a misunderstanding of their nature of their own commitments. Perhaps, also, they are frightened that modern cognitive methods and institutions will destroy their religion. That should not be the case, and will not be if the religion indeed has been put in the world by God. In principle, in any case, it should be—and sometimes, in the past, has been—precisely the devoutly religious who welcome argument from all quarters, are hungry for truth of all sorts, and will die rather than tell a lie. Rabbi Akiva, Thomas More, and Gandhi exemplify this attitude.

3. Turning now to specifically religious kinds of truth, I propose that believers can make use of a well-known Kantian distinction between public and private reasoning. John Rawls has given wide currency to the idea of public reason. As he uses the phrase, it refers to the mode of reasoning appropriate to the public realm: concerned with political matters, addressed by every citizen to every other citizen as a free and equal person, and conducted, therefore, according to norms that all citizens can accept. Rawls borrows the phrase, loosely, from Kant, who had designated all reasoning we offer simply as one human being addressing another "the public use of reason," in contrast with the reasoning we carry out as people with a specific social role or gender or way of life.[4] Rawls uses the phrase "non-public reason" for the reasoning we employ in our voluntary associations: our clubs and families, "churches and universities, scientific societies and professional groups" (PL 220). He denies that there is such a thing as a strictly private reason (PL 220n); reasoning, he indicates, is by definition directed towards some sort of social group. I am not sure how much rests on this point. Nonpublic reasons are *less* sharable than public ones, for Rawls, in the sense that they will not necessarily be convincing to people outside a particular voluntary association, and at the limit there could surely be reasons that we think, as individuals, we might in principle be able to share with others, but in fact find no others willing to share them.[5]

In any case, Kant does not so clearly rule out the possibility of private reasons. He does say that replacing our "communal sense" (*sensus communis*) with our "private sense" (*sensus privatus*) is a mark of insanity. Normally we correct the latter by the former. The person who refuses to do that is one who sees things "in broad daylight" that the people next to him do not see, or hears voices that no-one else hears. Relating our understanding to the understanding of others is "a subjectively necessary touchstone" of the correctness of our judgments, and we are on our way to madness if we "merely isolate ourselves within our own experiences." More generally, our private sense and understanding get better the more we test them against the judgments of others: public discussion is "the greatest and most useful means of correcting our own thoughts."[6]

But these claims do not amount to a denial that we have a private sense, or that we can base reasons on it. Kant calls *replacing* our communal sense with our private sense, not just *using* our private sense, a mark of insanity. Indeed he acknowledges that certain kinds of religious believers—"enthusiasts" or "fanatics"[7]—do base their beliefs on what they take to be personal experiences of God, and while he considers their views morally and politically dangerous, he does not suggest that they are mad.[8] His primary concern is just that we adjust our private reasons in some way to the norms of public reasoning, that we never lose sight of the latter even when employing the former. Kant offers us a general principle of all reasoning analogous to the categorical imperative on which he thinks morality is founded: that we never believe anything except on grounds we would be willing to uphold universally.[9] Call this Kant's "cognitive universalization test."

I'd like to propose a notion of private reasoning that I think can live up to that test. Crucial to its being a form of reasoning at all will be that we always be aware that it lacks the force of public reasoning: that we allow public reason to limit its role in our lives. That means, above all, that we recognize private reason as inadequate to supply us with *proofs*—the kind of arguments on which we can safely base scientific or moral conclusions—and keep it instead within the sphere of faith. It is nonetheless useful there; it is the sort of thinking appropriate to the reflective love with which we receive revelation. And for what we might broadly call political purposes—for the purpose of bringing our divine teachings into a social space that we share with non-believers—the idea of private reason will bring into sharp relief just how and why we cannot expect to impose our religiously-based beliefs on others, how and why the governance of our polis must be conducted on a purely public basis.

Drawing on a variety of suggestions in Kant, I'll sketch in what follows two different versions of private reason. The first is a very modest one, but it will enable us to see clearly the relations that need to hold between private and public reason. That will make it easier to see the shape of the second, more radical, but also more nebulous, version of the idea.

4. Most of us believe certain things despite the fact that the mainstream fact-gathering authorities in our day reject those beliefs. We know that our beliefs are rejected, but still think that someday we may turn out to be right. I remain inclined to think that going out with wet hair on cold days is likely to bring on a cold, even though I've read and heard many times that this is a myth. Other people I know still think that a conspiracy was involved in the Kennedy assassination, even though all official reports on the assassination deny this. And still others expect philosophers one day to embrace the medieval arguments for God's existence again, even though most reject those arguments now. We can call all these beliefs private reasons. They have been submitted to public reason and found wanting, but the believer nevertheless holds on to them in the hope that public reason will someday vindicate them. And that hope is not unreasonable, since the state of play among experts in science and history and even logic changes constantly; things once thought to have been refuted later on make a comeback.

So these private reasons involve reasoning, but they are private in the sense that we are reluctant to trot them out before large audiences, or in a scholarly forum. I am well aware that I am much too uninformed on medical matters to have a properly grounded belief about wet hair and colds, so I normally keep my opinion to myself, and quietly act on it without recommending it to others. Many of those who suspect that there was a conspiracy surrounding the Kennedy assassination are conscious enough of their limited skills as historians that they wouldn't insist on any such thing in public discussion. And many people who are drawn to arguments for the existence of God will admit that they don't know exactly how those arguments should go. A private reason in the sense I'm now describing it depends on experiences that we're not sure we can generalize or arguments that we have not yet worked out even to our own satisfaction. We therefore are or should be reluctant to offer such a reason, or anything that rests solely on it, as a contribution to scholarship or a basis for public policy.[10] We may be willing to discuss these views with a few intimate friends, who understand the tentativeness with which we hold them, but it would be irresponsible to represent them to a large group of others as if they had the sort of logical or empirical support that should compel the attention of any rational being.

It thus belongs to the nature of private reasons in this sense that we are aware of not understanding our own views fully, or not having a fully adequate defense for them. When we view our beliefs as a matter of private reason, we are conscious that they do not have the status of something proven, on par with the central claims of, say, quantum mechanics or evolution. We hold them as something that *might be* true, but cannot yet be *shown* to be true, that might one day be established by public reason, but are not so now.

To deny the rationality of maintaining beliefs of this sort would rule out many beliefs that may be useful to society, when better articulated or defended. Advances in science, for instance, practically always start out as someone's private reasons before they become public reasons. Copernicus and Einstein would not have effected scientific revolutions had they thought that their unusual views should be kept in their desk drawers. As a society, we therefore have good public reason to accept the category of private reason in the minimal sense I've described, and to apply the appellation "rational" to people who maintain beliefs of this sort. But we also have reason to insist that people deserve that appellation only if they understand *that* such reasons are private ones, and treat them as such: keep them to themselves, or share them only with intimate others, in the awareness that they do not yet live up to the standards of public reason. One need not be ashamed of private reasons, just unwilling to give them the status of full-blown, public reasons. There is a diffidence in private reasoning, a holding of one's arguments in reserve, an acknowledgment that they may not survive the kind of scrutiny by which we determine, publicly, whether to mark something as true or not.[11] This very unwillingness to impose private reasons on others, this very recognition of their weakness as reasons, amounts to an acknowledgment of the nature and status of public reason. To hold a belief *as* a matter of private reason is thus to affirm public reason. Private reason is disciplined by public reason. By participating in public reason, I find out what beliefs of mine I should keep private, or refine further before giving them a public hearing. Which is to say that I need to know and accept the canons of public reason even to understand the proper weight of what I keep in private reason.

But this modest notion of private reason is not what Rawls rejects as unintelligible, or Kant as dangerous. A person with private reasons of this sort still thinks that someday her grounds for belief could become a matter of public reason. The believer thus implicitly aims her beliefs towards the acceptance of public reason, even while realizing that the public does not currently accept them. What we need, if we want to make sense of a personal faith that *in principle* can't be brought into public reason is a rather more radical notion. We'll want to hold onto the idea that private reason respects the norms of public reason, as we develop this more radical version of private reasoning. But otherwise we are looking for something different. We need reasons that appeal to an intrinsically private kind of *experience*.

5. At various points, Kant indicates that aspects of our experience can be read as somehow representing the will or nature of a supernatural being—as symbolizing God—even if those experiences can also be given a perfectly good explanation in scientific terms.[12] Religious experience can be superimposed on ordinary experience, for Kant, can be understood as one layer of the experience that we also explain in non-religious terms. And he acknowledges that a "genius," a term he uses mostly in aesthetic contexts, may be able to channel such experiences into a form that inspires others—sparks their imagination to the same reflective joy that the genius herself had, in apprehending some aspect of the world. There seems to me a ready extension of this idea into religious contexts. We might react to a particular religious teaching with

reflective love, and the "geniuses" among us might be able to spark a similar love in others.[13] But we would never be able to *prove* that what we experienced in a case like this really did lie beyond nature. The convictions to which we come on the basis of such feelings would be intrinsically private, grounded in something that intrinsically eludes universal terms.

Suppose someone has an experience that she is inclined to regard as of what I have called "holiness"—a vision of the world as entirely beautiful and morally good—or indeed as a communication from God. This could be an apparent "miracle" (a voice from nowhere, a burning bush) or a vision or dream. But it could also be an otherwise ordinary event in which she sees extra-ordinary significance (she grants that she is talking to an ordinary human being, but thinks that God is nevertheless speaking through that person), or a feeling that God is present to her, or showing her what to do, at a time of great despair in her life. Any claim she makes to this effect will be, I want to say, a matter of private reason, in a strict sense of that term—something that could never be demonstrated in a way that would satisfy the standards by which human beings should judge in general. But as long as she grants that there is a perfectly adequate scientific account of what occurred,[14] and draws no inferences from it that conflict with her moral duties, that is not a problem. She must read her experience symbolically—as a representation of something not directly knowable, and that requires active interpretation to have anything to say to her. That still allows her to use her understanding of the experience to make some choices. As long as she stays within the limits of her moral duties, she may allow it to help her decide whom to marry, what job to take, or what to say to a troubled friend. Or she may engage in certain activities—prayer, meditation, a pilgrimage—that she would not have undertaken otherwise. What she may not do is treat her experience as an additional, special source of knowledge about science or morality. She gains no *knowledge* at all from these experiences, just a way of looking at her life that, if compatible with what else she knows about the good, she can hope will lead her closer to her highest end. She should not expect other people to be convinced by her on this basis—should indeed warn them *against* regarding her experiences as if they could contribute to knowledge— although of course she may have other arguments for her practical conclusions that meet the standards of public reason.

Now she may be able to share her special experiences, and the ways she has interpreted them, with a group of like-minded people who have had similar experiences, or are inclined to read experience in general in a similar symbolic way. Her imagination may spark theirs, or run along currents similar to theirs. The images that resonate with her may also resonate with them; or the readings she has of certain images may mesh with theirs. Perhaps this is because she and they already share a symbolic language—perhaps they already regard the same scripture or ritual tradition as sacred, or perhaps their emotional dispositions are similar, and they are therefore inclined to find the sacred in the same emotional settings. Then her religious experiences, and her interpretations of those experiences, will reinforce or shape theirs and theirs will reinforce or shape hers.

Or perhaps the import she takes from her religious experiences is one that leads her to *reject* all the religious traditions around her, and her gift for expressing these experiences, for cloaking them in imaginatively powerful, but comprehensible form—her "genius," as Kant would say—is so great that she comes to write a *new* scripture, which is taken up as such by a community. Then she is in the position of a founder of a religion. But the relationships between her and her followers will be of the same kind as those between members of an already existing religion. Her imagination sparks and informs theirs, they are drawn to what she says for that reason, and both she and they then come to find the sacred in similar events, and to develop rituals that can occasion such events or reflect on them.

One implication of this picture of religious communities is that they will be held together primarily by ways of feeling and imagining rather than by doctrines. They will have doctrines, of course, but those doctrines will always be more or less approximate ways of making sense of something that is at bottom a private experience, or symbol based on that experience. The community will share modes of figuration and inter-pretation, and thereby share attitudes about how a good human life should be led, far more than it will metaphysical or even moral propositions: they will share, primarily, an imaginative commitment or reflective love. And this is what does in fact define most religious communities. To be a Christian is first and foremost to have what one regards as a personal relationship to Jesus—whatever exactly that may mean. To be Jewish is to feel that one comes to God through the law of the Torah—whatever exactly *that* may mean. A Buddhist feels she has had intimations, through meditation and the cryptic teachings of the Buddha, of what Buddhist enlightenment may be like, but is normally quite unsure about how exactly to define that enlightenment: it is supposed to take more than a lifetime to grasp that properly. In each case, one feels strongly attached in the first instance to a particular experience and what it symbolizes, but a prime mark of one's faith in that experience and symbol is precisely that one will always be only on the way to understanding exactly what it means.

This is of course no more than the barest sketch of how religious groups may form and develop, and of the role that personal experiences taken to be of the divine play in the formation and life of such groups, but one point that I hope even the sketch makes clear is that the discourse of such groups will always remain "private," in the Kantian sense of that word. At no point does it become possible to offer public proof—proof capable of convincing any rational human being—that the experiences on which the group is based really come from the divine, or that the claims made on the basis of these experiences really enhance our ability to achieve the ultimate human telos. It doesn't matter how large the group gets. 500 million Catholics and a billion Muslims are still, for these purposes, a private group. They remain private because of the kind of grounds they offer for their shared claims. If they eschew the causal laws necessary to establish a claim as scientific, and the overlapping consensus necessary to establish a claim morally, their claims can never be public. That doesn't matter, as long as they are not *seen* as public claims. They must be preserved within the realm of private reason, which is to say presented as suggestions and prods that may spark the imaginations of like-minded individuals—and thereby lead those individuals, too, to what may be a communication from the divine—rather than something that any rational being, as such, should be expected to believe. This is what it is for private reason to be disciplined by public reason. We are aware, when we make such private claims, that they *are* private, and therefore keep ourselves and others from treating them as if they were public. Anything else would be group or individual madness. To think that a set of appearances to you, whether in dreams or waking life or via a scripture, constitutes a violation of the laws of nature is to substitute your private sense for the common one, to isolate yourself within your private experience rather than bringing it into a common world. And that, as Kant says, is just to lose the distinction between yourself and the world around you.

6. To remain sane, to remain in our common world, the believer must share his or her private reasons with a community of some sort. It is not easy to tell on one's own whether one's claims amount to private or public reasoning: one needs help from others to do so. It is not easy to tell whether any particular factual claim is a properly scientific one—what constitutes a "fact" cannot be delineated strictly, and the canons of scientific method are constantly shifting. Nor is it easy to tell whether a particular normative claim is a moral one: both moral and telic claims, after all, concern what makes for a good human life. But if religious modes of getting at the true and the good necessarily stand outside the science and morality that can be rationally defended to any and all human beings, it will take constant work to make sure we keep seeing them that way. No individual believer can keep himself from slipping into a purely private world unless he constantly checks his private sense against a communal sense.

For this he needs two sorts of community. The others he especially needs are people who can follow him in his private as well as his public reasoning, who share his revelation and therefore can assess the implications that he draws from it. But a community made up only of like-minded believers will be prone to group madness unless it is in turn in dialogue with wider groups that do not share its private views. Religious believers need a *reasonable* public against which to check their private reasons, and they will not achieve that unless they live in a double community of sorts: a like-minded religious one, and a secular and/or religiously mixed community that can correct for the errors or excesses of their religious group. Revealed religions usually in fact develop reasonable communities around themselves: they would not survive long otherwise. And any believer who holds a view of religion like the one in this book will think he ought to seek out such a community. He will see his fundamental vision as *of* the highest good for all humanity,[15] hence something that must make moral and pragmatic sense. To interpret it aright, therefore, he will need to integrate it with the way of the human world.

This need for reasonable community enables us to distinguish between reasonable religious traditions and mere cults. Consider Alison Lurie's novel *Imaginary Friends*, which gives a remarkably astute portrayal of a group of people who reinforce one another in the belief that they are in touch with beings on another planet.[16] These people's beliefs have a structure that public reason is very likely to condemn as irrational. But that is precisely because they have renounced the need to share their beliefs with a reasonable public.

This comes out, in the first place, in the way their beliefs conflict with science. They see themselves as making scientific claims of a sort—empirical claims analogous to the announcement that a new particle or planet has been discovered—but refuse to accept even obvious and overwhelming evidence against their claims. So they do not even try to heed the standards of the broader truth regime to which a reasonable person would submit claims of science. Were they to say, as mature religions typically do, that the experiences they take to be revelatory are to be seen as intimations from a supernatural realm only for the purposes of an ethical faith, their claims would lose much of what seems so lunatic about them. Religions often begin as rivals to science, making empirical claims that seem to upend everything we know about the natural world (a man has risen from the dead; a man has spoken to an angel). But over time they normally shift their emphasis to a vision of the human telos, reinterpreting their original empirical claims so that they become metaphorical for some ethical point, or at most represent an event for which there can be no scientific evidence.[17] My argument in this book has been that they are worthy of faith only when they make that shift.

But the unreasonableness of groups like the one in the Lurie novel comes out also in the way they lose grip on any sense of what constitutes an ethical faith. Religious claims must constitute an intelligible view of the human telos to become a proper part even of private reasoning. The central vision of a religion will not be fully articulable, on the account offered here, nor will it be shared universally. But it must at least be recognizable, both within and without its community of followers, *as* a vision of the human telos.[18] To some extent, the group in Lurie's novel meets this criterion—they interpret what they think the extraterrestrials are telling them to mean that we need as much as possible to shed our material ties and express our spiritual essence. But this is because they initially meld their weird beliefs with longer-standing traditions borrowed from various kinds of Christianity.[19] They do not, however, make ongoing efforts to integrate their revelation with the cognitive and moral practices of the world around them. This leads them into increasingly erratic, anti-social behavior. What goes wrong here is that they lack sufficient relationships with others to be part of a reasonable community. They have one another to talk to, but are largely isolated from any wider community. Lurie presents them, astutely, as a handful of misfits who withdraw increasingly from other human ties as their commitment to the group gets more intense. Far from welcoming the corrective of public reason, these people flee public reason, try to insulate their private beliefs from all possibility of being shaped by the broader human world. A healthy religious belief system—a sane and decent one, and one that has a chance of being passed down from generation to generation—requires of its adherents a far more open kind of community.

If this is correct, it is a great mistake for a religious group to isolate itself, or severely limit its interactions with people of other religions and no religion. Indeed, this is a mistake even insofar as religious groups try to maintain a vision that is distinct from the way of the world around them. Private reasons stand both apart from and in relationship to public reasons, and they get their distinctive character precisely by way of that relationship. Correspondingly, religious groups maintain their distinctive visions only if and to the extent that they are in constant contact with a science and morality from which to distinguish those visions. Only a relationship of this sort keeps a religious community sane and decent, but only a relationship of this sort, also, ensures that its religious vision remains truly of something outside the natural and ordinary—something *super*-natural and *extra*-ordinary.

7. The case I have offered for the possibility of a kind of private reason is itself supposed to satisfy the canons of public reason. If I am successful, it will be because even people who think no-one has spiritual experiences will be able to accept the claims made by people who believe in such experiences as intelligible, sane, and morally acceptable. Someone who maintained that they were engaged in private reasoning, but did not observe the strictures I have laid down for how that can take place, or who put forward private reasons as if they were public ones, would not be publicly accepted as reasoning at all—would indeed, if sane, have to doubt himself that that was what he was doing. This is another way in which public reason disciplines private reason: the case for the possibility of the latter must be made within the confines of the former.

So must the case for the *need* for private reason. I have tried in this chapter to show merely how private reason might be possible, not why we might need to engage in it. A strict Kantian, even if he accepted that case, might say we should avoid anything that smacks of private reasoning because it is morally and politically dangerous. The line between holding something privately and holding it publicly is hard to draw, as we have seen, and can become harder to draw in a large community of people who share the same mode of private reasoning. That's how we get the sort of group madness that leads to religious wars. So the defender of more personal or more traditional notions of religion than Kant allows needs to do more than show the *possibility* of private reasoning. To make her case; she needs also to make it plausible that such a thing could be *necessary* to us in some way. I have tried to make such a case in Parts III and IV of this book. It too must live up to the strictures of public reason. Only then can the private grounds it licenses serve as a general basis for belief—only then can we see how anyone with similar grounds could just as reasonably base beliefs on them.

But a private reasoning of that sort—a private reasoning that respects the publicness of science and morality, and shows why its peculiar mode of thinking might be ethically necessary—can live up to Kant's cognitive universalization test. Of course that test will need to operate on a meta-level here: what one universalizes is a ground for relying on *non*-universalizable grounds in certain carefully delineated cases. But that nevertheless makes room for a kind of private reason in the midst of Kant's public reason.

Once again, bringing our private thinking to the tribunal of public reasoning can enhance our faiths. By participating in public reason, we come better to understand what beliefs we should keep in a private realm. We need to know the canons of public reason even to understand the proper weight of what we keep in private reason. Public reason limits private reason, but also gives it its distinctive place, enables us to make sure that what belongs to faith remains a matter *of* faith.

And essential to keeping private reason properly private, to giving faith its distinctive role, is a recognition that it does not belong in the determination of scientific theories or public policy. It is a mistake for anyone to introduce into public debate a belief that he recognizes as having a justification only in his private reason.

Deuteronomy 4: 6: "[The laws of the Torah] are your wisdom and your discernment in the eyes of the peoples. Upon hearing all these rules, they will say, 'Surely this great nation is a wise and discerning people.'"
Isaiah 42: 6: "I the Lord . . . have set you to be a light unto the nations."

Does the whole of the Torah, then, translate into a way of the world? Is the whole special teaching we Jews treasure—the private faith we keep among ourselves—at bottom something that the entire world must be able to recognize, every human being see as "wisdom and discernment"? Well, it is at least a means for our achieving such a publicly sharable form of goodness, and that is at least one reason we were given it. Just before the revelation on Sinai, we are told we are to be "a kingdom of priests, a holy nation" (Exodus 19: 6). Surely that is the same as "a light unto the nations," and surely it is part of being such a light that we be recognizable to others as "wise and discerning." Light signifies what gives understanding, what allows for wisdom. We are to enlighten, and the terms of enlightenment must be shared by all human beings, not peculiar to us. It must be possible, then, for us to speak a public language, to come out of the hermetic shell by which we speak only to each other: to leave, if only for part of the time, the dancing shadow patterns of private revelation for the bright public realm of the Enlightenment.

2

Morality Again

8. The person who takes morality to be part of his or her religious commitments is likely to be something of a moral rigorist. If my obligation to tell the truth and to pay people what I owe them is an obligation to God, as well as to my fellow human beings, then I have no business waiving it when it seems to serve no human purpose.[1] On the other hand, the religious rigorist does not justify following rules as the strict Kantian does, just because practical reason demands rule-following. The religious rigorist respects rules as part of a path that expresses her commitment to a vision of the highest good, and helps her, and others, grasp the contours of that vision; she respects specifically moral rules insofar as they help maintain human community, which she regards as a necessary condition for the proper grasp of her revelatory vision. So the religious rigorist has a *purpose* for her rule-following, in the name of which she can allow exceptions to the rules (an act that destroys her community, for instance, would defeat the purpose of her rule-following), but a purpose remote enough from happiness, or anything else she could define on the basis of her own reasoning, that she is unlikely to grant such exceptions with the promiscuity of a utilitarian. Religious rigorism can therefore make a nice alternative to Kantian rigorism, conducing to trust-worthiness without the extremism to which Kantians are prone.

With this thought in mind, we can lay out the relationship between revelation and morality more precisely than we have before. The reception of revelation moralizes a religious teaching, because it must suit the revealed vision to a communal way of life. Because revelations are obscure, yet are supposed to show us how to live, they need interpretation; because human ways of life must be shared by a community, the mode by which these texts are interpreted must also be developed by a community, not carried out by each individual for him or herself. But a mode of interpretation developed by a community, and enabling its members to pursue a way of life as a community, will of necessity cohere, in general, with the principles enabling societies to survive that we identified as the core of our overlapping moral consensus. Of course, bringing revealed texts into accordance with morality is often not an easy task.

Communities often take many generations to figure out how to institute their guiding texts in ways that maintain justice and peace among their members, and in their relations with other societies. Again, this encourages us to regard revelations as being given to a tradition, a community of interpreters that works out the meaning of a divine teaching over time, rather than to individuals.

But if we look in the other direction, commitment to a revealed text can give people a new reason for morality. The religious person continues to believe that there are good reasons to be moral grounded in our self-interest, our desire to make other people happy, and our desire to be part of a community of free and equal individuals. But he or she layers onto all these reasons some additional ones: that morality can give us the solidarity by which, communally, we are fit to receive revelation, perhaps, and that it helps us more deeply to accept and understand our revealed vision. This is, I think, the best way to see the moral passages in revealed texts: the Ten Commandments, say, or the Sermon on the Mount. It is not that refraining from murder and theft, and loving your neighbor, are supposed to be something *new*, in these passages, something the audience has never heard before. Rather, these established moral demands acquire a new function in the context of the path laid out by the revelation. They become part of a discipline that helps the believer tame the selfish desires that interfere with properly understanding the revealed vision, or they help bring individual believers into a community of shared faith. And one thing that follows from this new function is that moral demands acquire a greater stringency than they have had before.

9. So there are good reasons why religious commitment can and should go together with great moral decency. But in practice religious believers are often far from moral paragons. Why not? I think the view I've laid out helps explain the otherwise rather puzzling fact that religious commitment leads some people to be more immoral than they might be without that commitment. Adam Smith says that "False notions of religion are almost the only causes which can occasion any very gross perversion of our natural [moral] sentiments" (TMS III.6.12; 176). While I don't think that is entirely true—false political ideologies often do the same thing—there is a large kernel of truth in it. And that should seem odd, given that religions generally claim to offer a deeper version of morality than we get by secular means alone.

On the account I have given, it is not so odd. The key to it is the distinction between the moral and the telic. Because they are separate, they are always potentially in competition with one another. So if religions primarily offer us a telic vision, their moral component, no matter how much they emphasize it, always stands in some tension with their primary purpose. There is always some temptation to a teleological suspension of the moral, among religious people, and that can lead to great danger.

More simply, there is a strain of selfishness in the forces that lead people to religious commitment. It's not uncommon to meet extremely self-centered religious people, more concerned with their own salvation than with helping other human beings. On my view it is not hard to see why that might be. What primarily draws a person to a religious vision is a set of worries she has about the pointlessness of her own life. She worries that her life is worthless, and comes to love a religious vision because it relieves that worry. It is not her ability to be kind or fair to others that worries her, but something that would trouble her even if there were no others, and that no human others can solve for her. The central source of her commitment is an intensely private, individualistic one: a concern that is, quite literally, "self-ish."

Yet religious commitment standardly demands that we not be selfish. Religions almost always call on their followers to transform themselves so that they can readily love others as themselves, or so they no longer feel a distinction between what they want for themselves and what they want for others. Indeed, most religions see the attainment of such a state as a necessary condition for achieving the worth one seeks for one's own life. And there is good reason to yoke the two together. When I fear that my life is worthless, in the existential sense that can lead me toward religion, I do not fear that my life *as opposed to yours* is worthless. I do not think you have something that I might have, something over which we might compete. If I thought that, I wouldn't be drawn to teleological visions. I'd just try to get what you have, whether by finding an equivalent for myself, or by taking yours. No, the fear of worthlessness that leads to religious commitment is a fear that *all* lives are worthless, yours and mine and everyone else's. The discovery that your life is worthwhile would actually be relieving to me: it would give me hope that mine could be as well. What I yearn for, when I seek telic balm, is something that I want for you as much as I want it for myself, something intrinsically shareable, and over which there could not possibly be competition. It makes good sense, then, that becoming the sort of person who cares about others in the way I care about myself might be a condition for achieving this end.

To call religious commitment "selfish" is thus too simple. We might better say that there is a certain structural similarity between religious commitment and selfishness. The religious seeker lives to a certain extent, like the selfish person, in his own world, withdrawn from the ordinary social sphere in which moral concerns are at home. The realm of the moral is, while the realm of the telic is not, sensitive to the demands of ordinary human interaction, and a person absorbed in telic concerns may therefore be inattentive to the demands of other human beings in just the way that a selfish person would be. That does not mean that the person absorbed in telic concerns fails to care about other human beings, much less fails to think he should care. It just means that the focus of his attention distracts him from that sort of caring—distracts him from all ordinary human needs, including his own. And a focus of this sort can lead him to set aside or override ordinary human needs in the name of the vision that he thinks bestows worth on life. In the realm of the telic we seek something that could require us to abandon ordinary human interaction, and even if it doesn't require that, it isn't identical with such interaction. There is a moment of isolation, of privacy, of radical individualism, in even the most socially oriented religions. And the danger that that moment may lead some committed believers to overlook or submerge the importance of the ordinary human realm is always there, even in religions that officially lay great stress on morality.

10. Some religious believers may feel that my view, on which morality is a pre-condition for religious commitment rather than the heart of that commitment, is overly aesthetic, that it deprives religion of its rightful moral power. "You are too concerned with what makes life interesting rather than boring, beautiful rather than ugly," this objector might say, "with the concerns that we have about an existence we can individually rejoice in or love, rather than our altruistic concerns for the dignity and well-being of others. What has happened, on your account, to the noble religiousness of an Albert Schweitzer or a Gandhi? To Ashraf Ma-ji, who protects battered women of all faiths in the name of Islam, or the rabbis who work for Palestinian rights as part of their reverence for God's image in humanity?[2] Does the power of revelation really lie in what it *adds to* morality, rather than what it teaches *about* morality? What kind of God would bring us into His presence only to tell us how to satisfy our yearning for a lovable existence, rather than how to achieve a righteous or compassionate one?"

This objection is understandable, but misguided. It arises from the stress I have placed on the secular self-sufficiency of morality. But the telic teachings that I attribute to revelation are supposed to be built upon morality. Ethics grows out of morality, on my view, and the maximal goodness or holiness that revelation offers us contains morality within it. There is no way to stand in God's presence (or to attain the vision of non-theistic religions) except through morality—that is indeed a criterion for a purportedly revealed text to *count* as a way to God—even if morality itself does not need to be revealed. So a religious person may well worship God in large part by promoting moral causes: together with other members of her religious community, or members of other religious communities, or secular people.

It is an advantage of my view, I believe, that it gives religious people good reason to promote moral values in solidarity with secular people. Of course the religious person will have somewhat different reasons—additional reasons—for her moral commitments than a secular person would have. Imagine a religious Christian or Jew who puts up with beatings and humiliation to work for the rights of Hispanic immigrants in America or Palestinians in Israel, or risks disease to work among the African poor. She may work alongside secular people committed to the same cause, she may do exactly what they do, and, drawing on the overlapping consensus that defines morality, she may give many of the same reasons for her actions: that the people she is trying to help deserve freedom and dignity, or that their suffering warrants our compassion, or that oppressing or ignoring these people de-humanizes us. But she may add that her ultimate aim is not to see her fellow human beings *merely* politically free and materially happy. Rather, she hopes they will one day be able to use their improved political and material conditions as a means to reach the ultimate human good. Perhaps she sees oppression and poverty as interfering with one's ability to achieve a fully free, reflective love for God. Or perhaps she sees the bringing of other human beings out of suffering and oppression as a means towards an ideal human condition in which we can reach enlightenment together. Or, again, she may see ending the suffering and oppression of other human beings as an expression of her love for God, and the image of God in other human beings. In any of these and many other ways, the religious person can have reason to take her moral duties as themselves religious duties, even if she thinks that the secular justifications for those duties would have been enough to motivate her on their own. She can affirm both religious and secular justifications for her moral duties, integrating the latter into the former. Moral duties can bring others to a divine teaching because freedom and well-being are good conditions, in general, for human reflection: hence good, in particular, for the reflective reception of divine teaching. Moral duties can express our love of God's image in humanity because they fulfill needs that all human beings, religious and secular, share. And moral duties can build the sort of community—free, friendly, and in which everyone has equal dignity—that would enable us to help each other achieve the highest good for all humanity. So the religious person can see her moral duties as a central mode of service to God. But she has no *distinctive* moral duties, and her distinctive religious reasons for being moral are grafted onto secular reasons for that commitment. It is therefore easy for her to carry out moral duties alongside secular people who do not accept her view of the function of morality.

This account of the relationship between religious and moral commitments has a number of advantages over accounts on which religion teaches us moral duties that we would never come to in a secular fashion. First, it allows us to have a notion of goodness in hand before we evaluate or endorse any particular conception of God or God's word. That makes it possible for us to call God "good" without circularity, and removes the danger of our interpreting God's word in an immoral way. Second, it enables religious and secular people, and people of different religions, to work together on moral projects, and to see themselves as primarily aiming at the same ends. It also gives religious people reason unqualifiedly to respect the decent people they know who are secular, or belong to a different religion, rather than having to insist that their co-religionists are morally better than anyone outside the faith. The sense that a fellow Christian or Jew or Muslim must be a better human being than anyone not of the faith is a source both of sectarian hatred and of an unwillingness to criticize one's co-religionists, or reform the institutions of one's religion.

Finally, the account I propose makes clear how religious commitment can transform one's view of morality without leading one to demand, on moral grounds, that others share that commitment. Helping battered women or oppressed minorities in the name of God can have a power that doing the same thing in the name of human happiness or freedom alone would not have.[3] But even one's ability to testify to this greater power will be greatest if one starts by recognizing that one shares a view of what moral duties are, and many reasons for those duties, with human beings generally. Only by starting from that point can one win respect for one's faith from people who do not share it— can one witness to it.

3

Politics

11. If revelation responds to telic questions rather than moral ones, believers in a revealed religion can allow political questions to be settled on a purely secular basis. If the way of the world is sufficient to define and ground morality, then it is sufficient to define and ground politics. Moreover, the religious believer, as I understand her, is well aware that her commitments cannot be reached by reason alone and that other people may either not share the sorts of experiences that aroused her faith or be led by them to a different faith. She will also be aware that the reflective love she holds for her own religious vision will be truly reflective only if she has been able to reach it freely, rather than having had it foisted on her by force or manipulation. She will be aware, that is, that a robust freedom of religion is a condition for the kind of religiousness she herself maintains. It follows that she will oppose attempts to use force to impose any religious vision, or to eradicate any religious visions or prevent people from considering them. She will have a *religious* interest in living in a society in which people are free to be religious or secular, and religious in any way they choose, as long as they conform to morality. She will also know that what counts as "morality" had better be determined independently of religion: that religious faith rests on imaginative commitments that can't readily underwrite a shared morality, and that the members of her community can therefore sustain their freedom only if they agree to elide those commitments when they enter the political arena. In this way, one can get by a religious route to what John Rawls calls "political liberalism": an approach to politics that prescinds from telic commitments.[1]

Indeed, the account I have offered of telic commitments may provide additional support for Rawls's position. On my view, both religious and secular views of what makes life worth living—"comprehensive [ethical] doctrines," as Rawls would call them—are based on faith. This makes them symmetrical in a way that helps justify Rawls's admonition to keep them both off the political table. Rawls's own defense of that admonition is not all that convincing. Rawls says that if we use the limited mode of reasoning that he recommends for fundamental political questions, eschewing appeal to our telic commitments, each of us will see our public discourse as "imperfect, ... falling short of the whole truth set out by our comprehensive doctrine" (PL 242). But we will know that all our fellow citizens "share with us the same sense of its imperfection, though on different grounds, as they hold different comprehensive doctrines and believe different grounds are left out of account" (PL 242–243). This shared sense of imperfection will thus work to assure us that our governing procedures are grounded in a way that respects the equality of all citizens. We need not feel at a relative disadvantage to citizens whose comprehensive views do figure in political discussion, for there are none. We need not feel, therefore, that we are less respected by our state than any of our fellow citizens.

This is an attractive view, but it is hard to make good sense of it using Rawls's rationalistic tools alone. Why should Kantian or utilitarian or Marxist views about how human beings should live not be given priority over religious views, one might ask? If we are seeking a reason-based politics, as Rawls clearly is, why should we not be able to favor purely rational over faith-based ethical views in public discourse? The equality of citizens follows from their equal capacity for rational argument, so anything that can be defended in purely rational terms, including rationalistic comprehensive views of life, should be fair game in political discussion. Kantians and utilitarians and Marxists eschew faith, in defending their views, and believe they can show any rational human being why they are right about how we should live. They also, often, believe that only a political sphere transformed in accordance with their comprehensive views will bring us true freedom or well-being. So cutting their views out of our political debates would seem unjustifiably to impoverish those debates.

Rawls has an answer to this challenge. The "burdens of argument," he says, make it unlikely that we will ever be able to reach a rational resolution of our differences over comprehensive views. These burdens include problems in assessing the empirical evidence for such views, the difficulty of commensurating our different values, the vagueness of many ethical terms, and a number of other considerations (PL 56–57).

But while these considerations do make it plausible that the superiority of any one comprehensive view over the others will be very *hard* to establish rationally, they fail to show that rationality *cannot* do the job. Many philosophers think Rawls is merely pessimistic about the reach of rationality. I disagree, but that's because I would add in factors that Rawls does not mention. For instance, his list of the burdens of judgment leaves out the possibility that ethical views may depend irremediably on metaphysical questions that cannot, in principle, be resolved by rational debate. But he says that his list is not complete (PL 56) and he might well allow for that possibility. What really goes beyond the sorts of considerations he has in mind is the possibility that a non-rational faith may be needed to make up the defects of rationality, when we commit ourselves to a comprehensive vision of the good life. If we add in this thought, central to the position I have defended here, then it is obvious why Kantian and utilitarian and Marxist comprehensive visions must come off the political table along with Christian and Muslim and Buddhist views. If the Marxist is relying on faith in his hope for a world in which species-being triumphs over individualism, if the utilitarian must rely on faith in her hope that a greater and more equitable distribution of pleasures would lead most of us to see our lives as worth living, then it is clear that a politics that depends only on reasons we can all accept, and favors the faith of none, cannot be based on such views. Rawls's removal of all comprehensive views from the grounds for constitutional principles thus makes better sense on the faith-based account I have given of such views than on his own attempt to include them in the scope of pure reason.

From this general sketch of how religious commitment, as I have construed it, goes along with political liberalism, let's turn to some practical questions. Liberals need to answer three central questions about religion and political practice:

1. May the state take direct efforts to promote a particular religion?
2. May laws or policies enacted by the state, if not intended to promote religion, be grounded in part on religious premises?
3. May the state take measures to help religions maintain their communal institutions?

We might picture these questions as the three prongs of a trident, which as a whole represents the challenge that religion poses to the liberal polity. My views on the first two accord closely with Rawls's, and I shall use materials drawn largely from him to respond to them. My view on the third departs from anything to be found explicitly in Rawls—notoriously, he did not attend much to the relationship between liberalism and community—although I will draw on the work of Will Kymlicka, a communitarian indebted to Rawls, when I come to it.

12. To begin, then, with the first prong of the trident: May a religious group, if it regards its vision as the way to the highest good for all humanity, try to use political power to bring others into its fold?

For a liberal, the answer to that question is "of course not," but different liberals arrive at this answer in different ways. Rawls derives the answer from the freedom and equality that is basic to democratic citizenship. I begin instead with a view of the nature of religious commitment. If religious commitment consists in reflective love, force cannot bring me to it. I cannot be forced to love something—that would not *be* love. Certainly, it would not be *reflective* love: a love I come to thoughtfully, and can alter if it seems misdirected.

This is a version of the position Rawls calls "free faith" (PL 145). As Rawls presents it, free faith is a position within certain religious worldviews, according to which the state should not use force to spread any religion because religious commitment cannot be achieved by coercion. Locke provides a good model for this position—Rawls uses him as such—although the view I am championing allows for a more full-blooded liberalism than Locke's. We can bring out the political implications of my view by comparing and contrasting it with Locke's.

For Locke himself, the case for religious freedom depends heavily on the claim that "no man can, [even] if he would, conform his faith to the dictates of another," that "religion consists in the inward persuasion of the mind, without which nothing can be acceptable to God" and that the understanding is such that "it cannot be compelled to the belief of anything by outward force."[2] Belief, reasoned belief at least, cannot be compelled. It is therefore pointless even to try to make people faithful by force. At best, one will get people outwardly to profess certain doctrines, while inwardly maintaining the beliefs one was trying to change. This is surely worse, in God's eyes, than an open profession of false but sincerely held beliefs. So the true believer, on Locke's view, must oppose the use of force to bring about belief in others.

On my view, faith consists in reflective love rather than reasoned belief, and the object of faith is a vision rather than a set of doctrines. This leads, I think, to yet stronger reasons to oppose using force to bring about faith than Locke has. But before we get to that point, we should consider a problem in Locke's argument.

The problem is that, as a matter of fact, belief *can* be compelled. When Locke says that "the nature of the understanding [is such] that it cannot be compelled to . . . belief," he presumably has in mind cases in which a person with a settled view on a topic is told to believe a contrary one or face punishment. In *such* cases the most the person could do is pretend to believe; the threat of punishment would not actually change his or her views. But this is not the only way in which force can be used to try to bring about belief. A governing power may instead use force to restrict what can be taught or said, such that children and hitherto uninformed adults who are developing their views of the world will have access only to information and arguments that incline them towards what the government wants them to believe. Thus citizens of the Soviet empire were presented with "facts" that made out their society to be far rosier than it was, and liberal capitalist societies to be far grimmer than they are. Thus children in doctrinaire Christian, Jewish, and Muslim schools are kept from historical criticism of their sacred Scriptures, and given pseudo-scientific presentations on subjects like evolution, so that at the end of the day "the inward persuasion of their minds" will conform with the doctrines their teachers want them to hold.

We might add that punishing dissent can be effective over time, even if not on a single occasion. When a variety of authority figures insist it is right to punish people who dissent from some doctrine (the dissenters are followers of Satan, one hears, or selfish individualists who want to undermine our glorious socialist state), when none of one's friends voice dissent from the doctrine, and when one must, oneself, affirm, teach, or argue for the doctrine to other people, one can very well come over time to believe it, if only to avoid the costs of cognitive dissonance.[3] Both totalitarian political regimes and totalitarian religious groups have made use of these psychological facts— putting potential dissenters or new converts into positions where they must teach the official line, for instance—to get the minds of the recalcitrant to yield to their doctrines.

Thus, even if compulsion cannot directly, and on single occasions, bring our under- standings to hold a belief against the weight of our reasons, an indirect and systematic program of indoctrination, underwritten by force, may convince us. Locke would surely consider these programs just as illegitimate as a direct use of force to compel belief, however, and he knew enough about how churches can control educational systems that he must have been aware of this possibility. How then can we re-read him so that his argument does not depend on the claim that as a matter of *fact* faith cannot be compelled?

I suggest that we attend closely to the qualifying phrase in the passage quoted above. "Religion consists in the inward persuasion of the mind, *without which nothing can be acceptable to God*," says Locke. That last phrase (together with the account of reasoning in the following paragraph) indicates that Locke's point is a normative rather than a factual one. The *sort* of "persuasion" suitable to religious belief, the sort that "can be acceptable to God," is not one brought about, either directly or indirectly, by force. Even the indirect use of force, on this view, is an obstacle to reason, and if our faith in God is supposed to come about by way of reason, the indirect use of force blocks faith as well. On this reading, Locke would be arguing that the sort of faith God wants from us is one in which we each ourselves freely "see," with the eye of our minds, the truths about God's existence and salvation. As directed at political and religious leaders who want to control how people come to religious belief, Locke's point would then be: a social order that fosters the sort of faith truly acceptable to God—free faith—is one in which everyone has as much access as possible to all facts and arguments available at a given time, and is able to affirm religious doctrines in the light of those facts and arguments. God wants a social order that allows everyone to reason freely, for Locke, even if that means that some people will decide not to come to God.[4]

One response to this sort of argument could be to say that the capacity to reason in some human beings is weak and that it would be better to ensure that those human beings come to the right conclusions about God, even if imperfectly, than to allow them to drift into an incorrect doctrine. The emphasis on reason in religious belief, that is, allows us to say that in principle there *are* "correct" and "incorrect" doctrines, and a political or religious leader may argue that his superior capacity for reasoning justifies him in using coercion of some kind to lead less capable human beings towards the truth. Locke could insist, as against this, that God prefers a fully free belief in (somewhat?) mistaken doctrines to a manipulated belief in the truth, but a case for this claim would likely depend on a very individualist version of Christian doctrine, rather than on premises shared by adherents of all religious beliefs. We will see shortly that this move against liberalism is not so easily made once reason is replaced, as the mainspring of faith, with reflective love.

13. It is at least as prima facie obvious that I cannot be compelled to love as that I cannot be compelled to believe, at least as obvious that "no man can, if he would, conform his love to the dictates of another." If I am told to love a person or thing or spirit on pain of imprisonment or death, I am likely to feel an *aversion* to that person or thing or spirit rather than love for it, whatever I may profess outwardly. Nor is being

put in a position where I need to teach others to love (say) a communist regime or a certain god likely to increase my feelings of love for that entity, or reduce my feelings of cognitive dissonance. Even the repeated pronouncements of people I respect to the effect that god X is lovable, and the unwillingness of my friends to dissent from these pronouncements, are unlikely to bring about love for X in me. The imperviousness of love to coercion is, if anything, greater than the imperviousness of reason to coercion.

That said, some indirect uses of coercion to induce belief will work just as well at inducing love. By controlling the flow of information—spreading falsehoods or with-holding truths about the worship of god X, or making sure that people are exposed to beautiful stories about this god from early childhood onwards—a governing power can create an environment in which people are likely to develop a love for god X from their own free will. We might say that this is not "real" love, but that would be an arbitrary restriction on the concept of love. People normally come to love whomever and whatever they love under conditions of limited, even distorted, information, and we don't normally consider them to love, say, their parents or spouses any the less for that. A more plausible objection is that this is not the *sort* of love that an all-good ruler of the universe would want from us. It is not a properly free love, and it is not directed, strictly speaking, *at* the god that is its purported object. If I love a distorted view of God then I do not properly love *God*. And we must suppose that God, who has no needs that could be satisfied by manipulating us, would want us to love Him, not a distorted view of Him.

Which is just to say that we must suppose that God wants us to have a reflective love for Him, and His way for us, not a blind or manipulated love. And to have a reflective love is to have a love that we scrutinize rationally, to ensure that it is not blind or manipulated, or the product of superstitions or prejudices. But no such reflective scrutiny can go on if we are filled with propaganda, or kept from relevant information or argumentative challenges. So the need to come to our religious visions by way of reflective love provides at least as good a ground for a demand that the political realm be free of religious coercion as the rationalist form of religion defended by Locke.

The route via love may in fact lead more unequivocally to liberalism about religion than the route via reason. For there is no parallel, on the love account of religious commitment, to the notion that some people may have a weak or confused capacity to reason, and therefore need guidance by their smarter peers. If I am aware that my commitment to the religious vision I favor is centrally a matter of love rather than reason, then I am less likely to think that I know better than you do what religious vision is right for you. I know, from the way love works in the aesthetic and erotic realms, that what arouses love in you may be something quite different from what arouses love in me, and if I believe in a God Who wants to be reached or must be reached via love, then I have every reason to believe that He (She, It) may appear differently to you than He does to me. I know that it is not primarily *argument* that might get you to share my views, or indeed enable me to assure myself that my view is superior to yours. There is therefore no way that I can plausibly say that my coercing you to follow the same path that I do is really something that you implicitly already agree to, or would agree to if you could only reason better. But liberalism is virtually defined by the proposition that force may only be used in ways to which all citizens agree, or would agree if they reasoned adequately. It follows that, on the love model of religious commitment, I cannot use any form of coercion, direct or indirect, to try to get you to share my religious commitments. My mode of trust in a religious vision imposes upon me a humility about the means by which people can be brought to such trust that undercuts any case for the legitimacy of force in religious matters.[5]

14. So much for the first prong of the religious challenge to liberalism. The second prong concerns the relationship between religious convictions and policy in areas that don't directly have to do with the fostering of religion itself. Here the question is whether a political agent in a liberal democracy—an elected official or candidate for elective office, even a citizen in her capacity as voter—may legitimately use religious reasons as the basis for her view of various laws: about, say, abortion or homosexuality or environmental policy.[6] An intense debate has raged over this question in recent years, both in the halls of academia and in the political arena, with some holding that political views should be grounded on reasons that all other citizens can share, whatever their religious convictions, while others maintain that we are truly free and equal only if we can bring to the political arena whatever reasons we have, regardless of their religious basis or whether we can expect others to share them.[7] My sympathies in this debate lie with the first group—the so-called "political liberals," like Rawls and Robert Audi. But the debate takes place at something of a tangent to the view of religion delineated in this book, since it rests on a presupposition that I have rejected: that our *moral* views may depend on our religious ones. Abortion and homosexuality cannot be morally wrong, on my view, unless there are adequate secular reasons showing them to be wrong,[8] nor can it be morally required of us to pursue a particular environmental policy unless there are adequate secular reasons for that policy. If morality already consists in a secular overlapping consensus among different approaches to how we should live—a consensus on norms for social life among people whose conceptions of the ideal human life differ widely—then there can be no moral objection to a politics based on such a consensus.

Indeed, an overlapping consensus account of morality can help disarm a common source of discomfort with Rawls's political liberalism. The main reason not to accept Rawls's overlapping consensus account of politics comes from a worry that we may thereby lead people away from their true good. Insisting that political arguments not be based on a comprehensive conception of the good will in all likelihood bring about a society in which people have rather less pleasure than utilitarians think they should have, are more heteronomous than Kantians think they should be, and are less committed to Christianity or Islam or Buddhism than adherents of these religions think they should be. That is a considerable evil, from each of these points of view. Rawls's argument that we should put up with that evil since the differences among comprehensive conceptions of the good will never be resolved, and the great values of politics trump the good that might be achieved by pressing for one of our comprehensive conceptions, has been very controversial. But if we start with an overlapping consensus view of morality, we will no longer have a single moral good for politics to achieve. We should therefore have no problem with an overlapping consensus approach to politics.

It's worth recalling that the need for an overlapping consensus in morality does not simply reflect the facts of life in modern, multicultural societies. Rather, even within each faith tradition, there are and have always been people with a great variety of moral views. There is a venerable tradition of Christian utilitarianism, for instance, but also a long tradition of Christian Aristotelianism, and over the past two centuries there have been many Christian Kantians. Today one will find examples of all three within a single Christian denomination, indeed within quite small churches. Radical, incommensurable pluralism is a pervasive and ineradicable feature of the moral life, historically and in the present, and there is no reason to expect it to disappear, short of a miracle (the "end of days") or a totalitarian regime that prevents people from teaching or advocating any moral view but its own. As I noted earlier,[9] this pluralism keeps alive debate over the ultimate human good, and our investigations into worth and revelation have given us additional grounds for valuing that debate. If the highest good is intrinsically obscure, or obscure as long as we remain in our natural condition, then we had better resist any attempt to settle the question of what that good is. Each religious tradition, certainly, has a strong interest in keeping secular people, and members of other religions, from closing down debate over the good. The value of a public realm in which there is open, vigorous controversy over the nature of the good will therefore indeed be great enough, in the eyes of each tradition, that it will have reason to refrain from pursuing its maximalist hopes for dominating the political realm. In both the moral and the political realm, religious and secular people alike have reason to promote an eclectic approach to moral argument, in which positions win only when they can command an overlapping consensus of different sorts of moral views.

But now we need to distinguish the two kinds of overlapping consensus. What marks off the public-reason arguments that Rawls delineates as a focus for a political overlapping consensus from the hodge-podge of arguments that, I want to maintain, support reasonable moral views in general? Well, one feature marking the political off from the moral is that in politics, but not in ordinary moral life, we use violence or the threat of violence to get people to do what we think they ought to do. We may issue harsh correctives to a rude or unkind person, we may not invite her over or give her a job in our family firm, but we won't call in the police to haul her off to jail. We call in officers of the law to handle only limited kinds of immoral action: generally, where the act in question itself uses violence or the threat of violence, or otherwise impinges on another individual's freedom. The powers we set up to protect freedom can themselves squelch freedom, so we limit the cases in which coercion may be used, and set a high bar for the justification of its use even in those cases.

And intrinsic to establishing that limit, and setting that high bar, is a requirement that the arguments for taking political action carry an especially high level of conviction across the spectrum of moral views in a society. If I am a fervent act-utilitarian in my private life, I may strike some of my neighbors as too willing to tell a lie, and if I am a staunch Kantian, people who know me may consider me rigid and unfeeling. But in neither case am I likely to harm anyone very much. As soon as public policy is made on such bases, by contrast, many people may be coerced to do things of which they greatly disapprove: may be harmed at the core of their moral identity. So we need to be far more careful, when considering political measures, about ensuring that the arguments for our positions can appeal to people of different moral orientations than we do as individuals in private life. We need a very broad consensus, ideally one that every member of our body politic can see as reasonable, on the kind of justification that should be given for the use of force.

This point applies in a yet stronger way if we broaden our conception of politics from the libertarian one I have offered thus far to one in which we see ourselves as entitled on occasion to pursue joint projects and ensure that even those who don't like the project contribute to it. Once a government has been established, even if its original mandate was to provide security against violence, it is generally seen as an appropriate agent to further certain common goods that individuals are unable to achieve on their own: providing roads, building cultural institutions, alleviating or ending poverty. On most views of politics, if projects of this sort are approved by a majority of a state's citizens, it is legitimate to raise money for them by way of taxes that everyone must pay. Some libertarians dissent from this claim, insisting that coercion may be used only to prevent greater coercion. Their view is not unreasonable: promoting the common good is less obviously a way of enhancing our freedom than is preventing violence. Like most political theorists, I think that some such projects nevertheless do enhance our freedom, and that it is generally reasonable to see citizens as consenting to these projects when they are democratically approved.[10] But the line between appropriate and inappropriate positive tasks for government is a fine one, so the bar for assessing what counts as the consent of the citizenry must be higher than it is when governments simply prevent violence. It follows that arguments in support of projects that promote the common good must yet more obviously command broad respect among citizens than arguments in support of coercion that simply prevents coercion. It would be a clear violation of individual freedom, and a misuse of the power we give to our governments, if that power were employed to promote the views or interests of some parts of the citizenry as against the rest. No theory of government that appeals to consent can make out a case that we have agreed, or would be willing to agree, to coercive projects that merely gratify the desires of some individuals among us, let alone that get us to follow practices of theirs, or avow beliefs of theirs, to which we have moral or spiritual objections. Indeed, we consent to the coercive powers of our governments so that they can protect us against precisely such incursions on our liberties. Consequently, it is crucial that positive political projects be designed to serve the *common* good, a good that we can all recognize as such.[11]

It follows that we need to be far more careful in politics than in ordinary private life to make use of moral arguments to which we can expect all reasonable members of our body politic to agree. When interacting casually with a few friends, I need not worry about giving a religious reason for doing something together even if I know that my friends don't share my religious premises. They are free, after all, to argue with me, or refuse to go along with my proposal. (And if they agree, they may do so for their own, quite different reasons, or be willing to compromise in the expectation that I will do the same for them on other occasions.) But when we need to make decisions as a body politic, and license our government to enforce those decisions, we can neither presume that all our fellow citizens share our religious (or anti-religious) premises nor allow everyone among us either to opt out from the policy or to present their opposing views in great depth. So we need to work from an argument base that abstracts from our individual differences, to which we can expect people to agree even if we don't get to hear their views in detail. That rules out, as Rawls says it does, the comprehensive ethical beliefs that divide us. Even if the moral overlapping consensus on which we rely in ordinary private life may include religious arguments (or, again, anti-religious arguments), the political overlapping consensus that defines a liberal regime cannot do that.

There is thus a difference between the kind of secularity I attributed to the moral overlapping consensus in Part II of this book and the kind of secularity I am attributing now to the political overlapping consensus. In Part II, the point was that religious reasons are *unnecessary* to a satisfactory resolution of moral questions, and unhelpful unless understood in conjunction with other, secular moral views. We can't make sense of God as loving us, for instance, or of our need to love God, unless we have an independent grip on what it is to love, and why love is a good thing. So religion isn't necessary to morality, and can enhance our moral views only by being grafted onto modes of action and evaluation that are adequate for most purposes on their own. Religious views can enter our moral overlapping consensus, but they need not, and if they do, they must be interpreted in accordance with other elements of that consensus.

Here the point is different. There are reasons for keeping religious reasons *out* of the discussions licensed by our political overlapping consensus. If politics concerns those aspects of the moral life that preserve our freedom to lead our individual lives, then anything that smacks of my using the powers of government to favor my religious views has no place in political argument. They may reasonably be aired, in the private sphere, to *support* the political consensus—it may even be reasonable for a public figure to try to show how a religious view can support the political consensus (see below, § 15)—but it is crucial, if governments are to respect the equal freedom of the individuals over whom they rule, that public policies not depend on religious premises. The political overlapping consensus needs to exclude religious reasons; the moral overlapping consensus does not.[12]

We can also distinguish the two types of consensus in a different way. For Rawls, one does not need an overlapping consensus view of morality to enter his overlapping consensus on politics. Single-minded Kantians, Millians, Catholic natural law theorists and others with no patience for an eclectic view of morality are all supposed to be able to agree with Rawls on the principles of political argument. His defense of public reason would be considerably less interesting if it depended on a prior acceptance of an overlapping consensus view of morality. Rawls does in fact describe something like my moral overlapping consensus model of morality—he calls it "a pluralist view" composed of an unsystematic "family of non-political values" (PL 145)—but as just one of the many sorts of views that can accept his political overlapping consensus.

So the moral overlapping consensus and the political overlapping consensus have much in common, but they are not identical.

15. Before leaving the subject of religious justifications for secular politics, I'd like to note that I do not entirely share Rawls's understanding of the place of religious discourse in the political realm, at least as that doctrine is often read. I can't see anything wrong, for instance, with a religious person illustrating the moral basis of her political beliefs by allusion to what she regards as sacred scriptures, even if she is a public figure, as long as she also provides adequate secular grounds for these beliefs. To call for an anti-poverty program in the name of freedom or fraternity and then add, "Justice, justice shalt thou follow!" (Deuteronomy 16: 20) in no way diminishes the ability of one's message to speak to citizens of all faiths and no faith, any more than a quotation from Cicero or Shakespeare would do that. Nor is there anything wrong with a religious person's explaining, to members of her religious community or to the public at large, how the policies she recommends on other, properly moral grounds also fulfill what she takes to be God's revealed commands in the Torah or Quran or Gospels. What would be offensive in the public square, what would imply that one expects one's polity to favor one's own faith over that of others, would be to defend a policy for which one's grounds, in one's own opinion, are unlikely to be shared by people of other faiths or no faith: to defend a policy primarily, let alone solely, on grounds derived from a sacred text or other source of religious authority. Religious language and arguments can appropriately enter political discourse, but only so long as they illustrate or supplement secular arguments that would alone be adequate—only so long as they provide a translation schema of an otherwise secular position into terms that religious citizens can accept. If they come into political discourse in that way, they can expand the reach of the secular arguments: speak to, and display respect for, a wider array of one's fellow citizens' beliefs than one would achieve by secular arguments alone. (An honest attempt to do this might include quotations from many different faith traditions, rather than just from one's own tradition: interfaith politics are less threatening to the freedom and dignity of all citizens than single-faith politics. But even interfaith politics will be offensive if they promote laws that cannot be defended on secular grounds.)

Robert Audi has laid out something like this position, saying that all citizens need what he calls an adequate "secular rationale" and "secular motivation" for their political positions, even if some also have a religious rationale and motivation for them.[13] The position is not far from Rawls's. For one thing, Rawls believes that we should keep religious (and other comprehensive) grounds out of one's justifications for public policy only on matters of "'constitutional essentials' and . . . basic justice" (PL 214). For another, he places no such restriction on what he calls "the background culture," which includes many venues for political discussion. The limits of public reason, he says, "do not apply to our personal deliberations and reflections about political questions, or to the reasoning about them by members of associations such as churches and universities, all of which is a vital part of the background culture. Plainly, religious, philosophical, and moral considerations of many kinds may here properly play a role" (215). The norms of public reason should govern us only when we come to vote, or advocate positions as public office-holders or candidates for public office. And even here, Rawls allows political leaders, on occasions in which they represent groups that are suspected of not being sincerely committed to the values of the political consensus, "to present in the public forum how their comprehensive doctrines do indeed affirm those [political] values" (249). But Rawls presents this relaxation of the strictures of public reason a bit reluctantly, and seems to think a crisis of confidence in the depth of one's fellow citizens' commitment to public reason will arise rarely in a well-ordered and just society. I suspect that crises of this sort are a permanent feature of public life, even in well-ordered and just societies. The tension between the telic aspect of religions and the morality that they share with secular ethical systems continually raises the worry that the former might demand a suspension or abrogation of the latter. At the same time, deep features of religious commitment require believers to give the moral way of the world priority over such telic demands in their political relationships. But that just means that the need to show how religious views can support secular political values is a never-ending one, and needs to be addressed again and again.

We might add that a great deal of political discourse, even when restricted to the public reason that Rawls recommends, involves translating arguments from one set of terms to another. One shows how a certain policy, hitherto touted for enhancing our security or improving our economic efficiency, also protects individual liberties, or works against racism or poverty. Republicans borrow the language of compassion from Democrats, and Democrats borrow an emphasis on fiscal conservatism from Republicans. Part of this effort at translation can surely include ways of demonstrating, to religious citizens, that what might seem to be purely secular policies actually fit in with their comprehensive ethical views as well—and demonstrating to secular citizens how certain religious remarks may make secular sense. To say, "the freedom of speech really protects the image of God within us," on the one hand, or "the sanctity of marriage really amounts to a healthy environment for child-raising," on the other, are perfectly admissible moves within liberal discourse. Even if one dislikes the policies thus advocated, or disagrees with the particular translation between secular and religious language being offered, one has to acknowledge that such efforts at translation are perfectly compatible with—indeed, a tribute to—the importance of couching the grounds for political proposals in secular terms. What is essential is that there *be* a translation schema. It is inadmissible to say "this policy is what God wants so I don't care if there are secular reasons for it."

Rawls may have recognized the acceptability of such translations. In one of his last writings, a supplement to *Political Liberalism* called "The Idea of Public Reason Revisited," Rawls amended his earlier view of public reason to include what he calls "the proviso." We may, he says here, "introduce into political discussion at any time our comprehensive doctrine, religious or non-religious, provided that, in due course, we give properly public reasons to support the principles and policies our comprehensive doctrine is said to support" (PL 453). It seems to me that this amounts to an endorsement of what Audi calls the principle of secular rationale.

So I see little daylight between Rawls and Audi, and think both are right to say that religion can enter political discourse as long as it never leads us to actions that we could not justify to secular as well as religious citizens. Indeed, I would go further than Rawls does in this regard. Rawls, remember, restricts the need to rely on public reason to matters of constitutional essentials and basic justice. He implies that ideally we might try to settle all political questions in this way,[14] but does not insist on that. In this respect I think he did not extend his views far enough. Partly because it can be hard to distinguish between matters of basic justice and more ordinary political issues,[15] and partly because the admission of faith-based grounds in one area of policy provides an opening for its use in other areas, I think we should bring the norm of "public reason," or "secular rationale and motivation," to all public policy. But that does not prevent us from illustrating secular arguments with quotations from religious writings, or showing religious citizens how secular positions make sense in their terms.

16. The third prong of the relationship between religion and liberalism concerns the degree to which governments may help a religious group preserve or foster its communal structure. This takes us into more difficult territory. I think governments may do something of this sort, but there is an obvious danger that it will lead them to promote religious doctrines or practices, and we ruled that out when we considered the first prong of our trident. The issue here is a tricky one and I am not as satisfied with what others have said on it as I am with what Locke and Rawls and Audi have said about our first two prongs. I'll therefore spend more time on it than I have on the other two issues.

Governments in fact preserve or foster religious communities in many different ways. Iran and Saudi Arabia are out-and-out theocracies, committed in principle as well as practice to a thoroughgoing enforcement of Islamic law; Egypt, Pakistan, Malaysia, Burma, and many other countries promote a particular religion to a lesser degree; in Thailand, Greece, Britain, and most Scandinavian countries, an official religion gets expressed in symbolic ways (state holidays and ceremonies, the design of the flag, restrictions on who can be monarch, etc.); Israel, Turkey, and Sri Lanka are secular states that nonetheless foster a particular religious/cultural community (we'll see in a bit that it's hard to separate religion from culture); and India and most European and Latin American governments are officially committed to treating all religious groups equally, but in fact often favor one religion over its rivals. The ubiquity of these arrangements suggests both that a purely secular politics is considerably rarer than the dominant political theories in academia might lead one to imagine, and that there may be deeply-entrenched needs or forces impelling religious communities to seek political protection, and political entities to seek a religious coloring. Nonetheless, liberals are right to be worried about the attraction between religion and politics. Many of the arrangements states make to favor a particular religious community have appalling consequences for dissenters from that community, or members of minority religions. The oppression of non-religious Muslims in officially Muslim states and the discrimination against non-Jews in Israel are perhaps the most discussed of such cases, but the ethnic cleansing that produced modern Greece, Turkey, Pakistan, and India, the wars that Thailand, Russia, and Sri Lanka have undertaken against their Muslim and Hindu minorities, and the discrimination against Muslims in China are just as striking examples of the violence and oppression to which religious favoritism leads. For a liberal, moreover, even the relatively mild ways in which some citizens are favored over others when a state observes Christian holidays, but no non-Christian ones, or recognizes religiously-sanctioned conceptions of marriage, but not gay marriage, are offensive. Even these relatively mild forms of discrimination set up invidious hierarchies among citizens, and give the state's implicit approval to one non-rational conception of the good over its rivals.

So in the ideal liberal world, there would be no Jewish or Christian or Muslim or Buddhist states, no state favoritism of any kind for a particular religious community. That is not the same as saying that states may not help preserve or foster religious communities: as long as they do so without favoring any particular religion, and in a way that is open to equivalent secular groups. In that case, they may still be doing something that has adequate secular grounds. The key to showing that they are doing that is to establish that religious communities can serve a basic human need, or provide a condition for individual freedom, shared by religious and non-religious people alike. Then, if a state fosters them, that will be simply part of its general duty to help its citizens in general to express their freedom and/or achieve a basic level of well-being. In what follows I lay out an account of one kind of religious community—or religiously-*based* community, to be precise—that can reasonably be seen as contributing to the greater well-being and freedom of religious and secular citizens alike. I then sketch how liberal states might legitimately foster such communities.

17. Let's start by bringing together the various roles we have seen for community, in religious commitment:

1. Insofar as our ultimate telos must be a telos for humanity, not just for our individual selves (Part III, § 5), any vision of the highest good must be given to a community, not just to individuals. Only then can we see it as offering more than selfish satisfaction. We apprehend the significance of the tao or the joy of the eternal sabbath *together*, not just as individuals, and any path designed to bring us to, or back to, this vision ought to include practices that we undertake together, in which we can develop our ability to feel that our ultimate goal is and must be shareable with all other human beings.

2. Insofar as revelations come with a path, an entire way of life, they must speak to the many respects in which human lives are socially embedded. The practices they give us need to be such that we can integrate them with having a spouse, raising children, engaging in business, etc, and they will affect our lives most if we can pursue them together with our spouses, children, business partners, etc.

3. Insofar as revelations need interpretation, they need a community of interpreters. Interpretation is essentially a social activity. We check our readings of a text against the opinion of fellow readers, we criticize or endorse readings proposed by our fellow readers, and our readings build on those of earlier readers. This is especially the case when we read a text not just for pleasure, but as the basis of shared practices. And it is yet more the case when the text requires humility of its readers. Only by humbling ourselves to the interpretations of others can we develop the humility towards the divine, or otherwise super-natural, author of a sacred text.

4. Finally, insofar as revelations need to be integrated with a moral and scientific way of the world, insofar as they give us private *reasons* rather than constituting a form of irrationality (§§ 3–6 of this Part), we need constant correction by others to ensure that we do not mix up what they say with claims that properly belong to morality or science. A reasonable community—a community that interacts freely with humanity at large—helps each believer interpret his revelation in this way.

For all these reasons, the paths associated with revelations are communal ones. Religious practices normally include communal worship, communal festivities and communal times of mourning, rituals marking the entry of adults into the community and marriages and births within the community, perhaps also modes of communal study and moral action. Kant, describing his religion of reason, acknowledges that even a purely moral church will need rituals in which individuals avow their commitment to their community, although for him these rituals are merely symbols of individual intentions (RWB 192–193). On my view, religion is a telic more than a moral matter, and its rituals are not mere symbols of but means to the end it presents to us, or the fuller comprehension of that end. In worshipping together, we envision our highest good more clearly and participate in it for a moment.

As a result, adherents of revealed religions need a variety of communal institutions. Communal worship and celebration often require and in any case are most conveniently carried out in communal buildings dedicated to them (churches, synagogues, mosques). A communal way of life also requires institutions for educating the young, training adults so that they can extend it and adapt it, and raising the material resources to carry out all the group's activities. Revealed religion is thus necessarily institutionalized. The notion of a purely individual revealed religion makes no sense—even if it is true, as I think it is, that the relationship each of us has with the religious teachings we accept is first and foremost an individual one, and that we do and should feel called on to criticize our communities if we think they fail to live up to the visions they are supposed to preserve. The relation between our commitment to a revealed religion and our membership in its associated community is a dialectical one, in which it is incumbent on each believer both to defer to the guidance and expectations of others in the community and to be willing to stand up to his co-religionists when he thinks that is required by the good that they are pursuing together. The trick, in building healthy religious communities, is to create institutions that preserve the communal dimension of the religion while retaining individual freedom within that community.

18. Religious communities find themselves best able to pull off this trick, and (relatedly) to maintain a healthy relationship between their teachings and the moral and scientific views of their members, when they consist of people with a variety of attitudes toward their central religious claims, and interact regularly with people who hold secular, even anti-religious attitudes. A community where Orthodox Jews mingle frequently with Reform and Reconstructionist Jews, and where the various subgroups themselves contain people with different viewpoints, is far more likely to give rise to thoughtful interpretations of Judaism than is an entirely homogeneous community— far more likely, moreover, to foster attitudes of flexibility and tolerance among the members of the community, and between them and their non-Jewish neighbors. We learn from co-religionists with different views from ours to find riches in our sacred texts that we would not have found on our own, and they can help check the more implausible or self-serving interpretations we come up with. Here as elsewhere the reasonableness and honesty of our thought is improved if we discuss our beliefs with others. We can improve the reasonableness and honesty of our interpretations yet further if we engage in discussion with secular people. If the interpretation of a sacred text must first and foremost be a moral one, then it can be especially useful to receive moral advice and rebuke from people outside the circle of our religious authorities and fellow congregants: they are less likely to confuse moral demands with a pious acceptance of official doctrine. If morality belongs to the way of the world, moreover, we should expect to share that aspect of our lives with our non-religious neighbors, and to be able to learn from them as well as our co-religionists.

But the capacity of discussions with secular people to improve our religious understanding increases greatly if those secular people have some residual attachment to the same texts and practices that we love. A formerly religious Jew or Catholic, or a Jew or Catholic who found her religious traditions aesthetically appealing as a child, is much more likely to help a religious Jew or Catholic think through her sacred text and path than is someone with an entirely different heritage. A formerly religious member of one's own religious tradition, and a secular person raised in that tradition as a cultural matter, is far more likely to share a certain respect for one's imaginative commitments and the values arising therefrom—to share a sense that the vision inspiring these commitments is at least an appropriate one with which to *struggle*—than someone wholly ignorant of one's revealed text, or left cold by it. Secular Christians often find the notion of God becoming human very powerful, even if they do not believe it happened, or are moved by stories of innocent people sacrificing themselves for a cause. Secular Hindus can similarly find the notion of karma or reincarnation fascinating and morally useful, even if they don't really believe in it, and secular Jews often take inspiration from the notion that great prophets rebuke their own people in the name of social justice, or from the high value that the Jewish tradition places on intellectual pursuits. For most secular Christians, the Gospels or the letters of Paul will also tend to be *the* religious text one should wrestle with, insofar as one thinks about religion at all—the religious teaching to reject: which is to say, the best candidate for a religious teaching to accept, if one were not secular—while the Quran and hadith function in that way for most secular Muslims, and the Torah and Talmud for most Jews. Secular Jews tend to find nothing appealing about the texts and symbols sacred to Christians and Muslims, while secular Christians and Muslims tend to find it equally mystifying that anyone could be drawn to the Torah or Talmud.

Around each religious community there thus tends to grow up a community of once-religious people who share the same point of religious orientation. "If one is going to be religious at all," they think, "the religion that makes sense is this one." And these secular dissenters are in many ways the best source of an outside corrective to people who are committed to the revelation. They share the same tradition of value: people committed to a religion and people raised with the remnants of that religion have the same picture of what *sorts* of things might make human life worthwhile.

Let's call a social group that combines these religious and once-religious people, with a shared tradition about value, a "telic community." Their sharing a tradition is a matter of their discussing it together, taking the same stories and symbols and ideas as starting-points for debates and conversations. Otherwise, some go to the synagogue or mosque while others are drawn mostly to the art or literature of the tradition, or hold political views that are informed by it. In various ways, then, many of them not religious, the projects expressing the ultimate values of the people in such a community will be inflected by the same vision and receptive tradition. A Mexican town where Catholic feast days are observed in the public square; a Hindu town like Palani or Canchipuram in India, partly but not wholly centered around religious shrines; a relatively open Muslim city like Istanbul or Lahore—these are all examples of telic communities. They were once the norm everywhere, and continue to make up most urban centers outside of the secular metropolises of Europe and North America, and the tightly-controlled towns in theocracies like Iran and Saudi Arabia. They are places where orthodox and heterodox, intellectual and anti-intellectual, gay and straight inheritors of the same religiously-rooted tradition can meet to talk and argue without violence, intermingle casually throughout their daily activities, and join together to celebrate or mourn on shared holidays or special occasions. The ability of a divine teaching to be shaped by a way of the world, and a way of the world to be informed by a divine teaching, is greatest in places where there are communities of this sort. Such communities enable people with the same telic heritage to live out their commitments with greater comfort and greater flexibility than they would have in either a social world where they are a dispersed minority, anonymous amid a sea of people with very different faiths, or immersed in the like-minded, surrounded by neighbors and authority figures who monitor their every move for its orthodoxy. Of course, interacting with a multicultural society can do yet more to ensure that their telic vision is checked against generally human cognitive and moral standards, and of course they will want to spend some of their time with people who share exactly their own kind of faith. But the in-between level of community, composed of people with different attitudes towards the same religious heritage, provides for many of us, religious and secular alike, the world in which we most want to *dwell*: in which we can best strike a balance between our private and our public kinds of reasoning, and best develop our commitment, if any, to our divine teaching in light of the way of the world.

It is this sort of open telic community that even a fully liberal state can support. Political theorists widely recognize, today, that liberal states can legitimately help people protect their cultural commitments, but telic communities are paradigms of what we mean by "culture," when we give it ethical significance. Many cultures consist of the heirs to a religious tradition, of people whose parents or grandparents raised their children to see a particular religious text and set of practices as definitive of a good human life. This is recognizably one kind of culture, and there are reasons to think it more or less fits all cultures: all cultures seen by their members as needing public expression, at any rate. It follows that states have reason to promote or preserve telic communities to exactly the extent that they do to promote or preserve cultures. And I believe they do have reason to promote and preserve cultures, although not to identify themselves with a culture (that's the mistake made by nationalism). A number of political theorists have argued that human beings can fully realize their freedom only if they live in communities in which they can publicly discuss and express shared memories and symbols, and that this gives liberal states a legitimate reason to foster cultural groups.[16] The arguments for this claim entail that liberal states also have reason to nurture religiously-based communities, and make sure they have a public space in which to express themselves.

In the remainder of this chapter, I'll sketch the reasons for seeing all cultures as having a religious root, then back off to the weaker claim that religiously-based communities are at any rate one species of the genus "culture," and deserve whatever political rights that cultures in general might reasonably have.

19. G. A. Cohen writes:

Individual Jews, like me, can be irreligious, yet we are Jewish only by virtue of connection with a people defined . . . by religion. The areligious cultural periphery cannot become the core, or even *a* core, of something new, and when I meet third- and fourth-generation secular American Jews whom I teach at Oxford, I observe, with regret, that the sense of connection to the Jewish past is decaying and that the special sensibility is disappearing.[17]

Cohen adds that this is meant to be a claim about Jewish culture in particular, not a claim about all cultures, but I think the general claim is true. It is virtually impossible to distinguish between culture and religion in aboriginal societies—whether in the Americas, Africa, Asia, or Australia—and not much easier to see how one can be fully Italian or Polish or Spanish without being Catholic, Greek without being Greek Orthodox, or Turkish without being Muslim. In general, it is religious traditions that provide the core of cultures, the structure of belief and practice that can define an entire life. Non-religious forms of every culture are peripheral to it, and tend to dominate only when the culture is dying.

Before the late eighteenth century, the form of group identity characteristic of human beings was almost everywhere a religious rather than a political or racial or linguistic one. Catholics and Protestants, in countries containing both groups, identified with their churches rather than their states; Shi'ites and Sunnis in the Middle East, Buddhists, Taoists and Confucians in China, and Hindus, Muslims, and Sikhs in India likewise saw themselves as united with their co-religionists far more than with their neighbors of different faiths. Sometimes there were alliances across religious lines, but these were *alliances*, not a blending of two groups into a single community. Often there were wars between political entities that shared a religious orientation, but these were considered fratricidal, and were frequently justified by portraying the enemy as failing to live up to its proper religious obligations. If we are looking for cultures in the premodern world—looking for groups of people who were, or saw themselves as, united in practice, outlook, and history—we will largely come across religions.

Furthermore, the notion of culture in the modern world has its roots in a religious vision and program, was then used by secular thinkers and activists in an attempt to displace religions, and is now being displaced in turn, in many parts of the world, by a return to explicitly religious modes of bonding. The word "culture" in its anthropological sense (the sense in which there can be "culture*s*," in the plural), was coined by followers of J. G. von Herder,[18] for whom the notion was very much part of a liberal religious project. Herder saw all peoples with a distinct history, language, and literature as reflections of God: Leibnizean monads that mirror the one ultimate Source of our universe, and express Its combination of unity and variety. The Leibnizean God, for Herder, is revealed *in* the multiplicity of cultures. This view of cultures went with an endorsement of cultural pluralism, and a liberal view of religion (Herder was himself a Lutheran pastor) by which the practices and history of a group could be as good a place to find a commitment to God as its belief system.[19]

Herder is an important ancestor of both modern anthropology and modern nationalism, and although many of his followers did not begin as explicitly as he did from a religious worldview, they tended to an uncanny degree to carry on his Leibnizean language, and understood cultures as monads, each of which reflects God in a different way. Fichte wrote that "[o]nly when each people, left to itself, develops and forms itself in accordance with its own peculiar quality . . . does the manifestation of divinity appear in its true mirror."[20] Ernst Renan called the nation "a soul, a spiritual principle"; Mazzini declared that "God has divided the human race into masses . . . evidently distinct; each with a separate tone of thought, and a separate part to fulfill."[21] For those who promoted the political expression of cultures—nationalism—it was of paramount importance to show not just *that* people form themselves into distinct groups, but that this splintering into groups was a good thing, and that the groups themselves deserved respect, perhaps even the degree of respect we are normally inclined to show to individual human beings. How better to ground these claims than by suggesting that the formation of cultures is divinely willed, and that the cultures themselves have the sort of "soul"—the sort of unifying, mental principle—we normally attribute to individuals? A religious view of cultures was thus a promising way to argue for the importance of cultures.

At the same time, Herder's followers, like Herder himself, were looking for a mode of religious expression less tied to doctrine, and to ecclesiastical structures, than traditional Christian ones. Gustav Klemm, who coined the term "culture" in its modern sense, hoped that nations would supplant "priestly dominion."[22] Mazzini wanted to forge an Italian identity that would reduce the role of the Catholic church in Italy. And the founders of modern India hoped that a secular state would reform Hinduism, and provide a way of being Indian that Muslims, Jains, Sikhs, Christians, and Jews, as well as Hindus, could embrace. Indeed, many nationalist programs have been hostile to religion. Most early Zionist leaders wanted to forge a non-religious identity for Jews, and Palestinian leaders in the 1960s and 1970s—often Christians who sought unity with their Muslim counterparts—called for a secular Palestinian identity. Nevertheless, in the almost mystical importance all these figures placed on their cultural groups, they implicitly endorsed something akin to a religious view of those groups. And a large part of their constituency—Hindus in the ranks of the Indian nationalist movement; Jews and Muslims in the ranks of the Zionist and Palestinian national movements—tended very much to see their group identity as a religious matter.

In any case, the hopes of secular nationalists have been sharply set back in the past few decades. From the reappearance of religious fault lines in India, Yugoslavia, Thailand, Russia, and Iraq, through the hardening of religious fault lines in Lebanon, Israel, and Palestine, to the rise of fervent religiously-based political movements among Muslims in Asia and Africa, and Christians in the United States, there have been signs all over that the hope for a world in which religious commitments will wither away, and human beings form communities on other bases, was severely misplaced. The idea of an Arab identity that would transcend differences between Christians and Muslims, of an Indian identity that would make the differences among Sikhs, Hindus, and Muslims seem unimportant, even of a non-Christian way of being Danish or Dutch, now seems far more naïve than it did a few decades ago.

Turning now from these historical points to the concepts "culture" and "religion," we should start by recalling that both terms have been extremely difficult to define. What to include in any such definition, and how to weight its various components, has been a subject of fierce controversy. A half century ago, two prominent social theorists (with the help of a young graduate student named Clifford Geertz) compiled a list of over 200 different definitions of the word "culture."[23] By now, there are many more. There is little more agreement over the notion of "religion"—and the debates here parallel, and are in part informed by, those over the meaning of "culture."

These disagreements over how to define basic terms are tied to deep problems in the very idea of a scientific theory of culture or religion. For if cultures and religions are supposed to represent our fundamental worldviews, the ground of our beliefs on all other subjects, then they must ground what we regard as theory and science itself, and the place we give to such theorizing in our moral and political practices. But in that case we can hardly expect to define the terms "culture" and "religion" without already committing ourselves, implicitly, to just one among the many competing worldviews that human beings hold: there will be no neutral place from which to construct such a definition. Of course, one can get out of this conundrum by denying that our various particular beliefs bottom out in a communally-held worldview at all—by upholding a foundationalist view of the form to be found in Descartes or Hume, for instance, in which reason or individual experience grounds everything else we believe. But those for whom "religion," and especially "culture," is a basic theoretical term have tended to reject foundationalist philosophies.

In the face of this sort of intractable disagreement, we are unlikely to succeed in agreeing on a definition of "culture" and "religion" except for specific theoretical or ethical purposes. Accordingly, the idea that they represent our fundamental values and way of life, our ultimate point of orientation in ethical space, will tend to go with a program of respecting as many different cultures or religions as possible, and preserving or fostering them if possible. Those who see culture as of supreme value to us will not accidentally give it the sort of ethical importance that I have attributed to religion—and will pick out such normally religious features of group life as a shared reverence for certain texts (oral or written), and shared practices related to those texts, as the essential components of culture. Those who want to demote cultural identity, on the other hand, and press a vision of human beings as essentially similar across groups, will define "culture" in a way that emphasizes more trivial aspects of the groups thus picked out, and see them as less homogeneous and as having a less coherent view of the world. So we may expect to find, as we do find, that nationalists and people who value cultural pluralism will understand culture much as I have here understood religion, whereas anti-nationalists, whether of a liberal cosmopolitan or Marxist variety, will use notions of culture that are further removed from any religious association. The more one sees culture as establishing a horizon of value, a comprehensive view of how to live, the closer one brings it to revealed or historical religion. Precisely when understood as something everyone should respect, cultures are similar if not identical to revealed religions.

20. For the purposes of the view of politics I am developing here, I can make do with a considerably weaker thesis: that there is at least a religiously-based species of the genus "culture," which deserves respect to the same degree that other species of this genus do. We can defend this thesis by way of the features of culture to which liberal communitarians and nationalists appeal.

The liberal communitarian and liberal nationalist positions that have been defended in recent years all start from the premise that human beings are inevitably shaped by the communities in which they grow up, and make their major decisions in life by reference to these communities. It is supposed to follow from this that we cannot respect individual freedom without allowing people to preserve and celebrate their communities. So liberals, for whom respect for individual freedom is definitive of decent politics, should also respect cultures. Will Kymlicka puts the point nicely: "Liberals should be concerned with the fate of cultural structures, not because they have some moral status of their own, but because it's only through having a rich and secure cultural structure that people can become aware, in a vivid way, of the options available to them, and intelligibly examine their value" (LCC 165–166). A culture, he says, serves "as a context of choice." For him, that is, cultures are not sets of fixed norms and practices handed down to us, but structures that help us make choices. Hence liberals can and should give moral importance to cultures. In order to respect individuals as choosing beings, we need to honor the conditions that make it possible for them to choose, and being raised in a cultural community is one of those conditions.

Now on the strong thesis about culture and religion that I explored in the previous section, the communities that Kymlicka is defending just *are* religiously-based. Thus baldly put, however, the claim seems vulnerable to obvious counter-examples. Anglicans and English Catholics, it might be said, are today much more united in their Englishness than separated by their religion. Christian and Muslim Arabs partake of an Arab identity that unites them with one another and distinguishes them from other sorts of Christians and Muslims. And the many different religious groups that meet in India's cosmopolitan centers, or in Sofia or Penang, share a cultural community that transcends their religious differences. Each of these apparent counter-examples can be questioned, with evidence to the effect both that religious differences divide the would-be cultural groups, and that their supposedly secular bonds remain inflected by a religious identity (English identity, even among English Catholics, by Anglicanism; Arab culture, even among Christian Arabs, by Islam; Indian culture, even among

Indian Muslims, by Hinduism). But let's suppose the counter-examples withstand this challenge, and that the communities in which many people are raised and develop their ethical identities today can be distinguished from any religious tradition. Even in that case, it is easy to show that the communities in which *other* people are raised, and develop their ethical identities, *are* rooted in particular religious traditions. So liberal communitarians or nationalists should support political efforts on behalf of religiously-based communities along with all other cultures.

This point needs to be made because some of the most prominent liberal communitarians and nationalists in recent years have suggested that liberal states may respect *only* communities based on language and history, not communities based on religion. Kymlicka maintains that it is "language and history" that makes our options vivid for us, and gives us a sense of their significance.[24] He also claims that French-Canadian identity—an example of great importance to him—shed its ties to Catholicism in the 1960s while remaining a culture in the morally significant sense (LCC 167). Clearly, he wants to maintain the significance of culture without tying it to religion; the liberal view of cultures that he advocates, as a context for choice rather than something that fixes choices, depends on this separation. Identifying cultures with language and history fits this view nicely. Language and history seem to offer an ethically neutral way of identifying groups. It seems easy for a state to favor a linguistic community that shares a history without favoring any comprehensive view about how to live.

But this puts a lot of pressure on the claim that language and history profoundly shape our choices, and that claim doesn't stand up to pressure very well. Language alone, certainly, seems severely to underdetermine a way of life. Britain and the US share a language, but certainly do not share a way of life, to any plausible degree of approximation. Nor does the fact that French is spoken in both France and Morocco unite the French and the Moroccans into a cultural whole. We can better approximate cultures by adding history to language, but that may be because "history" is vague, and we can tailor the history we consider relevant to just that history (often one that also tracks a religion) that matters to people's norms and ideals.

Kymlicka's defense for his claims about human nature is in any case remarkably weak. He cites a study purporting to show that language is a "marker of societal goals" (LCC 175), a carrier of values, without so much as raising the question of whether an issue of this sort can really be investigated empirically (what empirical evidence would show that languages carry values, rather than just being ways of communicating about whatever values we happen to have?). He also mentions history, without specifying what sort of history, as a marker of culture wherever a bare identification with language might seem implausible. And he doesn't so much as address the fact that French-Canadian culture, for all that it may have become less *devout* in recent years, remains tied tightly to the Roman Catholic community in Canada and is regarded with some suspicion by, for instance, the Jews of Montreal.

Now the great merit of Kymlicka's work is that he has tried to find a type of culture that can be fostered by states without infringing on individual rights (either of the members of those cultures or of other citizens). It goes with this project that he needs to walk the delicate line between upholding a thick and plausible view of cultures, but one on which their anti-individualist, choice-restricting features come to the fore, and upholding a liberally acceptable but implausibly thin view of cultures. He is right, I think, to insist that there is a significant form of culture lying between these extremes, but he errs a bit in the thin direction. It is hard to see how anyone can simultaneously uphold the importance of our communal identities and pick out the communities that have such importance primarily by language. Language when construed as a medium for communication is after all quite fungible—occasions in which a thought can be properly expressed in just one language are rare—and it would be something of a shame, but hardly a terrible tragedy, if all people came one day to communicate in a single language. It is only when a language is seen as holy, or the folk sayings and literature in that language are seen as tied to a comprehensive, usually religious, way of life, that people will make strenuous efforts to preserve it. That Hebrew and Arabic and Sanskrit are seen this way is obvious, but passionate Greek and German and Russian and English nationalists have long had a similar, often explicitly religious way of viewing their languages, and the languages of aboriginal groups all over the world are generally seen as divinely given, and the only appropriate medium for the group's religious rituals. At the very least, language, when valued highly, tends to be a proxy for texts or practices that a community regards as sacred.

Nevertheless, let us once again concede that Kymlicka and other liberal communitarians/nationalists are right about the importance of communities bound together primarily by language. My point is just that liberal states can and should respect communities held together by a shared religious heritage to the same degree that they respect linguistic communities. If language helps each of us "become aware, in a vivid way, of the options available to [us]," and "intelligently [to] examine their value" (LCC 165), then that is certainly true as well of religious heritage, whether or not one accepts the heritage as religious. And—because we are speaking of a heritage that may or may not be accepted *as* religious, rather than of religion *per se*—it is no less true that such communities thereby provide a context of choice, rather than specific prescriptions, to the individuals that live in them. Learning about one's ancestors' religious beliefs and practices, and discussing those beliefs and practices with people who share one's heritage—again: whether or not one decides to *follow* that ancestral path—can be and often is the primary context in which one comes to an identity as an individual, and decides how to lead one's life. So any argument that communities should be fostered because they help people make rich and meaningful choices will apply to religiously-based communities among others. Both religious and non-religious people have plausible liberal grounds on which to request political support for the survival of religiously-based communities. These grounds do not depend on the truth or decency of any religion. They are secular, like the appropriate grounds for other political measures, and they are grounds for the fostering of religiously-*based*, not strictly *religious*, communities.

21. What, now, do religiously-based communities need from the state? Well, the main thing they need is public space of some kind, in both a literal and a symbolic sense. Literally, communities cannot survive *as* communities unless significant numbers of their adherents live near one another, see one another on a regular basis (informally, at the grocery store; formally, at the church or mosque, or at talks or meetings at the local community center), and maintain communal institutions. For this to happen, members of the community will need to predominate in, minimally, villages or sections of a city, and it is not unreasonable to suppose that, to assure political protection for these minimal communities over the long term, they will need to predominate in rather larger regions than that, combining urban and rural populations and controlling some natural resources.

In addition to these material conditions, a community bound together by conversations about a vision of the good will need a symbolic public space, or some share of the public space that already exists where they live. This is partly a psychological matter. As many theorists have noted, it is difficult for individuals to maintain their self-respect, let alone a sense of confidence in what they are doing, if what they take to be their specific identity has no representation in the public realm around them: if the way of living associated with being gay, say, or Arab or Jewish or Native American, is a matter publicly treated with hostility or derision or even just indifference. Public attitudes are educative, and individuals who move in a public realm that attacks or dismisses what they take to be important come to feel as if they should do so as well, and suppress or change the identity that has hitherto mattered to them.[25]

There are also practical reasons for cultures to want a symbolic public space. To keep their traditions alive, again even for the purpose of discussion, communities need shared festival and mourning days and days of remembrance or study. They also usually want to place physical symbols of various kinds in public spaces, where they can occasion reflection and conversation. And they want their central stories and practices to be taught in the schools, and used as reference points in public speeches.

Now for many religiously-based groups, all this seems to happen naturally. There are many places where Christians of the same denomination, or Sunni or Shi'ite Muslims, make up the overwhelming majority of the population, and the public holidays, symbolic architecture, school curricula, and texture of political speech is inflected by these religious traditions. Anyone whose life is oriented in some way by Catholicism— including people whose lives are oriented by a critical view of Catholicism—can feel at home in Chile and Italy and Ireland and Poland. Lutherans can still recognize Germany and Denmark and Sweden as "their" countries. Buddhists dominate the public life of Thailand, Sri Lanka, Bhutan, Cambodia, and Burma. And the various states of India tailor their public holiday schedules, and public art and speech, to reflect the religious groups that predominate in them. In many of these cases, the public expression of a religious tradition goes far beyond what I have been advocating. Muslim nations often enforce religious law, penalizing people for acts that are not immoral on secular grounds; divorce and abortion law in Chile, Italy, and Ireland until very recently reflected Catholic doctrine more than secular morality; and Buddhist Thailand and Sri Lanka repress their Muslim and Hindu minorities. But even in places where the state as a whole is secular and liberal, local public life often provides a communal forum for a religiously-based community to express itself and debate its future.

This is not so for smaller, more dispersed groups, or for religious minorities. Zoroastrians and Bahais and followers of native religions in Australia or the Americas generally have no public realm to call their own, and certainly predominate in no state. (Lack of a public realm seems to be leading the Zoroastrians to extinction.) Non-Muslims in Muslim countries and non-Christians in Europe and the US often feel stifled, even where they are not oppressed, for lack of a public realm in which they can express and discuss their traditions. A case for liberal states to preserve or foster religiously-based communities needs to be concerned above all with *these* groups, the small, dispersed groups that cannot maintain a public realm on their own, and the minorities that feel stifled by the fact that the public realm around them expresses a religiously-based culture they do not share.

The claim that religiously-based communities make on public resources is thus strongest when these communities are small or dispersed or oppressed, when they do not otherwise have a public arena to call their own. This is especially so given that the fact that large, concentrated religiously-based groups are able to control public arenas is not really something "natural," but the product of a long history of conquest, expulsion, massacre, forced conversion, and official discrimination. Europe and the Americas did not become Christian, and central Asia and northern Africa did not become Muslim, by quiet efforts at convincing individuals that Christianity and Islam were better than their prior religions, and even the spread of Buddhism in Asia, while more peaceful, had a great deal to do with the political and socio-economic dominance of Buddhist elites, and the symbolic significance this gave to Buddhism in the eyes of the poor. Nor have grand cathedrals or central squares dominated by churches or mosques been built by private individuals. Public funds have been poured into such structures for centuries, and into city-planning that gave prominence to one religion over others. Nor again is it the choices of private individuals that have led to educational curricula in which the history of one religious group gets a lot of attention while others are ignored, or to the public enshrinement of the Christian festival calendar in Europe and the Americas, and the Muslim and Hindu calendars in the Arab world and India.

So to declare, in the twenty-first century, that we should allow public spaces to be dominated by whatever religiously-based group happens to make up the majority in a particular area, and not make any efforts to unsettle those majorities, or provide separate public spaces for excluded minorities, would be to endorse the long history of violence and injustice by which certain groups have come to their positions of public dominance, and to dismiss claims for similar rights by their victims. Liberal politics, concerned as it is to show equal respect to all human beings, cannot very well accept such an unjust status quo. Rather, it must either seek to undo *all* religiously-based domination over public spaces—to strip public spaces of all religiously-based group coloring—or make sure that the victories of majority groups are balanced as much as possible by an effort to establish political rights for the minorities over which they have triumphed. And the latter policy is more realistic than the former. It also better reflects the communal nature of human beings, and the communal features of their attempt to realize telic visions. Liberalisms concerned to make sure that all citizens can express their most dearly-held freedoms have good reason to allow states to promote and preserve telic communities, especially those telic communities that are disadvantaged in the competition for resources with their larger and better-established rivals.

It is on the basis of an argument like this one that liberals acknowledge the claim of cultures on the resources of the state—it is on the basis of this sort of argument, especially, that the case has been made for the group rights of indigenous peoples in various places[26]—and it is on the basis of this argument, therefore, that religiously-based communities have such a claim. On the other hand, religiously-based communities, like other cultural communities, can be oppressive to dissenters and outsiders. This provides a liberal basis for resisting their political claims. We have then a sort of standoff between two liberal claims, one resisting public expression for any cultural group, and the other accepting the public dominance of some cultural groups and compensating for it by establishing equivalent public arenas for less powerful such groups. I propose that the best solution to this standoff can be found by separating public expression as much as possible from the functions of a *state*, and limiting the arena for such expression instead to very small units. A telic community can be successfully realized, and for liberal reasons would best be realized, on a very local level—in villages or small towns—while the public realm in which crime and large-scale policy is defined, the realm of a state proper, is best stripped as much as possible of cultural coloring.

I can illustrate what I mean with an example from my own experience. I lived for several years in Williamstown, Massachusetts. Like many New England towns, this was and remains a strongly Protestant public space. Physically dominated by a Congregationalist church, rising high in white clapboard glory from the center of the town, it sponsored a yearly "Winter Fest" that was transparently a Christmas Fest, and the townspeople identified one another by which church they went to (disapproving, often, of Catholics, let alone Jews) until at least the 1970s. At first I found myself irritated by the ways in which I felt a less than equal citizen in this town, but I had to concede that the Protestant coloring of the public space had a lot to do with its beauty, and the sense of community that it fostered, and after a while I realized that I wouldn't object to its Protestant features at all if there were little villages equally dominated by Jews, Muslims, or Hindus right down the road. Indeed, if there were little communities all over the world as Jewish as Williamstown is Christian, I would imagine that many fewer Jews would see the need for a Jewish state. The almost universal support that the state of Israel has enjoyed among Jews since the 1940s and 1950s is intimately bound up with the destruction of Jewish communities, at that time, in most Christian and Muslim countries.[27]

Similarly, if all religiously-based communities could express themselves publicly in small arenas of this sort, there would be no need for states that are Buddhist or Muslim or Christian. A wholly neutral public realm in the center of large areas, combined with small public arenas with strong cultural coloring, would be the best way to navigate between the liberal case for and the liberal case against expressing telic communities in the public realm.[28]

It is important that the culturally-colored spaces be small. We may appeal to a famous aspect of Lockean political theory here: the "enough and as good" proviso he places on the claiming of private property in the state of nature. Locke thinks it obvious that individuals can claim hitherto unowned resources with which they have "mixed their labour" as long as they leave enough and as good over for others: "For he that leaves as much as another can make use of, does as good as take nothing at all" (ST V: 33). It is only with this proviso that Locke's account of property is plausible. Had he simply insisted that unclaimed goods with which a person mixes his labor must belong to that person, it would be easy to object that a rule of this sort gives unfair advantage to those lucky enough to find good natural resources. Once we add in the "enough and as good" proviso, these objections are answered. The fact that I happen to be able to claim this piece of the natural world does not limit your rights if there are just as good pieces out there for you to claim. Similarly, the fact that one cultural community claims a stretch of land for its public arena does not limit the rights of other cultural communities, or of individuals who would prefer to live in multicultural zones, as long as there are enough and as good regions for the latter to dwell in as well. Cultural communities must therefore be small.

In addition, even in small communities, the expression of cultural identity, whether religiously-based or otherwise, cannot be allowed to conflict with basic individual rights. Some argue for a regime in which small, illiberal communities could exist within a liberal state—imposing religious laws of various kinds, or promoting patriarchal or classist values.[29] At a minimum, to be compatible with liberalism such communities would have to grant their dissenting individuals full rights of exit, and the education and access to information that allows them to know about alternative ways of living. But I am doubtful that liberalism should license such exceptions to its norms, and they are in any case not part of the ideal for which it strives. What can be part of that ideal are small communities that express their cultural identity in purely symbolic and educational forms: in their holidays and public sculpture and architecture, in the literature and history they emphasize in their schools, in the events and discussions in their public forums. None of these activities need impose on what dissenters and outsiders do in the privacy of their homes. Nor do they involve coercing people into supposedly moral standards for which there is no secular reason, limiting anyone's speech, or limiting the opportunities of dissenters and non-members, in the state as a whole, for political or economic advancement. A liberalism that recognized the legitimacy of such communities could therefore accommodate the importance of culture without compromising individual rights.

The rationale behind this idea would also justify establishing public arenas for non-cultural groups that want to form a telic community. Communists, gays and lesbians, and all sorts of other people who feel they share a telic view of some sort may feel they can properly express and develop that view only if they live in an area mostly populated by like-minded others, and have public institutions in which to celebrate and discuss it and pass it down to their children. As long as they pick a small enough area for their public realm, and protect the individual rights of everyone under their jurisdiction, the argument I have offered on behalf of cultural communities will apply to them as well. And it is in the interest of all such communities that any government support they receive go out to religious and non-religious, cultural and non-cultural groups without discrimination—that it be based on features of the proposed community's *structure* (size, provision of exit rights, etc.) rather than its goal. No group wants government agents to determine whether they are "really" pursuing a telic vision or not, nor should liberal governments be keen to scrutinize their citizens' personal commitments in that way. So every telic community should want its public arena, if supported by the state, to be supported without direct attention to the telic vision it hopes to express: just as the US government is permitted to support religious institutions only if it does so in a way open to equivalent secular groups.

Of course, even if small telic communities flourished throughout a liberal state, members of any given group might prefer to live in a multicultural metropolis. There will always be some people who are more comfortable surrounded by people like themselves and others who prefer the anonymity of living among relative strangers, or who like the variety of a cultural melting pot. There are also some ethical advantages, on the account of community I have offered, to living in a multicultural environment: different telic communities can learn from one another's practices and beliefs, and provide each other with an outside view on themselves. Intense, intimate discussion of a particular telic tradition occurs best in a community made up mostly of people who were raised in that tradition, and certain kinds of institutions—academies for the study of the tradition, for instance, or for its artistic expression—are likely to thrive only there. But broader, more open discussions of science and morality are more likely to occur in a multicultural society, and institutions in which adherents to the tradition can learn from and gain respect for adherents to other traditions are likely to exist only there. Both kinds of discussion, and both kinds of community, contribute to the health of religious traditions, and an ideally liberal world would contain public spaces for both. A religious tradition is healthiest where its adherents can move fluidly between a "home" and a "diasporic" existence, and a society allows most fully for the freedom of its members where it allows them a choice between these different ways of living.[30]

So much for the ideals of liberalism. In the world we actually inhabit, many states brazenly flout individual rights in the name of cultural expression. Even if we set aside the authoritarian regimes that repress minority religious and ethnic groups, or purport to enact religious law, we have laws in generally liberal Turkey against "insulting Turkishness" by mentioning the Armenian genocide, official churches in Greece, Denmark, England, and many other places, government policies and official speeches promoting the flourishing of the Chinese majority, as against substantial Malay and Tamil minorities, in Singapore, and laws of "return," favoring the immigration of one particular religious or cultural group over others, in Bulgaria, Finland, Germany, and Israel, among other places. Israel is the bad conscience of this international regime. It has been artificially created, with the sanction of the United Nations, to realize goals that many other nations aim at as well, but that are also increasingly disapproved of and that the international world does not like to admit it promotes. Liberals should be uncomfortable with it, along with all states that favor one culture or religion over others, should hold up an ideal of complete cultural and religious neutrality on the state level. In the ideal world, there would be no Jewish state—but also no Christian or Buddhist or Muslim states, nor Arab or Malay or German or French states. But in our actual world, which is very far from that condition, it makes sense for liberals to pick their battles, and work primarily on rolling back the more egregious violations of individual rights to which nationalism has given rise. And in that actual world, where Jewish communities have been destroyed in almost every Christian and Muslim nation, where Jews can fully celebrate and wrestle with their own tradition only in the villages and towns of Israel, there is at least as much reason for a Jewish state as for any other religiously or culturally inflected state.[31] There is also a place for generally liberal Muslim and Buddhist states, like Turkey and Thailand, and for the hegemony that Christianity maintains in European countries. All these arrangements are far from ideal, and liberals should eventually work towards dismantling them, but they are not grossly unjust and may be necessary until better, more local public arenas for the expression of cultural identity can take their place.

22. To sum up this long chapter, on my view there is nothing essentially political about religious commitment, and nothing essentially religious about the politics of religious people.

Taking these points in order: Religious revelation is given in the first instance to individuals—albeit, perhaps, to individuals who see themselves as in community of some sort—rather than to a political entity. Revelation comes in after the public affairs that require shared reasons—truth-seeking and morality—are taken care of, and is accepted, as an answer to our individual variations on the question, "what makes life worth living?," by each of us in accordance with features of our individual imaginations, not on the basis of wholly sharable reasons. Moreover, the point of revelation is to inspire reflective love and that is not a condition that can be intelligibly attributed to social groups. We achieve it, if we do, each on our own. Revelation does need to be received by a tradition, and it thereby founds communities, but these are communities not well expressed in coercive laws; they are not polities. There is nothing political about the acceptance of revelation, nothing that makes it difficult for a revealed religion to be expressed at all if it is not expressed politically. Indeed, the fact that revelation is addressed primarily to individuals, and meant to inspire love in them, means that the attempt to express its teachings by way of coercive laws is likely to backfire, to distort the commitment of the faithful and squelch faith in people who might otherwise have come to it. Any social body formed out of people who share a faith is properly a wholly *voluntary* community, into and out of which individuals can move freely in accordance with their judgment of how well it lives up to the vision they think it should pursue. Religious people should indeed hope that their religious communities can be insulated from politics. By taking care of the issues that require coercion, secular governments can shelter religious communities from having to engage in that form of human interaction—can provide a space in which religious communities can afford to do entirely without coercion. The idea that religious commitment ought "to shape [our] existence as a whole, including... [our]... political existence," as Nicholas Wolterstorff suggests, does not fit my understanding of religion at all.[32]

If we look in the other direction, the political views of religious people are not normally, and should not be, marked by anything quintessentially religious. Religious people should resist attempts to suppress their beliefs by coercion, but they have grounds for this resistance that secular people can share. Religious people should not try to impose their comprehensive views of life by force, or enlist political powers in the service of teaching those views, but neither should secular people attempt to have their comprehensive views promoted by the state. Religious people should appeal to moral considerations in the defense of laws and policies, but so should secular people, and both need to take care in political discussion to use moral arguments that they think everyone in their society, whether religious or secular, can accept. And religious people may, and in some circumstances should, ask for aid from the states in which they live to set up or maintain small communities where their symbols and way of life can be publicly expressed—but their grounds for this request, too, are ones that secular people can share, and that can be used by secular groups as well. In each of these ways, then, the religious person need not venture outside the secular realm to ground his or her political positions, and can make alliances with citizens of different religions and no religion. There is no distinctive religious politics, on my view of religion, although members of a religious community who join together in a political cause may legitimately discuss what they are doing with one another in religious terms, or worship together in the course of carrying out their political work. There is nothing amiss if people go to a peace rally from a synagogue or mosque and then do their afternoon prayers together, but their doing this does not transform their properly political activity—their efforts at persuading their fellow citizens on matters that involve coercion—into something religious. Nor should it. Politics represents the way of the world par excellence. To bring a divine teaching into the political realm distorts both it and one's divine teaching.

Epilogue

Epilogue

1. What can religious people gain from living in a secular world? Well, for one thing, the fact that we have a community around us that is not dominated by our co-religionists allows us, if we ever decide that our religion is wrong or confused, to change it or become secular ourselves. The existence of a realm to which we don't need to bring our religious commitments allows us to examine those commitments freely, and alter them if we think necessary. The secular world provides a breathing space from religion, a place in which we can suspend our religious passions, and assess them in a cooler fashion. This breathing space leads some of us to stop being religious, or become religious in a more liberal way, or convert from one religion to another. Others just consider doing these things, and then return to the religious commitment they had with renewed fervor. But the mere fact that the opportunity is available, the mere fact that we can, if we want, drop our religious commitments or alter them, reassures us that the commitments we have, when we do not drop or change them, are freely chosen. The secular world thus guarantees the freedom of our religious beliefs. Which makes them more truly religious, less a product of fear or ignorance or habit.[1]

At the same time, the secular realm makes clearer to us, insofar as we do hold on to our religious commitments, what exactly those commitments amount to. It helps us interpret those commitments morally, relate them to, but also distinguish them from the science of our day, see how they differ from—add to, enhance, in any case contrast with—what secular people believe and do, and what we ourselves do in our secular capacities. There are a number of cognitive advantages for the religious project of living among secular people. Just as it is helpful to get the advice of an uninvolved outsider when trying to figure out what to do in a charged personal situation, so it can be helpful to get factual information, even on matters relevant to one's religious beliefs, from people who are not caught up in one's religious passions. I *want* to learn about physics and biology and history from people who are not committed to a religion (at least in their work on those subjects). I trust them to be more objective than I or my co-religionists would be about such matters. On all subjects other than the ultimate one of what our knowledge and practice is for, those of us who are religious seek information in ways that we share with all other human beings, and that are best pursued by abstracting from religious commitments.

In short, the secular world helps us make sure that our love for our revealed visions is truly a reflective one. In more religious terms we might say that God wants us to come to Him only through a community of humanity that He created as cognitive siblings: as creatures who need to work together, independently of their views about Him, to seek knowledge. Perhaps the religious significance of this humanistic cognitive process is that it will help us, eventually, bring everyone else to God. Perhaps it reminds us to recognize that the super-natural God we worship created the natural world. Or perhaps it leads us to recognize precisely that God is radically *different* from the natural world. I am not sure. But I am quite sure that God meant me to find most of my knowledge through the way of the world, not through His direct teaching—that the divine teaching He has given me, indeed, gains clarity and power by standing in and against the light of what I know in secular ways. Divine teaching shines forth most brilliantly, and most illuminates our lives, with a secular way of the world as background.

I am also convinced that God meant me to determine my relations to my fellow human beings primarily through the way of the world. We should determine how to treat others in accordance with what those others ask of us, not by turning to a source beyond us all. Nor could we expect to build a community of trust and friendship in which we can bring each other, freely, to the love of God unless we first had decent relationships with one another that were not predicated on a love for God. We cannot, indeed, maintain our *religious* communities without such pre-religious virtues. How else could we resolve disputes in our communities, over doctrine or practice, fairly and peacefully? Again, we can recast these points in a religious light. God, Who created us all and loves and respects us all, has good reason to want us to love and respect each other directly, not just as a consequence of our relations to Him, and to bring each other to Him out of that love and respect, not out of fear or shame or blind obedience. But to do that, we need to build a moral way of the world together that does not depend on belief in God. This is, moreover, the natural way to build human morality, and a way that can readily be informed by, and constructed alongside, the cognitive project that also proceeds with a suspension of religious belief. And a naturalistic, humanistic morality of this sort can again help bring out the significance of the non-naturalistic vision that breaks upon us in revelation. Divine teaching, again, is illuminated, and illuminates us, by contrast with a secular way of the world.

Revelation does not replace secularized reason. It grafts itself, rather, onto a way of thinking and acting that we develop independently, and that we need in order to receive it. Abraham is often cited as an example of someone who suspends all naturalistic moral and pragmatic concerns, when he offers up his beloved son to a super-natural God. But that same Abraham is figured in the Bible, earlier, as challenging God Himself to live up to an independent standard of justice: "Shall not the Judge of all the earth do justly?" (Genesis 18: 25). That same Abraham can also be read as breaking off a conversation with God in order to take care of what he thinks are three purely human guests.[2] These aspects of Abraham provide, I submit, a better model for religious commitment than the aspect by which he unquestioningly offers up his son. We first build a just and decent community with our fellow human beings, independently of revelation and religious belief. Only then does God appear to us.

That doesn't mean that the way of the world is adequate in itself. But what is missing in the way of the world, what it cannot accomplish, comes out clearly only when we give it free rein to demonstrate what it can accomplish. And only then does the true gift of divine teaching come out as well. God's Word is uncanny, sublime, "Other" to our ordinary human expectations, and it appears in its sublimity only when we allow it to set itself against our ordinary way of being.

2. Let's now return to some of the rabbinic passages about the way of the world (*derekh eretz*) with which we opened this book. The phrase from *Pirkei Avot* that I have adapted for my title—"Beautiful is Torah together with *derekh eretz*"—fits perfectly with the idea that divine teaching gains its significance by being simultaneously grafted onto and contrasted with the way of the world. But another passage we discussed may be even more useful: "If there is no Torah, there is no *derekh eretz*; if there is no *derekh eretz*, there is no Torah."[3] Here *derekh eretz* and Torah are interdependent, rather than the first being a pre-condition for the second. The medieval rabbi Jonah Gerondi understands this passage to teach that one needs to develop the virtues of *derekh eretz* before studying Torah—*derekh eretz*, for him, builds the community in which Torah study can take place—but he also says that "One who doesn't know Torah is incomplete as regards the virtues of *derekh eretz*."[4] The way of the world is not even morally self-sufficient, for him: one needs Torah to reach full virtue. Gerondi cites some of the Torah's admonitions to help the poor and be righteous in business dealings (Deuteronomy 15: 8, 14; Leviticus 19:36) to buttress this point. The implication is that secular moral theories (Aristotle's, for instance, with which Gerondi would have been familiar) do not mandate this level of compassion and righteousness.

Of course I resist this view of secular morality, and of revelation as serving a primarily moral function. Yet I agree that there is something missing in *derekh eretz* itself if one has no Torah (construed broadly, of course, to mean any divine teaching). A way of the world without a divine teaching will I believe be unable to provide a convincing picture of why our lives are worth living, of what our activities, including our cognitive and moral activities, add up to. Perhaps, without any such view, the way of the world itself may eventually decay. People may find it hard to commit themselves to science and virtue, however good the secular arguments for those pursuits are, if they see everything they do as in the end pointless. But in any case there will be something missing in a *derekh eretz* that points to no transcendent goal, no goal that can bestow absolute value on its activities. The way of the world will then be "all dressed up with nowhere to go." It will tell us *to* dress up, and how, without telling us why we should bother. *Derekh eretz* is intrinsically a referential system, something that points to a goal beyond itself. Deprive it of that goal, and there is something absurd about it. By providing such a goal, Torah reframes *derekh eretz*, puts it in a new light. *Derekh eretz* gives us means for achieving many different ends, but it does not give us an end. Torah gives us such an end, but without clearly specifying the appropriate means. The two must be brought together if we are to have a full understanding of how to live.

3. The combination of Torah with *derekh eretz* gives us a model for a thoughtful and decent religious life. We might call someone who exemplifies that model a worldly saint. I could pick Hillel or Thomas Aquinas or Ashraf Ma-ji or the current Dalai Lama as examples of the worldly saint, but it is simplest to come back to Abraham. For Abraham is *both* the other-worldly devotee who is willing to offer up all to God *and* the worldly fellow who travels to a strange land, builds a great clan, interacts with others politically and economically on terms independent of his religious commitments, and—except for that one shocking moment where he offers up his son—takes care of other human beings as well as, even before, his duties to God. Indeed, Kierkegaard, who focuses on the one shocking moment, also gives us an excellent portrait of the more complex believer that Abraham generally represents:

Here [is the knight of faith]. . . . The moment I set eyes on him I instantly push him from me, I myself leap backwards, I clasp my hands and say half aloud, "Good Lord, is this the man? Is it really he? Why, he looks like a tax-collector!" However, it is the man after all. I draw closer to him, watching his least movements to see whether there might not be visible a little heterogeneous fractional telegraphic message from the infinite, a glance, a look, a gesture, a note of sadness, a smile, which betrayed the infinite in its heterogeneity with the finite. No! I examine his figure from tip to toe to see if there might not be a cranny through which the infinite was peeping. No! He is solid through and through. His tread? It is vigorous, belonging entirely to finiteness; no smartly dressed townsman who walks out to Fresberg on a Sunday afternoon treads the ground more firmly, he belongs entirely to the world, no Philistine more so. One can discover nothing of that aloof and superior nature whereby one recognizes the knight of the infinite [resignation].[5] He takes delight in everything, and whenever one sees him taking part in a particular pleasure, he does it with the persistence which is the mark of the earthly man whose soul is absorbed in such things. . . . Toward evening he walks home, his gait is as indefatigable as that of the postman. On his way he reflects that his wife has surely a special little warm dish prepared for him, e.g., a calf's head roasted, garnished with vegetables. If he were to meet a man like-minded, he could continue as far as East Gate to discourse with him about that dish, with a passion befitting a hotel chef. As it happens, he hasn't four pence to his name, and yet he fully and firmly believes that his wife has that dainty dish for him. If she had it, it would then be an invidious sight for superior people and an inspiring one for the plain man to see him eat; for his appetite is greater than Esau's. His wife hasn't it—strangely enough, it is quite the same to him. On the way he comes past a building site and runs across another man. They talk together for a moment. In the twinkling of an eye he erects a new building, he has at his disposition all the powers necessary for it. The stranger leaves him with the thought that he certainly was a capitalist, while my admired knight thinks, "Yes, if the money were needed, I dare say I could get it." . . . He lives as carefree as a ne'er-do-well, and yet he buys up the acceptable time at the dearest price, for he does not do the least thing except by virtue of the absurd. And yet . . . this man has made and every instant is making the movements of infinity. With infinite resignation he has drained the cup of life's profound sadness, he knows the bliss of the infinite, he senses the pain of renouncing everything, the dearest things he possesses in the world, and yet finiteness tastes to him just as good as to one who never knew anything higher . . . [T]he whole earthly form he exhibits is a new creation by virtue of the absurd. He resigned everything infinitely, and then he grasped everything again by virtue of the absurd. He constantly makes the movements of infinity, but he does this with such correctness and assurance that he gets the finite out of it.[6]

On this picture, a worldly saint is a person who realizes how crazy it is, how utterly improbable, for there to be a God at the root of this petty, arbitrary, and thoroughly imperfect world, in which we live from disappointment to disappointment most of the time, yet who believes in that God anyway and, full of delight, sees His presence in every bit of the petty world that frustrates the rest of us. But to do this is to hold together, at all points in one's life, the ordinary human way of the world—with its cold, skeptical methods of inquiry, its dependence on the wheel of biological needs that keep us working without stop to stay alive, and its hard moral demand that we respect all our not-so-pleasant fellow human inquirers and need-satisfiers—with the hope or feeling that we are standing in the presence of an ideally good, transforming, loving Being, who can, or even currently does, give all this drudgery a joyous significance. There is something absurd about this sort of faith, but it shows most fully in a person who embraces our world like the sanest of folk at the same time that he stands beyond it: in the Abraham who builds a clan and fights wars even while worshipping a transcendent God, who talks to God but suspends the conversation to get bread and meat for some travelers. For religious as well as secular reasons, we need to render unto Caesar what is Caesar's and unto God what is God's. We need to give the way of the world its rightful respect, and not disdain its independence of religion, while still recognizing that it stands in need of revelation, and gains its true significance by becoming a tabernacle in which that divine teaching can find a home. The knight of faith enjoys his meat and his new buildings, but it is part of his faith to understand that faith itself does not make meat or buildings; the human community, religious and secular alike, does that.

Pace Kierkegaard himself, this means that a worldly saint cannot give up his moral commitments in the way he can give up his own hopes. His moral commitments belong to the human community, not to him: they are not his to give up. So, no, he cannot kill his beloved son, although he can be ready, in infinite resignation and infinite joy, to live with the loss of his son if God requires that. Kierkegaard's Abraham is thus not worldly enough—the worldly saint as I understand him recognizes that his moral commitments stand outside of and before his faith, belong to the world and not to him—but with that reservation, he is an admirably precise representation of how divine teaching and the way of the world fit together. The worldly saint seems first of all and most of the time indistinguishable from a wholly secular person. But his union with this finite world of ours comes about, as the secular person's does not, only because he constantly makes the movements of infinity.

Appendix I: Proofs of God

Today it is widely and I think rightly held that there are no good arguments for the existence of God—that at most we can show, with Kant, that there *might* be a God. Most philosophers would concede that the notion of God is not incoherent and that there are no conclusive arguments, on scientific or any other grounds, to show that God does *not* exist. Yet even this may be too much. It is possible to construct a plausible argument against the coherence of the notion of God. I'll sketch that argument here. Although in the end I am not convinced of it, I think it is plausible enough to make us skeptical of the project of coming up with proofs of God.

How sure are we that we can make sense of the notions of omniscience, omnipotence, and perfect goodness, especially if they are supposed to be connected to one another? To begin with omniscience: Does it entail that one knows all events in the universe, even before they happen, such that we need to presuppose that future events already exist in some form, or are strictly entailed by past and present events? Does it entail that one know the full extension of the square root of 2, which is in principle uncountable? Does it entail that one know how things look from the perspective of a more limited being, that one be able to enter into the finitistic knowledge, and biased or incorrect views, of beings like ourselves?

More deeply, knowledge is representational—as we usually understand it, and it is unclear whether we could understand anything else as knowledge—and it is hard to see what sense it makes to attribute representations to God. We human beings have knowledge if our judgments are true and we have the proper justification for them. It is a mistake to account for these representations in too mentalistic a way, or to describe knowledge too much as if there is a space of representation separate from the world it represents, but on practically any account of knowledge there is a gap between knowers and what they know, and we say of a person that he "knows" something only when he has done the appropriate work to cross that gap. Every knower is potentially someone who *fails* to know.

But this is a picture of knowledge suited to finite beings, who do *not* know everything and need a means to sort out false beliefs from true ones. How can such a picture be attributed to a Being who, by hypothesis, not only in fact knows everything, but *necessarily* knows everything—who cannot fail to know? God cannot possibly have false beliefs. Does He then have a use for the very notion of belief? For the notion of justification or good reason? Do *we* have a use for any of these notions in application to God? Surely it makes no sense to think of God as seeking justification for what He thinks is true and just happening always to find the right justifications. It makes little more sense to think of God as necessarily finding the right justifications for His beliefs—any being for whom that was true could not be described as "seeking" justification. But without the notion of seeking and finding justification, of having reasons for what one believes, and of believing as opposed to knowing, it is hard to see how we could give application to the notion of knowledge.

A traditional theological response to this sort of worry is to suggest that God knows in a radically different way from the way we know. He immediately intuits things, many say, where immediate intuition is supposed to get away from the need for justification. But it is unclear how this helps. If immediate intuition is supposed to be modeled, as it often is, on the way we human beings "see" the truth of fundamental logical principles, and understand their justification, then it is still a form of representational knowledge, with all the problems noted above when attributed to God. If immediate intuition is supposed to be entirely different from any cognitive state we ourselves enjoy—entirely different, *inter alia*, from the kinds of cognition that we normally call "intuition"—then it is a black box, which doesn't help explicate God's knowledge. And if, as is sometimes said, immediate intuition is identical with creating the objects of one's knowledge, so that God "knows" by bringing into being everything He knows, then it is really not a form of knowledge at all, and we should talk of God creating the world *rather than* knowing it.

A similar problem arises when we consider God's power. We normally attribute power to a thing or source of energy in relation to others. A is more powerful than B if A can crush or lift B. Perhaps we'll call A "powerful" full stop if its power is greater than a suitable range of objects. But what do we mean when we call something "all-powerful"? If a thing were *all*-powerful, then it would have to be the source both of the power in A that crushes B and of the power in B that enables it to hold out for however long it does against A. If God is the source of all power, then God is the source of the resistance to penetration in a piece of tissue paper as well as the source of the easy penetration many objects can effect in that tissue paper. But then God will be both weak *and* strong, the source of both the weakness of the tissue paper and the strength of the pen that pokes through it. Indeed, God will be *all*-weak as well as all-strong, the source of all weakness in the universe as well as of all strength. Power is something a thing has when it exists among other things with power. If there were an omnipotent thing, the distinction between having power and lacking it would break down.

Difficulties of this sort arise once again with God's goodness. Is God "good" for *all* the beings in the universe, or just for the human beings, or perhaps the sentient beings? If the former, then the distinctions between "good" and "bad" will break down. Everything that happens will be good, *ex hypothesi*—but sometimes it will be good *for* the snakes or bacteria that kill us off, rather than for one of us. Even if our universe is destroyed, that destruction will be good for the forces that destroy it. If God's goodness is limited to a concern for human or sentient beings, on the other hand, then it would seem to be a limited goodness, not the perfect goodness that allows us to see Him as providing or fulfilling the telos of everything in the universe.

A famous version of this last problem comes to the fore when we try to combine God's perfect goodness with His omniscience and omnipotence. In a world that had no evil, it is hard to imagine how anyone would come to use the word "good": things are called "good" by contrast with other things that are "bad." But how could an all-good Being be the source of a universe that contains bad things? Is God the source of the bad as well as the good? Then He would seem not to be all good. Does He, then, not *know* that the bad things are bad—or that certain things or events will lead to a bad result? Then He can hardly be all-knowing. Is He, in that case, not the source of the bad things? Do they arise on their own strength, or by the force of another, evil power? Then God is not omnipotent.

At the root of all these problems is the fact that we normally use our words to pick out limited facts about limited objects within our universe. We call an object "red" as opposed to "green" or "magenta"; we call it "powerful" as opposed to "weak," "good" as opposed to "bad." Our words operate within a field of contrasts. It is not clear, then, how we could use any word to describe an entity that is not supposed to be one object among others in the universe, but to underlie the entire universe. We can't simply take the notion of "power" or "knowledge" or "goodness" and extend it infinitely. These notions get their application by having limits, by *not* extending beyond all limits. We may literally not know what it means for anything to be all-powerful, all-knowing, or all-good.[1]

None of this amounts to a proof that the idea of God is incoherent. We should be suspicious, here and everywhere, of philosophers who purport to show that some long-standing element of our lexicon is nonsense. We are not working here in the realm of logic or mathematics, where well-defined rules establish the meaning of every term and it might be shown, for instance, that the phrase "rational square root of 2" is meaningless. Our ordinary terms are flexible and there is no *a priori* reason why a definition of "knowledge" or "power" or "goodness" might not someday be proposed on which "all-knowing," "all-powerful," or "all-good" makes clear sense. Alternatively, perhaps "all-knowing," "all-powerful," etc. can be shown to point to some deep truth about God, albeit not the ones they seem literally to express.

I doubt, indeed, that we can give a clear criterion for the inconceivable or unintelligible. To say what is inconceivable, one would need first to map out the entire territory of the conceivable. But how can we do that without knowing that territory from the outside? How can we tell where the border lies between the conceivable and the inconceivable without, as it were, looking in on the conceivable from the realm of the inconceivable? Of course, the idea of perching in the realm of the inconceivable doesn't make much sense, but that just reinforces the suspicion that the idea of a clear limit to the conceivable doesn't make much sense either. The very idea of the inconceivable, we might say, is inconceivable, or not clearly conceivable.[2]

Which leaves us with no good way of showing either that the idea of God is inconceivable or that it is conceivable. I think part of what a religious person takes on faith is that the idea of God is, or can someday be made, conceivable ("on that day the Lord shall be one and His Name one"). A religious person has faith both that the idea of God makes sense, and that there is a God to fit that idea. Nothing in the way of proof is available for either proposition, but nothing in the way of disproof for these propositions is available either. Reason makes space for belief in God, neither requiring it nor ruling it out. And faith goes to work precisely where there are spaces in reason, precisely where reason allows a certain belief, but cannot demand it.

Appendix II: Maimonides on the Evidence for Revelation

My understanding of what it is to stand at Sinai can be aligned quite nicely with Maimonides' reading of that event. Maimonides tells us in his *Guide* that not everyone at Sinai experienced the same event. "All saw the great fire, and heard the fearful thunderings," he says, "but only those of them who were duly qualified were prophetically inspired, each one according to his capacities."[1] So the fire and the sound—the apparently miraculous goings on—are not the important part of the event, and if one attended merely to them, or to anything else that can be picked up by the senses, one would miss the fact that God was speaking: one would not be "prophetically inspired." Maimonides is quite clear that prophecy, knowledge of what God has to say, depends on a *humiliation* of one's sensory faculties, on suspending one's senses and subduing the desires that come with sensation.[2] Prophecy is not possible until one has developed one's capacity for abstract understanding of God to a high degree, recognized the kind of commands God gives,[3] and broken the hold of one's natural tendency to trust the senses over the understanding. But then it is precisely a turning *away* from empirical evidence, and the tendencies in human nature that lead us to put our trust in such evidence, that allows us to "see" or "hear" God.

So what can Maimonides mean by saying, in the *Mishneh Torah*, that the Israelites believed in Moses, not because of miracles or signs, but because they "were themselves witnesses to the truth of [Moses's] prophecy"? What does he mean by saying that at Sinai the Israelites and Moses were "like two persons who saw an event together," that "each of them [was] a witness that the other [was] telling the truth"?[4] The comparison to witnessing, to testimony in a court, suggests that we are dealing with an empirical event here, which the Israelites directly experienced along with Moses.

Well, first we should note that Maimonides speaks repeatedly here of witnessing to, or "seeing and hearing," Moses's *prophecy*, or even the *truth* of that prophecy,[5] not to the events on Sinai, or the fact that Moses, or God, literally spoke this prophecy. It's not at all obvious how one could perceptually witness—see or hear—the truth of a prophecy; this is already a hint that the "seeing and hearing" are to be taken metaphorically.

Second, the way we grasped what happened at Sinai is supposed to remove all doubts we might have about its truth, unlike the way we might grasp a sign or miracle. Maimonides stresses that the Sinaitic event is supposed to remove all "lurking doubts" and "musings and speculation" about whether God really appeared to us or not.[6] But nothing we literally saw or heard could possibly remove such doubts, as Maimonides would have been the first to insist. If we may doubt whether the division of the Red Sea was produced by witchcraft, as Maimonides suggests earlier in this chapter,[7] then we may certainly doubt whether the voice and atmospheric show at Sinai were not also products of witchcraft.

And third, the chapter in the *Mishneh Torah* slips quietly between talking of what the Israelites *at Sinai* might have experienced and what *all* Jews—including the ones reading Maimonides's book—firmly believe. What are the grounds of our faith in Moses, Maimonides asks? "The standing at Sinai which *our eyes saw* and not [those of] a stranger, which *our ears heard* and not those of another." Later he tells us that we would know that a would-be prophet who claimed to refute Moses was wrong since "with our eyes and our ears we heard the divine Voice." But we didn't. We weren't there—at least if "being there" means literally being present at Sinai.[8] No reader of Maimonides is going to say, "Ah yes, I remember experiencing Sinai myself, so of course I am more certain of that than of any other prophecy."

So it seems clear that we can make best sense of the *Mishneh Torah* chapter, both in itself and in its relation to the *Guide*, if we understand what we "saw and heard" at Sinai as a metaphor for grasping the *content* of the Torah. Ultimately, for Maimonides, what shows that the Torah is divine is the fact that its law lives up to the criteria he lays out for what a divine law is supposed to accomplish.[9] So it is the content of the Torah, not its mode of transmission, in which its divinity lies. But that is something he believes we can know with certainty—as if we were seeing or hearing it—and that we can know today just as readily as anyone literally standing at Sinai could have known it. That is also something that, if we attain the highest moral and intellectual level, we can know *together with* Moses ("...like two persons who saw an event together...""). Standing at Sinai is standing in the space of the highest prophecy, attaining the highest knowledge of what God wants of us, and it is the ability to grasp the goodness of the Torah from that standpoint that all Jews are supposed to share.

Of course, Maimonides would not have approved of my view that it is our imaginations, more than our reason, with which we grasp the Torah's content. For him, imagination was a weak and misleading cognitive tool, in need of correction by reason.[10] But that, I think, is the source of all that is most disappointing, and threatening to traditional Judaism, in Maimonides' views: of the excessive rationalism by which he reduces Jewish law to Aristotelian ethics, to a degree that makes it hard to understand why a properly philosophical person need maintain the law at all. Maimonides is an ancestor of what I have called the "too-knowing adult's view" of revelation, the Kantian or Cohenian view that virtually eliminates it. I think we can embrace the understanding he offers us of what it is to stand at Sinai without accepting the excessively rationalistic way he reads the content of that experience.

Appendix III: Kant on Art and Natural Beauty

I argued in *A Third Concept of Liberty* that Kant's "play of the faculties" must be interpreted in an "inter-conceptual" rather than a "pre-conceptual" way. I now think that some aspects of Kant's aesthetic theory favor the pre-conceptual interpretation instead. The inter-conceptual reading is too talky, too directed to conversation, to get the phenomenology of our response to natural beauty right, however well it may work for our experience of art. We are not inspired by an hour's snorkeling in a great coral reef, or a view of a rich jungle, to engage in endless interpretation of what we have seen. We do not try out new concepts on the shapes in the reef or jungle in a never-ending attempt to make sense of what it is "saying." Rather, if we appreciate its beauty we fall into mute wonder, delighting in the rich array of sensory material without being inclined to talk about it at all. But natural beauty is Kant's official paradigm of all beauty, so if silent wonder is appropriate there, it may be appropriate to beauty in general.

I can incorporate something of the pre-conceptual approach to beauty into my own view. Not only in front of the jungle landscape, but also in front of a Pollock or Rothko, surely a part of the right reaction is to stand in silent admiration. The person who talks incessantly at operas and in museums is not a person who really loves art. But the kind of silence we have in front of the Pollock or Rothko is a silence that comes from, and eventually bursts forth into, a torrent of words. We are stumped, awed, by the mystery of the work; it tantalizes us by hovering just beyond what we think we understand; it holds out a promise that we will be able to grasp it, to make good sense of it, while ever deferring that promise. So if we are wise, we will hold our tongue to let it sink in before we try to get some sort of grip on it. The mystery in it is addressed to our understanding; it engages our understandings, even while eluding them. That is why this is a play of the facul*ties*, a body of richly sensuous material that we do not merely sink into, but try to reflect upon, that calls upon our capacity for reflection and not just our joy in certain kinds of sensation. It makes sense that a pre-conceptual moment is part of this reflection. If there is an inter-conceptual space, part of occupying that space will involve not knowing, at moments, what concepts to employ, feeling temporarily freed from the hold of any concept. But the pre-conceptual moment will be part of a larger inter-conceptual play, not the mark, on its own, of an experience of artistic beauty. Silent wonder, on its own, may be the appropriate response only to natural beauty.

I am, however, inclined to reject the aspects of Kant's view that favor natural beauty over the beauty in art. As it happens, there are independent reasons to question these aspects of Kant. First, the basic intuition driving Kant's account—that beauty is both subjective and something on which we demand agreement from others—seems not to hold in the case of natural beauty. Kant presents that intuition, toward the beginning of CJ (§ 7), by imagining two conversations. In one the first speaker says, "Canary wine is pleasant," and the second reminds him that he ought to say, "... is pleasant *to me*," while in the other, the first speaker says "This object [Kant's examples are a house, a coat, a concert, and a poem] is beautiful," and Kant says that it would be ridiculous in that case to end the sentence "... to me": the word "beautiful" demands the agreement of all other speakers. We should note that all Kant's examples here are of "art" of some kind, not of natural scenes. And in fact, in ordinary speech at least, exclamations of aesthetic delight about natural scenes fit the pattern of the first, not the second conversation. If I say that I love the jungles of Sumatra (an example Kant discusses in the remark following CJ § 22), you will feel free to say that you prefer desert landscapes, and I am unlikely to accuse you of bad taste. If I describe a certain flower as beautiful—another of Kant's own examples of natural beauty—I will not be shocked or think you lack taste if you disagree. It is only in the presence of certain *artworks*—Sophocles and Shakespeare, Bach and Beethoven—that I am likely to suppose you lacking in some way if you fail to share my taste.

Moreover, the general argument Kant gives for the normativity of beauty supports the priority of artistic over natural beauty. However one understands the play of the faculties, it is clear that it is supposed to be useful or even necessary for cognition. It is not a cognitive state, but it must foster cognition, else we could not see it as satisfying a need that any being with cognitive faculties like ours must have. But the impression that some kinds of natural scenes foster cognition better than others has got to be an illusion. Any natural object presents plenty of material onto which our cognitive faculties can fasten themselves, and no natural object is in itself more suited for cognition than any other. The shapes before us in a jungle, however variegated they may be, will not elude our concepts more than the shapes we see in a desert. We come to jungle and desert alike with a multitude of concepts intact, and know, even if the scene is very new to us, that we can in principle classify and explain practically everything we see. While we may have an immediate feeling, before some natural scenes, of a manifold that precedes and transcends all our skills at ordering, we know on reflection that this feeling is misleading. But the demand that others join us in hailing a scene as particularly conducive to the play of the faculties can surely not rest on a misleading feeling.

Kant wanted a unified account of beauty, explaining what we admire both in art and in the natural world and connecting these two kinds of beauty with one another. Unified accounts make sense in many philosophical areas, but here I think attention to our language about beauty militates against a unified account. What leads us to call a man or woman beautiful is quite different from what leads us to call a coral reef or desert landscape beautiful, and that is different again from what leads us to call a Rothko or Pollock beautiful. Perhaps there are further distinctions to be drawn—I suspect that what we find beautiful in art alone is a composite of many different factors—but in any case it seems an error to bring natural beauty and the beauty of art together. There are different kinds of beauty, and some either lack the normative element that Kant stresses or have it to a much lesser degree than others.

Notes

Introduction

1. BT Gittin 70a; Avot 6:6. Also, the first chapter of the minor tractate *Derekh Eretz* is devoted entirely to permissible and impermissible marriages and sexual relations.
2. They contain some cognitive advice also (see the beginning of *Derekh Eretz Zuta* ii)—which is of interest to me since I want to include cognitive norms in what I call "the way of the world."
3. Rabbi Samson Raphael Hirsch, the nineteenth-century founder of Orthodox Judaism, sums up the general meaning of the phrase as follows: "*Derekh eretz* includes all the situations arising from and dependent upon the circumstance that the earth [*eretz*] is the place where the individual must fulfill his destiny and dwell together with others . . . Accordingly [it] . . . is used primarily to refer to ways of earning a living, to the social order that prevails on earth, as well as to the mores and considerations of courtesy and propriety arising from social living and also to things pertinent to good breeding and general education." Hirsch, *The Hirsch Siddur* (Jerusalem: Feldheim Publishers, 1978) p. 434.
4. BT Eruvin 100b, Soncino translation, slightly altered. I've been helped, in translation and in argument, by Aharon Lichtenstein, "Does Jewish Tradition Recognize An Ethic Independent of Halakha?," in Marvin Fox (ed.), *Modern Jewish Ethics* (Ohio State University Press, 1975)—the best treatment I have seen of intimations of a natural law tradition in rabbinic thought.
5. See Christine Korsgaard, *Sources of Normativity* (SN), pp. 92–94.
6. Leviticus Rabbah 9:3.
7. There is a long-standing rabbinic view, which probably has some Greek sources, according to which the table is a place for discussion of Torah (see, for instance, Avot 3: 4): for fostering the Jewish idea of a proper community, which centers around intellectual and spiritual discussion. This is properly "human" eating, as opposed to the way animals eat. So R. Jannai means it literally when he calls his guest a "dog." And when he regrets the remark, he regrets it in part because he has realized that there are ways of achieving the wisdom that is part of humanity—and thereby earning a place at the table—independently of the Torah.
8. See Part IV, Chapter 6.
9. This reading makes better sense of Rabbi Elazar ben Azariah's remark, as a whole, which goes on to say, "If there is no wisdom, there is no reverence; if there is no reverence, there is no wisdom. If there is no knowledge, there is no discernment; if there is no discernment, there is no knowledge. If there is no bread, there is no Torah; if there is no Torah, there is no bread" (Avot 3: 17 [3: 22, in some editions]). Rabbi Elazar can't possibly mean to identify the two terms in each of these pairs fully with one another, or make them necessary conditions for one another. People notoriously have "bread"—make a living—without Torah, and study Torah without making much of a living. The relevant teaching must be something about how the fullest realization of each term requires the other term.
10. This is the effect of Article VI of the Constitution, which says that no religious oath may be required for public office—a much-debated clause in the state constitutional conventions, precisely because people saw it as an opening for Jews, Muslims, and "pagans" to occupy official positions. See the debates between Henry Abbott and James Iredell, and Rev. David

Caldwell and Samuel Spenser, in the North Carolina convention (Bernard Bailyn (ed.), *Debates on the Constitution* [New York: Library of America, 1993], Part II, 902–909) and Isaac Kramnick and R. Laurence Moore, *The Godless Constitution* (New York: Norton, 1997) for a nice account of this.

11. Adam Smith, *An Inquiry into the Nature and Causes of the Wealth of Nations*, ed. R. H. Campbell, A. S. Skinner, W. B. Todd (Oxford: Oxford University Press, 1976), p. 793.

12. Peter Gay, *The Enlightenment: A Modern Interpretation*, vol. I: "The Rise of Modern Paganism," (New York: Alfred A. Knopf, 1967). See pp. 8–9 for an explanation of the title phrase. But see also Fania Oz-Salzberger, "New Approaches towards a History of the Enlightenment," *Tel Aviver Jahrbuch für Deutsche Geschichte*, 2000: in place of Gay's monolithic antireligious Enlightenment, she says, contemporary intellectual historians have given us "a moderate Presbyterian Enlightenment in Scotland, a Latitudinarian Enlightenment in England, a radical Enlightenment of Spinozists and freemasons, a conservative Enlightenment which was largely Socinian [and] a Jesuit Enlightenment," among others (p. 175).

13. TMS 165–70. See my discussion of these passages in *On Adam Smith's Wealth of Nations* (Princeton: Princeton University Press, 2004), pp. 70–72.

14. See also TMS VI. ii. 3. At no point does he say that any of these claims are *true*, just that they are morally useful, and not clearly untrue.

15. "The magistrate should . . . provide proper instruction for all, especially for young minds, about the existence, goodness, and providence of God, and all the social duties of life, and the motives to them." Frances Hutcheson, *System of Moral Philosophy* (London: A. Millar, 1755), III.ix.1, volume II, p. 310.

16. Lessing, "On the Proof of the Spirit and of Power," in H. Chadwick (ed.), *Lessing's Theological Writings* (Stanford: Stanford University Press, 1956), p. 53.

17. The significance of this fact is a main theme of Part IV, Chapters 4 and 6, and Part V, Chapter 3.

18. I am skeptical of the very idea that proofs of God can be made compelling to reasonable unbelievers: see Appendix I.

19. On these terms in Kant, see Rachel Zuckert, "Kant on Practical Fanaticism," in B. Lipscomb (ed.), *Kant and the Supersensible* (Berlin: de Gruyter, forthcoming).

20. The excellent 19th-century editor of a standard edition of Locke's *Essay Concerning Human Understanding* mentions 14 different discussions of the topic, from the late 17th century onwards, in pamphlets, major works on epistemology by Henry More and Leibniz, and satires by Butler and Swift (Alexander Campbell Fraser, p. 432, note 1).

21. *Wealth of Nations*, 788–9, 793.

22. All quotations from "Of Superstition and Enthusiasm," in David Hume, *Selected Essays*, ed. S. Copley and A. Elgar (Oxford: Oxford University Press, 1993), pp. 38–43.

23. On this, see again Zuckert, "Kant on Practical Fanaticism."

24. WO? 8:141–142.

25. Although perhaps some experiential phenomena can subsequently be interpreted, in light of this notion, as marks of God's presence or will: "[N]o-one can *first* be convinced of the existence of a highest being through any intuition; rational faith must come first, and then certain appearances or disclosures could at most provide the occasion for investigating whether we are warranted in taking what speaks or present itself to us to be a Deity, and thus serve to confirm that faith . . . ." (ibid, 143).

26. ibid, 145.

27. ibid, 146. Kant discusses enthusiasm in several other places as well. See CJ 272–276, where he uses two different terms for it (*Enthusiasmus* and *Schwärmerei*), giving them slightly different meanings, and where he defines the latter (his usual term for it) as "a delusion of

being able to *see* something beyond all bounds of sensibility." The subject seems to have concerned him, in one form or another, for a very long time: the CJ passage makes use of distinctions that hearken all the way back to his 1766 *Dreams of a Spirit-Seer*.

28. An in-depth review of this issue can be found in Avi Sagi and Daniel Statman, *Religion and Morality* (Amsterdam: Rodopi, 1995).

29. Most modern Jewish philosophers either begin from the premises of Husserlian phenomenology, which I do not share, or argue for something much closer to "natural" or "personal" religion—to a religion one can arrive at through reason or personal experience, and that is at best *exemplified* by elements of the Bible or Talmud—than to the traditionalist view, bound to the authority of the Torah, that I want to defend.

30. This is perhaps a good point to note that the word "Judeo-Christian" largely represents Christian biases and distorts Judaism. There is no such religion as "Judeo-Christianity," except perhaps among some early Christian churches in Palestine. Since that time, attempting to hold on to Jewish practices has been regarded by Christians a sign that one has inadequate faith in Christ. And Jews regard accepting Jesus as the son of God as idolatry, and a renunciation of Judaism. The notion of a "Judeo-Christian" tradition makes as much sense as the notion of a "Christo-Islamic" or "Islamo-Bahai" or "Hindu-Buddhist" tradition. In each case, there is some historical basis for the assimilating phrase, but it suppresses the distinctive features of both religions, and mangles at least one of them. In each case, moreover, the assimilating phrase makes more sense from the perspective of one of the two religions than of the other—normally of the second one, which regards itself as containing whatever is good in the first (the exception is "Hindu-Buddhism" which might be acceptable to Hindus, who can accept the Buddha as another avatar of Krishna, but never to a Buddhist).

In any case, there is no good basis for the assimilation of Judaism to Christianity. Jews and Christians do not share ritual practices, differ vehemently over theology, agree no more on moral matters than either group does with members of other religions, are largely formed by different texts (the New Testament, in the Christian case, and the Talmud, in the Jewish one), and only dubiously have in common even the "Old Testament": never called that by Jews, read in Hebrew by Jews and in just about every language *except* Hebrew by Christians, attended to selectively with quite different selections being important to Jews than to Christians, and interpreted, of course, in radically opposing ways (with Christians indeed claiming, for much of their history, that Jews have a "veil" over their eyes such that they can't read their own text properly). The ubiquity of the phrase "Judeo-Christian" today is itself a reflection of the dominance of Christianity in Western discussions of religion.

31. Keith E. Yandell, *Philosophy of Religion: A Contemporary Introduction* (London: Routledge, 1999), pp. 17 and 23, footnotes omitted. I am grateful to Andrew Koppelman for directing my attention to this text.

32. I want to thank Brian Hosmer for urging me to make clear how my view applies to religions with oral rather than written traditions.

33. I am especially grateful to James Harris for pressing me on this point.

34. Charles Taylor provides a rich account of the rise of modern secularity in *A Secular Age* (Cambridge: Harvard University Press, 2007).

35. It's important to note that "secular" need not mean "anti-religious": certain leaders of the Catholic church are indeed designated as part of its "secular" arm. A distinction between secular and religious realms is a distinction between a realm in which religious commitments—faith-based ones, especially, and ones peculiar to particular religious traditions rather than shared by them all—are bracketed, and a realm to which they are central. This lines up well with a distinction between a realm in which we finesse or suspend the

commitments we have to our *revealed* religions and a realm in which we express and celebrate those commitments. Whether natural religion must also be excluded from the secular realm will depend on what people in a particular time and place believe reason alone can establish. In our own day, we do for the most part think of the secular as excluding natural as well as revealed religion. But that difference between us and our ancestors should not keep us from recognizing that they too, often, maintained a secular/religious distinction.

36. Alexander Altmann, translator's introduction to Saadya Gaon, "Book of Doctrines and Beliefs," in H. Lewy, A. Altmann, and I. Heinemann (eds), *Three Jewish Philosophers* (New York: Atheneum, 1985), pp. 13–14.

37. Georges Dreyfus, *Recognizing Reality: Dharmakirti's Philosophy and Its Tibetan Interpretations* (Albany: State University of New York Press, 1997), p. 15.

38. Walpola Rahula, *What the Buddha Taught*, 2nd edn (New York: Grove Press, 1974), pp. 4–5, 87–88.

39. I am indebted to an anonymous reader for pushing me to clarify this point.

Part I: Chapter 1

1. David Hare, *Gethsemane* (Faber & Faber, 2008), scene i.

2. Although the character turns out later on to have been guided all her life by the story of Gethsemane in the Gospels, from which the play gets its name. I assume that Hare intends this irony to encourage us to reflect critically on the knee-jerk suspicion of religious people to which he initially invited us.

3. Enq Chapter X.

4. Hume considers only the situation where we have to decide whether to accept *testimony* to a miracle, by other people, but the argument can easily be adapted to claims about miracles we are tempted to make on the basis of our own observations. We simply have to ask whether it is more reasonable to believe that we have really seen (say) a rod turn into a snake, or that our senses are confused or deranged, perhaps by physical or mental illness. Of course, if we *are* mentally ill, we may not get to the point of actually asking such a question, but this says nothing to the reasonableness of the question, and a person capable of asking it will respond. if he understands Hume's arguments, that any evidence he could have had for the occurrence of a miracle is necessarily outweighed by the evidence against it.

5. Enq 115–116/91. I have replaced "evidence" or "empirical evidence" in for Hume's "testimony." The point, as I argue in the previous note, is unchanged.

The distinguished philosopher of science John Earman has argued recently that this chapter is an "abject failure" on Hume's part, since it would rule out many kinds of evidence that actual working scientists do, and must, accept (Earman, *Hume's Abject Failure* [Oxford: Oxford University Press, 2000]). Hume, Earman argues, doesn't draw a sufficient distinction between the miraculous and the merely "extraordinary," but we need to be able to accept claims for the appearance of the extraordinary else the scientific enterprise itself cannot be carried out.

I think this misses Hume's point. Hume is not concerned with ordinary scientific procedure, just with claims that purport to over-ride science altogether. In a sentence that begins by "beg[ging]" us to remark the point it makes (but is also, unfortunately, buried towards the end of the chapter), Hume writes, "a miracle can never be proved, *so as to be the foundation of a system of religion.*" (Enq 127/99, my italics). He goes on explicitly to admit that there can be all sorts of "violations of the usual course of nature"—even a 3-day period of darkness over the whole earth!—but that none of these would suffice to show the plausibility of "a new system of religion" (Enq 128/99). Why not? Because the point of using violations of the usual course of nature to establish a system of religion depends precisely on those violations being, not just of the *usual* course of nature, but of the course of nature *tout simple*: the idea is precisely to show that there is a being, beyond nature, who can suspend all of nature at his will. And *that* is something that no evidence drawn from the course of nature itself—from past observations—could possibly demonstrate. We always have better reason to doubt our witnesses, or even our own senses, than to credit a purported observation of something that, if true, would abrogate the laws of nature.

6. Lessing, "On the Proof of the Spirit and of Power," p. 53.
7. ibid, 54–55.
8. See, respectively, Neil Gillman's "The Jewish Philosopher in Search of a Role," reprinted in his *Doing Jewish Theology* (Woodstock: Jewish Lights Publishing, 2008) and Norman Lamm's contribution to *Condition of Jewish Belief*, compiled by the editors of *Commentary* Magazine (Northvale: Jason Aronson, 1989). Gillman writes that "the uniquely modern collapse of the dogma of verbal revelation" leads inevitably to a collapse of "the sense that the Torah can serve as an explicit standard of authority on all matters of belief and practice." (*op. cit,* 102). For Lamm, "*That* God spoke [the words of the Torah to Moses] is of the utmost significance," (*op. cit,* 124).

   A more nuanced approach to the relationship between the Bible as an object of historical scholarship and the Bible as an object of traditional religious belief can be found in Jon Levenson's "The Eighth Principle of Judaism and the Literary Simultaneity of Scripture," in his *The Hebrew Bible, the Old Testament, and Historical Criticism* (Westminster: John Knox Press, 1993).
9. Evans, *Faith Against Reason* (Grand Rapids, MI: Wm. B. Eerdmans, 1998), p. 111.
10. Maimonides, *Guide for the Perplexed* (*Guide*), Part II, Chapter 25.
11. Simon Blackburn's *Truth: A Guide* (Oxford: Oxford University Press, 2005) provides a good introduction to these debates. For more detail, see the papers in S. Blackburn and K. Simmons, *Truth* (Oxford: Oxford University Press, 1999).
12. But modern science does not necessarily outdo traditional worldviews in all respects: see Robin Horton, "Tradition and Modernity Revisited," in M. Hollis and S. Lukes (eds) *Rationality and Relativism* (Cambridge: The MIT Press, 1982).
13. A sophisticated version of this line of argument, with a discussion of Calvin's sensus divinitatis, can be found in Alvin Plantinga, *Warranted Christian Belief* (Oxford: Oxford University Press, 2000). But Plantinga present his case for Christianity as a rival to scientific explanation: see, especially, pp. 386–387.

Part I: Chapter 2

1. See Introduction, § 8, p. 15.
2. See Part V, §§ 3–5.
3. Williams, *Truth and Truthfulness* (TT). I reviewed this book in *Ethics* (January, 2004)—what follows draws in part on that review.
4. Edward Craig, *Knowledge and the State of Nature* (Oxford: Clarendon: 1990), p. 11.
5. Occasionally, the Hebrew Bible does apply "true" to sentences: in I Kings 10: 6 and 17: 24, the word is used just as a modern philosopher might expect it to be used, with a speaker affirming a certain proposition after having verified it in her own experience. But even here, it serves as part of an affirmation that certain people (Solomon and Elijah, respectively) are reliable.

6. Largely in order to combat the oppression and injustice bred by the Catholic church's attempt to control inquiry, various early modern movements in Europe stood for the individual's right to investigate the world for himself and abjured trust in authorities as a mode of reaching truth. Recent work has demonstrated that that can be a mistake—C. A. J. Coady's wonderful book *Testimony* (Oxford: Clarendon. Press, 1992) brings out how much we need to rely on the authority of others even in science—but it was probably necessary as a corrective to the excessive reliance on authority that preceded it. And the remarkable history of Europe from 1500 onwards indicates that erring in this direction leads to far better science, and far freer political and social institutions, than had ever been achieved in more authoritarian societies.

   I suggest that the notion that truth paradigmatically attaches to sentences alone, rather than to speakers, goes with this modern cognitive individualism. The cognitive individualist does not want to trust speakers; he wants to test every sentence for him or herself. He wants to detach each sentence from its speaker, and take it home with him, as it were, to check it out for himself. The sentence is thus depersonalized, and anyone can use it or believe it or check it, regardless of his or her relationship to the person speaking it: it ceases to get its significance from a context in which its speaker offers to lead the listener on a certain path. But in a world in which people expect to check the truth of sentences on their own, it becomes crucial that each sentence be as accurate as possible, since people will be following the guidance of those sentences independent of the interpretation, and further speech, of those who have spoken them. If I am told, "Following the yellow brick road is the way to happiness" by a speaker who accompanies me, or reappears periodically, on my journey, I may learn over time that "the yellow brick road" is but a metaphor, or that "happiness" means something different from what I initially supposed. Or the speaker, while remaining trustworthy, may amend or retract the sentence as our relationship goes on. If I know simply that the *sentence* is true, however, then it had better be literally and strictly true, if it is going to guide me aright.

7. For one thing, as Alfred Tarski pointed out (Tarski, "The Semantic Conception of Truth," in Blackburn and Simmons, *Truth*, p. 137), there are cases in which we want to say that an infinite *range* of sentences is true and we cannot do that by uttering each of the sentences themselves. We want to say, for instance, "All sentences of the form, 'x=x,' are true," but we cannot replace that claim with an enumeration of all sentences of the form, "x=x." Or, to use Tarski's own example, we might want to say "All consequences of true sentences are true."

   Tarski also mentions cases in which our historical knowledge will prevent us from eliminating the word "true" from a sentence (his example: "The first sentence written by Plato is true"). I would add that there are cases in which one person wants to affirm the truth of what another person says, but cannot accurately repeat the other person's sentences. You announce a sophisticated logical or scientific discovery, and I, trusting you while lacking the technical skills even to repeat your sentence properly, tell the audience, "What he just said is true." "True" is emphatically not pleonastic here: but this is a paradigm of its ordinary use.

8. Or, presumably, "plain falsehoods": a plain falsehood is just something whose falsehood can be demonstrated with a plain truth.

9. As *we* would put it, of course: it is definitive of the state of nature that it does not include reflection on kinds of truth (see § 18 of this Part). As soon as one starts engaging in that kind of reflection, issues about what a theory of truth would look like will arise, and it is precisely the purpose of the state-of-nature scenario to hold these issues off until we have actual truths—paradigm cases of truth claims—in hand against which to measure our theories.

Part I: Chapter 3

1. It's important to note that this needn't coincide with the end of a political state of nature. Entering a governed condition need not lead to sophisticated uses of truth language, nor it is impossible that such uses might develop in a pre-political condition.

2. In this and the next few sentences, I follow Locke, ST §§ 7–13, 87–89.

3. This is analogous to what happens on the first order, where reports of observations go along with reports on and explanations of what makes someone a reliable informant about such matters. Information-sharing, at all levels, goes along with methods for assessing informants.

4. Foucault uses this phrase—see, for instance, *Power/Knowledge*, C. Gordon (ed.) (New York: Pantheon Books, 1980), p. 131: "Each society has its régime of truth"—but I do not mean it in quite the same way: I do not want to imply, for instance, that the acceptability of truth-claims is relative to a system of power. (There are nonetheless some affinities between the institutional account of truth-seeking I offer here and Foucault's concerns.)

5. Compare *Wealth of Nations*, 28–29.

6. See Kuhn, *The Structure of Scientific Revolutions* (Chicago: University of Chicago Press, 1962).

7. Kuhn, *Structure*, 23–24.

8. Michael Welbourne offers an account of "perversions and corruptions" of communal cognitive practices along somewhat similar lines in *The Community of Knowledge* (New Jersey: Humanities Press, 1986) pp. 66–70.

9. For instance: "From my childhood I have been nourished upon letters, and because I was persuaded that by their means one could acquire a clear and certain knowledge of all that is useful in life, I was extremely eager to learn them. But as soon as I had completed the course of study at the end of which one is normally admitted to the ranks of the learned, I completely changed my opinion. For I found myself beset by so many doubts and errors that I came to think I had gained nothing from my attempts to become educated, but increasing recognition of my ignorance. And yet I was at one of the most famous schools in Europe, where I thought there must be learned men if they existed anywhere on earth" *The Philosophical Writings of Descartes,* trans. J. Cottingham, R. Stoothof, and D. Murdoch (Cambridge: Cambridge University Press, 1985), vol. 7, pp. 112–13.

10. Enq 11–12.

11. See especially his essay on orientation, and the first part of the *Conflict of the Faculties*. Onora O'Neill interprets Kant's account of reasoning even in the first *Critique* as designed, as much as anything, to show the irrationality of appeals to authority: see chapters 1 and 2 of her *Constructions of Reason*, (Cambridge: Cambridge University Press, 1989).

12. Many have complained about this. Perhaps the most cogent version of the complaint can be found in Coady, *Testimony*. Coady's book is a major source for the rise, in recent years, of what has been called "social epistemology": see, for instance, the essays in Frederick Schmitt (ed.), *Socializing Epistemology* (Totowa, NJ: Rowman & Littlefield, 1994).

    Axel Gelfert has recently shown that the accusation that Kant ignored testimony, and the social aspects of cognition that go with it, is false: see Gelfert, "Kant on Testimony," *British Journal for the History of Philosophy* 14 (4), 2006.

13. Clifford, "The Ethics of Belief," in *The Ethics of Belief and Other Essays* (Amherst, NY: Prometheus Books, 1999), p. 86.

14. See Richard Boyd, "Scientific Realism," § 3.4 in the *Stanford Encyclopedia of Philosophy*: http://plato.stanford.edu/entries/scientific-realism/.

15. That is: We *in the West* have every reason to trust our experts on this. People in many other societies live under truth regimes that proclaim a scientific basis for religious belief of one kind or another. The truth regime of the modern West is a reliable one, however, while the truth

regimes of these other societies are not. We have every reason to regard our truth regime as highly reliable, especially on scientific matters, given both its political and cultural structure (the raucous debate that pervades it, the respect and protection given to scholars, the high level of education in the population at large), and the many ways in which we see, plainly, its success in helping us predict and control the world. The degree to which Western technology, and the science that underwrites that technology, gets borrowed by countries all over the world indicates that they too implicitly trust the scientific truth regime of the West, however much they may claim to oppose it. Individuals who live under these regimes also often realize that they are unreliable, and turn to Western societies instead for factual information.

16. See Dawkins, *The God Hypothesis* (Boston: Houghton Mifflin, 2006).
17. Plantinga, *Warranted Christian Belief* (Oxford: Oxford University Press, 2000), pp. 227–40.
18. I owe this example to Walter Edelberg.
19. Plantinga should concede, I think, that evolutionary naturalism can give a good account of how and why our everyday beliefs about everyday objects are likely to track the truth: evolutionary theory makes it very plausible that creatures survive only if they generally get right the sources of their food, the dangers around them, and the most suitable objects of sexual desire. But there is no good evolutionary reason for our *theories* about belief, or about anything else—including our naturalist theories—to be correct. The causal chains on which naturalistic epistemologists rely do not put us in good, regular contact with the vast number of objects that are needed to validate a scientific theory, nor is there any reason to think that the environment in which our brains developed most of their reasoning capacities, many millennia ago, selected for skills in developing accurate general theories—theories like that of evolutionary biology. (Nor, certainly, does the truth of metaphysical claims, like those of naturalism, affect anyone's ability to survive in their everyday environment.) And there is in fact plenty of reason to *doubt* that most general theories are true: as Dawkins and his ilk themselves stress, the theories of this sort that societies in the past have accepted have generally been false, by our modern lights. One can't look at the enormous array of conflicting supernaturalist theories about the nature of reality held by human beings in the past, and feel very confident that any theory of that sort we hold today, including our naturalistic theories, is likely to be true. (This is a version of what philosophers of science call "the pessimistic induction" (see Larry Laudan, "A Confutation of Convergent Realism," *Philosophy of Science* 48(1), 1981.) But even if they are wrong to run that induction over *scientific* theories—and I am not at all sure that they are wrong, although I suspect that the inference doesn't rule out progressive improvement in science—it would certainly seem entirely appropriate when applied to *metaphysical* theories.) So naturalism, while it may account fairly well for the likely truth of our everyday beliefs, makes its own truth look unlikely. And in that case it certainly is, just as Plantinga says it is, a self-defeating view.

Note, by the way, that if this line of argument makes a designed universe look more plausible than not—and I'm not sure it does: I'm inclined to think that theistic theories, when construed as a metaphysics of science, will be just as flawed as naturalism, that the proper stance we should have towards metaphysical theories, when construed as ways of accounting for the facts of science alone, is Humean skepticism (described quite well by Plantinga on pp. 218–220)—it does so from metaphysical considerations rather than scientific ones. Pope Benedict's recent attempt to argue that the best scientific evidence we have supports the idea that evolution is guided by a benevolent designer is incorrect; what *might* be true is that the best metaphysical account we have of the science by which we come up with evolutionary theories supports the idea of a designed universe. Again, I'm not sure that's true, but even if it is, it will be different from "intelligent design" construed as a scientific theory.

20. The idea that science proceeds on assumptions that rule out a God—that the metaphysics of science leave the question of God's existence indeterminate—and that our reasons for believing in a God, if any, can only come from the metaphysics of ethics is of course a Kantian one. I take that to be a recommendation of it.

Part I Chapter 4

1. Donald Davidson, *Inquiries into Truth and Interpretation* (Oxford: Oxford University Press, 1984), pp. 252–253.
2. "Poetry and Truth-Conditions" in Richard Eldridge (ed.), *Beyond Representation: Philosophy and Poesis* (Cambridge University Press, 1996).
3. The classic example involved the coronation of Edward VII, which was scheduled for June 26, 1902. Rooms with a good view of the procession were rented out for that date at inflated prices. Then Edward fell sick and the coronation was put off for 2 months. So there was a question about whether those who had rented the rooms had a right to their money back. The judges in this and similar cases have generally believed that they did, although they have also been reluctant to read terms into a contract that are not explicitly mentioned there.
4. Maimonides, *Guide* I: 54.
5. Alternatively, a Christian may retain the notion that Jesus was literally resurrected, but shift the *grounds* on which he or she believes it: faith alone, rather than historical evidence, comes to be the basis of that belief. That is still a shift in the status of the claim.
6. A basic feature, certainly, of religious language: "One of the great and most characteristic features of the history of religions is the ongoing reinterpretation of sacred utterances which are believed to be foundational for each culture. . . . [R]eligious change is characterized more often by revisions and explications of a traditional content than by new visions or abrupt innovations."—Michael Fishbane, "Inner Biblical Exegesis," in Geoffrey Hartman and Sanford Budick (eds), *Midrash and Literature* (New Haven: Yale University Press, 1986), p. 19.
7. Murdoch, *The Sovereignty of Good* (London: Routledge, 1970), and McDowell, "Virtue and Reason" in his *Mind, Value and Reality* (Cambridge: Harvard University Press, 1998).
8. I will not always include reference to non-theistic forms of religion in the main text, but I think the claims I make about God can virtually always be re-tooled to suit non-theistic religions instead.
9. Recall the need for each fact, in science, to fit together with all other facts: § 3 of this Part.
10. Coady, *Testimony*, p. 173, with sections in brackets added from 169. Coady's anti-reductionist view of testimony has also been challenged in subsequent literature on the subject. Sanford Goldberg and Jennifer Lackey, in different ways, argue that the debate between reductionists and anti-reductionists about testimony is misconceived: see Goldberg, "Reductionism and the Distinctiveness of Testimonial Knowledge" and Lackey, "It Takes Two to Tango: Beyond Reductionism and Non-Reductionism in the Epistemology of Testimony," both in Lackey and E. Sosa (eds), *The Epistemology of Testimony* (Oxford: Clarendon Press, 2006).
11. Coady, *Testimony* 129.
12. Revealed texts can also be authorities. That is indeed how best to understand what we mean when we call them "true," I believe: we regard them as true insofar as we regard them as trustworthy, reliable ethical guides. Of course, for someone committed to a theistic religion, the Person he or she is ultimately trying to trust is neither the guru or rabbi, nor the text for whom the guru or rabbi speaks, but God. She treats her sacred text and its spokespeople as authorities, but that is because she sees them as mediating God's own word to her, helping

her recognize God as a truth-teller, a Person with something to say to her, on Whom she can wholly rely. The cry, "The LORD your God is true" (cf. § 13 of this Part) may then be not just the highest use of "truth" for her, but its most representative one, the one that best expresses its meaning in other contexts.

13. This is in addition to the fact that a supernatural truth about the universe loses all credibility if it makes nonsense of natural truths. If God created this universe, and us with various faculties to find our way about in it, He presumably wants us to use those faculties as fully as possible when studying nature. Similarly, if the Buddha's claims express a deep truth about human life, rather than error or falsehood, what he says had better cohere with what we know naturally. Even a religion that presents the world around us as fundamentally an *illusion* had better get the details of that illusion right, else we have no reason to suppose that it truly sees through it to something deeper.

14. On this, see also Part V, Chapter 1.

Part II: Chapter 1

1. Something analogous holds for non-theistic religions. One way to understand the *tao*, and Buddhist nirvana, is that to say that they lie "beyond good and evil," that they show us, when we follow or attain them, the shallowness of our ordinary moral distinctions. Yet to make this point convincing, teachers of Taoism and Buddhism have long argued that the enlightenment they urge their followers to seek brings with it a vast increase in what people ordinarily consider virtue: that great Taoist or Buddhist sages will control or transcend the desires that lead lesser human beings into violence, deceit, or cruelty (the Buddhist sage is a model of compassion, in very much the ordinary sense of that term). So, once again, the higher goodness held out by a religious teaching is grafted onto the lower, more ordinary goodness by which people are drawn to that teaching.

2. Many would say they govern our relations with other animals as well, but this is controversial, and even those who believe we have direct duties to non-human animals tend to concede that our duties to our fellow human beings come first.

3. Frankfurt, *Taking Ourselves Seriously and Getting It Right* (Stanford: Stanford University Press, 2006), p. 28.

4. Kant, interestingly, thinks self-regarding duties provide the foundation of all duties (*Metaphysics of Morals* Ak 417–418), even though he characterizes ethics as a matter of interaction among rational beings.

5. Even if they do want to reflect it, moreover, the choice to do that is usually motivated by an ethical view: that our ethical norms are in decent shape as they stand.

Part II: Chapter 2

1. In addition to the works of Hutcheson, one can find emotivist systems played out in Hume (in part III of his *Treatise* and the second *Enquiry*, especially), Adam Smith's *Theory of Moral Sentiments*, Allan Gibbard's *Wise Choices, Apt Feelings* (Cambridge: Harvard University Press, 1990), and Simon Blackburn's *Ruling Passions* (Oxford: Clarendon Press, 1998).

2. See Bernard Williams, *Morality* (Cambridge: Cambridge University Press, 1972), pp. 20–25, for a trenchant critique of these claims.

3. A model of this kind of view can be found in David Gauthier, *Morals by Agreement* (New York: Oxford University Press, 1987).

4. Chronologically, that will be the primary meaning of the terms, the one we learn first. But logically, on this view, the priority must go in the other direction: one can justify this meaning of the terms only by starting from the egoistic one.

5. An egoist may of course grant that sometimes the spectacle of another's pleasure is itself pleasurable.

6. Very little that I will say bears on the *philosophical* views advanced, in contemporary literature, under the banner of divine command morality (DCM). It's an essential premise of practically all this literature that God would not ever command us to do something that runs seriously against our secular moral beliefs, and it is generally assumed, correspondingly, that what God wills that we do, in the moral realm, can be determined quite adequately by the reason and/or sentiments on which secular moralists rely. Philosophical DCM is thus quite unlike popular DCM, and is almost never presented as something that might lead you to suppose that we must find out how to act by way of the instructions in a sacred text. (See Adams, FIG 263 on this point.) Philosophical DCM does not particularly endorse a *scripturally*-based morality, and is concerned more with the metaphysics of morals than with concrete morality proper.

I suppose that in some sense I am myself a philosophical DCM theorist. I believe, as Robert Adams does, that moral obligations ultimately reflect facts about the will of God, that we obey or respect or honor God when we do what is right and disobey or show disrespect to God when we do what is wrong or evil. But for me this claim has very little impact on how, ordinarily, we should understand morality. For I also believe that what God commands human beings to do, as regards strictly moral matters, is to construct ideals and codes of action that will allow them to live together peacefully, and to preserve and foster their own freedom and material well-being, independently of their views about Him. I believe, that is, that God wants us to construct largely secular moralities. So we accord with God's will, morally, when we act in ways that make no direct reference to God's will, and do things that a non-believer could correctly describe as (simply) promoting peace, freedom, and happiness.

That doesn't mean that even such a thin divine command morality is irrelevant to our *religious* life. If we believe that moral commands reflect God's will, even in the thin sense I have proposed, that may tell us something about God and our relation to God. And a text that helps deepen our secular moral understandings may by that fact gain credibility as a text that more generally reflects the will of God. So a divine command morality may have significant theological implications even if it has no moral ones.

7. I am grateful to Tony Laden for urging me to clarify this point.

8. Introduction, §§ 1–2.

9. A *simulacrum* of it may, of course, have been realized where people have been coerced to avow a particular code, or way of speaking about moral issues.

10. "Morality needs absolutely . . . no end, either in order to recognize what duty is or to impel its performance; on the contrary, when duty is the issue, morality can perfectly well abstract from ends altogether, and ought to do so" (RWB 4).

11. My own work in the history of moral philosophy has focused on affinities between Kant and Adam Smith: see my "Philosophy in Moral Practice: Kant and Adam Smith," *Kant-Studien*, 82 (3) (1991) and *A Third Concept of Liberty: Judgment and Freedom in Kant and Adam Smith* (Princeton: Princeton University Press, 1999). Stephen Darwall, Christel Fricke, and Leon Montes have made similar points—see Darwall's and Fricke's contributions to Christel Fricke and Hans-Peter Schütt, *Adam Smith als Moralphilosoph* (Berlin: de Gruyter, 2005), and Leon Montes' *Adam Smith in Context* (London: Palgrave, 2004), chapter 4. Darwall also has a thorough and much-acclaimed book bringing out proto-Kantian elements in British moral philosophy from Cudworth through Hume: *The British Moralists and the Internal 'Ought'* (Cambridge: Cambridge University Press, 1995).

12. See Robert Louden, "Kant's Virtue Ethics," *Philosophy* 61 (1986), and the essays in Stephen Engstrom and Jennifer Whiting (eds), *Aristotle, Kant, and the Stoics* (Cambridge: Cambridge University Press, 1996).

13. Williams, *Morality: An Introduction to Ethics* (Cambridge: Cambridge University Press, 1972; Canto edition, 1993), p. 94.

14. Korsgaard (ingeniously) softens Kant's position on lying to murderers in "The right to lie," collected in her *Creating the Kingdom of Ends*. She also allows for suicide in some cases in SN 161–162, and works out duties to animals on Kantian grounds in "Fellow Creatures: Kantian Ethics and Our Duties to Animals," forthcoming in The Tanner Lectures on Human Values, edited by Grethe B. Peterson (Salt Lake City: The University of Utah Press), Volume 25/26. The so-called "philosophers' brief" in favor of assisted suicide was drawn up in part by the prominent Kantian John Rawls.

15. See, for instance, Rosalind Hursthouse, "Virtue Ethics and Abortion," in D. Statman (ed.), *Virtue Ethics: A Critical Reader* (Edinburgh: Edinburgh University Press, 1997).

16. Robert Adams brings out this point nicely: "The impact of ethical theory on common morality is limited because virtually everyone has more confidence in the central dictates of shared morality than in any ethical theory as such. An ethical theory of whose correctness I am persuaded may reasonably lead me to depart from the teachings of 'common sense' in a few cases. But if an ethical theory were to imply that lying, stealing, and killing people are not generally wrong—so much the worse for the theory. Ethical theorists are generally at pains to establish that their theories do not have such consequences, and if possible they try to show that they can explain the 'data' of common morality."—Adams, "Religious Ethics in a Pluralist Society," G. Outka and J. Reeder (eds), *Prospects for a Common Morality* (Princeton: Princeton University Press, 1993), p. 98.

17. See, e.g. Plato, *Republic*, trans. T. Griffith (Cambridge: Cambridge University Press, 2000), 442e–443a.

18. Mill, *Utilitarianism*, ed. G. Sher (Indianapolis: Hackett, 1979), p. 23.

19. I am grateful to Richard Kraut for stressing this point to me.

20. I say more about this later: see § 39 of this Part.

21. The word "eclectic" has been applied to some previous moral philosophies. Cicero is often described that way, and John Stuart Mill seems to have used the word at least of his views in the 1830s (see Mill, "Autobiography" (early draft), in John Robson and Jack Stillinger (eds), *Collected Works of John Stuart Mill* (Indianapolis: Liberty Fund, 2006), p. 156 and Michael Mathias, "Editor's Introduction," in Mill, *On Liberty*, ed. Mathias (New York: Pearson, 2007, pp. 11–12). I think Mill was an eclectic throughout his life. Despite his characterization of himself as a "utilitarian," he devoted much of his work to *revising* utilitarianism, so that it incorporated central themes in the ethics of Plato, Aristotle, and even Kant.

   Robert Adams defends a view very close to the one I offer here in "Religious Ethics in a Pluralistic Society." Common morality—the morality that most of us share and that enables our society to function—should be "conceived as the large area of overlap of the diverse moralities of different people and groups of people," he suggests, and as independent of the normative and meta-ethical theories that may be used to explain or justify it.

22. Compare TJ §§ 3–4, and PL § 4.

23. See PL, Lecture IV.

24. Mill, *Utilitarianism*, pp. 48–49.

25. Compare FIG 239–244 on the connection between guilt and alienation from other people.

26. This is what makes a view of morality like Kant's, on which it consists in principles that express our autonomy, or TM Scanlon's—on which it consists in principles we cannot reasonably expect other reasonable people to reject—so appealing.

27. See, e.g. PL xviii, 145, 157. But the fact that Rawls often speaks of comprehensive "religious" and "philosophical" doctrines, alongside comprehensive "moral" ones, and implies that many of us derive our values from the former, leads me to think that he might have been sympathetic to the idea that morality itself may not be free-standing, that it may depend in turn on a comprehensive view, or set of comprehensive views, from which it can be derived.

28. Consider, for instance, the comments of General William Heath on the fact that the Constitution maintained slavery, in the Massachusetts ratifying convention of 1788: "No gentleman within these walls detests every idea of slavery more than I do.... I ardently hope that the time will soon come, when our brethren in the southern States will view it as we do, and put a stop to it, but to this we have no right to compel them.... [S]hall we refuse to eat, or to drink, or to be united, with those who do not think, or act, just as we do, surely not."—*The Debate on the Constitution*, B. Bailyn (ed.) (New York: Library of America, 1993), p. 915.

29. One might respond that these are just the wrong *sorts* of moral systems, and that one can avoid all such absurd extremes by refusing to root morality in a single principle and adopting instead an intuitionist or a neo-Aristotelian moral system. But intuitionism too can look out of touch with the nature of morality: when, for instance, it leaves us without resources by which to challenge deeply-held cultural norms. And the neo-Aristotelian focus on virtuous character traits to the virtual exclusion of principles that might help people resolve contentious disputes not infrequently seems self-indulgent.

30. *Inter alia*, this makes their religion look amoral or immoral, rather than a real candidate for a vision of the ultimate good.

31. This point is not restricted to religious views. Any view of morality that sees actions as morally acceptable only when taken in the name of its own purported end for human life (e.g. a Marxist who sees no actions as good unless they are taken in the name of the proletarian revolution), and that therefore refuses compromise with other views, cannot enter into the eclectic mix with which I have identified morality. The mix is broad, but it cannot include within itself views that refuse to countenance eclecticism itself.

32. Although there are few if any verses in either the Jewish or the Christian Bible that say anything directly about abortion—and one (Exodus 21: 22) seems to *deny* that a fetus is a full human being.

33. I do not think these appeals are particularly *strong*, and they don't persuade many secular people of the wrongness of abortion. But they are aimed in that direction.

34. I disagree with this—see my *Short History of Distributive Justice* (Cambridge: Harvard University Press, 2004)—but do think passages from Amos, Isaiah, and the Gospels have helped inspire many modern activists on behalf of social justice. The sacred texts have been, I believe, re-read with modern moral concerns in mind. But that is perfectly appropriate, in a religious tradition. A revelation of eternal truths must have something to say to each generation, and the process of re-reading it is an integral part of how those with faith in it should receive it. See further, Part IV, Chapter 6.

35. See Scanlon, *What We Owe to Each Other* (Cambridge: Harvard University Press, 2000) and Habermas, *Moral Consciousness and Communicative Action*, trans. C. Lenhardt and S. Nicholsen (Cambridge: MIT Press, 1995).

36. I take James Tully's defense of Foucault against Habermas to make much the same point: see Tully, *Public Philosophy in a New Key* (Cambridge: Cambridge University Press, 2008), chapter 3.

37. See note 15 to pp. 487–488, above.

38. Which is to say, for many religious believers: a rejection of the structure of social life created by God.

Part II: Chapter 3

1. This way of presenting Kant owes much to Korsgaard's analysis of Kant's relation to his predecessors in SN.
2. Strictly: *may* have. We cannot prove that we are ever free (logic can't demonstrate facts, and if we try to prove it scientifically, we presuppose that freedom is a part of nature, hence that it follows causal laws: which is precisely what it is supposed *not* to do). But *if* we are ever free, we are free when and only when we use our reason.
3. See Christine Korsgaard, *Self-Constitution* (Oxford: Oxford University Press, 2009) for a brilliant defense of this view.
4. G 428–429, 435; CPrR 77–78.
5. Kurt Baier develops this idea in *The Moral Point of View* (New York: Random House, 1958). Alan Gewirth made use of a related principle—that claiming legitimacy for any of my own actions implicitly commits me to a certain freedom of action for everyone—throughout his writings.
6. See Thomas Nagel, *The View from Nowhere* (VN). Bernard Williams presents a trenchant critique of the analogy between practical and theoretical reason in ELP, chapter 4.
7. See SN, especially Lecture 3.
8. See Stephen Darwall, *The Second-Person Standpoint* (Cambridge: Harvard University Press, 2006).
9. See McDowell, "Virtue and Reason," and Jonathan Dancy, *Ethics Without Principles* (Oxford: Clarendon, 2004).
10. Frankfurt, *Taking Ourselves Seriously and Getting it Right* (Stanford: Stanford University Press, 2006), p. 21.
11. Ibid. 47–48.
12. The idea that many moral philosophers give "the wrong kind of reason" to be moral is a running theme of *The Second-Person Standpoint*.
13. A wonderful paper I received from Tafhim Rahman wonderfully laid out the arguments against a good God punishing anyone eternally.
14. They may, of course, want to say that the reason morality brings its own internal rewards (if they are Humean) or motivates us to act without reward (if they are Kantian) is that God has set up the world or human nature that way. But then there is nothing distinctly religious about their account of *what* motivates us morally; the distinctly religious contribution comes in after that has been established, as an explanation of how those motivations come about.
15. Beautiful versions of this view can be found in FIG Parts I and II, and Hermann Cohen, *Religion of Reason Out of the Sources of Judaism*, trans. Simon Kaplan (Atlanta: Scholars Press, 1995), chapter 9.
16. Compare Sagi and Statman, *Religion and Morality*, pp. 103–4.

Part II Chapter 4

1. On this phenomenon, see Daniel Statman, "Hypocrisy and Self-deception," *Philosophical Psychology*, vol. 10, No.1 (1997).
2. Plato, *Republic*, G. R. F. Ferrari (ed.), trans. T. Griffith (Cambridge: Cambridge Univ. Press, 2000), p. 293 (577e).

3. Freud, *Studies in Hysteria*, in J. Strachey (ed.) *The Standard Edition of the Complete Works of Sigmund Freud* (New York: Basic Books), vol. 2, p. 305.

4. Although many scholars of Marx, for a variety of reasons, would say that the position is attributed to Marx at the cost of serious *misinterpretation*: see Dan Brudney, *Marx's Attempt to Leave Philosophy* (Cambridge: Harvard University Press, 1998), pp. 337–347, Norman Geras, "The Controversy about Marx and Justice," Alex Callinicos (ed.) *Marxist Theory* (Oxford: Oxford University Press, 1989), and R. G. Peffer, *Marxism, Morality, and Social Justice* (Princeton: Princeton University Press, 1990), chapters 4–7.

5. Marx, C. J. Arthur (ed.) *The German Ideology* (New York: International Publishers, 1978), pp. 97, 99.

6. Ibid. 115.

7. See Allen Wood, *Karl Marx* (London: Routledge & Kegan Paul, 1981), chapter 10.

8. On Marx's critique of morality, see again Wood, *Karl Marx*, chapter 10. I would go further than Wood does, however. Wood argues that some aspects of bourgeois morality are salvageable from a Marxist perspective (pp. 153–156), and says "there is . . . some reason to say (as Engels does) that in future society there will be an 'actual human morality' in place of the false, ideological moralities of class society" (156). It seems to me that "human morality" would be something of a contradiction in terms for Marx himself. It belongs to the nature of anything regarded as a *morality* that it stands over us in a non-human, and dehumanizing, way. So while Marx would surely agree that "kindness, generosity [and] loyalty" would be respected in communist society, as Wood says (154), he would probably not expect these or other qualities to be treated as *moral* ones: and that shift in terminology is meant to reflect a crucial shift in our attitude toward these qualities.

9. I don't find the idea that we would all become kind to and respectful of one another if we overcame racial and gender hierarchies any more plausible.

10. Kierkegaard, *Concluding Unscientific Postscript*, trans. D. F. Swenson and W. Lowrie (Princeton: Princeton University Press, 1941), p. 70.

11. We may take "truth" here as the truth about ethical or religious matters, which is all that concerns Kierkegaard.

12. Ibid. 71–72.

13. G 425–426, 433–435, 454–455 and RWB 57–62.

14. See, for instance, Alan White, *Within Nietzsche's Labyrinth* (London: Routledge, 1990) or SN 158–60.

15. Which for Nietzsche, although not of course for Kierkegaard, means above all a *proud* spirit, bursting with self-esteem and contemptuous of Christian humility.

Part II: Chapter 5

1. Kierkegaard, *Fear and Trembling and the Sickness Unto Death,* trans. Walter Lowrie (Princeton: Princeton University Press, 1954), pp. 41, 67.

2. Jürgen Habermas draws a similar distinction in *Moral Consciousness and Communicative Action*.

3. He also has historical precedent for such a distinction. Hegel differentiated between *Moralität* and *Sittlichkeit*, including in the latter the social, historical, and political context that gives rise to our modes of evaluating people, and regarding the former as a system focused on freedom and obligation for which Kant was the paradigmatic spokesperson. Neither Hegel nor Williams *identifies* Kant's system with morality. Williams says, and Hegel would surely agree, that Kant merely gave voice to a tendency embedded in "the outlook of almost all of us."

4. The German title, *Grundlegung zur Metaphysik der Sitten*, could however equally well be translated "Groundwork for the Metaphysics of Ethics."

5. See, among others, Louden, "Kant's Virtue Ethics," Barbara Herman, "Making Room for Character," in Engstrom and Whiting, *Aristotle, Kant and the Stoics*, and Patrick Frierson, *Freedom and Anthropology in Kant's Moral Philosophy* (Cambridge: Cambridge University Press, 2003).

6. Thomas Hill, Jr provides a qualified defense of this view in chapters 1 and 2 of his *Autonomy and Self-Respect* (Cambridge: Cambridge University Press, 1991).

7. I deliberately leave open what counts as "others" here. Our duties are typically owed to other human beings, but we may also have them to other forms of life, possibly even to some inanimate things. The crucial point is that obligations to others, of any kind, are not necessarily identical with activities directed toward improving our *own* lives.

8. "Telic" comes from *telos*, the Greek word for any purpose or end, and could be used to characterize a relation to any sort of end: a "telic" description of my going downstairs might refer to my end of fixing myself some breakfast. But the Greek word is so often used, in English, in connection with our highest end that we court little confusion if we restrict it to that context.

9. NE Book I.

10. "Bentham's case for the principle of utility is that it can be applied uncontroversially, since it turns on empirically ascertainable facts, and that it can be expected to motivate since it concerns the 'two sovereign masters' of human motivation, pleasure and pain."—Stephen Darwall, *The Second-Person Standpoint* (Cambridge: Harvard University Press, 2006), p. 315.

11. Korsgaard construes Kantian maxims as making an ineliminable reference to the purpose of our actions (SN 107–108). But the purpose still figures only in an account of the action's form: we evaluate whether it would be universally acceptable for people to use *these* means for *these* kinds of purposes, not whether we should aim at the purpose at all.

12. But see Allen Wood, *Kant's Moral Religion* (Ithaca: Cornell University Press), pp. 51–60.

13. AV 219: "We have then arrived at a provisional conclusion about the good life for man: the good life for man is the life spent in seeking for the good for man, and the virtues necessary for the seeking are those which will enable us to understand what more and what else the good life for man is." It is important that this is a "provisional" conclusion, but MacIntyre never gives us a more settled or developed one.

14. See previous note.

15. In the situations in which we *are* morally required to answer it—when institutions must for instance determine policies about end-of-life decisions—we normally rely as much as possible on the Kantian or freedom-based aspects of our moral overlapping consensus: we try to allow individuals to make such decisions as much as possible on their own. This allows religious people to use their traditions' codes, while secular people make such decisions in entirely different ways. And this seems to me the right way to come to a shared view of such matters.

   For which reason I think it is also the right way to come to shared social views on abortion. As Ronald Dworkin has argued (*Freedom's Law* [Cambridge: Harvard University Press, 1996], pp. 104–110), abortion decisions belong in the hands of the mother because the way we settle moral issues like this one is tied closely to our freedom of religion. Only telic views—whether religious or non-religious—can tell each of us how to define human life at its margins. But it is essential to our retaining a shared morality that we abstract from these telic views. So the morally correct settlement of an issue that requires us to advert to our telic views is one that allows each of us to decide that issue, as much as possible, on our own.

16. *Moralische Glaube* or *Vernunftglaube*, which can be translated just as moral or rational *belief*. But Kant makes clear that he uses these terms to mean something quite different from "belief" as a component of knowledge (see CJ 470 or CPrR 126)—this sort of belief is incapable of being given the sorts of grounds by which it could ever be transformed into knowledge.

17. There may nevertheless be resources in Kant's *speculative* philosophy by which to criticize some of these claims.

18. What it means to say that a belief is "practically necessary" is of course unclear. There are several different possibilities for what Kant has in mind here: I sketch them below.

19. CPrR 119–121, 133–134.

20. Reading CPrR 120 together with 141, and recalling that a "canon" of reason, in CPR, is a procedure for taking up the conclusions of speculative reason for practical purposes.

21. And Kant talks very much as if speculative reason *has* a choice to make here: practical reason "offers [speculative reason certain propositions] for its acceptance," he says, and the latter can either do that or "stubbornly . . . reject[. . .]" them (CPrR 120).

22. This second reading gains support from the fact that Kant argues in several places that speculative reason is ultimately driven by concerns about the objects of practical reason—is there a God? is there free will? is there immortality?—and that practical reason can help speculative reason clarify its concepts of these objects. See CPR B 7, A798=B826, A804–819=B832–47, CPrR 132–133.

23. CPrR 143 and 143n and CJ 469–470. In addition to the argument I present in the main text, Kant distinguishes practical reason's posit of the highest good and its presuppositions from the attribution of reality to imaginary entities on the grounds that practical reason, in its concern with our ultimate end, is "pure," rather than "pathologically conditioned": in its claim that the highest good is necessary, it relies not on our empirical desires, but on the nature of reason itself (CPrR 120–121). If we posit the existence of something we merely happen to desire (of a merely imagined beautiful lover, in the example posed to Kant by Thomas Wizenmann (143n)), we would also have empirical grounds on which to explain the posit *as* a fantasy. Our knowledge of empirical psychology, thus of the human tendency to fantasy, would allow us to see that the object posited is unlikely to exist. But if the object is posited by reason itself, then we have no empirical reason to deny its reality. And we have as much reason to believe in it—it is posited *by* reason, after all—as we could possibly have not to believe in it.

24. Allen Wood misses this point. Wood defends the view that the belief in the highest good, for Kant, is "morally necessary" in the sense that without it one will cease to be moral. To make his case for this interpretation, he relies heavily on a passage in Kant's lectures on philosophical theology, according to which a person who denies moral faith "is brought *ad absurdum practicum*" (Kant, *Lectures on Philosophical Theology*, trans. A. Wood and G. Clark [Ithaca: Cornell University Press, 1978], 122–123; quoted by Wood on p. 29 of *Kant's Moral Religion*, and referred to often throughout that book). This is supposed to parallel a theoretical argument ad absurdum, except that in the practical case the consequence of denying a certain proposition is not a logical contradiction, but becoming "a scoundrel." Without moral faith, according to this passage, we will give up on morality. And Kant says something similar in CPR, telling us that we must "regard the moral laws as empty figments of the brain" if we abandon a belief in the highest good, and the God and afterlife that make that highest good possible (A 811=B 839).

But these claims occur in works written before Kant arrived at his mature view of moral motivation, and are linked to his earlier view that we need religious belief for such motivation. A few paragraphs after the passage from the first *Critique* that I have just cited, Kant says that "without a God and a world that is now not visible to us, but is hoped for, the majestic ideas of morality are ... objects of approbation and admiration, but not incentives for resolve and realization" (CPR A813=B841). He insists that we don't need the idea of God or a future life to come up with the *content* of morality (A807–808=B 835–806)—we derive the laws of morality, here as elsewhere in Kant's critical writings, from reason alone— or to recognize that we are *obligated* to follow moral laws (A818–819=B846–847). But we will find ourselves unable to live up to that obligation unless we posit a God and a future life. If so, then of course we will become "scoundrels," give up on morality, if we lack moral faith. On the view Kant holds from the time of the *Groundwork* onwards, however, reason is its own incentive and needs no external help to motivate us. (Jerome Schneewind says that "it was only when working out the [*Groundwork*] that Kant came to his final motivational theory" (*The Invention of Morality* [Cambridge: Cambridge University Press, 1998], p.492 n18. See also text thereto and Frederick Beiser, "Moral Faith and the Highest Good," in Paul Guyer (ed.), *The Cambridge Companion to Kant and Modern Philosophy* [Cambridge: Cambridge University Press, 2006], pp. 614–616.) It is indeed a central theme of the *Groundwork* and *Critique of Practical Reason* that reason, by itself, can "be practical." Although we cannot explain *how* reason can motivate us (constructing such an explanation, says Kant, would be tantamount to giving an empirical cause for freedom: G 459-63), we nonetheless must believe that it does. But if morality is the expression of reason, and reason needs no external incentive to motivate us, then we no longer have grounds to suppose that a person who lacks a belief in God and a future life must become a scoundrel. And in fact we find no such suggestion in Kant's works from the *Groundwork* onwards. On the contrary, Kant is at pains to stress that "on its own behalf morality does not need" the idea of a highest good (RWB 4), and that a person who "cannot convince himself" of the existence of God would still be fully able to recognize the demands of the moral law (CJ 450–451; see also Beiser, *op. cit.*, p. 606).

25. Kant writes of "the virtuous Epicurus" (CPrR 115) and "a righteous man (like Spinoza)" (CJ 452). Indeed he describes Spinoza as an especially outstanding example of a virtuous person: of a person who pursued the good "unselfishly," for its own sake rather than for any personal advantage, and who was "honest, peaceable and benevolent" (ibid.) And he says that Hume was "unblemished in his moral character" (CPR B 774).

26. CJ 450–451, 469.

27. Compare: "I have reason to bring out the voicing when I play the Bach Chaconne, even if I have no reason to play the violin." (I am grateful to Kyla Ebels Duggan for pressing an objection of this kind on me.) That does sound strange, but I think it is true. Rome is burning, and I am fiddling. So I shouldn't be fiddling. But if I *am* fiddling, then—*qua* fiddler—I still have reason to fiddle well. The reasons I have not to fiddle at all are not reasons to fiddle badly. Perhaps we should say: *all things considered,* I have no reason to be careful about the voicing in the Chaconne. But even this sounds wrong. Instead, my all-things-considered and my local reasons are incommensurable here.

   This is a not uncommon feature of practical reasoning. I find advertising a dishonest business, but I am good at it and take a job with an advertising firm despite my qualms. Now my job gives me reasons to do all sorts of things, and as long as I stick with that job, those are reasons for my actions: even if, on some level, I still harbor doubts about whether I should be holding the job at all. Or I participate in a hobby that looks ridiculous to outsiders—I am a Trekkie, say—and am perhaps able to take up that outside perspective on the hobby myself, at some points. Then I will have strong reason for all sorts of local tasks—how could I *not* go to a conference in which the original Starship Enterprise will be on display?!—even while recognizing that I may lack reason for the whole project in which those tasks are nested. And how do I handle this incommensurability, this threat of incoherence, in my reasoning? Well, I try not to think about the project as a whole, keep myself immersed in its details to distract myself from such holistic thoughts, and surround myself with like-minded enthusiasts, rather than people who will urge the outside perspective on me.

I see no reason for supposing that the grand projects of all of our lives could not be like this, and it seems to me more likely than not that for the most part we deal with the threat of incoherence that that possibility raises by not thinking about our lives as a whole, immersing ourselves in local tasks, and surrounding ourselves with like-minded friends who cheer us on.

28. "The Metamorphosis," in Kafka, *The Complete Short Stories* (New York: Schocken, 1971), p. 91. Kafka's stories are in fact replete with argument. The creature in "The Burrow," obsessed with security even though it has built itself an enormous underground dwelling, incessantly argues to itself that it is rightly so concerned, and appeals to notions like "deduction," "validity," "*a priori* assumptions" and "hypotheses" throughout its internal debates (344, 353–354). "The Problem of Our Laws" does nothing but describe some specious reasons that a society gives itself for keeping its laws secret (437–438). And *The Trial* and *The Castle* are filled with arguments over all sorts of trivia, while their bizarre overall scenarios go virtually unmentioned. Over and over, Kafka's characters argue, cogently and clearly and in all apparent seriousness, but over issues that avoid rather than confronting the main concerns of their lives. A firm sense of what is worthwhile in life, a commitment to some sort of telos or system of value, Kafka implies, does not come through argument. See my "Religious Questions: Kafka and Wittgenstein on Giving Grounds," *Sophia*, April 1982.

29. "...the dusk...the strain...waiting...I confess...I imagined....for a second"—Beckett, *Waiting for Godot* (New York: Grove Press, 1964), p. 16.

30. Beckett, *The Unnamable* (New York: Grove Press, 1958), p. 414.

31. At one time, it was quite common to see Kant as anticipating such figures. "Kant is often claimed as a backer of the existentialist view," said Iris Murdoch (*The Sovereignty of Good*, p. 30). I doubt anyone would say that Kant is "often" seen this way today, but compare again Beiser: "[Kant's] ultimate worry [should there be no highest good] is (for lack of a better word) *existential*: the despair that comes from believing that all our moral efforts and strivings in the world are vain. No less than Camus, Kant is haunted by the figure of Sisyphus, who rolls his boulder up the hill only for it to roll back down" ("Moral Faith...," p. 616).

32. Exactly what balance between simplicity and adequacy to the evidence is "best" in scientific explanation, for instance, is very hard to pin down; it is, indeed, hard to figure out exactly how "simplicity" alone should be defined.

33. A properly scrutinized ethical faith will not give us license to posit any supernatural being or event we like: there is reason to do that only when the posit is essential to our telic vision.

This leaves open the degree to which such a faith should allow miracles. The founding texts of many revealed religions include stories of miraculous happenings of some sort or another; certain miracles are central to many faiths. Indeed, revelation itself, if it occurs at all, would be a miracle: it is in essence a communication from God to us, or at least a description of a supernatural principle grounding the universe, or a supernatural condition human beings can achieve. And if revelation itself is possible, there is no reason to rule out other ways in which the supernatural might somehow appear within our natural lives. A God who can reveal himself is a God who can appear in history. So it should be no surprise that revealed religions tend to include a belief in miracles. The crucial point, on my view, is that we can have *only* ethical reasons to maintain a faith in such things. The reason to believe in a miracle is because one sees it as necessary to the telic vision in which one has faith, not because one supposes there to be empirical evidence for it. A believer in Jesus's resurrection may legitimately say, "I don't know how it happened, and I'm willing to concede that there's lots of empirical evidence that it didn't happen, but I still believe that Jesus of

Nazareth was raised from the dead—I couldn't see God as saving me otherwise." And a Jew or Muslim might say, "I believe in the divine authorship of the Torah or Quran because I can't see how *halakha* or *sharia* can bring me into God's presence otherwise." (A belief in miracles can *follow from* an ethical faith; it never appropriately *grounds* such faith. Hume was right that a miracle can never be proven *so as to ground any religion*: "I beg the limitations here made may be remarked, when I say, that miracle can never be proved, so as to be the foundation of a system of religion" (Enq 127). No experiential evidence could establish a violation of the laws of experience. If one has *other*, independent reasons to believe in a supernatural being, however, the possibility of miracles cannot be ruled out.)

But neither Christian nor Jew nor Muslim needs to believe that Joshua stopped the sun, or that the world was once populated by half-human, half-angelic beings, or any of the other marvelous events that appear in their sacred texts. Metaphorical explanations of such stories have been around for centuries, and no-one thinks that the telic vision of these religions depends on their having literally occurred. The telic core of Judaism lies in its claim that God wants Jews to follow the law of the Torah; of Christianity, that God has redeemed us from our sins by suffering, in human form, with us; of Islam, that God requires us to submit to Him via an acceptance of the Quran as His supreme teaching. It is not clear that *any* historical event has to have occurred for these claims to be true—the Torah could be God's will for Jews even if there never was an exodus or a Moses; God could have suffered with us and saved us even if there never was a Jesus; and the Quran could be God's supreme teaching even if nothing recorded historically about Mohammed is true—and they certainly do not require the occurrence of all the supernatural events recounted in the Hebrew Bible and Gospels. Before the modern age, many of these events were indeed probably not seen quite as "supernatural": a looser notion of "nature" prevailed, by which magical events and entities might be features of everyday experience. On such views, it was less difficult to suppose that everything recorded in the Jewish and Christian Bibles had literally occurred. As conceptions of nature—of science—have changed, it is reasonable for religious believers to interpret many of these events in different ways; revealed texts must anyway be opened to a very wide range of interpretations (see Part IV, Chapter 6).

I am grateful to Bob Fischer for conversations that greatly helped clarify these issues.

34. Ken Seeskin has raised the first objection in conversation with me; Lewis White Beck and Yirmiyahu Yovel present the second one: Beck, *A Commentary on Kant's Critique of Practical Reason* (Chicago: University of Chicago Press, 1960), 270–271, and Yovel, *Kant and the Philosophy of History* (Princeton: Princeton University Press, 1996), 113.

35. To the first: If we don't set moral perfection as our goal, we are essentially saying that we may rest satisfied with our imperfections, and not try to improve ourselves. But that is surely an objectionable picture of morality. Instead, "being as good as we can be" itself entails realizing at every moment that we could still improve our characters further. But that's just to say that the real goal is perfection—and lies beyond us at every moment of the moral life.

To the second: Yovel says that Kant's argument would seem to lead to an additional postulate of the immortality of the *body*, which he calls "a strange Schellingian notion that could never have entered Kant's mind" (*loc. cit.*). But a notion of this sort could well have entered Kant's mind. Lessing, who anticipated and probably influenced much of Kant's picture of moral faith, speculated about the possibility of reincarnation at the end of his "Education of the Human Race." Kant may similarly have seen a future life as possibly embodied, rather than bodiless (at points, his language indeed suggests such a thing: see, for instance, RWB 68 and 77). In any case, as Wood points out (*Kant's Moral Religion*, 123–124), Kant's epistemology rules out the possibility of our knowing anything about what happens to us after death, which allows both for the possibility of our continuing in some altered bodily state, and for our being disembodied, but nevertheless—somehow—able to work on our characters.

36. Thaddeus Metz brings out a deep connection between believing in immortality, and believing in God's existence—and provides a better argument than Kant's for the belief in immortality—in "The Immortality Requirement of Life's Meaning," *Ratio* 16 (2003).

37. We might think that a merciful God would grant us happiness beyond what we deserve.

38. See, among other sources, CPR A813=B841; G 393, 396; CPrR 110, 130; CJ 450; RWB 4–5, 36.

39. CPrR 110; see also 124.

40. I discuss Kant's debt to Smith, and its connection to judgment, in *A Third Concept of Liberty*.

41. There are arguments that one could give for a highest good composed of happiness together with virtue. We might say, as Allen Wood does, that happiness is our actual end, as finite, natural beings, and that reason must therefore incorporate it, along with its own end—virtue—into any overall end it sets for us. Or we might interpret Kant's "happiness," as Stephen Engstrom does, so that it is close to Aristotle's "eudaimonia": an intrinsically rational and active condition of which virtue is a constituent part. (Engstrom, "Happiness and the Highest Good in Aristotle and Kant," in Engstrom and Whiting (eds), *Aristotle, Kant, and the Stoics*.)

But these arguments are open to serious challenges. To the first, we might respond that Kantian reason, in its transcendental freedom, is supposed to be able to suspend all actual facts about us, and change them if necessary. Ought implies can, for Kant, entails that no mere fact about us—even our mortality—can be regarded as fixed if morality requires that it not be fixed. So the mere fact that happiness is our natural end, the mere fact that we have certain desires and they set certain goals for us, cannot dictate anything about our *proper* end.

And to the second we might say that Engstrom's happiness, even if it is what Kant meant by that term—there is reason to doubt that, given Kant's insistence on the heterogeneity of virtue and happiness—no longer coincides with what nature sets as our end. But if our goal in seeking happiness is not fixed by our empirical nature, then it is hard to see why we could not defy that nature more dramatically, and pursue only ends set for us by reason.

42. See, for instance, G 393, 418, CJ 434n, RWB 58, 67, 134–135.

43. See my "Smith und Kulturrelativismus," in Fricke and Schütt (eds), *Adam Smith als Moral Philosoph*.

44. Can we just allow "happiness" to include nirvana, the beatific vision, etc.? Not if "happiness" means, as it does for Kant, the satisfaction of the desires we naturally have. No-one naturally desires nirvana, on the Buddha's teachings; the point rather is to *overcome* what we naturally desire. And many Christians and Jews say the same about the beatific vision or *kedushah*: that we can attain them only by overcoming our yearnings for what we ordinarily call "happiness," not by satisfying those yearnings. Nachmanides, for instance, describes *kedushah* as a separation from our natural desires: *Commentary on the Torah*, "Leviticus," trans. Rabbi Charles Chavel (New York: Shilo Publishing House, 1974), pp. 282–284.

45. This means that it cannot be *contrary* to virtue—we cannot have moral reason to believe in an immoral telos—and that we must will it for all rational beings, not just for ourselves and our friends. But it also means that there should be some plausible case that our telos is *dependent on* virtue, attainable only by way of virtue. As Wood points out (*Kant's Moral Religion*, 125–126), Kant understands the highest good as involving, not simply virtue and happiness somehow added together, but a *systematic* connection between the two such that virtue is the *ground* of the happiness we seek. But the two components as Kant conceives them have too little in common for one to ground the other. Virtue expresses and preserves the conditions for freedom, not happiness, and happiness arises from the satisfaction of sensuous inclination, not

from virtue. So there is reason, within Kant's own system, for moving away from regarding "happiness," as Kant conceives it, as the second component of the highest good.

46. Susan Wolf elaborates this point in "The Meanings of Lives," in J. Perry, M. Bratman, J. Fischer (eds), *Introduction to Philosophy: Classical and Contemporary Readings* (Oxford: Oxford University Press, 2007).

47. As we saw in § 46 of this Part, Kant himself appeals to the approval of an impartial spectator when constructing his *summum bonum*.

48. Kant says that the Stoics were wrong to think that virtue is enough to make for a satisfying life: CPrR 118, 127.

49. See Wood, *Kant's Moral Religion*, 83–84, 125–126.

Part III: Introductory text

1. The degree to which religious teachings vindicate the value of non-religious lives varies, in different religious traditions. Some religions teach that only a life according to their path is worth living. Others see the creation of the world by a loving God, or its rootedness in a sublime *tao*, as giving worth to the lives of all human beings, at least as long as they achieve a certain level of moral virtue. These are matters of specific religious doctrine, rather than the shape of revealed religion in general—of the content rather than the form of revelation. I don't think philosophy can say much for or against them.

2. "It is easy to decide what sort of value life has for us if it is assessed merely by *what one enjoys* (the natural end of the sum of all inclinations, happiness)[:] Less than zero" (CJ 434n).

3. Anyone with a view of the human telos must deny the adequacy of alternative views (that comes with having a view, in general). Even a person who thinks we can achieve our telos in a wide variety of ways does so on the basis of a specific account of how all those kinds of life achieve the human telos, and such accounts inevitably contradict one another. This is not to say that people with one view of the human good must see people with different views as by that fact failing to *achieve* the good. A secular person might see a religious person as leading a worthwhile life insofar as the latter's commitments lead her to build close communal bonds, contribute to social justice, or enjoy the music, architecture, and other aesthetic goods that come with religious traditions. But this is to translate the goods of the religious life into something non-religious: a religious Christian or Buddhist or Jew herself would not be able to view the goods of her life in (just) the same light. Similarly, a religious person might see a secular person as achieving many of the goods of a religious life unknowingly: as properly venerating the image of God in other human beings by pursuing social justice, say, or properly loving the image of God in the beauties of art or nature. But again, the secular person will not see the goods he or she is pursuing in the same light—*could* not do so without giving up his or her distinctive conception of the human telos. Religious and secular people can respect one another's lives, but they cannot accept one another's understanding of those lives.

Part III: Chapter 1

1. There has been considerable writing in recent years on the "meaning" of life—which I regard as a less happy formulation of the question I am trying to pursue. (See Thaddeus Metz, "Recent Work on the Meaning of Life," *Ethics* 112 [July 2002]. Metz does not regard the "meaning" and the "worth" of life as equivalent.) But most of this literature is content to draw on the intuitions we already have about what makes a life worthwhile, while I regard those intuitions as unreliable.

One contemporary philosopher unsatisfied with intuitions alone is Thomas Nagel (in "The Absurd," in *Mortal Questions* [Cambridge: Cambridge University Press, 1979], and in chapter XI of VN). I agree with a good deal that Nagel says, but it is worth noting two central differences between my approach and his. First, Nagel does not place the problem of finding an objective point for our lives in an historical framework. For him, life has always looked meaningless from the objective stance. This misses a significant feature of modernity, I believe, and makes it hard to explain why premodern thinkers, in a variety of cultures, had views according to which life was not objectively meaningless at all—had instead a definite, objective goal.

Second, and relatedly, I do not agree with Nagel that questions about whether life is worth living are independent of our daily deliberations. ("Relatedly," because the pre-modern thinkers who thought there was an objective point to or lives believed that that point needed to play a central role in our everyday decision-making.) Nagel sees the problem about what he calls "the meaning of life" as arising solely when we take up an objective, or "external", viewpoint on our lives (VN 209-210, 217). From the subjective or internal standpoint, he believes, values appear to us as real; and doubts about whether there is anything worth doing cannot arise: "To the subjective view, the conditions that deter-mine whether life makes sense are simply given, as part of the package" (215). And the subjective view is the view of deliberation: "When you are considering a career, marriage, children, or even whether to go on a diet, review a book, or buy a car, the external standpoint is excluded and you face the matter . . . from the internal standpoint of ordinary life" (VN 218). Consequently, for him, the apparent absurdity of life is irrelevant to the decisions of ordinary life. But I don't think this is true. The prompting scenarios I lay out below are meant to demonstrate how questions about the worth of life can at many points break into decisions about precisely "whether to go on a diet . . . or buy a book," let alone about whether to enter, or leave, a career or marriage.

2. The pluralism, I take it, is an offshoot of the appeal to common sense. Common sense—today, at least—tells us that there are many different kinds of good lives.

3. Some would say that the existentialists did. I don't think that's the best reading of their position, however: see § 27 of this Part. (The absurdists—Kafka, Ionesco, Beckett, Albee—did hold such a view. But they tended to be novelists and playwrights rather than philosophers.)

4. Prioritization can of course be a *moral* problem—do I keep my promise to meet my friend or do I help the accident victim in front of me?—and I don't mean to diminish the interest of these questions. But I am not talking about morality here.

5. Ludwig Wittgenstein, *Philosophical Investigations*, trans. G. E. M. Anscombe, 3rd edn (New York: Macmillan, 1958), § 38.

6. Similarly, if Green rejects what we consider to be common sense, her reasons for doing that will presumably mirror Olive's reasons for *accepting* it. And for us, sitting in philosophical judgment of Green and Olive, it's helpful to remember that we can't dismiss Green without losing our ability to defend Olive: that we will have to *argue* Green out of the choice she seems about to make if we want to help argue Olive into the choice she is inclined to make.

7. "For me to see anything as enhancing my life, I must see it as enhancing life in a generally intelligible way, in a way that pertains to *human* life and not just to my particular life." James Griffin, *On Human Rights* (Oxford: Oxford University Press, 2008), p. 114.

8. I consider reasons supporting this thought in § 23 of this Part.

9. Indeed, we essentially reject *his* subjective attitude, which requires reasons for a thing to be worthwhile.

10. Compare Sabina Lovibond: "[T]here is a difficulty with . . . thinking of the ['subjective'] as logically isolated from that part of our mental life which is regulated by external reality.

The difficulty is that 'subjective' dispositions, thus represented, are liable to flag when too much attention is fixed upon them. The part they are asked to play is embarrassingly naive—as if we were to be asked to relive the experience of some early childhood birthday party, where we were expected to gurgle enthusiastically over our presents, but under the benign scrutiny of a band of adult spectators, were awkwardly unable to mount the required show of glee."— Lovibond, *Realism and Imagination in Ethics* (University of Minnesota Press, 1983), p. 9.

11. Simon Blackburn suggests that the significance of life depends on our moods, and that a person who doubts whether life has meaning "needs a tonic more than an argument." (Blackburn, *Being Good* [Oxford: Oxford University Press, 2001], p. 80.) It's hard to imagine that he would say the same about someone who asks whether there is a God, or if human beings will ever overcome their propensity to oppress and kill one another. Cheerfulness is no substitute for getting the facts right, on any subject where there are facts. So presumably Blackburn would say that there are no facts of the matter where the meaning of life is concerned. But for those who link the question about the value of their lives to beliefs in God, or an afterlife, or the need to annihilate our sense of selfhood, there certainly are facts of this matter. And those people may be wrong, but their beliefs are not unintelligible. So to prescribe a tonic for them, instead of responding to their factual concerns, is to misunderstand the nature of their questions.

12. See Clifford Geertz, "Common Sense as a Cultural System," in Geertz, *Local Knowledge* (New York: Basic Books, 1983).

13. The psychologist Daniel Gilbert demonstrates how in some circumstances false beliefs can spread through a society more effectively than true ones. Imagine a game, he suggests, in which teams spoke to each other for a while on the phone and at the end got one point for every accurate belief that the team shares, and lost one point for every inaccurate belief it shares. What would happen if one team came to accept the false belief that "Talking on the phone all day and night will ultimately make you very happy"? This belief in itself will not help the team win the game—indeed it will deprive them of a point—but "it may have the compensatory effect of keeping [the team's members] on the telephone for more of the time, thus increasing the total number of accurate messages they transmit.... The lesson to be learned . . . is that inaccurate beliefs can prevail in the belief-transmission game if they somehow facilitate their own 'means of transmission'" (Gilbert, *Stumbling on Happiness* [New York: Vintage Books, 2005], p. 238). But the belief that life is worthwhile, and that it is especially worthwhile if lived so as to sustain and promote one's society's practices, obviously facilitates its own means of transmission in precisely the way that Gilbert's telephone claim does. Claims of this sort are excellent examples of what he calls "super-replicating false belief[s]" (239), and indeed close to the examples that he goes on to give.

14. Wittgenstein, *Tractatus Logicus-Philosophicus*, trans. D. F. Pears and B. F. McGuinness (London: Routledge and Kegan Paul, 1961), § 6.521.

15. Wittgenstein, *Philosophical Investigations*, § 124.

16. I should say that as far as I know the later Wittgenstein did not say anything directly on my question. The argument I shall consider is one some of his followers might construct from what he said on other issues, not one he made himself.

17. Nagel puts this sort of position well: "It may be objected that the standpoint from which these doubts are supposed to be felt does not exist . . . If we retain our usual standards of what is important, then questions about the significance of what we are doing with our lives will be answerable in the usual way. But if we do not, then those questions can mean nothing to us, since there is no longer any content to the idea of what matters, and hence no content to the idea that nothing does." (Nagel, "The Absurd," in *Mortal Questions*, p. 17. See also

VN 216). Nagel rejects the objection, as I do, although not for quite the same reasons. See also David Cooper, "Life and Meaning," *Ratio* 18 (2005).

18. Or at least that they each *can* be worthwhile if they are done right, where ordinary criteria will determine what counts as doing them right (loving someone who is honest and loves you back, pursuing political causes that serve the common good, and not just your own welfare or a personal vendetta).

19. See McDowell, "Virtue and Reason," 61.

20. On the crude verificationism of Alfred Ayer, all of these notions—as well as claims that life is or is not worthwhile—are indeed meaningless: see Ayer, "The Claims of Philosophy," in E. D. Klemke (ed.), *The Meaning of Life* (New York: Oxford University Press, 2000). But Wittgenstein was opposed to such verificationism.

21. Such a response sounds like G. E. Moore's unfortunate proof of the external world, derided by Wittgenstein in *On Certainty*, in which my everyday acceptance of the reality of my hands is supposed to answer the philosophical skeptic who doubts the existence of the external world. Wittgenstein rightly says that the beliefs of common sense can't bear so much philosophical freight. They are all right as they stand, but they don't answer questions about reality in the way that philosophers ask such questions. Our ordinary discourse about the worth of everyday choices and activities will similarly not have the structure to bear up in the face of someone who wants to question whether that entire everyday way of living is a waste of time or not. If someone doubts that pleasure or even survival is a good or not, it is of no help to say that she has in the past regarded things as good that conduced to her pleasure or survival.

22. See Thomas Nagel's "Death" for an excellent discussion of the issues involved here.

Part III: Chapter 2

1. Most of the recent philosophical literature on "the meaning of life" seems to start from intuition. (See for instance, the papers collected in Thaddeus Metz (ed.), "Special Issue: Meaning in Life," *Philosophical Papers*, 34 (2005).) The assumption that intuition is an adequate basis for an account of the meaning of life rarely if ever receives any defense. There also seems to be an assumption that life *must* be meaningful, and the task of philosophers is just to figure out where that meaning lies. I don't share either of these assumptions.

2. PE §§ 53–55, 112–113.

3. Jonathan Dancy, correctly I think, describes Moore's method of absolute isolation as "just too bizarre to stand as an appropriate test" for value, adding that many things that seem to have intrinsic value, like a happy marriage, couldn't possibly exist in isolation (*Ethics Without Principles*, p. 166). Dancy is, however, more sanguine than I am that Moore's test has disappeared from the philosophical scene: he does not, for instance, consider the similarities between Moore's test and Nozick's "experience machine."

4. "I agree both with Professor Moore's account of what is implied in a value's being intrinsic, and with what I take to be his view, that goodness, in its most fundamental meaning, . . . is intrinsic" (W. D. Ross, *The Right and the Good* [Oxford: Clarendon, 1930], p. 116). The "account" here referred to is from an essay by Moore in *Philosophical Studies*, not from *Principia Ethica*, and the long passage Ross quotes from that essay makes no explicit mention of the method of absolute isolation. But Moore's point in the passage is much the same as the one he had made earlier by way of the isolation method.

5. E.g.: "[I]f any one is inclined to doubt [my claim for the intrinsic goodness of virtue] and to think that, say, pleasure alone is intrinsically good, it seems to me enough to ask the question whether, of two states of the universe holding equal amounts of pleasure, we should really think no better of one in which the actions and dispositions of all the persons in it were thoroughly virtuous than of one in which they were highly vicious" (ibid. 134).

6. Smart, in J. J. C. Smart and Bernard Williams, *Utilitarianism: For and Against* (Cambridge: Cambridge University Press, 1973), p. 27.

7. Ibid. 18–22.

8. It is remarkable that Smart simply slips right out of the subjunctive voice in which he has couched his scenario, at this point: he does not even attempt to imagine what our feelings of approval and disapproval *would* be in a world that contained such machines, but appeals to the feeling we have now about the scenario. According to his own usual way of dealing with things, the proper test even of many objects of value in the actual world depends on feelings we *would* have under certain conditions—conditions in which we were bound less by tradition and superstition, and in which we had better information about the effects of the object under consideration—not on the feelings we *actually* have.

9. This is exactly the same as Smart's scenario, in fact, except that the machine provides us with a full life, with pains and pleasures in whatever proportion one chooses to put into it, rather than just with pleasure.

10. True intimacy was also one of Moore's absolute goods.

11. I confess that I also don't share Moore's intuitions. On an intuitive level, I don't find anything implausible about attributing value, even supreme value, to the "consciousness of pleasure exist[ing] . . . by itself," nor do I see, offhand, why the pleasurable contemplation of beauty, or the enjoyment of intimate affections, should be so much better than pleasure by itself. The life of pleasure "by itself," to the extent that I can make sense of such a thing, seems quite appealing to me. And I certainly don't see why a world containing beautiful things, but with no-one around to experience them, should be in any way superior to a world containing ugly things, with no-one around to experience them. I am uneasily aware that these intuitions may simply mark me as a shallower and perhaps less decent person than G. E. Moore, although I take some comfort in the fact that no less refined, and by all accounts deeply decent, a person than Henry Sidgwick seems to share my, rather than Moore's, intuitions on this matter. More seriously, the fact that two such highly intelligent, and otherwise similar, people as Moore and Sidgwick should have sharply different intuitions on these matters suggests that "intuition" is not a good test for value.

   In addition, when I am asked to compare pleasure alone with pleasure in the contemplation of beauty, I am aware of strong pressures to opt for the second because that way I will look more sophisticated to others. I would be ashamed to admit that I am so shallow as to be satisfied with a life of mere pleasure, unconnected to an active use of my reflective capacities, and so selfish as to be satisfied with pleasure unconnected to intimate relations with other people. But it is likely that Moore, too, was affected by this embarrassment about plumping for pleasure alone, and that everyone who has agreed with him has been similarity affected. It is a mystery to me what leads people to believe that they have successfully set this feeling aside when answering Moore's question.

12. These points, of course, should make us reluctant to put too much trust in any supposed intuition into intrinsic or absolute goodness.

13. Indeed if, as is not implausible, a world of Smart's electrode operators would be a world without war or violent crime (if we can satisfy all our desires by plugging into a pleasure-machine, what would ever lead us to violence?), it would seem—on Smart's own principles—that we *should* prefer the machine-made lives.

14. In the Smart and Nozick versions of the test, we of course have to choose *whether* to be hooked up to the electrodes or machine. But *what* we choose, if we do opt for the electronic stimulation, is a life in which there will be no further choices and that makes this very unlike our usual choices. In the normal situation of choice, I need to pick some good or goods with an eye out for the choices I might make later on, and make sure that I have access to the goods I am likely to need for those choices (the goods, for instance, that I need to make choices at all: which will include knowledge of reality).

15. Moore asks after our "judgment" of them (PE § 55), but he gives us no way of judging except by appeal to feelings.

16. Storage is of course a potential cost here. I won't take an extra refrigerator if I have no place to put it.

17. One could draw from this the lesson that religious belief is in fact rational: see Adams, FIG, chapter 2, for an elegant "inference to the best explanation" argument for God. But I am in the end unconvinced by Adams's argument—as I am by other attempts to demonstrate God's existence rationally (see Appendix I). I would say instead that the belief in objective goods is at least as *non*-rational as belief in God, that it requires the same sort of faith, the same sort of move beyond rational grounds.

    For an interesting "inference to the best explanation" argument for objective goods, see Charles Larmore, *The Autonomy of Morality* (Cambridge: Cambridge University Press, 2008), chapters 3 and 5. Charles Taylor also offers such an argument in *Sources of the Self* (Cambridge: Harvard University Press, 1989), but Taylor is a theist who would not, I think, resist the comparison between arguments for objective goods and arguments for God.

18. A term Finnis would dislike: he rejects the word "intuition" for the kind of non-inferential insight he is describing at FE 51 (see also FE 22). But what he calls "insight" fits, I think, under "intuition" as I am using the term.

19. I owe this observation to Patrick Frierson, who rightly thinks it brings out something important about the project in which both are engaged. Finnis's list can be found at NLNR 86–89 and Nussbaum's in Nussbaum, "Defense of Aristotelian Essentialism," *Political Theory*, May 1992, pp. 217–218. Finnis does say that "sexual intercourse may be play, and/or expression of love or friendship, and/or an effort to procreate" (NLNR 86), where play and love or friendship are basic goods for him and procreation is a form of the basic good "life." But, under his way of looking at things, this means that sexual intercourse is just one form of or means to a more basic goal for us, which allows for it to be replaced by other forms of play or friendship. This gives Finnis room for the view that a celibate life can be a perfectly good life, which is important to his arguments, elsewhere, against homosexuality and pre-marital sex (presumably it also helps him defend the goodness of the life of Catholic priests and nuns).

20. NLNR 53–54, 71–72; FE 57–60.

21. Especially, but not exclusively: the national and international enforcement of basic human rights, the measurement of welfare, and the provision of aid, in accordance with this measurement of welfare, by each country to its citizens and by NGOs and wealthy nations to the poor in nations that do not adequately serve their own citizens.

22. McDowell, "Virtue and Reason," pp. 57–58.

23. This is a central theme of Elizabeth Anderson's *Value in Ethics and Economics* (Cambridge: Harvard University Press, 1993).

24. Frances Kamm, *Morality, Mortality,* Volume I (New York: Oxford University Press, 1993), p. 31.

25. On whether honor-killings, or terrorism for certain causes, should be exempted from the former, say, or on what sort of property regime best expresses the latter.

508 NOTES TO PAGES 198-206

26. Not exclusively so: social pressures can also lead us to believe in factual propositions (the existence of witches) and false scientific theories (Nazi or Soviet biology, creationism).

27. See J. Baird Callicott, *Beyond the Land Ethic* (Albany: State University of New York Press, 1999), and discussion in Patrick Frierson, "Smithian Intrinsic Value," in V. Brown and S. Fleischacker, *Essays on Adam Smith's Moral Philosophy* (London: Routledge, 2010).

28. See David Velleman, "Well-Being and Time," in John Fischer (ed.), *The Metaphysics of Death* (Stanford: Stanford University Press, 1993).

Part III: Chapter 3

1. One might think that this enlightenment need not be supernatural. But it must be. In the first place, it is supposed to be a position in which I can reconcile myself with the entire natural order. And in the second place, it is supposed to be a position in which my desires no longer succeed one another in an endless train, the satisfaction of one just breeding a new kind of dissatisfaction. But everything we know about human biology suggests that we need this structure of desire in order to keep on struggling for survival. The idea, in Buddhism, that we need a series of reincarnations in order to achieve nirvana, reflects the supernatural quality of its vision of enlightenment.

   I want to emphasize, however, that I have deliberately described supernatural enlightenment vaguely enough that it need not coincide with the telos of Buddhism alone. Reconciliation with some ultimate world-spirit, or with a *tao* underlying the universe, or indeed with some Jewish and Christian and Muslim understandings of God—as "source" or "ground" of the world (*mekor ha'olam*)—may take much the same form. But faith that this reconciliation is possible is required by all these religious claims, and is not significantly more rational than faith in an afterlife. The supposedly naturalistic versions of religion that have become so popular in the last century or so, when not just a colorful way of encouraging people to be virtuous, do not have great metaphysical advantages over the supernatural versions they replace—they are not, indeed, all that naturalistic, in the end.

2. It's perhaps important to note that I do not take these views to rely primarily on intuition, like the views canvassed in the previous chapter. Rather, they are defended by appeal to metaphysical claims or supposed empirical facts (sometimes *mixed* with appeals to intuition). I want to suggest that these appeals are of much the same quality as the ones commonly used to defend religion.

3. The two claims I've just made are rooted in Marx's and Freud's own writings, but in what follows I'll use the labels "Marxist" and "Freudian" rather loosely: as a shorthand for what a socio-political and a psychoanalytic explanation of the phenomena in question *might* look like. For a deep investigation into the challenge that psychoanalysis poses to any teleological account of our lives, see Jonathan Lear, *Happiness, Death, and the Remainder of Life* (Cambridge: Harvard University Press, 2000).

4. Unsurprisingly, sexual passion is used in many religions as a metaphor for commitment to God—think of *Song of Songs* or the vision of Teresa of Avila or the erotic imagery in Jain temples—while religious metaphors are often used to enhance erotic poetry. It is also unsurprising that the struggle between secular liberals and religious traditionalists today turns so centrally on sexual mores: with liberals complaining about the repression of women and gay people among the traditionalists (the repression of women being based, often, on a fear of encouraging "loose" sexuality), while traditionalists cite liberal attitudes towards sexuality as among the gravest threats to their religious commitments.

5. And even being in love involves some propositional attitudes. Lovers admire one another, and can give reasons for why they maintain their relationship—each supposes, for instance, that neither she nor her partner is in it purely for financial or social gain. Even if they don't expect to be together forever, they will look back on their moments of delight in each other with distaste if they come to think they were wrong about these propositions. The feeling of delight itself, I think we can say, is committed to these propositions. Even if you aren't explicitly thinking, when looking into your lover's eyes, that very unthinking delight is implicitly dependent on a number of beliefs about what your lover is like, and can fade quickly if you change those beliefs.

6. This kind of love is probably more healthy—more likely to endure, certainly—than a love between people primarily committed to love itself.

7. These are just the questions that religious believers need to ask often, and are expected to answer positively if they retain their faith.

8. See the quotation from James Griffin in note 7 on p. 503.

9. "[T]he senses of the social man are *other* senses than those of the non-social man. Only through the objectively unfolded richness of man's essential being is the richness of subjective *human* sensibility (a musical ear, an eye for beauty of form—in short *senses* capable of human gratification, senses confirming themselves as essential powers of man) either cultivated or brought into being" ("Economic and Philosophic Manuscripts of 1844," in *The Marx-Engels Reader*, R. Tucker (ed.), 2nd edn [New York: Norton, 1978], pp. 88–89). It is perhaps obvious that this eschatological vision of politics requires faith.

10. Thanks to Andrew Koppelman for describing this strip to me. Thomas Nagel also puts this point well: "If no one's life has any meaning in itself, how can it acquire meaning through devotion to the meaningless lives of others?" (VN 217).

11. If I make someone's life less worthwhile, I can't be said to be "helping" her, even if I fulfill her desires. It isn't "help" if, for instance, I sell her a drug to which she is addicted.

12. See, for instance, Anthony Laden, "Evaluating Social Reasons: Hobbes vs. Hegel," *Journal of Philosophy* 102: 7.

13. See the quotation from a seventeenth century response to Galileo in Charles Taylor, "Rationality," in Martin Hollis and Steven Lukes (eds), *Rationality and Relativism* (Cambridge: MIT Press, 1982), p. 94, and Taylor's comments on the passage on pp. 93–94.

14. Dickens, *Bleak House* (London: Thomas Nelson & Sons, 1930), p. 39.

15. This idea has some merit: we'll return to it, as an element of religious views, in Part IV.

16. See George Dickie, *Art and the Aesthetic: An Institutional Analysis* (Ithaca: NY: Cornell University Press, 1974) and *Art Circle: A Theory of Art* (Chicago: Spectrum Press, 1997).

17. In *A Third Concept of Liberty*, I give an account of Mill's argument for higher pleasures that does not rely on Aristotelian metaphysics (pp. 116–118, and more generally in Chapter 5), but there I am concerned only with the *political* advantages of an emphasis on higher pleasures, not whether they are intrinsically better than lower ones.

18. See G. E. Moore's critique of this claim in PE §§ 29–34.

19. "I think we cannot expect naturalistic (for instance, biological) investigations of 'human nature' to answer . . . questions [about what constitutes excellent human activity] convincingly. Even if Aristotle's biological teleology had given him more of an answer to [these questions] than I think it did, we cannot today expect help on this point from biology. If there is a teleology intrinsic to *our* biology, it is one in which the *telos* served in fact by evolving organisms is the propagation of their genes; and efficacy in serving *that telos* has, I think, no plausibility as a measure of ethical virtue."—Robert Adams, *A Theory of Virtue* (Oxford: Clarendon Press, 2006), p. 51.

20. Blackburn, *Being Good*, 42–43.

21. Compare Gibbard, *Wise Choices, Apt Feelings*, pp. 28–29: "[I]t is crucial to distinguish human goals from the Darwinian surrogate of purpose in the 'design' of human beings. Darwin's achievement was to show how the appearance of purpose and intricate design in living things . . . could be explained without supposing purposeful design. The Darwinian evolutionary surrogate for divine purpose is now seen to be the reproduction of one's genes. That has not, as far as I know, been anyone's goal, but the biological world looks as if someone quite resourceful had designed each living thing for that purpose. Let me call this surrogate purpose, the reproduction of an organism's genes, its evolutionary *telos*. . . . My evolutionary *telos*, the reproduction of my genes, has no straightforward bearing on what it makes sense for me to want or to act to attain. Specifically, that something would fulfill my *telos* is neither a reason for wanting it to come about nor a reason for wanting it not to do so."

22. Which in my own experience has felt more like an intrinsically valuable activity than anything else. But how could this alone make life worth living? Imagine telling your children: "Nothing you do in life will be intrinsically worthwhile except raising your own children." Won't that undermine your ability to raise them? Surely it's hard to accept that it's worthwhile for human beings to raise children just so that the children can raise children, who in turn will raise more children . . . Not only does this leave the childless without any reason to stay alive, but it doesn't give the children we're trying to raise anything much to strive for.

    In addition, this is of course about the easiest of our candidates to see as something to which we are inclined for purely biological reasons—something that serves our genes rather than our whole selves—and that our societies might encourage us to believe regardless of whether it serves our individual needs.

23. It is, moreover, a matter of common experience that we often find the strong commitments other people have to a particular activity or project hard to understand, and explain them as a matter of irrational obsession, even while having commitments ourselves that others find incomprehensible. So the idea that the human world is filled with people all of whom have a blind faith in the importance of some project or another while finding the projects and faith of their neighbors absurd should not be a surprising one.

24. Alasdair MacIntyre famously sees our current moral language as but a collection of remnants of an earlier, Aristotelian worldview in which these terms made much better sense, and claims that used them could be properly debated. Rational discourse about ethics will only be possible again, he maintains, if we return to some version of Aristotelianism. I am saying something similar about our language games of "ultimate worth," except that, with many of MacIntyre's critics, I do not believe we can return to Aristotle. MacIntyre proposes a sociological replacement for Aristotle's teleological biology, but after the rejection of "final causes" that defines modern science, and especially after Darwin, I do not think we can return to any view according to which it is supposed to be a factual matter that human beings have purposes.

Part III Chapter 4

1. A number of philosophers have also stressed the narrative shape of lives: see, for example, AV, chapter 15, Velleman, "Well-Being and Time," and Wolf, "The Meanings of Lives."
2. Compare Robert Adams: "You may be very virtuous, you may be brilliant, beautiful, successful, rich, and famous; but if you do not enjoy your life, it cannot plausibly be called a good life *for you*. We may think of this as the kernel of truth in hedonism, or as the important truth to be found in the neighborhood of hedonism." FIG 95. Adams also regards

enjoying one's life as a necessary, but not sufficient criterion of its worth on 93–94. He allows, however, for an excellent life to include features that are not enjoyed at all on 101.

3. An excellent discussion of the relation between pleasure and time can be found in FIG 96–97.

4. From here we can see why we might want to exist eternally. Our consciousness does not brook limits: it wants at each moment to continue to the next one. As Thomas Nagel says, "Observed from without, human beings obviously have a natural lifespan and cannot live much longer than a hundred years. A man's sense of his own experience, on the other hand, does not embody this idea of a natural limit. His existence defines for him an essentially open-ended future, containing the usual mixture of goods and evils that he has found so tolerable in the past. . . . [H]e finds himself the subject of a *life*, with an indeterminate and not essentially limited future. Viewed in this way, death, no matter how inevitable, is an abrupt cancellation of indefinitely extensive positive goods." (Nagel, "Death," in *Mortal Questions* [Cambridge: Cambridge University Press, 1979], pp. 9–10).

5. Compare Kant: "[P]leasure and pain . . . are both included in the temporal series [of our past experience], and disappear with it; they do not constitute a totality with the present enjoyment of life, but are rather displaced by it as it succeeds them" (RWB 70n).

6. On this, even Hume agrees: "[T]he prospect of past pain is agreeable, when we are satisfy'd with our present condition; as on the other hand our past pleasures give us uneasiness, when we enjoy nothing at present equal to them" (T 376).

7. And if each moment does encompass whatever was of value in past moments and surpass them, then it is quite reasonable that at each moment we want to continue to the next one. (See note 4, above.)

8. FIG 88–89. See also Kraut, *What is Good and Why* (Cambridge: Harvard University Press, 2007), 34, 120–126, and Ronald Dworkin, *Sovereign Virtue* (Cambridge: Harvard University Press, 2000), 18, 41–44, 291–292.

9. Compare Korsgaard: "[T]he notion of happiness is just as obscure as the notion of the good. In fact we can interpret 'happiness' so broadly that it means pretty much the same thing as the final good." ("The Origin of the Good and Our Animal Nature," p. 11).

10. Leon Kojen clarified this point in a wonderful lecture on NE 1.7 at Williams College.

11. AV chapter 14; McDowell, "Virtue and Reason"; Kraut, *What is Good and Why*, pp. 5, 90, 106, 133. Korsgaard also compares goodness to health, understanding the final good of conscious animals to be "something that constitutes or contributes to the [well-functioning] condition of something that can experience its own condition as a good" (ibid. 34; see also 21–24, on the relationship of goodness to health). I am inclined to ask both Korsgaard and Kraut, "Is it then *nonsensical* to view one's health as getting in the way of a higher good—say, nirvana, or closeness to God? Are ascetic Hindus and Christians, and martyrs in any faith, making a mistake about the meaning of the word 'good'? And if not, what sort of mistake are they making? How would you convince them of your naturalistic, biologically-oriented view?"

12. *Third Concept of Liberty*, chapter 5.

13. Compare AV, chapters 9 and 18.

14. For a thoughtful reading of Nietzsche along these lines, see Alexander Nehamas, *Nietzsche: Life as Literature* (Cambridge: Harvard University Press, 1985), especially chapter 6.

15. Compare Taylor, *A Secular Age*, pp. 586–587.

16. TJ, § 65, pp. 432–433.

17. "Persons, character and morality," in Williams, *Moral Luck* (Cambridge: Cambridge University Press, 1981), pp. 10–13; "The Makropoulos Case," *Problems of the Self* (Cambridge: Cambridge University Press, 1973), pp. 85–88.

18. "Persons, character and morality," pp.10-11.

19. "Persons, character and morality," pp. 10–12.

20. Williams considers the fear of death to be irrational. I'm not sure why. He gives the Epicureans' famous argument that death is nothing to us, but that seems to me entirely unconvincing, and should surely be so to him, given that he considers it rational to care about things that will happen after our deaths ("Persons, character and morality," p. 13). But if it is rational for me to care about events that happen after I die, why would it be irrational for me to care about the fact that I will not be aware of those events (to care about the event, we might say, *of* my not being aware of future events)? Why should it be irrational for us to care about simply being aware of things? That, it seems to me, is precisely what we want when we want to go on existing eternally: we want never to have to stop being aware of what goes on.

21. Williams, "Critique of Utilitarianism," in Smart and Williams, *Utilitarianism: For and Against*, pp. 112–113, 116.

22. ibid, p. 116.

23. Is it a matter of the *time* one spends on one's projects? But we spend more time preparing meals, probably, than on anything else . . . Or of the *feelings* we have about our projects? But those, surely, can be misleading.

24. See the essays in Amelie Rorty (ed.) *Explaining Emotions* (Berkeley: University of California Press, 1980), and Ronald de Souza, *The Rationality of Emotions* (Cambridge: The MIT Press, 1990).

25. The hard determinism on which Spinozism depends is probably also undemonstrable, something one can accept only on faith. But without hard determinism, the argument that all suffering must happen the way it does falls away, and reconciliation with the world becomes correspondingly harder: one loses all reason to accept suffering rather than fighting against it.

26. See quotation from Lovibond above, note 10 on pp. 503–504.

Part III: Chapter 5

1. Compare Korsgaard, "Aristotle and Kant on the Source of Value," in her *Creating the Kingdom of Ends* (Cambridge: Cambridge University Press, 1996). Paul Guyer also provides evidence that Kant saw rational agency—freedom—as providing ultimate value to our lives in *Kant's Groundwork for the Metaphysics of Morals* (London: Continuum, 2007), pp. 12–15.

2. Kant identifies humanity with Christ at RWB 60–67 and 74–76; he uses the first-cause proof of God to demonstrate the possibility of free will in the Third Antinomy of CPR—as if each act of free will were like the creation of a new universe (A 444–451=B476–488); and he proposes that we see ourselves as if we were creating an entire universe when we determine moral principles, in the Typic of the second *Critique* (CPrR 69–70; we are also, of course, supposed to see ourselves as lawgivers to the world according to the *Groundwork*: G 433–436). And in "Theory and Practice," Kant explicitly says that insofar as we act morally, we may see ourselves "on analogy with divinity" (Ak 8:280n).

3. See, for example, Bernard Williams in ELP, and Alasdair MacIntyre in AV, both of whom begin with the work of Alan Gewirth.

4. The last of these claims is made explicit in her more recent book, *Self-Constitution*. See especially chapter 9.

5. Wittgenstein, *Philosophical Investigations*, trans. G. E. M. Anscombe (New York: Macmillan, 1958), §§ 1, 87, 217; and *On Certainty*, ed. G. E. M. Anscombe and G. H. von Wright, trans. Denis Paul & Anscombe (Oxford: Basil Blackwell, 1977), §§ 192, 253.

6. I return to this point later: see Part IV, § 7.

7. Never mind valuing the humanity of others, which I think does follow readily from valuing humanity in oneself. Even Korsgaard's arguments from the publicity of reasons in Lecture IV strike me as more than what is needed to establish this point.

8. Guyer also points this out, and uses it as an objection to Korsgaard's account of Kant, in *Kant's Groundwork*, pp. 109–111.

   I do, however, think that Kant uses something like the same regress to which Korsgaard appeals in his account of worth in *Groundwork* II (see below, §§ 36–38). It seems to me that what both Kant and Korsgaard should be saying is that reason faces an antinomy over whether to value itself. Antinomies tend to arise, on Kant's account, when we reach a foundational point in some area of our thinking; Kant's antinomies all represent ways in which our thought both demands and refuses to accept an ungrounded ground at the root of some mode of grounding other claims. But the claim that our reason is intrinsically valuable is supposed to be precisely such an ungrounded ground at the root of our mode of grounding evaluative claims. So we should expect to find an antinomy over whether it is true or not—there should be, as I think there are, good arguments both for and against valuing our own reason.

9. Korsgaard introduces a voice making this sort of argument, and rightly says that it shows that no evolutionary theory could possibly justify morality (SN 14–16). But she seems to think that such a theory *could* satisfactorily explain morality: "The case of the evolutionary theory shows that a theory could be adequate for the purposes of explanation and still not answer the normative question" (SN 16). The proper response to the threat of this voice, for her, is to draw a sharp distinction between explanation and justification, and to ignore determinism when we engage in the latter. This understates what the voice has to say, overlooking precisely its suggestion that we need to bring the perspective of explanation to bear on how we justify our actions.

10. But contrast Hud Hudson, *Kant's Compatibilism* (Ithaca: Cornell University Press, 1994).

11. This notion, and the "reflective love" introduced later in this chapter, have obvious affinities with themes in the work of Harry Frankfurt. See especially the title essay and "Identification and Wholeheartedness" in his *The Importance of What We Care About* (Cambridge: Cambridge University Press, 1988), "Autonomy, Necessity, and Love" and "On Caring," in his *Necessity, Volition and Love* (Cambridge: Cambridge University Press, 1999), and the whole of his *The Reasons of Love* (Princeton: Princeton University Press, 2004). I retain more of the Kantian emphasis on rationality than Frankfurt does, however.

12. Tony Laden is currently working out a conception of reason along these lines: see his *Proposals for Rational Creatures* (Oxford: Oxford University Press, forthcoming).

13. Compare Guyer, *Kant's Groundwork*, 20–21, 112–114, 171.

14. This point is made explicit only in G 435–436. But without the connection between rationality and autonomy, the claim on 428 that the nature of rational beings "marks them out as an end in itself" makes no sense.

15. Of course, evaluating things is an essential *part* of determining action.

16. "That which serves the will as the objective ground of its self-determination is an end" (G 427); "An end is an *object* of free choice, the representation of which determines it to an action . . . Every action, therefore, has its end . . . [S]ince there are free actions, there must also be ends to which, as their objects, these actions are directed." Kant, *Metaphysics of Morals*, trans. Mary Gregor (Cambridge: Cambridge University Press, 1991), Ak 384–385.

17. Kyla Ebels Duggan has pointed out to me that Kant doesn't think he's yet shown that rational action is possible at this stage in the *Groundwork*: that's something to be shown in Part III (and then later in the second *Critique*). But the work Kant thinks still needs to be done is demonstrating that we have free will, which is not my concern here. It seems clearly

possible that we could have free will and still lack any goal of absolute worth; it even seems not impossible that we could lack free will, but have a goal of absolute worth. So Kant's concern about his own position is not mine: what Kant says in *Groundwork* III neither helps nor hurts the regress from relative to absolute worth.

18. Kant himself had to acknowledge this point, to make sense of how we could be responsible for immoral actions: in RWB, he uses the term "Willkür" rather than "Wille" to describe the process that leads to less-than-fully rational behavior.

19. In this I agree with Korsgaard: "the concept of goodness, in the final sense of goodness, has a kind of *reflexivity* about it: nothing can be a final good if it cannot be perceived as a final good, and indeed the final good is, as it were, made complete by its own perception." ("The Origin of the Good and Our Animal Nature," Lecture given at the University of Illinois-Chicago on November 5 2007, pp. 31–32).

20. *Metaphysics of Morals*, 381.

21. I will treat conscious thought as requiring rationality throughout. I think it is pretty clear that awareness, at least in the sense we humans are acquainted with it, requires the ability to form and use concepts, to make inferences, and to regard propositions as more and less justified. But I don't think it much matters if someone wants to dispute this (perhaps on behalf of animals, or infants, who seem to have some kind of awareness without rationality). The Kantian argument I am considering turns on our ability to *choose*, not on our merely having awareness, and for that rationality is surely necessary.

22. For Berlin's views see, among other sources, *The Crooked Timber of Humanity* (New York: Vintage, 1990), chapter 1; for Taylor's, see "The Diversity of Goods," in his *Philosophy and the Human Sciences* (Cambridge: Cambridge University Press, 1985).

23. Alasdair MacIntyre has argued (AV 207–209, 217) that the notion of a discrete action is actually an abstraction from the notion of a history or narrative, in which the narrative as a whole has an intelligible point. If he were right, my talk of nesting actions within one another to form a system would get things backward: the system as a whole must come first and the individual actions are a construction out of that. But MacIntyre's insistence on teleology goes too far. As he himself almost admits on pp. 212 and 214, it is not *impossible* for life to consist in fairly unconnected events that do not add up to a story (at least a "realist" story: if our lives have stories the way Buñuel films have stories, would that be enough narrative for MacIntyre?). It may be an unhealthy social system that encourages such a fragmented life, and a shallow or otherwise limited person who lives one. But to utter that condemnation is to presuppose that such a life is possible. So the question remains of how to *bring* our potentially scattered actions together in a unity—even if, from the perspective of that unity, we would not want to differentiate these actions into isolated bits.

24. Again, see the writings by Frankfurt cited in note 11 above.

25. Indeed, Kant himself seems to recognize this point, when he comes to write RWB. In their ultimate end "human beings seek something that they can *love*," he says, while reason, and reason's law, offers them something that "only inspires *respect* in them" (7n: Kant's emphasis). I don't think that the highest good as Kant construes it will inspire love in us, but he sets up the criterion for such a good nicely here.

26. See note 2 above.

27. Marx expounds on a passage from Goethe's *Faust* in the "Economic and Philosophic Manuscripts" (*Marx-Engels Reader*, 102–103), and may allude to its closing lines in the *Communist Manifesto* (ibid, 476: "All that is solid melts into air . . ."). He acknowledges an early debt to Kant in his 1837 letter to his father (ibid, 7), that shows, I think, in his deep commitment to critique—albeit of a kind different from Kant's—throughout his early writings.

28. Metamorphoses—caterpillar to butterfly, and any attempts at analogous transformations on the part of humans—present a problem for this line of thinking, but they can be explained away: (1) The caterpillar seeks to remain what it is until, driven by forces beyond itself, it dies and is replaced by a butterfly. Or: (2) The butterfly is actually just a version of the caterpillar, and we should see the metamorphosis as part of the survival mechanism of one organism.

29. The idea that a temporal thing could become eternal "to some degree" is hard to understand, but the idea that reason becomes like what it reasons about is not so strange—it makes for a neat answer to the problem of how knowledge connects with its objects, for one thing. In any case, both ideas are taken over from Plato by Aristotle.

30. Even if one does not accept the ontology, the account makes good sense of why mathematicians and other abstract thinkers take such joy in what they do. It is not at all implausible that we love things that enable us to forget our mortality, and that thought about abstractions helps us do that. There is, however, a crucial difference between *forgetting* mortality and *overcoming* it. There is also an enormous difference between regarding abstract ideas as mere human tools for understanding the universe and regarding them as basic elements *of* the universe. Because we now hold the first rather than the second view, Plato's account no longer suffices to show that philosophy is the most valuable of human activities.

31. See, especially, CJ §§ 78–79.

Part III: Chapter 6

1. Would the feeling then be a "reason" for accepting the view? Well, feeling drawn to a view is not a way of demonstrating its truth logically, nor a piece of empirical evidence for it, nor something that shows it has pragmatic or ethical advantages. So if it is a reason for a view, it is an odd sort of reason.

2. As sketched in Part I of this book, for instance.

3. "It would strike me as ridiculous to want to doubt the existence of Napoleon; but if someone doubted the existence of the earth 150 years ago, perhaps I should be more willing to listen, for now he is doubting our whole system of evidence."—Wittgenstein, *On Certainty*, § 185.

4. A possibility not at all lost on Hume himself: see his comparison of the levellers to religious fanatics, at Enq 193.

5. Perhaps we inevitably hold some such view, but we could still treat it as an intellectual illusion on the model of optical illusions—the bent stick in water—and keep our tendency to endorse the illusion at a distance from ourselves.

6. The discussion that follows is in good part derived from a wonderful presentation on what we can hope given at UIC in November, 2009 by Andrew Chignell. See his *For What Can We Hope?* (London: Routledge, forthcoming).

7. This leaves room for hoping for miracles. The suspension of the entire natural order is not logically impossible, and a religious person's hopes may in part depend on such miracles. Kant's own hope for an afterlife falls into that category.

8. W. K. Clifford, *The Ethics of Belief* (New York: Prometheus Books, 1999), 77. Hume held much the same view, albeit with less vehemence: "a wise man . . . proportions his belief to the evidence" (Enq 110). Much of the Clifford essay looks back to Hume (see, for instance, p. 95: "No evidence . . . can justify us in believing the truth of a statement which is contrary to, or outside of, the uniformity of nature.")

9. Adams makes a powerful case for the idea that robust realism about the good makes best sense if one identifies the good with God in FIG, chapters 1 and 2: see especially pp. 44–45, and 77–82.

10. There is no direct parallel to this point in Buddhism, which does not see the world as designed by a God, and where the effort is, if anything, to get beyond our yearning for objective purposiveness. But in Buddhism too, as I have noted repeatedly, there is a sense that our natural state is such that we cannot get beyond our illusions and that enlightenment comes only if we can stand beyond our own nature. I don't think this view is significantly less dependent on a rejection of the scientific monopoly on factual truth than the views of theistic religions.

11. Alternatively, it requires us to get beyond the notions of purposes that lead us to seek objective purposiveness. Non-theistic religions may be understood as trying to do this. But that means that they require that we reach a point at which we can see our empirical nature as imposing illusions on us—which in turn means they need to posit a supernatural position, if not a supernatural entity or force, from which to survey our natural lives. A Buddhist can thus make use of the reasons for favoring religious views of the highest good that I describe here, although she would have to change some of the terms in which I couch it.

12. In his *Sources of the Self*, chapter 3.

13. See FIG, chapter 2.

14. And some, but not all, of these religious views include an explanation *of* the fact that there are many different kinds of faith: see Part IV, Chapter 7.

15. Alvin Plantinga describes nicely how a devout Christian might arrive at such a best account:

> She reads Nietzsche, but remains unmoved by his complaint that Christianity fosters a weak, whining, whimpering, and generally disgusting kind of person: most of the Christians she knows or knows of—Mother Teresa, for instance—don't fit that mold. She finds Freud's contemptuous attitude towards Christianity and theistic belief backed by little more than implausible fantasies about the origin of belief in God . . . and she finds little more of substance in Marx. She thinks as carefully as she can about these objections and others, but finds them wholly uncompelling.
>
> On the other side, although she is aware of theistic arguments and thinks some of them not without value, she doesn't believe on the basis of them. Rather, she has a rich inner spiritual life . . . ; it seems to her that she is sometimes made aware, catches a glimpse, of something of the overwhelming beauty and loveliness of the Lord; she is often aware, as strongly it seems to her, of the work of the Holy Spirit in her heart, comforting encouraging, teaching, leading her to accept the "great things of the gospel" . . . , helping her see that the magnificent scheme of salvation devised by the Lord himself is not only for others, but for her as well. After long, hard, conscientious reflection, this all seems to her enormously more convincing than the complaints of the critics (*Warranted Christian Belief* 100–101)

This is exactly what I mean by a "best account" of the ethical. As against Plantinga, however, I would want to urge that such reflections are not necessarily appropriate to cognition in general. Plantinga has a tendency to treat Christian beliefs as if they were of the same sort as our common-sense and scientific factual beliefs, but I see no reason to think that the sort of reflection he describes is adequate for deciding matters like whether Barack Obama was born in the United States, say, or Darwinian evolution provides a good account of the development of various life-forms. We need to maintain a sharp distinction between the scientific and the ethical, and to determine empirical facts, and accept theories and expertise about those facts, in different ways and for different purposes than we seek ethical guidance. That said, the reflections of Plantinga's Christian are an excellent example of how one might integrate a telic vision with one's moral and empirical beliefs.

16. See Part II, § 43.

17. It's worth stressing that what we are now beginning to develop is a case for the reasonableness of putting one's faith or trust in a religious *text* or oral teaching, not (just) in an inarticulate experience of awe, wonder, or mystery that one takes to have supernatural significance of some sort. It is hard to see how the latter could have a determinate enough content to guide our actions, or fit the telic aspects of our good together with its moral aspects. We will need something quite articulate to show us how to find worth in our lives, not simply an impressive feeling.

    These considerations are, I hope, enough to justify proceeding for the moment as though revelation must take a verbal form; I will try to offer some deeper reasons for that point later on (Part IV, §§ 37–43).

18. See especially Robert Paul Wolff, *Kant's Theory of Mental Activity* (Gloucester: Peter Smith, 1973).

19. See, for instance, the discussion of how our reactions to sensory stimuli precede our being able to identify them, in Gilbert, *Stumbling on Happiness,* pp. 61–62, and the experiments mentioned therein. Split brain experiments have also shown that the right side of our brain can use or point to an object without being able to name it, while the left side can name objects without having as much ability to use them.

20. Alexander Gerard describes imagination as "presenting" or "exhibit[ing]" ideas to us in his *Essay on Taste* (London: A. Millar, 1759) pp. 156–157; Kames details this process beautifully in his account of "ideal presence": Henry Home, Lord Kames, *Elements of Criticism*, ed. Peter Jones (Indianapolis: Liberty Fund, 2005), pp. 66–71. These authors make clearer what Hume may have meant by "imagination," and look forward to Kant, whose distinction between the reproductive and the productive imagination is crucial to what I say here: as is the connection Kant draws between the two, such that there is never, even in immediate experience, reproductive imagination without at the same time a process of producing images.

21. Smith, TMS, Part I, especially chapter 1. See also my "David Hume and Adam Smith on Sympathy: A Contrast, Critique and Reconstruction," in Dagfinn Føllesdal (ed.), *Intersubjectivity in Adam Smith and Edmund Husserl* (Frankfurt: Ontos Verlag, forthcoming).

22. Compare Gilbert on what he calls "nexting": *Stumbling on Happiness*, pp. 6–9.

23. In this it is, again, akin to hope, which is a component of religious faith. And hope too depends on the imagination.

24. It's important to remember that Rawls describes the theory of the good he develops in this stretch of TJ as the "thin" theory of the good, and says that "its purpose is to secure the premises about primary goods required to arrive at the principles of justice" (TJ 396) and to "defend [. . .] justice as fairness against various objections" (TJ 397; see also 433–434). With this purpose in mind, it makes good sense that anything a rational and well-informed person aims at will count as her good. That is the only way to guarantee a liberal political system, in which each person can search for the good on her own, rather than being coerced to pursue a particular conception of the good by her government. We should not, however, suppose that Rawls intends his thin theory of the good to answer what I call "telic" questions.

25. The tediousness of Kantian goodness has struck his readers from the beginning. Here is an early, and for a time very enthusiastic, reader writing to him on the subject:

    I feel that a vast emptiness extends inside me, and all around me—so that I almost find myself to be superfluous, unnecessary. I'm tormented by a boredom that makes life intolerable. Don't think me arrogant for saying this, but the demands of morality are too easy for me. I would eagerly do twice as much as they command. They only get their prestige from the attractiveness of sin, and it costs me almost no effort to resist that.

I comfort myself with the thought that, since the practice of morality is so bound up with sensuality, it can only count for this world. I can hope that the afterlife won't be yet another life ruled by these few, easy demands of morality, another empty and vegetating life.

Letter to Kant from Maria von Herbert, January, 1793, as quoted in Rae Langton, "Duty and Desolation," (1992), *Philosophy* 67, p. 493. Langton brings out wonderfully the depth of this challenge to Kant's moral philosophy.

Part IV: Chapter 1

1. See HH Price, "Faith and Belief," and Norman Malcolm, "Is it a Religious Belief that God Exists?" in John Hick (ed.), *Faith and the Philosophers* (New York: St Martin's Press, 1964). I am grateful to Amelie Rorty for directing me to these sources.
2. The similarities and differences between an "I-you" relationship with God, and an I-you relationship with a fellow human being, are considered interestingly in Darwall's *The Second-Person Standpoint*, pp. 104–115 and Gary Watson's review of that book in *Ethics*: "Morality as Equal Accountability," *Ethics* 118 (1) (October 2007), pp. 40–47. See also Darwall's response to Watson in the same issue of *Ethics*, pp. 65–69.
3. James Rachels misses this point, and misreads the Abraham story—saying that Abraham's willingness "to challenge God" in the Sodom and Gomorrah story shows that Abraham fails there fully to understand what worship is, and that he understands this better when he offers up his son unquestioningly: see Rachels, "God and Human Attitudes," in Paul Helm (ed.), *Divine Commands and Morality* (Oxford: Clarendon Press, 1981), pp. 42–44. There is no reason to ascribe this view to the author of Genesis, as Rachels does on p. 42, and as a philosophical matter, it depends on a tendentious conception of "worship." Many rabbinic commentators have read this story in precisely the opposite direction: seeing Abraham's argument with God over Sodom and Gomorrah as exemplary of a true worshipper, and his unquestioning acceptance of the proposed sacrifice of Isaac as displaying a certain failure of true religious commitment. This goes with a view, pervasive in the rabbinic tradition and with roots in many Biblical passages, that God welcomes our willingness to argue with Him.
   Similarly, Hugo Grotius maintains that "God suffers himself to be judged of according to [right reason]," citing a variety of Old and New Testament passages as prooftexts. (Grotius, *The Rights of War and Peace*, ed. Richard Tuck (Indianapolis: Liberty Fund, 2005), Book I, chapter 1, § X.5, p. 156.
4. Of course this deliberate respect can also bring her to reject the trusting relationship or to feel oppressed by it. There is a delicate balance between ways in which intelligence and independence can enhance and ways in which it can threaten a trusting relationship.
5. Mendelssohn, *Morgenstunden*, ch. X, in *Sämmtliche Werke* (Ofen: P. Burian, 1819), vol. 3, pp. 140–141. Fred Beiser summarizes the dream in Beiser, *The Fate of Reason* (Cambridge: Harvard University Press, 1987), p. 99.
6. Ibid. 100. See also p. 99: "[T]he extension of Mendelssohn's 'common sense' and Jacobi's 'faith' is the same. Both terms are used in a broad sense, so that they refer to all the fundamental beliefs of morality, religion, and everyday life."
7. Ibid. 100.
8. Ibid. 100.
9. "Of Superstition and Enthusiasm," in Hume, *Selected Essays*, ed. Stephen Copley and Andrew Elgar (Oxford: Oxford University Press, 1993), p. 39; *Enquiry Concerning Human Understanding*, 11."
10. *Wealth of Nations*, 793, 796.

11. As Beiser says: "[W]hat is this figure of reason that so blithely settles the conflicts between speculation and common sense? If it is a faculty of criticism, a faculty that demands to know the reasons for our beliefs, then it amounts to nothing more than speculation. If, however, it is an intuitive faculty, a faculty that judges all issues according to 'a natural light,' then it is little more than common sense" (*Fate of Reason*, 101).

12. But see the Jäsche *Logic*, where Kant attributes an "orienting" function to common sense (Ak 9:57).

13. CPrR 119–121. See the discussion of this passage above, Part II, § 42.

14. And which also contains a condemnation of *Schwärmerei*: Ak 272–275.

15. Maimonides, for instance, describes prophecy as an overflow of the divine into the imagination (*Guide* II.36, 38, 47) that at the same time is channeled into legislation for the good of a community (*Guide* II.39–40). The product is a work of morality rather than of art, but otherwise the process seems very similar.

    See also Milton Nahm, *The Artist as Creator* (Baltimore: Johns Hopkins Press, 1956), N. Kershaw Chadwick, *Poetry and Prophecy* (Cambridge: Cambridge University Press, 1942), and—for a somewhat critical view of the comparison—Abraham Joshua Heschel, *The Prophets* (New York: HarperCollins, 2001), chapter 11.

16. This passage was much admired—and somewhat misunderstood—by Hannah Arendt: see her *Lectures on Kant's Political Philosophy*, ed. Ronald Beiner (Chicago: University of Chicago Press, 1982), pp. 70–75 and my *Third Concept*, note 14 on pp. 316–317.

17. See Harry Frankfurt, "Descartes on the Creation of the Eternal Truths," in his *Necessity, Volition and Love* (Cambridge: Cambridge University Press, 1999).

18. I discuss this in my "A Fifth Antinomy," *Philosophia*, May, 1989.

19. See Heidegger, *Phenomenological Interpretation of Kant's Critique of Pure Reason*, trans. P. Emand and K. Maly (Bloomington: Indiana University Press, 1997), especially pp. 189, 234–236, 244, 250–255, 265.

20. If not *as* passive as sensibility: which helps explain the Heideggerian reading.

21. Ibid. 250.

22. Ibid. 235.

23. Faith is also, like spontaneous receptivity, a state primarily of the imagination rather than the understanding. Heidegger makes this point in Kantian terms, stressing the way the imagination contains and shapes time for Kant, and drawing from that his own theory about how we, with our temporality—the limited time-frame within which we make our plans, and which ends in our death—face a universe with a very different temporality. We make ourselves open to things, let givenness occur, for Heidegger, when we face our temporality honestly, allow being-towards-death to shape our worlds. I am not so interested in this existentialist point, but I agree with Heidegger that it is precisely by imagining the world that we can prepare ourselves for objectivity. Objectivity occurs when we allow our imaginative visions to be *broken into*, when we take note of the ways the world, for good or ill, is other than how we imagine it. But for our imaginative visions to be broken into, we need first to *have* such visions, to hold them before us for the breaking. Revelation, as we shall see, both gives us such a vision and urges us to prepare for it to be constantly broken, constantly re-made or made new. And faith in revelation is then an imaginative commitment both in the sense that it is a commitment to something that appeals to our imagination and in the sense that it is a commitment to the workings *of* our imagination, to the legitimacy of holding something true primarily because it appeals to our imagination, rather than to our reason.

24. *Midrash Rabbah* on *Song of Songs*, trans. Maurice Simon (London: Soncino Press, 1939), I, 1, 8. I am grateful to Rabbi Michael Balinsky for drawing my attention to this source and the rich irony of its teaching.

25. WO? 134–138.
26. Kant himself brings them quite close at times: see for instance CJ § 57.
27. Rudolf Otto's phenomenology of the holy brings out this point wonderfully: see his *The Idea of the Holy*, trans. J. Harvey, second edition (Oxford: Oxford University Press, 1950) chapters 3–6.
28. I am not concerned here with the possibility of an "evil God" (that's ruled out by the hypothesis that God must be "all-good"). We can readily imagine that even a good God might demand the sacrifice of our career, our marriage, and other things we care about.
29. See, for instance, Psalm 115:4, 135:15, Isaiah 2:8, 40:18–20 and 44:10–18.
30. Many thought they were: Blake, Scriabin, and Joyce, to take but a handful.
31. This dovetails with Kant's suggestion that that harmony somehow represents the supersensible: see again CJ § 57.

Part IV: Chapter 2

1. The two moments I have described correspond to two famous Midrashim about the giving of the Torah on Sinai, one in which God holds Mt. Sinai over the people and threatens to bury them there if they do not accept the Torah, and one in which he asks all the peoples of the world if they will accept the Torah and gives it to the Israelites because they alone say yes (BT Shabbat 88a and Sifre Devarim 343, respectively).
2. Butler, *Five Sermons*, S. Darwall (ed.) (Indianapolis: Hackett, 1983), pp. 30, 33, 41.
3. Hinduism may be a partial exception: there a transcendental self *is* supposed to be the revelatory speaker to our empirical selves. But the Hindu transcendental self is an entity that is supposed to govern the universe, not the epistemic position Kant says we must assume to engage in reason, much less the cooler versions of our ordinary selves that Butler and Smith were talking about. So I think devout Hindus would see the Enlightenment interpretation of revelation we have been discussing as an anemic reduction of what they believe.
4. As we will see in chapters 3 and 6, this leaves room for a moral interpretation of the text. But such readings retain the notion that the text itself does not contain errors.
5. Kierkegaard, *Authority and Revelation*, trans. Walter Lowrie (Princeton: Princeton University Press, 1955), pp. 107–108, 110–113.
6. Ibid. 111–112. See also Kierkegaard's *Philosophical Fragments*, which is concerned throughout with the paradox of a God who can come into relationship with human beings.
7. By "paradox" I don't mean an outright contradiction. Perhaps Kierkegaard meant that, but he was writing against the background of Hegel's philosophy, in which logic could tolerate contradictions, even be propelled forward by them. Today, we regard contradictions as necessarily false. But "paradox" has a somewhat broader and gentler hue than "contradiction." A claim or text or vision is paradoxical if it contains tensions that *threaten* to amount to a contradiction. A paradoxical claim or text is puzzling, worrying, mysterious. It provokes us to work hard at interpreting it, at giving it a sense that preserves the tensions while not entailing a contradiction. If it is deeply paradoxical, it may require us to redo that work over and over. Each of our efforts may be unsatisfactory, either resolving the tensions too easily (ignoring some of the details giving rise to the tensions) or continuing to threaten a contradiction. And to be deeply paradoxical in this sense may be the only way of being deeply mysterious. A merely unsolved problem is not deeply mysterious, simply in wait of a solution, and something wholly unintelligible does not yet amount to a claim at all. Only the deeply paradoxical contains a mystery that we may fear, or hope, will never be wholly resolved. It is that sort of mystery that we expect to find in revelation.

8. Speaking with a Buddhist monk, Heidegger said: "I consider only one thing to be decisive [in religion]: to follow the words of the founder. That alone—and neither the systems nor the doctrines are important. *Religion is succession*" (quoted in Mark Wrathall, "Between the earth and the sky," in Wrathall (ed.), *Religion After Metaphysics* (Cambridge: Cambridge University Press, 2003), p. 85.

9. We may take the fact that our sensory perceptions are said to have been confused at Sinai— we are said to have "seen" the thunder (Exodus 20:15)—as an indication that the truth conveyed there had to be grasped by ethical, not sensory, perception. Maimonides says that "All saw the great fire, and heard the fearful thunderings, but only those of them who were duly qualified were prophetically inspired, each one according to his capacities." Given Maimonides's view of the nature of divine law, and of sensory evidence, I think this line is best interpreted as endorsing an ethical account of the evidence for revelation very much like the one I have suggested. See Appendix II for an interpretation of Maimonides along these lines.

10. Its unexpectedness was, as we shall see, crucial to its revelatory power. By being unexpected, a revelatory teaching holds out the promise to its recipient of an ever-unexpected world, a world in which we can keep encountering new views or truths—and a good part of the joy of the maximally good world that we hope for would come by its being constantly new to us. That is how it overcomes the boredom that we fear if our naturalistic teloi are satisfied.

11. Akira Kurosawa depicts such a person beautifully in his film *Scandal*.

12. Easwaran, Introduction, *The Upanishads*, trans. Easwaran (London: Penguin, 1987), p. 8.

13. Eboo Patel, *Acts of Faith* (Boston: Beacon Press, 2007), pp. 136–137.

14. Gita Meta, *A River Sutra* (New York: Vintage, 1993), pp. 31–32.

15. Of course, there is a limit to *how* new the message can be. The teaching would not be greeted as revelation at all if it did not seem, once pronounced, to be true, and the fact that the hearers so understand it implies that they must have some access to truth, in moral matters, even before they hear the revelation. Which is to say, the moment of revelation cannot be as radically new as it may at first seem, and what it teaches must be integrated with what its receivers already take to be true before they come to this moment. That sets up a dialectic between the giving and the receiving of revelation that is central to any revealed religion.

Part IV: Chapter 3

1. The only ones, on many traditional Jewish accounts, that all the Israelites are said to have heard: the medieval commentator Rashi, following on a midrash in the Mechilta, takes the fact that Exodus 20: 2–6 have God speaking in the first person, while the rest of the commandments use the third person for God, to indicate that only the first two commandments were given directly to the Israelites. The others are supposed to have been declared by Moses.

2. See Psalms 115 and 135, or Isaiah 2, 40, or 44.

3. This is, of course, much too thin an interpretation of the famous passage in Exodus. What exactly the framing verse to the ten commandments ("I am the LORD ... ") is doing has been a matter of debate for centuries, and saying that it serves as a slap against Pharaoh's claims to divinity, and a warning against worshipping Moses, while I think true, does not do justice to the many other meanings that that verse can take. Still, we will have to make do with this reading for the purposes of our moral exploration of revelation. As long as we interpret revelatory texts as moral guides, we need some central, fairly clear and simple

message. The point of revelation as a moral matter, after all, is to provide us with a clue for the overcoming of evil, so we need (a) something we can use as we *act*, not something we have to interpret endlessly, and (b) something we can *all* act on, not something too obscure for the less literarily skilled among us. This is a limitation on the understanding of revelation in a moral light, a hint that revelatory texts do not serve moral purposes alone. We will be able to restore the richness of sacred texts when we see them as aiming at holiness rather than morality.

4. This may mean that I see for the first time how the Torah provides a solution to my moral problems—that I have a revelation, I stand at Sinai, I (re)-commit myself to traditional Judaism—or simply that I find it morally useful to me, at a particular moment or recurrently, in the course of a life already dedicated to the Torah.

5. The latter is Lessing's proposal for the ideal revelation. But he is fully aware of how platitudinous it sounds, and gives it power by presenting in the context of a larger narrative. See "The Testament of John," in Chadwick (ed.), *Lessing's Theological Writings*.

6. See § 14 of this Part.

7. What follows is a loose commentary on OWA 52–53.

8. All this is especially true in moral matters. Familiar norms and attitudes go unquestioned and thereby preserve sources of ill-will and error, for all the good they may also do.

   Heidegger himself was notoriously uninterested in morality, but he does seem concerned in OWA with truth in the sphere of practical reason, broadly speaking: "He who truly knows what is, knows what he wills to do in the midst of what is" (OWA 65; see also 43, 53, 61).

9. On the difficulties in achieving cosmopolitanism, see Fonna Forman-Barzilai, *Adam Smith and the Circles of Sympathy* (Cambridge: Cambridge University Press, 2010).

10. "The person who seeks to learn *from* the Bible is smaller than the text; he crouches at its feet, waiting for its instructions or insights. Learning *about* the text generates the opposite posture. The text moves from subject to object; it no longer speaks, but is spoken about, analyzed, and acted upon. The insights are now all the reader's, not the text's and anyone can see the results" (James Kugel, *How to Read the Bible* [New York: Free Press, 2007], p. 666).

   Kugel—a great historical scholar of the Bible himself—puts here in a nutshell what is problematic about using historical insights to explain away the difficult passages in one's sacred texts. Why not say, "This text was written by people who lived long before the rise of modern science and liberal values, and who consequently made factual errors and had what we now consider to be a confused, harsh or bigoted moral sense?" Because such an approach removes the revealed or authoritative quality of the text. One no longer sees oneself as *following* the text, being guided by it, but instead regards one's own conscience or reason, or perhaps the collective norms around one, as the highest source of ethical wisdom. Perhaps one takes one's own conscience or reason, or the way of life of one's community, to be the true voice of God. This is not revealed religion anymore; it's more a species of rational or personal religion. And in fact the progressive or liberal denominations that have grown up in Judaism and Christianity over the past two centuries have I think become varieties of rational or personal religion. Justifications for this sort of religion will not run through the value of a sacred text. They have to show instead how our reason, or an internal sense, can alone help us find value in our lives—have to carry out the sort of demonstration that, in Part III, I suggested may be impossible. I am therefore skeptical that religion in this vein is likely to be successful, and unsure why one would prefer it to a purely secular approach to telic questions.

   That said, one advantage of the progressive or liberal varieties of religion is that they can deal easily with morally problematic aspects of sacred texts. The historicism they invoke in doing so is not available to one who takes the revealed status of such texts seriously. Nevertheless, even those of us who refuse to relativize the meaning of our Scriptures themselves to history can insist on a progressive *reception* of Scripture. Our revealed or sacred texts, to remain revealed and sacred, must be regarded as standing beyond time and human error; the way by which we *receive* those texts, interpret and implement them in our lives, can and should change over time, and reflect the different circumstances, and developments in moral understanding, of different human communities. That means that it is essential *not* to fix the reception of Scripture in the way Scripture itself is fixed—that element of many traditional communities should be resisted. As a reader for this book has pointed out, the Talmud too, and not just the Torah, has "pockmarks": morally disturbing passages that reflect its history. The Talmud, however, need not be regarded as given by God. It can and I think should instead be regarded as a human attempt to receive God's word, a stage in the ongoing project, by the Jewish community, to make sense of the text that it believes God has given them.

11. In the book mentioned in the previous note, Kugel makes a powerful case for this difference between historical and religious readings of Scripture. One of his critics within the Jewish community has responded in part by arguing that, since Jews are "commanded to serve God with all one's mind [and] all one's soul," it would be *religiously* wrong to accept biblical scholarship as a historical matter while rejecting it as a contribution to theology:

    [A] Jewish response [cannot] be to bifurcate, so that one has a Jewish soul and a secular mind, coexisting uneasily in a single body, but not communicating with each other. . . . A Jew whose intellect believes that biblical criticism makes valid claims, but whose religious self pretends otherwise is not enjoying secondary naivete; that Jew, it seems to me, is rendering God service that is fragmented and defective. (Benjamin Sommer, "Two Introductions to Scripture: James Kugel and the Possibility of Biblical Theology," *Jewish Quarterly Review*, 100.1 [2010], p. 174)

    But this is confused. To accept biblical criticism when doing science while setting it aside in religious practice is not to "bifurcate" one's self; it is simply to recognize the appropriateness of different criteria for different activities. Just as one might find the history of math interesting, but irrelevant to the correctness of a mathematical proof, or a biography of Shakespeare interesting, but irrelevant to what one learns from *King Lear*, so the history of the Bible is irrelevant to its religious interpretation. There *is* a sharp bifurcation of great importance to religious believers, but it runs between science and telic faith, not down the middle of one's soul. Indeed, we risk our personal integrity if we *fail* to recognize the bifurcation between science and telic faith. It is foolish to try to find a God (or *tao* or state of enlightenment) in a nature that could not possibly contain any such thing, and believers who try to do that wind up deceiving themselves about either the real implications of science or the real nature of their religious commitments. To render God wholehearted rather than fragmented service in the modern world is to treat what one takes to be His revelation as if it were wholly written by Him, now, for our ethical enlightenment, regardless of how it was produced historically—and, in that context, to do one's best to give its historical pockmarks a moral interpretation.

12. Matthew 12: 46–50; 21: 18–19 (and parallel passages in Mark and Luke); Matthew 23; John 8: 44.

13. Matthew 5: 31–32 and parallel passages; Colossians 4: 18, 22–24.

14. On the dangers of Christianity's premature universalism, see Marc Shell, "Marranos (Pigs), Or From Coexistence to Toleration," *Critical Inquiry* 17 (Winter 1991).

15. *Tov me'od*: see Nachmanides on Numbers 6: 24 (*Commentary on the Torah*, "Numbers," p. 58), and the Midrash from Bereishit Rabbah quoted therein.

Part IV: Chapter 4

1. See *Faust* I.1700 and II.11575–82.
2. Paul Guyer traces the history of this notion of beauty in his forthcoming history of aesthetics.
3. Plato talks of our wanting to "procreate" with the Forms, but that turns out to mean having (true) thoughts in their presence. Kant's play of the faculties is just as geared towards coming up with new thoughts.
4. T 471; Enq 242; TMS 25, 188, 192, 238.
5. Cf. Part III, § 23.
6. The aesthetic, on my view, is not just *analogous* to religious experience, as Kant might have it: it is a *component* of religious experience. The holy is a form of the beautiful and/or the sublime, and one that holds out to us the promise that we can reach a condition that will be eternally beautiful or sublime—what Christians call "the beatific vision"—or in which the beauty of what we see will be sufficient for us to relinquish our selves, and all their other longings.
7. "Good" here is on my view not primarily a moral term. For Plato himself, of course, morality itself depends on this ultimate purpose, but that is a piece of his thought I don't want to accept; on my view, morality can function very well while setting aside the question of our ultimate end. Moral goods may be subsumed in, or illuminated by, our highest good, but we can grasp the former without having perceived the latter. (I am grateful to Sally Sedgwick for pushing me to clarify this point.)
8. And if it were, we wouldn't know it, since ex hypothesi our state of awareness of the universe would be exactly the same as well: we couldn't be aware, at the second of the moments, that it *was* a repetition of the first one.
9. There is a parallel here, of course, to the tension between the angled and the comprehensive quality of revelation that we noted when considering revelation in a moral light: see §§ 20, 25–27, above.
10. Wittgenstein: "The sense of the world must lie outside the world.... *[I]n* it no value exists." *Tractatus Logicus-Philosophicus* 6.41.
11. *Tao te Ching*, chapter 25, trans. by Jennifer Oldstone-Moore, in Michael Coogan (ed.) *Eastern Religions* (Oxford: Oxford University Press, 2005), p. 228.
12. "Taitiriya Upanishad" II.8–9, as translated by Eknath Easwaran in *The Upanishads*, p. 145. See also "Chandogya Upanishad" 14.4, p. 178 (among many other places).
13. "Examination of Self and Entities" (chapter xviii), verses 5 and 7, *The Fundamental Wisdom of the Middle Way*, trans. Jay Garfield (New York: Oxford University Press, 1995), pp. 48–49. See also the quotation from the Dalai Lama in translator's note 126 to p. 325: "The ultimate nature of things—emptiness—is ... unknowable, ... one cannot comprehend it."
14. Psalm 19:1–4.
15. The seven steps of the *Tractatus* echo the seven levels of Bonaventura's *Mind's Road to God*, as does the ladder imagery at the end of the book, and the fact that silence marks the highest level of understanding.
16. Wittgenstein, *Tractatus*, 6.45 and 6.421.
17. See Anthony Savile, *Kantian Aesthetics Pursued* (Edinburgh: Edinburgh University Press, 1993), chapter 3.
18. Much of the next few paragraphs appeared earlier in my "Poetry and Truth-Conditions" (*op. cit.* in note 3 on p. 529), and chapter 2 of my *Third Concept of Liberty*.
19. On my view these are identical: the faculties engage in a harmonious play. Other readings see the harmony of the faculties as arising out of the play of the faculties.

20. And that a movement among concepts—an inter-conceptual condition—satisfies the cognitive need to which Kant alludes. The harmony of the faculties, on my reading, is pre-cognitive because it is inter-conceptual. I elaborate this idea below.

21. There are a number of passages supporting such a reading. For instance: "The animation of both faculties (imagination and understanding) to an activity that is indeterminate, but yet . . . in unison . . . is the sensation . . . postulated by the judgment of taste" (§ 9). See also "First Introduction," § VII (Ak 20: 220–221): "If, then, the form of a given object in empirical intuition is so constituted that the *apprehension* of its manifold in the imagination agrees with the *presentation* of a concept of the understanding (though which concept be undetermined), then in the mere reflection understanding and imagination *mutually agree* for the advancement of their business . . . " (my emphasis on "mutually agree"). Section VIII goes even further: what we consider in the relationship of the two faculties "is how one *helps or hinders* the other in the very same representation" (Ak 20: 223). Consider also the following remarkable excerpt from a transcript of lectures Kant gave on aesthetics in the winter of 1794/95: "[Understanding and imagination] are like two friends who dislike but can't relinquish each other, for they live in a continuous fight and yet can't do without each other" (quoted in Dieter Henrich, *Aesthetic Judgment and the Moral Image of the World* [Stanford: Stanford University Press, 1992], pp. 52–53).

22. Paul Guyer gives a thorough account of the evidence for both sorts of readings in "The Harmony of the Faculties Revisited," (in Guyer, *Values of Beauty* [Cambridge: Cambridge University Press, 2005]). He uses the terms "precognitive" and "multicognitive" for the two sorts of reading: I prefer "pre-conceptual" and "inter-conceptual" in part because I think both readings see the harmony of the faculties as a pre-cognitive state. See Appendix III for further discussion of Kant's aesthetics.

23. This is not an isolated passage: the word "definite" or "determinate" appears again and again in similar discussions in the *Critique*. For instance: "Flowers, free designs, lines aimlessly intertwined in each other under the name of foliage, signify nothing, do not depend on any *determinate* concept, and yet please. The satisfaction in the beautiful must depend upon reflection on an object that leads to some sort of concept (*it is indeterminate which*), and is thereby distinguished from the agreeable, which rests entirely upon sensation" (CJ 207; my emphases). See also CJ 222, 241, and "First Introduction" 220.

24. See the previous three notes.

25. What I say here expands on pp. 26–28, and the footnotes thereto, in my *Third Concept of Liberty*.

26. It's worth noting two features of the account I give: (1) It neither identifies concepts with linguistic entities, nor renders them entirely independent of language—any fine-grained use of concepts will certainly require language, but I've left open the possibility that non-language users may also have some concepts. And (2) it neither identifies concepts with anything purely mental nor gives encouragement to materialistic reductions of the mental. These are reasons, I think, to regard my account as a minimal one, something on which philosophers who otherwise differ about concepts might agree.

27. Wittgenstein, *Philosophical Investigations*, § 72.

28. One might object to this sort of view that on it there can be no "first" concept—either in the sense that a child might be said to have a "first" concept or in the sense that some concept provides a ground for all other concepts. I think this is in fact correct and not an objection (compare Wittgenstein, *Philosophical Investigations*, § 157 on reading a "first" word).

29. See McDowell, *Mind and World* (Cambridge: Harvard University Press, 1994).

30. CJ § 19. "Woo" is Hannah Arndt's translation: see "The Crisis in Culture," in Arendt, *Between Past and Future* (Hammondsport: Penguin, 1968), p. 222.

31. Hermann Cohen, *Religion of Reason Out of the Sources of Judaism*, pp. 10, 63–64, 69. See also Cohen, *Logic der reinen Erkenntnis* (Berlin: Bruno Cassirer Verlag, 1914), pp. 31–38, 79–93.

32. Kierkegaard, *Philosophical Fragments*, trans. D. Swenson, N. Thulstrup and H. Hong (Princeton: Princeton University Press, 1962), p. 46. This is also the key to Kierkegaard's understanding of revelation as essentially paradoxical: see § 14 above.

33. I expand on why I apply an otherwise Kantian view of the aesthetic paradigmatically to artworks in Appendix III.

34. Similarly: "[N]o description of *nibbana*, even in terms of simple existence or non-existence, was ever held to be true .... To use my own metaphor, the denial of self in whatever can be experienced or conceptualized ... serves to direct the attribution of value away from that sphere. Instead of supplying a verbalized notion of what *is* the sphere of ultimate value, Buddhism simply leaves a direction arrow, while resolutely refusing to predicate anything of the destination, to discuss its relationship with the phenomenal person, or indeed to say anything more about it." Steven Collins, *Selfless Persons* (Cambridge University Press, 1982), 82–83.

35. Proust, *In Search of Lost Time*, trans. C. K. Scott-Moncrieff and Terence Kilmartin, revised by D. J. Enright (New York: Modern Library, 1998), volume I (*Swann's Way*), p. 252. A few sentences later, these experiences get linked to something much like Kant's play of the faculties: "they gave me an unreasoning pleasure, the illusion of a sort of fecundity of mind" (cf. CJ 222). Richard Moran discusses these passages in "Kant, Proust, and the Appeal of Beauty" (unpublished).

36. Paul Celan, "All Souls," in *Poems of Paul Celan*, trans. M. Hamburger (New York: Persea Books, 1988), p. 129.

37. But finding the world beautiful is a problematic goal for the lives we lead *within* the world. Nagel notes that the kind of "non-egocentric" attention to the particular that he describes "doesn't blend well with the complex, forward-looking pursuits of a civilized creature." (VN 223) He says that it is therefore hard to know whether we could "sustain [this] attitude consistently" in everyday life, and speculates that perhaps we could if we radically changed the way we live. I think his insight into the incompatibility of the aesthetic attitude with the kinds of lives we have is correct, but goes deeper than he realizes: *no* life with "forward-looking pursuits" is compatible with an attitude of standing back and taking in particulars. We are creatures that need to find food and shelter, and that crave the companionship of other creatures like ourselves, and therefore find ourselves with a large number of obligations to family and neighbors. We could not survive if we rid ourselves of all our forward-looking projects, and we certainly could not maintain our moral commitments. Even those with the resources to live a life of pure aesthetic attention would do so at the cost of abandoning those who suffer or are oppressed among their fellow creatures. A life of such self-indulgence would be immoral, and, for that reason, not worthwhile.

   Which is to say that a state of pure attention to the particular is suited to a *non-bodily, eternal existence*, could wholeheartedly satisfy only a creature who did not need to survive as we do in this world, and who did not have obligations to help other, similar creatures. Once again, the possibility of some sort of existence after our deaths seems essential to an adequate answer to our telic questions.

38. Ever anew, because absorption in just one particular, forever, would not be absorption in a particular at all: particulars need limits in space and time to be particular.

39. We see now why revealed religions must be historical even if the stories they tell need not be historically *accurate* (see Introduction, § 5).

40. "The Torah can only be acquired in partnership (*b'havurah*)" (BT Berakhot 63b).

41. "Resh Lakish said: 'Great is repentance, for because of it premeditated sins are accounted [by God] as errors'" (BT Yoma 86b). See also Soloveitchik, *On Repentance*, ed. and trans. Pinchas Peli (New York: Paulist Press, 1984), pp. 248–256.

42. Of course, the beauty in this scene may draw in part on "properly" religious revelations that influenced Mozart: moments of loving forgiveness in Jesus's life, in traditional Christian portrayals of Mary, and in the lives of Christian saints, surely stand behind the Countess's noble gesture. But so much could be said of "properly" religious revelations themselves: there are ancient Near Eastern influences on the Hebrew Bible, and Jewish influences on the Gospels and Quran. These influences do not take away from the newness of the Torah or Gospels or Quran, and the Christian influences on *Figaro* do not take away from what is new in it: its ability to speak to people regardless of their commitment to Christianity, for instance, or the fact that it puts its central point in a musical rather than verbal form, thus in a form that gives priority (in characteristic 18th-century fashion) to our sentiments over our rationality.

43. Mozart more than da Ponte, since it is the music far more than the plotting or the lines that carries the dignity here, and the air of almost-religious transfiguration.

44. As Thomas Reid says, according to Peter Kivy, what awes us when we encounter the *Iliad* or the *St. Matthew Passion* is the sense that we have been "somehow put[...] in contact with a mind of massive dimensions: an intellect far beyond our own, and magnificent in its workings and proportions. We are directly communicating with a mind far beyond our own and vicariously experiencing through its creation what the mind itself experienced.... For a while we are coming as close as we possibly can to *being* Bach."—Kivy, "Reid's Philosophy of Art," in T. Cuneo and R. van Woudenberg (eds.), *The Cambridge Companion to Thomas Reid* (Cambridge: Cambridge University Press, 2004), p. 284.

45. See the discussion of "inspiration" models for the composition of the Torah, and the discomfort therewith, in Heschel, *The Prophets*, chapter 11, Dorff (ed.), *Conservative Judaism*, pp. 114–115, 122–123, or the first article of the *Niagara Bible Conference Creed*, a statement of principles by conservative Christian biblical scholars in 1883: "We believe 'that all Scripture is given by inspiration of God' [2 Timothy 3: 16], by which we understand the whole of the book called the Bible; nor do we take the statement in the sense in which it is sometimes foolishly said that works of human genius are inspired, but in the sense that the Holy Ghost gave the very words of the sacred writings to holy men of old" (quoted in Kugel, p. 766, note 22).

46. In Dorff, p. 115.

47. In Dorff, p. 123.

48. See M. I. Finley, *The World of Odysseus* (Harmondsworth: Penguin, 1979), pp. 41–42, and Thaddeus Zielinski, *The Religion of Ancient Greece* (Oxford: Oxford University Press, 1926), p. 194.

49. This is not to remove a legitimate role, within such preservation, for a moral wrestling with the Torah: see chapter 6 of this Part.

50. See "...Poetically Man Dwells ...," in *Poetry Language, Thought*, p. 214.

51. Maimonides, *Guide*, Introduction and II.45, and MT, *Book of Knowledge*, "Laws of the Foundation of the Torah," chapter VII.

Part IV Chapter 5

1. One thing this means is that engaging in practice leads one to change one's understanding of the terms of the vision. Just as Aloysius's advisee realizes after his actions that the literal sense

of what Aloysius said doesn't convey his real point, that he must reinterpret Aloysius's words, so in general the effect of putting doing before understanding is to require us constantly to reinterpret our revelation. We will see the significance of this point in Chapter 6.

2. Joseph Soloveitchik, *Halakhic Man*, trans. Lawrence Kaplan (Philadelphia: JPS, 1983), pp. 23, 20–21. I should note that Soloveitchik would resist the aesthetic way in which I understand halacha. He prefers to draw comparisons between halachic categories and mathematical ones, or the categories of Kant's epistemology. I think this is a result of an impoverished understanding of aesthetics, and an overly Platonic picture of the truth that mathematical and philosophical abstractions might reveal.

3. See McDowell, "Virtue and Reason," "Two Sorts of Naturalism" (also in *Mind, Value and Reality*), and "Deliberation and Moral Development" (in Engstrom and Whiting, *Aristotle, Kant and the Stoics*).

4. See McDowell, "Virtue and Reason," and Iris Murdoch, *The Sovereignty of Good*.

5. It is this need for humility that accounts for the importance of the declaration "It is written," in religious language-games. What disturbed Kant (Introduction, § 8), and the character from *Gethsemane* that I quoted in the beginning of this book (Part I, § 1) about the reverence with which religious believers regard their sacred text is essential to the ability of revelation to transform us morally, and show us something radically new. "It is written" is not a dispositive move in the language game, as Kant supposes, since it is always possible to dispute exactly *what* is written in a sacred scripture (we'll see more about this in chapter 6), but it is an important one, that can never simply be dismissed.

6. This language runs through the second half of his *Concluding Unscientific Postscript* (Part II, chapter IV).

7. Mundaka Upanishad, III.i, in Easwaran, p. 115.

8. *loc. cit.* Compare: "[I]n putting himself last, the sage puts himself first, and in giving himself up he preserves himself. / If you aren't free of yourself, how will you ever become yourself?"—*Tao te Ching* 7, trans. by David Hinton (New York: Counterpoint, 2002), p. 9.

9. See §§ 14, 41.

10. For a different—but, I think, compatible—account of divine commands, see FIG, chapters 10 and 11. Adams understands commands in general as necessary to social bonds, and divine commands as ways by which we build social bonds with God. I like this view of social bonds, and agree with Adams about the importance of coming into community with God. But there are other aspects to the command structure of religious discipline (aspects that, for one thing, make sense even in non-theistic religions), and I stress one here that fits well with the idea that our ultimate telos is partly obscured from us.

11. Kant, RWB 172.

12. RWB 171; see also 176 and 166n, which speaks of replacing the "yoke" of Jewish ritual with the yoke of "profession of faith in sacred history, which, for the conscientious, is an even more onerous burden."

13. See Kugel, *How to Read the Bible*, 667–672.

Part IV: Chapter 6

1. See John Boswell, *Christianity, Social Tolerance and Homosexuality* (Chicago: University of Chicago, 1980), pp. 233–9 and *Selected Poems of Shmuel HaNagid*, ed. and trans. Peter Cole (Princeton: Princeton University Press, 1996), pp. 15–19 and notes on 167–168.

2. After a Protestant movement that insisted on a particularly literalist reading of Scriptures. The term is not well-suited to ultra-conservative Jews, Muslims, or Catholics.

3. That is: people who do not embrace the revelation must still be able to see how it gives a plausible answer to the people in our prompting scenarios, incorporates morality as a condition for its highest end, and allows for reflection as well as love in its followers. The tradition adhering to the revelation need not represent it as something that all human beings must *accept*. Some religions do insist on that, but many do not. And they need not do that; they need just to see their vision as something that outsiders could in principle recognize as good. Otherwise they cannot say that it is *of* the highest good for humanity.

What can it mean to say that a vision is of the highest good for all humanity, if not that every human being should accept it? Here are a few possibilities:

(1) The vision is an example or model of the highest good for everyone. It is, let's say, a way of being ascetic and in order to satisfy his or her telic yearnings, everyone ought to be ascetic in some way, or it is intellectually challenging and everyone needs to be intellectually challenged, or it develops our love for all sentient beings, and everyone needs somehow to develop such love. Thus Jews stress the reverent study of their sacred texts, but allow that a similar such study can take place in other traditions, and Islam opposes all forms of idolatry, but acknowledges that other traditions also resist idolatry.

(2) The vision contributes to the bringing about of a condition in which all human beings will find their telic yearnings satisfied, but does not do the whole job of bringing about that condition. By promoting a strong commitment to justice or non-violence, say, or a rigorous version of monotheism, a particular group helps the rest of humanity get closer to a situation in which justice and mercy and integrity will reign everywhere, and at that point God will let us see how all our telic questions are properly answered.

(3) The vision does lead all human beings to achieve their highest good, but only some human beings will be aware that that is how they are reaching their end. On some Christian views, for instance, Christ's death and resurrection provides salvation to everyone whether they realize that or not. The works of grace by which Christ shows up in people's lives may then not be explicitly Christian ones: the worship of a devout Jew or Hindu may, for such Christians, be expressions of God's salvation even though the Jew or Hindu doesn't see what she is doing, explicitly, as having to do with Christ.

A revelation can, that is, be understood as just one way of imagining or realizing the highest good for all humanity, or as realizing just a part of that end. What it cannot do is maintain that its telos is the end just of an individual or member of a limited human group. We are led to revelation by questions about whether human beings in *general* have an end, and an answer to those questions must respond to us *as* human beings, not just as individuals or groups: to the features we share with all humanity. So any revelation needs to hold that its vision and path is at least one way by which any human being can attain the highest good, and that those who follow this way will contribute to, rather than obstructing, the good of all other human beings. In that sense, all revealed visions must be universal. There is no need for them to be universal in the stronger sense that they hold out their vision as the sole correct representation of the highest good, or the sole way to achieve that good.

4. As earth and world, and poetry and philosophy, do for Heidegger (OWA 47–48, 216).

5. Kugel, 682.

6. Which for Kugel is the fourth assumption that the interpreters shared—I leave it off the list because I think it should be treated as dependent on the other three. Moreover, Kugel thinks that for a while ancient interpreters held the first three assumptions without regarding the text as divinely authored (15n). Rather, the idea that the entire Bible was divinely authored arose after a process of interpreting it in accordance with the three assumptions I have listed had been going for some time. (Kugel, 14–16; my claim that being cryptic is essential to

sacredness contradicts Kugel's footnote on 15, although elsewhere he indicates that a text that is supposed to address readers over many generations may have to be cryptic: see the last paragraph on 667, for instance).

7. Ibid. 679–682.
8. Ibid. 137.
9. "The person who seeks to learn *from* the Bible is smaller than the text; he crouches at its feet, waiting for its instructions or insights. Learning *about* the text generates the opposite posture. The text moves from subject to object; it no longer speaks, but is spoken about, analyzed, and acted upon. The insights are now all the reader's, not the text's and anyone can see the results" (Kugel, 666).
10. The seminal book on this subject is Michael Fishbane, *Biblical Interpretation in Ancient Israel* (Oxford: Oxford University Press, 1985). For a short introduction, see Fishbane, "Inner Biblical Exegesis," in his *The Garments of Torah* (Bloomington: Indiana University Press, 1992). Fishbane offers convincing evidence for seeing many passages in the Bible as containing editorial modifications inserted by scribes. But I see no theological reason for calling the latter "human" additions to "divine teachings" ("Inner Biblical Exegesis," p. 26). Why suppose that the scribes either intended any less to channel God's voice than the oracles they were transcribing, or succeeded any less well in doing that? Moreover, the history of traditional Jewish and Christian interpretation shows that the original, more oracular material and its later revisions can readily be understood to form one seamless text. And on the view of revelation I am urging here, the Bible must be so read, if it is to be revelatory at all.
11. See quotation in note 9.
12. BT Sanhedrin 68b–72a.
13. Ibid. 71a.
14. Ibid. 45b.
15. Ibid. 112a.
16. Ibid. 71a.
17. By inference from Deuteronomy 12: 3–4, where the Torah commands the destruction of objects of idolatry and then immediately adds, "Do not do so to the Lord your God." (The most straightforward reading of the passage would not join these verses, however.)
18. BT Sanhedrin 45b.
19. BT *Baba Kamma* 83b–84a.
20. Mishnah Makkoth 1: 10 (BT Makkoth 7a).
21. When it tells us that all human beings are formed in the image of God (Genesis 1: 27).
22. It's worth noting here that—for all the difficulty of finding justice and mercy explicitly laid out in the Torah—the rabbis interpreted Torah law so as to bring their society far closer to what today we consider justice and mercy than practically any other premodern culture. Roman law allowed parents the right to execute their children, and made frequent, careless use of capital punishment. Almost all Christian societies have executed people with abandon until recent times, and the United States, one of the most strongly Christian nations in the modern world, continues to do so. Rights of women to divorce were not present in many societies, including again most Christian ones, until quite recently, and in many places, women either were not asked at all, or asked only nominally, for their consent before entering into marriage. This is not to say that rabbinic Judaism overcame sexism—it was and is very sexist in many respects, and even the rights it established for women as regards marriage and divorce were inadequate, and often honored more in the breach than in the observance. But it is remarkable how much the rabbinic world, often pilloried by Christian writers even in modern times as the paradigm of a hidebound, bigoted culture, in fact

recognized certain Enlightenment ideals long before most other parts of the world came to them.

23. By "the mainstream Jewish tradition" I mean to exclude Philo, who was read by Christians far more than by Jews.

24. BT Sotah 49b (cf. BT Menachoth 99b, Baba Kamma 82b, and Menachot 64b). An exception is made for prominent Jews, who might use such wisdom to influence the non-Jewish ruling powers: but this makes philosophy just a tool for political manipulation.

For a very different view of this passage, see Saul Lieberman, *Hellenism in Jewish Palestine* (New York: Jewish Theological Seminary, 1962), pp. 100–105. Lieberman notes that it is teaching Greek wisdom to one's children that is forbidden, not studying it oneself, but makes nothing of what it might mean that such study would be restricted to people capable of engaging it on their own. He also notes that the rabbis put an age restriction on studying Greek (see p. 103, n. 24), but doesn't comment on the fact that this makes it like the study of the so-called *Ma'aseh Mercava* (mystical teachings). And he accepts uncritically a statement in the Palestinian Talmud to the effect that the restrictions on teaching Greek wisdom were designed to prevent people from becoming informers (101–102). But it is very hard to understand how *that* reasoning would lead to a minimal age for learning Greek wisdom: surely no-one would fear that *children* would become informers. The age-restriction, the concern that studying Greek wisdom competes with Torah study, and the restriction of such study to people learned enough to master it on their own, fit far better with a fear that the content of this material might conflict with one's commitments to Torah.

Lieberman never mentions such a possibility, nor does he discuss the other sources I bring below. Some of these omissions—BT Avot 3: 23, in particular (on astronomy and geometry)—are surprising in a book on Hellenism in Jewish Palestine. Indeed, the book as a whole, while wonderful when it comes to Hellenic influences on the grammar, hermeneutics, attitudes towards idolatry, and natural science of the rabbis, is very disappointing as regards rabbinic attitudes towards Greek and Roman philosophy. Plato doesn't appear in the index, nor does "Stoicism" or "Epicureanism" (Lieberman does not even address the rabbinic use of the word "Epicurean" [*apikoros*] for a heretic), and the citations from Aristotle are almost entirely from his empirical observations on animals.

25. The fourth was Rabbi Akiva, who "came out whole", but who also, it would seem, renounced any further philosophical investigations; he certainly never uses philosophical argument in his halachic reasoning. Rabbi Akiva's peremptory dismissal of any conflict between free will and determinism, in BT Avot 3: 19, and insistence, in Avot 3: 18, that our belief in creation comes to us only by revelation, can also be read as a polemic against any attempt to derive fundamental religious principles by reason.

26. Bereishit Rabbah I.10, in *Midrash Rabbah*, trans. H. Freedman (London: Soncino, 1939), volume I.

27. Philosophers are also treated as (somewhat foolish) challengers to Judaism in a series of stories at BT Avodah Zarah 54b–55a.

28. The phrase the rabbis tend to use for someone who has been led by philosophy away from Jewish faith is that such a person is *kofer b'ikar*: one who "denies the essential." Usually, "the essential" here is either the existence of God (that is what the *apikoros*—Epicurean—is said to deny) or the divine origin of the Torah.

29. They left some room, after all, for the study of mathematics and physics—Rabbi Elazar may call geometry and astronomy "peripheral" to wisdom, but he does not claim that one should avoid them altogether.

30. See Rashi and Ramban *ad locorum* (*Pentateuch with Rashi's Commentary*, trans. M. Rosenbaum and A. M. Silberman [Jerusalem: Silbermann Family, 1933], vol. 5, p. 39, and Nachmanides, *Commentary on the Torah*, "Leviticus," pp. 282–284).

31. Tikvah Frymer-Kensky has argued that the Jewish Bible was actually quite *anti*-sexist in the context in which it was written: see her *In the Wake of the Goddesses* (New York: Free Press, 1992).

32. This is to say nothing of hermeneutical techniques like *gematria*, used by all sorts of different Jewish groups, which employ the numerical value of words in the Hebrew text to come up with meanings very distant from the literal one. Or consider the view that the Torah is fundamentally just a collection of letters, not words, that can be re-arranged into entirely different patterns of meaning if God so chooses:

> Because of Adam's sin, God arranged the letters before Him into the words describing death and other earthly things, such as levirate marriage. Without sin there would have been no death. The same letters would have been joined into words telling a different story. That is why the scroll of the Torah contains no vowels, no punctuation, and no accents, as an allusion to the Torah which originally formed a heap of unarranged letters. The divine purpose will be revealed in the Torah at the coming of the Messiah, who will engulf death forever, so that there will be no room in the Torah for anything related to death, uncleanness, and the like. For then God will annul the present combination of letters that form the words of our present Torah and will compose the letters into other words, which will form new sentences speaking of other things. This is the meaning of the words of Isaiah (51: 4): "A Torah will proceed from me," which was already interpreted by the ancient rabbis to mean: "A new Torah will proceed from me." Does this mean that the Torah is not eternally valid? No, it means that the scroll of the Torah will be as it is now, but that God will teach us to read it in accordance with another arrangement of letters, and enlighten us as to the division and combination of the words (quoted from the 18th-century mystic Rabbi Eliyahu Kohen Ittamari of Smyrna, by Gershom Scholem in *On the Kabbalah and Its Symbolism* (New York: Schocken, 1965, pp. 74–75).

On such a view, of course, the text could mean just about anything. Jewish mystics in fact avoided the most radical implications of views like this in practice, constraining what they attributed to the Torah in accordance with the norms of Jewish law. And Eliyahu Kohen himself says that the radical re-reading of the Torah his view opens up will only be available to us in the days of the Messiah: when we are given a new revelation. But in principle he allows for a wholesale reinterpretation of the Torah.

33. Compare Gershom Scholem: "One cannot but be fascinated by the unbelievable freedom with which Meister Eckhart, the author of the *Zohar*, or the great Sufi mystics read their canonical texts, from which their own world seems to construct itself.... But how can [the mystic] case aside the literal meaning while still recognizing the authority of the text? This is possible because he regards the literal meaning as simply non-existent or as valid only for a limited time. It is *replaced* by a mystical interpretation."—ibid. 13.

34. *On Certainty*, §§ 124, 149. See also §§ 126, 128–132, 139–140, 150, 156, 232, 492–494, 519, and (for the link between "judgment" and "interpretation," and for the general philosophical view on which I am relying here) *Philosophical Investigations*, §§ 28, 34, 198, 201–202 and 241–242.

35. The same goes for the supposedly literal ways of reading the text favored by critical Bible scholars. They, too, must fit in with general theories of history, and prior readings that have been accepted in the discipline.

36. One might ask why an all-good God would allow His will for us to be put in such obscure ways, and perhaps in multiple texts, rather than giving us a single, clear text that spells out exactly how we should live, and that is clearly superior to any other candidate for revelation. Immoral interpretations of sacred texts have been a source of many cruelties and injustices, and the struggle among people who uphold different texts as sacred, or different interpretations of the same purportedly sacred text, has been one of the greatest causes of war. Why would a good God not avoid such evils by making His will for us crystal clear?

    One answer to that is that there is no such thing as a "crystal clear" text. The process of interpreting even such a straightforward document as the American Constitution has been a difficult and much-contested one, and that is only to be expected if the application of general terms and principles to specific cases is something that no general term or principle can determine. If the human telos is inherently obscure, moreover, no text purporting to present that telos can be remotely as clear as the American Constitution.

    Another answer to this objection is that the exercise of our hermeneutic capacities is itself a great source of freedom and joy, and that one can hardly imagine an all-good God loving us as autonomous beings unless He (She) allowed us to receive His (Her) teachings in full use of those capacities.

    But these answers may seem inadequate in the face of the extreme cruelty, injustice, and violence to which religious controversy has given rise. When the objection is put this way, I would simply say that the problem of why an all-good God would allow us obscure and/or multiple revelations is no different from—is indeed part of—the problem of evil. It is very difficult to explain why a good God would allow us to commit any of the cruel and unjust and violent acts we regularly perform, let alone countenance the natural horrors we face: many people, understandably, abandon religion for precisely that reason. But if one remains religious, maintains a faith, especially, that this world flows forth from an all-good Being, then one perforce has faith that there is some answer or set of answers to the problem of evil. And if there is an answer to that problem in general, then there will also be an answer to the problem of how a God could permit the evils of obscure revelations in particular.

37. A famous Mishnah in Pesahim limits the degree to which one needs to root out leavened substances before the Passover holiday, despite the great importance that that process is given (BT Pesahim 9a); the Day of Atonement, which involves a 25-hour fast, was never doubled, even though the other holidays were; the command to remit all debts every seventh year was modified so that poor people could get loans.

38. Mishnah Hagigah 1:8 (BT Hagigah 10a).

39. A major early rabbi, known for his choleric temperament.

40. One of the most important early rabbis, known for his patience and kindness—this story is told primarily to illustrate how much better a teacher Hillel was than Shammai.

41. BT Shabbat 31a.

42. BT Baba Mezia 59b, Steinsaltz translation, slightly revised: Adin Steinsaltz (trans. and commentator), *The Talmud*, Tractate Bava Metzia, vol. III, pp. 235–237.

43. See the passage from *Seder Eliyahu Zuta* cited in Dorff, p. 76.

44. The notion, as Davidson points out (*Inquiries*, xvii), originally comes from Neil Wilson, "Substances Without Substrata," *Review of Metaphysics* 12 (1959).

45. Davidson, *Inquiries*, 197.

46. *Inquiries*, 200–201.

47. *Inquiries*, 196.

48. See, e.g. BT Berakhot 31b and Keritoth 11a.

49. G. W. F. Hegel, *Phenomenology of Spirit*, trans. A. V. Miller (New York: Oxford University Press, 1977), ¶ 784, p. 475.

50. See my "Poetry and Truth-Conditions."

51. See Song of Songs Rabbah I.i.8 and Bamidbar Rabbah XIII.15 (in *Midrash Rabbah*, vol. VI and vol. IX, p. 10). The issue of Scriptural polysemy in rabbinic teaching is well discussed in David Stern, "Midrash and Indeterminacy," *Critical Inquiry* vol. 15, no. 1 (August 1988).

52. Indeed, the debates in the Talmud gave rise to centuries of further debates, and those debates are included in medieval and modern editions of the Talmud.

53. As I hope I have made clear, I don't think the revelatory status of the Torah hangs on Mosaic authorship—I don't think the historical circumstances that the Torah gives for its own production need be even approximately correct. But we don't have to go into that issue here. In fact, it strengthens the case against seeing the oral Torah as just like the written one if we grant Mosaic authorship to the latter. It then becomes paramount to ask what reason Moses could possibly have had for not writing down the former—what reason, indeed, *God* could possibly have had for not ordering Moses to write down the former—given the likely corruption of transmission in the absence of a written text.

54. Hence their strict laws about how to write a Torah scroll: with indelible ink, on strong materials on which ink is unlikely to become blurry, etc.

55. Certainly, that doesn't match the sorts of arguments one finds in the *Mishnah*, which codified the oral law. The rabbis in the Gemara quite often cite material from the Mishnaic period, passed down orally and not included in the Mishnah itself, and questions about the reliability of this material, or its proper sources, do come up. But this is a type of debate that arises *after* the oral law had been codified, not a debate that characterizes the oral law itself. It is a debate about the reliability of historical memory between the Tannaitic and Amoraic periods, not about the reliability of historical memory between Moses and the Tannaim.

56. For instance, some think that the juxtaposition of two verses can be used to derive legal conclusions while others reject that notion.

57. BT Eruvin 10b.

58. BT Menahot 29b.

59. Compare Abraham Joshua Heschel, *God in Search of Man* (New York: Farrar, Straus & Giroux, 1955), pp. 186–199.

60. Kant, *The Conflict of the Faculties*, trans. Mary Gregor (Lincoln: University of Nebraska, 1979), Ak 63. Compare RWB 87, 187.

61. Some paths mandate such practices for a special class of adepts in the society—Max Weber called them religious "virtuosi"—while allowing most people to pursue a milder version of the religious ideal.

62. For this reason it represents a deep confusion about the nature of revelation when historical scholars insist that a purportedly revealed text be understood in accordance with the intentions of its likely human authors. Marc Brettler, for instance, insists that many ritual texts in the Torah "lack an ethical or moral component, and we misunderstand (or 'anachronize') them if we claim that such a component is implicit" (Brettler, *How to read the Jewish Bible* [Oxford: Oxford University Press, 2005], 83). But insofar as one regards the true author of the text as God, there is no anachronism in reading it as if it were given to one right now, and no misunderstanding about presupposing that the practices it mandates contain an ethical or moral component. Brettler consistently takes a historical understanding of the Bible to be the *correct* one (see for instance 93, where he brings historical materials to prevent the "error" of holding certain theological views about Deuteronomy), even though he describes himself as a religious Jew, and in that context recognizes the importance of non-historical modes of interpretation (see 279–283). What he says about squaring his scholarly and his religious views is unsatisfying; I think he simply does not know how to bring his inclination to view history as giving us the truth about texts together with his religious

commitments. More successful attempts to do that can be found in Kugel, *How to Read the Bible*, and Levenson, "The Eighth Principle of Judaism and the Literary Simultaneity of Scripture."

Part IV: Chapter 7

1. See Zohar II:99a–b.
2. Gotthold Ephraim Lessing, *Nathan the Wise*, trans. Bayard Morgan (New York: Frederick Ungar, 1955), Act III, scene 7, lines 112–120, p. 79.
3. Ibid., lines 125–141, pp. 79–80. I've slightly revised the translation of lines 131–132.
4. Act III, scene 7, ll 1978–1986. I discuss the importance of parental love to Lessing's understanding of religion in *The Ethics of Culture* (Ithaca: Cornell University Press, 1994), pp. 117–118. For a rich examination of Lessing's theology, see Henry Allison, *Lessing and the Enlightenment* (Ann Arbor: University of Michigan Press, 1966).
5. And again, conversion to a different religion, if it is not a reaction to one's family, can often be explained either by revulsion towards the community of one's upbringing or by one's having been raised in a community that showed little love for its own traditions.
6. The five commandments that concern relations between human beings and God, rather than between one human being and another.
7. *Inter alia*, this makes sense of how we can read the Bible as the word of God even after the discoveries of historical criticism: we can say that even as God made use of human ways of speaking, so He made use of the earlier cultural traditions by which ancient Israelites understood the religious realm. In order to "speak in human language," God had to graft His teaching to the Israelites onto the rituals and institutions and laws they shared with their neighbors elsewhere in the Near East. Only a text that came about in that manner could speak to the emotional and conceptual formation of the ancient Jewish people.

   This is rather different from the view, once popular among liberal Protestants and Reform Jews, on which the Bible comes increasingly to represent God's will as it comes to be written by increasingly rational Israelites, with the sophisticated civilization by which to transform the crude myths of their past into a properly moral conception of God. On my view, God must speak in *any* historical time and place—including a "sophisticated," rationalistic one— through images and commands that resonate with the emotional yearnings that history and culture have made salient to that people at that time, not through an ahistorical reason alone. It is not the more rationalistic writings of the prophets and sages, but the insistence on reading all the materials of the Bible as expressing God's will that marks the formation of Judaism, as a powerful religious vision, out of its spiritually and morally shallower past. The Jews transformed their old tales into a vision of God by embracing them as expressions of God's will, and humbling themselves to the attempt to find an appropriately divine meaning for them, not by surveying those materials from above, and pruning them in accordance with an independent philosophical theory about what God is likely to say. The latter approach, advocated by Plato and followed by religious rationalists ever since, makes a shambles of revelation. For such rationalists, there can really be nothing revealed aside from the contents of reason. An approach that centers on imaginative commitment, on the other hand, can grant that revelation requires a spontaneous (rational) reception *of* that revelation while stressing at the same time that we need to receive something from outside ourselves, to see ourselves as not already containing everything a God might want to tell us.
8. Maimonides, *Mishneh Torah*, "Laws of Kings and Wars," chapter 10, law 9.

9. See David Stove, *The Plato Cult* (London: Wiley-Blackwell, 1991). The Druze are said to this day to regard Plato as a prophet.

10. This seems precisely what happened to, at least, the *Song of Songs*, and perhaps much else in the Hebrew Bible: see Kugel, pp. 514–518, 667–672.

11. But I am even more inclined to think that the idea of a single right religion is just part of what Lessing calls the "pious madness... to have the better God, and to impose this better God as best on the whole world" (*Nathan*, Act II, scene v, 1959 translation, slightly revised).

12. Note that these considerations are all ethical ones. Revelation answers the Kantian question, "for what may we hope?" and so we select among possible revelations primarily in accordance with what we hope, not with our factual beliefs (although factual beliefs to some extent constrain what we hope: see Part III, § 50). One revelation, you may feel, holds out a morally inappropriate hope to its followers; another holds out too small a hope or a shallow picture of what would satisfy our hopes. It is these considerations, and not the pseudo-scientific arguments often used to make one tradition seem more plausible than another (better evidence for the resurrection of Jesus than for the revelation on Mount Sinai, say, or better reason to trust the history in the Hebrew Bible than in the Quran), that should, and generally do, lead people to choose one tradition over another: to convert, or to stick with their own tradition after having considered conversion.

Part V: Chapter 1

1. Marxists, for instance, sometimes urge the unconvinced to trust in communist teachings on the promise that after the proletarian revolution they will see the transformative value of a wholly egalitarian society. Many Freudians similarly tell those who resist psychoanalysis to trust the process, promising that they will eventually see why their trust was merited. Both Marxists and Freudians of this stripe call their teachings "true" in much the way that religious people do: by doing so, they ask their listeners to trust in a certain path.

   It's not a coincidence that Marxism and Freudianism are varieties of what we called transformative ethical projects in Part II, chapter 4. Revealed religions are also modes of transformative ethics, and the nineteenth century gave rise to many secular equivalents precisely because it was the first period in human history in which religious faith had widely lost its hold.

2. Cf. Part II, § 25.

3. To the extent that that conflict arises: many revealed religions allow for deceit in certain dire cases.

4. "The determination of the private horizon," he tells us in his *Logic*, "depends on various empirical conditions and special considerations, e.g. age, sex, position, way of life and the like" (Ak 9:41; English in Kant, *Logic*, trans. R. Hartman and W. Schwarz [New York: Dover, 1974], p. 46)—features of what today we might call our "identity," which can limit our thought or guide it towards limited aims. From the absolute or universal horizon, by contrast—the public horizon—we are concerned with the question, "What can the human being, *as* a human being, ... know?" (*loc. cit.*).

5. Imagine someone who regards a particular claim as reasonable, but is joined in this view by others only after her death; an argument for which she was derided in her lifetime finally receives wide acclaim. We surely would not want to deny that such a person had reason for her claim during her lifetime; the claim could not *become* a reason unless it had always been one.

6. All quotations in this paragraph from Kant, *Anthropology from a Pragmatic Point of View*, trans. V. Dowdell (Carbondale: Southern Illinois University Press, 1978), p.117 (Ak 7: 219).

7. See Introduction, § 6.

8. In WO?, he even suggests that personal experience might legitimately play some role in religious faith, once the foundations of that faith are laid elsewhere: "[N]o-one can *first* be convinced of the existence of a highest being through any intuition; rational faith must come first, and then certain appearances or disclosures could at most provide the occasion for investigating whether we are warranted in taking what speaks or present itself to us to be a Deity, and thus serve to confirm that faith" (Ak 8: 143).

9. "To make use of one's own reason means no more than to ask oneself, whenever one is supposed to assume something, whether one could find it feasible to make the ground or the rule on which one assumes it into a universal principle for the use of reason" (WO? 146–147n).

10. Rawls's "non-public" reason is not co-extensive with private reason in this sense. In the "universities, scientific societies and professional groups" (PL 220) to which I belong, I would be loath to rely on the private reason I have described. Public reason, in Kant's sense of that phrase, is the default currency in most large and diverse social settings; we depart from it only where we are confident that our interlocutors share certain experiences and vocabularies that we ourselves regard as largely private, peculiar to our individual lives. This sort of discourse constitutes a small part of what Rawls would regard as non-public reason.

11. As Kant says, public discussion is "the greatest and most useful means of correcting our own thoughts" (*Anthropology*, Ak 219).

12. See "Dreams of a Spirit-Seer" Ak 2:338–9, in conjunction with CJ §§ 49, 57, and 59, and RWB 65n. "Dreams" is an early and much-disputed text, but the idea, in the passage I have cited, that certain images can function as "symbols" of God, and that concepts of God need "a corporeal cloak in order to present themselves in a clear light" runs through the later passages as well.

13. Compare the discussion of geniuses and prophets in Part IV, § 49.

14. She may, nevertheless, consider it a miracle. Any believer in a revealed religion sees God as intervening in human history, and it would be strange to suppose that He could appear at Sinai or Golgotha, but cannot affect our lives today. Once one supposes that there is a supernatural Being beyond and in control of the entire natural order, there is no great difficulty in supposing that that Being can manipulate the natural order, or make His presence known in it, at various points. The problem comes if we suppose that apparent cases of such intervention—apparent miracles or signs of God's presence—can be used as *evidence* for God's existence. That, as Hume demonstrated, goes against the very nature of empirical evidence.

15. See note note 3 on p. 529.

16. Lurie, *Imaginary Friends* (London: Heineman, 1967). I am grateful to Ken Alder for suggesting this novel to me in connection with the notion of private reason I am discussing here.

17. See Part I, § 29–30.

18. Again, see note 3 on p. 529.

19. One of the finest aspects of the novel is the way Lurie presents her cult as syncretic, borrowing elements constantly from its members' churches of origin.

Part V: Chapter 2

1. There may still be room for judicious rather than strict rigorism here. I may be able to view the rules God wants me to keep as those that serve the needs of the human institutions and

communities that establish them, and therefore to say that they cease to exist when a representative of the relevant institution or community waives them.

2. See Patel, *Acts of Faith*, pp. 98–100, 109, and the website of the organization *Rabbis for Human Rights*: http://www.rhr-na.org/.

3. Something similar can happen among purely secular moralists. Kantians may respect the character and projects of utilitarians while feeling that carrying out moral duties in the name of human freedom is nobler than carrying them out in the name of human happiness.

Part V: Chapter 3

1. What Rawls calls "comprehensive conceptions of the good life."

2. Locke, "A Letter Concerning Toleration," in David Wootton (ed.), *Political Writings of John Locke* (New York: Penguin, 1993), pp. 394–395.

3. A good analysis of this process can be found in Daniel Statman, "Hypocrisy and Self-Deceit."

4. We may, indeed, be able to use Locke's epistemology to justify the claim that Mill made, later on, to the effect that each of us can truly believe something—hold it while fully understanding it and recognizing its implications, rather than holding it as a barely-understood prejudice: as a "living truth," rather than a "dead dogma" (Mill, *On Liberty*, chapter 2)—if we live in a social order in which we face vigorous opposition to our views, in which every imaginable argument against our views is trotted out before us.

5. Paul Weithman offers a somewhat similar argument: see "Why Should Christians Endorse Human Rights?" in Terence Cuneo (ed.), *Religion in the Liberal Polity* (Notre Dame: University of Notre Dame Press, 2005).

6. These are the most talked-about examples of issues in which religious premises might be used to support political claims: see, for instance, Kent Greenawalt, *Religious Convictions and Political Choice* (Oxford: Oxford University Press, 1988), chapters 5–7, and FIG 327, 347–349.

7. The debate is nicely laid out in Robert Audi and Nicholas Wolterstorff, *Religion in the Public Square* (London: Rowman & Littlefield, 1997).

8. They could be *ritually* wrong: forbidden, by a particular rite, as part of what it takes to perceive or achieve a particular religious vision. Some religions encourage celibacy, some require heterosexual, monogamous marriage, some mandate polygamy or orgiastic festivals as part of their paths to salvation, the perception of God, the annihilation of the self, or whatever else they take to be the true human telos. (Similarly, a particular religious rite may regard a stringently reverent attitude towards fetal or animal life as requisite to achieving its particular vision, and may therefore forbid abortion or mandate vegetarianism.) But when seen in this light, these are clearly telic rather than moral demands. There is therefore no way to argue that a liberal state should enforce them.

9. Part II, Chapter 2.

10. I argued in *A Third Concept of Liberty* that freedom has more conditions than most libertarians allow—we do not have freedom, I held, unless we have a certain degree of material security (basic levels of food, shelter, and health care), a decent education, and a certain amount of leisure time—so welfare programs need to be included among the protections of freedom that a liberal state will carry out. I continue to hold this view of freedom, but would add now that a liberal *democratic* state can legitimately carry out some projects unrelated to freedom. As long as the burden of taxation is not stifling, I no longer think there is anything coercive about using tax monies to carry out religiously and morally neutral projects that the majority of the population supports. If the majority of a city is willing to support politicians who promise them a new football stadium or park, I see no objection on liberal premises to

the use of tax monies for such purposes. If the majority of the citizens are willing to support a space program or farm subsidies, that too seems to me legitimate (if ill-advised)—as long as these projects do not take away from the liberty-enhancing policies, including the liberty-enhancing welfare policies, that states have a duty to support. The principles guiding liberal democracy can underwrite a mix of liberty-enhancing and utilitarian policies, I now think, although the emphasis should be on the ones that foster liberty. Investment in a space program or new stadium can never rightly come at the cost of police protection, or of adequate housing, food, health care, and education for the poor.

11. This is not the place to lay out my position in detail, but I mean to allow for the possibility that the "common good" can include tradeoffs. I'll pay taxes for a new football stadium that you want if you'll pay taxes for a new park that I want. We agree to these tradeoffs if we want governments to carry out any projects of this sort (it will never be possible to get unanimity on a given project, so we are willing to fund a bunch of them, in the hope that we can thereby get the ones we each care about off the ground). What is important is that we avoid doing things for one sub-group of the population at the expense of everyone else, and that none of our projects offend against the principles of the people paying for them.

12. It is important to be precise here. Religious arguments can certainly be used to *arrive at* the principles on which the political overlapping consensus converges: that is a feature on which Rawls insists, and without which he could not plausibly claim to be resolving differences among religious and secular people. But *what* one thereby arrives at is a view according to which religious arguments are removed from public reason, at least on constitutional essentials and matters of basic justice.

13. See Audi's contribution to *Religion in the Public Square*.

14. "Some will ask: why not say that all questions in regard to which citizens exercise their final and coercive political power over one another are subject to public reason? . . . To answer: my aim is to consider first the strongest case where the political questions concern the most fundamental answers. . . . Should [the limits of public reason] hold here, we can then proceed to other cases. Still, I grant that it is usually highly desirable to settle political questions by invoking the values of public reason" (PL 215).

15. In the eyes of many, rights to abortion and gay marriage are matters of basic justice; in the eyes of others, they are ordinary political issues. In the eyes of some, basic justice requires public education and public health care for all; in the eyes of others, how the government should be involved in education and health care is an ordinary political issue.

16. See Will Kymlicka, *Liberalism, Community, and Culture* (LCC); Charles Taylor, "The Politics of Recognition," in *Multiculturalism*, ed. Amy Gutmann (Princeton: Princeton University Press, 1994); Yael Tamir, *Liberal Nationalism* (Princeton: Princeton University Press, 1993); and Daniel Bell, *Communitarianism and Its Critics* (Oxford: Oxford University Press, 1993).

17. Cohen, *If You're Egalitarian, How Come You're So Rich?* (Cambridge: Harvard University Press, 2000), p. 39.

18. See my *Ethics of Culture* (Ithaca: Cornell University Press, 1994), chapter 5.

19. I defend this reading of Herder, and develop a notion of culture along these lines myself, in *The Ethics of Culture*, especially ch. 5, and "The Moral Interpretation of Culture," in Michael Barnhart (ed.) *Varieties of Ethical Reflection* (Lanham: Lexington Books, 2002).

20. Quoted in Boyd Shafer, *Nationalism: Myth and Reality* (New York: Harcourt, Brace, 1955), 19.

21. Quoted in ibid. 26, 20.

22. Quoted in Robert Lowie, *The History of Ethnological Theory* (New York: Farrar & Rinehart, 1937), pp. 11–12.

23. Alfred Kroeber and Clyde Kluckhohn, *Culture: A Critical Review of Concepts and Definitions* (Cambridge: Peabody Museum of American Archaeology and Ethnology, 1952).

24. LCC 165, 175–176. This emphasis on language and history continues throughout Kymlicka's later writings. But he does not give it any more thorough defense there. See, for instance, his *Multicultural Citizenship* (Oxford: Clarendon Press, 1995), pp. 82–93, and *Politics in the Vernacular* (Oxford: Oxford University Press, 2001), pp. 53–55.

25. See Iris Young, *Justice and the Politics of Difference* (Princeton: Princeton University Press, 1990), Taylor, "The Politics of Recognition," and Tamir, *Liberal Nationalism.*

26. This is a central concern of Kymlicka's work. See also Tully, *Public Philosophy in a New Key,* vol. I, chapters 7 and 8.

27. The Holocaust is not the only relevant piece of this history. Large, ancient Jewish communities in Iraq, Syria, Yemen, Libya and Egypt were brought to an end by pogroms and official persecution from the 1930s through the 1980s. No-one can address the Israel/Palestine conflict fairly without taking into account the fierce anti-Semitism, fanned by Zionism, but by no means wholly caused by it, that has spread throughout the Muslim world since the mid-19th century.

    On the other hand, Zionism made the mistake of all nationalisms in aiming for a state, rather than just thriving Jewish communities. Some early Zionists did see cultural rather than political nationalism as the movement's proper aim, and Chaim Gans has recently defended such a view: see his *A Just Zionism* (Oxford: Oxford University Press, 2008). I lay out my own views in an online series on Normblog called "A Cool Hour on the Israel-Palestine Conflict."

28. See Robert Nozick, *Anarchy, State, and Utopia* (New York: Basic Books, 1974), Part III, for a proposal along these lines.

29. See Nozick, *op. cit.,* pp. 320–323, and Mark Rosen, "Illiberal' Societal Cultures, Liberalism, and American Constitutionalism," 12 *Journal of Contemporary Legal Issues* 803 (2002).

30. We might compare this proposal with what Nahum Goldman called "diaspora Zionism": the idea that the ideal Jewish condition would be one with a fluid movement between Israel and the diaspora. Goldman's suggestion that Jews should think of the diaspora as part of their permanent condition, and a good thing rather than a regrettable one, stuck in the craw of many other Zionists, and nationalists in many other communities have similarly wanted to end the diaspora of their people, rather than maintain it alongside a national entity. But I think a diaspora can contribute positively to any culture. There are advantages for a committed Jew or Muslim of living in a non-Jewish or non-Muslim community. And the fact that some of their members live in a condition like this also has advantages for the wider Jewish and Muslim communities: the "diasporic" members bring information and viewpoints from outside the community's horizons back to its center, even as the center provides a deeper and more vibrant understanding of the tradition to the diaspora. Every religious tradition gains from having members in both conditions.

31. Although not for a Jewish state that oppresses its non-Jewish minorities. Standing against Israel's oppression of Palestinians and Israeli Arabs is something every liberal ought to do; standing against the very existence of a Jewish state is not.

32. Audi and Wolterstorff, *Religion in the Public Square,* p.105.

Epilogue

1. Compare Weithman, "Why Should Christians Endorse Human Rights?," pp. 105–106.
2. See Genesis 18:1–2 and BT Shabbat 127a.

3. BT Avot 3: 17 (3:22, in some editions).
4. *Perushei Rabeinu Yonah MeGerondi al Mesechet Avot*, ad locum, my translation (Jerusalem: Machon Torah Shlema, Tashchat).
5. Kierkegaard's figure for the religious ascetic, willing to give up everything for God, but unable fully to achieve the faith that God will—absurdly—return it all to him.
6. Kierkegaard, *Fear and Trembling*, trans. W. Lowrie (Princeton: Princeton University Press, 1954), pp. 49–51.

Appendix I

1. Leibniz complained, about Descartes's version of the ontological argument for God, that one needs to show first that God is *possible* before going on to show that He is necessary (and, consequently, actual). Leibniz then thought he had addressed that problem by preceding his own version of that argument with the obscure sentence, "Nothing can hinder the possibility of [a] substance which contains no limits, no negation, and hence no contradiction" (*Monadology*, § 45, as translated in P. Schrecker and A. M. Schrecker, *Monadology and Other Philosophical Essays* [Indianapolis: Bobbs-Merrill, 1965]). So if the absence of limits makes the idea of God incomprehensible, then on Leibniz's terms the ontological argument cannot get off the ground.
2. I learned to think about these issues from Jonathan Lear (although he puts them rather differently). See "The Disappearing We," and "Transcendental Anthropology," in his *Open-Mindedness: Working Out the Logic of the Soul* (Cambridge: Harvard University Press, 1998).

Appendix II

1. Maimonides, *Guide*, II.32.
2. *Guide* II.41, 36, and 40.
3. See the end of *Guide* II.39.
4. MT I.i.viii.2; 44a.
5. They were *edim al nevuato shehi emet*.
6. MT I.i.viii.2; 44a.
7. MT I.i.viii.1; 43b.
8. There is a famous Midrashic tradition to the effect that we were all at Sinai. But Maimonides is here trying to provide foundations for all Jewish belief, so he cannot appeal to Midrash. Anyone still trying to figure out why he should believe the Torah is not going to be convinced that he experienced something he can't remember on the basis of a Midrash.
9. See the whole of *Guide* III, but especially chapters 27–28.
10. See, for instance, *Guide* I.2 and II.12, 36–37.

Index Locorum

Index